Lecture Notes in Computer Science 11569

More information about this series at http://www.springer.com/series/7409

Sakae Yamamoto · Hirohiko Mori (Eds.)

Human Interface and the Management of Information

Visual Information and Knowledge Management

Thematic Area, HIMI 2019
Held as Part of the 21st HCI International Conference, HCII 2019
Orlando, FL, USA, July 26–31, 2019
Proceedings, Part I

Editors
Sakae Yamamoto
Tokyo University of Science
Tokyo, Japan

Hirohiko Mori
Tokyo City University
Tokyo, Japan

ISSN 0302-9743 ISSN 1611-3349 (electronic)
Lecture Notes in Computer Science
ISBN 978-3-030-22659-6 ISBN 978-3-030-22660-2 (eBook)
https://doi.org/10.1007/978-3-030-22660-2

LNCS Sublibrary: SL3 – Information Systems and Applications, incl. Internet/Web, and HCI

This Springer imprint is published by the registered company Springer Nature Switzerland AG
The registered company address is: Gewerbestrasse 11, 6330 Cham, Switzerland

Foreword

The 21st International Conference on Human-Computer Interaction, HCI International 2019, was held in Orlando, FL, USA, during July 26–31, 2019. The event incorporated the 18 thematic areas and affiliated conferences listed on the following page.

A total of 5,029 individuals from academia, research institutes, industry, and governmental agencies from 73 countries submitted contributions, and 1,274 papers and 209 posters were included in the pre-conference proceedings. These contributions address the latest research and development efforts and highlight the human aspects of design and use of computing systems. The contributions thoroughly cover the entire field of human-computer interaction, addressing major advances in knowledge and effective use of computers in a variety of application areas. The volumes constituting the full set of the pre-conference proceedings are listed in the following pages.

This year the HCI International (HCII) conference introduced the new option of "late-breaking work." This applies both for papers and posters and the corresponding volume(s) of the proceedings will be published just after the conference. Full papers will be included in the *HCII 2019 Late-Breaking Work Papers Proceedings* volume of the proceedings to be published in the Springer LNCS series, while poster extended abstracts will be included as short papers in the HCII 2019 *Late-Breaking Work Poster Extended Abstracts* volume to be published in the Springer CCIS series.

I would like to thank the program board chairs and the members of the program boards of all thematic areas and affiliated conferences for their contribution to the highest scientific quality and the overall success of the HCI International 2019 conference.

This conference would not have been possible without the continuous and unwavering support and advice of the founder, Conference General Chair Emeritus and Conference Scientific Advisor Prof. Gavriel Salvendy. For his outstanding efforts, I would like to express my appreciation to the communications chair and editor of *HCI International News,* Dr. Abbas Moallem.

July 2019 Constantine Stephanidis

HCI International 2019 Thematic Areas and Affiliated Conferences

Thematic areas:

- HCI 2019: Human-Computer Interaction
- HIMI 2019: Human Interface and the Management of Information

Affiliated conferences:

- EPCE 2019: 16th International Conference on Engineering Psychology and Cognitive Ergonomics
- UAHCI 2019: 13th International Conference on Universal Access in Human-Computer Interaction
- VAMR 2019: 11th International Conference on Virtual, Augmented and Mixed Reality
- CCD 2019: 11th International Conference on Cross-Cultural Design
- SCSM 2019: 11th International Conference on Social Computing and Social Media
- AC 2019: 13th International Conference on Augmented Cognition
- DHM 2019: 10th International Conference on Digital Human Modeling and Applications in Health, Safety, Ergonomics and Risk Management
- DUXU 2019: 8th International Conference on Design, User Experience, and Usability
- DAPI 2019: 7th International Conference on Distributed, Ambient and Pervasive Interactions
- HCIBGO 2019: 6th International Conference on HCI in Business, Government and Organizations
- LCT 2019: 6th International Conference on Learning and Collaboration Technologies
- ITAP 2019: 5th International Conference on Human Aspects of IT for the Aged Population
- HCI-CPT 2019: First International Conference on HCI for Cybersecurity, Privacy and Trust
- HCI-Games 2019: First International Conference on HCI in Games
- MobiTAS 2019: First International Conference on HCI in Mobility, Transport, and Automotive Systems
- AIS 2019: First International Conference on Adaptive Instructional Systems

Pre-conference Proceedings Volumes Full List

1. LNCS 11566, Human-Computer Interaction: Perspectives on Design (Part I), edited by Masaaki Kurosu
2. LNCS 11567, Human-Computer Interaction: Recognition and Interaction Technologies (Part II), edited by Masaaki Kurosu
3. LNCS 11568, Human-Computer Interaction: Design Practice in Contemporary Societies (Part III), edited by Masaaki Kurosu
4. LNCS 11569, Human Interface and the Management of Information: Visual Information and Knowledge Management (Part I), edited by Sakae Yamamoto and Hirohiko Mori
5. LNCS 11570, Human Interface and the Management of Information: Information in Intelligent Systems (Part II), edited by Sakae Yamamoto and Hirohiko Mori
6. LNAI 11571, Engineering Psychology and Cognitive Ergonomics, edited by Don Harris
7. LNCS 11572, Universal Access in Human-Computer Interaction: Theory, Methods and Tools (Part I), edited by Margherita Antona and Constantine Stephanidis
8. LNCS 11573, Universal Access in Human-Computer Interaction: Multimodality and Assistive Environments (Part II), edited by Margherita Antona and Constantine Stephanidis
9. LNCS 11574, Virtual, Augmented and Mixed Reality: Multimodal Interaction (Part I), edited by Jessie Y. C. Chen and Gino Fragomeni
10. LNCS 11575, Virtual, Augmented and Mixed Reality: Applications and Case Studies (Part II), edited by Jessie Y. C. Chen and Gino Fragomeni
11. LNCS 11576, Cross-Cultural Design: Methods, Tools and User Experience (Part I), edited by P. L. Patrick Rau
12. LNCS 11577, Cross-Cultural Design: Culture and Society (Part II), edited by P. L. Patrick Rau
13. LNCS 11578, Social Computing and Social Media: Design, Human Behavior and Analytics (Part I), edited by Gabriele Meiselwitz
14. LNCS 11579, Social Computing and Social Media: Communication and Social Communities (Part II), edited by Gabriele Meiselwitz
15. LNAI 11580, Augmented Cognition, edited by Dylan D. Schmorrow and Cali M. Fidopiastis
16. LNCS 11581, Digital Human Modeling and Applications in Health, Safety, Ergonomics and Risk Management: Human Body and Motion (Part I), edited by Vincent G. Duffy

17. LNCS 11582, Digital Human Modeling and Applications in Health, Safety, Ergonomics and Risk Management: Healthcare Applications (Part II), edited by Vincent G. Duffy
18. LNCS 11583, Design, User Experience, and Usability: Design Philosophy and Theory (Part I), edited by Aaron Marcus and Wentao Wang
19. LNCS 11584, Design, User Experience, and Usability: User Experience in Advanced Technological Environments (Part II), edited by Aaron Marcus and Wentao Wang
20. LNCS 11585, Design, User Experience, and Usability: Application Domains (Part III), edited by Aaron Marcus and Wentao Wang
21. LNCS 11586, Design, User Experience, and Usability: Practice and Case Studies (Part IV), edited by Aaron Marcus and Wentao Wang
22. LNCS 11587, Distributed, Ambient and Pervasive Interactions, edited by Norbert Streitz and Shin'ichi Konomi
23. LNCS 11588, HCI in Business, Government and Organizations: eCommerce and Consumer Behavior (Part I), edited by Fiona Fui-Hoon Nah and Keng Siau
24. LNCS 11589, HCI in Business, Government and Organizations: Information Systems and Analytics (Part II), edited by Fiona Fui-Hoon Nah and Keng Siau
25. LNCS 11590, Learning and Collaboration Technologies: Designing Learning Experiences (Part I), edited by Panayiotis Zaphiris and Andri Ioannou
26. LNCS 11591, Learning and Collaboration Technologies: Ubiquitous and Virtual Environments for Learning and Collaboration (Part II), edited by Panayiotis Zaphiris and Andri Ioannou
27. LNCS 11592, Human Aspects of IT for the Aged Population: Design for the Elderly and Technology Acceptance (Part I), edited by Jia Zhou and Gavriel Salvendy
28. LNCS 11593, Human Aspects of IT for the Aged Population: Social Media, Games and Assistive Environments (Part II), edited by Jia Zhou and Gavriel Salvendy
29. LNCS 11594, HCI for Cybersecurity, Privacy and Trust, edited by Abbas Moallem
30. LNCS 11595, HCI in Games, edited by Xiaowen Fang
31. LNCS 11596, HCI in Mobility, Transport, and Automotive Systems, edited by Heidi Krömker
32. LNCS 11597, Adaptive Instructional Systems, edited by Robert Sottilare and Jessica Schwarz
33. CCIS 1032, HCI International 2019 - Posters (Part I), edited by Constantine Stephanidis

34. CCIS 1033, HCI International 2019 - Posters (Part II), edited by Constantine Stephanidis
35. CCIS 1034, HCI International 2019 - Posters (Part III), edited by Constantine Stephanidis

http://2019.hci.international/proceedings

Human Interface and the Management of Information (HIMI 2019)

The full list with the Program Board Chairs and the members of the Program Boards of all thematic areas and affiliated conferences is available online at:

http://www.hci.international/board-members-2019.php

HCI International 2020

The 22nd International Conference on Human-Computer Interaction, HCI International 2020, will be held jointly with the affiliated conferences in Copenhagen, Denmark, at the Bella Center Copenhagen, July 19–24, 2020. It will cover a broad spectrum of themes related to HCI, including theoretical issues, methods, tools, processes, and case studies in HCI design, as well as novel interaction techniques, interfaces, and applications. The proceedings will be published by Springer. More information will be available on the conference website: http://2020.hci.international/.

General Chair
Prof. Constantine Stephanidis
University of Crete and ICS-FORTH
Heraklion, Crete, Greece
E-mail: general_chair@hcii2020.org

http://2020.hci.international/

Contents – Part I

Data Visualization and Analytics

Information, Cognition and Learning

Information, Empathy and Persuasion

Knowledge Management and Sharing

Contents – Part II

Haptic and Tactile Interaction

Information in Virtual and Augmented Reality

Machine Learning and Intelligent Systems

Human Motion and Expression Recognition and Tracking

Medicine, Healthcare and Quality of Life Applications

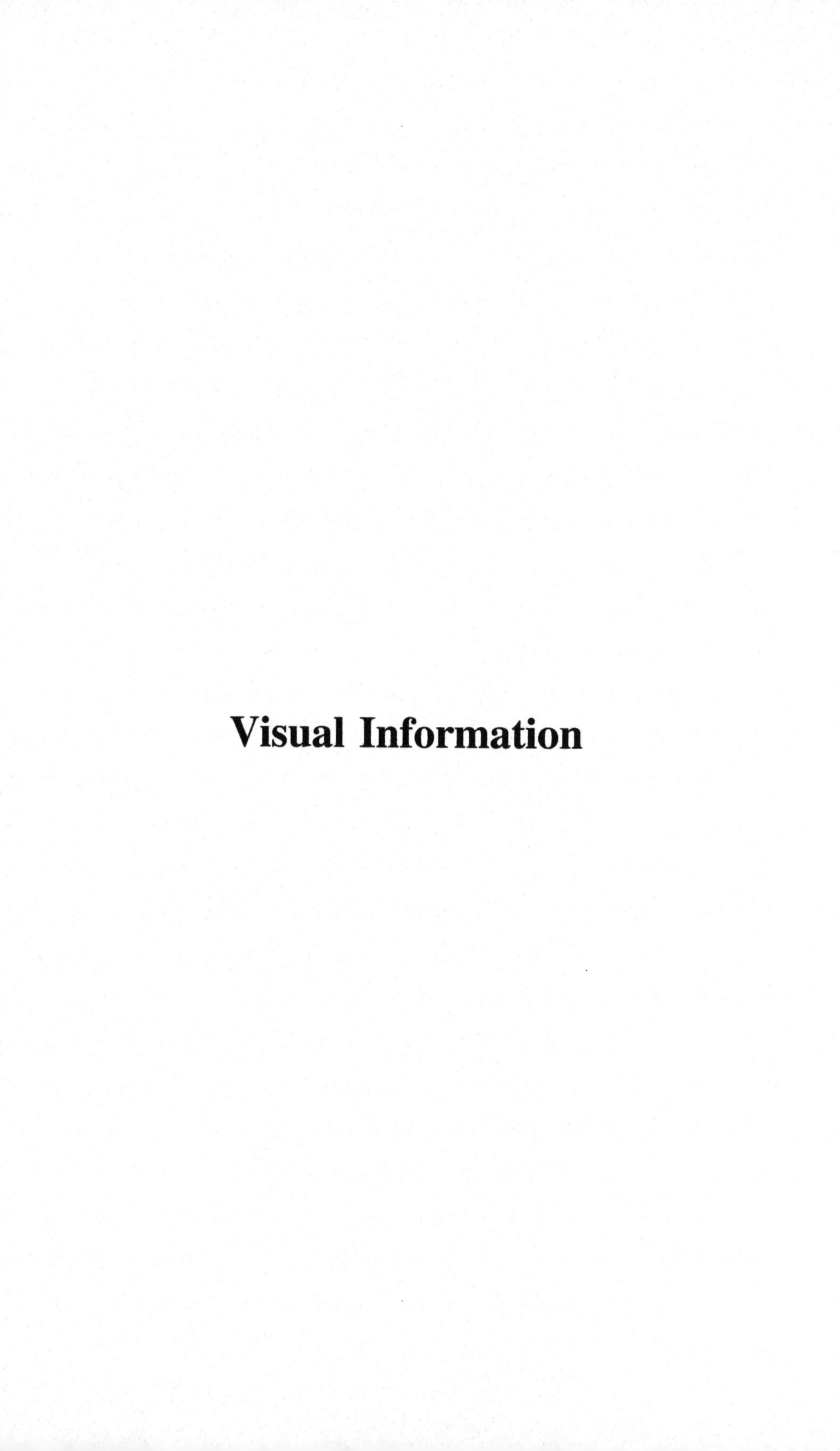

Visual Information

Customization: The Path to a Better and More Accessible Web Experience

Ryan Fritz, Kim-Phuong L. Vu(✉), and Wayne E. Dick

California State University, Long Beach, CA 90840, USA
RYFRITZ2006@yahoo.com, Kim.Vu@CSULB.edu,
WAYNEEDICK@gmail.com

Abstract. The ever-increasing prevalence of electronic information online has provided a medium that allows for greater access to a wider range of users. It is important that user groups such as older adults, or individuals with visual impairments or disabilities, have an equal level of access to electronic information as do individuals without visual impairments or disabilities. This study examined whether allowing older adults the ability to customize various aspects of text would improve their reading performance and subjective usability ratings, while reducing the level of reported visual fatigue for online reading. Data from 16 older adult participants (age range 49 to 69) and 16 younger adult participants (age range 18 to 22) were analyzed. Participants were asked to read text passages using a big or small screen size, and answer reading comprehension questions under conditions where they were able to customize text or not able to customize text. Reading performance and ratings of usability and visual fatigue were obtained. Results showed an interaction between customization condition and age group. In the customized reading conditions, younger adults were more accurate than older adults in answering reading comprehension questions, but their performance did not differ significantly in the non-customized reading conditions. There was no effect of screen size on any of the dependent measures. Implications of these findings are discussed.

Keywords: Web-accessibility · Text-customization · Older adults

1 Introduction and Literature Review

Reading performance varies depending on whether an individual is reading from printed materials or from electronic sources. When reading from a computer screen, people typically take longer compared to when reading the same information from a printed source [1]. Despite the difference in reading speed, reading comprehension does not appear to differ across printed or electronic resources, suggesting that electronic content can be understood just as well as printed materials [2]. Although reading comprehension is similar, whether the electronic document can be useful depends on a variety of factors that impact usability and accessibility including, properties of the materials (font size, accessibility features), user characteristics (age, impairments, fatigue), and viewing conditions (mobile or desktop, lighting). In the following sections, an overview of the importance of usability and accessibility will be presented

S. Yamamoto and H. Mori (Eds.): HCII 2019, LNCS 11569, pp. 3–21, 2019.
https://doi.org/10.1007/978-3-030-22660-2_1

followed by a literature review on factors that influence user performance with reading electronic text on the web. Finally, results from an experiment conducted that examined user performance and preferences with electronic material that can be customized versus material that cannot be customized is presented.

1.1 Usability and Accessibility

Many aspects of our society such as education, banking, and healthcare have turned to the web as an additional medium through which organizations can interact with greater numbers of people. With this ever-increasing availability of information that can be obtained online, and its growing prevalence in our everyday lives, it is essential that individuals are able to access the information regardless of their mental or physical limitations. According to the United Nations Convention on the Rights of Persons with Disabilities, access to information and communication technologies including the web should be a basic human right [3]. In the United States, accessibility is required in design by national law according to Sect. 508 of the Rehabilitation Act of 1973. According to the World Wide Web Consortium (W3C), an international community that develops web standards, accessibility means that information can be obtained by all individuals regardless of hardware, software, language, location, or physical or mental capabilities [4]. In accordance with these standards, Web Content Accessibility Guidelines (WCAG 2.0) have been developed as part of the W3C to help ensure that web content is accessible.

There are a variety of web accessibility tools available that can assist designers in determining whether a website meets accessibility guidelines and standards [5]. Sun, Vu and Strybel [6] found that electronic content that was ranked high in accessibility resulted in better ratings of user experiences compared to electronic content ranked as low in accessibility. Sun, Manabat, et al. found that chapters from eBooks that were rated to be higher in accessibility were considered by participants to be more usable. Participants also indicated greater levels of satisfaction with books rated higher in accessibility compared to those rated lower in accessibility. Accuracy on reading comprehension questions was unaffected for participants without visual impairments. However, for visually impaired participants, accuracy was higher for books with non-STEM (science, technology, engineering or math) content compared to STEM content. Thus, the findings of Sun, Manabat, et al. demonstrated that web content that adheres to accessibility guidelines and standards could increase the subjective usability experience and performance of users with visual impairments.

According to the Nielson Norman Group, usability is an attribute that determines how easy an interface is to use, and is defined by learnability, efficiency, memorability, accuracy, and user satisfaction [7]. Usability is important regarding design in that if the interface or website is not usable, it will likely also be less accessible. Yesilada, Brajnik, Vigo, and Harper [8] found that accessibility standards were viewed as being highly related to usability. Although usability and accessibility are similar in design goals and approaches, the difference between the two is that usability does not focus specifically on individuals with restricted use due to disabilities or physical limitations. According to the Web Accessibility Initiative, the best method for developing websites is to incorporate both usability and accessibility standards and guidelines into the design process [4].

Websites that adhere to accessibility standards may also consider aspects of usability in the design process. Hallett, Dick, Jewett, and Vu [9] found that screen magnification techniques that utilized text wrapping (Responsive Web Design [RWD]) resulted in better user experience scores compared to standard screen magnification (SMS) software that did not allow for text wrapping. This is because SMS enlarges text onscreen in a manner that results in text becoming cutoff and requires horizontal scrolling which decreases usability [10]. Responsive web design wraps the enlarged text within the margins of the visible portion of the screen, making it more usable compared to SMS. Moreover, participants reported significantly higher usability ratings for the RWD than SMS condition, as measured by the System Usability Scale (SUS) [11]. Performance was measured by time-on-task and accuracy to reading comprehension questions. Although both methods (SMS and RWD) yielded similar accuracy scores on the comprehension questions, and received ratings that were within the acceptable range of the SUS, RWD had an average score equating to an "A," while SMS had an average score representative of a "C" [9]. Hallett et al.'s findings demonstrate that adhering to accessibility standards may improve the subjective usability of the system with which the interaction is occurring. Participants stated that they were more comfortable, and that it was more enjoyable to read the passages that used text wrapping (RWD condition). This is because RWD eliminated horizontal scrolling, which is a usability guideline recommendation.

Research has also demonstrated that the use of accessibility guidelines benefits not only individuals with disabilities but also individuals without disabilities. A recent study by Schmutz, Sonderegger, and Sauer [12] examined the level of adherence to accessibility standards and found that as more accessibility standards were implemented within a website, the percentage of tasks that were completed increases. Subjective measures obtained showed that participants gave higher ratings for usability, trustworthiness and aesthetics, and lower ratings of workload to more accessible sites [12]. These findings suggest that designing websites with high adherence to the WCAG 2.0 accessibility guidelines may benefit both users with and without disabilities.

With this in mind, it is important to study user groups that are not considered to be disabled but may have trouble in accessing content online. One such user group would be the elderly. According to the Web Accessibility Initiative, accessibility standards can also assist the elderly population who struggle with decreases in vision, hearing, and fine motor movements [13]. While it seems apparent that accessibility standards that deal with aspects of decreasing vision (color contrast, text size adjustment), fine motor movements (keyboard navigation), and hearing (closed captions, audio transcripts) can aid the elderly user in accessing web content, there has been little research demonstrating that high adherence to accessibility standards benefits the elderly. Aside from this, the implementation of accessibility standards into newly designed websites is slow moving, and in many cases, poorly integrated in the development process [4].

Yesilada et al. [8] found that those who are novices in the field of web accessibility may hold a popular view, not supported by experts and research, that implementing accessibility standards into the design of new websites is not worth the effort. Yesilada et al. found that the typical person feels that although web accessibility guidelines are beneficial to some users, they may not necessarily provide added benefit to users without disabilities, such as the elderly. Respondents were considered to be experts in the field of web accessibility if they spent at least 20% of their working hours dealing with accessibility, and have been working in the field of accessibility for seven or more years. Level of expertise was found to have an effect on responses where individuals with higher expertise agreed more with statements indicating that there was an added benefit to certain groups (such as those with low vision or the elderly) compared to responses from non-experts. These results show that, in general, the population with less expertise or experience in web accessibility may not see the necessity of following accessibility standards in web development.

Another view or idea that may be hindering the implementation of accessibility standards in designing websites is that by designing for accessibility, there could be a risk of creating usability issues for users without disabilities. However, research has shown this suggestion to be unfounded. Schmutz et al. [12] tested whether high adherence to accessibility standards would result in disadvantages to users without disabilities and found no observable differences. Yesilada, Brajnik, and Harper [14] had 76 college students evaluate websites according to accessibility standards to identify barriers that were common to both mobile device users and users with disabilities. They found that accessibility standards that help individuals with visual impairments and motor control issues access the web also help the standard user with accessibility of the web on a mobile device.

However, a study conducted by Hart, Chaparro, and Halcomb [15] found that design for accessibility by itself may not be beneficial. They conducted a study in two parts. The first part consisted of the identification of 40 websites that were checked against a set of heuristic design standards for accessibility. The second part consisted of participants browsing through three of those websites, ranging in adherence levels to accessibility standards, to discover any issues in the websites' usability. Hart et al. found that websites which had higher adherence to accessibility standards resulted in higher task success. However, they did not find any significant differences in task efficiency, user satisfaction, or preference from sites that were rated lower in adherence to accessibility standards. This suggests that although accessibility standards were implemented in the design of the websites, the usability of the website was overlooked. Curran, Walters, and Robinson [16] conducted an evaluation on various websites (including government, university, shopping, and charitable websites) to determine the level of adherence to accessibility standards and guidelines. Curran et al. found that although adherence to the accessibility guidelines is a matter that is becoming more important, many websites still fail to implement all recommendations. Moreover, most failed to even meet the most basic conformance level. This finding suggests that there is a lack of, or inadequate, implementation of accessibility guidelines, and demonstrates the importance of conducting usability and accessibility evaluations.

1.2 Age

The elderly, ranging in age from 50 and above, are the fastest growing group of internet users in society [15]. With age-related declines in vision and motor movement being experienced by this user group [17], it is important that accessibility not only aid the disabled, but also individuals such as the elderly who also have accessibility issues. Aside from the growing population of elderly internet users, there are still many elderly adults that do not use the internet. It is important to understand the reasons behind the disuse of the internet that still exists in the elderly population to determine if they can be overcome. Although the reasons for non-use vary, the top reasons for elderly individual's disuse of the internet (aside from cost of hardware and internet providers) include functional impairments and ergonomic barriers, such as small font sizes being hard to read due to visual deficits [17]. Websites that follow accessibility standards in design and that would allow for customization in such areas as text size adjustment could provide conditions that are beneficial to those who do not use the internet due to the lack of such capabilities.

Age-related issues involving vision are possibly the most common among the elderly. Fozard [18] found that declines in vision, visual acuity, and contrast sensitivity can begin to be noticed during the mid-40s. However, visual impairments typically occur at age 50, resulting in difficulty focusing on near objects, discriminating fine detail, or noticing changes in illumination. The ability of the older adults to differentiate between different hues of color, especially between blue-green, decreases because of reduced sensitivity to color [19–21]. Another visual factor that degrades as one ages is the ability to process visual information [17]. The effects of aging on the decline in cognitive functioning typically begin during midlife, but do not have a striking effect until age 70 and beyond, when very noticeable declines can occur [22, 23].

Another deficit that occurs as age increases is a decline in auditory functioning [17]. This can impede the use of electronic information by elderly internet users, especially when the information is presented in an audio format. The decline in auditory perception in the elderly is important to accessibility because information presented via sound, without the use of captioning or text transcripts, could be lost. This places a heavier reliance on visual information.

1.3 Screen/Font Size

It has been suggested that adults, 65 and older, may benefit from text that is displayed in less complex styles, such as sans serif, and with a font size in the 12- to 14-point range [24]. This suggestion was developed from the results of a series of surveys conducted across a 10-year period looking at the use of electronic devices by individuals 65 and older. Morrell and Echt [24] found that using a sans serif font type resulted in faster reading rates, and were reported as being easier to read by participants, as were larger character sizes between 12- to 14-point font. A study conducted by Ellis and Kurniawan [25] also found that the san serif font type, black Arial with a character size of 14, was preferred by elderly participants. Moreover, it was reported as being more appealing, and subjectively easier to read, compared to other font types such as Times New Roman. A more recent study conducted by Lin, Wu, and Cheng [26] found similar results to the study conducted by Ellis and Kurniawan [25]. However, screen size was also varied in Lin et al.'s study, using a color LCD e-reader. In this study, 60 Taiwanese students with normal or corrected-to-normal vision completed search tasks on pseudo-text. Their task was to identify target words as quickly and accurately as possible. Search time for words, accuracy, and visual fatigue were measured. Lin et al. found that search time for words varied significantly depending on screen size and character size. They found that as screen size increases from 6″ to 9.7″, when using 10- and 12-point font, search time significantly decreased. The same was observed for 8- and 14-point font size, but there was no significant change observed in search time from 8″ to 9.7″ screen size. In regards to the decrease in search time, Lin et al. found that 12-point font had the fastest word search time, followed closely by 14- and 10-, and finally 8-point font size. Lin et al. also found that screen size did not have a significant effect on accuracy, but font size did. They found that increasing the font size led to better accuracy, with 12- and 14-point font having the highest accuracy. It was also found that participants' reports of visual fatigue decreased as the size of the screen and font size increased. However, the results of this study were obtained using a younger population (i.e., high school students), and the results may not generalize to an older population.

Another study looking at the effect of screen size of mobile phones on college students' reading comprehension found that the screen size had no significant impact on user comprehension in terms of accuracy [27]. However, screen size did significantly impact reading time and ease of reading characters, in such that as screen size increased, the easier it became to read the characters. A study by Lee, Shieh, Jeng, and Shen [28] looked at the effect of font size on the legibility of electronic paper in search time for letters. College students completed a series of 12 conditions where they were required to scan alphanumeric pseudo text, and identify the target letter "A" as accurately and quickly as possible. Lee et al. found that as font size increased, the time it took to search for and locate desired information decreased. These findings suggest that the use of devices with smaller screens and font sizes may result in lower accuracy and longer search times for letters, unless the font size is able to be adjusted to a larger size.

1.4 Lighting/Contrast

The effects of age-related visual deficits regarding visual acuity are typically worsened in a dimly lit room. It has been found that even elderly individuals who had similar visual acuity to younger individuals in well-lit areas experienced significant reduction in visual acuity in low lit areas [29]. In a study that looked at the effect of lighting on the legibility of electronic paper, it was observed that accuracy increased as illumination increased [28]. A visual search task, conducted by Lee, Ko, Shen, and Chao [30], using letters as targets, looked at the effect of display type, light source, ambient illumination, interline spacing, and character size on visual performance and fatigue. Lee et al. found that search time decreases significantly, as illumination is increased from 300 to 1500 lx, for college participants who had completed visual scanning of three paragraphs for target letters. A study by Benedetto, Carbone, Drai-Zerbib, Pedrotti, and Baccino [31] looked at the effect of luminance and ambient illumination on visual fatigue and arousal during a reading task with college-aged participants. They found that elevated levels of light intensity from screen luminance reduce the number of eye blinks, which is one of the leading causes of visual fatigue. Benedetto et al. also found faster reading times for higher levels of luminance, but comprehension was not observed to be affected by the level of luminance or ambient illumination.

1.5 Visual Fatigue

As the use of computers and electronic devices have increased, so have a prevailing tendency of eye-related symptoms such as eyestrain, tired eyes, irritation, burning sensation, redness, blurred vision, and double vision [32]. These symptoms as relating to the use of computers and electronic devices have been termed Computer Vision Syndrome (CVS) [32]. The leading cause of CVS is dry eye brought on by the reduced tendency of the user to blink, which has also been shown to be related to elevated levels of illuminance [31, 32]. These symptoms result in the user experiencing visual fatigue. This is the state in which the visual mechanism, after operating in less than optimal conditions, ceases to function with maximum efficiency [33]. Visual fatigue does not primarily result from prolonged exposure or extensive involvement in reading, but from eye strain, which is greatly determined by illegibility due to inadequate illumination and color contrast [33].

According to Blehm et al. [32], there are several factors that could assist users in reducing the effects of visual fatigue. These factors include better lighting and less glare, optimal screen refresh rates, and proper screen positioning. In regards to lighting, reducing the intensity of lighting in the reading area will increase the readers blink rate, which in turn will reduce the level of dry eyes. The refresh rate of the screen on which individuals are reading from should be set at a high level to reduce the amount of flickering [32].

1.6 The Need for Customization

It is important to understand the difference between system driven personalization, user driven personalization, and customization. System driven personalization places control in the hands of the website. It delivers content and functionality to the user that matches his or her needs or interests based on users' past behaviors, without the user having to do anything [34]. An example of system driven personalization would be the ability of the website to make suggestions based on previous search inquires or interactions with the website. User driven personalization gives control to the user through customization, and allows the user to make changes to the physical layout, content, or functionality of the website to meet the individual's needs [35]. An example of this would be the ability of the user to change the color contrast of a website, adjust the size of the text displayed, or even move icons or images around on the website.

The idea of customization is important to website accessibility and usability. There are currently 56.7 million people in the United States who are classified as having a disability, which is roughly 1 out of every 5 people in our nation's population [36]. Allowing the user to have the ability to make customized changes to the web browser, or directly to the website, can greatly improve the accessibility of the web content to that individual [37]. In addition, adults can experience deficits in visual functioning as they age. There are over 28.8 million elderly internet users in the United States [36]. Ellis and Kurniawan [25] examined factors that should be taken into account in the development of a website specifically designed for use by the elderly population. They found that the most common features that participants wanted to customize were related to page visibility and legibility, or more specifically, font size, font type, and the color scheme. The ability to adjust text size, font type, and the color contrast can help older adults see well.

The goals of the present study were to determine if website customization for accessibility would lead to an increase in task performance and perceived usability of the system for older adults. In addition, the study examined whether customized text would reduce the reported level of visual fatigue when interacting with electronic content over a period of time. There has been little research on web customization, which can be due in part to the lack of platforms that allow the user to make customized changes to the webpage. A collaboration of departments at California State University Long Beach, along with the Knowbility organization, are developing a platform tool, called TRx. The TRx allows users to customize various aspects of the webpage to enhance the usability, accessibility, and user experience of the web. The TRx allows the user to make customized selections regarding: foreground-background color, font type and size, as well as, spacing parameters including line, letter, and word spacing. After the user selects the desired customization parameters, the TRx generates a stylesheet that can be incorporated into the internet browser, and it applies the desired selections.

This study examined the effects of customization and screen size on user performance, subjective usability, and reported levels of visual fatigue for online reading of older adults. We looked at performance in terms of reading time and accuracy, as measured by reading comprehension questions. Usability was determined by participants' responses to a SUS, and the level of user visual fatigue was assessed using a Visual Fatigue Questionnaire. We tested older adult participants who were between the ages of 50 to 69 years old. The ideal population would be users with visual disabilities, however, this population was selected due to the relative ease in obtaining participants for the study. Individuals with low vision have, in the past, been difficult to obtain for participation. The older adult participant sample for this study, although being one of convenience, was likely to have some visual problems associated with aging. We limited our older adults to participants less than 70 years old because of the cognitive decline typically found in participants 70 year or older [22, 23]. Since the reading passages are academic test passages, and not general reading materials, and the older adults may not be used to reading these types of passages, we ran a group of younger adult participants, who were between the ages of 18 to 22. The younger adults performed the reading tasks under customized and un-customized conditions to serve as baseline performance measures.

We developed a set of hypotheses based on previous research and they are: H1: Customization will lead to a decrease in reading time, but not in accuracy to reading comprehension, which has been shown to be insensitive [6, 9, 28]. H2: Customization will result in higher ratings of subjective usability. Allowing the user to customize webpage elements, such as, the ability to increase the font size, and select the font type, should result in higher user preferences. This has been shown in related studies conducted by Hallett et al. [9] and Ellis and Kurniawan [25], which were discussed previously. H3: Finally, customization is predicted to result in lower levels of reported visual fatigue from reading online content over a period of time. Previous research has supported this point in that increased font size, and better color contrast, has been shown to reduce reports of visual fatigue [26, 31, 33].

2 Methods

2.1 Participants

Thirty-four individuals participated in this study. Data for one participant in the older adult age group was excluded from the analysis and replaced due to extensive reading response times that were more than three standard deviations from the mean, for customized conditions, and more than two standard deviations from the mean for non-customized conditions. Data for one participant in the younger adult age group was excluded and replaced due to having low accuracy scores (20%) for the passage comprehension questions. Thus, the final data set consisted of data from 32 participants, 16 in each age group. All participants had normal or corrected-to-normal vision. All older adult participants indicated that they do not experience difficulty in typing or in using a mouse for cursor movement and selections. The older adults (5 males, 11 females) were 49 to 67 years old, with an average age of 57.5 years. The younger adults (1 male, 15 females) were 18 to 22 years old, with an average age of 18.6 years. Older adult participants were selected by means of convenience sampling, utilizing flyers and word-of-mouth recruitment. Younger adult participants were recruited by mean of the California State University Long Beach's Psychology 100 Subject Pool. Older adult participants received $15 for their participation in the study, while the younger adult participants received one credit towards their course research participation requirement.

Older adults were required to take the Mini-Mental State Examination to determine if any cognitive impairments were present that would interfere with the study's results. All results were in the normal range of cognitive functioning, with a mean score being greater than the 24-point criteria ($M = 28.94$, $SD = .99$). Older adult participants' computer proficiency was obtained from responses to the pretest demographics questionnaire. Responses were made based on a 5-point scale where participants rated their agreement to the statement, "I am proficient in using a computer," where 1 represented "Strongly Disagree" and 5 represented "Strongly agree". Older adults indicated that they were proficient in using the computer ($M = 4.06$, $SD = 1.39$). Older adult participants also indicated agreement with the statement that the use of a computer is essential in daily activities ($M = 4.12$, $SD = 1.36$), using a 1 to 5 scale. Both older and younger adult participants rated their level of proficiency in using the web browser Google Chrome on a scale of 1 to 7, with 1 representing "Not Proficient" and 7 representing "Very Proficient". Participants were all shown to be proficient in using Google Chrome (older adults: $M = 4.23$, $SD = 1.42$; younger adults: $M = 5.56$, $SD = 1.03$).

2.2 Materials

The current study was reviewed and approved by the university's Institutional Review Board (IRB). A standard Dell desktop computer, using a Windows 7 operating system, was used in this study. The monitor used was a Dell model U2312HM, with a 1920 × 1080 Pixel Resolution and 24-in. LCD display. The active screen size was scaled down to 7.5 in. for the small screen display conditions, and the full screen was used for the big screen display condition. The screen was not titled and was positioned perpendicular (90°) to the table. A Visual Fatigue Questionnaire was used to assess participants' levels of reported symptoms of fatigue. The questionnaire was administered before and after each reading condition completed during the study. Participants responded to the questionnaire by indicating their agreement to statements regarding visual fatigue symptoms on a scale that ranged from 1 (strong disagreement) to 5 (strong agreement). Although the scale was used in previous studies [9, 31], metrics regarding its reliability and validity were not available.

The TRx program was modified by the experimenters to allow participants to create customized selections of various elements of the reading material. Sample text was provided to each participant showing the effect of each customized selection made. Participants were given the opportunity, after viewing the sample text, to return and change any customized selection previously selected. The total time taken to complete all customized selections was less than ten minutes. A SUS was given to each participant to determine overall usability of the reading tasks with and without customization. The SUS consists of a 10-item questionnaire with a range of five response choices ranging from strongly disagree to strongly agree. Scores were normalized to create a percentile ranking. A score above 68 is considered above average, while anything below 68 out of 100 is below average [38]. A post experiment questionnaire was used to obtain participants' preferences relating to customization for both the big and small screen size, as well as responses relating to levels of visual fatigue.

A set of four reading passages, and two medical prescription passages, were used to assess participant performance in terms of accuracy to reading comprehension questions. The four reading passages average 557 words, and were obtained from online sixth-through eighth-grade standardized practice tests for reading comprehension. The medical prescription passages have 209 words for medicine A and 199 words for medicine B. The medical prescription passages have a seventh grade comprehension level, and were also obtained from online sixth- through eighth-grade standardized practice tests for reading comprehension. Participant reading times included the amount of time it takes to read each passage, plus the time it takes to answer the corresponding set of comprehension questions. Participants were allowed to refer to the reading passage when answering the comprehension questions, which removed any need for reliance on memory for passage content.

2.3 Design

The study employed a 2 (Customization: Customization vs. No Customization) × 2 (Screen Size: Big: 24 in. vs. Small: 7.5 in.) × 2 (Age Group: Younger vs. Older Adults) mixed design, with age group serving as the between-subjects variable, and customization and screen size being within-subjects variables. Half of the participants were randomly assigned to start in the customization condition first, and the other half started with the non-customization condition first. The order of the different passages was counterbalanced between participants. The dependent variables included performance (accuracy and time), subjective usability/preference ratings (SUS and Post Experiment Questionnaire) and reported levels of visual fatigue (Visual Fatigue Questionnaire).

2.4 Procedure

All participants were tested in the same lab environment. Participants were tested individually in a well-lit room with constant overhead lighting throughout the study. The lighting level did not produce any glare on the computer screen. When participants showed up for the study session, they were greeted and given an informed consent form. The informed consent included information regarding risks, benefits, and incentives associated with the study. After signing the consent form, participants were seated approximately 20 in. in front of the computer. The participant then completed a visual fatigue scale, which served as our baseline measure. Then they performed two reading tasks and one medical prescription passage within the customization or non-customization condition. Again, the condition the participant received first was counterbalance between participants. For each condition, the participants were given task instructions.

In the customized condition, the participants were given the opportunity to explore the TRx program. The experimenter showed the participants the different customization options and allowed them to select the setting that was most comfortable for them. Once all the customized settings were selected, the experimenter saved the settings and transferred the stylesheet containing the selections into Qualtrics. Qualtrics is an online survey platform that was used to display the reading passages and record the answers for the reading comprehension questions. Participants performed one reading passage within the customized condition with the big screen and one with the small screen. The order of screen size was counterbalanced between participants. After completing both reading passages, the participant was given the prescription task. Once the participant completed the prescription task, they were asked to fill out a paper-based VFS and SUS surveys. For the non-customized condition, the participants were given the task instructions and presented with the reading passages from Qualtrics. As with the customized condition, participants performed one reading task with the small screen and the other with the large screen (order counterbalanced between subjects) prior to performing the prescription task and filling out the paper based VFS and SUS.

After completing all experimental tasks, older adult participants were given the post experiment questionnaire. The post experiment questionnaire asked participants about their user preference for using customized text compared to non-customized text and level of agreement to statements relating to visual fatigue. The questionnaire consisted of a total of seven items: three to capture user preferences, three to capture users' agreement ratings with specific statements, and one open-ended question for user comments. Younger adults were not given the post questionnaire since we only intended to use their reading performance data as a baseline. Once the study was completed, participants were given a debriefing form and thanked for participation.

3 Results

All participants made customized selections in the customization condition. Each condition, customized and not customized, took approximately 20 min to complete with an overall task completion time of about 40 min.

3.1 Accuracy

Reading Task. A 2 (Customization vs. No Customization) × 2 (Screen size: Big vs. Small) × 2 (Age group: Younger Adults: vs. Older Adults) repeated measures ANOVA was performed. Age group was entered as the between-subjects variable, and accuracy on the reading passages was the dependent measure. Accuracy was determined by the percent of responses that a participant answered correctly (out of a total of five reading comprehension questions). Table 1 lists the mean accuracy for each condition by age group. There were no significant main effects found for customization, screen size, or age group. However, there was a significant interaction between age group and customization, $F(1, 30) = 8.62$, $MSE = 0.03$, $p < .01$, partial $\eta 2 = .22$ (Fig. 1). Tests of simple effects were performed by customization condition. For the customized condition, younger adults were more accurate ($M = 91.9\%$, $SD = 3.2\%$) compared to older adults ($M = 76.9\%$, $SD = 3.2\%$), $p = .002$. However, for the non-customized conditions, there was no significant difference in accuracy between older adults ($M = 86.3\%$, $SD = 3.4\%$) and younger adults ($M = 82.5\%$, $SD = 3.4\%$). Tests of simple effects by age group showed that younger adults tended to be more accurate in the customized condition compared to the non-customized condition, $p = .055$, but there was no difference in accuracy rates for older adults by condition, $p = .17$. No other significant interaction effects were found.

Table 1. Mean percent correct on reading comprehension passages by age group

Age group	Screen size	Customization	Reading accuracy	
			Mean	Standard error
Younger adults	Big	Customized	88.8%	5.1%
		Not-Customized	88.8%	4.8%
	Small	Customized	95.0%	3.9%
		Not-Customized	81.3%	4.9%
Older adults	Big	Customized	78.8%	5.1%
		Not-Customized	86.3%	4.8%
	Small	Customized	75.0%	3.9%
		Not-Customized	86.3%	4.9%

Prescription Task. A separate 2 (Customization vs. No Customization) × 2 (Age group: Young Adult: vs. Older Adults) repeated measures ANOVA was conducted, with age group serving as the between-subjects variable. The accuracy of responses to the prescription passages was the dependent measure. Overall, accuracy was high. The mean accuracy for young adults was 93.8% in both the customized and non-customized condition. The mean accuracy for older adults was 92.5% in the customized condition and 96.3% in the non-customized conditions. This ANOVA yielded no significant effects.

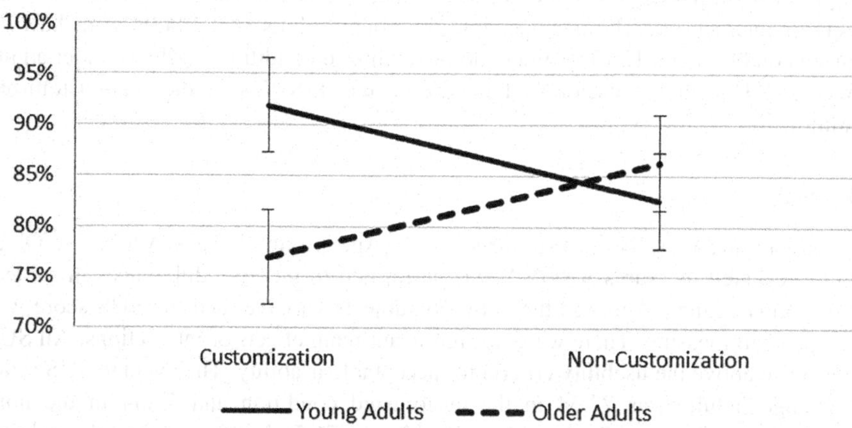

Fig. 1. Mean accuracy percentage. Accuracy in the customization condition was higher for younger adults compared to older adults whereas no differences were found for the non-customized condition.

3.2 Reading Time

Reading Task. A 2 (Customization vs. No Customization) × 2 (Screen size: Big vs. Small) × 2 (Age group: Young Adult: vs. Older Adults) repeated measures ANOVA was performed. Age group was the between-subjects variable, and reading time (reading passages and answering comprehension questions) was the dependent measure. The analysis did not yield any significant main effects or interaction effects (see Table 2 for means).

Table 2. Mean time on task (in Seconds) for reading comprehension passages by age group

Age group	Screen size	Customization	Reading time	
			Mean	Standard error
Younger adults	Big	Customized	267.87	14.67
		Not-Customized	282.31	15.03
	Small	Customized	268.25	17.24
		Not-Customized	270.94	16.91
Older adults	Big	Customized	284.00	14.67
		Not-Customized	262.06	15.03
	Small	Customized	296.81	17.24
		Not-Customized	278.75	16.91

Prescription Task. A separate 2 (Customization vs. No Customization) × 2 (Age group: Young Adult: vs. Older Adults) repeated measures ANOVA were performed.

Again, age group was the between-subjects variable, and reading response time for the two prescription passages was the dependent measure. There were no significant main effects or interactions. The average time for young adults was 144.94 s in the customized condition and 126.75 s in the non-customized condition, while for older adults it was 141.31 s in the customized condition and 118.25 s in the non-customized condition.

3.3 SUS

A 2 (Customized vs. Non-Customized) × 2 (Age group: Young Adult: vs. Older Adults) repeated measures ANOVA was performed to measure differences in subjective usability ratings. Age was the between-subjects variable, and the SUS score was the dependent measure. There were no significant main effects or interactions. All SUS scores were above the usability criteria for acceptable usability. The average SUS score for younger adults was 72.34 in the customized condition and 77.34 in the non-customized condition, while for older adults it was 76.56 in the customized condition and 76.87 in the non-customized condition.

3.4 Visual Fatigue

Visual fatigue was measured by an average score to Likert-like questions about visual fatigue, where 1 reflects low levels of visual fatigue, and 5 reflects high levels of visual fatigue. Since we were interested in how visual fatigue changed over the course of the study, a change score was obtained by subtracting both the customized and non-customized conditions visual fatigue averaged scores from the baseline score.

A 2 (Customized vs. Non-Customized) × 2 (Age group: Young Adult vs. Older Adults) repeated measures ANOVA was performed using the change in VFS score as the dependent measure. Age group served as the between-subjects variable. Overall, mean fatigue ratings were low, being less than 2, on a 5-point Likert Scale. There were no significant main effects or interactions.

3.5 Post Experiment Questionnaire

A post experiment questionnaire was given to participants in the older adult age group. For the first three items, participants indicated preference using a scale from 1 (using non-customized text) to 7 (using customized text), with 4 representing no preference. For the last three items, participants stated their level of agreement using a scale ranging from 1 (Strongly Disagree) to 7 (Strongly Agree), with 4 representing neither agreement nor disagreement. Individual one-sample T-tests were performed on Questions 1 to 3 to determine whether the preference for customization was significantly higher from the rating of 4, which represented no preference. Results indicated that participants' preference for using customization in the big screen conditions was significant, $t(15) = 3.67$, $p < 0.01$, while preference for using customization in the small screen, $t(15) = 1.78$, $p = 0.10$, and prescription, $t(15) = 1.85$, $p = 0.08$, conditions were non-significant (see Fig. 2). For Questions 4 to 6, descriptive analysis also showed a slight agreement that customized text decreased visual fatigue overall for both big and small screen reading tasks, as well as for the prescription tasks (see Table 3 for post experiment questionnaire means).

1. To perform the reading tasks using the **Big** screen, I preferred: 5.50

1	2	3	4	5	6	7
Using non-customized text			No Preference			Using customized text

2. To perform the reading tasks using the **Small** screen, I preferred:

1	2	3	4	5	6	7
Using non-customized text			No Preference			Using customized text

3. To perform the **Prescription** tasks, I preferred:

1	2	3	4	5	6	7
Using non-customized text			No Preference			Using customized text

Fig. 2. Post experiment questionnaire customized preferences.

Table 3. Mean ratings given by older adults to the post experiment questionnaire

Older adult preference	Mean	Standard deviation
Big screen (preference for customization)	5.50	1.63
Small screen (preference for customization)	5.00	2.25
Prescription (preference for customization)	5.00	2.16
Decrease visual fatigue: big screen	5.38	1.63
Decrease visual fatigue: small screen	4.94	1.98
Decrease visual fatigue: prescription	4.88	1.75

4 Discussion

The present study evaluated whether reading tasks that utilized customized text elements would result in better performance, higher usability ratings, and decreased reports of visual fatigue for older adults. Performance was determined by accuracy (the percent of correct responses to reading comprehension questions) and reading/response time (the time it took participants to read each passage and answer the comprehension questions). The older adults' performance on the reading tasks were compared to those of younger adults.

The results showed only one significant interaction involving Customization and Age Group for accuracy on the reading passages. The customized reading passages resulted in higher accuracy rates for younger adults, but not older adults. In fact, older adult participants had numerically lower accuracy for the customized conditions compared to the younger adult participants. These findings do not support our hypothesis that customization will lead to a decrease in reading time but not in accuracy to reading comprehension questions. In fact, contrary to our hypothesis, we found that customization improved accuracy to reading comprehension questions for younger adults. Previous findings have shown that sans serif font types and font size between 12 and 14 point led to reduced reading times [24, 26]. When making the customized text selections participants were free to choose what they felt would be best for their online reading experience. However, after final customized selections were made, participants were not permitted to make changes to customized selection choices. Thus, customization selections were made only once and could not be optimized for the different screen sizes being tested.

For our younger adult group, 38% of participants customized their text to be 15 points and 43% of participants set their text to be 18 points or greater. For the older adult group, 43% of participants customized their text to be 15 points and 57% of participants set their text to be 18 points or greater. The lack of a difference in reading times may have resulted from the individual customized selections made by the participant. Larger text can be easier to read, but enlarging text can add to the reading task because participants will have to spend more time scrolling through the passages. Task demand was relatively low for the reading passages and comprehension questions. Pilot testing of the reading passages indicated that task completion times were all under 10 min for each passage and accuracy to the reading comprehension questions was above 80%. Because the sample size was small, and participants made different selections, there was not enough data available to meaningfully compare the reading times for each of the font sizes that were selected.

According to Tullis and Albert [11], SUS scores that are less than 50 are considered to be unacceptable, scores between 50 and 70 are considered to be marginally acceptable, and scores greater than 70 are considered to be acceptable in terms of usability. We found the SUS scores to be above 70 for all conditions. There were no significant differences in reported subjective usability observed between older adults and younger adults in either customized or non-customized reading conditions. Although our hypothesis stating that customization will result in higher rating of usability was not supported, both the customized and the non-customized reading conditions appeared to be within the acceptable range of usability according to participants from both age groups. The fact that customization did not reduce the usability ratings of the system is consistent with previous findings that showed designing for accessibility does not reduce system usability [12, 14].

Although previous studies have shown that visual fatigue may be decreased by increasing font size and improving color contrasts [26, 32, 33], there were no significant differences in participants' reported levels of visual fatigue found in the current study. These results do not support our hypothesis that customization will result in lower levels of reported visual fatigue. The changes in visual fatigue observed in the present study were small. The visual fatigue questionnaire used in the current study consisted of questions with a 5-point rating scale, which had a minimum score of 1 (representing low visual fatigue) and a maximum score of 5 (high visual fatigue). Baseline visual fatigue levels suggested that participants were not fatigued at the beginning of the study (mean visual fatigue scores were below a score of 2). Participants did not report significant increases in visual fatigue levels by the end of the study, and the means for all conditions were still under 2.0. Chi and Lin [39] found that changes in visual fatigue, as measured by the visual fatigue scale, were evident for reading tasks lasting about 60 min. The participants in the current study were able to finish the study within an hour. Thus, the time spent on the reading task may not have been long enough for detection of visual fatigue. In fact, in the post questionnaire, older adults only showed moderate levels of agreement with statements indicating that the customized conditions decreased their visual fatigue.

The lack of significant findings of the current study may be a result of the small sample size, which was limited by the availability of older adults. The observed power for all non-significant effects was between the range of 0.05 to 0.375, which reflects low power. Further research with a larger sample size is needed to increase the power, and to determine if the current results are representative.

Prior research has shown that to improve the accessibility and usability of the online experience, websites should be designed with the user in mind and allow for customizations of text elements including font family and size, color contrast, and spacing parameters [25]. Websites that incorporate the ability to customize are more likely to aid individuals with disabilities or populations without disabilities, such as older adults, that may experience difficulty in accessing electronic information. Based on findings from the current study, designing websites that allow for customization may lead to an increase in the younger population's ability to accurately answer reading comprehension questions. However, allowing for unlimited combinations of color for foreground and background text might not be an optimal design for electronic text. Further research should be conducted to determine what color combinations would work best for customized electronic text. Future research should also look at predetermined selections regarding font size, screen size, and color combinations to determine if allowing users to make unrestricted customized selections is more beneficial compared to the use of preset selections.

Another limitation of the current study is that, as noted earlier, participants were not able to make changes to the customized selections after they started the reading task in the customized condition. In practice, users may set an initial customize scheme, and then change the settings as they perform the task. That is, users may like a certain font size or color contrast setting at the start of the task, but after performing the task, they may want to make adjustments. Users may have also wanted to select different customization schemes based on the small versus large screen. Although the current implementation of the TRx customization software allowed users to see the changes in the text as a function of the customized selections, once the customized settings were finalized, the experimenter had to generate code for the selections and upload the code into Qualtrics. This process did not permit adjustments to be made for a single aspect in real time. It could be the case that a platform that allows users to customize in real time would lead to better performance, and future research should explore this possibility.

Acknowledgments. We thank the students in the Center for Usability in Design and Accessibility (CUDA) for help in proof reading and formatting the paper.

References

1. Mayes, D.K., Sims, V.K., Koonce, J.M.: Comprehension and workload differences for VDT and paper-based reading. Int. J. Industr. Ergon. **28**, 367–378 (2001)
2. Porion, A., Aparicio, X., Megalakaki, O., Robert, A., Baccino, T.: The impact of paper-based versus computerized presentation on text comprehension and memorization. Comput. Hum. Behav. **54**, 569–576 (2016)
3. United Nations. Convention on the Rights of Persons with Disabilities: Articles (2007). https://www.un.org/development/desa/disabilities/convention-on-the-rights-of-persons-with-disabilities/convention-on-the-rights-of-persons-with-disabilities-2.html
4. World Wide Web Consortium (W3C). Accessibility (2016). https://www.w3.org/standards/webdesign/accessibility
5. Sun, Y.T., Manabat, A.K., Chan, M.L., Chong, I., Vu, K.-P.L.: Accessibility evaluation: manual development and tool selection for evaluating accessibility of e-textbooks. In: Hale, K., Stanney, K. (eds.) Advances in Neuroergonomics and Cognitive Engineering. AISC, vol. 488, pp. 327–337. Springer, Cham (2017). https://doi.org/10.1007/978-3-319-41691-5_28
6. Sun, Y.T., Vu, K.-P.L., Strybel, T.Z.: A validation test of an accessibility evaluation method. In: Ahram, T., Falcão, C. (eds.) AHFE 2017. AISC, vol. 607, pp. 625–633. Springer, Cham (2018). https://doi.org/10.1007/978-3-319-60492-3_59
7. Nielson, J.: Usability 101: Introduction to usability (2012). https://www.nngroup.com/articles/usability-101-introduction-to-usability/
8. Yesilada, Y., Brajnik, G., Vigo, M., Harper, S.: Exploring perceptions of web accessibility: a survey approach. Behav. Inf. Technol. **34**(2), 119–134 (2013)
9. Hallett, E.C., Dick, W., Jewett, T., Vu, K.-P.L.: How screen magnification with and without word-wrapping affects the user experience of adults with low vision. In: Ahram, T., Falcão, C. (eds.) AHFE 2017. AISC, vol. 607, pp. 665–674. Springer, Cham (2018). https://doi.org/10.1007/978-3-319-60492-3_63
10. Sherwin, K.: Beware horizontal scrolling and mimicking swipe on desktop. Nielsen Norman Group (2014). https://www.nngroup.com/articles/horizontal-scrolling/
11. Tullis, T., Albert, B.: Measuring the User Experience: Collecting, Analyzing, and Presenting Usability Metric, 2nd edn. Morgan Kaufmann, Waltham (2013)
12. Schmutz, S., Sonderegger, A., Sauer, J.: Implementing recommendations from web accessibility guidelines: would they also provide benefits to nondisabled users. Hum. Factors **58**(4), 611–629 (2016)
13. World Wide Web Consortium (W3C). Social factors in developing a web accessibility business case for your organization (2012). https://www.w3.org/WAI/bcase/soc#groups
14. Yesilada, Y., Brajnik, G., Harper, S.: Barriers common to mobile and disabled web users. Interact. Comput. **23**(5), 525–542 (2011)
15. Hart, T.A., Chaparro, B.S., Halcomb, C.G.: Evaluating websites for older adults: adherence to 'senior-friendly' guidelines and end-user performance. Behav. Inf. Technol. **27**(3), 191–199 (2008)
16. Curran, K., Walters, N., Robinson, D.: Investigating the problems faced by older adults and people with disabilities in online environments. Behav. Inf. Technol. **26**(6), 447–453 (2007)
17. Hawthorn, D.: Possible implications of aging for interface designers. Interact. Comput. **12**(5), 507–528 (2000)
18. Fozard, J.: Vision and hearing in aging. In: Birren, J., Sloane, R., Cohen, G. (eds.) Handbook of Mental Health and Aging, pp. 150–170. Academic Press, San Diego (1990)

19. Echt, K.: Designing web based health information for older adults: visual considerations and design directives. In: Older Adults. Health Information and the World Wide Web, pp. 61–88 (2002)
20. Helve, J., Krause, U.: The influence of age on performance in the Panel-D15 colour vision test. Acta Opthalmologica **50**, 896–901 (1972)
21. Weale, R.: Retinal illumination and age. Trans. Illum. Eng. Soc. **26**, 95–100 (1961)
22. Aartsen, M.J., Smits, C.H., van Tilburg, T., Knipscheer, K.C., Deeg, D.J.: Activity in older adults: cause or consequence of cognitive functioning? A longitudinal study on everyday activities and cognitive performance in older adults. J. Gerontol. **57**(2), 153–162 (2002)
23. Vestergaard, S., Thinggaard, M., Jeune, B., Vaupel, J.W., McGue, M., Christensen, K.: Physical and mental decline and yet rather happy? A study of Danes aged 45 and older. Aging Mental Health **19**(5), 400–408 (2015)
24. Morrell, Q., Echt, K.: Designing written instructions for older adults learning to use computers. In: Fisk, A., Rogers, W. (eds.) Handbook of Human Factors and the Older Adult, pp. 335–361. Academic Press, San Diego (1996)
25. Ellis, D.R., Kurniawan, S.H.: Increasing the usability of online information for older users: a case study in participatory design. Int. J. Hum.-Comput. Interact. **12**(2), 263–276 (2000)
26. Lin, H., Wu, F.-G., Cheng, Y.-Y.: Legibility and visual fatigue affected by text direction, screen size and character size on color LCD e-reader. Displays **34**, 49–58 (2013)
27. Ghamdi, E.A., et al.: The effect of screen size on mobile phone user comprehension of health information and application structure: an experimental approach. J. Med. Syst. **40**(1), 11:1–11:18 (2016)
28. Lee, D.-S., Shieh, K.-K., Jeng, S.-C., Shen, I.-H.: Effect of character size and lighting on legibility of electronic papers. Displays **29**, 10–17 (2008)
29. Kline, D., Scialfa, C.: Sensory and perceptual functioning: basic research and human factors implications. In: Fisk, A., Rogers, W. (eds.) Handbook of Human Factors and the Older Adult, pp. 27–54. Academic Press, San Diego (1996)
30. Lee, D.-S., Ko, Y.-H., Shen, I.-H., Chao, C.-Y.: Effect of light source, ambient illumination, character size and interline spacing on visual performance and visual fatigue with electronic paper displays. Displays **32**, 1–7 (2011)
31. Benedetto, S., Carbone, A., Drai-Zerbib, V., Pedrotti, M., Baccino, T.: Effects of luminance and illuminance on visual fatigue and arousal during digital reading. Comput. Hum. Behav. **41**, 112–119 (2014)
32. Blehm, C., Vishnu, S., Khattak, A., Mitra, S., Yee, R.W.: Computer vision syndrome: a review. Surv. Ophthalmol. **50**(3), 253–262 (2005)
33. Demilia, L.A.: Visual fatigue and reading. J. Educ. **151**(2), 4–34 (1968)
34. Schade, A.: Customization vs. personalization in the user experience. Nielsen Norman Group (2016). https://www.nngroup.com/articles/customization-personalization/
35. World Wide Web Consortium (W3C). Personalization Semantics Explainer 1.0 (2018). https://www.w3.org/TR/personalization-semantics-1.0/
36. U.S. Census Bureau. Fact for features: older Americans, May 2016. https://www.census.gov/newsroom/facts-for-features/2016/cb16-ff08.html
37. World Wide Web Consortium (W3C). Better web browsing: tips for customizing your computer. Web Accessibility Initiative (2010). https://www.w3.org/WAI/users/browsing
38. U.S. Department of Health and Human Services. System Usability Scale. Usability.gov (2017). https://www.usability.gov/how-to-and-tools/methods/system-usability-scale.html
39. Chi, C., Lin, F.: A comparison of seven visual fatigue assessment techniques in three data-acquisition VDT tasks. Hum. Factors **40**(4), 577–590 (1998)

Users' Interpretation of *Pictograms* and *Pictures* for Conveying Instructions and Warnings on Pharmaceutical Labels

Destyn Jones[1(✉)], Sabrina Moran[2(✉)], Jaime Sanchez[2(✉)], Amber Latham[2(✉)], and Kim-Phuong L. Vu[1,2(✉)]

[1] Building Infrastructure Leading to Diversity (BUILD) Program, California State University, Long Beach, Long Beach, CA 90815, USA
Destyn.Jones@student.csulb.edu, Kim.Vu@csulb.edu
[2] Center for Usability in Design and Accessibility (CUDA), California State University, Long Beach, Long Beach, CA 90815, USA
Sabrina.N.Moran@gmail.com, AmberLatham@gmail.com, Jaime7529@att.net

Abstract. Pharmaceutical pictograms are figures that provide a visual representation of medication instructions and warnings. Pictograms were created in order to lower the continuously rising problem of poor medication adherence due to patients misunderstanding what is being instructed on medication labels. Research on pictograms show that their use could increase patients' comprehension of medication instructions, but the comprehension rates are still low. Researchers have argued that in order to improve the effectiveness of pictograms, they must be more concrete, simple, meaningful, and familiar. Pictures have these properties. Thus, the goal of this study was to examine if the use of pictures (i.e., real images) provide a better representation of what is being instructed to users on medication labels than pictograms. We hypothesized that real images would lead to a better understanding of the instructions and warnings for taking medication, and in turn, users would have higher comprehension levels. Participants completed an online survey evaluating the meaning of either pictograms or pictures. Both quantitative and qualitative data analyses were conducted on free responses to the questions and on users' ratings of the "goodness" of the stimuli. The results showed that participants were moderately accurate (74%) in their interpretation of pictograms, and the use of pictures did not improve their comprehension.

Keywords: Pictograms · Pictures · Real images · Medication instructions · Medication adherence · Comprehension levels

1 Introduction

According to the Institute of Medicine, nearly every individual living today has taken or will take medication at some point in their lifetime. Specifically, approximately four out of five U.S. adults will use prescription medicines, or other drugs received over-the-counter, on a weekly basis [1]. These medications are meant to be beneficial to consumers; however, they can be harmful if the medication is not taken appropriately [2].

S. Yamamoto and H. Mori (Eds.): HCII 2019, LNCS 11569, pp. 22–33, 2019.
https://doi.org/10.1007/978-3-030-22660-2_2

Errors in taking prescription medicine are more common than expected. For example, Brown and Bussel [3] indicated that 50% of people who are prescribed pharmaceutical prescriptions do not take them correctly. Of these people, 58% of these errors are due to inadequate medication labeling [4]. In efforts to prevent errors caused by insufficient labeling, the Food and Drug Administration (FDA) established guidelines for the labeling of substances and filling prescriptions. Under Title XXI, companies are required to include the pharmacy name, address, prescription serial number, date of initial filling, name of the patient, name of the practitioner issuing the prescription, drug name and dosage, as well as the directions for use and cautionary statements on all medication labels [5]. This information is helpful; however, it may not be enough to allow users to understand all of the information they need to know regarding the medication. In order to further build upon the standards set by the FDA, Pharmacopeia and the Institute for Safe Medicine Practices suggested that labels should contain:

1. Words that are typed and easy-to-read in 12-point font
2. Warnings that are typed directly onto labels in large font
3. The generic and brand name of the drug
4. Images or physical descriptions of the pills in the container
5. No extra zeros
6. Pharmacy information at the bottom of the label

Herron and Vu [6] conducted a study to determine whether the Pharmacopeia and the Institute for Safe Medicine Practices recommendation for adding images or physical descriptions of the pills in the container would help people in identifying the correct medication to take. Herron and Vu included conditions wherein participants were asked to identify the medication in a container by viewing labels that had a black and white picture of the medicine, a color picture of the medicine, or text description of the medicine. They found that participants were faster and more accurate at identifying the correct medication with the labels that had a color depiction of the medication compared to ones that had a text description or a black and white picture of the medicine. Based on this finding, they recommended that if a pharmacy were to employ pictures of the medication, they do so only if they can provide color pictures of the medicine on the labels.

One reason that pictures and symbols are recommended on pharmaceutical labels is that illiterate patients are 3.4 times less likely to comprehend prescription labels correctly [7]. Patients' inability to understand the instructions given on pharmaceutical labels compromises the medications' outcomes and increases the risk of side effects. To improve patients' understanding of pharmaceutical instructions, pictograms were created. Pictograms give a visual representation of the instructions listed on pharmaceutical labels. Although, people interpret pictograms with higher accuracy than text [7], pictograms have not been shown to result in high levels of comprehension [8]. Nevertheless, as previously noted, pictograms can be particularly beneficial for users with low literacy.

To make pictograms more effective, pharmaceutical pictograms should be visible and easy to interpret, make direct connections to familiar things, be concrete [8], and be semantically close [9]. Semantic closeness can improve interpretations of pictograms by making them more accessible and relatable [9]. Furthermore, the picture superiority effect [10] states that pictures are more likely to enhance memory than words through top-down processing. Top-down processing theorizes how individuals use their general knowledge to understand new information. Pictures are commonly used amongst individuals; therefore, top-down processing should allow them to better understand what is being depicted in pictures. As a result, pictures are used in many contexts as memory aids.

The purpose of this study was to examine if real images that depict instructions and warnings lead to better comprehension of what is being instructed to patients than pictograms. Participants were recruited from Amazon Mechanical Turk (mTurk) to complete an online survey in which they interpret the meaning of a pictogram or picture that depicts a medical instruction or warning that would be found on a pharmaceutical label. After participants provided their interpretation of the stimuli, the intended meanings of the pictograms or pictures were provided, and participants were asked to rate the stimuli's ability to capture the intended meaning. It was hypothesized that participants would be more accurate in their interpretation of the intended meaning of the instruction or warning when the stimuli were pictures rather than pictograms.

2 Methods

2.1 Participants

Overall, 236 participants were recruited from mTurk to participate in this study. Participants were U.S. residents who were 18 years of age or older, self-identified as fluent in English, and had a 95% or higher approval rating on mTurk. The demographics for participants in each experimental condition are described below for each survey type.

Pictogram Survey. There were 120 participants who completed the pictogram survey, (M_{age} = 36.40, *SD* = 11.36). Seventy-six were female (63%) and 44 were male (37%). Ninety-one of the participants self-identified as White (76%), 10 as Hispanic (8%), 14 as Asian (12%), and five as Black or African American (4%). Sixty participants reported that their yearly income was over $50,000 a year (50%), with seven specifically reporting their income was over $100,000 a year (12%). Twenty-four participants had a high school diploma or equivalent (20%), 28 had an Associate's degree (23%), 55 had a Bachelor's degree (46%), and 13 had a Master's degree (11%).

Picture Survey. There were 116 participants who completed the picture survey, (M_{age} = 37.74, SD = 11.48). Sixty-four were female (55%) and 52 were male (45%). Ninety participants self-identified as White (78%), six as Hispanic (5%), seven as Asian (6%), eight as Black or African American (7%), and five as other (Native American, Pacific Islander, etc.; 4%). Fifty-two participants reported that their yearly income was over $50,000 (45%); out of those participants, eight reported a yearly income of over $100,000 (16%). Seventeen participants had a high school diploma or equivalent (15%), 16 had some four-year college (14%), 19 had an Associate's degree (16%), 48 had a Bachelor's degree (41%), 10 had a Master's degree (9%), and six had a Ph.D. or M.D (5%).

2.2 Design

The study utilized a between-subjects design, with survey type (Pictogram vs. Picture) as the independent variable. The dependent variables were the accuracy scores in interpreting the stimuli and rating scores for the "goodness" of the stimuli. Accuracy scores were determined in two ways. First, responses were classified as correct, partially correct or incorrect. Second, a numeric value was assigned to the answer given by the participants based on their accuracy in generating the intended meaning of the picture or pictogram. Rating scores reflected how well the picture or pictogram aligned with its intended meaning once participants were told its meaning.

2.3 Materials

Pictogram Stimuli. The pictograms used in the study were extracted from the U.S. Pharmacopeial Convention (USPC). The USPC is "a scientific nonprofit organization that sets standards for the identity, strength, quality, and purity of medicines, food ingredients, and dietary supplements manufactured, distributed and consumed worldwide" [5]. Enforced by the FDA, the USPC creates standard pharmaceutical pictograms that companies can use on their medication labels in order to convey their medication instructions. Not all companies utilize the USPC's pictograms, as they are not mandated to do so. However, if companies choose to include pictograms, they must select the pictograms from the selection offered through the USPC.

Picture Stimuli. The pictures used in the study were gathered from Google images or taken by experimenters. Picture stimuli were manipulated in order to be as close as possible to their pictogram counterpart (see example below in Fig. 1).

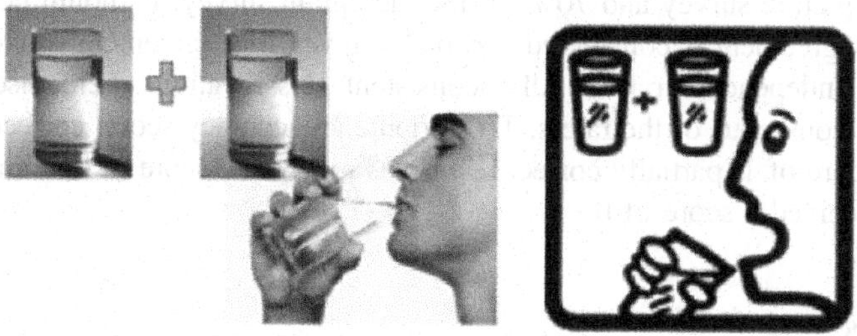

Fig. 1. An example of a picture and pictogram stimuli portraying "drink additional water."

Surveys. Two versions of an online survey were constructed in Qualtrics, an online survey platform. Each survey consisted of 3 blocks of questions. The first block included open-ended questions that asked, "What does the following image mean to you?" and was presented with a stimulus (either a pictogram or picture, depending on the survey type). Participants responded by typing answers into a response box. The second block consisted of rating questions. The rating questions asked participants to rate from 1 to 5, with 1 being "strongly disagree" and 5 being "strongly agree," how well the stimuli (i.e., pictogram or picture) aligned with its intended meaning. Each question was presented one at a time in randomized order within the block. The last block consisted of demographic questions. On average, it took participants 30 min to complete each survey. Data collection was completed in one day.

2.4 Data Coding

In order to compute the accuracy of the participants' responses to the stimuli, a content analysis was performed on the open-ended responses. Participants' responses were grouped based on similarities in semantic meaning. These groups of responses were then classified as being correct, partially correct, or incorrect. Whether a response was correct, partially correct, or incorrect was determined by an agreement across eight independent raters. For example, for the stimuli depicting: "if this medication makes you dizzy, do not drive," correct responses included, "medication may make you dizzy, do not operate motor vehicles after taking" and "do not drive if this medication makes you dizzy." Examples of partially correct responses for this stimulus included: "do not operate heavy machinery," "do not drive," "potential dizziness," or "may cause dizziness." These responses were considered partially accurate because only one aspect of the intended meaning of the stimuli was stated. As another example, for the stimuli depicting, "take with additional water," correct responses included: "drink two glasses of water with medication" and "take with plenty of water." Responses that stated, "take with water" were considered partially correct because these responses do not indicate drinking more or "plenty" of water (which the raters defined as drinking more than one glass of water).

Interrater reliability was determined by the percentage of agreement amongst all raters in deciding whether participants' responses to each stimulus was correct, partially correct, or incorrect. The percent of questions with agreed coding from all raters was 79% for the picture survey and 70% for the pictogram survey. It should be noted that this level of agreement is considered acceptable given that agreement was determined across eight independent raters. All inconsistent classifications were discussed and classified by consensus of the raters. To compute an accuracy score, correct responses received a score of 1, partially correct responses received a score of 0.5, and incorrect responses received a score of 0.

3 Results

3.1 Accuracy

Accuracy was analyzed in two ways: one based on the frequency of correct, partially correct, and incorrect classifications through a chi-square analysis, and one based on an accuracy score through t-tests.

For the frequency analysis, a chi-square test was performed on the 26 stimuli that shared the same meaning between the picture and pictogram surveys to see if the frequency of response accuracy classification differed between the two surveys. Results showed that there were significant differences in response categorization for 18 stimuli,

Table 1. The significant difference between pictures and pictograms sharing the same meaning. C = correct; PC = partially correct; M_{score} = mean accuracy score

Stimulus # and Meaning	Pictogram	Picture	Test Statistics
#2 Avoid Salt	 C = 80.49% PC = 12.19% $M_{score} = 0.53$	 C = 18.33% PC = 73.33% $M_{score} = 0.55$	X^2 (2, $N = 243$) = 100.77, $p < .001$ $t(241) = 0.70$, p = .484
#3 Do not crush, break, or open capsule	 C = 83.74% PC = 5.69% $M_{score} = 0.87$	 C = 69.17% PC = 14.17% $M_{score} = 0.76$	X^2 (2, $N = 243$) = 7.77, $p = .021$ $t(241) = -2.28$, p = .023
#4 This medicine may make you dizzy, do not drive	 C = 60.16% PC = 37.40% $M_{score} = 0.79$	 C = 19.17% PC = 73.33% $M_{score} = 0.56$	X^2 (2, $N = 243$) = 42.95, $p < .001$ $t(241) = -6.84$, p < .001
#5 Do not share with others	 C = 39.84% PC = 30.89% $M_{score} = 0.55$	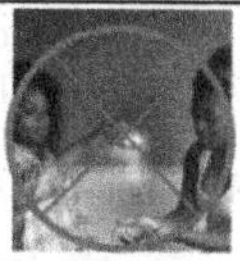 C = 40.00% PC = 2.50% $M_{score} = 0.41$	X^2 (2, N = 243) = 40.23, $p < .001$ $t(241) = -2.42$, p < .016
#7 Take in the mornings	 C = 68.30% PC = 25.20% $M_{score} = 0.81$	 C = 84.17% PC = 0.00% $M_{score} = 0.84$	X^2 (2, $N = 243$) = 37.01, $p < .001$ $t(241) = 0.76$, p = .449

(*continued*)

#9 Take by mouth	 C = 65.04% PC = 24.39% M_{score} = 0.77	 C = 45.00% PC = 34.17% M_{score} = 0.62	X^2 (2, N = 243) = 10.50, p = .005 t(241) = -3.24, p = .001
#10 Check pulse	 C = 85.36% PC = 1.63% M_{score} = 0.86	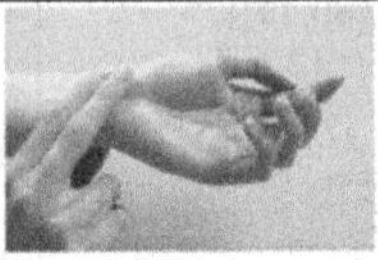 C = 70.00% PC = 10.00% M_{score} = 0.75	X^2 (2, N = 243) = 11.04, p = .004 t(241) = -2.33, p = .021
#13 Store medication in the refrigerator	 C = 91.06% PC = 0.81% M_{score} = 0.91	 C = 74.17% PC = 0.00% M_{score} = 0.74	X^2 (2, N = 243) = 14.53, p = .001 t(241) = -3.68, p < .001
#15 Take three times a day with food	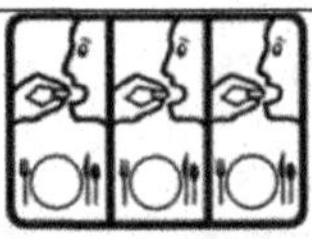 C = 69.92% PC = 24.39% M_{score} = 0.82	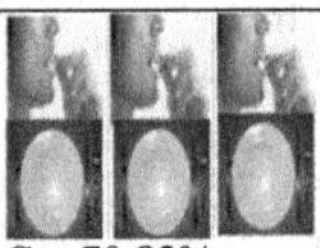 C = 70.83% PC = 15.00% M_{score} = 0.78	X^2 (2, N = 243) = 7.14, p = .028 t(241) = -2.28, p < .023
#16 Take two hours after eating	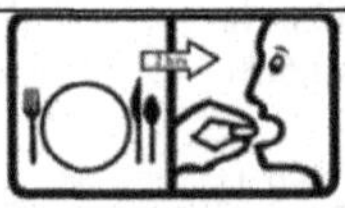 C = 92.68% PC = 2.44% M_{score} = 0.94	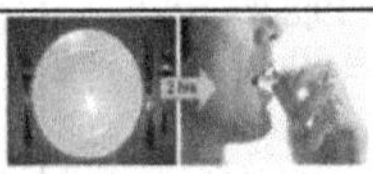 C = 85.45% PC = 0.91% M_{score} = 0.79	X^2 (2, N = 243) = 6.07, p = .048 t(241) = -0.89, p = .375

(*continued*)

#17 Take an hour before eating	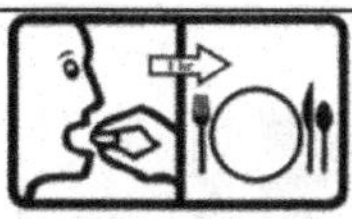 C = 80.49% PC = 7.32% M_{score} = 0.84	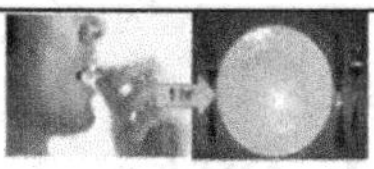 C = 67.50% PC = 2.50% M_{score} = 0.69	X^2 (2, N = 243) = 13.41, p = .001 t(241) = -2.98, p = .003
#18 Do not give to children	 C = 75.61% PC = 17.89% M_{score}= 0.85	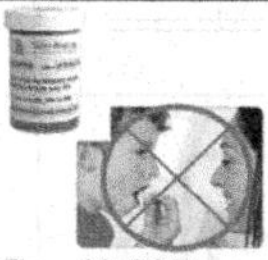 C = 60.83% PC = 21.67% M_{score} = 0.78	X^2 (2, N = 243) = 8.54, p = .014 t(241) = -1.62, p =.106
#19 Do not refrig-erate	 C = 85.36% PC = 4.88% M_{score} = 0.88	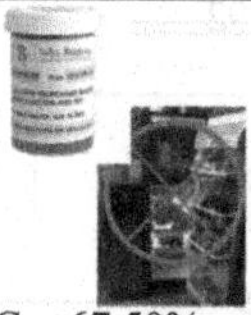 C = 67.50% PC = 3.33% M_{score} = 0.69	X^2 (2, N = 243) = 14.72, p = .001 t(241) = -3.75, p < .001
#20 Dissolve in water	 C = 82.93% PC = 0.00% M_{score} = 0.83	 C = 66.67% PC = 0.00% M_{score} = 0.67	X^2 (2, N = 243) = 8.54, p = .003 t(241) = -2.96, p = .003
#21 This medica-tion may cause drowsiness	 C = 85.36% PC = 9.76% M_{score} = 0.88	 C = 80.83% PC = 0.83% M_{score} = 0.81	X^2 (2, N = 243) = 18.73, p < .001 t(241) = -1.46, p = .147

(*continued*)

#22 Do not give to babies	 C = 67.48% PC = 26.83% M_{score} = 0.81	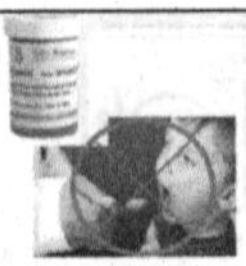 C = 67.50% PC = 22.50% M_{score} = 0.72	X^2 (2, N = 243) = 1.90, p = .386 t(241) = -2.09, p = .038
#23 Do not take before bed	 C = 91.87% PC = 0.00% M_{score} = 0.92	 C = 82.50% PC = 2.50% M_{score} = 0.84	X^2 (2, N = 243) = 6.17, p = .046 t(241) = -1.97, p = .050
#24 Avoid exposure to sunlight	 C = 35.77% PC = 56.10% M_{score} = 0.48	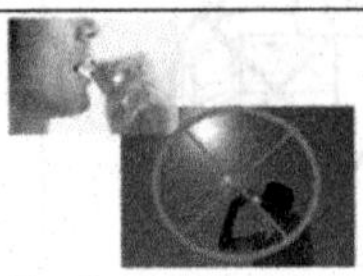 C = 29.17% PC = 10.83% M_{score} = 0.35	X^2 (2, N = 243) = 86.12, p < .001 t(241) = -3.00, p = .003
#26 Do not take with food	 C = 70.73% PC = 22.76% M_{score} = 0.82	 C = 56.67% PC = 29.17% M_{score} = 0.71	X^2 (2, N = 243) = 6.31, p = .043 t(241) = -2.53, p = .012

which are shown in Table 1. For the pictogram survey, the percent of correct responses was 74.33%, with 16.34% classified as being partially correct and 9.33% as incorrect. For the picture survey, the average correct response was 60.81%, with 16.67% classified as partially correct and 22.52% classified as incorrect. Thus, participants were more accurate with interpreting the stimuli in the pictogram survey than the picture survey.

Accuracy scores for the pictogram and picture stimuli were further compared using independent-sample t-tests (see last column in Table 1 for accuracy scores). The overall accuracy score was 0.80 for the pictogram survey and 0.69 for the picture survey. The accuracy score for 14 stimuli were significantly different based on the survey type.

Pictograms had higher accuracy scores than pictures for 12 of the 14 stimuli (86%); pictures had a higher accuracy than pictograms for 2 of the 14 stimuli (14%).

The results from the chi-square and t-test analyses converged. The chi-square tests were more sensitive and found more differences in stimuli responses between the survey types (pictogram vs. picture) than the *t*-tests revealed.

3.2 Rating Scores

One-way analyses of variance (ANOVAs) were performed for each stimulus to determine participants' ratings of how well the pictures or pictograms aligned with their intended meaning, see Table 2. The independent variable was the stimuli type (pictogram or picture) and the dependent variable was the rating score that each stimulus received. Overall, participants rated the stimuli as being good, with the average rating for pictograms being 4.57 out of 5, and the average rating for pictures being 4.54 out of 5. Nine stimuli showed significant differences in participants' rating scores as a function of the survey type. The pictogram was rated to be better than the picture in 8 out of 9 cases (89%).

Table 2. The rating scores for the effectiveness of the picture and pictogram stimuli performed through an ANOVA test.

Stimulus # and meaning	Mean rating	F-statistic
#5 Do not share with others	Pictogram $M = 4.30$ Picture $M = 3.38$	$F(1, 237) = 25.61, p < .001$
#13 Store medication in the refrigerator	Pictogram $M = 4.75$ Picture $M = 4.43$	$F(1, 238) = 7.49, p = .006$
#17 Take an hour before eating	Pictogram $M = 4.67$ Picture $M = 4.37$	$F(1, 239) = 6.29, p = .013$
#18 Do not give to children	Pictogram $M = 4.66$ Picture $M = 4.43$	$F(1, 237) = 3.88, p = .050$
#20 Dissolve in water	Pictogram $M = 4.63$ Picture $M = 4.29$	$F(1, 238) = 6.77, p = .010$
#22 Do not give to babies	Pictogram $M = 4.61$ Picture $M = 4.19$	$F(1, 239) = 11.59, p = .001$
#23 Do not take before bed	Pictogram $M = 4.63$ Picture $M = 4.27$	$F(1, 238) = 7.33, p = .007$
#24 Avoid exposure to sunlight	Pictogram $M = 4.22$ Picture $M = 3.33$	$F(1, 238) = 30.20, p < .001$
#26 Do not take food	Pictogram $M = 4.66$ Picture $M = 4.38$	$F(1, 237) = 4.83, p = .029$

4 Discussion

The purpose of this study was to determine if real images would provide users with a better understanding of medication instructions and warnings than pictograms. Contrary to the hypothesis, participants were better at interpreting the meaning of pictograms compared to pictures. However, participants' comprehension for pictogram stimuli were still low, with only 74% of responses being classified as correct interpretations.

A potential reason why pictures were not more understandable than the pictograms could be that when viewing the pictures, participants fixated on the specific details presented in the pictures which led them to more specific, literal interpretations. This was detrimental as some of the pictures used in the study contained additional, irrelevant details that may have served as distractors. For example, for the picture stimuli, "avoid exposure to sunlight," a red "x" covers the picture of a man dressed in active wear, drinking water in the sun. Due to the picture depicting a man wearing active wear outdoors, many participants focused on this irrelevant cue when interpreting the meaning of the picture. This was seen in participants' responses, with some being, "do not drink fluids or be outside when taking medication", "do not exercise after taking this," and "do not take with water." Similar misinterpretations occurred with the picture stimuli, "do not share with others," as the glare from the sun made the medication bottle and pills used in the stimuli hard to recognize. As a result, some of the responses received were "light prohibited", "do not apply it to your skin," "do not play with fire," and "do not touch hot liquid." Thus, due to the lack of clarity in the picture stimuli selection, the benefits of the pictures were reduced. Future research should focus on developing better, more simplistic picture stimuli that do not have any distractor. In addition, future research could investigate whether individuals would understand pictures better than pictograms if the pictures were generated to depict the intended meaning rather than be replications of pictograms. These improvements to the picture stimuli could potentially render higher comprehension levels for pictures.

Acknowledgements. Gratitude is extended to graduate students in the Center for Usability in Design and Accessibility (CUDA) lab for assisting with the qualitative data coding. Also, the National Institute of Health (NIH) (grant numbers: 5UL1GM118979; 5TL4GM118980; 5RL5GM118978), for providing the funding needed to carry out this research.

References

1. Health and Medicine Division (2015). http://www.nationalacademies.org/hmd/Reports/2006/Preventing-Medication-Errors-Quality-Chasm-Series.aspx. Accessed 10 Apr 2018
2. McGinley, P., Rashidee, A., Hart, J., Chen, J., Kumar, S.: Data trends: high-alert medications: error prevalence and severity (2009). https://www.psqh.com/analysis/data-trends-july-august-2009/. 10 Apr 2018
3. Brown, M.T., Bussell, J.K.: Medication adherence: WHO cares? (2011). https://www.ncbi.nlm.nih.gov/pmc/articles/PMC3068890/. Accessed 23 Oct 23 2017

4. Jeetu, G., Girish, T.: Prescription drug labeling medication errors: a big deal for pharmacists (2010). https://www.ncbi.nlm.nih.gov/pmc/articles/PMC3035877/. Accessed 27 Sept 2018
5. Work at the United States Pharmacopeial Convention. (n.d.). https://www.careerbuilder.com/company/the-united-states-pharmacopeial-convention/C8S05668H22YDHCWJ0Y. Accessed 10 April 2018
6. Herron, M., Vu, K.L.: The value of including a picture of the medicine on pharmaceutical labels. Proc. Hum. Factors Ergon. Soc. Annu. Meet. **57**(1), 688–692 (2013). https://doi.org/10.1177/1541931213571149
7. Davis, T.C.: Low literacy impairs comprehension of prescription drug warning labels (2006). https://www.ncbi.nlm.nih.gov/pmc/articles/PMC1831578/. Accessed 10 Apr 2018
8. Chan, A.H., Chan, K.W.: Effects of prospective-user factors and sign design features on guessability of pharmaceutical pictograms. Patient Educ. Counsel. **90**(2), 268–275 (2013). https://doi.org/10.1016/j.pec.2012.10.009
9. Dowse, R., Ehlers, M.: Pictograms for conveying medicine instructions: comprehension in various South African language groups (2004). https://journals.co.za/content/sajsci/100/11-12/EJC96165. Accessed 17 Oct 2017
10. Stenberg, G.: Conceptual and perceptual factors in the picture superiority effect. Eur. J. Cognit. Psychol. **18**(6), 813–847 (2006). https://doi.org/10.1080/09541440500412361

Chinese Pinyin Input Method in Smartphone Era: A Literature Review Study

Guanlong Li and Yueqing Li(✉)

Department of Industrial Engineering, Lamar University,
Beaumont, TX 77705, USA
{gli,yli6}@lamar.edu

Abstract. This study conducted a literature review on the latest academic publications concerning smartphone-based Pinyin input method. The objective is to explore what academic endeavors have been made to address the key concerns of today's Pinyin input method. Results show that much work has been concentrated in advancing Pinyin-to-character conversion, by forging a more powerful algorithm more capable of tolerating, detecting and correcting error. Besides, a serial of interface layout optimization attempts have been tried. Based on the analysis of the review result, comments of the existing work and suggestions for future research direct are proposed.

Keywords: Pinyin input method · Usability · Interaction design · Layout · User behavior

1 Introduction

1.1 Background

If there is a behavior most Chinese today would do in their daily life, that would definitely be the use of smartphone. Indeed, according to Statista, in 2017 China has around 663.37 million smartphone users, a number greater than the whole population of USA and Brazil combined. The widespread application of smartphone has brought the whole Chinese nation into an unprecedented social media era when interpersonal communication has been dramatically facilitated regardless of space and time limits.

To support such frequent and effective communication, many smartphone-based social media tools are playing key roles. Take the most successful one: WeChat as an example, it is a mobile instant messaging (text and voice) communication service invented by Tencent (腾讯) in 2011. WeChat bridges the communication between millions of users by means of text messages (SMS), hold-to-talk voice messages, group chat, video conferencing, free voice call, location sharing, contact sharing and Moments (photo and video sharing). Among these communication methods, text message is undoubtedly the most widely and frequently used function. Consequently, the need for a convenient way to input Chinese text messages becomes increasingly important [1].

S. Yamamoto and H. Mori (Eds.): HCII 2019, LNCS 11569, pp. 34–43, 2019.
https://doi.org/10.1007/978-3-030-22660-2_3

1.2 Pinyin Input Method

To edit a piece of Chinese message on a smartphone, Chinese input methods are always needed. Basically they are categorized into two types, as seen in Table 1:

1. Pronunciation based input method; 2. Structure based input method.

Table 1. Examples of some famous Chinese input methods

Pronunciation based	Structure based
Pinyin 拼音	Wubizixing 五笔字型
Shuangpin 双拼	Wubihua 五笔划
Jianpin 简拼	Cangjie 仓颉
Bopomofo 注音	Sucheng 速成
	Sanjiao 三角
	Dayi 大易

Among various Chinese input methods, Pinyin input method is apparently the most popular means. In 2014, 76.7% of Chinese smartphone users choose Pinyin input method [2]. Pinyin (Pinyin Romanization (https://en.wikipedia.org/wiki/Romanization)) is a system that transcribes the pronunciation of Chinese characters into a string of Roman letters [3]. The mechanism of Pinyin input method is that by typing Pinyin, computer will automatically recognize and match all possible corresponding Chinese characters, phrases, and sentences for user. For example, one wants to input "兽医" (veterinary) on a smartphone. First, he needs to type the Pinyin of 兽医, which is "shouyi". Then smartphone will list a cluster of candidate Chinese characters and phrases that are pronounced as "shouyi", such as:

手艺 craftsmanship; 受益 benefit; 收益 earnings; 兽医 veterinary; 寿衣 shroud.

Finally, a user completes the texting by just tapping characters "兽医" (see Fig. 1).

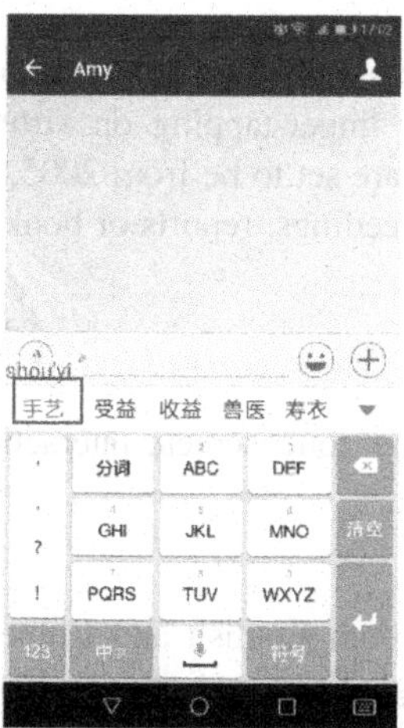

Fig. 1. An example of how to input Chinese character with Pinyin input method (T9 Pinyin keyboard).

1.3 Research Question

Pinyin input method was born to confront with a sheer challenge: Modern Chinese has merely less than 500 pinyin syllables that disproportionately represent over 6,000 commonly-used Chinese characters, which leads to serious ambiguities for pinyin-to-character mapping [4]. Therefore, lasting efforts are still required both from academia and industry to continuously improve the efficiency of pinyin-to-character conversion.

The advent and widespread of touchscreen technology revolutionarily change human behavior of texting. While typing on a physical QWERTY keyboard is one thing, typing with a virtual keyboard on a smartphone touchscreen is another story. Instead of using all ten fingers, tapping on a soft keyboard only requires one or two thumbs. In this sense, people may optimistically believe that this radical change facilitates user's typing behavior since no touch typing would ever be needed. However, scientific study has found that the speed and accuracy of Pinyin typing would be significantly reduced when using a smartphone virtual keyboards due to the difficult nature of tapping small targets on virtual keys [5]. Hence, more rigorous research is needed to seek optimal layout design of a Pinyin input method interface.

The fact that smartphone-based Pinyin input method use is so widespread in today's China and no systematic work has been done to review related academic research makes the present research extremely important and motivated. By reviewing the latest academic works, the present study tries to explore what academic efforts have been spent:

1. To improve the functionality and usability of Pinyin input method?
2. To better understand user behaviors during the interaction with Pinyin input method interface?

As a result, a summary in forms of tables will be proposed as a guideline for future Pinyin input method development.

2 Methodology

2.1 Literature Criteria

Academic studies that discussed smartphone-based Chinese Pinyin input method (The input of Pinyin is achieved by finger-tapping on virtual keyboard based on touchscreen). Candidate publications are set to be from 2005, in forms of either peer review journal articles, conference proceedings, reports or books. They can be both written in Chinese and English.

2.2 Keywords

Pinyin input method, smartphone, touchscreen, interaction design, layout, usability.

3 Results

Initially, thirty publications in both English and Chinese have been found from the following online database: Google Scholar, Springer, ELSEVIER, IEEE Xplore Digital Library and Research Gate. After carefully sieving, 13 articles have been eventually selected and a summary covering their basic information such as author, year, problem, solution, result has been established in the form of Table 2, as shown below.

Table 2. Summary of literature review

Authors	Functions	Problems/Defects	Solutions	Results
Zheng, Li, and Sun [6]	Mistyping detection and correction	Current IME is inefficient to recognize and correct typos	A novel error-tolerant IME "CHIME", (CHinese Input Method with Errors) Mechanism: Finding Similar Pinyins -> Ranking Similar Pinyins - > | Pinyin-to-Chinese Conversion with Typos	*Metric* | *CHIME* | *Sougou* *DectER* | *37.40%* | *70.62%* *CorrER* | *52.43%* | *91.19%* *ConvER* | *53.56%* | *91.75%*
Wu, Kato, and Yang [7]	Frequent typos advice function	Indication function needed to avoid frequent spelling error	Advice prompt on frequent spelling error 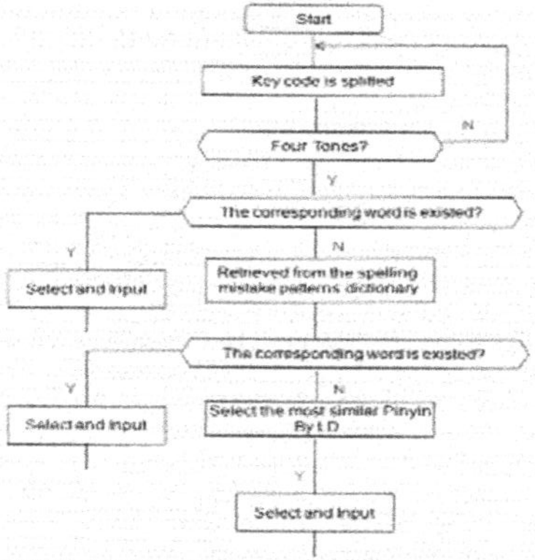 Start Key code is splitted Four Tones? N Y The corresponding word is existed? Y Select and input N Retrieved from the spelling mistake patterns dictionary The corresponding word is existed? Y Select and input N Select the most similar Pinyin By LD Y Select and input	Prompt advice on patterns of frequent spelling errors

(*continued*)

Table 2. *(continued)*

<table>
<tr><th>Authors</th><th>Functions</th><th>Problems/Defects</th><th>Solutions</th><th>Results</th></tr>
<tr><td>Jia and Zhao [4]</td><td>(1) Pinyin-to-character conversion
(2) Typo correction</td><td>Inefficient to correct a typo and generate the expected sentence, which often requires extra user's corrective effort and thereby leads to a poor user experience.</td><td>Jointed graphic model (Markov Hidden Model and K-shortest paths)</td><td>The new model outperformed both academic systems and existing commercial IME in reducing conversion error</td></tr>
<tr><td>Yang, Zhao, Wang, and Lu [8]</td><td>Pinyin-to-character conversion</td><td>Serious ambiguity of Pinyin-to-character corresponding</td><td>A monotone phrasal SMT based approach</td><td>The new Machine Translation (SMT) approach outperformed in whole sentence accuracy and time cost
<table>
<tr><th>Model \ Dataset</th><th>10K</th><th>100K</th><th>1M</th></tr>
<tr><td>ME</td><td>0.075</td><td>0.169</td><td>0.302</td></tr>
<tr><td>SMT</td><td>0.402</td><td>0.429</td><td>0.454</td></tr>
</table></td></tr>
<tr><td>Chen, Zhao, and Wang [9]</td><td>Predictive performance</td><td>Neural network language models (NNLMs) fails to support real-time human machine interaction due to its heavy computational cost nature</td><td>Recalculating the probabilities of n-grams in the BNLMs with NNLMs:
(1) A BNLM and a NNLM are respectively trained on the same corpus.
(2) Extract all the n-gram from the BNLM and calculate the probability of them with the NNLM
(3) Rewrite the BNLM with the probability computed by NNLM
4) Re-normalize the probabilities of BNLM</td><td>New method effectively improved the predictive performance of pinyin IME in terms of hit rate of the first candidate sentence (HRF) with no extra time cost
<table>
<tr><th>Test</th><th>Models</th><th>HRF</th><th>HRF10</th><th>CA</th></tr>
<tr><td>10K</td><td>Baseline</td><td>74.72</td><td>89.92</td><td>96.80</td></tr>
<tr><td>10K</td><td>Our model</td><td>75.71</td><td>90.14</td><td>96.80</td></tr>
<tr><td>400K</td><td>Baseline</td><td>67.02</td><td>86.08</td><td>95.46</td></tr>
<tr><td>400K</td><td>Our model</td><td>67.68</td><td>86.45</td><td>95.59</td></tr>
</table></td></tr>
<tr><td>Yang, Zhao, Wang, and Lu [8]</td><td>Pinyin spelling checking</td><td>Ineffective Pinyin-to-Hanzi (character) translation and recommendation function which leads to a wrong decoding of a Pinyin</td><td>A hybrid model (mini-path + LM) incorporating Minimized-Path Segmentation and Statistical Criteria</td><td>F-score (F = 2RP/(R + P)), a common measure of spelling checking system's performance) achieved a 12% improvement over the baseline, it also performed much better in Precision and Recall</td></tr>
</table>

(continued)

Table 2. *(continued)*

<table>
<tr><th>Authors</th><th>Functions</th><th>Problems/Defects</th><th>Solutions</th><th>Results</th></tr>
<tr><td>Zhang [10]</td><td>Pinyin-to-character conversion</td><td>Big space for conversion efficiency to be improved.</td><td>(1) New approach based on large scale hybrid language model and word lattice decoding algorithm
(2) Integrating dynamic information such as recent context, recent user profile, automatic prediction algorithm and machine learning technology</td><td>Accuracy of conversion significantly improved<table><tr><th></th><th>First character accuracy</th><th>First page accuracy</th></tr><tr><td>New model</td><td>92.1%</td><td>96.2%</td></tr><tr><td>MS Pinyin</td><td>87.6%</td><td>94.9%</td></tr></table></td></tr>
<tr><td>Suzuki and Gao [11]</td><td>Online spelling correction</td><td>Existing input methods fail to identify and correct minor typos to the desired target Chinese characters</td><td>(1) Substring-based spelling correction using a log-linear model
(2) A unified model enabling character conversion with spelling correction (Noisy channel model)</td><td>The proposed method outperforms all these baselines to reduce the CorrER to 7.12:
A 35% reduction VS no correction baseline,
A 20% reduction VS Zheng's design
A 10% reduction VS noisy channel baseline</td></tr>
<tr><td>Authors</td><td>Interface designs</td><td>Problems/Defects</td><td>Solutions</td><td>Results</td></tr>
<tr><td>Liu, Chen, Wang, Zhang and Li [12]</td><td>Soft keyboard</td><td>Optimal layout for soft keyboard designed for Pinyin input has not been explored.</td><td>A pie-menu augmented soft keyboard</td><td>(1) Slower text entry rate
(2) Slightly fewer errors
(3) Users better remember the layout of pie menu</td></tr>
<tr><td>Liu, Ding, and Liu [13]</td><td>Virtual keyboard</td><td>To test the usability of new Pinyin virtual keyboard VKB</td><td>VKB: a consonant keyboard with a vowel keyboard to complete a pinyin</td><td>(1) Lower error rate
(2) Significantly slower text entry rate
(3) Significantly fewer the keystrokes per character (KSPC)</td></tr>
</table>

(continued)

Table 2. *(continued)*

Authors	Interface designs	Problems/Defects	Solutions	Results
Wu and Xi [14]	Interface layout	Seek optimal layout design user visual search behavior	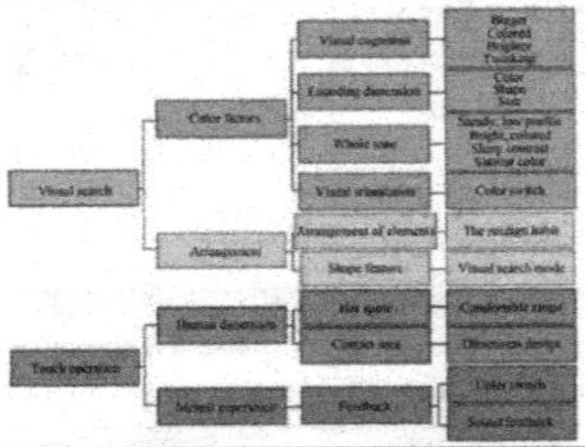	General rules regarding three factors: dimension design, color features and arrangement of elements have been established for future HCI development.
Zhou, Rau and Salvendy 2014 [3]	Interface layout design	(1) The distance between candidate characters area and the keyboards area (d1) is too short (2) The distance between candidate characters area the input field area (d2) is too long	(1) Recommend 7 in. and 9.7 in. display size (2) Enlarge the Pinyin script area to be sufficiently big 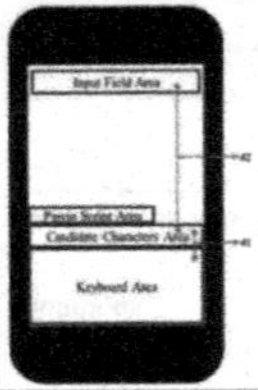	(1) Participant successfully completed more tasks on 9.7 in. display size than on 3.5 in (2) Participants perceived the 9.7 in. display size much more user-friendly than the 3.5 in
Bi, Smith, and Zhai [15]	Visual keyboard layout	Optimal keyboard layout design for Pinyin input is needed	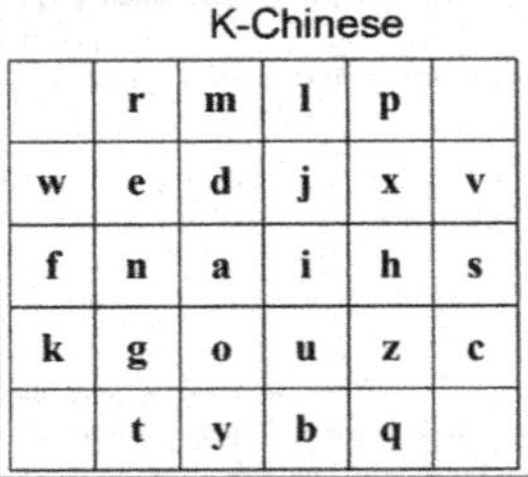 K-Chinese r m l p w e d j x v f n a i h s k g o u z c t y b q	(1) Reduces the average movement distance from QWERTY's 3.85 keys to K5's 1.5 keys (2) Significantly reduced completion time and Fitt's time (3) Improves the input speed by 24% over QWERTY

4 Discussion

For convenience, two tables have been developed to separately discuss the literature review result Table 3 in two aspects: functional characteristics and design characteristics.

Table 3. Discussion regarding functions

	Functions
Comments	Pinyin-to-character conversion has drawn extensive attention from academia and substantial work has been done to enhance its efficiency by: Enhancing typos detection and correction ability Advancing error-tolerant in-built model Much more theoretical and practical endeavors are needed to further improve the existing Pinyin IME's prediction function, which matches the conclusion from the iiMedia Research Report that prediction is among the top usability concerns from Pinyin IME user's perspective [16]
Suggestions	The prediction function needs to evolve to be more intelligent. Thereby recommendations of developing following abilities are given: Predict characters from complete Pinyin acronyms: For example, by typing 'bjsdgjjc' instead of its full Pinyin 'bei jing shou du guo ji ji chang', Pinyin IME will be able to match the correct characters "北京首都国际机场" (Beijing Capital International Airport). This ability facilitates Pinyin typing of long proper noun (e.g. place name, people name and terminology) and common Chinese phrase Further, predict characters from incomplete Pinyin acronyms: For example, after typing 'gysqs', short for 'gong yu shan qi shi', corresponding "工欲善其事" (To Do A Good Job), Pinyin IME will automatically predict the rest part of this idiom "必先利其器" (One has to first sharpen his tool) without manual typing of its corresponding Pinyin. This function would greatly save user' effort in typing multi-phrase Chinese idiom and poetry Intelligent prediction of future characters based on conversation context: For example, given the first part of sentence "我还会做" (I can also cook), Pinyin IME could envision that the rest of the characters should relate to some kind of food, in this sense, when 'cf' is further typed, only character candidates meaning food will be listed, such as "炒饭" (full Pinyin as chao fan) Actually, the idea of context-based character prediction is the most innovative idea proposed by the present study. It is a fresh and inspiring example of machine learning application on human texting behavior. This ability enables Pinyin IME to understand human's language, thus being able to predict what human want to say next, and finally assist human by providing more precise range of candidate characters In addition, corpus needs to be further enriched by: Responsively adopting newly-born phrases such as popular Chinese Internet slang Memorizing characters based on recently-typed Pinyin

4.1 User Behavior

Analyzing user behavior provides novel perspective and is thus helpful in improving user experience and performance of Pinyin input method [17]. The result in this study reveals that users desire a Pinyin input method that could, to maximum extent, lesson human's physical (typing, visual searching) and mental (recognizing) loads and if better, could further understand the meaning and the logic of human language and thus be able to intelligently assist human in texting (Table 4).

Table 4. Discussion regarding interface design

	Interface design
Comments	Previous research primarily focuses on layout optimization of virtual keyboard by means of either rearranging keyboard elements or designing innovative new keyboard with irregular shape
Suggestions	More interface-related issues are pending to be explored such as: further simplifying layout, size-adjustable keyboard, color effect on user visual perception and other novel typing methods such as gesture typing and eye typing

5 Conclusion

The present study conducted a literature review regarding smartphone-based Pinyin input method. While thirty publications have been found, thirteen of them was eventually selected and summarized. As a result, it is found that much efforts have been implemented to enhance Pinyin-to-character conversion by integrating more powerful algorithm addressing issues over error detection and correction. For design issue, lots of work has been done to optimize visual keyboard layout to improve typing speed and accuracy. In the last, suggestions for future work such as strengthening prediction function, introducing size-adjustable keyboard and innovative typing methods have been proposed.

References

1. Ge, Y., Guo, F., Zhen, L., Chen, Q.: Online Chinese character recognition system with handwritten Pinyin input. In: Document Analysis and Recognition, Washington DC (2005)
2. China Mobile Input Method Research Report (2014)
3. Zhou, J., Rau, P.-L.P., Salvendy, G.: Older adults' text entry on smartphones and tablets: investigating effects of display size and input method on acceptance and performance. Int. J. Hum.-Comput. Interact. **30**(9), 727–739 (2014)
4. Jia, Z., Zhao, H.: A joint graph model for Pinyin-to-Chinese conversion with typo correction. In: Proceedings of the 52nd Annual Meeting of the Association for Computational Linguistics, Baltimore (2014)

5. Po, L.M., et al.: Dynamic candidate keypad for stroke-based Chinese input method on touchscreen devices. In: 2011 IEEE Symposium on Computers & Informatics (ISCI), Kuala Lumpur (2011)
6. Zheng, Y., Li, C., Sun, M.: CHIME: an efficient error-tolerant Chinese Pinyin input method. In: International Joint Conference on Artificial Intelligence, Barcelona (2011)
7. Wu, J., Kato, T., Yang, D.: Development of a smart classroom for Chinese language learning using a smartphone & tablet. Educ. Technol. Res. **36**(1–2), 153–165 (2013)
8. Yang, S., Zhao, H., Wang, X., Lu, B.: Spell checking for Chinese. In: The International Conference on Language Resources and Evaluation, Istanbul (2012)
9. Chen, S., Zhao, H., Wang, R.: Neural network language model for Chinese Pinyin input method engine. In: 29th Pacific Asia Conference on Language, Information and Computation, Shanghai (2015)
10. Zhang, S.: Solving to the Pinyin-to-Chinese-character conversion problem based on hybrid word lattice. Chin. J. Comput. **30**(7), 1145–1153 (2007)
11. Suzuki, H., Gao, J.: A unified approach to transliteration-based text input with online spelling correction. In: Proceedings of the 2012 Joint Conference on Empirical Methods in Natural Language Processing and Computational Natural Language Learning, Jeju Island, Korea (2012)
12. Liu, Y., Chen, X., Wang, L., Zhang, H., Li, S.: PinyinPie: a pie menu augmented soft keyboard for Chinese Pinyin input methods. In: Proceedings of the 14th International Conference on Human-Computer Interaction with Mobile Devices and Services, San Francisco (2012)
13. Liu, Y., Ding, K., Liu, N.: Immediate user performances with touch Chinese text entry solutions on handheld devices. In: Proceedings of the 11th International Conference on Human-Computer Interaction with Mobile Devices and Services, Bonn (2009)
14. Wu, X., Xi, T.: Study on design principle of touch screen with an example of Chinese-Pinyin 10 Key input method in iPhone. In: Rebelo, F., Soares, M. (eds.) Advances in Ergonomics in Design. AISC, vol. 485, pp. 639–650. Springer, Cham (2016). https://doi.org/10.1007/978-3-319-41983-1_58
15. Bi, X., Smith, B.A., Zhai, S.: Multilingual touchscreen keyboard design and optimization. Hum.-Comput. Interact. **27**(4), 352–382 (2012)
16. 2015-2016 China Mobile Phone Input Method Annual Research Report. http://iimedia.cn/1453087394023n2nii.pdf
17. Zheng, Y., Xie, L., Liu, Z., Sun, M., Zhang, Y., Ru, L.: Why press backspace? Understanding user input behaviors in Chinese Pinyin input method. In: Proceedings of the 49th Annual Meeting of the Association for Computational Linguistics: Short Papers, Portland (2011)

Research on Layout Design of Main Interface of Stadium Monitoring System Based on Gestalt Psychology

Biying Li and Ying Cao(✉)

Huazhong University of Science and Technology, Wuhan, People's Republic of China
150110363@qq.com

Abstract. The venue monitoring interface design has a large amount of information, and many features of the visual graphics classification area module. The interface layout design needs a suitable method for distinguishing and expressing between different functional partition modules. Gestalt is a graphic theory from psychology. From the psychological point of view, Gestalt psychology emphasizes the characteristics of the human visual system to see the overall organization of knowledge and simplification of things, and connects people's psychology and vision. Gestalt psychology helps designers to organize, simplify and unify the interface information structure as a whole, making the interface more user-friendly, and facilitating users to read key information and complete task requirements. Based on the interface design project of the stadium monitoring system, this paper starts from the four directions of the basic principles of Gestalt psychology, the similarity, similarity, closure and **simplicity**, and studies how to combine the visual perception law with the human-machine interface design. A rational way to create a more coordinated interface layout design ideas and methods that are easy for users to understand. Thereby, the main interface layout design of the actual project is carried out to verify the theoretical results.

Keywords: Gestalt psychology · Gestalt · Interface design

1 Introduction

1.1 Research Background

In the information environment, the interface is the carrier for information analysis and processing by users, and is the medium for transferring and exchanging information between people and machines. The interface becomes the initial level of user contact with the product, and the interface design is the outermost representation of the interaction design. Interface design is a kind of design extension and extension with visual perception design as the core. It is a design language with visual consciousness as its expression form. It has a certain influence on the user's initial perception and user experience.

S. Yamamoto and H. Mori (Eds.): HCII 2019, LNCS 11569, pp. 44–55, 2019.
https://doi.org/10.1007/978-3-030-22660-2_4

This paper is based on the interface design project of the stadium monitoring system, and analyzes the interface layout as the background. The venue monitoring interface has problems such as large amount of information and messy information. How to enable users to quickly recognize information and obtain demand information in a short period of time becomes a major problem affecting the user experience. Gestalt psychology is an important theory of cognitive psychology. It connects people's perception and visual perception and has a key influence in visual design. Therefore, starting with Gestalt psychology, the Gestalt principle can provide a theoretical basis for the layout of the interface design and design criteria that are more user-friendly.

1.2 Related Literature Review

Gestalt psychology is one of the main schools of modern Western psychology. The concept of "formatting tower quality" was first proposed by the Austrian philosopher Christian von Ehrenfels in the 1890 paper "On Gestalt Qualities". In 1912, German psychologists Marx Wertheimer, Kurt Koffka and Wolfgang Kohler published their paper "Experimental Studies of the Perception of Movement" to discuss their findings. This marked the rise of the school of Gestalt psychology, and Wertheimer, Kaufka and Kohler became the three founders [1].

Kurt Koffka introduced Gestalt psychology in detail in the book Principles of Gestalt Psychology. Through systematic analysis and analysis of Gestalt psychology principles, it laid a solid foundation for this study and became the strong support of the theoretical part of this article [2]. The German scholar Rudolf Arnheim's "Art and Visual Perception" first applied the theory of Gestalt psychology to the field of art vision. He believes that the process of perception is actually the physiological process of the cerebral cortex according to the organization principle (proximity, similarity, closure, directionality), transforming visual stimuli into an organized whole process [3]. In "Cognition and Design: Understanding UI Design Guidelines," Johnson Jeff talks about the relationship between Gestalt psychology principles and interactive interface design, and the important principles of Gestalt principles, pointing out the use of Gestalt principles to perceive interfaces. It allows us to understand things and events faster. Combining methodologies in the field of psychology and behavioral science can effectively improve the design level of products and services and enhance the user experience [4]. Wang Peng, Pan Guanghua and others wrote "The Gestalt of Experience: Gestalt Psychology", which systematically introduces the development process of the Gestalt School and summarizes its ideological viewpoints, theoretical systems and research methods. development trend. It is of great inspiration to apply the Gestalt principle to interface design in this paper. In "Human Interface: Interactive System Design", Jeff Ruskin proposed to introduce the principle of cognitive psychology into interface design, and rethink the interface design method from the aspects of interface unification, quantification and navigation [5].

1.3 Research Content and Architecture

The article is divided into four parts: The first part is the introduction, which discusses the research background, related literature review and research content, etc. The second part is an overview of Gestalt psychology, Gestalt psychology and interface design. The relationship and its basic principles are summarized, including the definition of Gestalt psychology, from the two parts of perception and perception, visual perception, analysis of Gestalt, the specific analysis of the four basic principles of Gestalt, and the following The actual design application leaves the foundation; the third part is to apply the four basic principles of Gestalt psychology to the layout design of the main interface of the stadium monitoring system; the fourth part is a summary of the theoretical viewpoint of this article. The overall framework of the article is shown in Fig. 1.

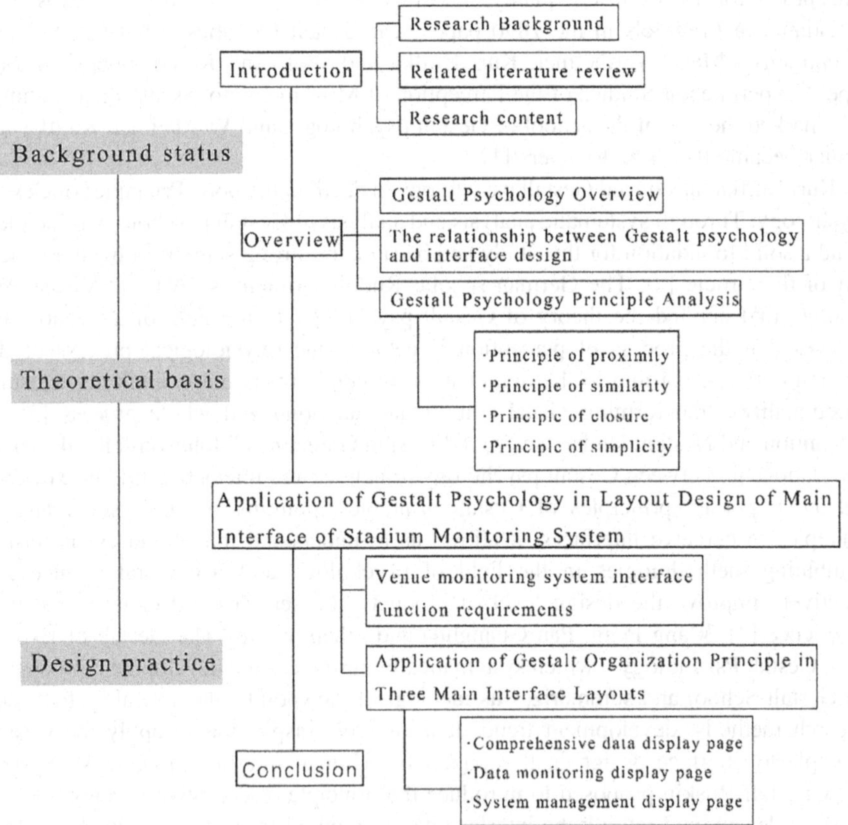

Fig. 1. Article overall architecture diagram (Source: Editor's self-painting)

2 Overview

2.1 Gestalt Psychology Overview

Gestalt Psychology was founded in the 20th century and provides the basis for modern perception research. Gestalt is intended to mean a form, a shape, or a whole that is visually separated. The theory emphasizes the overall, the nature of the overall decision part, and partly depends on the whole. The starting point of Gestalt psychology research is based on "shape", but it is not limited to the general form or shape, but also the whole of the experience organized by the perceptual activity. Therefore, the translation is "whole or gestalt", so Gestalt psychology is also called gestalt psychology [6]. Gestalt psychology emphasizes the initiative of perceptual activities and the integrity of psychological phenomena. The basic theory is that human visual systems can automatically input and construct structures, and organize visual elements such as shapes, figures and objects, rather than a single element is analyzed [7].

Gestalt Psychology advocates the study of direct experience and behavior, emphasizes the integrity of behavior and direct experience, and advocates the use of overall motivation to observe and study psychological phenomena. In the development of Gestalt psychology, Gestalt psychologists have summarized many organizational principles applicable to visual graphics. The "Pinguistic Tendency Principle" is the most important and basic organizational principle. The "finished tendency principle" refers to the tendency for those organizations to be poor, untidy, ambiguous, and complex. Perception has a tendency to transform the best, most symmetrical, and simplified graphics into the organization [8].

Gestalt psychology can be understood from two parts: perception and perception, and perception. First of all, it is perception and feeling. Feeling is the direct reflection of the human body on the physical and psychological aspects of the object. It is the basic reaction to the individual attributes of the object, including visual, auditory, olfactory, taste, and skin feeling. Perception is the reaction of the human body to the overall attributes of things, and it is a comprehensive and holistic reaction that combines various sensations organically. Feeling and perception are two inseparable basic psychological processes. Generally speaking, they appear at the same time, which are direct reflections on objective things. Objective things act on the senses, and perceptions will occur. Second, it is visual perception. Visual perception is the observation of the information received through the eyes, through the brain to perceive the characteristics of things, to understand and analyze things, to abstract, combine, separate, simplify and other comprehensive processing, and evolve into a process of thinking.

2.2 The Relationship Between Gestalt Psychology and Interface Design

Interface design is the visual representation layer in human-computer interaction, which is an important aspect to determine visual perception. The interface design is based on the visual experience. The basic purpose is to meet the user's usage habits, to obtain the user's demand information more quickly and effectively, and to make the user have a good user experience in the interface interaction process. Rudolf Arnheim, a representative of Gestalt theory, believes that the combination of visual research and the study of art forms, visually becomes the sensory ability to grasp the overall structural style of visual objects [9]. Gestalt psychology has a key influence in visual design. It mainly studies human body visual information reception process with human perception and visual perception. It is an important theory of cognitive psychology. Gestalt aesthetics is a scientific interpretation of the perception of human visual aesthetics. Therefore, based on this principle, the principle of introducing and applying the psychology of the format tower in the interface design is systematically analyzed and discussed.

2.3 Gestalt Psychology Principle Analysis

Gestalt theory puts forward four basic principles through the physiological research on visual perception: the principle of proximity, the principle of similarity, the principle of closure, and the principle of **simplicity**.

Principle of Proximity. The principle of proximity means that the parts that are close in distance tend to form a whole. It is believed that the distance between elements affects people's perception of their state. Elements that are adjacent to each other and relatively close to each other are easily perceived as a whole object; conversely, elements that are not adjacent to each other and far away from each other are easily separated by perception. As shown in Fig. 2, elements of the same size, color, and shape are arranged together, and visually distinctly divided into two parts according to the distance.

Fig. 2. The brief illustration of proximity law (Source: Editor's self-painting)

The principle of proximity is usually used to classify content elements for interface design. The general application is embodied by grouping the content elements of the interface by using the edge of the interface area, and creating different element unit groups according to the distance of the relative distance. In this way, the design interface has no visible boundary or separation frame, which not only reduces the visual clutter in the interface design, but also makes the overall planning of the interface more standardized and easy to identify, and more fully satisfies the audience's clear and complete interpretation of the interface content information demand.

Principle of Similarity. The principle of similarity means that parts that are similar in one aspect tend to form a whole. That is, when other factors are the same, people tend to regard visual objects having similar shapes, sizes, colors, materials, and the like as a whole or a combination. As shown in Fig. 3, in the case where the distance distribution of each element is the same, elements of different shapes and colors are visually clearly divided into four groups.

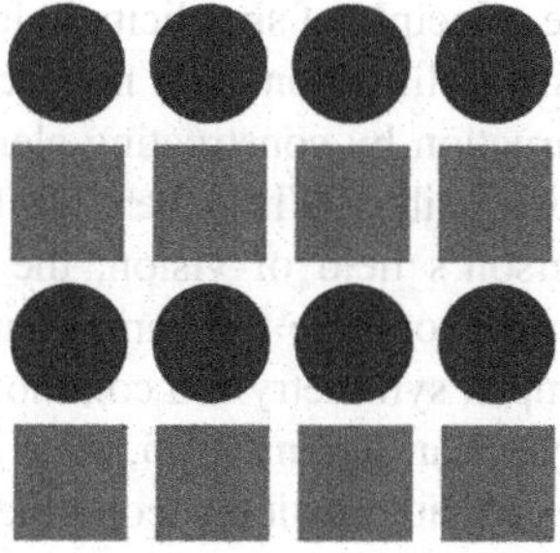

Fig. 3. The brief illustration of **similarity** law (Source: Editor's self-painting)

The principle of similarity is often used for the division of elemental regions of interface design. The area is divided by categorizing the element size, background color, shape, structural features, and the like. By designing the interface in this way, the picture can be neat and unified, and the grouping of different style elements can be highlighted, so that the user can find the relevant information required in a large amount of information.

Principle of Closure. The principle of closure means that when the element is incomplete or obscured, the human perception system automatically fills in the obscured or missing part according to past experience and perceptual tendency to approach the integrity, so that the element looks complete. Overall. As shown in Fig. 4, the graph consists of four incomplete circles with a blank space between the four circles, but the human visual system automatically fills the blanks into a white square. At the same time, the visual system will automatically judge that the circle is blocked by a square, rather than being incomplete.

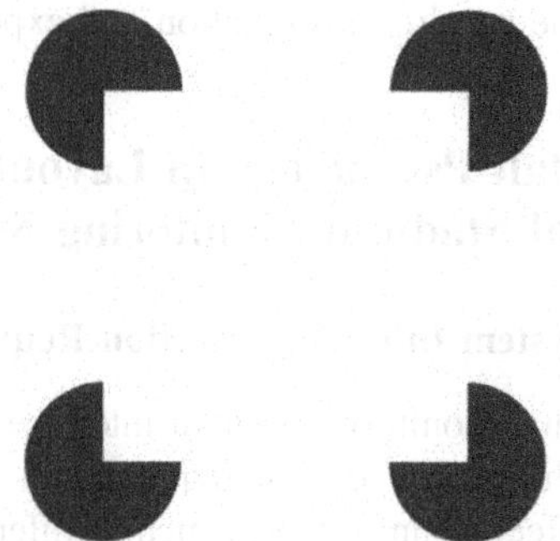

Fig. 4. The brief illustration of **closure** law (Source: Editor's self-painting)

The principle of closure is often applied in interface design. This "complete form" trend helps users to transform visual elements that are not easily perceived into familiar ones. This design method can make the interface clear and clear, and not too many elements, and follow the user's usage habits.

Principle of Simplicity. The principle of simplicity holds that human perception has a tendency to "simplify". This simplification does not mean simplicity, but rather the tendency to organize the construction by constructing elements that are perceived and accepted in as simple a way as possible. When there are too many visual elements or cognitive possibilities in a person's field of vision, the visual system will actively simplify the graphic elements and combine the various units to make them a perceptually sensible whole. For example, symmetry is a common form of organization in the "simplification" tendency. As you can see in Fig. 5, there are six positive and negative "c" elements, and the vision system automatically combines the graphical elements into three sets of symmetrical graphics.

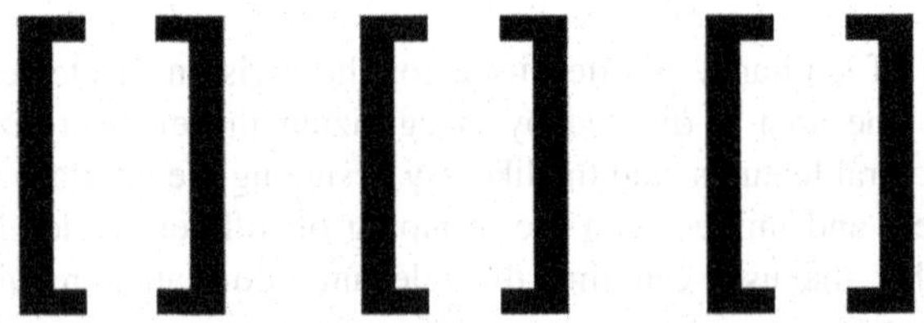

Fig. 5. The brief illustration of **simplicity** law (Source: Editor's self-painting)

This simplification tendency, in the application of interface design, generally uses symmetrical, balanced or appropriate proportions of the composition method, which can simplify the process of user cognitive page layout, highlight key points, and speed up the user identification information.

Flexible use of the four basic principles, has an important guiding role in the interface design, can more rationally design the interface layout structure, clarify the primary and secondary relationship of each interface element, thereby designing the user to more easily obtain the required information and experience a better interface.

3 Application of Gestalt Psychology in Layout Design of Main Interface of Stadium Monitoring System

3.1 Venue Monitoring System Interface Function Requirements

The article relies on the venue monitoring system interface design project for design and application research. The project design requirements have the following three points: the interface visual effect is innovative, which is different from the conventional interface and effect; the interface style needs to reflect digital, scientific and intelligent; The user experience of the interface system is good. When there is important information, the user can be reminded at any time, and the function menu is convenient and eye-catching. At the same time, the human-machine interface of the stadium monitoring system has many characteristics of visual information elements and complex visual information. According to the design requirements and characteristics of the interface in the project, here are mainly the three main interfaces - comprehensive data display, data monitoring, system management, combined with the basic principles of Gestalt introduced in the above analysis to study the layout design of the main interface of the stadium monitoring system.

3.2 Application of Gestalt Organization Principle in Three Main Interface Layouts

Comprehensive Data Display Page (First Page). As a comprehensive data display page, as the home page of the system interface, the information to be presented is more complicated, including temperature and humidity, people flow, operation status of major equipment, current energy consumption, the situation of each branch, and schedule. Therefore, in the layout design, the interface should summarize and sort out various information, and provide users with a variety of modules for finding information, thereby highlighting the hierarchicalization of information and making the interface expression clearer. As shown in Fig. 6 is a comprehensive data display interface. The overall interface layout utilizes the principle of simplicity, and the grid layout is formed by the distribution ratio of the sizes of different regions to form a layout frame structure. This attributes elements of different content, color, form, size, format, and so on to a unified and orderly grid, and ensures that as many of them are displayed in an effective space. Cleverly reduces interference between elements, greatly improving visibility [10] will highlight the module of information in its central location, simplifying the process of user-aware page layout, highlighting key points, reducing visual confusion and speeding up user identification.

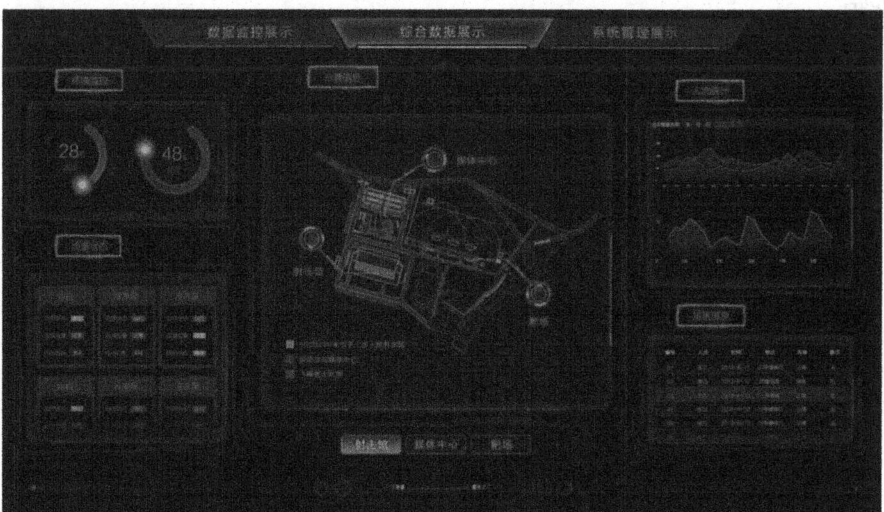

Fig. 6. Integrated data display interface (Source: Editor's self-painting) (Color figure online)

The navigation bar at the top of the interface contains multiple function panels, each of which contains a large number of information display modules. The diversity of functional interfaces increases the complexity of the design. In order to make the interface simple and convenient, and the information transmission is clear, according to the principle of similarity, three different functional modules are arranged in a line, and the whole blue light-emitting wire frame is used to attract the line of sight, highlighting the digitization, technology sense and intelligence. The interface style, on the one hand, is grouped with elements that are emphasized in a uniform frame. It is illuminated on the background of the selected function module, which reflects the interactivity and brings comfort to the user. It conforms to the user's first use of the navigation function classification and then pay attention to the usage habits of the content. The environment monitoring system module interface in the upper left corner of the interface, in which the ring graphic uses incomplete ring graphics combined with small light spots to represent information data and functions. According to the principle of closure, we can see the incomplete ring visually, but it does not strongly feel the fragmentation of the ring figure, and automatically fills in the blank part in the perception, so that the information transmission is clear and clear.

Data Monitoring Display Page. Figure 7 is the data monitoring display interface. On the left side of the interface, because this interface needs to display the monitoring interface display of various functions such as building automation, elevator system, HVAC, public lighting, video monitoring, etc., the diversity of functions is often Will increase the complexity of the design [11]. According to the principle of similarity, the information of these different functions is expressed in the same blue wire frame to unify the picture. Each function module is distinguished by size and brightness, and at the same time, the selected function information is illuminated and the form is enlarged to highlight its state. Make the overall functional area, the information is orderly and clear.

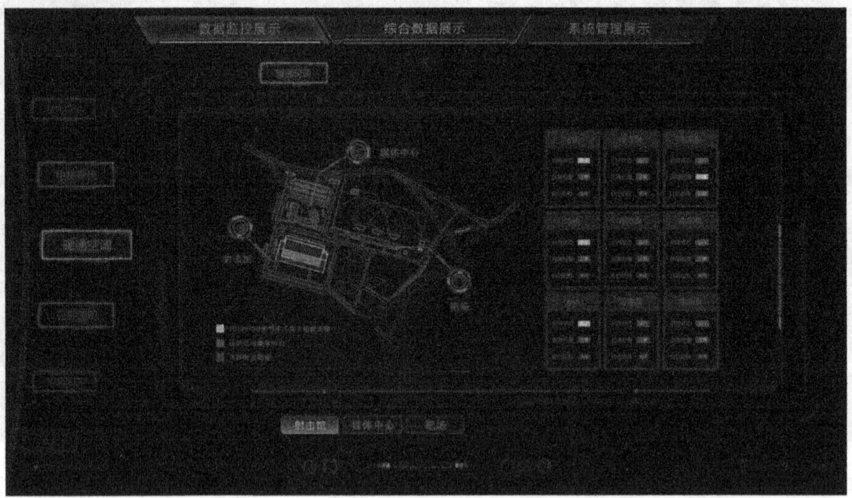

Fig. 7. Data monitoring interface (Source: Editor's self-painting) (Color figure online)

On the machine state display interface at the right end of the interface, using the principle of similarity, the shape and arrangement of different mechanical categories are consistent, so that the interface remains neat and orderly, and that each module has the same properties. However, the colors of different states in the module are distinguished from each other. During the use, the user can clearly understand the different state feedback of the machine represented by each color, and meet the requirement of quickly obtaining information.

System Management Display Page. The system management display interface is shown in Fig. 8. The layout information module is located in the middle of the interface. The entire module interface does not use segmentation lines to distinguish each piece of information. Instead, the proximity number is used to adjust the number, personnel, time, and location. The left and right spacing of information such as content, notes, etc., allows the user to clearly know the corresponding top information. Using the principle of similarity, the bottom color distinguishing module is used at the top, and the function of the top navigation is distinguished while the same form of expression. In the same way, the light color background color is used at the lower end to indicate the effect of the information selection, so that the interface is clear and clear.

Fig. 8. System management interface (Source: Editor's self-painting)

4 Conclusion

Firstly, the paper analyzes and introduces the research background, and at the same time puts forward the problems existing in the monitoring interface of the stadium. Through the reading and research of related literatures, the feasibility and necessity of applying Gestalt psychology to the interface of the stadium monitoring system is theoretically determined. Secondly, it summarizes the psychology of Gestalt, analyzes the relationship between Gestalt psychology and interface design, and analyzes the four organizational principles of Gestalt theory. Thirdly, the specific design requirements of the actual project main interface design are put forward. Based on the Gestalt psychology theory, the basic principles are applied to the interface design of the stadium monitoring system, and the Gestalt psychology theory is analyzed and verified. The interface design information is more clear and clear, and the user can quickly and conveniently obtain the demand information, so that the user has a good user experience in the interface interaction application process. The main conclusions of the study include:

- Based on Gestalt psychology, this paper analyzes the characteristics of the human visual system to understand and simplify the overall organization of things. Analysis of human-machine interface design has learned that its fundamental purpose is to enable users to obtain demand information more quickly and efficiently, and to provide a good interactive experience. The principles of the two are just right, so the enlightenment of applying the basic principles of Gestalt psychology to the interface design of the stadium monitoring system is generated;
- According to the design requirements of the venue monitoring system interface, the basic framework of its main interface layout is derived;
- Through the analysis and summary of the four principles of Gestalt psychology: the principle of proximity - element classification, similarity principle - regional division, closed principle - complete form, concise principle - highlight key points, Apply these four aspects to the actual case interface, and analyze and verify the Gestalt psychology theory.

Through the discussion of this article, although many knowledge about Gestalt psychology and interface design has been enhanced, based on the format tower psychology, the layout design of the main interface of the stadium monitoring system is studied, but there are many shortcomings. It is hoped that the relevant research results can provide some theoretical basis and reference for the venue monitoring interface design.

References

1. Behrens, R.R.: Art, Design and Gestalt Theory. Decoration **299**, 32–35 (2018). https://doi.org/10.16272/j.cnki.cn11-1392/j.2018.03.008
2. Koffka, K.: Principles of Gestalt Psychology. Peking University Press, Beijing (2010). Li, W. Trans.
3. Arnheim, R.: Art and Visual Perception, pp. 64–73. Sichuan People's Publishing House, Chengdu (1998). Teng, S. Trans.
4. Johnson, J.: Designing with the Mind in Mind: Simple Guide to Understanding User Interface Design Guidelines, 2nd edn. People Post Press (2011). Zhang, Y. Trans.
5. Jeff, R.: The Human Interface: New Directions for Designing Interactive Systems. Addison Wesley, Boston (2000)
6. Wang, P., Pan, G., Gao, F.: The Gestalt of Experience, pp. 1–2. Shandong Education Publishing House, Shandong (2009)
7. Dong, Q.: Design thinking of the visual gestalt theory. Packag. Eng. **32**(6), 25–26 (2011)

8. Ning, H.: Study on the dynamic theory of Ahnheim's visual perception form, p. 42. People's Publishing House, Beijing (2009)
9. Zhang, X.: Western Aesthetics in the 20th Century, p. 46. Wuhan University Press, Wuhan (2009)
10. Norman, D.A.: Design Psychology. China Citic Press, Beijing (2015). Xiao, K. Trans.
11. Xia, Y.: Simple or unnecessary method in interface design for digital products. Decoration **5**, 98–99 (2013)

The Impact of Information Presentation on Visual Inspection Performance in the International Nuclear Safeguards Domain

Laura E. Matzen(✉), Mallory C. Stites, Heidi A. Smartt, and Zoe N. Gastelum

Sandia National Laboratories, Albuquerque, NM 87123, USA
{lematze,mcstite,hasmart,zgastel}@sandia.gov

Abstract. International nuclear safeguards inspectors are tasked with verifying that nuclear materials in facilities around the world are not misused or diverted from peaceful purposes. They must conduct detailed inspections in complex, information-rich environments, but there has been relatively little research into the cognitive aspects of their jobs. We posit that the speed and accuracy of the inspectors can be supported and improved by designing the materials they take into the field such that the information is optimized to meet their cognitive needs. Many in-field inspection activities involve comparing inventory or shipping records to other records or to physical items inside of a nuclear facility. The organization and presentation of the records that the inspectors bring into the field with them could have a substantial impact on the ease or difficulty of these comparison tasks. In this paper, we present a series of mock inspection activities in which we manipulated the formatting of the inspectors' records. We used behavioral and eye tracking metrics to assess the impact of the different types of formatting on the participants' performance on the inspection tasks. The results of these experiments show that matching the presentation of the records to the cognitive demands of the task led to substantially faster task completion.

Keywords: Visual inspection · Situational awareness · Information visualization

1 Introduction

International nuclear safeguards are measures that provide assurance to the global community that nations are using nuclear technologies for peaceful purposes. The International Atomic Energy Agency (IAEA), which operates under the auspices of the United Nations, is the agency tasked with verifying States' safeguards agreements. A State declares nuclear materials and facilities and the IAEA periodically verifies those declarations to ensure that nuclear materials are not being diverted from known (safeguarded) facilities and that safeguarded facilities are not being misused for undeclared nuclear purposes. They also attempt to detect any undeclared nuclear activities within a State.

S. Yamamoto and H. Mori (Eds.): HCII 2019, LNCS 11569, pp. 56–75, 2019.
https://doi.org/10.1007/978-3-030-22660-2_5

The basic verification method used by the IAEA is nuclear material accountancy (NMA), which is achieved through nuclear materials measurements and examination of records and reports. The IAEA also inspects nuclear facilities to determine operational status, design, and production capacity. Containment and surveillance technologies, such as seals and cameras, are applied to maintain continuity of knowledge for nuclear materials between inspection intervals.

During a facility inspection, IAEA inspectors complete tasks such as verifying that seals have not been tampered with, verifying the inventory of nuclear material by checking seal numbers against the IAEA and facility records, comparing the facility's records to their declarations to the IAEA, taking material measurements, and looking for any anomalies in a facility that may indicate misuse. Safeguards inspections are physically and cognitively demanding [1]. The inspectors are working under time pressure in an industrial environment that may be loud, hot, and/or cramped, in addition to containing radiological hazards. For many aspects of the inspections they must wear protective gear which makes it more difficult to manipulate the tools they need to take samples and record observations. They may not share a common language with the facility operators and are often dealing with jet lag on top of the demands of the working environment. While working in this challenging environment, the inspectors must take care to record accurate data and notes, while also being on the alert for any subtle discrepancies or indications of unusual activity in the facility.

Despite the importance of an IAEA inspector's role and the cognitive demands of the job, there has been very little application of cognitive science research to this domain [2]. To address this gap, our research team conducted an evaluation of key safeguards inspection tasks to identify where cognitive science research methods could be applied to support the inspectors' cognitive processing in the field [3]. One of the areas that we identified was visual inspection. IAEA inspectors must complete several types of visual inspection tasks, including paper-based tasks, such as comparing the facility's inventory and shipment records to State declarations and records from prior inspections, and object-based tasks, such as finding seal numbers on containers of nuclear materials and checking them against IAEA records.

There has been a great deal of research on visual search in general [4], as well as visual search of lists [5, 6] and visual inspection in industrial contexts [7–12]. These studies have shown that factors such as the work environment [9, 12], task structure [9, 11], feedback [7], list formatting [5] and other types of job aids [8] impact visual search and inspection performance. Although safeguards inspectors do not have control over many of these factors, it may be feasible to format their own records and inspection-related materials in ways that make their visual inspection tasks faster and easier. We conducted a series of experiments to test the impact of changing the formatting of the inspector's materials on the speed and accuracy of their inspection performance.

In our first study in this area [13], we developed a computer-based mock inspection task. Participants saw two lists of seal and container numbers displayed side-by-side on the screen. One of these lists was designated the "inspector's list" and one was the "facility's list." Participants were tasked with checking all the items on the inspector's list against the facility's list and marking which seals were present, which were missing, and which (if any) were anomalous in other ways. While the facility's list was always presented in a random order, we altered the presentation of the inspector's list by changing its order and color coding, two factors long known to impact visual search performance [5, 14–17]. The experiment found that participants had equally high accuracy across all of the list presentation conditions, but very different response times. Participants were fastest when the order of the seals on the inspector's list matched the order of the seals on the facility's list. When the order did not match, participants benefited from having color coding to narrow their search of the facility's list, which significantly improved their response times.

Given the results of this study, we expanded this line of research to other types of inspection tasks. In [13], participants were tasked with verifying all of the seals on the facility's list. However, in real-world IAEA inspections, it is common for inspectors to check a randomly determined, statistically representative subset of the seals in a facility during each inspection. Checking a subset of the full list may change how the inspectors use the lists, which may in turn impact which list presentation conditions lead to the biggest benefits to the inspectors' performance. The work presented here addresses this scenario.

Experiment 1, like our prior study, involved a list-to-list comparison activity, except that participants were only looking for a subset of the seals in the facility's list. Experiments 2 and 3 represented inspection activities in which the inspectors must walk through a facility to check a list against physical items, such as sealed containers. Although these were computer-based tasks, they were designed to mimic list-to-item inspection activities. In Experiment 2, participants had a list of seals to verify but could only view one sealed container at a time, mirroring the process of checking a subset of the sealed containers in one room of a facility. In Experiment 3, participants used a map to navigate between different "rooms" in a facility. Across all three experiments, the information provided to the participants was manipulated to determine the impact of list order and different types of information about a seal's likely location on the speed and accuracy of the inspection.

2 Experiment 1

In Experiment 1, participants were given a mock safeguards inspection task in which they were asked to compare two lists to ensure that the information matched. The "inspector's list" contained a subset of half of the items on the "facility's list," mimicking a paper-based inspection task in which inspectors verify a representative subset of a facility's records. The order and color coding of the inspector's list was manipulated across six conditions and participants were assessed in terms of their accuracy and response times for each condition. Eye tracking data were collected to identify any differences in inspection strategy across the list presentation conditions.

2.1 Method

Participants. Nineteen participants were recruited from the employee population of Sandia National Laboratories and were compensated for their time. Four participants were later excluded from the analysis due to dropped or noisy eye tracking data. The remaining 15 participants (10 female) had an average age of 32 years. Four of the participants held a high school degree, three held a bachelor's degree, four held a master's degree, and three held a PhD.

Materials. As in our prior study [13], the experimental materials consisted of six sets of lists containing seal numbers and container numbers. The inspector's list, presented on the left side of the computer screen, contained 18 pairs of seal and container numbers arranged in two columns. The facility's list, presented on the right side of the screen, contained 36 pairs of seal and container numbers arranged in four columns. See Fig. 1 for an example.

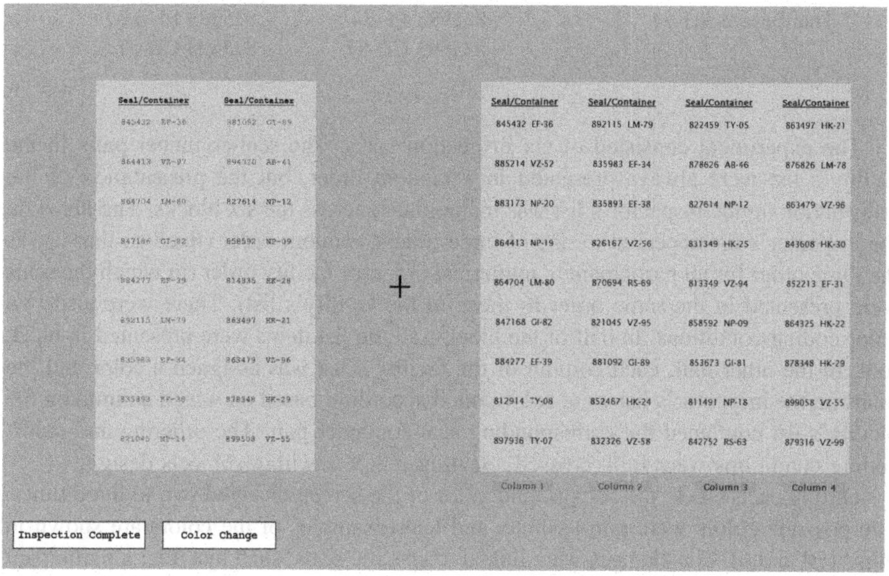

Fig. 1. Example of the screen layout used in Experiment 1. This example shows the color-coded facility order condition. (Color figure online)

The seal numbers were six-digit numerical strings. Within each condition, the first digit of the seal number was always the same and the five final digits were pseudorandomly generated such that every digit (0–9) appeared approximately the same number of times in each position. This was done to avoid any patterns within the seal numbers that could have made some numbers more memorable than others. The container numbers consisted of two letters and two numbers, separated by a hyphen, such as "AB-37." Each container number was unique, although the same letter pairs appeared in multiple container numbers.

On the facility's list, there were 20 filler items that did not appear on the inspector's list. The remaining items corresponded to the conditions outlined in Table 1. Some of the conditions contained transposed digits, which were intended to make the inspection more difficult. If participants did not pay close attention, they could mismatch or mis-categorize these items, which could lead to confusion later in the inspection process. The types of transpositions were the same as in [13].

Table 1. Conditions and example items for Experiment 1.

Condition	Number of items	Examples	
		Inspector's list version	Facility list version
Match	8	845432 EF-36	845432 EF-36
Wrong container	2	864413 VZ-97	864413 NP-19
Missing	2	894320 AB-41	N/A
Transpose	2	847186 GI-82	847168 GI-82
Transpose match	4	835983 EF-34 835893 CD-57	835983 EF-34 835893 CD-57

The experiment consisted of six inspection tasks. The seal-container pairs in the facility's list were always presented in a random order, but the presentation of the information on the inspector's list was manipulated across the six blocks. The items on the inspector's list appeared in one of three orders: random order (fixed so that it was the same order for all participants), numerical order, or facility order (in which the seals were presented in the same order as those in the facility's list). There were also two color-coding conditions. In half of the blocks, all the list items were presented in black font. In the other half, each column of the facility's list was assigned a color and the items on the inspector's list were color-coded according based on which column on the facility's list contained the corresponding seal-container pair. The ordering and color-coding conditions were fully crossed, creating a 3 × 2 within-subjects design.

During each block, the background color of the screen changed two to three times. The possible colors were purple, blue, and teal (examples of the colors are shown in Figs. 1, 4 and 6). The changes were linked to specific seals, such that after a participant clicked on that seal, the background color would change on the next trial. The seals that triggered the color changes were different for each block. The color change detection task was included to encourage participants to maintain their situational awareness by attending to a secondary task while completing their primary inspection task. This mimics the work of safeguards inspectors, who must maintain their overall situational awareness in addition to completing their inspection tasks. There were relatively few color changes per block, so the participants' accuracy on the color change detection task was not analyzed separately for the different inspection conditions.

Procedure. After giving their informed consent, participants were seated in a dimly lit, sound attenuating booth so that their eyes were 80 cm from the computer monitor. Participants completed a practice session that explained the task and allowed them to complete a shortened version of the inspection. After the practice block, the eye tracker was calibrated. Eye tracking data was collected with a Fovio eye tracker and recorded and analyzed with EyeWorks software. The participants completed a five-point calibration sequence, and then the accuracy of the calibration was assessed by the experimenter and repeated if necessary. The calibration process was repeated prior to each block.

The participants completed the six blocks of the experiment in a counterbalanced, pseudorandom order. Each block began with a description of how the inspector's list would be organized. The participants were instructed to check off each item on the inspector's list. When they clicked on an item in the inspector's list, four response choices appeared in the center of the screen. The choices were "Seal present, correct container," "Seal present, incorrect container," "Seal missing" and "Other issue." Participants clicked on one of the four choices to indicate their response for that seal. After a response was recorded for a seal, that seal was grayed out on the inspector's list to indicate that it had been checked off. Following each response, a fixation cross was presented in the center of the screen for 1.5 s, initiating the next trial.

Participants were instructed to click on a button labeled "Color Change" as soon as they noticed a change in the background color. Clicking on the "Color Change" button also initiated a new trial. Once participants had checked off all the seals on the inspector's list, they clicked the "Inspection Complete" button. Then they were asked how many times the background color changed during the inspection task. Their choices ranged from zero to four.

Finally, participants were asked to describe their search strategy. The instructions stated: "Please give a brief description (2–3 sentences) of the strategy that you used for this inspection task. For example, which list did you start from? What visual cues were you looking for? Did you ever switch to a different strategy during the task, and if so, what was it?" The participants typed their answer in a text box on the screen. Upon finishing each inspection task, participants were given a short break. In total, the experiment lasted 1–1.5 h, depending on how fast the participants completed each task.

2.2 Results

Accuracy. Across all blocks, the participants detected an average of 61% (*SD* = 41%) of the background color changes in real time and 79% (*SD* = 21%) of the color changes when asked at the end of the inspection to report the total number of changes that had occurred. The participants were not penalized for overestimating the number of color changes. These results indicate that the participants generally maintained their awareness of the secondary task.

For the primary task, the seal checking task, participants performed near ceiling on all inspection conditions, correctly identifying which seals were present, missing, or paired with the wrong container number. For items in the Transpose condition, the responses "Seal Missing" and "Other Issue" were both counted as correct. The average percentage of seals categorized correctly ranged from 95% to 97%. A 3×2 repeated measures ANOVA showed that there were no significant main effects or interactions for the different list presentation conditions (all $Fs < 1$).

Response Times. In contrast with the accuracy results, the participants had very different response times across the six inspection conditions. For each trial, the participants' response time was calculated as the time from trial onset to the time the participant clicked on one of the seals on the inspector's list. The average response times across all trials for each condition are shown in Fig. 2. A 3 × 2 repeated measures ANOVA showed that there was a significant main effect of list order ($F(2,70) = 25.42, p < 0.001$), a significant main effect of color coding ($F(1,70) = 41.25, p < 0.001$), and a significant interaction between the two ($F(2,70) = 11.67, p < 0.001$).

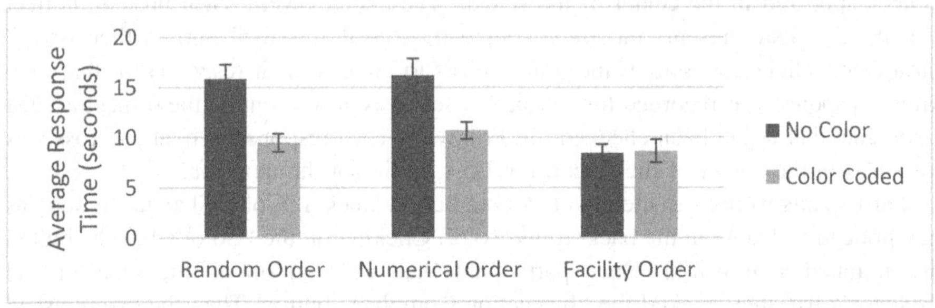

Fig. 2. Average response time for each trial for each of the six conditions in Experiment 1. Error bars represent the standard error of the mean in all figures.

Post-hoc paired t-tests showed that participants responded significantly faster when there was color coding in the random ($t(14) = 7.24$, $p < 0.001$) and numerical order conditions ($t(14) = 3.55, p < 0.01$). Color coding did not have a significant effect in the facility order condition ($t(14) = 0.21$). Paired t-tests were also used to compare across the list order conditions. When the lists did *not* have color coding, participants were significantly faster for the facility order condition than for the numerical order ($t(14) = 6.58$, $p < 0.001$) and random order conditions ($t(14) = 7.48$, $p < 0.001$). The numerical and random order conditions did not differ significantly from one another ($t(14) = 0.53$). For the conditions with color coding, there were no significant differences in response times across the three list order conditions (all $ts < 1.69$, all $ps > 0.11$).

Eye Tracking Data. The eye tracking data showed that the length of the participants' visual search process was the driving factor behind the differences in response times across the six inspection conditions. The average number of fixations per trial in shown in Fig. 3. A 3 × 2 repeated measures ANOVA showed that there was a significant main effect of list order ($F(2,70) = 11.09, p < 0.001$), a significant main effect of color coding ($F(1,70) = 23.00$, $p < 0.001$), and a significant interaction between the two ($F(2,70) = 3.23$, $p < 0.05$).

The gaze data were used to determine how many items the participants scanned as they were searching for each seal number. The seal-container pairs on both lists were labeled as regions of interest (ROIs) and we calculated the average number of ROIs containing gaze data points on each trial. These data are also shown in Fig. 3. Once again, there was a significant main effect of list order ($F(2,70) = 14.25$, $p < 0.001$), a significant main effect of color coding ($F(1,70) = 30.98$, $p < 0.001$), and a significant interaction ($F(2,70) = 8.41, p < 0.01$). The patterns seen in both eye tracking analyses mirrored the pattern observed in the response time data.

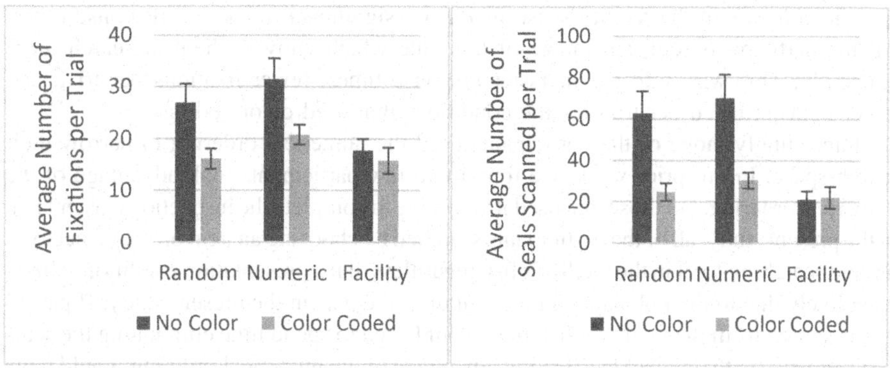

Fig. 3. Average number of fixations (left) and average number of ROIs containing gaze data (right) per trial for each of the six conditions in Experiment 1.

Search Strategy. After completing each inspection task, participants were asked to describe the search strategy that they had used during the task. Across all inspection conditions, all of the participants reported that they started from the inspector's list and searched for the items in the facility's list. When there was color coding available, all 15 participants reported using the colors to constrain their search to the appropriate column on the facility's list. For example, one participant wrote "I looked at the color on my list and then found the right column, then scanned for the first two numbers and then if I found the first two numbers matching I looked to see if the rest matched."

When the inspector's list was in the same order as the facility's list, but with no color coding, 13 of the 15 participants reported that they used the matching order to constrain their search. For example, one participant reported "Since the lists were in the same order, I simply looked at the number on the left and looked to see if there was a match on the right side, below the previous match." The other two participants did not specify whether they used this information.

When the inspector's list was in numerical order, participants could have used the order information to constrain their search. If they started from the facility's list, they could have used the numerical ordering of the inspector's list to quickly match or eliminate seals. However, none of the participants reported using this strategy, nor did the behavioral or eye tracking results indicate that any participants used this strategy. Only one participant mentioned the numerical ordering, saying "It was really not helpful for me to have my list in number order, having the facility list in number order would have been better."

2.3 Discussion

The results of the partial-to-full list comparison in Experiment 1 were generally consistent with those for the complete list-to-list comparison used in our prior work [13]. Participants were equally accurate across all of the list presentation conditions, but they had faster response times when their list was ordered to match the order of the items on the facility's list. The use of color coding to narrow the participants' search space to specific columns in the facility's list also had a significant impact on response times. All the participants took advantage of this cue, which allowed them to search more efficiently. This was reflected in faster response times, fewer fixations per trial, and fewer items scanned per trial for the conditions that used color coding.

Interestingly, none of the participants used the numerical ordering to narrow their search space. In our prior work, we found that few participants took advantage of the numerical ordering, but those that used it were able to complete the inspections faster [13]. In the present study, all of the participants searched by choosing an item on the inspector's list and searching for it in the facility's list, regardless of list presentation condition. This is most likely due to the imbalance in the length of the lists in the present study. If participants started from the facility's list, they would need to spend time eliminating the seals that were not on their checklist. Taking advantage of the numerical ordering would have made the search process more efficient but would have increased the number of items that participants needed to search for.

3 Experiment 2

In Experiment 2, we built on the findings of Experiment 1 by extending the experimental paradigm to another aspect of safeguards inspections. In addition to comparing inventory lists to one another, safeguards inspectors must also physically check the seals on containers to verify their presence within a facility and to ensure that the seals have not been tampered with. In this case, inspectors must navigate through a facility to find and check the seals on their list. Unlike the list-to-list comparisons, where all of the information can be placed side-by-side, in this list-to-seal comparison, inspectors are only able to look at one seal at a time.

This scenario changes the dynamics of search process, which may also change which types of list presentation conditions are most helpful. Thus, in Experiment 2 the inspector's lists were the same as in Experiment 1, but instead of checking the inspector's list against a second list, the participants checked the list against images of sealed containers which could only be viewed one at a time. In this scenario, we hypothesized that participants would start by looking at the image of the sealed container, then search for the seal or container number in their list. Searching in this manner should lead more participants to take advantage of non-color cues on the inspector's list, such as numerical ordering.

3.1 Method

Participants. Twelve participants were recruited from the employee population of Sandia National Laboratories and were compensated for their time. The participants (4 female) had an average age of 41 years. One of the participants held a high school degree, one held an associate degree, five held bachelor's degrees, and five held master's degrees. One participant reported a diagnosis of colorblindness.

Materials and Procedure. The seal-container pairs were the same as those used in Experiment 1 and included all of the same seal conditions (Match, Wrong Container,

Missing, Transpose, and Transpose Match). As before, the inspector's list, containing 18 items, was presented in two columns on the left side of the computer screen. Participants checked the list against 36 sealed containers in the "facility." The right side of the screen showed an olive green square representing a container and a yellow circle representing a seal. Buttons labeled "Previous" and "Next" allowed participants to reveal the sealed containers in sequence. Below the container, a text box tracked which seal-container pair was being shown (i.e., "Seal 9/36"). When participants clicked on the buttons to move to another container, there was a short delay (500 ms) before the new container was displayed. This delay simulated physically moving to see the next seal. An example of the screen layout is shown in Fig. 4.

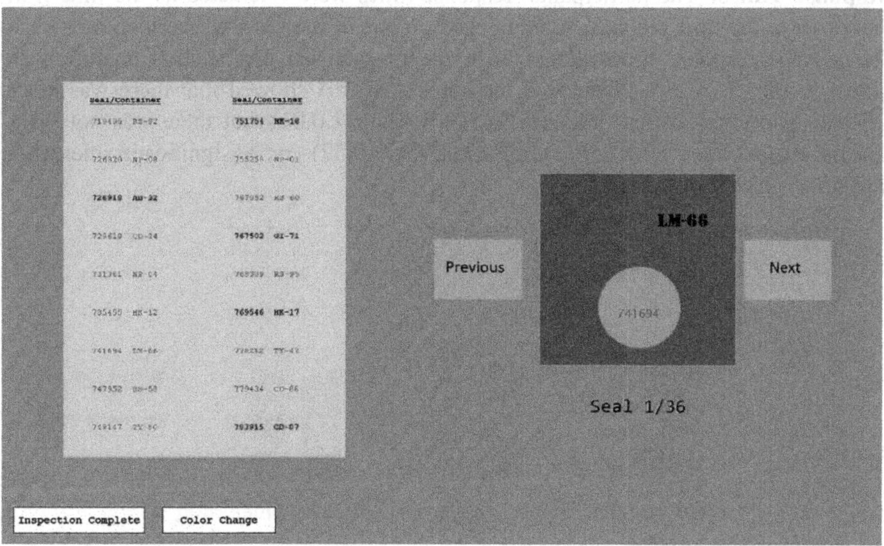

Fig. 4. Example of the screen layout used in Experiment 2. This example shows the color-coded numerical order condition. The box and circle on the right side of the screen represent a container and seal. (Color figure online)

The experiment consisted of six blocks and used the same six variants of the inspector's list that were used in Experiment 1. In this case, the color coding corresponded to the order in which the seals appeared in the facility. Participants were instructed that seals 1–9 in the facility would be presented in red text on the inspector's list, seals 10–18 in teal, seals 19–27 in blue, and seals 28–36 in purple.

The procedure was the same as in Experiment 1, except that eye tracking was not used for this experiment.

3.2 Results

Accuracy. Across all blocks, the participants detected an average of 73% (*SD* = 33%) of the background color changes in real time and reported an average of 75% (*SD* = 33%) of the changes when asked for the total number that had occurred during each inspection. There was one participant who did not report seeing any color changes. For the primary task, the participants performed near ceiling on all inspection conditions. The average percentage of seals categorized correctly ranged from 93% to 97%. A 3 × 2 within-subjects ANOVA showed that there were no significant main effects (all *F*s < 1), nor was there a significant interaction ($F(2,55) = 2.94$, $p = 0.06$).

Response Times. The participants' response times were calculated as the time from trial onset to the time the participant clicked on one of the seals on the inspector's list. The average response times across all trials for each list presentation condition are shown in Fig. 5. A 3 × 2 repeated measures ANOVA showed that there was a significant main effect of list order ($F(2,55) = 7.63$, $p < 0.01$), but there was not a significant main effect of color coding ($F(1,75) = 0.52$), or a significant interaction ($F(2,55) = 2.33$, $p = 0.11$).

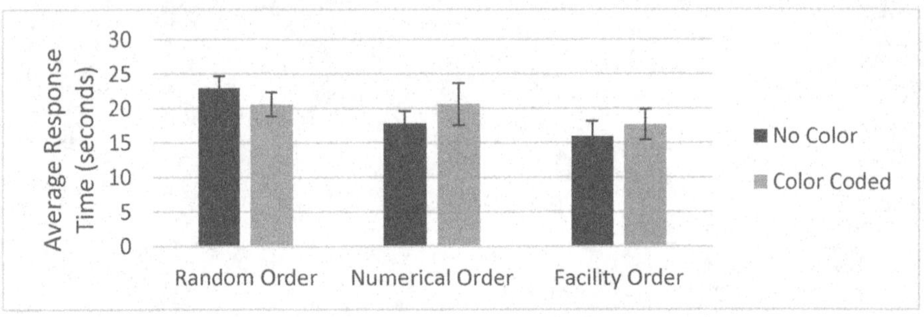

Fig. 5. Average response time for each trial for each of the six conditions in Experiment 2.

Post-hoc paired t-tests were used to compare the list order conditions, collapsed across color coding conditions. The average response time per trial of 21.9 s (*SD* = 5.7) for the random order conditions was significantly longer than the average response time of 19.1 s (*SD* = 7.4) for the numerical order conditions ($t(11) = 2.20$, $p < 0.05$) and 16.7 s (*SD* = 6.6) for the facility order conditions ($t(11) = 4.10$, $p < 0.01$). The difference between the numerical order and facility order conditions was not significant ($t(11) = 1.94$, $p = 0.08$).

Search Strategy. Eleven of the twelve participants stated that they searched by looking at the seal or container number on the right side of the screen, then scanning the inspector's list for that item. The twelfth participant did not specify how s/he searched.

In contrast to Experiment 1, nine participants reported that they used the numerical ordering to constrain their search in one or both numerical order conditions. Five of the participants reported using the color coding to constrain their search, but two other participants complained that it was distracting and difficult to remember. Six participants reported that they used the ordering of the inspector's list to constrain their search in the facility order condition. Interestingly, in the condition with numerical ordering and color coding, five participants mentioned using the order to help them, while only one participant mentioned the color coding. The rest of the participants did not specify which constraint they used in that condition, if any.

3.3 Discussion

In Experiment 2, we confirmed our hypothesis that a list-to-item comparison would lead to different search strategies than a list-to-list comparison. When participants could only view one seal at a time, they started with the seal and compared it to their list rather than starting from their list as they did in Experiment 1. Both experiments had twice as many items in the "facility" as on the inspector's list. In Experiment 1, this prevented the participants from starting from the facility's list, even when doing so would have been more efficient, as in the numerical order conditions. In Experiment 2, the extra effort required to move between seals flipped the direction of the comparison.

The change in the direction of the participants' search led them to use the cues provided by the inspector's list in different ways. In contrast to Experiment 1, the participants used the numerical ordering to their advantage, leading to performance that was quite similar across the numerical order and facility order conditions. On the other hand, the color coding was not as helpful for this type of search. The analysis showed no main effect of color coding, and on average the participants were numerically slower in the numerical order and facility order conditions when there was color coding. This indicates that the color coding was neutral at best and distracting at worst.

4 Experiment 3

Experiments 1 and 2 indicated that participants benefit from list organization conditions that support their visual search process. In Experiment 3, we tested two additional types of information that could support the search process. First, we replaced the color coding with room numbers. In both of the prior experiments, the color coding provided information about the expected location of each seal. In Experiment 1, the color coding told participants which column of a list would contain the seal (if present), and participants successfully used that information to constrain their searches. In Experiment 2, the color coding told participants which group of seals (1–9, 10–18, etc.) would contain the items from their list. In this case, the participants were beginning their search from the seals rather than from their list and did not derive much benefit from the color coding. They may also have found the color coding more difficult to interpret or to remember. In Experiment 3, we used room numbers rather than color coding to provide location information. The 36 seal-container pairs in the "facility" were divided into four different "rooms." In some of the inspection conditions, the inspector's list included room numbers to indicate which room should contain each seal-container pair. Unlike the color coding used in the other experiments, which was always accurate for seals that were present in the facility, the room number list was sometimes incorrect. Our goal was to assess the impact of a different method for providing location information as well as the impact of occasional inaccuracies in that information.

In addition to the presence or absence of room numbers, we also manipulated the way in which the participants moved from one container to another. To move between the four "rooms" in the facility, the participants clicked on a room map that depicted each of the rooms. Then they clicked on a seal map which represented each of the nine seals in that room. Clicking the icons on the seal map revealed the seal-container pair at that location. This mimicked the process of an inspector walking to different rooms in a facility and then finding the correct seals within each room. In half of the inspection conditions, the seal map updated throughout the inspection, indicating which seals had already been checked off of the inspector's list. Our goal was to test the impact of dynamic updating on the participants' ability to track their progress and find the remaining seals. With new and emerging technologies, it may be possible to provide safeguards inspectors with progress tracking or other dynamic updates while they are in the field, but it is not yet known if this will benefit their performance. Experiment 3 represents an initial test in this area.

4.1 Method

Participants. Eighteen participants were recruited from the employee population of Sandia National Laboratories and were compensated for their time. Two participants were later excluded from the analysis due to dropped eye tracking data for one of the experimental blocks. The remaining 16 participants (four female) had an average age of 34 years. Two of the participants held a high school degree, one held and associate degree, five held a bachelor's degree, seven held a master's degree, and one held a PhD.

Materials and Procedure. The seal-container pairs were the same as the items used in Experiments 1 and 2. As before, the inspector's list was presented in two columns on the left side of the computer screen. The right side of the screen had a representation of a container and a seal similar to the one in Experiment 2. However, instead of using "Previous" and "Next" buttons to move between seal/container pairs, the participants had to navigate between virtual "rooms" to view the seals in each one. Below the representation of the container, there was a grid of nine seals which we referred to as the seal map. Below the seal map was the room map, which consisted of a row of four light gray squares labeled Room A, Room B, Room C, and Room D. See Fig. 6 for an example.

When participants clicked on one of the rooms in the room map, a message saying "Walking to Room X" appeared on the screen for two seconds and the room that they had clicked on turned dark gray, indicating that they were "in" that room. Participants could then click on the seals in the seal map, which made the corresponding seal and container numbers appear on the screen.

This experiment also had six conditions, but the manipulations were different from the other two experiments. There were three variants of the list presentation. The first

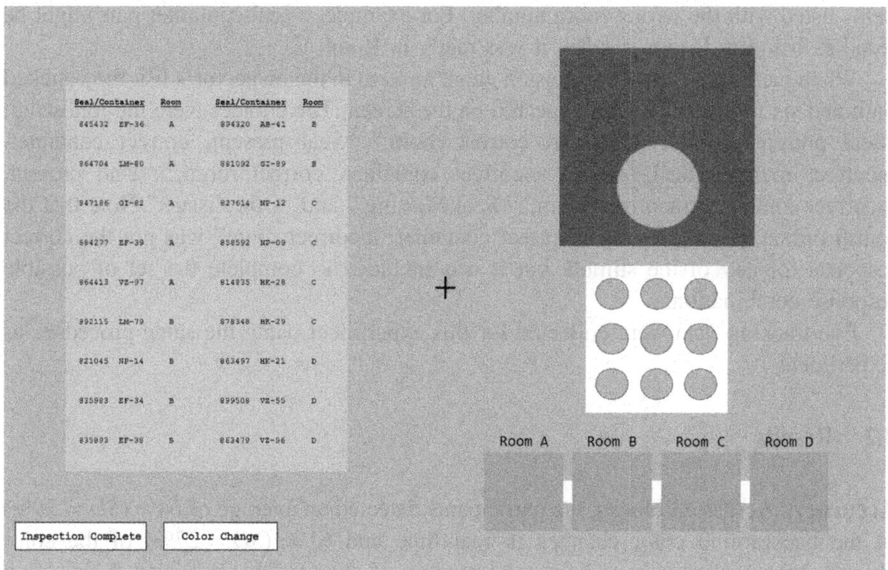

Fig. 6. Example of the screen layout used in Experiment 3. This example shows the room number condition, where the expected room was listed next to the seal/container pair in the inspector's list. In the dynamic map conditions, the yellow seals in the 3 × 3 "seal map" turned gray as participants checked off the corresponding seals from their list. (Color figure online)

variant corresponded to the facility order condition in the prior experiments. The seal-container pairs were listed in the order in which participants would encounter them if they moved through the rooms and seals in the facility in order (row by row on the seal map) from Room A to Room D. The room in which the seal should be located was listed next to the seal-container pair in the inspector's list. In the second variant of the lists, the seal-container pairs were listed in random order, but the room was listed with them. This was referred to as the room number condition. In the third variant, the seal-container pairs were listed in random order and no room information was provided. This was referred to as the random condition. In addition, there were two variants of the seal map, which could be static or dynamic. In the static condition, the seal map stayed the same throughout the inspection task. In the dynamic condition, the seal map updated based on which seals had been checked off of the inspector's list. When seals were checked off, they were grayed out both on the list and on the map, so that participants could see at a glance which seals in each room had already been checked off. The list and map conditions were fully crossed, creating a 3 × 2 within-subjects design.

As in Experiments 1 and 2, there were eight items in the inspector's list that were in the Match condition, two in the Wrong Container condition, two in the Missing condition, two in the Transpose condition, and two in the Transpose Match condition. These items were pseudorandomly assigned to the rooms such that there were never two of the same type of error in the same room. In addition, for the list conditions in which the room information was presented in the inspector's list, there were two Match items listed with the wrong room number. For example, a seal-container pair might be listed as being in Room A when it was really in Room C.

When participants made a decision about an item in the inspector's list, they clicked on it and six response choices appeared on the screen. The choices were the following: "Seal present, correct container, correct room," "Seal present, correct container, incorrect room," "Seal present, incorrect container, correct room," "Seal present, incorrect container, incorrect room," "Seal Missing," and "Other issue." Note that the fourth option, "Seal present, incorrect container, incorrect room" was not the correct response for any of the stimuli, but it was included to complete the set of possible response combinations.

Eye tracking data were collected for this experiment using the same procedure as Experiment 1.

4.2 Results

Accuracy. Across all blocks, the participants detected an average of 64% (*SD* = 29%) of the background color changes in real time and 61% (*SD* = 27%) of the color changes when asked to report the total number of changes that occurred during each inspection task. There was one participant who failed to report any of the color changes.

As in the other experiments, the participants performed near ceiling on all inspection conditions. The average percentage of seals categorized correctly ranged from 94% to 96%. A 3 × 2 within-subjects ANOVA showed that there were no significant main effects or interactions (all *F*s < 1).

Response Times. For each trial, the participants' response times were calculated as the time from trial onset to the time the participant clicked on one of the seals on the inspector's list. The average response times across all trials for each list presentation condition are shown in Fig. 7. A 3 × 2 repeated measures ANOVA showed that there was a significant main effect of list order ($F(2,75) = 9.00$, $p < 0.001$), and a significant main effect of map type ($F(1,75) = 9.08$, $p < 0.001$), but there was not a significant interaction between the two ($F(2,70) = 0.79$).

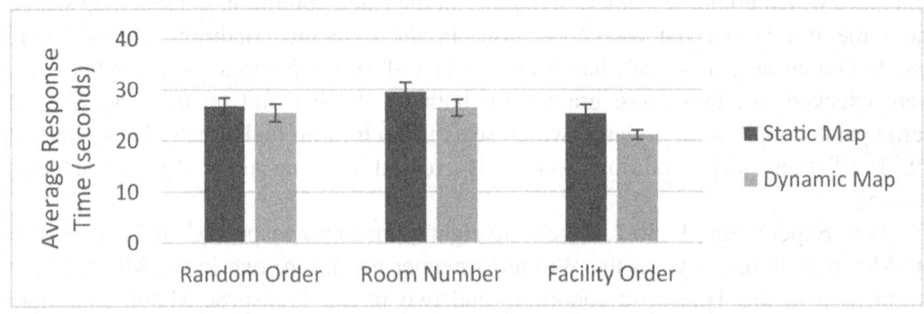

Fig. 7. Average response time for each trial for each of the six conditions in Experiment 3.

Post-hoc paired t-tests were used to assess the main effects. When participants had a dynamic map rather than a static map (collapsed across list order conditions), they had significantly faster response times ($t(15) = 3.18$, $p < 0.01$). Comparisons of the three list order conditions (collapsed across map type) showed that participants had significantly faster response times in the facility order condition than in the room number ($t(15) = 3.73$, $p < 0.01$) or random ($t(15) = 2.52$, $p < 0.03$) conditions. The participants had slightly faster response times in the random condition than in the room number condition, and the difference between the two was marginally significant ($t(15) = 2.08$, $p = 0.05$).

Search Strategy. All of the participants indicated that they searched by starting from one of the rooms and then searching the list for all of the seals in that room before moving on to the next room. An analysis of the number of times participants switched rooms indicated that there was not much variability across conditions, with the average number of switches per condition ranging from 6.1 to 7.4.

Seven of the participants mentioned the dynamic maps (or lack thereof) when describing their search strategies. Two participants wrote that they used the mouse to keep track of their place in the room when the maps did not update. Five of the participants mentioned that they double checked all of the seals in each room when the map did not update. For the dynamic maps, three participants wrote that they did a second pass through each room, checking only the seals that were not already greyed out. An analysis of the number of clicks on the seal map in each condition indicated that participants made many fewer clicks in the conditions with dynamic maps. These data are shown in Fig. 8. A 3×2 repeated measures ANOVA showed that there was a significant main effect of map type ($F(1,75) = 50.10$, $p < 0.001$), but not a significant main effect of list order ($F(2,75) = 0.51$), nor was there a significant interaction ($F(2,75) = 0.89$).

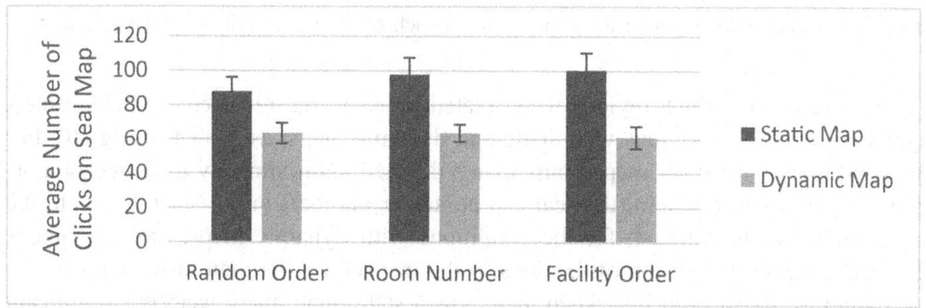

Fig. 8. Average number of seal views, as indicated by clicks on the seal map, for each of the six conditions in Experiment 3.

Eye Tracking Results. The ROIs in Experiment 3 consisted of each seal-container pair on the inspector's list, each room number on the inspector's list (when present), the container number and seal number in the "facility," the seal map, and the room map. The average proportion of fixations to each ROI was calculated for each participant in each of the inspection conditions. This analysis revealed that the participants rarely fixated on the room numbers in their list, even though this information would have helped them to narrow their visual search of the list. The average percentage of fixations to the room numbers ranged from a low of 3% (*SD* = 3%) to a high of 4% (SD = 2%). The proportion of fixations to the seal map was also quite similar across all conditions, ranging from a low of 19% (*SD* = 7%) to a high of 20% (*SD* = 7%).

The average number of fixations per trial (defined for the eye tracking analysis as the time between participants' clicks on the screen, whether those clicks were on the list or on the maps) is shown in Fig. 9. A 3 × 2 repeated measured ANOVA showed that there was a significant main effect of list order ($F(2,75) = 11.25$, $p < 0.001$) and a significant main effect of map type ($F(1,75) = 7.90$, $p < 0.01$), but not a significant interaction between the two ($F(1,75) = 0.72$). Post-hoc paired t-tests showed that the dynamic map conditions had more fixations per trial in ($t(15) = 2.95$, $p < 0.01$), while the facility order condition had fewer than the other order conditions (both *t*s > 2.87, *p*s < 0.02). The room number and random conditions did not differ significantly from one another ($t(15) = 1.89$, $p = 0.08$).

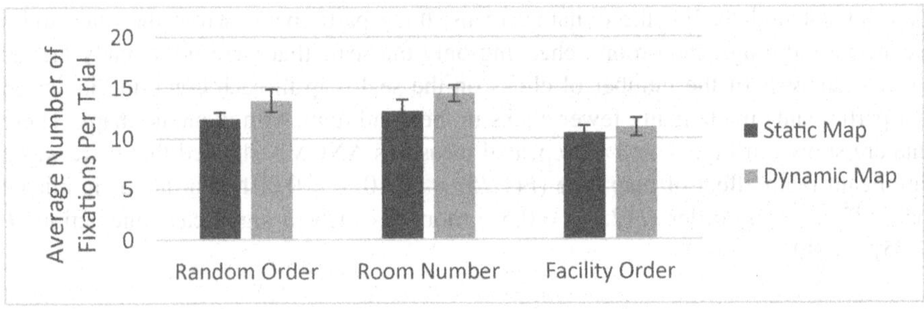

Fig. 9. Average number of fixations per trial for each of the six conditions in Experiment 3.

An analysis of which regions were fixated on each trial revealed a notable difference between the conditions with static and dynamic maps, as shown in Fig. 10. For the conditions with static maps, participants devoted approximately the same proportion of fixations to the item (the seal and container number) in the "facility" as to the inspector's list. In contrast, for the conditions with dynamic maps, the participants devoted a higher proportion of fixations to the inspector's list than to the item.

Paired t-tests showed that when there was a static map, there were not significant differences between the proportion of fixations to the item and the proportion of fixations to the list for the random or room number conditions (both *t*s < 1), although the difference approached significance for the facility order condition ($t(16) = 2.02$, $p = 0.06$). When participants had a dynamic map, there was a significantly higher proportion of fixations to the list for all list order conditions (all *t*s > 5.51, all *p*s < 0.001).

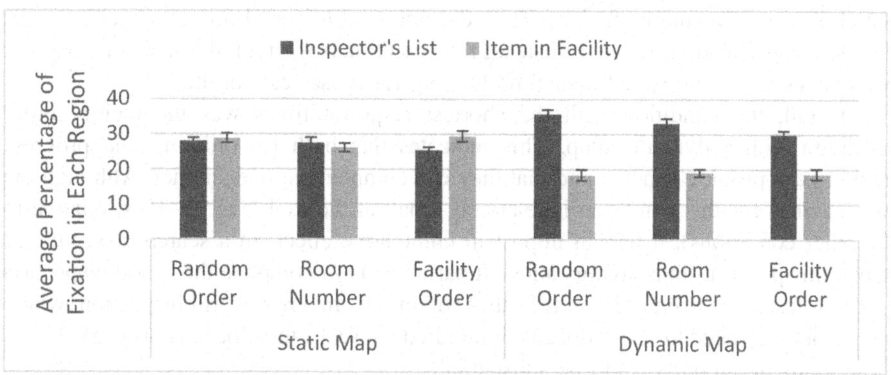

Fig. 10. Average percentage of fixations in each region per trial in Experiment 3.

4.3 Discussion

The results of Experiment 3 mirrored those of Experiment 2 in the sense that the list-to-item comparison led participants to search by looking at the item and then searching for a match in the list. Even though half of the items did not appear in the list at all, the participants universally used this search strategy rather than selecting an entry on the list and searching for it in the "rooms." The participants generally did not take advantage of the room number information, which could have constrained their visual search of the list (or their search of the rooms, had any of them chosen to start their search from the list). This also mirrored the results of Experiment 2, where participants did not benefit from the presence of color coding in the list as an indicator of a seal's location. We had predicted that participants might find room numbers easier to use than an arbitrary color code, but the participants did not seem to use this constraint. It is possible that checking the room numbers as they scanned the list for a specific seal or container number could have disrupted their ability to maintain the seal or container number in working memory. In addition, the room numbers were inaccurate for two items on every list, so the inaccuracies may have led the participants to mistrust the room numbers in general.

In the end, the room number condition had somewhat slower response times than the random order condition. The room numbers did not provide any benefit to the participants, yet they had to take the additional step of checking to make sure that the room numbers were correct. In the random condition, where no room numbers were listed, participants had fewer pieces of information to track for each item, leading to somewhat faster performance.

Although the list order conditions did not have a large impact on the participants' search process, the map conditions did. Participants navigated from one seal to another by clicking on a seal map to reveal each item in a "room." When participants had a map that updated to track which seals they had already checked off of their list, they made many fewer clicks on the seal map, made more fixations between clicks, and devoted a higher proportion of their fixations to the inspector's list. At the same time, they were significantly faster to check the seals off of their list. This indicates that their visual search process was more efficient. They did not need to spend time re-checking seals that they had already inspected. Instead, they could narrow in on the seals that had not been checked off and spend their time looking for those seals in the list.

Overall, the condition with the shortest response times was the facility order condition with a dynamic map. This indicates that both list ordering and progress tracking can provide benefits and that they can complement one another. Although the time savings for this condition is relatively small at the trial level (5–10 s, relative to the other conditions), it has an important cumulative effect. In a search task with 18 items, this per-trial time savings allowed participants to complete the entire inspection 1–2 min faster, on average, than the other conditions. In a real-world inspection, where inspectors may need to check dozens or hundreds of seals, the time savings provided by these kinds of supports could be substantial.

5 General Discussion

The experiments described in this paper demonstrate that list presentation can impact speed and efficiency for list-based visual inspection tasks. When participants are comparing two lists, as in Experiment 1, they tend to work from the shorter list and can take advantage of visual cues, such as color coding, that constrain which portions of the longer list they need to search. When participants are comparing a list to a set of items that must be viewed sequentially, as in Experiments 2 and 3, they tend to begin from the items and then search for them in the list, even if this means extra search time devoted to items that are not included in the list. In this situation, participants are better able to take advantage of list organization cues such as numerical ordering, whereas encodings of spatial information are less useful. When searching for an item in the list, participants have already located that item, and using that location information to narrow their search of the list would place an additional burden on their working memory. As a result, the participants generally ignored the encodings of spatial information, whether color coding or room numbers, and searched all of the remaining entries in the list. In all of these experiments, the inspector's list was fairly short, containing only 18 items. It is possible that inspectors would be more likely to take advantage of spatial cues if the list were longer, making the visual search more onerous.

In Experiment 3 we provided an additional support to the participants by providing them with dynamic information about which seals they had already inspected. This progress tracking made participants more efficient in their search and led to a considerable reduction in the number of times they viewed the seals, in addition to a reduction in their overall inspection time relative to other conditions.

Both sets of findings have important implications for the international nuclear safeguards domain, as well as other domains that involve list-based inspections. Although the IAEA inspectors do not have control over the materials provided to them by facility operators, they could change the formatting of their own materials to provide better support for their inspection process. The inspectors conduct both list-to-list and list-to-item checks, and the results of these experiments indicate that they are likely to use different search processes for these two types of tasks. Formatting their materials accordingly and using new technologies to allow them to track their progress, when possible, will enable faster, more efficient inspections.

References

1. A day in the life of a safeguards inspector. https://www.iaea.org/newscenter/news/a-day-in-the-life-of-a-safeguards-inspector. Accessed 28 Jan 2019
2. Gastelum, Z.N., Matzen, L.E., Smartt, H.A., Horak, K.E., Moyer, E.M.: Brain science and international nuclear safeguards: implications from cognitive science and human factors research on the provision and use of safeguards-relevant information in the field. ESARDA Bull. **54**, 62–69 (2017)
3. Gastelum, Z.N., Matzen, L.E., Smartt, H.A., Horak, K.E., Solodov, A.A., Haass, M.J.: Testing human performance in simulated in-field safeguards information environments. In: Proceedings of the 58th Annual Meeting of the Institute of Nuclear Materials Management (2017)
4. Wolfe, J.M.: Guided search 2.0 a revised model of visual search. Psychon. Bull. Rev. **1**(2), 202–238 (1994)
5. Bednall, E.S.: The effect of screen format on visual list search. Ergonomics **35**(4), 369–383 (1992)
6. Ojanpää, H., Näsänen, R., Kojo, I.: Eye movements in the visual search of word lists. Vis. Res. **42**(12), 1499–1512 (2002)
7. Gramopadhye, A.K., Drury, C.G., Sharit, J.: Feedback strategies for visual search in airframe structural inspection. Int. J. Ind. Ergon. **19**(5), 333–344 (1997)
8. Hall, R., et al.: An evaluation of a job-aiding tool for an inspection task. Proc. Hum. Factors Ergon. Soc. Ann. Meet. **47**(18), 1987–1990 (2003)
9. Megaw, E.D.: Factors affecting visual inspection accuracy. Appl. Ergon. **10**(1), 27–32 (1979)
10. Megaw, E.D., Richardson, J.: Eye movements and industrial inspection. Appl. Ergon. **10**(3), 145–154 (1979)
11. Gallwey, T.J., Drury, C.G.: Task complexity in visual inspection. Hum. Factors **28**(5), 595–606 (1986)
12. Taylor, W., Melloy, B., Dharwada, P., Gramopadhye, A., Toler, J.: The effects of static multiple sources of noise on the visual search component of human inspection. Int. J. Ind. Ergon. **34**(3), 195–207 (2004)
13. Gastelum, Z., Matzen, L., Stites, M., Smartt, H.: Cognitive science evaluation of safeguards inspector list comparison activities using human performance testing. In: Proceedings of the 59th Annual Institute of Nuclear Materials Management (INMM), 59th Meeting, Baltimore, MD (2018)
14. Carter, R.C.: Visual search with color. J. Exp. Psychol. Hum. Percept. Perform. **8**(1), 127 (1982)
15. Green, B.F., Anderson, L.K.: Color coding in a visual search task. J. Exp. Psychol. **51**(1), 19 (1956)
16. Smith, S.L.: Color coding and visual search. J. Exp. Psychol. **64**(5), 434 (1962)
17. Williams, L.G.: The effect of target specification on objects fixated during visual search. Percept. Psychophys. **1**(5), 315–318 (1966)

Caught in Eye Trackers' Blind Spots: Adapting Vision Studies to Ethnographic Field Research

Larry S. McGrath(✉), Lindsay A. Carrabine(✉), and Ranjan Nayyar(✉)

Design Science Consulting, Inc., Philadelphia, USA
{larry.mcgrath,lindsay.carrabine, ranjan.nayyar}@dscience.com

Abstract. Although eye tracking has been used to analyze user interfaces, the technology poses numerous challenges when applied to environments in which people move, work, and interact. Aren't eye trackers limited to studying two-dimensional planes? How might the device help to understand activities that are not exclusively visual? These questions are integral to ethnography, the observational study of peoples' interactions with products, processes, and places. We offer answers by way of two bodies of research. The first was conducted to optimize Instructions for Use (IFUs) for medical devices. The second was an exploratory study conducted to adapt eye trackers to manual tasks. The objective was to cultivate interpretive methods for evaluating visual and non-visual perception in eye-tracking data (i.e., fixation duration, gaze plots, heat maps). We suggest that the latter body of research illuminates new opportunities for ethnographic fieldwork to examine how medical professionals move their bodies when simultaneously carrying out procedures and viewing visual systems.

Keywords: Ethnography · Vision · Medical devices · User experience · Design human factors · Instructions for Use · Hospitals

1 Introduction

Technological advancements in eye-tracking technology has contributed to widespread vision studies of user interfaces, particularly in human factors research. At Design Science, we use mobile eye trackers to support the design of Instructions for Use (IFUs). Medical devices and products are sold with IFUs, which inform users and lay caregivers about proper uses, risks, and benefits. Eye trackers generated insights into how people actually use a given set of instructions—revealing what the users see, what they skip, and where they stumble. We have used the results to produce intuitive and readable IFUs.

We are now revamping our eye-tracking methods in an effort to incorporate the device into our ethnographic field research in hospitals and clinics. Many researchers, however, have been slow to use eye trackers as a part of their toolkit because questions linger about the utility, methodology, and value of conducting visual research in medical environments where people move, work, and interact. Why would devices

S. Yamamoto and H. Mori (Eds.): HCII 2019, LNCS 11569, pp. 76–88, 2019.
https://doi.org/10.1007/978-3-030-22660-2_6

designed to record superficial visual interfaces be useful in three-dimensional contexts? Given that medical professionals employ multiple perceptual systems when interacting with devices, how could eye tracking be adapted to examine modes of perception other than vision? Answers remain fleeting. As a result, ethnographic research gets lost in the blind spots of eye tracking.

In this paper, we show that this needn't be the case. Eye trackers stand to enrich ethnographic inquiry by empowering researchers to examine peoples' visual, tactile, and spatial interactions with medical devices.

Our goal is to outline interpretive methods to make eye tracking impactful in immersive contexts where users don't make use of visual perception alone. We do so by drawing on two bodies of research carried out at Design Science, in which researchers reconfigured vision studies for IFU optimization into experimental ethnographic models. Along the way, we found that the constraints of eye trackers in conventional visual-interface research generate criteria for improving ethnographic fieldwork.

The first body of research on IFUs identified what users read (and didn't) when performing tasks with medical devices. Eye trackers buoyed our reiterative research process, which serves to compare multiple versions of IFUs. Eye-tracking data made it easier for us to answer usability questions, such as:

- Which aspects of an IFU lead to use errors and difficulties?
- What elements of an IFU stand out to users?
- Do users rely more on images or text to comprehend an IFU?
- When confusion arises, is it due to the IFU or to the device?

Our human factors engineers and graphic designers used the results to eliminate design flaws and to reorganize IFUs' visual architecture for intuitive reading. We found, however, that the studies were suited to scenarios in which users primarily relied on vision to navigate superficial interfaces. Ethnography presents different parameters. In an effort to understand immersive contexts in which users do not only look *at* a visual field, but also interact with objects *in* the visual field, our researchers sought to devise alternative methods for ethnographic observation.

The second body of research is of users' interactions with various devices using visual and haptic feedback. In our study, tasks were designed to emulate interventional procedures in which, for example, pulmonologists or neurosurgeons engage with patients' bodies directly via medical devices (i.e., bronchoscopes and spinal screwdrivers) and indirectly via visual interfaces (i.e., bronchoscopy and fluoroscopy). By tracking participants' pupil movement while they performed manual tasks and observed a visual interface, our researchers tackled questions that are crucial to using eye trackers in future ethnographic research, such as:

- How is pupil movement indicative of users' spatial and tactile navigation of medical spaces?
- At which point do users shift their concentration from visual to tactile perception?
- How could users strike the right balance between tactile and visual engagements with medical devices?
- Which aspects of devices induce users to rely on perceptual systems other than vision?

The results demonstrated that tasks involving continuous physical exertion prompt users to diminish visual perception and instead to rely on tactile perception. By contrast, tasks that involve spatial coordination induce users to rely more on visual perception. Moreover, eye-tracking data can be interpreted to reveal both modes of perception. We suggest that distinct fixation patterns are associated with continuous physical exertion and spatial coordination. These results will empower our ethnographic researchers to use eye trackers in order to explore medical professionals' embodied interactions with interventional procedures for the sake of generating device design recommendations.

For both bodies of research, we used the Tobii Pro Glasses 2. This mobile eye tracker rests on the nose and ears like normal glasses. The glasses weigh 45 g and feature four sensors, which emit infrared light to the retinas at a 100-Hz sampling rate. A high-definition scene camera is attached to the bridge and directed outward to the visual field.

2 Visual Studies for Optimizing IFUs

2.1 Conventional Eye-Tracking Metrics vs. Customized Analysis

Usability testing is critical to creating effective IFUs. Observing users as they read and carry out simulated tasks helps to optimize the layout. By adding eye-tracking technology to traditional usability testing, we followed participants' optical behaviors using conventional metrics as well as our customized analyses (see Table 1). The results combine quantitative reports and qualitative insights to facilitate the design of intuitive and readable IFUs.

Table 1. Eye-tracking data

	Conventional metrics	Custom analysis
Data types	• Heat maps • Gaze plots • Fixation duration	• Parallel scan path visualizations • Reading-rate comparison • Task completion association
Key insights	• Length of time participants observe IFU elements • Order in which participants navigate IFU content	• Relation of use errors to gaze patterns • Relation of gaze patterns to IFU layout • Relation of reading rate (i.e., skimming vs. reading thoroughly) to IFU content

Out-of-the-box eye tracking generates gaze plots and heat maps, which visualize the IFU areas observed by users (see Figs. 1 and 2). These conventional metrics convey helpful information, yet they fail to provide a full context with meaningful clues to help optimize IFUs (see Table 2).

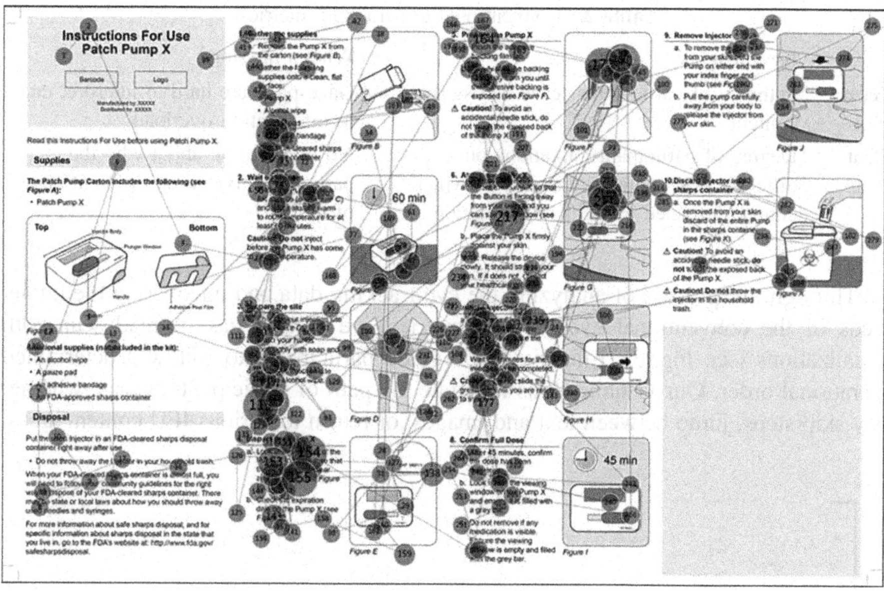

Fig. 1. Gaze plot

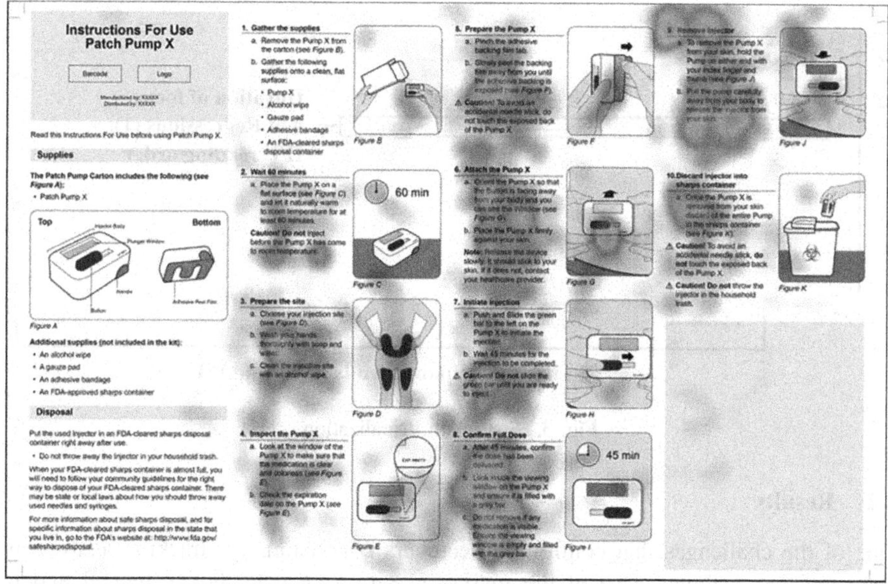

Fig. 2. Heat map

Table 2. Conventional eye-tracking metrics

	Key insights	What's missing?
Gaze plots	Pathway of participants' gaze across IFU content	Gaze plots are hard to interpret due to information overload
Heat maps	Degree of participants' fixations on different IFU content indicative of which content attracted participants' attention	No information about why the participant fixated on different areas of the IFU

Through our process of analyzing the eye-tracking data and uncovering the unmet needs of the conventional eye-tracking metrics, we created easy-to-read scan path visualizations (see Fig. 3). Effective IFUs guide participants to follow a determined operational order. Our visualizations illustrate the path of participants' gazes: whether they skip steps, jump between text and images, or return to various IFU content areas.

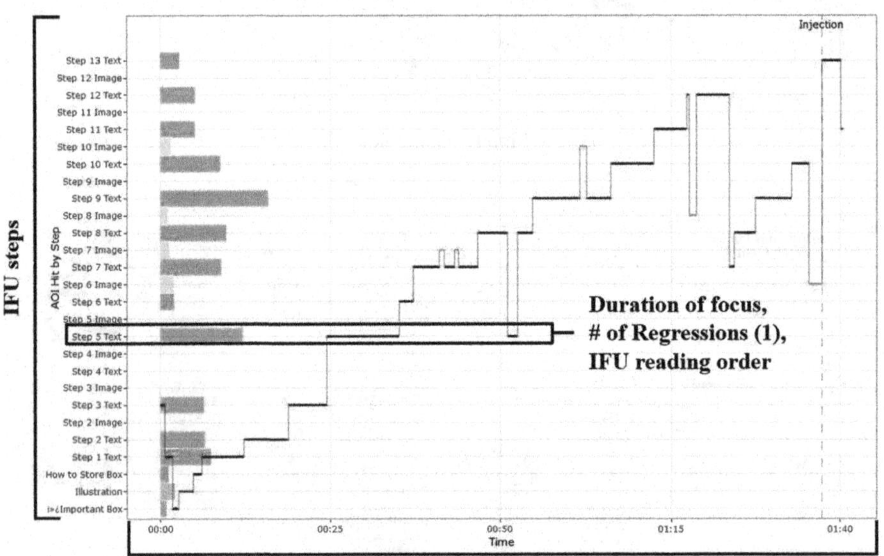

Fig. 3. Scan path visualization

2.2 Results

One of the challenges that confronts researchers conducting eye-tracking analysis is choosing and making sense of the myriad eye-tracking data. For a general understanding of participants' use of an IFU, heat maps and gaze plots are useful because they are easy to generate and interpret. However, when the aim is to diagnose a recurrent issue, such as when participants make a mistake at a specific instructional step, it can be useful to look at scan path visualizations, fixation metrics, and raw video from the eye tracker.

Upon review of the customized scan path visualizations, we generated concrete design recommendations to improve the IFU (see Table 3).

Table 3. Examples of IFU design recommendations

Gaze pattern behavior	Usability result/feedback	IFU design implication
• User skims over Steps 10–13 • User does not observe images at Steps 10–13	Use difficulty at Step 11: • User is confused by needle guard and assumes something has gone wrong	• Highlight critical tasks in Step 10–13 • Improve illustration to highlight specific device element
• User skips step 4 (image and text) while reading IFU	Use error at Step 4: • User does not mention anything about waiting 30 min before giving the injection	• Improve layout and bring location of Step 4 from top of the page closer to the center • Highlight critical information at Step 4 • Repeat critical information located in Step 4 (wait 30 min before injecting) at Steps 6, 7

3 Visual Studies for Embodied Research

Although eye trackers generated insightful data for optimizing IFUs, we found that different considerations were in order when conducting vision studies with users who manually engage with devices. In such contexts, users do not rely exclusively on sight. Indeed, rarely do people use only their eyes when navigating everyday spaces. How, then, might eye trackers account for visual perception as well as sensorimotor modes of perception? We sought to answer the question by creating an experimental vision study in which eye-tracking data were used to track not only the pupils' movement but that of the body as well.

We observe these contexts in Design Science's field research. For example, neurosurgeons conduct spinal fusions by watching fluoroscopic images to orient the manual placement of pedicle screws. In so doing, neurosurgeons navigate multiple modes of perception: both the fluoroscopic imaging and the tactile impression of the screw driver in patients' vertebrae. We have found that neurosurgeons enjoy direct haptic feedback of the vertebrae, though only indirect visual feedback from the imaging. We have also found that pulmonologists encounter a similar perceptual asymmetry. When conducting lung biopsies, for instance, pulmonologists manipulate a bronchoscope through patients' airways and enjoy direct haptic feedback via the device, yet indirect visual feedback from bronchoscopic visualizations on a screen. Both scenarios are ripe for eye tracking. Neurosurgeons, pulmonologists, and potentially other medical professionals stand to benefit from a better understanding of the intimate and imbricated interactions between visual and tactile perception. This is especially the case for younger medical professionals, who have yet to develop the delicate sense of balance when manipulating devices in patients' bodies and simultaneously watching images of patients' bodies.

Designing an experimental eye-tracking study to emulate medical professionals' perceptual asymmetry poses challenges. In lived experience, vision seamlessly complements tactility. Isolating distinct modes of perception is not straightforward. Instead of isolating either perceptual mode, we interpreted eye-tracking data to be indicative of both bodily and ocular activities. The pupils' movement reflects not only the eyes, but also an ensemble of embodied activities such as holding the head in place, shifting weight, and manipulating the hands [1]. We accounted for these activities by approaching eye-tracking data (notably, fixation durations, heat maps, and gaze plots) as indices of tactile perception. The gaze is one aspect of embodied movement.

3.1 Experimental Setup

For the study, 14 participants performed simple manual tasks with devices hidden under a box. Although the participants could not look directly inside the box, they could see indirectly via a video feed projected onto a television screen (see Fig. 4). This served as the visual interface. Akin to the parameters of interventional procedures mentioned above, participants encountered an asymmetry between visual and tactile perception.

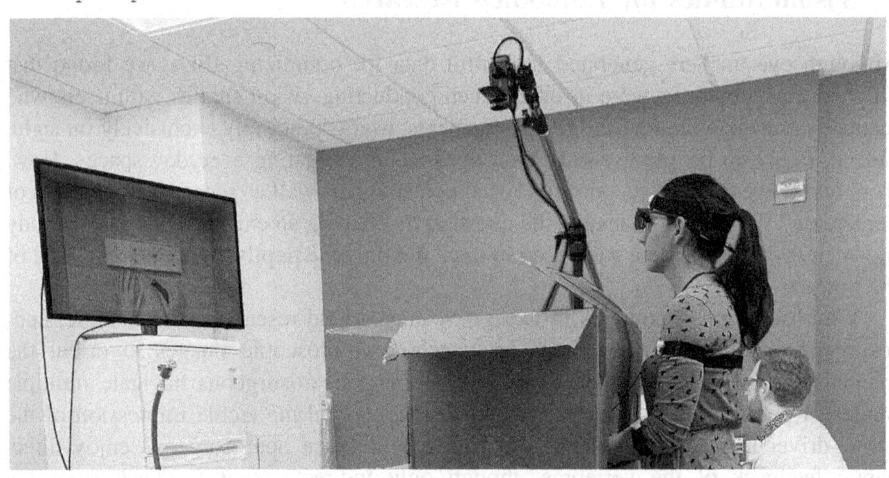

Fig. 4. Study setup for Scenarios 1 and 2

In the first scenario, participants were presented with a screwdriver and wood block with eight holes, four of which had Philips-head screws. The moderator asked the participants to un-screw and re-screw (in a different hole) each of the screws.

Scenario 1 involved two distinct kinds of manual activities: spatial coordination and continuous physical exertion. In the image below, a participant performs the former. She coordinates her hands in space, aligning them with a screw (Fig. 5).

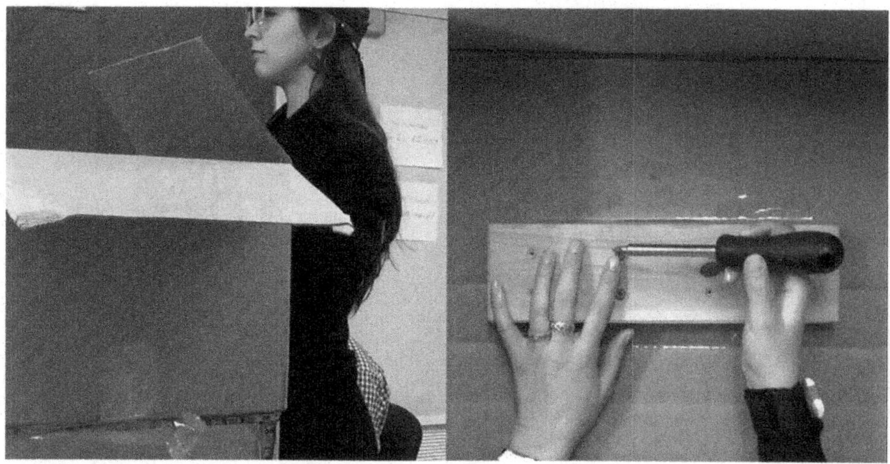

Fig. 5. Scenario 1 spatial coordination

For the second kind of manual activity, participants exercised exertive force to unscrew and re-screw using the screwdriver (see Fig. 6).

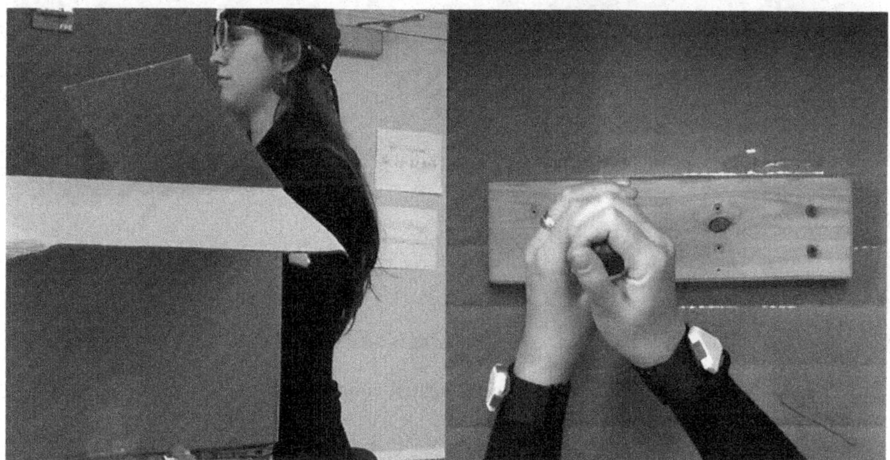

Fig. 6. Scenario 1 physical exertion

In the second scenario, participants were presented with a pill organizer. It had eight compartments, each of which contained three pills (see Fig. 7).

The moderator prompted participants to open select compartments, remove a specified number of pills, and arrange them in two rows along dotted lines. Unlike Scenario 1, the second scenario emphasized one manual activity: spatial coordination. Participants identified, selected, extracted, and arranged small objects (see Fig. 8). There was little expectation to exert sustained physical force.

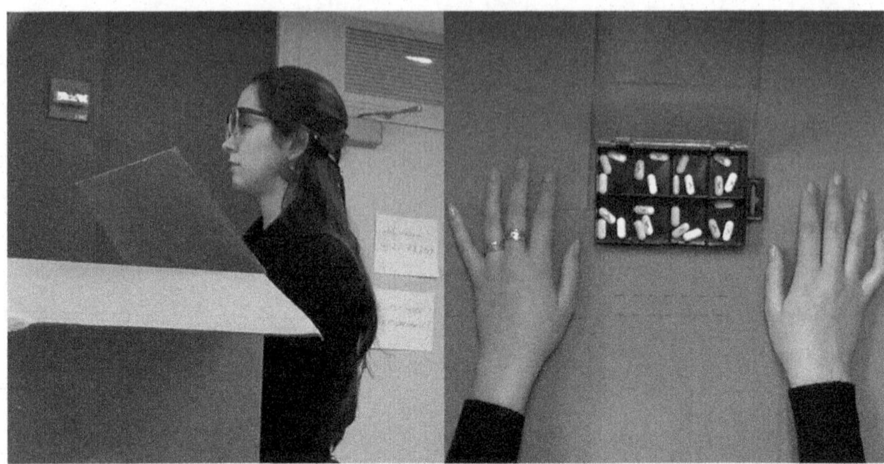

Fig. 7. Scenario 2

Fig. 8. Scenario 2 spatial coordination

Given the divisions between vision and tactility are porous in lived experience, we interpreted visual and tactile perception as heuristic categories. Neither are pure. Our focus was the moments at which participants shifted their attention from visual to non-visual perception: namely, when they looked away from the screen to perform a manual task. By having participants perform distinct kinds of manual tasks (i.e., coordinative and exertive), we compared tactile and visual perception relatively. Neither was wholly tactile nor visual; they differed according to their respective degrees of emphasis.

3.2 Results

Our results revealed that participants in Scenario 2 spent 84.65% of their time, on average, fixating on the screen. By contrast, the same participants in Scenario 1 spent 69.27% of their time, on average, fixating on the screen. Moreover, the difference was statistically significant; every participant spent more time looking away from the screen during Scenario 1 (p=.006 according to a two-tailed t-test).

Closer examination of the eye-tracking results reveals distinct fixation patterns associated with the Scenarios. Each involved different manual activities: spatial coordination and continuous physical exertion. When prompted to locate objects, participants directed their gaze at the screen in order to gather spatial information and to coordinate their hands. By contrast, participants tended to direct their gaze away from the screen when performing manual tasks involving intensive exertion.

The fixation pattern associated with spatial coordination was pronounced in Scenario 2. Participants identified, selected, and extracted pills from the small compartments of a pill organizer. Those participants' fixation patterns were confined to a narrow region on the screen around the visualization of manual activity. This is likely because the region offered the spatial information required to execute tasks.

A divergent fixation pattern associated with continuous physical exertion was peculiar to Scenario 1. Like Scenario 2, participants identified and selected screws, while the participants also observed the screen in order to gather spatial information. Once participants anchored a screw in place, however, they proceeded to apply exertive force to the screwdriver and shift their gaze beyond the screen. Moreover, the region to which participants directed their gaze remained consistent for each individual (though not across individuals).

What is the nature of this fixation pattern? Its purpose, we hypothesized, was not primarily visual. Participants in Scenario 1 did not aim to collect spatial information but instead to facilitate embodied effort. Just how the fixation pattern helped them in doing so demanded explanation.

3.3 Eye-Tracking Visualizations

Heat maps and gaze plots help to clarify the distinct perceptual modes involved in each fixation pattern. These visualizations represent the distribution of fixations across the visual field. Heat maps illustrate the concentration of fixations. Gaze plots illustrate their pathway. Together, the visualizations allowed us to make sense of the characteristics unique to each fixation pattern.

Participant 9 was exemplary. She fixated on the screen for 88% of the time during Scenario 2, which involved more coordination, and for only 70% of the time during Scenario 1, which involved more exertion.

The gaze plot of the participant's pupil movement in Scenario 2 illustrated that her gaze centered on the region of manual action in which she identified, located, and extracted pills from compartments of a pill organizer. This region offered ample visual resources for the coordination of the participant's manual tasks. The gaze plot of the same participant's pupil movement in Scenario 1 illustrated that her gaze repeatedly shifted above the screen and slightly to the left (see Figs. 9 and 10).

Fig. 9. Scenario 1 gaze plot

Fig. 10. Scenario 2 gaze plot

Whereas the gaze plot of Scenario 2 illustrates constrained pupil movement around the region of manual action, the gaze plot of Scenario 1 illustrates a mobile fixation pattern between two regions: the region of manual action on the screen as well as a relatively consistent region above the screen and to the top left. The latter region coincides with moments when the participant exerted force to manipulate the screwdriver. Embodied strain, and minimal spatial coordination, was involved.

Moreover, the fixation pattern associated with continuous physical exertion did not occupy a stable point (see Fig. 9). Pupil movements transitioned back-and-forth between the region of manual activity (the screw) and a region beyond the screen. The fixation pattern, therefore, involved a mobile circuit of visual perception.

3.4 Discussion

We interpret these divergent fixation patterns to represent a shift in emphasis between competing modes of perception: visual and tactile. Fixating on the screen was associated with visual perception, which participants emphasized to draw spatial information about the location of small objects. Shifting the gaze away from the screen was associated with tactile perception, which participants emphasized to concentrate on the screwdriver's haptic feedback. The latter scenario is representative of those we encounter in ethnographic observations of interventional medicine. For example, when straining to screw in a pedicle screw during spinal fusion procedures, neurosurgeons look away from key visual interfaces – such as fluoroscopic images – in order to concentrate on the task's tactile demands. Novice neurosurgeons stand to benefit from understanding the delicate balance struck by expert neurosurgeons when navigating overlapping perceptual systems.

Moreover, we found that the distinctive fixation pattern exhibited in Scenario 2 reflects participants' "attentional anchors" [2]. These are emergent (and not pre-given) constructs of vision. They offer a visual pivot point, as it were, upon which people exert perceptual leverage in order to concentrate on the exertive demands of manual tasks. The selection and formation of attentional anchors—that is, the range of space beyond the screen where participants fixated—was unique for each participant. Nonetheless, patterns emerged. In 9 of 11 cases (for which complete gaze plots were generated), participants' range was positioned on the side of the visual field opposite their dominant hand (i.e., right-handed participants tended to shift their gaze to the left of the screen). Numerous interpretations are possible. Because attentional anchoring secured embodied leverage, the associated fixation pattern may have facilitated the centrifugal force with which participants drove the screwdriver's handle. Alternatively, because the attentional anchor reflected repeated sensorimotor activity; its selection and location may have aligned with the diagonal movement of participants' bodies when applying continuous exertion to the screwdriver. In either case, the fact that fixation patterns tended to intersect with a region of the visual field opposite of participants' dominant hands suggests that the eyes' movement derived from the body's. Tactile perception lead; visual perception followed.

4 Conclusion

Different contexts call for different approaches to eye tracking. Not all usability challenges present the same parameters for vision studies. By comparing the distinctive aspects of two bodies of research, we hope to have shown that eye tracking is a malleable tool adaptable to diverse usability contexts. When examining IFUs, eye trackers facilitate a reiterative approach that optimizes their arrangement of information and visual architecture. The result is more intuitive instructions for the sake of effective medical device use. When it comes to the manual practices by which people interact with devices, eye tracking can—and should—be interpreted for modes of perception that are not exclusively visual. By interpreting eye-tracking data as an index of tactile perception, ethnographic researchers can better adapt vision studies to the immersive contexts in which interactions between users and devices takes place. The results, we hope, will illuminate what has remained in eye trackers' *blind spots:* the embodied skillsets with which people exert force and coordinate movement when performing manual tasks.

References

1. Solman, G., Foulsham, T., Kingstone, A.: Eye and head movements are complementary in visual selection. R. Soc. Open Sci. **4**, 160569 (2017)
2. Abrahamson, D., Bakker, A.: Making sense of movement in embodied design for mathematics learning. Cogn. Res.: Princ. Implic. **1**(1), 33 (2016)

A Study of Optimum Representation of Digital Contents on Smart Phones

Guo-Peng Qui[1], Chien-Nan Chen[2], Yi Gui Li[1], and Ming-Chyuan Lin[1(✉)]

[1] College of Arts and Design, Sanming University, Sanming, Fujian, China
644021962@qq.com, 342037137@qq.com, mingchyuan1688@gmail.com

[2] Department of Industrial Design, National Cheng Kung University, Tainan, Taiwan, China
jasperview2002@gmail.com

Abstract. Currently, smart phones are widely used in the world. The way of display representation on digital contents is usually a combination of pictures, characters, voices and dynamic images. Since characters can communicate accurate information to people, the presentation of characters plays an important role in displaying information. As such, the research objective is to explore the optimum digital contents display for smart phones that can help users improve better viewing and operating. In this research, character contents of smart phones including (1) color matching of character and the corresponding background, (2) spacing between lines, (3) spacing between words, (4) character size, and (5) typeface are considered in the experimental design for analysis and evaluation. To conduct the study, the research divides the development procedure into three stages. They are (1) definition of experimental parameters and design of simulation display for building experimental environment, (2) implementation of experimental design for data collection, and (3) analysis of back-propagation neural network process for determining suitable character contents. The result showed that 12 to 16 pts for character size, line distance, and word distance will be preferred. In addition, DFKai-SB, PMingliU, Arial, and Times New Roman of Chinese and English typefaces are recommended. As to colors for character and background, a mixed black and white color is preferred. The research may need to make further investigation on the color issue. It is expected that the implementation of this research will provide designers with design references.

Keywords: Smart phones · Digital content · Character visual representation · Back propagation neural network

1 Introduction

The progress of Internet technology has made the hand-held intelligent devices become the mainstream of 3C (Computer, Communication, and Consumer Electronics) electronic products. Most of these kinds of products, especially the smart phones are operated by senses of fingertip and finger touch and seeing based on a touch screen. The factors that

S. Yamamoto and H. Mori (Eds.): HCII 2019, LNCS 11569, pp. 89–102, 2019.
https://doi.org/10.1007/978-3-030-22660-2_7

affect the tactual identification will include shape, texture, and size [1]. To accurately and efficiently operate a hand-held intelligent device, the user needs to pay more attention to his or her hand activity and will cause safety problems especially when the user is in walking or driving situation [2]. In general, a smart phone has a touch screen with 5 to 6 in. of size to display human-computer interaction information for the user. The information is presented in specific digital contents which make the user can view and operate according to its instantaneous message display. Most digital contents are represented in multimedia types including pictures, characters, voices and dynamic images that enrich the satisfaction of user requirements. Even though picture images can present direct, subjective, emotional and visual feelings, characters which present abstract and objective message can help transmit accurate and complicated information to the user [3]. Stone et al. [4] indicated that some factors such as typeface, type size, letter spacing, line spacing, line length and color will affect the legibility of text in current digital displays. It appears that the characters share a large portion in digital contents and also become an important factor in the human-computer interaction process. Jung and Im [5] recommended that character icons with suitable touch area and desirable hit rate be important guidelines for a smart phone user interface design. Crundall et al. [2] observed that larger text sizes will have high relatively short glances, whereas smaller text will lead to have long glances. Preece et al. [6] suggested that a good design should optimize the user's interaction with a usable interactive product system in a way of easy to learn, effective to understand and enjoyable to use. However, any poor design of digital contents in characters and color matching of the corresponding background can cause problems in legibility and cognition.

Since the designer has his or her own subjected opinion, the integration of knowledge Since most information interfaces in digital contents are primary an image-based design, it will be worthy of exploring a better form of character representation for serving an auxiliary information communication. In addition, determining the optimum combination of characteristic levels is a known issue in research. It is also noted that the concept of the back-propagation algorithm in neural network (NN) research offers a useful search tool for engineering optimization problems. The back-propagation algorithm requires a sufficient number of correct and efficient training samples to complete the training process and calibrate the system such that it will have suitable prediction capacity [7]. The application of NN has gradually turned towards design improvement [8, 9]. This improvement could greatly enhance the quality of digital content design, especially for determining more precise settings of the characteristic values in character design. Therefore, it might be possible to more effectively develop "better" character design by providing designers with a neural network approach that can recommend more suitable character design. As such, the objective of this research is to proceed with an integrated study of neural network approach on the legibility of characters in digital content representation for the smart phones to help identify the most suitable mode of parameter combination in interaction interface design. The character properties to be considered in this research will include (1) color matching of character and the corresponding background, (2) spacing between lines, (3) spacing between words, (4) character size, and (5) typeface [10]. The proposed concept of the optimum experimental training, simulation, and inference procedure on character representation research will be able to apply in various hand-held intelligent products that provide users with greater viewing comfort.

2 Development Procedure

According to the research objective, the proposed approach will use interactive experiments to obtain the optimum operational data of character representation from smart phone tested subjects. The collected data will then be forwarded to the back propagation neural network training, simulation, and inference for recommending the optimum parameter combination of character representation. To conduct the experimental procedure, the research has three stages of development. They are (1) definition of experimental parameters, (2) development of simulation displays and conduction of experimental design, and (3) back propagation neural network process for optimum character representation. At the first stage, the research will collect and summarizes characteristics of character contents from a variety of current smart phone representation displays to figure out threshold values of common characteristics for designing a representative display in the experimental design. Note that several pairs of colors regarding character/background color matching, current character attribute values including candidate spaces between lines and words, typeface and character sizes are also collected. The second stage includes definition of experimental interface, development of experimental programming, conduction of optimum character display experiment, and collection and summary of experimental data. At this stage, the research develops an interactive interface for the experimental design and arranges the tested subjects to perform the experiment. During the experimental process, the tested subjects input their characteristic data and get into the adjustable interface to choose typeface, character/background color matching, character size, spaces between lines and words based on their preferences. The inputted data will be stored in the file of Microsoft Excel 2007. As to the third stage, the research applies the concept of back propagation neural network in the process of data manipulation and analysis to explore the optimum combination of character attribute values. At this stage, the research will use Microsoft Visual Basic 6.0 to establish an input interface for retrieving characteristic data of tested subjects. Besides, the software of MATLAB 7.0 will be used for the back propagation neural network training and simulation process. The output data of the simulation results will be restored and adjusted to represent the optimum combination of character attribute values. Figure 1 shows the overall development procedures for the exploration of optimum representation of digital contents on smart phones.

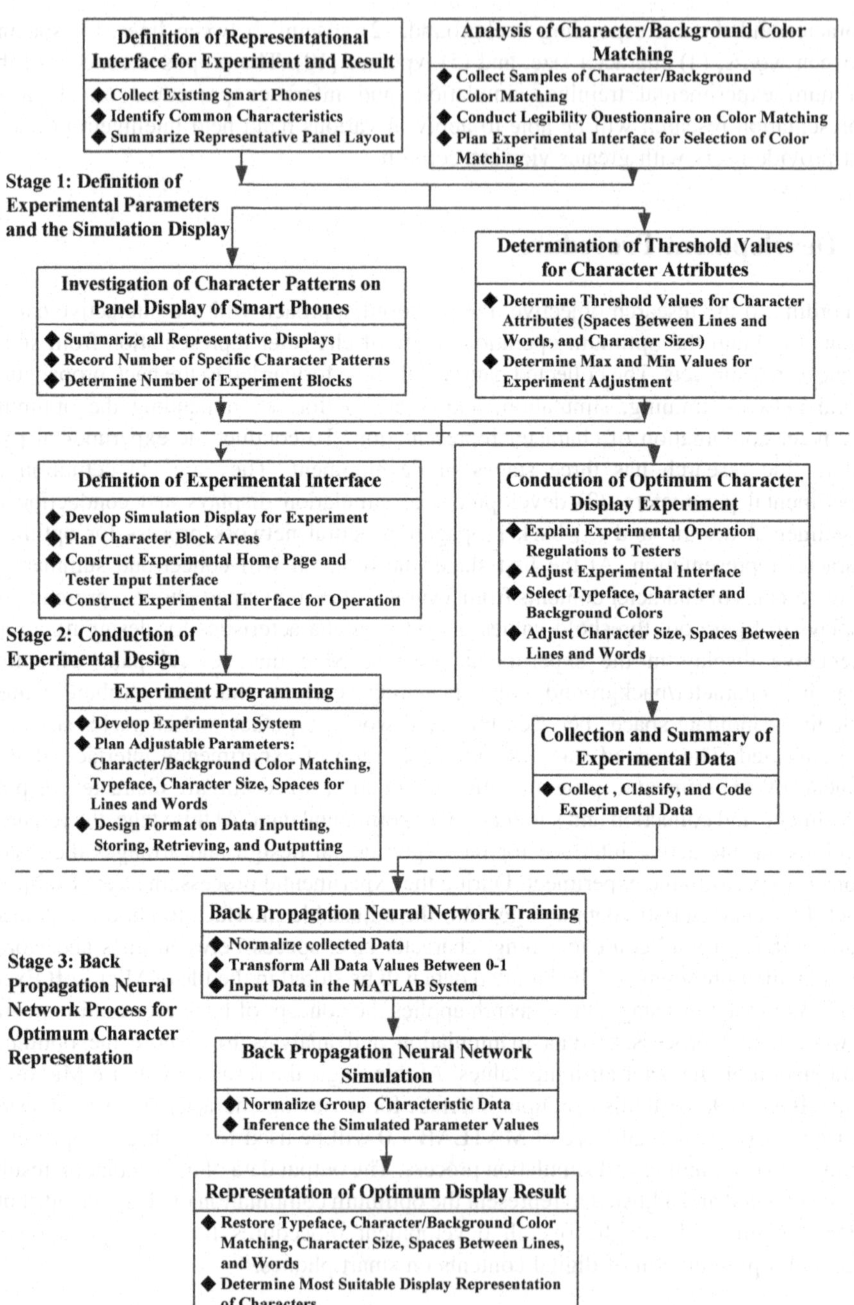

Fig. 1. A conceptual development framework for the proposed approach

3 Definition of Experimental Parameters

To construct an optimum inference system for exploring the most suitable character representation of smart phones, the research collected 55 existing types of smart phones from Websites of different brands. Since 31 of 55 types of smart phones have sizes equal or larger than 5.5 in., this research decided to use the most popular size of 5.5 in. as a representative display and computer software of Illustrator CS 6 to help develop a simulation environment for further experimental design. The research also collected characteristics of character contents from these 31 types of smart phones. Note that the collection of character/background color matching is based on the measurement of RGB (R: red; G: green; B: blue) index values directly from smart phone display interfaces. The tools for use in measuring the RGB values include (1) use the software AdobeIllustrate CC to measure RGB values directly from sample displays, and (2) use APP free software Pixel Picker to measure RGB values directly from smart phone build-in trim picture function. Figure 2 illustrates a targeted orange color background that is measured to have a RGB value of (255/149/0) from a sample display when using the Pixel Picker in App. As to the character characteristics, the research directly extracted samples both Chinese and English from smart phone pictures and placed them in categories to determine representative character characteristics. The definition of threshold values for character parameters is based on the collection of 234 display pictures of current smart phones. Figure 3 illustrated some extracted samples of display pictures from collected smart phones.

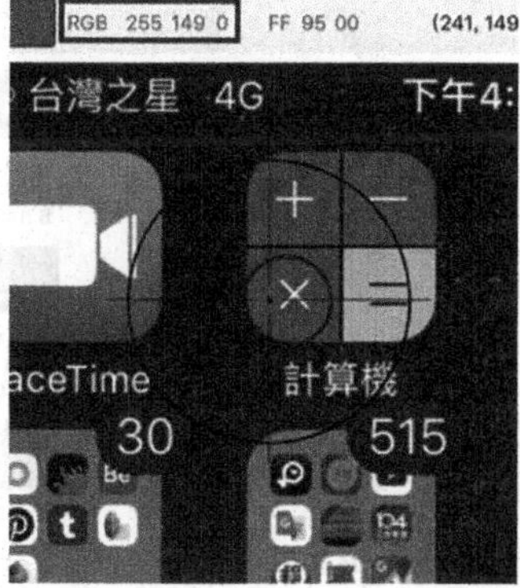

Fig. 2. Measurement of display RGBs by the Pixel Picker in App (Color figure online)

3.1 Definition of Colors for Character and Background Color Matching

Statistical analysis of pair-wise colors on characters associated with backgrounds found that close color matching is frequently used. This situation made the RGB value cannot be measured separately. As such, the research first asked 7 experienced designers to record 63 types of character/background RGB values and then summarized to 20 representative color blocks for the experiment. Figure 4 illustrates the identified 20 colors of characters and backgrounds.

Fig. 3. Extraction of display pictures from collected smart phones

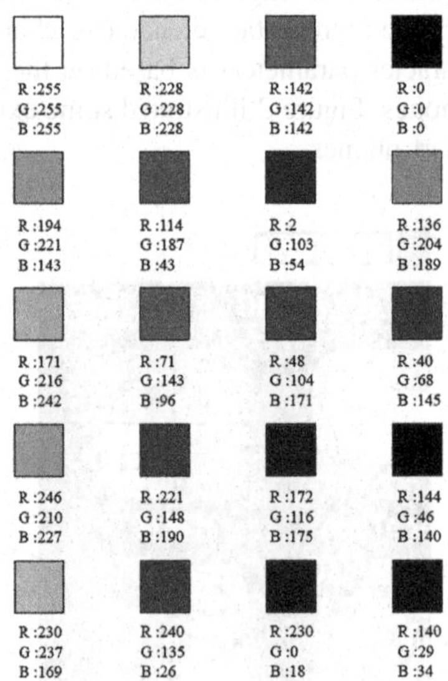

Fig. 4. Illustration of identified colors for character/background color matching (Color figure online)

3.2 Definition of Spaces Between Character Lines

The research invited 124 people (67 males and 57 females) between ages 13 and 65 years to choose acceptable ranges of line spaces from 124 extracted displays of 5.5″ smart phones. Figure 5 illustrates the distribution of line spaces based on character size 12 pt of Microsoft JhengHei with fixed 12 pt of word spaces. According to the survey result shown in Fig. 5, the research decided to use 12, 14, 16, 18, 20, 22, and 24 pts of line spaces for the experiment.

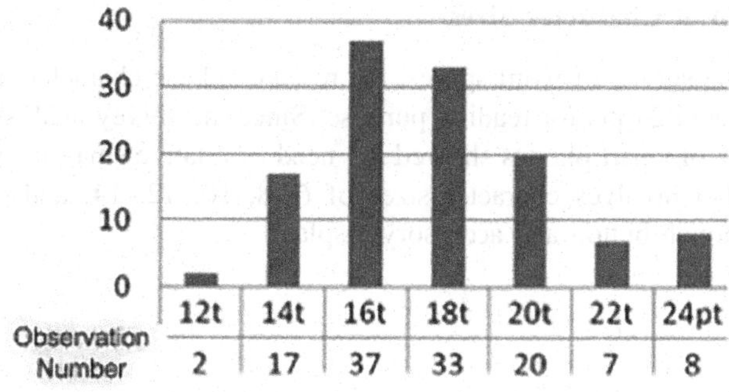

Fig. 5. Distribution of character line space survey

3.3 Definition of Spaces Between Words

A similar survey of spaces between character lines is used to define spaces between words. Figure 6 defines the word space for Chinese words. The character size 12 pt of Microsoft JhengHei with fixed 16 pt of line spaces is considered. The survey result is illustrated in Fig. 7. Note that current smart phones have built-in functions to increase or reduce the space between words based on the increase or reduce of character/word size. In other words, the space between two words is flexible and will depend on the size of the words. Based on the result shown in Fig. 7, the research also decided to use 12, 14, 16, 18, 20, 22, and 24 pts of word spaces for the experiment.

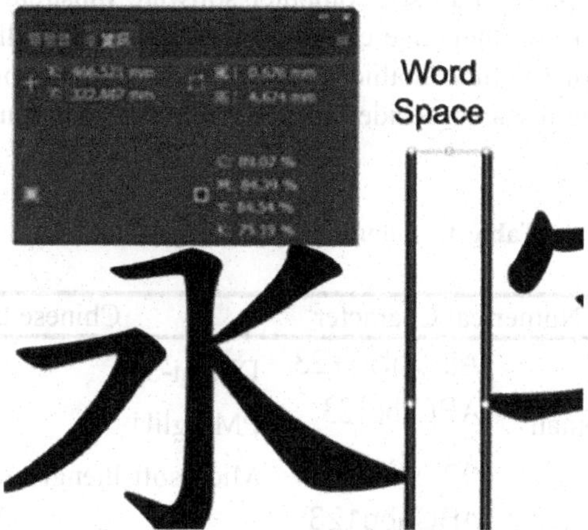

Fig. 6. Definition of word space in Chinese

3.4 Definition of Character Sizes

According to the survey of word spaces, the research chose character sizes of 12, 14, 16, 18, 20, 22, and 24 pts for reading purpose. Since the survey analysis regarding in the icon display of smart phones showed the need of relative small of character sizes, the research also involves character sizes of 6, 8, 10, 12, 14, and 16 pts for the experiment of touch button and accessory display.

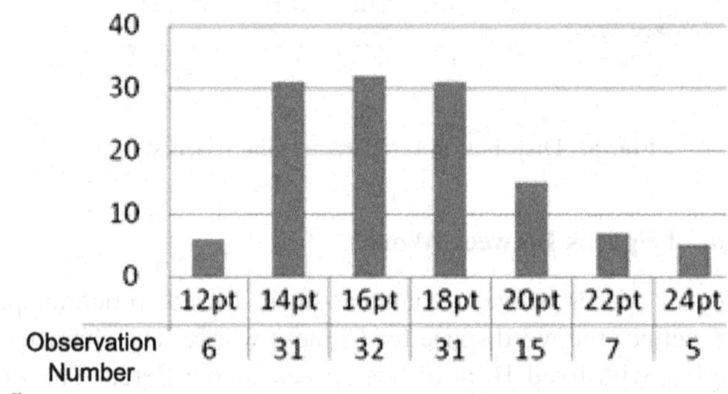

Fig. 7. Distribution of word space survey

3.5 Definition of Typefaces

To choose representative typefaces for experiments, the research extracted 234 pictures from smart phone displays and used computer software Illustrator CS6 built-in character typefaces to make an inductive comparisons. The result is illustrated in Table 1. Since the typefaces of Century Gothic, Gadugi, Arial, and Calibri do not make significant difference, the research decided to use Arial as a representative typeface.

Table 1. Summary of popular typefaces

English/Numerical Character		Chinese Character	
Century Gothic	ABCabc123	DFKai-SB	永字八法
Times New Roman	ABCabc123	PMingliU	永字八法
Gadugi	ABCabc123	Microsoft JhengHei	永字八法
Arial	ABCabc123		
Calibri	ABCabc123		

4 Development of Simulation Displays and Conduction of Experimental Design

The framework of the operational interface is developed based on the definition of character contents. To insure that the experiment can be fitted to the real situation, the research designed an APP operational interface display corresponding to a 5.5″ of smart phone. The research defined 20 RGB color codes for character and background color matching, set the line space around 12–24 pts, the word space around 0.6 mm–1.0 mm (refer to 12–24 pts), and the character size around 12–24 pts (regular reading) and 6–16 pts (touch button and icon display), respectively. The legibility questionnaire is designed with a five-scale evaluation form and its contents are based on user preference, aesthetic color matching, appropriate color matching, viewing habit and reading cognition. Note that Chinese typefaces of DFKai-SB, PMingliU, and Microsoft JhengHei and English typefaces of Arial and Times New Roman are chosen respectively for further experiment. In this operational interface design, three major interface displays in Chinese mode are illustrated in Figs. 8, 9, and 10, respectively. They are (1) recommendation of character size, (2) recommendation of line space and word space, and (3) recommendation of character color and background color and submission of final survey result.

Since current smart phones are popular to the young people, the research chose a total of 36 tested subjects including 12 male and 24 female college students to be voluntarily invited to participate in this experiment. All tested subjects have at least some sort of experiences on using hand-held intelligent products especially the smart phones and corrected normal visual acuity. Each tested subject is first asked to input personal data and then sequentially measures the character size, line space, word space, and character color/background color matching. During the experiment, the tested subject can adjust each character content attribute value based on his or her visual preference and cognition. All tested subjects should be able to easily adjust the

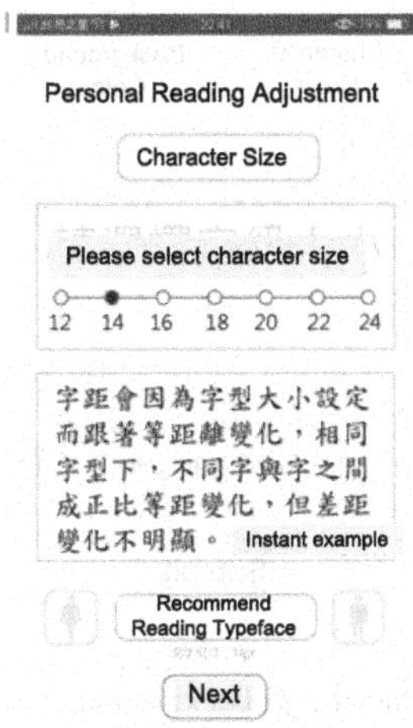

Fig. 8. Interface display of Chinese character size selection

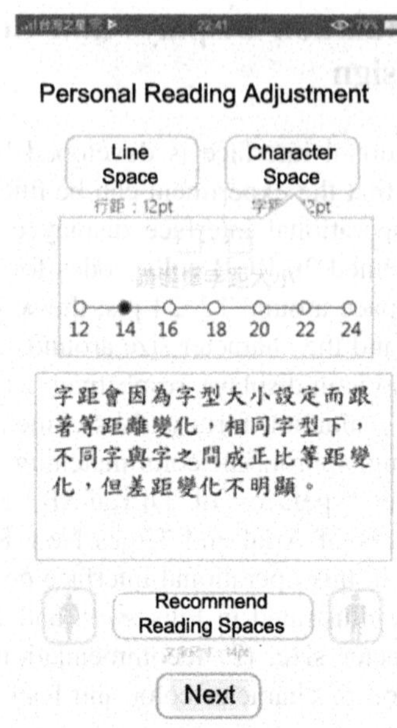

Fig. 9. Interface display of Chinese line and word spaces selection

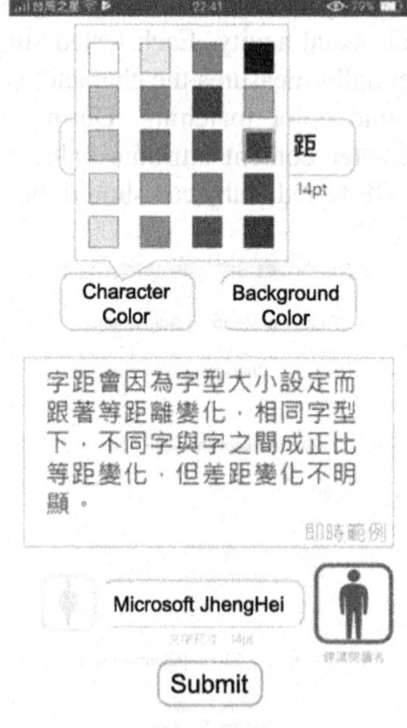

Fig. 10. Interface display of character and background color selection (Color figure online)

character-blocks in the simulated display by the system of optimum experiment and re-adjust the character-blocks until the optimum display is determined. Having finished the experiment, the tested subject is asked to do a five scale of satisfactory questionnaire. Each run of the experiment, the adjusted values of character contents will be stored in the tables of Microsoft Excel 2007. The information of subjects' features and experimental data will be applied in the training-stage of neural network to generate an optimum display of character contents.

5 Exploration of Optimum Character Content Representation

In the third stage, the information of users' features and experimental data will be applied in the training and simulation stages of the back propagation neural network to generate an optimum display of character characteristics representation. The frame development of training and simulation in neural networks include type of network, input data, target data, training function, number of layer, adapting learning function, performance function, and number of neurons. According to the collected data characteristics of tested subjects and character contents, a three- layer of back propagation neural network with multiple input neurons is selected [10]. Table 2 illustrates a list of neural network function configuration. In this research, the prediction of character typeface, size, line space and word space has 4 input neurons, 2 output neurons and 3 hidden neurons, while the prediction of character/background color has 22 input neurons, 2 output neurons and 2 hidden neurons [9, 11].

To simplify the study, 36 tested subjects are divided into male and female groups. Figure 11 shows the input data of tested subjects. Note that the data illustrated in Fig. 11 are transformed into numerical values for the purpose of statistical manipulation The computer software Matlab 7.0 is used for the analysis of back-propagation neural network training and simulation. In Matlab 7.0, the research defined transfer function, number of neurons and transfer function variable settings as illustrated in Fig. 12. As to the expected goal values, they are all defined as less than 0.05. Having finished the training and simulation process of back propagation neural network, the research derives the optimum combination of character contents as presented in

Table 2. List of neural network function configuration

Propagation functions configuration				Network configuration	
Epoachs	1000	Mu_dec	0.1	Input range	[0,1]
Goal	0.001	Mu_inc	10	Training function	LMTRAIN
Max_fail	5	Mu_max	1e+010	Layer1 neuron	3
Mu_reduc	1	Show	25	Layer1 transfer function	TANSIG
Min_grad	1e−010	Time	inf	Layer2 neuron	2
Mu	0.001			Layer2 transfer function	PURELIN

	Sex	Age	Typeface	size	Line space	Word space	Character Color	Background Color
1	2	20	1	14	14	14	1	10
2	2	20	2	14	18	14	1	4
3	1	20	2	14	18	14	1	4
4	1	20	2	14	14	14	4	18
5	2	20	2	12	14	14	11	1
6	1	20	2	14	16	12	4	1
7	2	20	1	14	18	14	4	5
8	1	20	1	14	14	14	1	9
9	2	20	2	14	18	12	1	10
10	1	19	2	12	14	14	4	1
11	2	19	2	12	14	12	4	2
12	2	19	2	12	18	16	1	3
13	2	19	2	12	16	14	11	1
14	2	19	1	14	16	16	4	1
15	2	19	2	14	16	14	1	10
16	2	19	2	12	18	14	1	3
17	2	19	2	12	16	14	1	11
18	2	19	2	14	18	12	1	7
19	2	20	1	12	16	14	14	10
20	2	20	1	12	14	14	14	10
21	1	19	2	12	18	14	4	1
22	2	19	2	14	16	12	4	1
23	2	19	2	12	18	12	4	1
24	2	19	2	14	16	14	1	4
25	2	19	2	14	14	12	4	13
26	1	19	1	14	18	12	1	10
27	1	19	2	12	16	12	4	10
28	1	19	2	12	16	14	4	18
29	2	19	2	14	14	14	4	1
30	2	19	2	12	18	14	18	4
31	2	19	2	12	14	14	1	12
32	1	20	1	12	14	12	1	4
33	1	19	2	14	14	14	2	1
34	2	19	2	12	14	12	4	1
35	2	19	1	12	14	12	1	4

Fig. 11. Input data of tested subjects

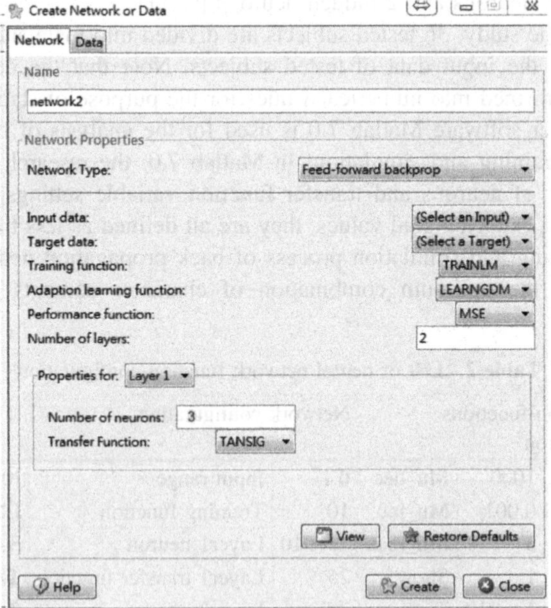

Fig. 12. Example showing Matlab functional settings

Table 3. Summary of recommended character contents

Optimum combination of character parameter values				
Character type	Typeface	Character size (pt)	Line space (pt)	Word space (pt)
Chinese	DFKai - SB	12	14	12
	Microsoft JhengHei	14	16	14
		16	18	16
English	Arial	12	12	12
	Times New Roman	14	14	14
		16	16	16

Table 3. The analysis of Chinese and English legibility prediction obtained 77.2% and 66.2% of accuracy on character typeface, character size, line space, and word space, respectively. However, only 13.3% of average accuracy on character and background color matching.

6 Conclusion

Smart phones have become part of our daily essentials. People whoever they are young or old, female or male use smart phones all the time. In general, the ease of setting conditions will affect the operation time of uses. It appears that the user always needs to spend more time in adapting interface operation for different brands or models of smart phones. The research proposed an integrated procedure to explore an optimum combination of character parameters including character and background color matching, space between lines, space between words, character sizes, and typefaces. The parameter values for the above mentioned character characteristics are identified and defined for designing an experimental simulation display. The tested subjects were selected from experienced voluntarily male and female college students. In the experiment, data including basic information of tested subjects and preferable settings of character values are forwarded to the process of back-propagation neural network training and simulation. It is noted that the outcomes of this research are all experiment-oriented so that the optimum character contents are highly objective. However, more experiment data collection and validation are needed for further studies so that the final results can be more reliable and useful. It is expected that the result of exploration of character contents on smart phones this will provide designers with design references in (1) designing a more suitable interaction interface connection between character contents and users, (2) organizing an optimum structure of character contents in operation performance, and (3) developing an appropriate mode of character content information display. In addition, this research will help user reduce the time in setting attributions of character contents and establish users' awareness on the digital content information interface so that the human-computer interaction can be more humanized and intelligent.

Acknowledgements. The authors are grateful to the Fujian University Humanities and Social Science Research Base-Product Design Innovation Research Center, China for supporting this research.

References

1. Tomioka, K.: Study on legibility of characters for the elderly-effects of character display modes on legibility. J. Physiol. Anthropol. **26**(2), 159–164 (2006)
2. Sanders, M.S., McCormick, E.J.: Human Factors in Engineering and Design, 7th edn. McGraw-Hill Inc., New York (1993)
3. Preece, J., Rogers, Y., Sharp, H.: Interaction Design: Beyond Human-Computer Interaction. Wiley, Hoboken (2002)
4. Stone, D., Jarrett, C., Woodroffe, M., Minocha, S.: User Interface Design and Evaluation. Morgan Kaufmann Publishers, San Francisco (2005)
5. Jung, E.S., Im, Y.: Touchable area: an empirical study on design approach considering perception size and touch input behavior. Int. J. Ind. Ergon. **49**, 21–30 (2015)
6. Crundall, E., Large, D.R., Burnett, G.: A driving simulator study to explore the effects of text size on the visual demand of in-vehicle displays. Displays **43**, 23–29 (2016)
7. Holland, J.H.: Adaptation in Natural and Artificial System. University of Michigan Press (1992)
8. Hsiao, S.-W., Chiu, F.-Y., Lu, S.-H.: Product-form design model based on genetic algorithms. Int. J. Ind. Ergon. **40**(3), 237–246 (2010)
9. Lin, M.-C., Lin, Y.-H., Lin, C.-C., Chen, M.-S., Hung, Y.-C.: An integrated neuro-genetic approach incorporating the Taguchi method for product design. J. Adv. Eng. Inform. **29**, 47–58 (2015)
10. Lin, M.-C., Lin, Y.-H., Liu, S.-F., Wang, M.-H.: A study of interaction interface design of digital contents on hand-held intelligent products. In: Yamamoto, S. (ed.) HIMI 2017. LNCS, vol. 10273, pp. 235–247. Springer, Cham (2017). https://doi.org/10.1007/978-3-319-58521-5_19
11. Jung, J.-R., Yum, B.-J.: Artificial neural network based approach for dynamic parameter design. Expert Syst. Appl. **38**, 504–510 (2011)

Research on the Information Layout of HMDs Based on Flight Missions and Visual Cognition

Jiang Shao[1,2(✉)], Jun Yao[1], Kun Zhang[1,2], and Ketong Yan[1]

[1] School of Architecture & Design, China University of Mining and Technology, Xuzhou 221000, China
shaojiangseu@qq.com

[2] Engineering Research Center for Innovative Design of Industrial and Intelligent Equipment, Xuzhou 221000, China

Abstract. The study on the rationality of the layout of the interface information presented by HMDs (helmet-mounted Display Systems) during different flight missions was conducted, mainly for the purpose of solving the problem that the position of the alarm information displayed on HMDs interface was not reasonable, and the pilot was unable to timely react to the decision. The HMDs warning information rendering area is divided in detail. Behavioral experiments were designed based on the visual cognitive mechanism of pilots. The priority of warning information in different regions was analyzed through comparative analysis of task response time, which provided experimental basis and scientific criteria for HMDs alarm information layout coding.

Keywords: Helmet-mounted Display Systems · Augmented reality · Information identification

1 Introduction

With the rapid development of aviation technology and computer technology, a fighter avionics system becomes more and more complex and data information generated by the system rises explosively so that a pilot has to receive much more information in a short period of time. HMDs interface is an augmented reality (AR) interface. In comparison with the traditional avionics system, whose display interface is featured by single and limited data sources, fixed interaction modes and low-dimensional information visualization, the information sources of HMDs are diversified; its information is real-time and dynamic; its information presentation is characterized by overlapping, multi-dimensionality and spatiality. For different flight missions, the pilot needs to acquire and focus on the information importance. If alarm information during different mission phases is scientifically designed and effectively hinted, the situational awareness ability of the pilot will be significantly improved to avoid accidents.

Many scholars at home and abroad have carried out relevant researches on the interface layout and information presentation of avionics systems such as HMDs. For the development of optical principles and the visual expression of interfaces of HUD and HMDs, Collinson et al. made comprehensive researches to ensure a pilot can perform missions safely and efficiently [1]. Rolland et al. conducted holographic

S. Yamamoto and H. Mori (Eds.): HCII 2019, LNCS 11569, pp. 103–121, 2019.
https://doi.org/10.1007/978-3-030-22660-2_8

waveguide HMD experimental researches on the improvement of imaging quality of HMDs [2]. Zhang et al. performed experimental researches on depth perception of HMDs, analyzed and summarized factors affecting the optimal retro-reflection screen [3]. For an unfixed-wing fighter in extreme environments such as fog, dust and darkness, Doehler et al. researched the interface navigation design of HMDs [4]. By right of ways of highlighting including brightness and flashlight, Van Orden et al. experimented symbol shapes and colors and probed into their influences on searching time [5]. For the design and development of graphical user interfaces, Hackos and Redish (1998) put forward effective user demand analysis methods and user models easily applied by software developers [6]. Also, some researchers, with regard to the specific designs of graphic user interface elements such as window layout, graphic design, pointer design, menu form, color and symbol, etc., proposed instructional design principles and empirical methods. Based on experimental observation, Fleetwood and Byrne found out the factors affecting user's visual searches, namely, the first factor is the number of icons, the second one is the target region boundary and the last one indicates the quality and definition of icons [7]. Wu et al. brought forward a video image processing method to detect the azimuth and pitch angle of HMDs relative to the fighter and optimize the current angle of HMDs tracking head [8]. Peinecke adopted a multi-sensor information fusion to enhance the visual display effect of HMDs [9]. In order to raise the situational awareness of a helicopter pilot under low visibility situations, Knabl et al. developed a symbolic system suitable for demonstrations, covering obstacles, route information and threat areas [10]. During the HMPP (Human Measures and Performance Project) study, NASA especially focused on the color security and availability design displayed in the various complex graphic interfaces [11]. Yeh and Wickens experimentally studied how to better present information about combats in a chaotic environment [12]. Montgomery and Sorkin made some experimental researches on impacts of brightness on the interface information identification [13]. Tullis and Schum researched the identification efficiency of digital display and graphic display information coding [14, 15]. Monnier made a comparative experiment on colors and positions by the experimental paradigm of digital delay search mission [16].

In accordance with Chinese military standards, navigation standards and USA military *standards, etc., HMDs* interface *is divided into several major areas in this paper. As shown in* Fig. 1, *extending out from the center, the core area is regarded as an aiming display area, which displays no symbols and icons in principle to avoid sheltering any aiming target; the upper part of this interface is classified as heading indicating area, which is relatively intuitive, so that the pilot can conclude the current heading and target heading information when he or she observes the interface directly; the left side of this interface is classified as speed indicating area; the left side is a height indicating area; the lower part of this interface is an attitude indicating information area. For the division* of icons, HMDs interface information layout is divided into 5 parts according to guiding principles for the layout specified in Chinese military standards.

Where, area 1 indicates localizer deviation area, area 2 indicates speed indicating area, area 3 indicates attitude and guidance area, area 4 indicates height indicating area and area 5 shows aiming display area. The upper edge and lower center of this interface are white reserve areas (the flight mode announcement area is placed on the upper part

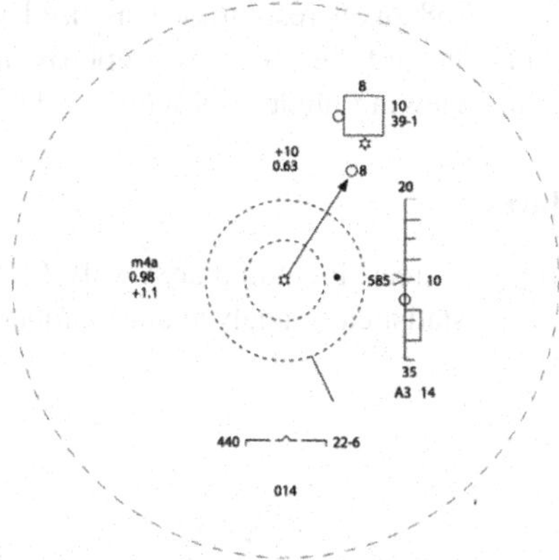

Fig. 1. Typical schematic diagram of HMDs interface

of the localizer deviation area, which lies on the upper edge of the whole interface, the lower white reserve area is an attitude indicator presentation area, as shown in Fig. 2).

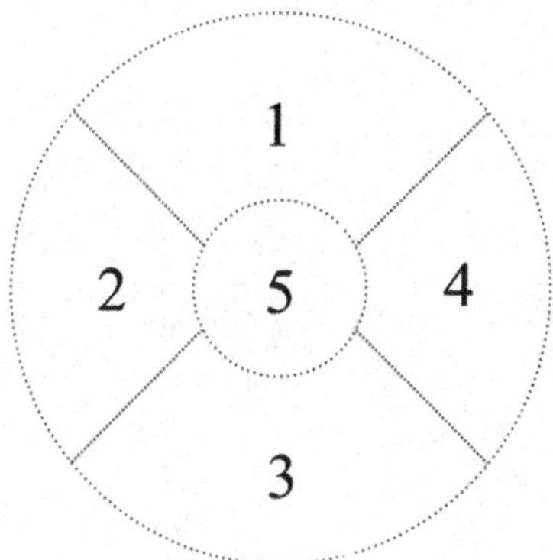

Fig. 2. Division diagram of HMDs interface layout

2 Materials and Methods

2.1 Participants

Twenty subjects (11 males and 9 females) were present undergraduates ($n = 6$), postgraduate ($n = 8$) and doctoral candidates ($n = 6$) from China University of Mining and Technology. They ranged in age from 20 to 35 years, with a mean age of 24 years. They had no color blindness, with the corrected visual acuity over 1.0. They were required to practice and train to know the experimental procedure and operation requirements. Each participant put on electrode cap and sat in a comfortable chair in a soft light and soundproofed room, and eyes gazed at the center of the screen. A 17-in.

CRT monitor with a 1024 × 768 pixel resolution was used in the experiment. The distance between participant eyes and the screen was approximately 60 cm, while the horizontal and vertical picture viewing angle was within 2.3°.

2.2 Tasks and Procedures

HMDs interface is divided into 4 areas, including area A, B, C and D, the division basis is as shown in Fig. 3, so as to statistically analyze and number the experimental data.

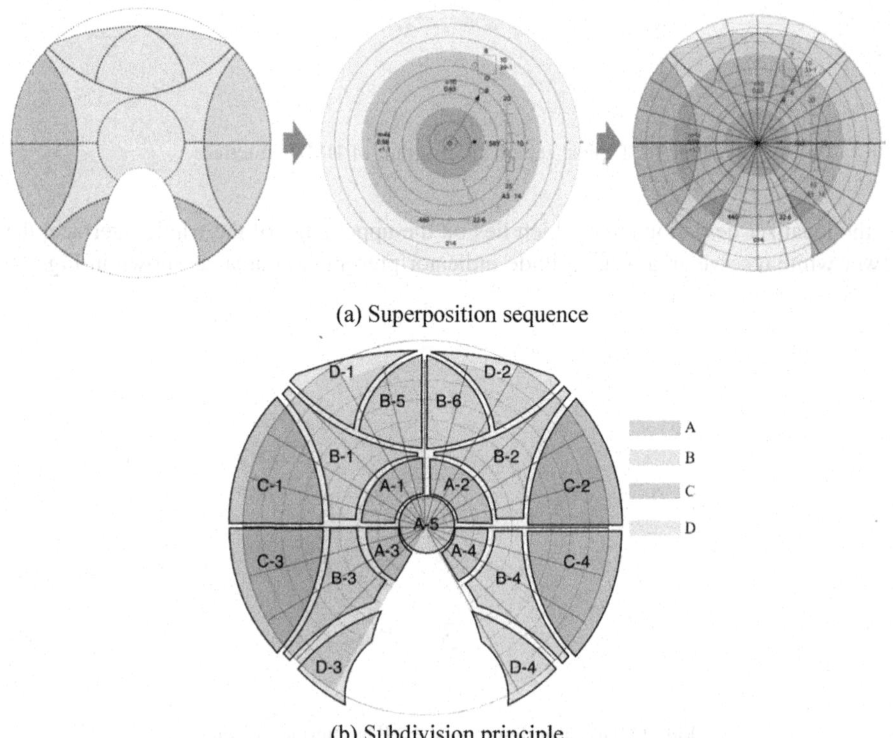

(a) Superposition sequence

(b) Subdivision principle

Fig. 3. Subdivision diagram of HMDs alarm information presentation areas

Four areas mentioned above are subdivided, area A is subdivided into 5 parts, which focuses on the interface aiming area; area B is subdivided into 6 parts, which aims at the fighter heading reminder area and secondary center area; area C is subdivided into 4 parts, which mainly considers the presentation position of speed instrument and height meter; area D is subdivided into 4 parts, which mainly considers the division of edge area and secondary center area in the upper visual field displayed by HMDs. Accordingly, there are 19 subareas in total, so as to statistically analyze and number the experimental data.

The experiment is the simulation of four flight missions of the aircraft, which is the experimental factor one. Each state has A/B/C/D large regional variables, which is the experimental factor two. In each group of experiments, warning information was presented randomly in the regional variables. In order to test whether there was any difference among different factors, the factorial experimental design was used. After the start of each group of experiments, the observation tasks at each stage were given to the subjects, such as the take-off stage, which required them to constantly observe the speed, height, load and other information degrees, as shown in Fig. 4. Then the alarm information is presented suddenly at an uncertain time, and the position is random. The subjects are required to accurately find the alarm information and press the response key to enter the detection interface. The subjects need to match the alarm information observed just now, press the A key if it is correct, and press the L key when it's wrong. There were four sets of experiments, each with 19 small areas, each of which was repeated three times, for a total of 228 times. Through the random arrangement of the order, keep the attention of the subjects. Based on the typical flight state and mission of the aircraft, the experiment is divided into four parts, which are the four typical flight stages of the aircraft, and are carried out in sequence. In each part of the experiment, the subjects read the instructions and started the experiment with any key on the keyboard. Firstly, the center of the screen showed the gaze point "+" 500 ms, and then randomly presented the alarm-free information interface. The subjects were observed according to the task requirements. The alarm information interface will be presented randomly, and the subjects will react, record the reaction time, and enter the matching judgment interface after a delay of 300 ms. After the judgment, the subjects will press "A" and "L", and the statistical accuracy rate will be correct. After the completion of each part of the experiment, there was a rest time of 2 min. It took about 0.5 h for each person to complete the whole experiment.

Fig. 4. Descriptions of experimental tasks

3 Results

The data of accuracy rate and reaction time of experiment on test subjects are statistically analyzed to eliminate extreme data. As for the accuracy rate and reaction time of test subject regarding alarm information for different areas, refer to Figs. 5 and 6.

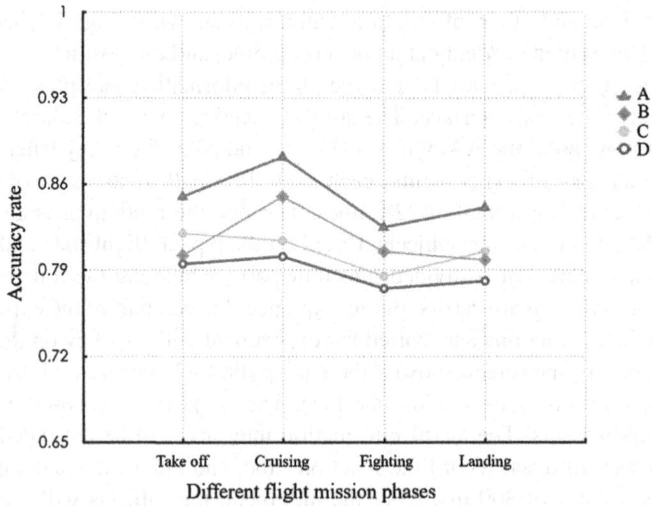

Fig. 5. Statistics of accuracy rate of test subjects

A variance analysis of this accuracy rate (*F* shows significant difference level and *P* indicates test level) indicates that alarm information presents insignificant main effects of different areas ($F = 0.722$, $P = 0.203 > 0.05$).

As shown in Fig. 6, the variance analysis of reaction time shows that alarm information presents significant main effects of different areas ($F = 18.857$, $P = 0.001 < 0.05$). Under the missions for four flight phases of the fighter, obviously, different presentation areas of alarm information show significant effects on the cognitive speed of test subjects; but no significant effects on the visual cognitive capacity and accuracy of the test subjects.

As for the test and analysis of multiple comparisons of the minimum significant difference method for main effects of different alarm information presentation positions on reaction time of test subjects, the result is as shown in Table 1.

The reaction time of both area A and B has no significant difference; that of area C and D has no significant difference; there are significant differences among area A, B and C; significant differences are available among area B, C and D. The reaction time relationship of four areas is D > C > B > A; the accuracy rate relationship is A > B > C > D. As a result, During the HMDs interface alarm information presentation design, area A more easily attracts the attention of test subjects, while area D uneasily causes the reactions of test subjects. In different flight missions, HMDs interface information that the pilot requires paying attention to is different, some areas, as key

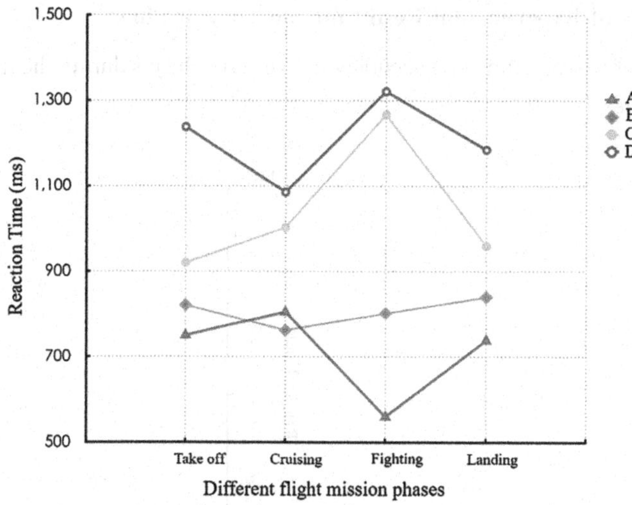

Fig. 6. Statistics of reaction time of test subjects

Table 1. Test on multiple comparisons of the minimum significant difference method

Evaluation index	Area division		Stage		
	I	*J*	Average error (*I* − *J*)	Standard error	*P*
RT	A	B	−46.215	30.275	0.078
		C	−113.317*	30.275	0.007
		D	−135.209*	30.275	0.004
	B	A	46.215	30.275	0.078
		C	−67.102*	30.275	0.031
		D	−88.994*	30.275	0.011
	C	A	113.317*	30.275	0.007
		B	67.102*	30.275	0.031
		D	−21.892	30.275	0.306
	D	A	135.209*	30.275	0.004
		B	88.994*	30.275	0.011
		C	21.892	30.275	0.306

I and *J* respectively stand for any two of four areas; "*" indicates significant level, the average error is at level 0.05, which is significant.

areas, may be unfit for presenting alarm information, deep analyses are thereby conducted in this paper according to information presentation requirements for specific flight missions.

3.1 Analysis of Experimental Result for the Takeoff Phase

The statistics of reaction time and accuracy rate of test subjects during the takeoff phase is shown in Fig. 7.

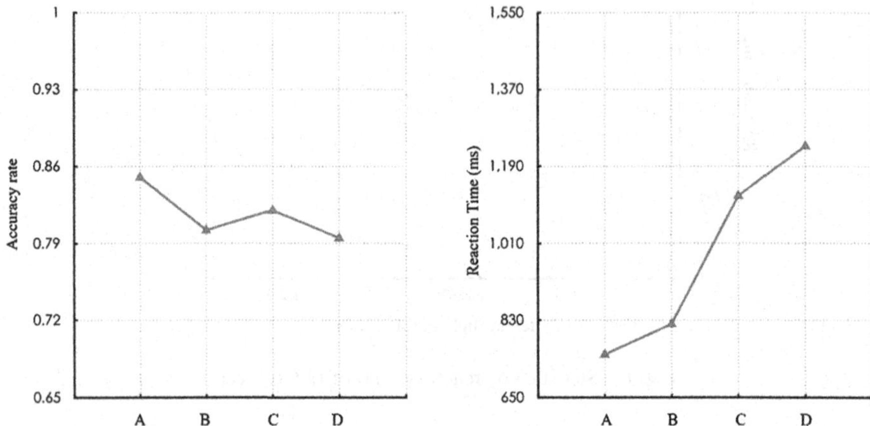

Fig. 7. Statistics of accuracy rate and reaction time of test subjects during the take-off phase

As shown in Fig. 7, the accuracy rate relationship of four areas is A > C > B > D; the reaction time relationship is D > C > B > A. During the takeoff phase, the pilot must focus on the speed and height changes. In order to ensure the smooth takeoff of the fighter, the pilot needs to retract the landing gear and flaps at the specified height, adjust the pitch angle and pay attention to the fighter load. It is required to eliminate these necessary information presentation areas and main presentable areas of alarm information of the fighter during the takeoff phase are referred to Fig. 8 (Area No.: A-1, A-2, A-3, A-4, A-5, A-6, B-1, B-2, B-5, B-6).

A statistical analysis is conducted for reaction time of test subjects against such 9 subdivision areas, as shown in Fig. 9.

In the flight mission of fighter during the takeoff phase, according the statistical analysis in Fig. 9, the reaction time of test subjects is the shortest when alarm information is presented in area A-5 while it is the longest when presented in area B-6. As a whole, reaction time of test subjects presenting alarm information in the interface center is generally shorter, which indicates that visual cognitive reactions of test subjects are the most sensitive to the central visual area but comparatively weaker to the upper visual area. During the takeoff phase, the priority ranking of presentation of alarm information for different position areas is as follows: area A-5, area A-1, area A-2, area B-1, area B-2, area A-3, area A- 4. Area B-5, area B-6.

In summary, as shown in Fig. 10, test subjects prefer to choose a priority visualization presentation of information for different position areas during the takeoff phase. The preferred area is expressed by red system, the secondary area is expressed by orange system and the alternative area by yellow system. Apparently, the information presentation position area easily found by test subjects tends to the upper center of

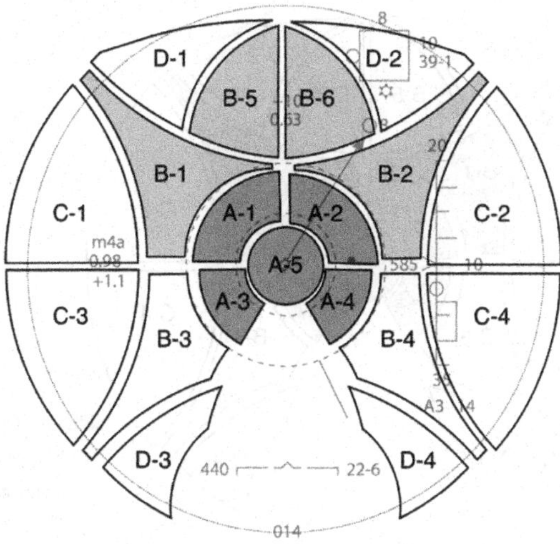

Fig. 8. Presentable areas of alarm information during the takeoff phase

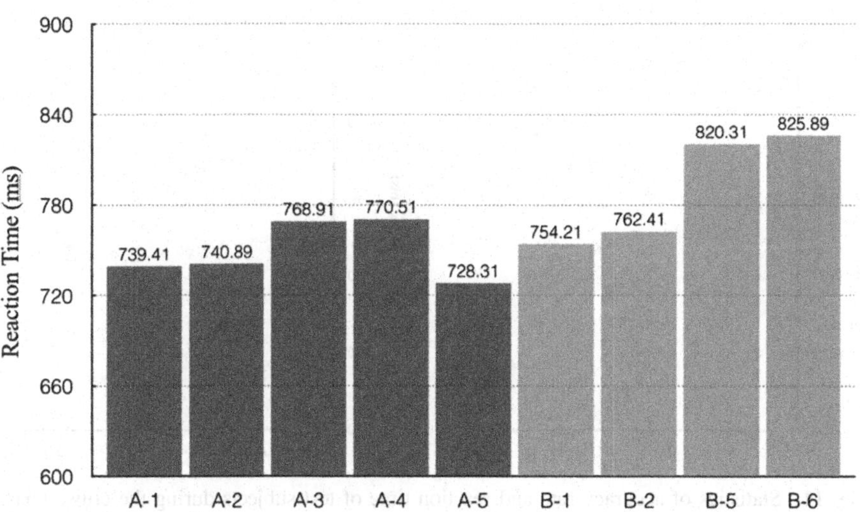

Fig. 9. Reaction time analysis of test subjects against presentable areas during the takeoff phase

HMDs interface during the takeoff phase. As for the selection of important alarm information presentation position during takeoff phase of the fighter, it is necessary to give priority to the upper middle position of this interface, especially area A-5.

3.2 Analysis of Experimental Result for the Cruise Phase

As for the reaction time and accuracy rate of test subjects during the cruise phase, refer to Fig. 11.

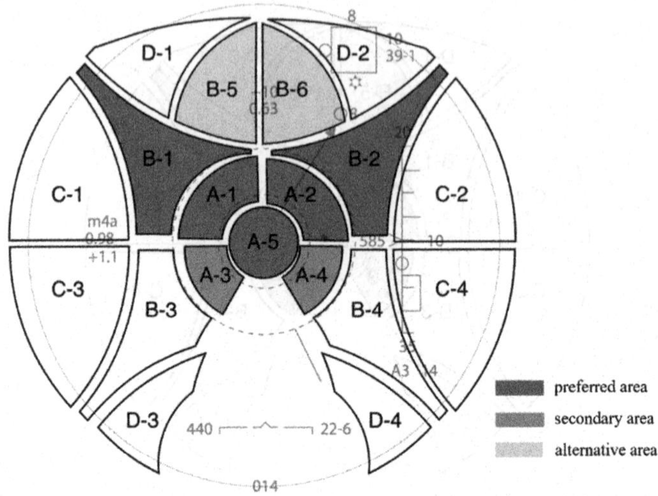

Fig. 10. Priority division of presentation areas of alarm information during the takeoff phase (Color figure online)

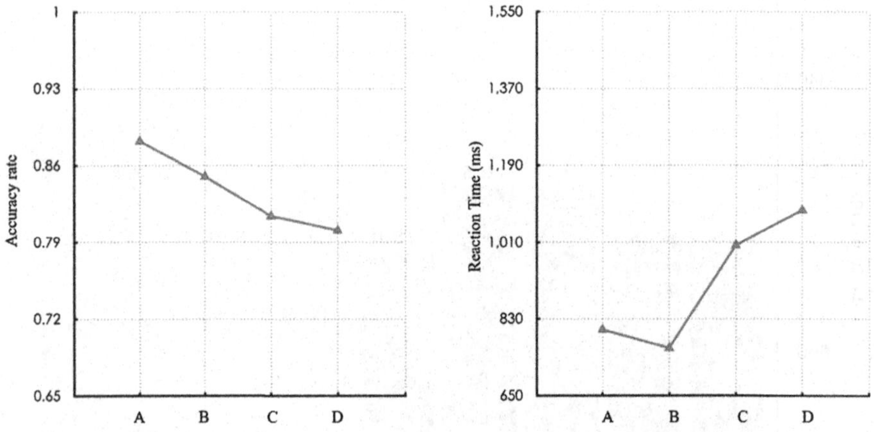

Fig. 11. Statistics of accuracy rate and reaction time of test subjects during the cruise phase

As shown in Fig. 11, the accuracy rate relationship of four areas during the cruise phase is A > B > C > D; the reaction time relationship is D > C > A > B. In accordance with the universal display information classification and typical flight mission analysis of fighter, the pilot, during the cruise phase, needs to not only focus on the flight speed, height and attitude of fighter but also adjust information such as fighter heading and height according to specified information so as to reach the specified cruise destination. Therefore, it is required to eliminate these necessary information presentation areas and main presentable areas of alarm information of the fighter during the cruise phase are shown in Fig. 12 (Area No.: A-1, A-2, A-3, A-4, A-5, B-1, B-2, C-4).

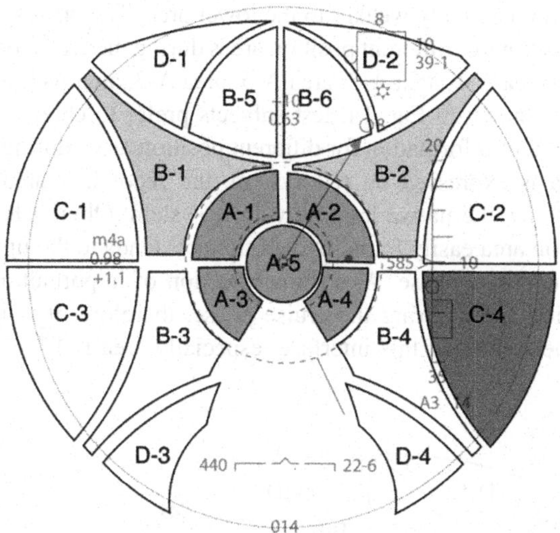

Fig. 12. Presentable areas of alarm information during the cruise phase

A statistical analysis is conducted for reaction time of test subjects against such 8 subareas, as shown in Fig. 13.

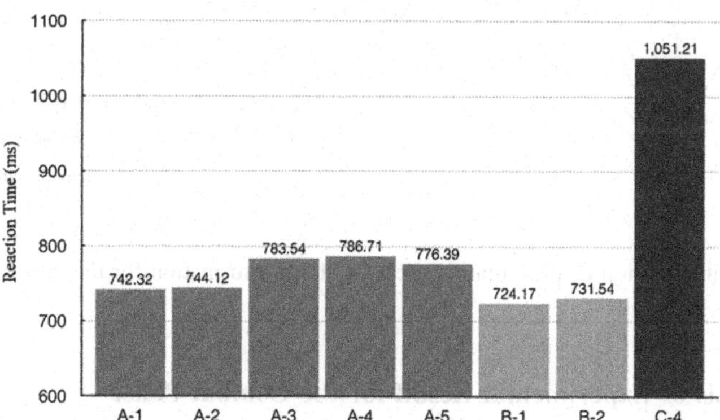

Fig. 13. Analysis of reaction time of test subjects for presentable areas during the cruise phase

During the cruise flight mission of the fighter, in accordance with the statistical analysis in Fig. 13, the reaction time of test subjects is the shortest when alarm information is presented in area B-1 while it is the longest when presented in area C-4. As a whole, the reaction time of test subjects presenting alarm information in the upper middle area and the upper left middle area of this interface is generally shorter, which indicates that visual cognitive reactions of test subjects are the most sensitive to the upper center of this interface but comparatively weaker to the lower area. The priority ranking of alarm information presentations of different position areas during the cruise phase is as follows: area B-1, area B-2, area A-1, area A-2, area A-5, area A-3, area A-4, area C-4.

In summary, as shown in Fig. 14, test subjects prefer to choose the priority visualization presentation of information for different position areas during the cruise phase. The preferred area is expressed by red system, the secondary area is expressed by orange system and the alternative area by yellow system. Obviously, the information presentation position area easily found by test subjects tends to the upper left of HMDs interface during the cruise phase. As for the selection of important alarm information presentation position areas during the cruise phase, therefore, it is necessary to give priority to the upper center of this interface, especially area B-1.

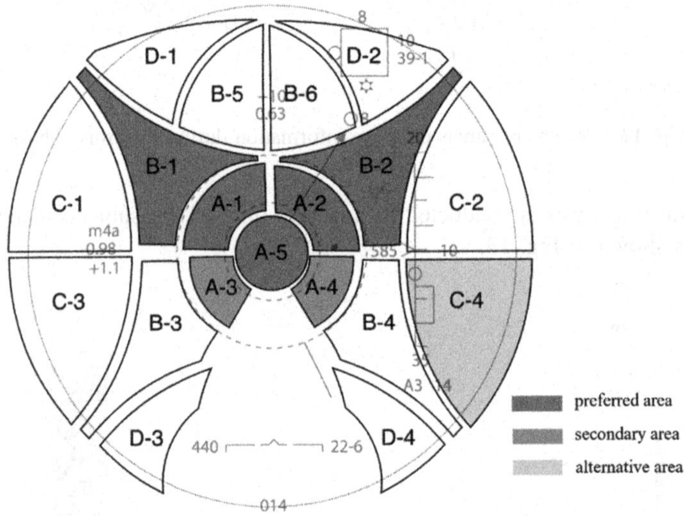

Fig. 14. Priority division of presentation areas of alarm information for the cruise phase (Color figure online)

3.3 Analysis of Experimental Result for the Combat Phase

As for the statistics of reaction time and accuracy rate of test subjects during the combat phase, refer to Fig. 15.

As shown in Fig. 15, the accuracy rate relationship of four areas during the combat phase is A > B > C > D; the reaction time relationship is D > C > B > A. In accordance with the universal display information classification and typical flight mission analysis of fighter, HMDs for the combat phase is slightly different from that for other flight phases. During the combat phase, how to find out a hostile plane as early as possible and accurately predict its intention of action for ultimate destruction is an important mission of the pilot, so HMDs interface during this phase mainly displays such information as combat command, weapon status, target information and fighter

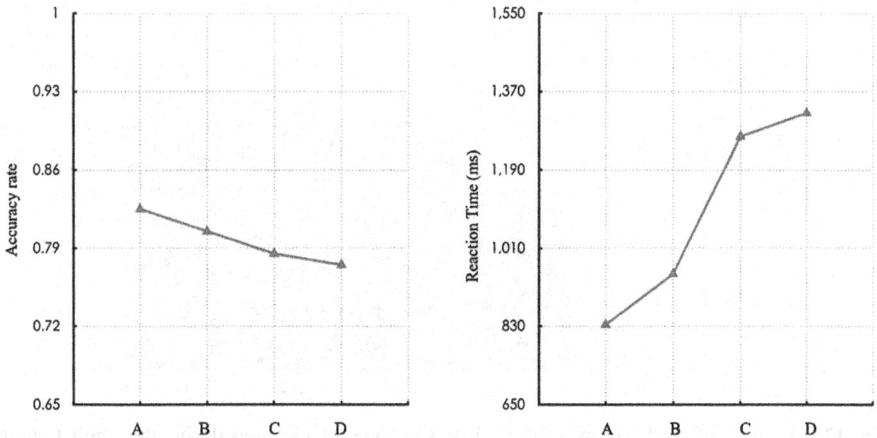

Fig. 15. Statistics of accuracy rate and reaction time of test subjects during the combat phase

information. However, the pilot needs real-time control over basic parameters, including flight speed, height and attitude. Therefore, it is required to eliminate these necessary information presentation areas and main presentable areas of alarm information are shown in Fig. 16 (Area No.: B-3, D-1, D-2, D-3, C-4).

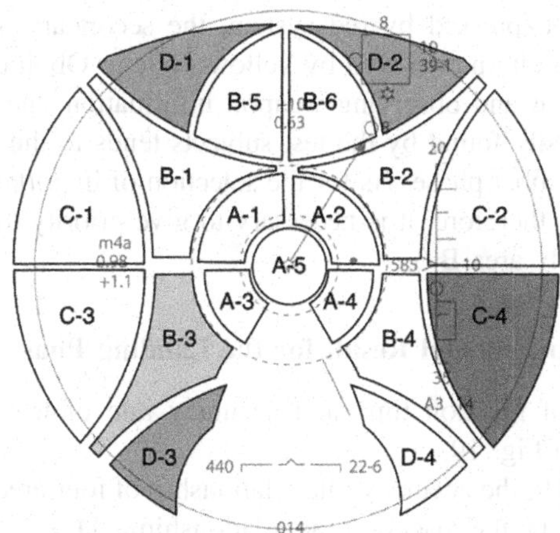

Fig. 16. Presentable areas of alarm information for the combat phase

As for the statistical analysis of reaction time of test subjects against such five subareas, refer to Fig. 17.

During the combat flight mission of the fighter, according to the statistical analysis in Fig. 17, the reaction time of test subjects is the shortest when alarm information is presented in area B-3 while it is the longest when presented in area D-3. As a whole, the reaction time of test subjects presenting alarm information in the left center and

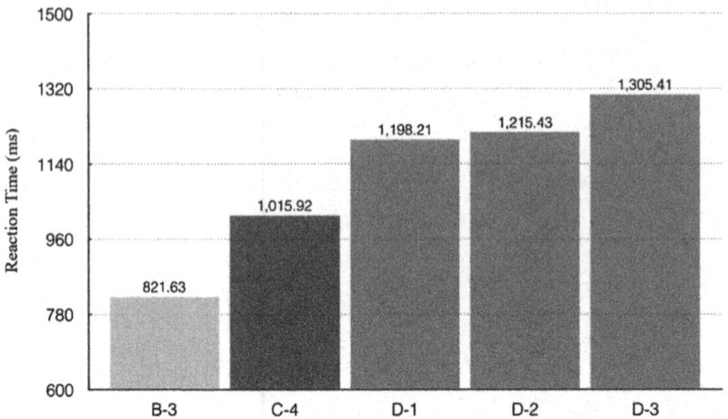

Fig. 17. Analysis of reaction time of test subjects for presentable areas during the combat phase

lower left center of this interface is generally shorter, which indicates that the visual cognitive reactions of test subjects are the most sensitive to these areas and comparatively weaker to the edge areas. The priority ranking of different alarm information presentation position areas during the combat phase is as follows: area B-3, area C-4, area D-1, area D-2, and area D-3 (The remaining position areas are not recommended).

In summary, as shown in Fig. 18, test subjects prefer to choose priority visualization presentation of information for different position areas during the combat phase. The preferred area is expressed by red system, the secondary area is expressed by orange system and the alternative area by yellow system. Obviously, considering the pilot needs to aiming at and observing weapon information, the information presentation position area easily found by the test subjects tends to the lower left of HMDs interface during the combat phase. As for the selection of important alarm information presentation positions, therefore, it is necessary to give priority to the lower center of this interface, especially area B-3.

3.4 Analysis of Experimental Result for the Landing Phase

As for the statistics of reaction time and accuracy rate of test subjects during the landing phase, refer to Fig. 19.

As shown in Fig. 19, the accuracy rate relationship of four areas during the landing phase is A > C > B > D; the reaction time relationship is D > C > B > A. During the landing phase, the main mission of the pilot is to safely land in the specified time, when the runway benchmark must be displayed except the flight speed, height and attitude. According to rules in Display Symbology for Head up Display of Aircraft, the runway benchmark is used for mobilization and landing modes, which are displayed during use of an instrument landing system and indicate the aiming point and earthing point of the runway. The length, width and angle of symbol form a perspective relationship corresponding to the actual runway. Therefore, it is required to eliminate these necessary information presentation areas and main presentable areas of alarm information of the fighter are shown in Fig. 20 (Area No.: B-1, B-2, B-3, C-3, C-4).

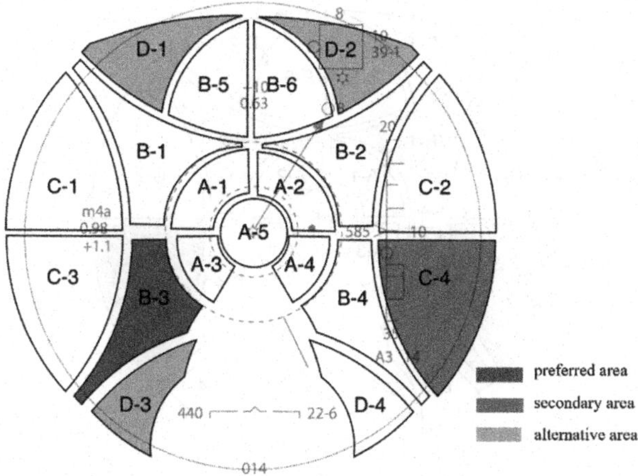

Fig. 18. Priority division of alarm information presentation areas during the combat phase (Color figure online)

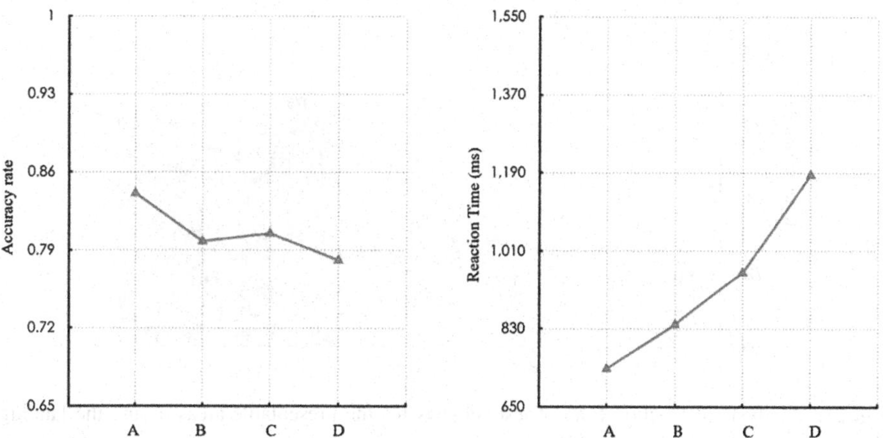

Fig. 19. Statistics of accuracy rate and reaction time of test subjects during the landing phase

A statistical analysis is conducted for reaction time of test subjects against such five subareas, as shown in Fig. 21.

During the landing flight mission of the fighter, according to the statistical analysis in Fig. 21, the reaction time of test subjects is the shortest when alarm information is presented in area B-1 while it is the longest when presented in area C-4. As a whole, the reaction time of test subjects presenting alarm information in the left center and upper center of this interface is generally shorter, which indicates that visual cognitive reactions of test subjects are the most sensitive to these areas and comparatively weaker to the left and right edge areas. The priority ranking of different alarm information

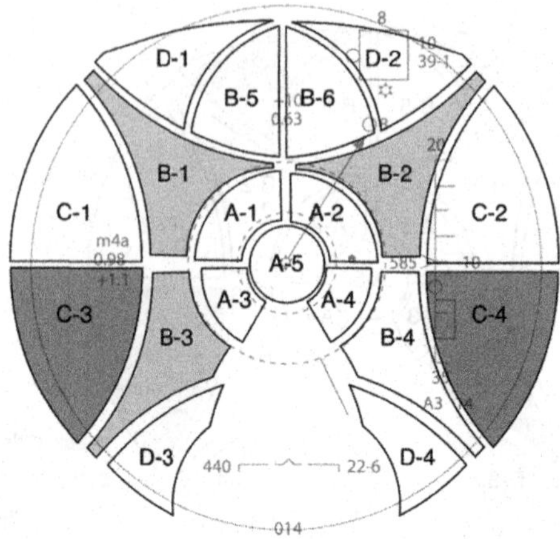

Fig. 20. Presentable areas of alarm information for the landing phase

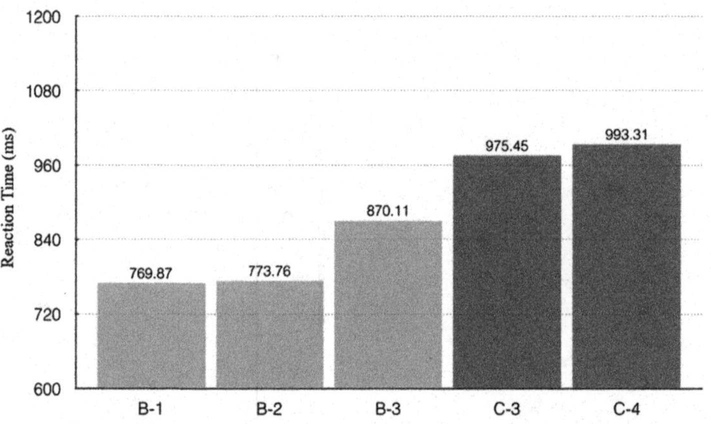

Fig. 21. Analysis of reaction time of test subjects for the presentable areas during the landing phase

presentation areas during the landing phase is as follows: area B-1, area B-2, area B-3, area C-3 and area C-4 (other position areas are not recommended).

In conclusion, as shown in Fig. 22, test subjects prefer to choose priority visualization presentation of information for different position areas during the landing phase. The preferred area is expressed by red system, the secondary area is expressed by orange system and the alternative area by yellow system. Obviously, the information presentation position area easily found by test subjects tends to the upper left of HMDs interface during the landing phase. For the selection of important alarm information presentation area during the landing phase, therefore, it is necessary to give priority to the upper left of this interface, especially area B-1.

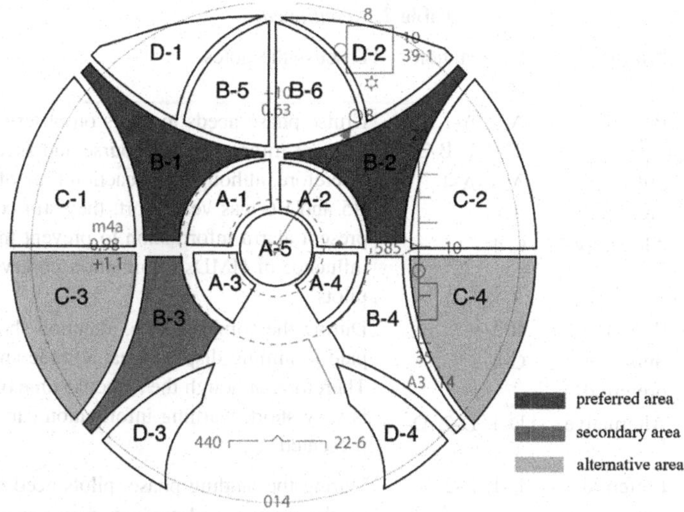

Fig. 22. Priority division of alarm information presentation areas during the landing phase (Color figure online)

4 Discussion

Based on the statistical analysis of the experimental data in three stages of the fighter, the visual perception priority ranking of the specific subdivision region is summarized, and the information presentation requirements in different flight stages are discussed. The preferred, sub-preferred and alternative regions of the alarm information in the three stages of takeoff, cruise and landing are summarized. The experimental results are shown in Table 2.

Table 2. Statistical table of experimental conclusions

Flight phase	Priority	Presentation area	Discuss the notes
Take off stage	Preferred	A-5, A-1, A-2, B-1, B-2	During the take-off phase, attention should be paid to the load, speed, attitude, runway status and so on. Therefore, although the response time of some areas is very short, warning information can not be presented to prevent the pilot from observing HMDs information
	Sub-preferred	A-3, A-4	
	Alternative	B-5, B-6	

(continued)

Table 2. (*continued*)

Flight phase	Priority	Presentation area	Discuss the notes
Cruising stage	Preferred	A-5, A-1, A-2, B-1, B-2	Cruise phase needs to focus on observing the relevant information of course and speed. Therefore, although the reaction time of C1, C2, B5 and B6 was very short, they still could not present alarm information to prevent the influence of HMDs information observed by pilots
	Sub-preferred	A-3, A-4	
	Alternative	C-4	
Combat stage	Preferred	B-3	During the combat phase, attention should be paid to aiming display area, attitude and so on. Therefore, although the response time of A areas is very short, warning information can not be presented
	Sub-preferred	C-4	
	Alternative	D-1, D-2, D-3	
Landing stage	Preferred	B-1, B-2	During the landing phase, pilots need to focus on the runway and navigation information, as well as speed, altitude status and so on. Therefore, although the response time of A region and C-1, C-2 is not high, it is not appropriate to present alarm information
	Sub-preferred	B-3	
	Alternative	C-3, C-4	

5 Conclusion

This paper classifies and discusses the general display information of aircraft, summarizes the priority of information presentation of avionics system, and summarizes the information presentation requirements of typical mission phases such as takeoff, cruise and landing. The HMDs information layout interface is divided into 4 large areas and 19 subdivisions according to the experimental requirements. Based on the research basis of flight missions and visual perception cognition, combined with the division of HMDs information layout, the experiment of HMDs interface alarm information distribution was carried out. The experimental data are analyzed in detail, and the preferred, sub-preferred and alternative regions of alarm information in takeoff, cruise and landing phases are summarized. The research results of this paper provide experimental basis for HMDs interface information layout coding, and will effectively improve the efficiency of the system.

Acknowledgement. This paper is supported by Basic Research Program of Xuzhou, 2017 (No: KC17071).

References

1. Collinson, R.P.G.: Displays and man-machine interaction. In: Collinson, R.P.G. (ed.) Introduction to Avionics Systems, pp. 17–96. Springer, Boston (2003). https://doi.org/10.1007/978-1-4419-7466-2_2
2. Rolland, J.P., Hua, H.: Head-mounted display systems. Encycl. Opt. Eng. 1–13 (2005)
3. Zhang, R., Hua, H.: Effects of a retroreflective screen on depth perception in a head-mounted projection display. In: 2010 9th IEEE International Symposium on Mixed and Augmented Reality (ISMAR), pp. 137–145. IEEE (2010)
4. Doehler, H.U., Schmerwitz, S., Lueken, T.: Visual-conformal display format for helicopter guidance. In: SPIE Defense+ Security. International Society for Optics and Photonics, pp. 90870 J–90870 J-12 (2014)
5. Van Orden, K.F., Divita, J., Shim, M.J.: Redundant use of luminance and flashing with shape and color as highlighting codes in symbolic displays. Hum. Factors **35**, 195–204 (1993)
6. Deaton, M.: User and task analysis for interface design. Tech. Commun. **45**(3), 385–388 (1998)
7. Fleetwood, M.D., Byrne, M.D.: Modeling icon search in ACT-R/PM. Cogn. Syst. Res. **3**(1), 25–33 (2002)
8. Wu, W., Sun, J.: Research on the orientation method of HMD based on image processing. In: 2012 10th World Congress on Intelligent Control and Automation (WCICA), pp. 4160–4162. IEEE (2012)
9. Peinecke, N., Knabl, P.M., Schmerwitz, S., et al.: An evaluation environment for a helmet-mounted synthetic degraded visual environment display. In: 2014 IEEE/AIAA 33rd Digital Avionics Systems Conference (DASC), pp. 2C2-1–2C2-7. IEEE (2014)
10. Knabl, P., Többen, H.: Symbology development for a 3D conformal synthetic vision helmet-mounted display for helicopter operations in degraded visual environment. In: Harris, D. (ed.) EPCE 2013. LNCS (LNAI), vol. 8019, pp. 232–241. Springer, Heidelberg (2013). https://doi.org/10.1007/978-3-642-39360-0_26
11. MIL-STD-1787B (USAF): Aircraft Display Symbology. The Department of Defense of United States of America (1996)
12. Yeh, M., Wickens, C.D.: Attentional filtering in the design of electronic map displays: a comparison of color coding, intensity coding, and decluttering techniques. Hum. Factors **43** (4), 543–562 (2001)
13. Montgomery, D.A., Sorkin, K.D.: Observer sensitivity to element reliability in a multi element visual display. Hum. Factors **38**(3), 484–494 (1996)
14. Tullis, T.S.: An evaluation of alphanumeric, graphic, and color information displays. Hum. Factors **23**(5), 541–550 (1981)
15. Schum, D.A.: The weighting of testimony in judicial proceeding from sources having reduced credibility. Hum. Factors **33**(2), 172–182 (1991)
16. Monnier, P.: Redundant coding assessed in a visual search task. Displays **24**(1), 49–55 (2003)

An Investigation of Placement of Textual and Graphical Information Using Human Performance and Eye Tracking Data

Chao Shi[1], Ayala Cohen[2], Ling Rothrock[1(✉)], and Tatiana Umansky[2]

[1] Department of Industrial and Manufacturing Engineering, Pennsylvania State University, State College, USA
{cxs1063, lrothroc}@psu.edu

[2] Faculty of Industrial Engineering and Management, Technion-Israel Institute of Technology, Haifa, Israel
ieayala@g.technion.ac.il, ieumansk@technion.ac.il

Abstract. This paper reports the findings of a human-machine system (HMS) experiment, which was conducted to explore how to combine textual and graphical information in an interface. Specifically, this paper explored how the location of textual and graphical information would influence response time, accuracy and eye movement. We also explored the effectiveness of three different configurations (9, 16, and 25 points). Our findings suggest that if the accuracy was the highest priority, the textual information should be placed at the left side of the screen and the graphical information should not be placed at the center of the screen. If a quicker response time was the highest priority, the graphical information should not be placed at the corners and bottom right margins. Finally, if an interface includes both textual and graphical elements, graphical information could be placed at corner and margin areas and textual information could be placed at corner areas to facilitate the efficiency of information processing. From the perspective of response accuracy and response time, the 9-point configuration was most appropriate for the calibration process.

Keywords: Human-computer interaction · Perception · Information displays · Industrial ergonomics

1 Introduction

Information processing is a key component of human performance. As users are faced with the need for more information through the use of complex visual displays, there are increasing demands in developing design strategies to facilitate effective information seeking behavior. Moreover, as users require more and more information to do their jobs, display complexity has greatly increased. This complexity makes it difficult for people to correctly interpret the information displayed and project what is likely going to happen (Salvendy 2012). There are two major ways to represent information, textually and graphically. As computer interfaces have become more complex, the questions of using either graphics or alphanumeric texts to display information

S. Yamamoto and H. Mori (Eds.): HCII 2019, LNCS 11569, pp. 122–136, 2019.
https://doi.org/10.1007/978-3-030-22660-2_9

(Tullis 1997) has become moot. Instead, combining graphics and alphanumeric texts in an interface to facilitate information seeking behavior becomes an important issue, (Aigner et al. 2011; North 2006; Spence 2007 and Steele and Iliinsky 2010).

As the need for combining graphical and textual elements grows, some researchers compared graphical displays with textual displays to find which display is easier and quicker for information notification. For example, (Ottensooser et al. 2012) reported that subjects with textual representations showed significant improvement in understanding business processes without training beforehand, while training is still required for graphical representations to show significant improvement. Some researchers have found that subjects spent more time and effort in graphical representations, which challenges the general assumption that graphical representations are easier than textual representations, (Cepeda and Guéhéneuc 2010). Moreover, some research emphasizes the importance of combining graphical with textual tasks together. For example, Bederson et al. (2004) used focus and context mechanisms to develop the temporal information presentation of calendars on small handheld devices. If the display space is large enough, calendar entries are shown in textual form. Otherwise, calendar entries are indicated by bars. The present study will explore how to combine graphical and textual information in different display configurations.

Eye tracking is a technique that measures individual's eye movements. It can help to understand visual and display-based information processing and the factors that may influence the usability of system interfaces, (Poole and Ball 2006). An eye tracker requires calibration before a session is started. Calibration is a procedure in which data are gathered from the coordinates of the subject's pupils and corneal reflections in the eye video coordinate system, to represent his or her eye fixations in the stimulus space. A common procedure is to have the subject fixate nine points in a rectangular calibration grid, (Kliegl and Olson 1981 and Blignaut et al. 2014) although 16 and 25-point systems are also used. The fact that calibration points consists of equally spaced points extending to the boundaries of the stimulus field provides a structure for an experiment to examine the placement of textual and graphical information.

The configurations of the 9, 16, and 25-point calibration systems occupies 37 different locations on the screen. In the present study, we used an arithmetic task and a gauge task to investigate the effect of locations. The arithmetic task represented the textual task and the gauge task represented the graphical task. In this study, response time, response accuracy and root mean square (RMS) of fixations, representing the magnitude of the distance from the center of the target to the fixation point, were analyzed. The results from this study can be used to help interface designers to locate the different types of information more effectively and also to help eye tracker experimenters to choose the most appropriate calibration points.

2 Methods

2.1 Participants

Thirty participants (Mean age = 22.5, 13 male and 17 female) were recruited from the Pennsylvania State University and were paid $10 each. Because prescription eye glasses affect the accuracy of the eye tracker, recruits were screened through reading 11.25 pt Arial regular font text at a distance of 25 in. without wearing eye glasses (contacts were allowed).

2.2 Apparatus

The study was conducted on a standard PC (Windows 7 installed) and a 20″ monitor (ST2010, Dell Inc., LOCATION), which was set to a resolution of 1600 × 900 pixels and placed 24.5 in away from the participant. An eye-tracker (Mirametrix S2 Eye Tracker, Montreal, QC, Canada) was used for recording the participants' gaze data at a sampling rate of 60 Hz within 1° of accuracy. A chin rest was used to minimize head movement and the vertical viewing angle and the horizontal viewing angle was controlled to 0° to −24.5° (below eye level) and −21.53° to 21.53°, respectively, to ensure that participants could see the entire screen (Van et al. 1972; Fig. 1).

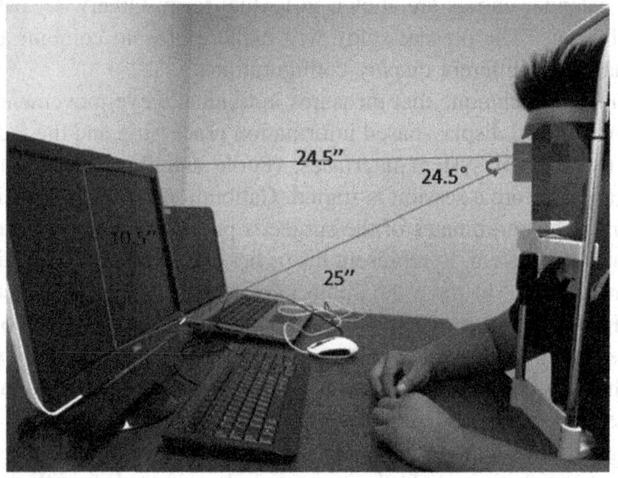

Fig. 1. Participant position.

2.3 Stimuli and Task

To evaluate the performance of textual and graphical tasks and to give advice on how to display two types of information on an interface, two types of tasks were prepared, the arithmetic and gauge task. The arithmetic task consisted of presenting participants with textual stimuli, which were arithmetic equations (Arial font, regular, 11.25 point, white) placed inside black circles (80 × 80 pixels; Fig. 2). Participants were required to determine whether the equations were incorrect or correct by pressing 'F' or 'J', respectively.

The gauge task consisted of presenting participants with graphical stimuli, which were semicircle gauges (80 × 40 pixels; Fig. 3). Participants were required to determine whether the indicator arrow was on the left or right by pressing 'F' or 'J', respectively.

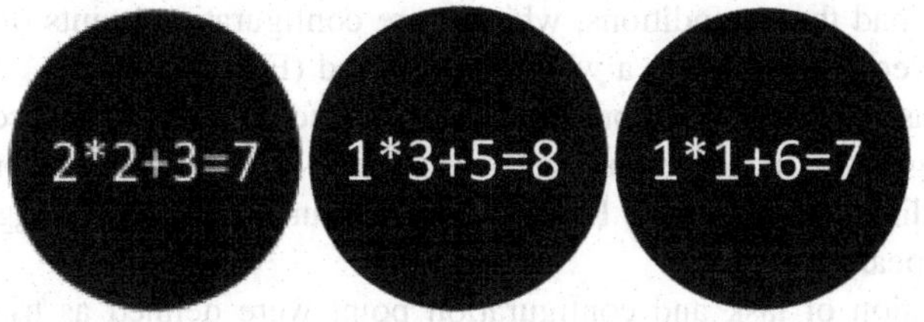

Fig. 2. Examples of the equations presented in the arithmetic task.

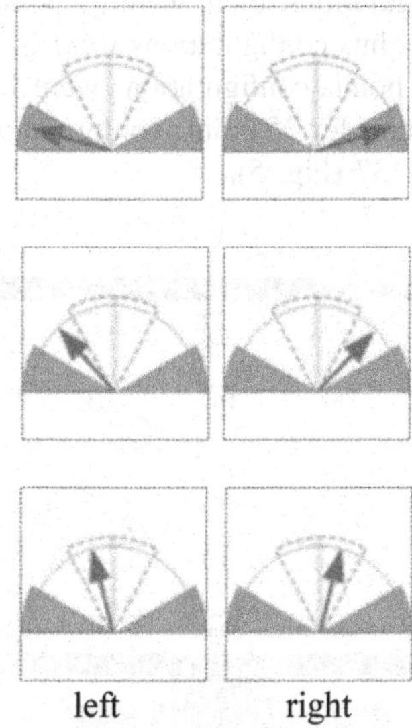

Fig. 3. Examples of the semicircle gauges presented in the gauge task.

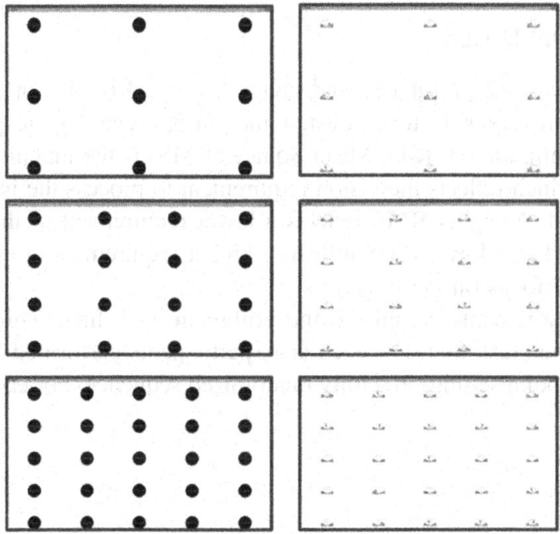

Fig. 4. The arithmetic and gauge task with 9, 16, or 25 configuration points.

Both tasks had three conditions, which were configuration points of 9, 16, or 25, and all tasks were presented on a white background (Fig. 4).

For both tasks, stimuli were presented one-by-one on the screen (according to the task and configuration point setting) and participants were required to press ‘F’ or ‘J’ based on the displayed stimulus. Response to the current stimulus triggered the next stimulus to appear.

A combination of task and configuration point were defined as trials. Each trial required participants to respond to either 9, 16, or 25 stimuli. Stimuli did not appear more than once on the same location per trial.

Combining all three configurations, there were 37 possible locations for each task. The possible locations for 9 points configurations were 1, 4, 7, 17, 19, 21, 31, 41, 47. The possible locations for 16 points configurations were 1, 3, 5, 7, 13–16, 22–25, 31, 33, 35, 37. The possible locations for 25 points configurations were: 1, 2, 4, 6, 7, 8–12, 17–21, 26–30, 31, 32, 34, 36, 37 (Fig. 5).

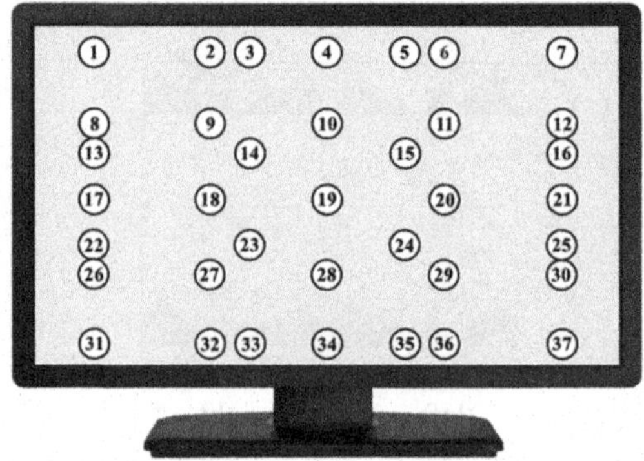

Fig. 5. The locations of points.

2.4 Experimental Design

The experiment was a 2 (arithmetic and gauge task) × 3 (9, 16, or 25 configuration points) repeated measures factorial design measuring accuracy, response time, and RMS for each configuration. Root Mean Square (RMS) is the magnitude of deviation from the target, which reflects the vision requirement to process the information in the current experiment. A higher RMS reflects a lower requirement of the eye to process the information, while a lower RMS reflects a higher requirement of the eye to process the data and more focus on the target.

Half of the participants completed the arithmetic task first, while the other half completed the gauge task first. For each task, participants performed 24 trials (8 trials per configuration point setting) in a fully randomized sequence. For each configuration, the number of correct/incorrect or left/right stimuli were equally divided and the sequence was also fully randomized. Combining all three configurations, there were 37 possible locations for each task.

2.5 Procedure

Prior to arrival, the participants completed an online demographic questionnaire to provide background information to make sure that they could read 11.25 pt Arial regular font text at a distance of 25 in without wearing eye glasses (contacts were allowed). After an introduction, participants provided informed consent. Each experiment started with instruction of each task. Next, they were instructed to put their chin on the chin rest with the thighs roughly parallel to the floor, and were asked to maintain a roughly upright sitting posture (Woo et al. 2015). Then, participants started the experiment by pressing the SPACE button, and the white board showed up. When they pressed the SPACE again, the first target stimulus appeared and the participants were asked to respond as quickly and accurately as possible. After they finished the first part (either arithmetic and gauge) of the experiment, each participant was required to take a five-minute break, and then continue to the second part with the same procedure as the first part. After they finished all parts, they were given a post-experiment questionnaire asking them for feedback about their experience and additional suggestions. Finally, they were compensated.

2.6 Statistical Analysis

Regression models were fitted for each of the response variables: Correctness (proportion of correct answers), Response time, and RMS. The Mixed model was used for RMS and also for the log of the response time, while GLIMMIX (Generalized Mixed Model) was used for correctness. Pvalues were adjusted to allow for the multiple comparisons, using the Sidak correction.

In all analyses, p-values less than 0.05 were considered statistically significant.

3 Results

For each dependent variable, the model was fitted first to find whether configuration points was accompanied by elevated calibration accuracy, shorter response time and higher response accuracy. Then, pairwise comparisons among different locations were conducted to test which locations caused the significant results. The points that located at the four corners were examined first, followed by the examination of the points located at the marginal places. Finally, the points located at the center place were examined. Points that differed from only two or fewer other points were excluded, because it did not form a pattern. These statistically significant differences were interpreted as random effects.

3.1 Accuracy

The generalized mixed model showed that the tasks and configuration points had a significant effect on accuracy ($F(1,121.5) = 57.26$, $p < .0001$). Post hoc analysis with Sidak correction showed that the accuracy in the gauge task was significantly higher than in the arithmetic task for all three configuration points (all $p < .05$). The accuracy in the 25 configuration point of the arithmetic task was significantly lower than in both the 9 configuration point ($p < .001$) and the 16 configuration point ($p < .001$; Table 1). Two trials were discarded due to high error rate (> 3 standard deviations from the mean).

Table 1. Mean (SD) accuracy for each task and each resolution.

Task type	Configuration points		
	9	16	25
Arithmetic	.9569 (.095)	.9596 (.053)	.9040 (.142)
Gauge	.9782 (.059)	.9776 (.047)	.9692 (.041)

The fitted model showed that the interaction between task and location was significant ($F(36,1044) = 8.608$, $p < .001$). Thus, pairwise comparisons of locations were conducted for each task separately. The significant results were summarized below (Tables 2 and 3).

Table 2. Significant location results for the arithmetic task.

Stimulus	Direction	Stimuli
4	<	2, 14, 16, 22, 24, 31, 32, 33, 35
6	<	1, 2, 3, 5, 7, 9, 11–16, 18, 21–24, 26, 27, 31–35, 37
17	<	2, 5, 14, 18, 21, 22, 27, 31–35
19	<	2, 14, 22, 27, 31, 33, 35
20	<	1–3, 5, 9, 11, 12, 14, 16, 18, 21, 22, 24, 26, 27, 31–35, 37
29	<	1–3, 5, 7, 9–16, 18, 21–24, 26, 27, 31–35, 37
30	<	1–3, 5, 7, 9, 11, 12, 14–16, 18, 21–24, 26, 27, 31–35, 37
36	<	1–3, 5, 7, 9, 11, 12, 14–16, 18, 21–24, 26, 27, 31–35, 37

Table 3. Significant location results for the gauge task.

Stimulus	Direction	Stimuli
19	<	1–4, 7, 10, 14–18, 20–23, 25, 27, 28, 32, 34–37

3.2 Response Time

According to the fitted mixed model, the tasks and configuration points had a significant effect on response time (F(1,38.8) = 681.3, $p < 0.0001$). Post hoc showed that the mean response time for the gauge task was significantly lower than the arithmetic task for all three configuration points (all $p < .05$). For the gauge task, a significantly small mean was found for the 25-point configuration compared with the other 2 configurations (Table 4). One trial was discarded due to high error rate (>3 standard deviations from the mean).

Table 4. Mean (SD) response time (msec) for each task and each resolution.

Task type	Configuration points		
	9	16	25
Arithmetic	2158.5199 (857.309)	2118.4341 (563.496)	2149.0825 (491.015)
Gauge	772.9065 (102.857)	763.5732 (100.796)	743.5745 (84.499)

It was also found that the interaction between task and location was significant (F (36,1044) = 3.205, $p < .001$). Pairwise comparisons of locations were conducted only for the gauge task (Table 5). The location effect was not significant for the arithmetic task.

Table 5. Significant location results for the gauge task.

Stimulus	Direction	Stimuli
1	>	9, 20, 27, 28
7	>	4, 9, 17–20, 27, 28, 30
21	>	19, 27, 28
31	>	4, 6, 8, 9, 11, 17–20, 26–30
35	>	9, 19, 27, 28
37	>	1–4, 6, 8, 9, 11, 13, 14, 16–24, 26–30, 33, 35, 36

3.3 RMS (Root Mean Square)

The fitted mixed model showed that the tasks and configuration points had a significant effect on RMS (F(1,155.7) = 116.8, $p < 0.0001$). Post hoc analysis showed that the gauge values were significantly larger than the arithmetic values for all resolutions. For the gauge task, a significant large mean was obtained for the 9 points (p adjusted < 0.001; Table 6).

It was also found that the interaction between task and location was significant (F (36,684) = 2.890, $p < .001$). Thus, the pairwise comparisons of locations were conducted for each task separately (Tables 7 and 8). Because the point 20 and point 35 are too close, they were considered as one location point for the arithmetic task.

Table 6. Mean (SD) RMS (pixel) for each task and each resolution.

Task type	Configuration points		
	9	16	25
Arithmetic	234.4311 (118.110)	237.9664 (90.396)	219.6488 (97.833)
Gauge	429.7662 (200.110)	368.0321 (135.231)	389.4911 (111.995)

Table 7. Significant location results for the arithmetic task.

Stimulus	Direction	Stimuli
1	>	10, 14, 18–20, 28
7	>	2, 4, 5, 10, 11, 14, 18–20, 23, 27, 28
31	>	18–20, 27, 28
37	>	10, 11, 14, 15, 18–20, 23–29, 34, 36
30, 25	>	14, 19, 20, 23, 29

Table 8. Significant location results for the gauge task.

Stimulus	Direction	Stimuli
1	>	2, 3, 9, 10, 14, 15, 19, 23, 24, 27, 28,
7	>	2–5, 9–11, 14–16, 19, 20, 22–24, 27–29, 32–34, 36
31	>	3, 9–11, 14, 15, 19, 20, 23, 24, 27, 28
37	>	2–4, 9–11, 14–16, 18–20, 22–24, 27–29, 32–34, 36
10	<	1, 4, 7, 17, 18, 21, 25, 26, 31, 37
14	<	4, 6, 17, 21, 25, 26, 34, 35
19	<	4, 17, 21, 25, 26

4 Discussion

In this experiment, task type × configurations analysis was first conducted to find whether more configuration points are accompanied by elevated calibration accuracy, shorter response time and higher response accuracy. Next, task type × locations analysis was conducted to find the influence of locations on task performance.

When looking at the results of accuracy of different configurations (Table 1), the accuracy in the 25-point configuration of the arithmetic task was significantly lower than in both the 9-point and the 16-point configurations with 9-point the highest. Moreover, although the configuration results for the gauge task was not significant, the accuracy in the gauge task was the highest in the 9-point configuration, followed by 16-point and 25-point. This indicated that more configuration points did not facilitate the information processing accuracy, which may lead to the suggestion that fewer configuration points would be more accurate. Finally, A more detailed analysis on locations of the arithmetic task was conducted and summarized in Fig. 6 (accuracy of red points is significantly smaller than many of the other points). Results of the arithmetic task showed that the accuracy was more influenced by the points that were

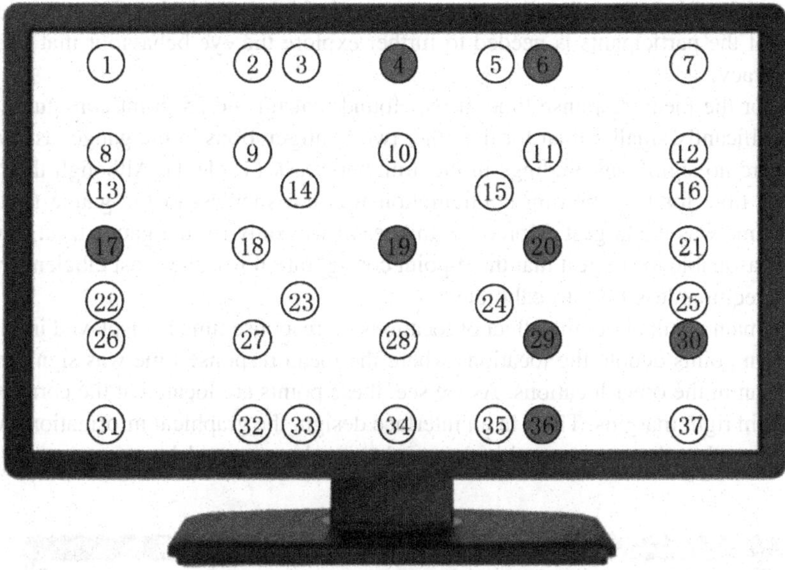

Fig. 6. The accuracy result for the arithmetic task. (Color figure online)

located at the right side of the screen, indicating that in the interface design, textual information should be placed at the left side of the screen. Results of the gauge task (Fig. 7) showed that the accuracy of the 19-point was significantly smaller than many of the other points. This result was counterintuitive because the participants seated in front of the center of the screen, and they were supposed to see the stimuli in the center

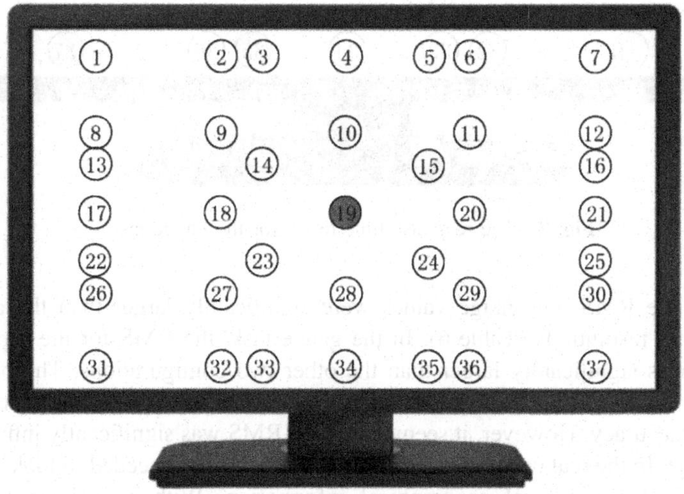

Fig. 7. The accuracy result for the gauge task.

much quicker than the stimuli in the corners. A further analysis of the eye search pattern of the participants is needed to further explore the eye behaviour that affected the accuracy.

As for the mean response time, it was found that for the 25-point configuration it was significantly smaller than for the other two configurations in the gauge task, while there were no significant findings in the arithmetic task (Table 4). Although the mean response time for the 25-point configuration was the smallest in the gauge task, the overall time was the largest. Moreover, this result was only for the gauge task. Thus, it seems reasonable to suggest that the 9-point configuration was the most efficient choice since it requires less time to calibrate.

The main result about the effect of locations on response time is displayed in Fig. 8. The green points denote the locations where the mean response time was significantly larger than in the other locations. As we see, these points are located at the corners and the bottom right margins. Thus, in an interface design, the graphical information should not be placed at the corners and bottom right margins to avoid longer response time.

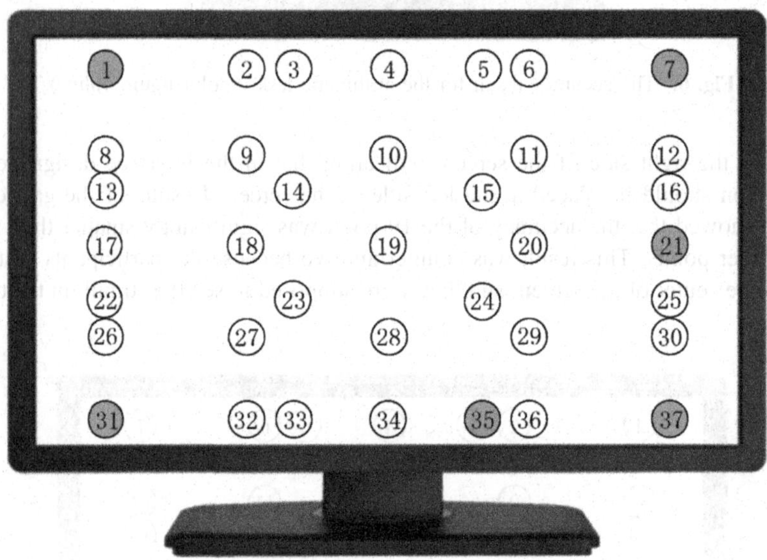

Fig. 8. The response time result for the gauge task.

As for the RMS, the gauge values were significantly larger than the arithmetic values for all resolutions (Table 6). In the gauge task, the RMS for the 9-point configuration was significantly larger than the other two configurations. The purpose of calculating RMS was to find whether more calibration points would lead to elevated calibration accuracy. However, it seemed that the RMS was significantly influenced by the task type. In the real calibration process, the subjects only needed to look at specific points without any textual or graphical information. With such huge differences between the two types of tasks, it was very difficult to conclude which configuration would facilitate the calibration accuracy. The results on locations are displayed in Figs. 9 and 10. The accuracy which is denoted by red points is significantly smaller than many of the other points and the accuracy marked by green points is significantly larger than many of the other points. An analysis of the locations of the arithmetic task

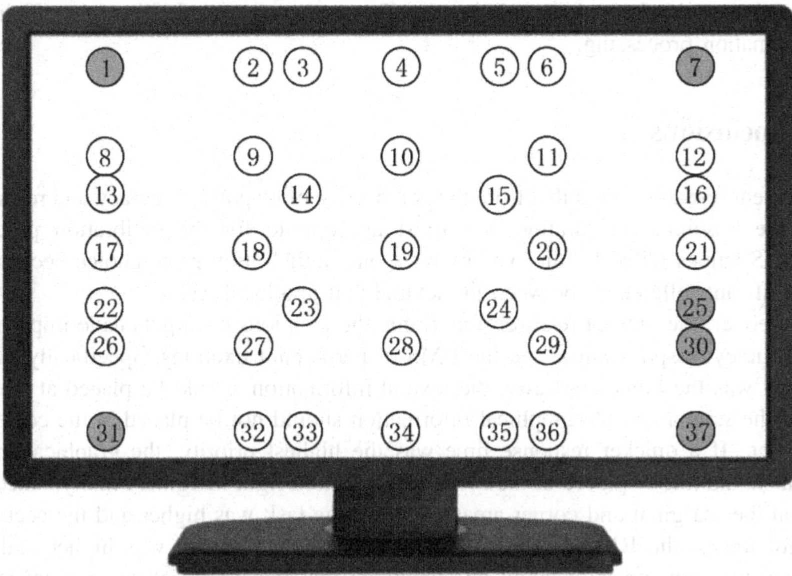

Fig. 9. The RMS result for the arithmetic task.

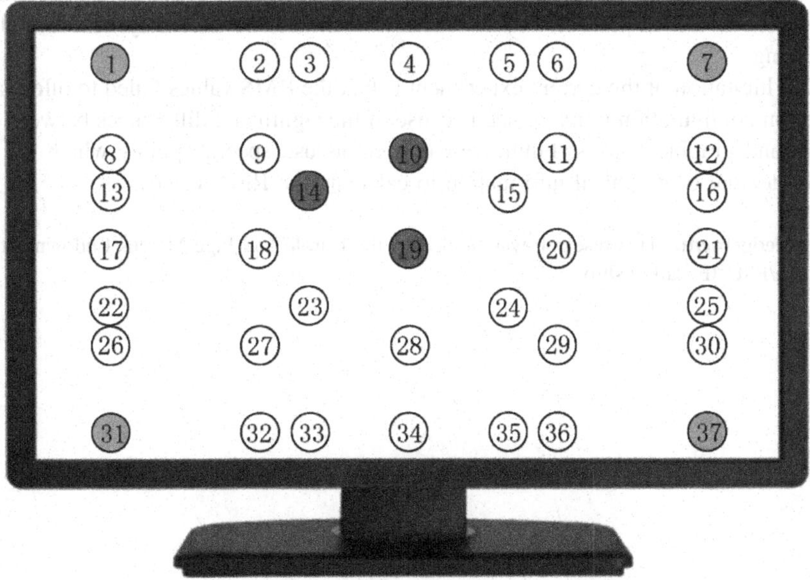

Fig. 10. The RMS result for the gauge task.

(Fig. 9) found that the corner points have larger RMS. Larger RMS was also significant for the corner points in the gauge task, (Fig. 10). These results indicate that the participants could process the corner textual and graphical information correctly without a high vision acuity. Also, the participant could process the margin graphical information correctly without a high vision acuity. Thus, when an interface includes both textual and graphical elements, graphical information could be placed at margin and corner areas and textual information could be placed at corner areas to facilitate the efficiency of information processing.

5 Conclusions

The present research found that from the perspective of response accuracy and response time, the 9-point configuration was most appropriate for the calibration process. The RMS values failed to offer valid advice on configuration point choice because of the significant differences between the textual and graphical tasks.

Moreover, the present research found that the locations of targets have impacts on task accuracy, response time and the RMS of participant fixations. Specifically, if the accuracy was the highest priority, the textual information should be placed at the left side of the screen and the graphical information should not be placed at the center of the screen. If a quicker response time was the highest priority, the graphical information should not be placed at the corners and bottom right margins. Finally, since the RMS at the marginal and corner areas of the gauge task was higher and the accuracy was not lower, the RMS at the corner areas of the arithmetic was higher and the accuracy was not lower, it could be concluded that the graphical and textual information could be processed without a high visual acuity. Thus, if an interface includes both textual and graphical elements, graphical information could be placed at corner and margin areas to facilitate the efficiency of information processing and textual information could be placed at corner areas to facilitate the efficiency of information processing.

One limitation of the current experiment is that the RMS values failed to offer valid advice on configuration point choice because of the significant differences between the textual and graphical tasks. Future research could use specific points which do not include textual or graphical information to calculate the RMS values.

Acknowledgement. This research was funded by the Harold and Inge Marcus Endowment for Technion/PSU IE Partnership.

Appendix 1 Coordinates of the 37 points

Point number	X coordinate (pixel)	Y coordinate (pixel)	Point number	X coordinate (pixel)	Y coordinate (pixel)
1	160	70	20	1120	450
2	480	70	21	1440	450
3	586.66	70	22	160	576.66
4	800	70	23	586.66	576.66
5	1013.32	70	24	1013.32	576.66
6	1120	70	25	1440	576.66
7	1440	70	26	160	640
8	160	260	27	480	640
9	480	260	28	800	640
10	800	260	29	1120	640
11	1120	260	30	1440	640
12	1440	260	31	160	830
13	160	323.33	32	480	830
14	586.66	323.33	33	586.66	829.99
15	1013.32	323.33	34	800	830
16	1440	323.33	35	1013.32	829.99
17	160	450	36	1120	830
18	480	450	37	1440	830
19	800	450			

References

Aigner, W., Miksch, S., Schumann, H., Tominski, C.: Visualization of Time-Oriented Data. Springer, London (2011). https://doi.org/10.1007/978-0-85729-079-3

Bederson, B.B., Clamage, A., Czerwinski, M.P., Robertson, G.G.: DateLens: a fisheye calendar interface for PDAs. ACM Trans. Comput. Hum. Interact. (TOCHI) **11**(1), 90–119 (2004)

Bennett, K.B., Nagy, A.L., Flach, J.M.: Visual displays. In: Salvendy, G. (ed.) Handbook of Human Factors and Ergonomics, 3rd edn, pp. 1191–1221. Wiley, New York (2006)

Blignaut, P., Holmqvist, K., Nyström, M., Dewhurst, R.: Improving the accuracy of video-based eye tracking in real time through post-calibration regression. In: Horsley, M., Toon, N., Knight, B.A., Reilly, R. (eds.) Current Trends in Eye Tracking Research, pp. 77–100. Springer, Cham (2014). https://doi.org/10.1007/978-3-319-02868-2_5

Cepeda Porras, G., Guéhéneuc, Y.-G.: An empirical study on the efficiency of different design pattern representations in UML class diagrams. Empir. Softw. Eng. **15**(5), 493–522 (2010). https://doi.org/10.1007/s10664-009-9125-9

Jeong, H.: A comparison of the influence of electronic books and paper books on reading comprehension, eye fatigue, and perception. Electron. Libr. **30**, 390–408 (2012). https://doi.org/10.1108/02640471211241663

Kieras, D.E.: GOMS models for task analysis. In: Diaper, D., Stanton, N. (eds.) The Handbook of Task Analysis for Human-Computer Interaction, pp. 83–116. Lawrence Erlbaum Associates, Mahwah (2004)

Kim, J.H., Rothrock, L., Laberge, J.: Using signal detection theory and time window-based human-in-the-loop simulation as a tool for assessing the effectiveness of different qualitative shapes in continuous monitoring tasks. Appl. Ergon. **45**(3), 693–705 (2014). https://doi.org/10.1016/j.apergo.2013.09.008

Kliegl, R., Olson, R.K.: Reduction and calibration of eye monitor data. Behav. Res. Methods Instrum. **13**(2), 107–111 (1981)

Liversedge, S.P., Findlay, J.M.: Saccadic eye movements and cognition. Trends Cogn. Sci. **4**(1), 6–14 (2000)

Nikolic, M.I., Sarter, N.B.: Peripheral visual feedback: a powerful means of supporting effective attention allocation in event-driven, data-rich environments. Hum. Factors: J. Hum. Factors Ergon. Soc. **43**(1), 30–38 (2001)

North, C.: Information visualization. In: Salvendy, G. (ed.) Handbook of Human Factors and Ergonomics, 3rd edn, pp. 1222–1245. Wiley, New York (2006)

Ottensooser, A., Fekete, A., Reijers, H.A., Mendling, J., Menictas, C.: Making sense of business process descriptions: an experimental comparison of graphical and textual notations. J. Syst. Softw. **85**(3), 596–606 (2012)

Plocher, T., Rau, P.L.P., Choong, Y.Y.: Cross-cultural design. In: Handbook of Human Factors and Ergonomics, pp. 162–191 (2012)

Poole, A., Ball, L.J.: Eye tracking in HCI and usability research. Encycl. Hum. Comput. Interact. **1**, 211–219 (2006)

Proctor, R.W., Proctor, J.D.: Sensation and perception. Handb. Hum. Factors Ergon. 59 (2012)

Rayner, K., Inhoff, A.W., Morrison, R.E., Slowiaczek, M.L., Bertera, J.H.: Masking of foveal and parafoveal vision during eye fixations in reading. J. Exp. Psychol. Hum. Percept. Perform. **7**(1), 167 (1981)

Salvendy, G.: Handbook of Human Factors and Ergonomics. Wiley, Hoboken (2012)

Sanders, M.S., McCormick, E.J.: Human Factors in Engineering and Design, 7th edn. McGraw-Hill, New York (1993)

Shneiderman, B., Plaisant, C.: Designing the User Interface: Strategies for Effective Human-Computer Interaction, 5th edn. Addison Wesley, New York (2010)

Spence, R.: Information Visualization: Design for Interaction, 2nd edn. Prentice Hall, New York (2007)

Steele, J., Iliinsky, N. (eds.): Beautiful Visualization. O'Reilly Media Inc., Cambridge (2010)

Tullis, T.S.: Screen design. Handb. Hum.-Comput. Interact. **2**, 503–532 (1988)

Thorpe, S.J., Gegenfurtner, K.R., Fabre-Thorpe, M., BuÈlthoff, H.H.: Detection of animals in natural images using far peripheral vision. Eur. J. Neurosci. **14**(5), 869–876 (2002)

Tullis, T.S.: Screen design. In: Helander, M.G., Landauer, T.K., Prabhu, P. (eds.) Handbook of Human-Computer Interaction, 2nd edn, pp. 503–531. Elsevier Science Publishers, Amsterdam (1997)

Van Cott, H.P., Kinkade, R.G.: Human Engineering Guide to Equipment Design, Revised edn (1972)

Wickens, C.D.: Multiple resources and performance prediction. Theor. Issues Ergon. Sci. **3**(2), 159–177 (2002)

Woo, E.H.C., White, P. and Lai, C.W.K.:. Ergonomics standards and guidelines for computer workstation design and the impact on users' health–a review. Ergonomics (just-accepted), 1–46 (2015)

Use of Customized Text Can Be Beneficial to Students Who Read Online Materials Under Constrained Visual Conditions

Kim-Phuong L. Vu[1(✉)], Amber Latham[1], Timothy Diep[1], Jonathan Van Luven[1], Ryan Fritz[1], and Wayne E. Dick[1,2]

[1] California State University Long Beach, Long Beach, CA, USA
Kim.Vu@csulb.edu, {Amber.Latham, Timothy.Diep, Jonathan.VanLuven, Ryan.Fritz}@student.csulb.edu, Wayneedick@knowbility.com
[2] Knowbility, Austin, TX, USA

Abstract. The use of digital materials, such as eBooks and other online content, has become increasingly popular among diverse groups of users due to their portability, ease of access, and cost effectiveness. However, individuals with disabilities and individuals without disabilities, who access the materials under constrained conditions (e.g., dim lighting), have different user needs. The ability to customize text is a potential solution for allowing users with different needs to optimize their online reading environments. The present study examined whether the ability to customize text would improve reading performance and reduce visual fatigue associated with online reading in two experiments. In addition, subjective ratings were obtained to evaluate the perceived usability of a system that allowed for customized text. Experiment 1 provided participants with limited experience with reading text on big or small screens under customizable and non-customizable conditions, and in either normal or dim lighting. In this experiment, we did not find any performance differences, but participants indicated that the use of customized text reduced their visual fatigue and showed a slight preference for using customized over non-customized text. In Experiment 2, participants performed the reading tasks over a longer period of time in a dimly lit room using either a big or small screen. Participants were more accurate in answering reading comprehension questions in the customized text condition. They also indicated agreement with statements about the use of customized text to reduce visual fatigue, and they wanted the option to customize text. Thus, overall, this study showed that the use of customized text could help users read and comprehend information better, as well as mitigate the effects of visual fatigue under constrained viewing conditions.

Keywords: Accessibility · Web accessibility · Customization · Customized text

S. Yamamoto and H. Mori (Eds.): HCII 2019, LNCS 11569, pp. 137–150, 2019.
https://doi.org/10.1007/978-3-030-22660-2_10

1 Introduction

Originally, web accessibility was thought to be primarily important for people with disabilities because it allows this group of users to perceive, understand, navigate, and interact with online materials. However, it has been shown that improving web accessibility not only benefits people with disabilities, but also other groups of people, including older users [1] and users accessing information under constrained conditions [2]. Examples of common constrained reading conditions include reading in dimly lit environments or on devices with smaller screen sizes. Lee, Ko, Shen, and Chao [3] found that search time for target letters decreased as illumination increased from 300 to 1500 lx. Benedetto, Carbone, Drai-Zerbib, Pedrotti, and Baccino [4] also found that students produced faster reading times in conditions with higher levels of luminance compared to lower levels. In addition, Lin, Wu, and Cheng [5] found that increasing font sizes on smaller screens (i.e., 6 to 9.7 in.) resulted in better search performance by students for targeted words. Thus, having the ability to customize properties of text can be beneficial to users by allowing them to tailor display properties to meet their specific needs.

Most universities in the United States are increasingly adopting electronic components as part of their educational practices. For example, at many universities, syllabi and other course materials are made available to students online through course management systems. The use of electronic documents not only increases the portability of the material, but it also reduces the costs associated with printing the materials. Use of electronic materials also has the potential for making the content more accessible if the content can be customized to meet the users' specific needs. In 2013, the California State Legislature enacted a bill that was intended to make higher education more affordable to students through the use of online teaching materials. As a result, the California State University system established a California Digital Open Source Library (CDOSL) and a California Open Online Library for Education (COOL4ed) to help faculty find and adopt online course materials at little or no cost to students. However, the online course materials must be accessible for the students to maximize their potential use. Sun et al. [6] and Chan et al. [7] evaluated the accessibility of 140 eTextbooks available at that time on the COOL4ed website and found that only about 60% of the books passed their accessibility evaluation. Moreover, many textbooks were in fixed formats (e.g., PDF files) that could not be customized for formatting and displaying the content on different devices. Thus, there is a need to improve the accessibility of electronic contents that are intended for use by students with and without disabilities.

As noted earlier, making text customizable may be the best way to improve accessibility for a broad range of users because the text can be adjusted to meet the specific needs of the individuals, the devices used to access the materials, or environmental conditions under which tasks are performed. Unlike personalization, which allows websites to provide content intended to suit the users' needs or interests without any intervention from the users, customization gives users control over the look and feel of the website, as well as the ability to make changes to the layout, functionality, or properties of text [8]. Many typographic properties have been identified as factors that improve reading for various groups of people with low vision [9, 10], including:

1. Font size and face
2. Color foreground and background
3. Spacing between lines, words, and letters
4. Borders and spacing between and around blocks of text
5. Width of blocks of text and line length
6. Word-wrapping, hyphenation, and justification
7. Typographic differences used to distinguish between paragraphs, headings, lists, etc.

As noted earlier, these same text properties should also improve reading for users with normal vision, especially in constrained conditions [3–5].

One tool that is being developed that allows for customized typographic properties is a "Typometric Prescription" Style-Picker program, which is called the TRx for short [11]. The current version of the TRx allows users to adjust the font size, foreground/background colors, and the spacing between lines and between words/letters, and other features of webpages. The present study used this tool to evaluate whether the ability to customize text improves reading comprehension of online text by students under different visual conditions (dim vs. regular lighting; small vs. big screens). Two experiments were conducted that used a combination of TRx and Qualtrics, an online survey software, to present reading passages to participants and to record their responses. In Experiment 1, a mixed design was used where participants were provided with limited experience with reading text on big and small screens under customizable and non-customizable conditions. Half of the participants performed the reading tasks in a brightly lit room and half in a dimly lit room to examine whether the benefits of customization occur in standard viewing conditions or constrained conditions. Because participants were only provided limited experience with viewing customized text in Experiment 1, a complete between-subjects design was used in Experiment 2, where participants performed the reading tasks over a longer period of time in a dimly lit room using either a big or small screen. We hypothesized that the use of customized text would improve participants' reading performance and reduce their visual fatigue.

2 Experiment 1

2.1 Methods

Participants. One hundred and eleven participants were recruited from the Introductory Psychology Participant Pool at California State University Long Beach (CSULB). Participants were given experimental credits toward their course research requirement for their participation. Data from 15 participants (13.5%) were excluded due to low accuracy scores (under 60%) for the reading comprehension questions. The final data set consisted of 96 participants (70 female, 26 male; Mean Age = 18.6 years).

Participants self-identified as Hispanic/Latino (47%), White/Caucasian (12%), Asian/Asian-American (34%), Black/African American (6%) or Other (1%) as their racial/ethnic background on the demographic questionnaire.

All participants reported having normal or corrected-to-normal vision. Computer proficiency was obtained from a demographic questionnaire. Participants were asked to indicate the type(s) of device(s) they typically use to access and read online content (e.g., smartphone, tablet, laptop or desktop computer), and how many hours they spend per week on each indicated device. Most participants indicated the use of a phone/mobile device (83%) and/or laptop (85%) as their typical device for reading online content. However, some also reported using a tablet (50%) or desktop computer (17%) to perform online reading.

Of the participants who reported typical use of a phone/mobile device to read online content, 6% reported spending 5 h or less per week, 28% reported spending between 5 and 10 h per week, 24% reported spending between 10 and 15 h per week, and 42% reported spending 20 or more hours per week reading on the device. Of those who reported typical use of a laptop to read online content, 12% reported spending 5 h or less per week, 33% reported spending between 5 and 10 h per week, 40% reported spending between 10 and 15 h per week, and 15% reported spending 20 or more hours per week reading on the device.

Materials. This study was conducted on Dell desktop computers running Windows 7 as the operating system. The 24-in. (18.46 × 53.70° visual angle) LCD monitors had a 1920 × 1080-pixel resolution. For the small screen conditions, the functional screen size was scaled down to reflect viewing on a 7.5-in. display (8.58 × 17.76° visual angle) on a black background. For the big screen conditions, the full screen was used. The monitor was positioned perpendicular to the table, and the participant sat about 20 in. away from the screen.

The reading task consisted of four brief passages ($M = 557$ words) and two medical prescriptions ($M = 204$ words) obtained from online standardized practice tests for reading comprehension at the 6th to 8th grade level. Each reading passage was accompanied by five comprehension questions that were displayed on the same page so that participants could reference the passage when answering the questions. Visual fatigue was measured using a visual fatigue questionnaire used in previous studies [1, 4, 12]. The questionnaire asked participants to indicate their agreement to statements regarding visual fatigue symptoms on a scale that ranged from 1 (strongly disagree) to 5 (strongly agree).

Usability was assessed using the System Usability Scale (SUS) questionnaire [13]. The SUS is a 10-item questionnaire, where participants rate their agreement to statements designed to assess the usability of a system on a 5-point scale, ranging from 1 (strongly disagree) to 5 (strongly agree). The post-experiment questionnaire consisted of questions designed to capture participants' preferences for customization in the different conditions using a 1 (prefer non-customization) to 7 (prefer customization) scale, as well as statements about customized text reducing visual fatigue in the different conditions using a 1 (strongly disagree) to 7 (strongly agree) scale.

Design. A 2 (Condition: customization or non-customization) × 2 (Screen Size: big or small) × 2 (Lighting Level: normal or dim) mixed design was implemented, with

Lighting Level being the only between-subjects factor. Participants were randomly assigned to a lighting level condition, which remained constant throughout the experiment. They were also randomly assigned to begin in either the customization or non-customization condition. Within each customization condition, participants were given two reading passages, one using the big screen and the other using the small screen. Afterwards, participants were given one of the prescription passages, performed using the big screen. The order for screen size within each condition was counterbalanced between subjects. In addition, the order of the four reading passages and two prescription passages was counterbalanced across the different experimental conditions.

Procedure. The procedures used in the present study were approved by the institutional review board (IRB) at CSULB. The experiment was conducted in a laboratory

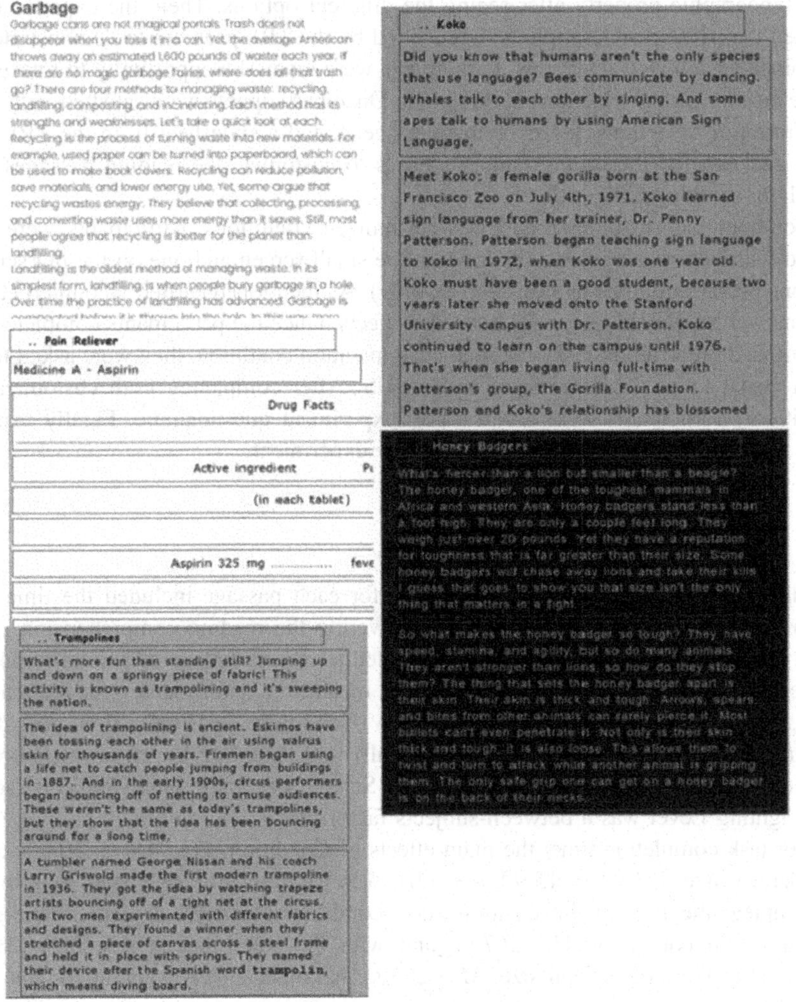

Fig. 1. Examples of customized text using TRx

environment, with each participant being tested individually. Half of the participants completed the experiment in a well-lit room and the other half completed it in a dimly-lit room. Participants began by reading and signing a consent form. Then, they were asked to complete a pre-questionnaire which consisted of demographic and computer preference and proficiency questions. Participants also filled out a pre-test visual fatigue questionnaire.

After completing the questionnaire, participants were seated approximately 20 in. from the computer screen and were presented with instructions for completing the reading tasks. In the customized condition, the experimenters assisted participants with setting their customized preferences. To do so, the experimenters used the TRx program to show the participants the different selections of font size and face, color foreground and background, as well as spacing between lines, words and letters. The selections were demonstrated one at a time, and participants made their selections for each typographic property after seeing the different options. Then, the experimenters showed the participants sample text generated by the TRx program to demonstrate the combined customized selections. Participants were given the opportunity to revise any of the customization selections at this point. Once participants were satisfied with their customization selections, the experimenters generated a stylesheet from the TRx program and inserted the settings into Qualtrics to customize the reading passages (see Fig. 1 for sample text).

For both the customized and non-customized conditions, participants were presented with two reading passages (one on the small screen and one on the big screen) and one prescription passage (big screen only). As mentioned earlier, a counterbalance scheme was employed to control for order effects. Once the participants completed the reading and prescription tasks for each customization condition, they were asked to fill out a visual fatigue questionnaire and a SUS. After completing both customization conditions, participants were given a post-experiment questionnaire. Finally, participants were debriefed at the conclusion of the experiment.

2.2 Results

Reading Tasks. The task completion time for each passage included the time participants spent reading the passage and answering the reading comprehension questions. Accuracy for each passage was calculated as the percentage of correct responses to the reading comprehension questions. The mean time and accuracy for the reading tasks were submitted to separate 2 (Condition: customization or non-customization) × 2 (Screen Size: big or small) × 2 (Lighting Level: normal or dim) repeated measures ANOVAs. Condition and Screen Size were within-subjects factors and Lighting Level was a between-subjects factor.

For task completion time, the main effects of Condition, $F(1,94) = 5.70$ $p = .019$, and Screen Size, $F(1,94) = 15.90$, $p < .001$, were significant. Participants took longer to complete the task in the customization condition ($M = 281$ s) than in the non-customization condition ($M = 267$ s), and with the small screen size ($M = 284$ s) compared to the large screen size ($M = 265$ s). No other effects were significant.

For accuracy, there were no significant effects or interactions. The overall accuracy was acceptable, averaging 82% (see Table 1 for means by condition).

Table 1. Reading accuracy (9% of correct responses) as a function of customization condition, screen size and lighting condition

Reading accuracy				
Condition	Screen size	Lighting	Mean	Standard deviation
Customized	Big	Dim	85.4%	20.9%
		Normal	83.3%	22.0%
	Small	Dim	85.0%	19.1%
		Normal	82.1%	18.1%
Not-customized	Big	Dim	81.3%	19.5%
		Normal	81.7%	22.5%
	Small	Dim	79.6%	21.6%
		Normal	80.4%	21.6%

Visual Fatigue. Visual fatigue was measured three times: at pre-test (baseline) and after the reading tasks in both the customized and non-customized conditions. These scores were submitted to a 3 (Condition: baseline, customized, non-customized) $\times$ 2 (Lighting Level: normal or dim) repeated measures ANOVA, with Lighting Level being the between-subjects factor. The main effects of Condition, $F(2,188) = 3.49$, $p = .03$, Lighting Level, $F(1,94) = 7.79$, $p = .006$, and the interaction between the two variables, $F(2,188) = 3.27$, $p = .04$, were significant.

Visual Fatigue scores were lowest at baseline ($M = 1.87$), intermediate after reading customized text ($M = 1.93$), and highest after reading non-customized text ($M = 2.03$), see Fig. 2. Bonferroni pairwise comparisons indicate that the difference between baseline and the non-customized text conditions was significant. Visual fatigue scores were also lower in the normal lighting condition ($M = 1.79$) than in the dim lighting condition ($M = 2.10$).

Tests of the simple effects were performed to investigate the interaction between Condition and Lighting Level. They showed little difference in visual fatigue across the three conditions in normal lighting, but visual fatigue scores differed for the three conditions in dim lighting, see Fig. 3. For dim lighting, visual fatigue scores were lowest at baseline ($M = 1.96$), intermediate after reading customized text ($M = 2.08$), and highest after reading non-customized text ($M = 2.27$). Bonferroni pairwise comparisons indicate that the difference between baseline and the non-customized text conditions was significant.

Subjective Usability Ratings. SUS scores were normalized to create a percentile ranking. Scores of 68 and above are considered above average, while scores of 68 or below less than average [14]. SUS scores were analyzed using a paired *t*-test (Condition: customization or non-customization). Both conditions resulted in above average SUS scores, being 73 in the customization and 75 in the non-customization condition. The difference between the two conditions was not significant.

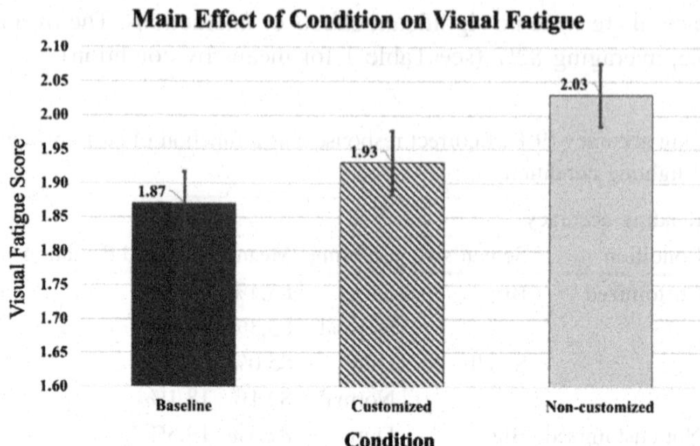

Fig. 2. Main effect of condition on visual fatigue scores. Visual fatigue scores were lowest at baseline, intermediate after reading customized text, and highest after reading non-customized text.

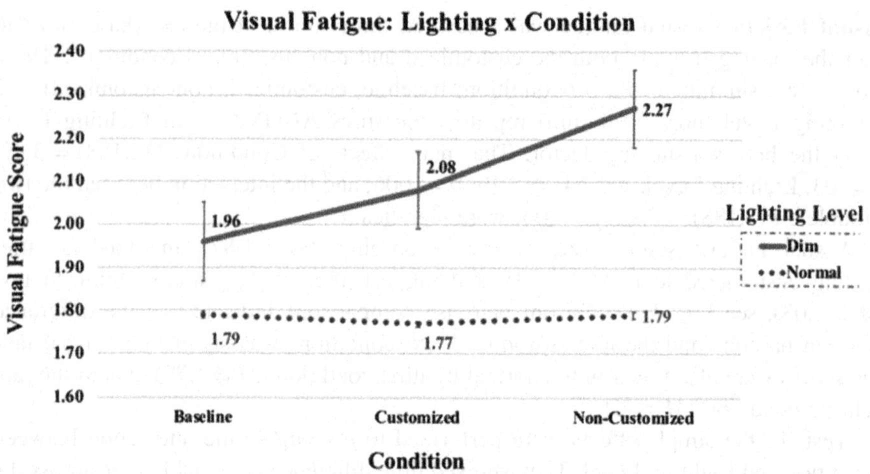

Fig. 3. Interaction between condition and lighting on visual fatigue scores. Visual fatigue scores were lowest at baseline, intermediate after reading customized text, and highest after reading non-customized text.

Post-questionnaire. Mean ratings for the questions on the post-experiment questionnaire are shown in Table 2. For the first three questions, one sample *t*-tests on the test value of 4, which indicated no preference, showed that participants preferred customization over non-customization for reading passages in both the small ($M = 4.59$), $p = .005$, and big ($M = 4.75$), $p < .001$, screen conditions. However, participants showed no preference for customization to perform the prescription task, which was only presented on the big screen.

For the three statements about whether customization decreased visual fatigue, one sample t-tests using the test value of 4, which indicated neither agree or disagree, showed that participants slightly agreed that using customization decreased their visual fatigue for the reading passages on both the small ($M = 4.64$), $p = .001$ and big ($M = 4.66$), $p < .001$, screens. However, participants neither agreed or disagreed with the statement for the prescription task, which was only presented on the big screen.

Table 2. Mean ratings given to the post experiment questionnaire

Question	Mean	Standard deviation
1 = using non-customized text, 4 = no preference, 7 = using customized text		
To perform the reading tasks using the Big screen, I preferred	4.59	2.02
To perform the reading tasks using the Small screen, I preferred	4.75	1.89
To perform the Prescription tasks, I preferred	3.63	2.05
1 = Strongly Disagree, 4 = Neither Agree or Disagree, 7 = Strongly Agree		
Using customized text decreased my visual fatigue when performing the reading tasks with the Big screen	4.64	1.84
Using customized text decreased my visual fatigue when performing the reading tasks with the Small screen	4.66	1.69
Using customized text decreased my visual fatigue when performing the Prescription tasks	3.95	1.69

2.3 Discussion

Experiment 1 showed that customization had little influence in terms of enhancing users' comprehension of the reading passages or the information in the prescription task. However, customization did help mitigate visual fatigue, especially with dim lighting, and despite the fact that participants spent a longer amount of time reading and answering questions in the customized condition. These findings indicate that there is some value in allowing users to customize text for online reading. Moreover, participants did not rate the customization condition to be lower in usability than the non-customization condition. This latter point is important because it indicates that use of customization features does not decrease the usability of a system.

The lack of strong effects of customization in the present experiment may be due to the fact that participants were only given limited experience with the customization condition (i.e., were only provided with two passages, one on a big screen and one on a small screen). Thus, Experiment 2 examined whether any performance benefits would appear for customized text if participants performed the reading task for a longer period of time.

3 Experiment 2

3.1 Methods

Participants. Sixty-six students were recruited from the same subject pool to participate in Experiment 2. Data from two participants (3%) were excluded and replaced due to low accuracy scores (under 60%) on the reading comprehension questions. The final data set consisted of 64 participants (32 female, 32 male; Mean Age = 19.5 years). These participants self-identified as Hispanic/Latino (32%), White/Caucasian (29%), Asian/Asian-American (27%), Black/African American (9%) or Other (3%) as their racial/ethnic background on the demographic questionnaire.

Similar to Experiment 1, most participants indicated that they typically use a phone/mobile device (83%), and/or laptop (71%), as opposed to a tablet (32%) or desktop computer (18%) to view online materials. Of the participants who reported typical use of a phone/mobile device to read online content, 7% reported spending 5 h or less per week, 25% reported spending between 5 and 10 h per week, 36% reported spending between 10 and 15 h per week, and 31% reported spending 20 or more hours per week reading on the device. Of those who reported typical use of a laptop to read online content, 19% reported spending 5 h or less per week, 35% reported spending between 5 and 10 h per week, 27% reported spending between 10 and 15 h per week, and 19% reported spending 20 or more hours per week reading on the device.

Materials, Design and Procedure. The materials used in Experiment 2 were the same as those used in Experiment 1, with the exception of the post-questionnaire. In addition, participants only performed the experiment in the dim lighting condition, and with a single screen size (half with the small screen and half with the big screen). Similar to Experiment 1, participants were presented with all four reading passages. Thus, they performed the reading task over a longer period of time in their assigned condition. The prescription passage was not used in the present experiment. Thus, this experiment used a 2 (Condition: customization or non-customization) × 2 (Screen Size: big or small) between-subjects design.

Participants were randomly assigned to one of the four conditions (i.e., the customization small screen, customization big screen, non-customization small screen, or non-customization big screen condition). As noted above, participants performed all four reading passages in their assigned condition. The order of the reading passages was counterbalanced across participants. Similar to Experiment 1, the visual fatigue questionnaire was administered before the test (baseline), after reading the first two passages, and after reading all four passages. The SUS was administered at the end of the session, prior to the post-experiment questionnaire.

3.2 Results

Reading Task. The mean time and mean accuracy on the four reading passages were calculated for each participant. Mean task completion time and accuracy scores were

submitted to separate 2 (Condition: customization or non-customization) x 2 (Screen Size: big or small) ANOVAs. All factors were between subjects.
For task completion time, no effects were significant.

For accuracy, there was a main effect of Condition, $F(1,60) = 6.98$, $p = .011$, where accuracy was higher in the customization condition ($M = 88.0\%$) than in the non-customization condition ($M = 80.9\%$), as seen in Fig. 4. No other effects were significant.

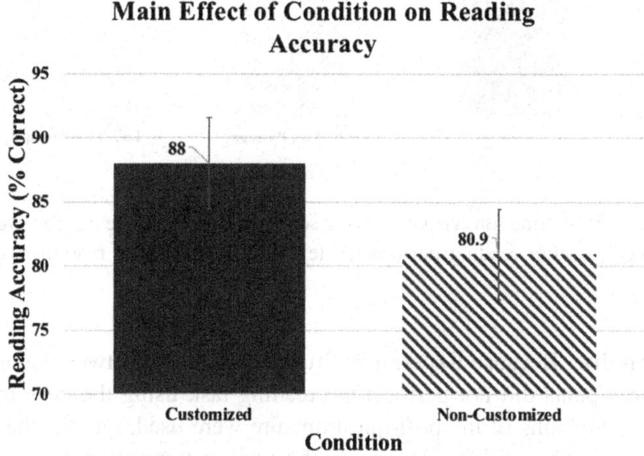

Fig. 4. Main effect of customization on reading accuracy. Accuracy was higher in the customization condition than the non-customization condition.

Visual Fatigue. Visual fatigue scores were submitted to a 2 (Condition: customization or non-customization) × 2 (Screen Size: big or small) × 3 (Time: baseline, after reading the first two passages, and after reading all four passages) ANOVA. Only the main effect of Time was significant, $F(2,120) = 4.62$, $p = .012$, as seen in Fig. 5. Visual fatigue scores were lowest at baseline ($M = 1.78$), intermediate after the first two reading passages ($M = 1.85$), and highest after reading the last two passages ($M = 1.97$). Bonferroni pairwise comparisons indicate that the difference between baseline and the last two passages was significant.

Subjective Usability Ratings. SUS scores were submitted to a 2 (Condition: customization or non-customization) × 2 (Screen Size: big or small) ANOVA. The main effects of Condition, $F(1,60) = 4.71$, $p = .034$, and Screen Size, $F(1,60) = 6.93$, $p = .011$, were significant. Participants rated the non-customized condition as higher in usability than the customized condition ($M = 78.2$ vs 70.9, respectively) and the condition with larger screen size as higher in usability compared to smaller screen size ($M = 79.1$ vs 70.2, respectively). The interaction of Condition × Screen Size was not significant.

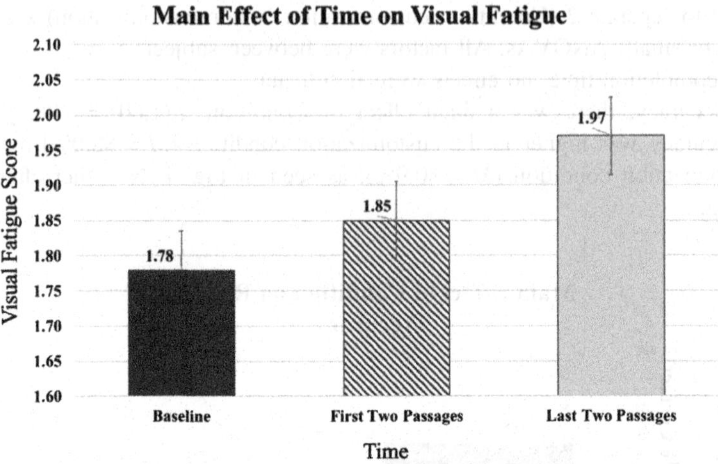

Fig. 5. Main effect of time on visual fatigue scores. Visual fatigue scores were lowest at baseline, intermediate after reading customized text, and highest after reading non-customized text.

Post-questionnaire. Because Experiment 2 used a complete between-subjects design, half of the participants did not perform the reading task using the customization features. Thus, two versions of the post-questionnaire were used, one for the participants in the customization condition and one in the non-customization condition. For the customization group, participants were asked whether they agreed with statements about using customized text to decrease visual fatigue and wanting to have the option of using customized text on a 1 (strongly disagree) to 7 (strongly agree) scale.

For the non-customization group, participants were shown the customization features at the end of the session and asked, "Now that you have seen what the customization program can do, please rate your agreement with the following statements." The statements that followed were similar to the statements shown to the participants in the customization condition. A mean perceived value of customization score was computed based on the ratings given to the 5 statements, and this mean rating was submitted to a 2 (Condition: customization or non-customization) × 2 (Screen Size: big or small) ANOVA. There were no significant effects or interactions. The average rating was 5.4, and this value was significantly different from a test value of 5 using a one-sample *t*-test, $p < .05$. Thus, participants agreed that the customization features were valuable through either direct experience or after demonstration of the customization features.

3.3 Discussion

Experiment 2 used only the dim lighting condition to examine the effects of reading customized text over a longer period of time. In this experiment, use of customized text did result in higher accuracy on the reading comprehension questions. However, unlike in Experiment 1, there was no evidence of customization leading to lower levels of visual fatigue. Although usability scores showed that the customization condition was in the usable range, participants rated the customization condition to be lower in usability than the non-customization condition. However, in the post-questionnaire, users agreed with statements that indicated that customized text reduces visual fatigue, and users wanted the option to customize text.

4 Conclusion

Taken together, the results of Experiment 1 and Experiment 2 show that use of customized text could be beneficial to users performing online reading tasks, even if those users do not have visual impairments. Use of customized text can also help mitigate the effects of visual fatigue under some conditions. Given that the participants in this study were young adults, the results are promising in terms of promoting the capability of providing users, especially those with visual impairments, the ability to customize text.

Acknowledgement. We thank Allen Chen, Andrea Flores, and Jaime Sanchez for their assistance with running participants in the study.

References

1. Fritz, R., Vu, K.-P.L., Dick, W.: Customization: the path to a better and more accessible web experience. In: Yamamoto, S., Mori, H. (eds.) Human Interface and the Management of Information: Visual Information and Knowledge Management. LNCS, vol. 11569, pp. 3–21. Springer, Heidelberg (2019)
2. Caldwell, B.B., Vanderheiden, G.C.: Access to web content by those with disabilities and others operating under constrained conditions. In: Handbook Human Factors Web Design, vol. 2 (2011)
3. Lee, D.-S., Ko, Y.-H., Shen, I.-H., Chao, C.-Y.: Effect of light source, ambient illumination, character size and interline spacing on visual performance and visual fatigue with electronic paper displays. Displays **32**, 1–7 (2011)
4. Benedetto, S., Carbone, A., Drai-Zerbib, V., Pedrotti, M., Baccino, T.: Effects of luminance and illuminance on visual fatigue and arousal during digital reading. Comput. Hum. Behav. **41**, 112–119 (2014)
5. Lin, H., Wu, F.-G., Cheng, Y.-Y.: Legibility and visual fatigue affected by text direction, screen size and character size on color LCD e-reader. Displays **34**, 49–58 (2013)
6. Sun, Y., Manabat, A.K.M., Chan, M., Chong, I., Vu, K.-P.L.: Accessibility evaluation: manual development and tool selection for evaluating accessibility of e-textbooks. In: Hale, K., Stanney, K. (eds.) Advances in Neuroergonomics and Cognitive Engineering. Advances in Intelligent Systems and Computing, vol. 488. Springer, Cham (2016). https://doi.org/10.1007/978-3-319-41691-5_28
7. Chan, M., Sun, Y., Tesoro, A., Vu, K.-P.L.: Development of a scoring system for evaluating the accessibility of eTextbooks (2016). https://www.researchgate.net/publication/304995934_Development_of_a_Scoring_System_for_Evaluating_the_Accessibility_of_eTextbooks

8. Schade, A.: Customization vs. personalization in the user experience. Nielsen Norman Group website, 10 July 2016. https://www.nngroup.com/articles/customization-personalization. Accessed 08 Jan 2019
9. Legge, G.E.: Psychophysics of Reading in Normal and Low Vision. Lawrence Erlbaum Associates, Mahwah (2007)
10. W3C Low Vision Accessibility Task Force: Accessibility Requirements for People with Low Vision (2016). https://www.w3.org/TR/low-vision-needs/. Accessed 27 Jan 2019
11. Dick, W., Gadberry, D., Monge, A.: Adjusting typographic metrics to improve reading for people with low vision and other print disabilities. In: Barnard, I., et al. (eds.) Annual International Technology and Persons with Disabilities Conference, pp. 36–45. California State University, Northridge (2013)
12. Tullis, T., Albert, B.: Measuring the User Experience: Collecting, Analyzing, and Presenting Usability Metrics, 2nd edn. Morgan Kaufmann, Waltham (2013)
13. Hallett, E.C., Dick, W., Jewett, T., Vu, K.-P.L.: How screen magnification with and without word-wrapping affects the user experience of adults with low vision. In: Ahram, T., Falcão, C. (eds.) AHFE 2017. AISC, vol. 607, pp. 665–674. Springer, Cham (2018). https://doi.org/10.1007/978-3-319-60492-3_63
14. U.S. Department of Health and Human Services: System Usability Scale. Usability.gov website (2017). https://www.usability.gov/how-to-and-tools/methods/system-usability-scale.html

Data Visualization and Analytics

A Coordinated Multi-channel Information Presentation Framework for Data Exploration

Zev Battad[1(✉)], Jeramey Tyler[1], Hui Su[2], and Mei Si[1]

[1] Department of Cognitive Science, Rensselaer Polytechnic Institute, 110 8th St, Troy, NY 12180, USA
{battaz,tylerj2,sim}@rpi.edu

[2] Cognitive Horizons Network, IBM Research, Austin, USA
huisuibmres@us.ibm.com

Abstract. As the information age changes the world around us, humans are interacting with ever-increasing amounts of data. While it can be difficult to remember details from data, presenting it in a coordinated manner can aid in its retention and recall. In this work, we investigate whether placing a greater degree of emphasis on elements of coordination in a multi-channel presentation system aids in recall of information. The interface described in this paper presents three coordinated channels of information: a pair of interactive time-series graphs, a text narrative and its vocalization, and salient external search data. 36 subjects were asked to use the interface to explore stock market data in one of two groups. For subjects in the increased-emphasis group, the interface color-coordinates related data across visual elements to emphasize the coordination between channels of information. Subjects in the control group received the same interface with no color coordination. It was hypothesized that increasing emphasis on coordination would produce a positive effect on recall of information from the interface. Subjects in the increased-emphasis group exhibited significantly greater accuracy than the control group when attempting to recall dates, but only for graph patterns presented with more detailed descriptions. However, subjects in both groups exhibited significantly worse accuracy when attempting to recall graph patterns that were presented with more detailed descriptions than those presented with simpler ones. Thus, increasing emphasis on coordination only helped accuracy of recall for dates, and only when the patterns associated with those dates were more difficult to recall to begin with.

Keywords: Data visualization · Information presentation · Multimodal interaction

1 Introduction

Data is constantly being collected around us. Data is collected in increasing amounts when we make purchases, visit the doctor, or browse the internet.

S. Yamamoto and H. Mori (Eds.): HCII 2019, LNCS 11569, pp. 153–173, 2019.
https://doi.org/10.1007/978-3-030-22660-2_11

However, data is rarely collected without purpose; there is usually the expectation that someone will eventually examine it. As more data is collected, less skilled people find themselves in the position of examining it. Difficulties are also encountered by those learning new subjects or doing individual research. Much of the data that is encountered will not be relevant, and much of the relevant data will not be easy to identify. Remembering the relevant details and/or relocating their positions in the data can be difficult, and those with little experience may not be able to overcome these challenges.

These challenges are not exclusive to digital data; they present themselves with physical data as well. Humans have developed strategies for coordinating detailed physical data. It is common to see students use colored highlights to draw their attention to specific passages of text. If similar approaches are applied to digital data, would they provide similar benefits?

Multi-modal information presentation has proven itself as an effective method of human communication across various applications [1,2]. Instructional environments [3] and domain-specific decision making [4] have utilized coordinated multi-channel, or multi-source, data presentation. It has also been shown to aid in learning and comprehension [5] with paired textual/verbal [6] and textual/visual sources [7,8]. Successfully presenting multiple channels of information requires them to be coordinated. It is thought that this coordination may help offset the cognitive load of engaging with additional information [3].

In this work, we investigate whether increasing the degree of emphasis on coordination in a multi-channel data presentation system increases memory of information. The system described in this paper presents users with stock market data via three coordinated channels of information: visualizations of time series data, a textual and vocalized description of patterns in the data, and salient external data. Channels are mainly coordinated using critical points, which are dates of significant changes in graph trends which appear throughout the data. Critical points define stock patterns, are referenced by the narrative, and define the search parameters for salient data search. We hypothesize that increasing the degree of emphasis on data coordination between channels will help individuals remember information more accurately from each channel. To investigate this hypothesis, a human subject study was performed. Subjects were asked to explore stock market data using a version of our interactive interface with either increased emphasis on coordination between channels or not. Afterward, they were quizzed on details of the information that they explored. While subjects in both groups showed significantly worse recall for patterns presented with more complex descriptions, subjects in the increased-emphasis group showed significant improvement over the control group for recall of specific dates associated with those patterns.

2 Related Work

The system and experiment for coordinated multi-channel information presentation described in this paper draws mainly from three sources of information.

Our usage of explicitly linked and redundant information is motivated by experimental work on the presentation of multiple types and modes of information in learning scenarios. Our use of narrative, and method for narrative generation, build off of previous work in narrative systems with coordinated information presentations, and literature on the memorability of narrative. Our method for graph pattern recognition is based largely off of existing work on automated stock pattern recognition.

2.1 Learning and Multi-channel Information Presentation

Presenting multiple channels of information has been shown to help individuals learn and retain information [1,2]. However, there exists an apparent contradiction. Presenting more channels of information in parallel splits attentional resources and demands an increase in information processing commensurate with each additional channel. According to models of working memory, splitting and increasing an individual's commitment of cognitive resources should hinder rather than help learning of information [9].

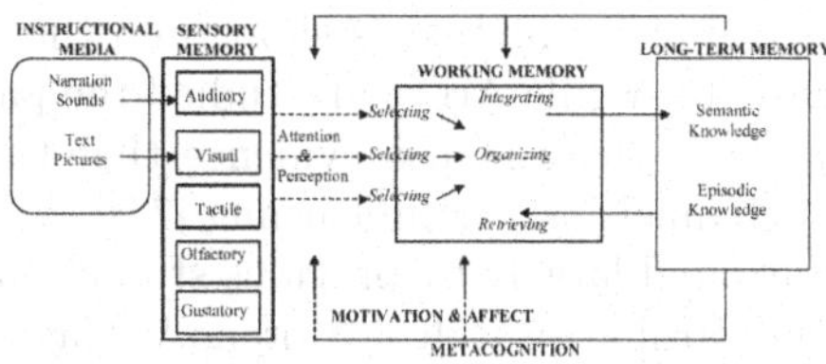

Fig. 1. Moreno & Mayer's model for learning in multimedia learning environments [3].

Moreno & Mayer offer a cognitive-affective model of learning in multimedia learning environments that helps explain this apparent contradiction (Fig. 1). In the model by Moreno & Mayer, one crucial component of learning is dedicating cognitive resources to the process of "selecting, organizing, and integrating new information" from the instructional media exposed to an individual. In learning tasks, Moreno & Mayer make a distinction between extraneous processing and essential processing. Essential processing consists of the commitment of cognitive resources to tasks required for learning, such as selecting, organizing, and integrating information. Extraneous processing consists of the use of cognitive resources for tasks outside of those required for learning new information. Tasks that cause extraneous processing often arise from the learning environment, such as shifting attention between visual displays or cross-referencing items between channels of information, and detract an individual's limited cognitive resources from essential processing [3].

Providing multiple channels of information inherently increases extraneous processing. However, coordination between channels of information such that they provide complimentary redundant information, explicitly link information, or both, seems to have a positive effect on remembering information that offsets these increased extraneous cognitive processing costs.

Several studies have explored the coordination of multiple overlapping and complementary channels of information as a presentation technique that contributes positively to human learning and comprehension of information. Presenting complementary information through separate, coordinated channels of information can help in understanding domain-specific information. Bloomfield et al. studied the effects of presenting complimentary sets of information about company finances to credit analysts tasked with making credit downgrade decisions. Information was either explicitly linked in the text, or simply presented together on the same page. Though both groups came to the same decisions, analysts who received linked information displayed a better understanding of the underlying material. They were able to give better projections of company profit margins and justifications for credit downgrade decisions [4].

Additionally, using different channels of information to present redundant information can have a positive effect. In their study on the effects of pairing verbal descriptions with on-screen text in a college-level learning scenario, Ari et al. found that redundant on-screen text had a positive effect on comprehension and recall. However, they also specify that the effect was only seen when the studied material is complex, the text is short, and the subject controls the pace at which they study [6]. While Ari et al. studied the pairing of textual and verbal information channels, there is also evidence that the pairing of textual and visual information channels assists in learning [7,8].

Our experiment is inspired largely by previous studies on coordinated multichannel information and learning, as well as Moreno & Mayer's model of learning in multimedia environments. Previous studies varied the coordination of information by adding or detracting redundant channels of information [6–8] or explicitly linking channels of information [4], showing the positive effects of both on comprehending and learning information. According to Moreno & Mayer's model, one of the key factors to learning information is attending to, selecting, and organizing it [3]. It follows that attending to the coordination between channels of information may be important to benefit from that coordination. In our experiment, the degree to which coordination is emphasized between channels of information is varied.

The system described in this paper coordinates three channels of information, which are explicitly linked and providing redundant information. Through the dates of critical points on the graph, the visualization of a company's stock data is explicitly linked with a narrative description of the graph's shape and salient external data pertaining to the company. Redundant information is presented in both visualizations of stock data and narrative descriptions of stock patterns. Users control the pace of their exploration by way of the interface's interactions.

2.2 Narrative Generation

Narrative has long been used as a constellation of natural and memorable techniques for information exchange [10–12]. The use of narrative as a channel of information in this system draws mainly from previous work by Battad and Si on generating narratives from data. Battad and Si demonstrated a system for generating stories from large, online information networks [13,14]. Narratives in their system formed a structure from which a multi-channel information display with descriptive text and data visualization operated. In more recent work, Battad and Si presented a system for general graph-based narrative pattern description [15]. Pattern descriptions describe visible patterns in graphs and how they are skewed, using skew as an element of narrative abnormality. Abnormality in narrative has been observed in oral storytelling traditions [16] and in experimental settings [17] to have a positive effect on memory of information in a narrative, and is used in their system to increase memorability of graph-based information.

The system described in this paper uses a modified version of the narrative generation system for graph-based pattern description by Battad and Si [15]. The system is specialized to describe stock price graph patterns, a regular occurrence in stock market data analysis. Additionally, the generated narrative description is color-coordinated to match critical points and patterns on the visualization, as well as those shown in the headers of the salient data results.

2.3 Pattern Recognition

To present information about stock price graph patterns, a method was required for recognizing said patterns amongst stock price data. Three main methods were considered: a multi-classifier based approach for detecting Elliott wave patterns by Volna et al. [18], a genetic algorithm based method for detecting patterns by Parraccho et al. [19], and a method for detecting a discrete set of common stock price graph patterns by Dover [20].

The methods by Volna et al. and Parraccho et al. are both learning-based methods, and primarily aim to predict stock price changes based on one specific pattern. Volna et al.'s method was focused on Elliott wave recognition. Elliott waves are a repeating pattern of stock price changes characterized by a discrete set of rise-and-fall patterns which have shown utility in forecasting stock price changes. Using a back-propagation neural network, Volna et al.'s method is able to recognize Elliott wave patterns and use them for the purposes of prediction [18]. While Elliott waves have proven useful for stock price forecasting, they are less known in common stock price graph analysis. More common shapes were preferred for more convenient predefined descriptions. Parraccho et al. instead focuses on the profile of upwards trends in stock price graphs. In Parraccho et al.'s method, a genetic algorithm is used to maximize the profitability of investment strategies based on characteristics of upwards trend patterns, such as normal buy and sell windows and the direction of the graph after the upwards trend [19]. Upward trends are certainly common stock price patterns. However, a method that could offer more variety in recognizing different, common, distinguishable stock price graph patterns was preferred.

Our approach to pattern recognition is an extension and implementation of recent work by Dover [20]. In her work, Dover provides a simple set of

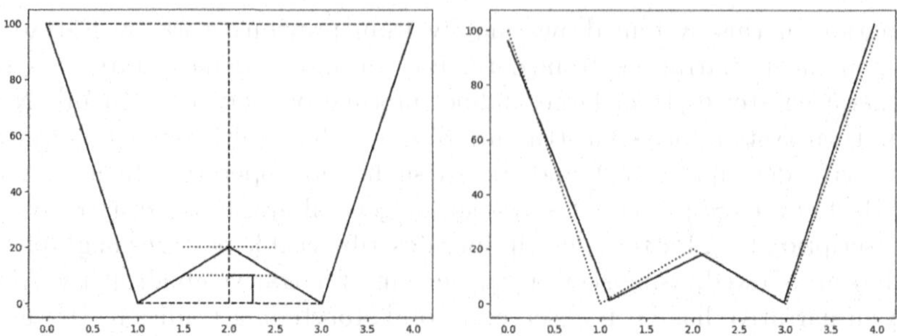

Fig. 2. A perfect 'W' in contrast with an imperfect 'W'.

mathematical bases for a number of patterns used in stock data analysis. These bases provide a useful mechanism for describing how abnormal a pattern is when compared to a perfect version of itself. Each basis represents a set of common mathematical relationships. Since their definitions and transformations are commonly known, these relationships provide convenient predefined descriptions.

3 System Overview

The system described here is modeled off of work by Battad and Si [15]. In their work, Battad and Si utilize narrative and storytelling to describe time-series data. Our works extends theirs in three ways; additional input, additional output, and coordination across elements in the interface.

Our system is composed of three high level modules: pattern recognition, narrative generation, and salient data search (Fig. 3). Stock closing data is provided courtesy of the IEx Finance API [21]. Data is coordinated between modules using *critical points*. In pattern recognition, critical points form the local extrema of a pattern. In narrative generation, critical points are used to identify the location of patterns in a graph. In salient data search, they are used to generate query terms.

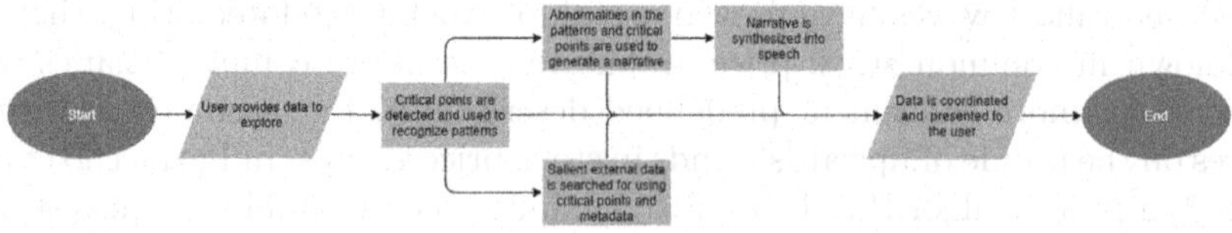

Fig. 3. System overview

3.1 Critical Points

In order to coordinate multiple channels of information, there must be some commonality. In our system, this commonality takes the form of critical points. In this section, we discuss how critical points are found and coordinated between modules.

Critical Point Identification. A critical point represents a place where the trajectory of the data changes dramatically, resulting in a local extrema. These extrema are identified in the pattern recognition module. Sequences of local extrema in the stock data are identified and examined. If a sequence proves to be a valid pattern, the dates of its extrema are used as critical points to coordinate data presentation. Due to the highly volatile nature of stock data, patterns found by this method tend to span short time periods. To combat this, the stock data is progressively smoothed. As the data is smoothed, the less pronounced extrema vanish, while the more pronounced extrema remain present. This produces extrema that are farther apart temporally, resulting in patterns that span greater ranges of time. This process may cause extrema to shift to dates for which no actual data exists, e.g. days when no trading occurred. In these instances, the nearest date with trading data is used.

Critical Points in Narrative Generation. In the narrative generation module, critical points serve two roles: they provide a mechanism for measuring a pattern's time span, and a way to reference its location in the graph. Critical point mentions are highlighted in the narrative to draw the user's attention and are color-coordinated to match the patterns for which they are associated.

Critical Points for Salient Data Search. Critical points are utilized a final time in the salient data search module. Each critical point in a given shape is used to programmatically generate an internet search query term. Query terms are generated by concatenating the name of the company with a corresponding critical point. A Google custom search engine processes the query terms, and their results are displayed as a series of nested menus, grouped by critical points. The outermost set of menus correspond to patterns, while the inner menus correspond to their critical points (Fig. 6).

3.2 Pattern Recognition

The basic components of our pattern recognition module are critical point identification, data smoothing, and pattern validation. Iteratively searching for critical points and smoothing the data via Gaussian Process, a la Dover [20], allows us to recognize patterns over large spans (Fig. 4). Patterns can be easily located by searching for sequences of local extrema. For example, a 'W' shape is composed of the following extrema sequence: maxima, minima, maxima, minima, maxima. Our system implements the set of patterns from Dover's original work: double top, double bottom, and head and shoulders [20]. Additionally, we provide our own implementations for uptrends and downtrends.

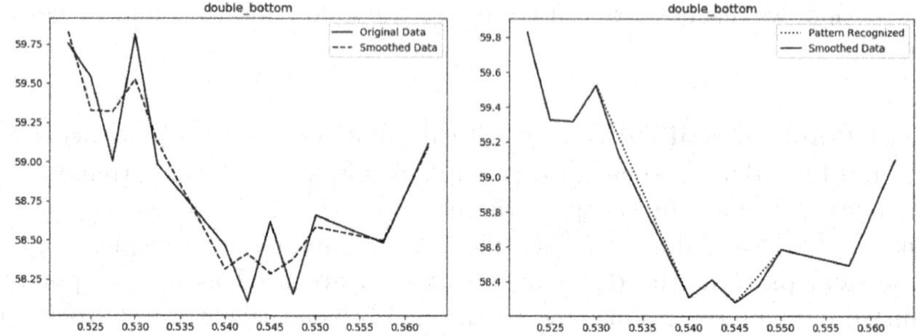

Fig. 4. Data smoothed by Gaussian process and the 'W' it predicts

Patterns are validated by examining the relationships between vectors, as in Dover [20]. Relationships like parallelism and perpendicularity can be used to define an ideal version of the pattern (Fig. 2, left). By measuring the difference between the expected values of relationships and the actual values, we can measure how abnormal a pattern is and set thresholds for acceptable deviation.

Some level of deviation needs to be allowed for pattern recognition to function. Real data is unlikely to produce many perfect patterns, so if the pattern validation is too rigid, it will rarely detect patterns other than uptrends and downtrends. In addition, Humans are able to recognize patterns that are distorted, exhibiting a tolerance to minor deviations in the pattern. In Fig. 2, the right hand image shows an imperfect 'W' with a perfect 'W' superimposed. Although an AI could easily find these differences, they are minor to a human; by setting a threshold for ignoring minor deviations, our system is able to recognize and describe patterns in a similar manner to humans.

The subset of the initial data that the subject has selected is displayed as a time-series graph, with recognized and validated patterns highlighted. Each pattern is assigned a color for coordination; uptrends are green, downtrends are red, double bottoms are blue, double tops are orange, and head and shoulders patterns are purple. All references to a particular pattern in the interface are color-coordinated. This is done to aid subjects in quickly finding coordinated data in the interface. For each pattern, a series of vector relationships are calculated [20]. These vector relationships are normalized to a 0–1 scale, with 0 being the perfect relationship and 1 being the worst relationship. These calculations, or abnormality measures, are used by narrative generation to select topics and generate detailed descriptions. The three patterns with the smallest average abnormality measures are select for narrative generation. By restricting the number of patterns presented to the subjects, we are able to limit the length of descriptions.

3.3 Narrative Generation

Patterns, their critical points, and their abnormality measures are passed from the pattern recognition module to the narrative generation module. Based on previous work by Battad and Si on general graph-based narrative shape description [15], the narrative generation module produces a description of the visible patterns in the graph and their abnormalities. Descriptions are made in terms of dates for critical points, creating a narrative that links visual patterns in the data with salient external data related to the company. This helps users associate where relevant events occur on the company's stock graph.

To limit the size of the narrative, only one pattern receives a fully detailed description. The pattern with the more detailed description is designated the *detailed pattern* while the other patterns are designated as *non-detailed patterns.* Currently, the pattern with the longest date range that is not an uptrend or downtrend in each set of patterns is designed as the detailed pattern. For the detailed pattern, the abnormality measures with the highest values are chosen to be included in the description. Currently, the top two abnormality measures are chosen for each detailed pattern. Then, a narrative plan is generated that includes the name of the pattern, start and end critical points of the pattern, the critical points and pattern line segments associated with the abnormality measures chosen, and the abnormality measures themselves. An example of a detailed pattern description can be see in the description for the double bottom pattern in Fig. 5. For non-detailed patterns, the narrative plan includes only the name of the pattern and the start and end critical points of the pattern. An example of a non-detailed pattern description can be seen in the description for the downtrend and uptrend patterns in Fig. 5. A more detailed overview of the narrative generation method can be found in [15].

Narrative plans allow for templates to be employed, providing the potential for domain-specific narratives. A template is provided for each pattern, supplying a text description for each critical point, line segment, and abnormality measure. Once a narrative description is generated, its vocalization can be synthesized. The narrative is displayed to the subject and its vocalization plays automatically. The visual narrative highlights all mentions of a pattern or its critical points, and color-coordinates them to match their respective patterns (Fig. 5). By highlighting the mentions in the narrative, we are able to draw the subject's attention to the most important aspects of the narrative. By color-coordinating them, we provide an easy way to associate mentions in the narrative with their locations in the graph and their salient data search results (Fig. 10).

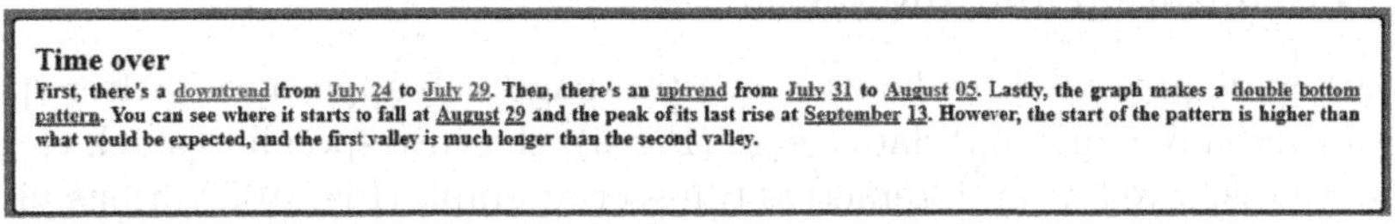

Time over

First, there's a downtrend from July 24 to July 29. Then, there's an uptrend from July 31 to August 05. Lastly, the graph makes a double bottom pattern. You can see where it starts to fall at August 29 and the peak of its last rise at September 13. However, the start of the pattern is higher than what would be expected, and the first valley is much longer than the second valley.

Fig. 5. Shape and date mentions are colored to match the graph.

3.4 Salient Data Search

In an effort to associate real events with recognized patterns, our system autonomously performs a salient data search for each critical point. Salient data can be described as any external data that is relevant to the data we are examining. By programmatically generating a query term from a critical point, salient data is gathered via a Google Custom Search Engine (CSE). For each critical point in a pattern, a query term is generated by combining the name of the company with the critical point, e.g. "Tesla July 29, 2018". The CSE results for a particular critical point are presented in a collapsible menu. The results are grouped by their respective patterns and nested in another set of collapsible menus (Fig. 6), and the headers of the menus are color-coordinated to match their corresponding patterns. Displaying salient data search results allows us another avenue to test a subject's memory retention and recall.

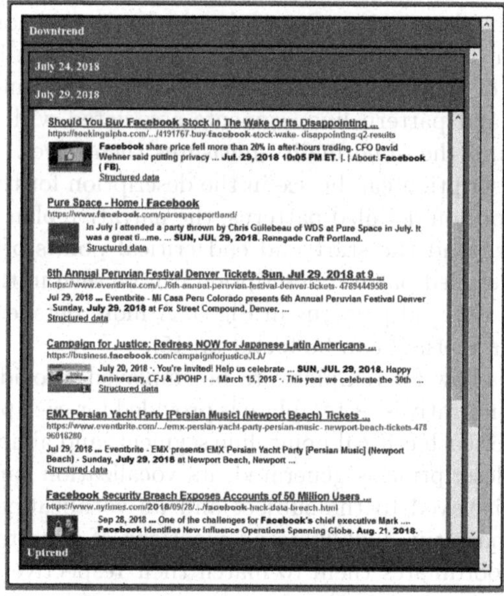

Fig. 6. News results are displayed according to their shape and date. Colored headers provide and additional level visual coordination.

3.5 Visualization and Interaction

Our system is presented to the user as a two-page web application. After specifying a company name and date range (Fig. 9), the corresponding stock closing prices are displayed as an interactive time-series graph (Fig. 10). Various visual elements are added to the graph to aide the user. Vertical tick marks graduate the time-series into quarter-year segments. A reticule and vertical line accompany the mouse's x position on the graph. Next to the reticule, the *date* and *price* values are displayed. This is done so that the user does not have to search for the axes values, as they will always be near the mouse pointer.

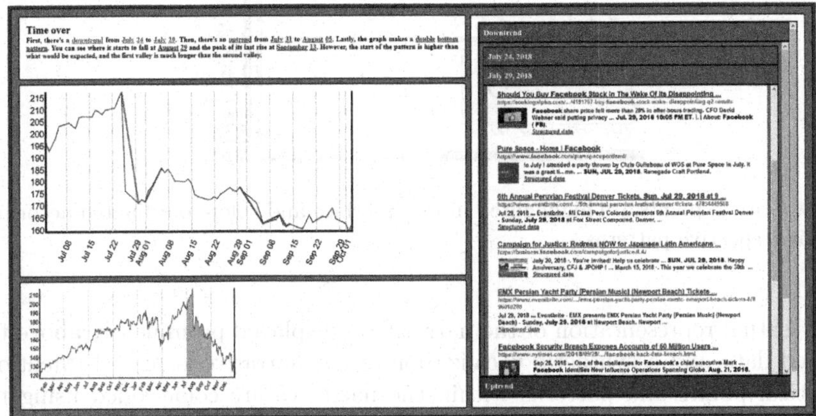

Fig. 7. Highlighted sections of the graph are presented to the user in a coordinated manner.

Coordination. As mentioned previously, critical points are the common link that coordinates our data, and play a pivotal role in coordinating the presentation of our multiple disparate channels of information. In this section, we give an explanation of how critical points are used to coordinate each channel. Our system currently must coordinate the following channels: *interactive data visualization*, *textual and vocalized narrative*, and *salient data display*.

Data visualization and presentation is handled by generating interactive graphs within a web page. Data is displayed as is, with no pattern matching, etc. visible. Vertical and horizontal markers provide visual indicators of axis values. Selecting a section of the graph initializes pattern recognition and salient data search. A second graph is generated with the same interactions, focusing on the selected section. Critical points within the data, and the patterns which they comprise, are visually indicated in the new graph. Each pattern is assigned a color and all instances of the pattern are colored accordingly. New selections of the graph may be made, in which case the second graph will be generated anew with the updated selection.

Salient data search terms are generated by combining critical points and meta-data. Results of salient data searches are displayed next to the narrative, grouped according to their critical points and presented as a series of collapsible panels. Currently, our system displays the top search results of a Google custom search engine, sorted by Google's relevancy algorithm.

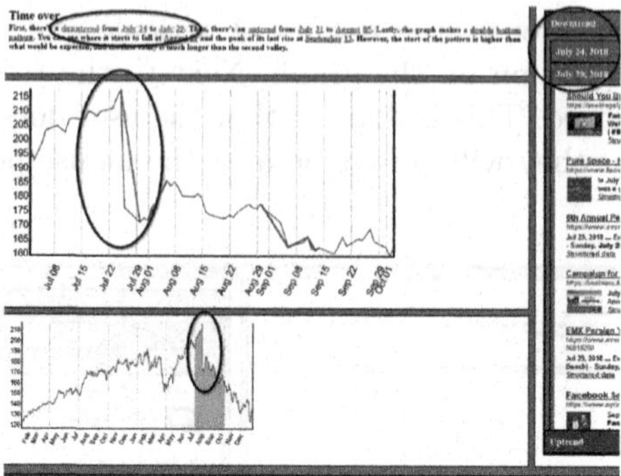

Fig. 8. Critical points are highlighted in the interface and color-coordinated according to their respective patterns.

A textual representation of the narrative is displayed prominently above the selected data and a synthetic vocalization of the narrative is played. Mentions of critical points and patterns within the narrative are color-coded using the same scheme as described above (Fig. 8). This provides synchronized visual indicators of the narrative's elements in the interface. A full view of the coordinated elements of the interface can be seen in Fig. 7.

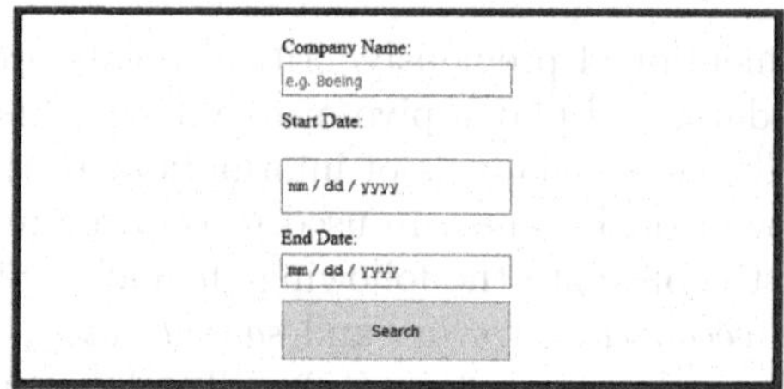

Fig. 9. Subjects can search for stock data by providing a company name and date range. A set of radio buttons indicate whether or not the data is to be coordinated.

4 Empirical Evaluation

The objective of the following experiment was to investigate the hypothesis that emphasizing coordination between multiple channels of information within the system presented in this paper helps people remember more information from those channels.

To test this hypothesis, two versions of the system were prepared with varying levels of emphasis on coordination between channels of information. The *increased-emphasis*, version is the full system as described in this paper. In the *control* version, no color-matching is done between patterns, description text referencing those patterns, and media menu headers associated with those patterns, and color-matched pattern line overlays are not present in the zoomed-in graph.

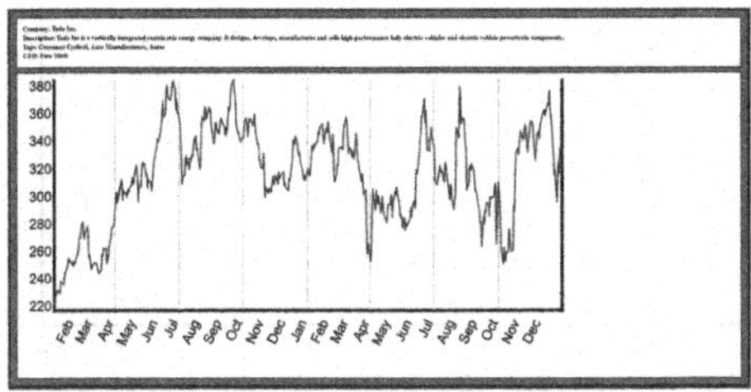

Fig. 10. Stock closing prices are presented to the user as an interactive time-series graph.

To gauge memory of information, recall was tested on what patterns appeared on the graph, the dates of the start and end critical points of those patterns, and what news headlines associated with the company appeared in the salient data panel. As pieces of information that were present across multiple channels of information, appearance of patterns and dates of critical points were expected to be more susceptible to changes in emphasis on coordination. To give more equal coverage to recall of information from the salient data panel, news headline recall was included as a third measure.

4.1 Method

Participants. 36 college students were recruited for the study from the Cognitive Science subject pool at Rensselaer Polytechnic Institute. Subjects were tested in groups of one to three subjects per session. Each session was randomly assigned to one of two experimental groups corresponding to each version of the system: the increased-emphasis group and the control group. All subjects in the same session were assigned to the same experimental group. 18 served in the increased-emphasis group and 18 served in the control group.

Materials and Apparatus. Materials consisted of a questionnaire and a recall quiz. The questionnaire asked for a self-assessment of prior experience with financial analysis and stock price patterns. The questionnaire consisted of three questions: "Do you have any experience with financial analysis? (coursework counts)", "If so, from what?", and "Are you familiar with standard stock price pattern shapes (e.g. double-top, double-bottom, head-and-shoulders)?"

The recall quiz was separated into one part for each one-quarter year interval of each company studied. Each part of the quiz consisted of an image of the zoomed-in stock price graph for the interval without pattern lines overlain, the name of the company, the start and end date of the interval, and two questions (Fig. 11).

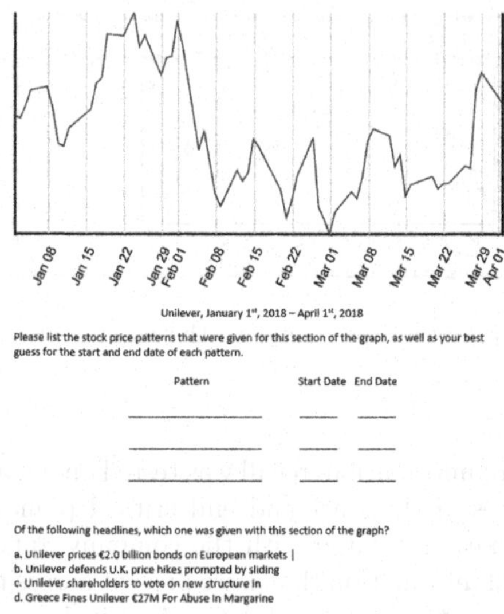

Fig. 11. The recall quiz part for the first quarter of Unilever.

Question 1 solicited recall for pattern names and start and end dates for each pattern. Three rows were provided, one for each of the three patterns that appeared in the interval. Question 2 was a multiple choice question with four options. Each option consisted of the text of a news headline exactly as it appeared in the salient search results panel. The correct option was a headline randomly chosen from the same interval. The three incorrect options were headlines randomly chosen from different intervals. To help filter news headlines from other results, headlines were chosen such that each headline contained a verb and the name of the company. No headline chosen appeared in more than one interval.

The apparatus consisted of a workstation with a monitor, mouse, keyboard, headphones, and a computer running the version of the system corresponding to the subject's experimental group. Workstations were placed such that subjects were not facing each other's monitors.

Procedure. First, subjects were given the questionnaire. Subjects were allowed to fill out and submit the questionnaire on their own time. After all subjects had submitted their questionnaire, the experiment administrator gave oral instructions. Subjects were told that their goal was to study the stock price graphs and news headlines for several companies using the interface on the computer in front of them. Subjects were asked to study the stock price graphs and related news headlines for one year's worth of data for five different companies. The same five companies were studied by each subject: Unilever, General Electric, McDonald's, Sony, and Walgreens. The order in which companies were studied was randomized for each subject.

For each company, subjects were asked to search from January 1st, 2018 through December 31st, 2018 in the initial search window. Subjects were directed to examine each company's stock price graph in one-quarter year intervals, demarcated on the overall stock price graph with vertical grey lines, from the earliest interval to the latest interval. Subjects were given one minute to explore the information for each interval, including listening to its narration, reading its description, looking at its stock price graph, and looking at its headlines. In each interval, the system presents exactly three patterns. Subjects were asked to take the full minute to study each interval, and to proceed to the next interval as soon as their time was over. After finishing the last interval for one company, subjects were asked to return to the initial search window and were given the name for the next company.

Before beginning, subjects were given a short walkthrough of the system's interface using an example company, Facebook. An overview of each panel of information and a thirty-second period of free exploration was given to each subject. After the thirty-second period, all subjects were asked to return to the initial search window, and each subject was told the name of their first company.

After all subjects had finished studying their last company, the recall quiz was given. The recall quiz was given in five sections, with one section for each company. Each section consisted of the quiz parts for all four intervals of a single company, from the earliest interval to the latest. After a subject finished the quiz section for one company, the quiz section for the next company was given to the subject. Quiz sections were given to each subject in the same order that companies were studied by that subject. Each subject was given thirty minutes total to complete the recall quiz.

Scoring. Subject memory of information from each interval was evaluated using three primary measures: pattern recall accuracy, date recall error, and headline recall accuracy. Pattern recall accuracy is measured as the percentage of patterns correctly recalled in Question 1 of the recall quiz. For each correctly recalled pattern, date recall error is measured as the total difference, in days, between the start and end dates given by the subject and the actual start and end dates of the pattern. Headline recall accuracy is measured as the percentage of multiple choice questions answered correctly in Question 2 of the recall quiz.

4.2 Results

Of the 36 subjects, 12 self-reported some experience with financial analysis. Of those, 6 reported that their experience came from personal trading, and 6 reported that their experience came from an introductory economics class. 2 of the 12 self-reported familiarity with stock price pattern shapes. No significant effect was found between any of the three primary measures and experience with financial analysis or familiarity with pattern shapes.

Table 1. Mean and standard deviations of primary measures by level of emphasis on coordination.

	Pattern recall accuracy (%)		Date recall error (Days)		Headline recall accuracy (%)	
	m	std	m	std	m	std
Increased-emphasis	51.5	8.64	15.2	4.01	35.0	10.6
Control	51.1	7.96	16.8	5.68	30.0	9.54

Table 1 shows the overall mean and standard deviation of all three measures by level of emphasis on coordination. The data were analyzed using pairwise tests for significance between increased-emphasis and control groups for each measure. No significant effect was found. To investigate if population size was appropriate for the study, the effect size of each measure between groups was calculated (Cohen's d). It was found that for date recall error ($d = -0.627$) and headline recall accuracy ($d = 0.622$), the effect size is medium. For pattern recall accuracy ($d = 0.284$), the effect size is small.

Table 2. Mean and standard deviations of primary measures by level of emphasis on coordination and by pattern detail.

		Pattern recall accuracy (%)		Date recall error (Days)	
		m	std	m	std
Increased-emphasis	Detailed	30.3^1	16.4	11.4^3	6.46
	Non-detailed	58.3^1	9.06	14.9	4.05
Control	Detailed	23.1^2	14.3	17.7^3	9.22
	Non-detailed	57.5^2	12.0	18.0	5.75

Significant differences: 1 - $p < 0.001$, 2 - $p < 0.001$, 3 - $p < 0.05$.

To further explore the data, it was investigated whether certain patterns were recalled better or worse than others. As discussed in Sect. 3.3, one pattern in each set of patterns is chosen as a detailed pattern. Thus, for each interval, a more complex and detailed description is generated for one of the three patterns. The data for each group were separated by whether patterns were detailed or non-detailed during description generation (Fig. 12). Table 2 shows the mean and standard deviation of pattern recall accuracy and date recall error by level of emphasis and by level of pattern detail. Headline recall accuracy was not analyzed in this way, as each headline recall question gauges an entire interval rather than a single pattern. One-way ranked ANOVA (Kruskal-Wallis H-test) with level of emphasis and level of pattern detail as independent variables showed $p < 0.001$. Post-hoc pairwise comparison showed that pattern recall accuracy was significantly lower for detailed patterns than for non-detailed patterns in both the increased-emphasis ($p < 0.001$, $d = 2.11$) and control ($p < 0.001$, $d = 2.61$) groups. Thus, in both groups, subjects were less likely to recall patterns with more detailed descriptions than less detailed descriptions. In addition, date recall error for detailed patterns was found to be significantly lower in the increased-emphasis group as compared to the control group ($p < 0.05$, $d = 0.78$). Thus, for patterns with more detailed and complicated descriptions, subjects more accurately recalled specific dates in the increased-emphasis group than in the control group.

One possible explanation for the difference in pattern recall accuracy between detailed and non-detailed patterns is the length of the descriptions generated. To investigate this, description length was analyzed by pattern detail. Detailed patterns were found to have significantly longer description length ($m = 216$ characters, $std = 19.2$) than non-detailed patterns ($m = 47.4$ characters, $std = 4.75$), due to their description generation procedure ($p < 0.001$, $d = 15.9$). However, no significant correlation was found between description length and whether a pattern was recalled correctly amongst detailed shapes, non-detailed shapes, or both.

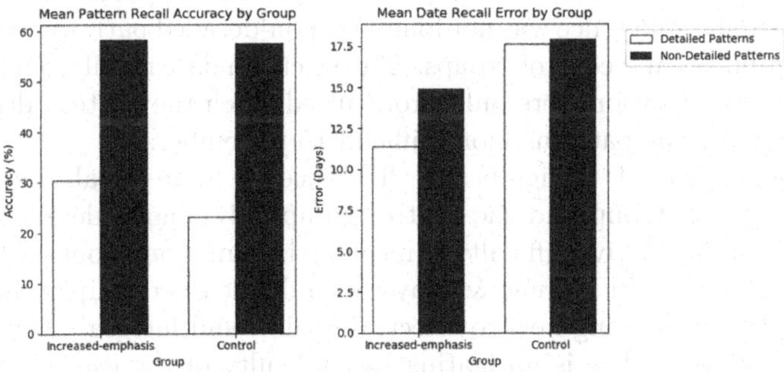

Fig. 12. Mean pattern recall accuracy (left) and date recall error (right) by experimental group and level of pattern detail.

5 Discussion

5.1 Experiment Results

Increased description detail seemed to have a significant negative effect on whether subjects recalled a pattern. Since patterns with detailed descriptions were those that leveraged narrative abnormality, which is thought to have a positive effect on recall of information in stories [16,17], it was expected that those patterns would be better recalled overall. However, the opposite was true. In terms of Moreno & Mayer's model for multimedia learning, the increased extraneous processing cost of reading, listening to, and comprehending a more detailed description of a pattern may have been detrimental to remembering information about that pattern past any positive effect on memory conferred from leveraging narrative abnormality [3].

Given the lack of correlation between description length and pattern recall, the increase in extraneous processing cost for patterns with detailed descriptions appears to be more complicated than simply an increase in reading or listening time. Descriptions for detailed patterns present more dates for subjects to attend to, and direct them to more areas of the graph than descriptions for non-detailed patterns do. If subjects were being overwhelmed with dates to remember in detailed descriptions, then a significant increase in date recall error between detailed and non-detailed patterns would be expected. However, no significant difference was found. A deeper analysis on the relationship between subject recall of information and the complexity of pattern descriptions besides those that leverage narrative abnormality would be necessary to explore this difference.

For detailed patterns, subjects in the increased-emphasis group were able to recall start and end dates with higher accuracy than those in the control group. This is thought to be due to the presence of color-matched pattern overlay lines in the increased-emphasis version, drawing attention to the coordination between patterns on the graph and specific dates mentioned in the pattern's description. However, a similar difference was not found for non-detailed patterns between the increased-emphasis and control groups. The effects on date recall from increasing emphasis on coordination were only pronounced when the pattern descriptions were detailed and the patterns more difficult to remember.

The appearance of a significant difference in date recall between the increased-emphasis group and the control group only among detailed patterns could be due to the relative difficulty of recalling information about patterns with detailed descriptions. In Moreno & Mayer's model, learners employ metacognitive strategies for choosing how to select, organize, and integrate new information (Fig. 1). Part of that is mitigating the difficulty of the learning task with the strategies employed to perform the task [3]. Dates presented for patterns with non-detailed descriptions may be easy enough to process that subjects did not use the elements of the interface that increased emphasis on coordination. Detailed patterns, on the other hand, may have had descriptions difficult enough to process that subjects had to use other elements of the interface, such as those elements that increased emphasis on coordination.

5.2 Future Work

For future work, we see two main directions that are not necessarily orthogonal: extension of the interface and further experimentation.

The modules of the interface presented in this paper do not represent a fully fleshed-out system, and the system is currently limited to the specific domain of financial analysis and the specific application of stock market pattern exploration. A more matured system may be more capable of affecting elements related to coordination, and moving the system to different types of data can help explore the generalizability of both the modules of the system and the effects of future experiments on coordination in multichannel information presentation environments.

For further experimentation, several questions raised during analysis of the results can be addressed. While some significant effect was found on date recall error, it was measured only for the start and end critical points of each pattern. Further assessment of recall for intermediary critical points besides the start and end points is necessary to explore the question of recall for critical point dates further. Additionally, the issue of what exact elements of the interface subjects use to help learn information remains unresolved. Tracking attentional foci through the experiment through eye-tracking software or screen mouse capture would provide a first step in this direction, and may shed more detail on what parts of the interface subjects attended to for which patterns. Finally, the small effect size for pattern recall accuracy between increased-emphasis and control groups ($d = 0.284$) indicates that the population size may not have been sufficient to measure pattern recall accuracy between the groups. Future iterations of the experiment would benefit from a larger sample size.

6 Conclusion

In this work, we investigated the effects of emphasizing coordination in a multi-channel data presentation on memory of information. In the system presented in this paper, data is coordinated across visual elements by identifying and color coordinating critical points, important dates that appear in the data. It was hypothesized that increasing the degree of emphasis on coordination between channels of information in the interface would help individuals remember information from those channels more accurately. To investigate the hypothesis, 36 college students participated in a human subject evaluation. Subjects were divided into increased-emphasis and control groups. For subjects in the increased-emphasis group, critical points are color-coordinated, while no color coordination occurs for subjects in the control group. Using our interface, subjects in the increased-emphasis group showed greater recall accuracy over subjects in the control group for dates that were presented as part of descriptions with greater detail. For subjects in both groups, recall accuracy was significantly decreased for patterns that were presented with more detailed descriptions compared to patterns presented with less detailed descriptions. Increasing the degree of emphasis on coordination only helped individuals more accurately remember specific dates when those dates were part of a pattern that was already more difficult to recall.

Acknowledgements. This work is partially sponsored by the Cognitive and Immersive Systems Lab, a research collaboration between IBM and Rensselaer Polytechnic Institute. We would like to thank our lab mates, IBM research collaborators, undergraduate researchers, faculty, staff, and Matthew Peveler in particular for their support and assistance.

References

1. Sarter, N.B.: Multimodal information presentation: Design guidance and research challenges. Int. J. Ind. Ergon. **36**(5), 439–445 (2006)
2. Rousseau, C., Bellik, Y., Vernier, F., Bazalgette, D.: A framework for the intelligent multimodal presentation of information. Signal Process. **86**(12), 3696–3713 (2006)
3. Moreno, R., Mayer, R.: Interactive multimodal learning environments. Educ. Psychol. Rev. **19**(3), 309–326 (2007)
4. Bloomfield, R., Hodge, F., Hopkins, P., Rennekamp, K.: Does coordinated presentation help credit analysts identify firm characteristics? Contemp. Account. Res. **32**(2), 507–527 (2015)
5. Dubois, M., Vial, I.: Multimedia design: the effects of relating multimodal information. J. Comput. Assist. Learn. **16**(2), 157–165 (2000)
6. Ari, F., Flores, R., Inan, F.A., Cheon, J., Crooks, S.M., Paniukov, D., Kurucay, M.: The effects of verbally redundant information on student learning: an instance of reverse redundancy. Comput. Educ. **76**, 199–204 (2014)
7. Carney, R.N., Levin, J.R.: Pictorial illustrations still improve students' learning from text. Educ. Psychol. Rev. **14**(1), 5–26 (2002)
8. Eitel, A., Scheiter, K.: Picture or text first? explaining sequence effects when learning with pictures and text. Educ. Psychol. Rev. **27**(1), 153–180 (2015)
9. Baddeley, A.: Working memory: An overview. In: Working Memory and Education, pp. 1–31. Elsevier (2006)
10. Neumann, B., Nünning, A.: An Introduction to the Study of Narrative Fiction. Klett, Stuttgart (2008)
11. Bruner, J.: Self-Making and World-Making. Narrative and Identity: Studies in Autobiography, Self, and Culture, pp. 25–37 (2001)
12. Mateas, M., Sengers, P.: Narrative Intelligence (1999)
13. Si, M.: Tell a story about anything. In: Schoenau-Fog, H., Bruni, L.E., Louchart, S., Baceviciute, S. (eds.) ICIDS 2015. LNCS, vol. 9445, pp. 361–365. Springer, Cham (2015). https://doi.org/10.1007/978-3-319-27036-4_37
14. Battad, Z., Si, M.: Using multiple storylines for presenting large information networks. In: Traum, D., Swartout, W., Khooshabeh, P., Kopp, S., Scherer, S., Leuski, A. (eds.) IVA 2016. LNCS (LNAI), vol. 10011, pp. 141–153. Springer, Cham (2016). https://doi.org/10.1007/978-3-319-47665-0_13
15. Battad, Z., Si, M.: Apply storytelling techniques for describing time-series data. In: Rouse, R., Koenitz, H., Haahr, M. (eds.) ICIDS 2018. LNCS, vol. 11318, pp. 483–488. Springer, Cham (2018). https://doi.org/10.1007/978-3-030-04028-4_56
16. Rubin, D.C., et al.: Memory in Oral Traditions: The Cognitive Psychology of Epic, Ballads, and Counting-out Rhymes. Oxford University Press, New York (1995)
17. Bower, G.H., Black, J.B., Turner, T.J.: Scripts in memory for text. Cogn. Psychol. **11**(2), 177–220 (1979)
18. Volna, E., Kotyrba, M., Jarusek, R.: Multi-classifier based on Elliott wave's recognition. Comput. Math. Appl. **66**(2), 213–225 (2013)

19. Parracho, P., Neves, R., Horta, N.: Trading in financial markets using pattern recognition optimized by genetic algorithms. In: Proceedings of the 12th annual conference companion on Genetic and evolutionary computation, pp. 2105–2106. ACM (2010)
20. Dover, K.: Pattern Recognition in Stock Data (2017)
21. IEX: Iex. Data provided for free by IEX. View IEX's Terms of Use (2018). https://iextrading.com/api-exhibit-a/

Creating a User-Centric Data Flow Visualization: A Case Study

Karin Butler(✉), Michelle Leger, Denis Bueno, Christopher Cuellar, Michael J. Haass, Timothy Loffredo, Geoffrey Reedy, and Julian Tuminaro

Sandia National Laboratories, Albuquerque, NM 87123, USA
{kbutle,maleger}@sandia.gov

Abstract. Vulnerability analysts protecting software lack adequate tools for understanding data flow in binaries. We present a case study in which we used human factors methods to develop a taxonomy for understanding data flow and the visual representations needed to support decision making for binary vulnerability analysis. Using an iterative process, we refined and evaluated the taxonomy by generating three different data flow visualizations for small binaries, trained an analyst to use these visualizations, and tested the utility of the visualizations for answering data flow questions. Throughout the process and with minimal training, analysts were able to use the visualizations to understand data flow related to security assessment. Our results indicate that the data flow taxonomy is promising as a mechanism for improving analyst understanding of data flow in binaries and for supporting efficient decision making during analysis.

Keywords: Visualization · Data flow · Vulnerability analysis · Reverse engineering · Taxonomy development · Requirements · Binary analysis

1 Introduction

1.1 Background

Society increasingly relies on software that both interacts with security-critical data and communicates with external networks (e.g., in the military, in medicine, in education, and at home). Further, software complexity, size, variety, and modification rate continue to increase. More efficient and effective processes that will assure that software does not have vulnerabilities are needed [1].

Ideally, automated tools would assess and protect binary software statically, without executing the program. Static binary analysis avoids (1) needing access to all of the supporting systems required to run the binary, (2) missing vulnerabilities introduced during the translation from source code to binary [2], and (3) introducing threats from actually running the code. Unfortunately, automatic static binary analyses do not scale to real-world software [3].

S. Yamamoto and H. Mori (Eds.): HCII 2019, LNCS 11569, pp. 174–193, 2019.
https://doi.org/10.1007/978-3-030-22660-2_12

Currently, experts assess and protect systems by performing binary vulnerability analysis manually with assistance from automated tools [4]. These experts use extensive domain knowledge of binary code, operating systems, hardware platforms, programming languages, and vulnerabilities; they engage in reverse engineering to understand binary programs [5], combining their extensive knowledge, and that of their colleagues, with automated tool results and line-by-line analysis. Binary vulnerability analysis is cognitively demanding, requires persistent attentional resources, and lacks prescribed approaches or tools. Binary code analyst support tools must be effectively integrated into their workflows to support their decision-making processes [6].

Current analyst tools have been developed and optimized to support understanding program *control flow*, the order in which individual statements, instructions, or function calls are executed or evaluated in a program. However, as the capability to detect control flow vulnerabilities has improved, attackers have started to take advantage of how data passing through program functions influences other program data and program decisions [7]. Programmers write source code, using comments and variable and function names to explain the purpose of parts of the code and to help model the control flow and data flow. When translating from source to binary code, compilers remove these comments, they may remove all names, and they change the code to make it faster or smaller or safer—and usually less understandable.

Unfortunately, data flow is difficult to understand, particularly when working from a binary. Analysts find that the current set of tools for understanding data flow is inadequate.

To begin to fill this gap in the analyst toolset, we used human factors methods to derive requirements for an analyst-centric interprocedural data flow visualization to assist binary reverse engineers in identifying and mitigating vulnerabilities in code. Working with experienced binary analysts, we used a rolling discovery process to derive our requirements through semi-structured interviews, applied cognitive task analysis knowledge audits, cognitive walkthroughs, and a two-stage modified sorting task. Our contributions include:

- a description of a modified sorting task, a human factors method to achieve consensus about mental models used across diverse tasks (Sect. 2.2),
- a taxonomy of essential features to support vulnerability analyst understanding of data flow in static analysis of binary code (Sect. 3),
- and an informal evaluation of the static requirements of our taxonomy, through proof of concept and analytic evaluation (Sect. 4).

1.2 Related Work

Current Inadequate Data Flow Visualizations. Traditional static data flow analyses use unwieldy mathematical representations for computation [8]. Most visualizations of these analyses overlay data flow or other information onto a control abstraction, the control flow graph (CFG) [9–11], the call graph [12,13], a file view [14] or a condensed text-based view of the code [15,16]. The former two sets of visualizations do not provide fine-grained interprocedural views; the latter set does not support interactive updates from the analyst (e.g., correcting the disassembly). Several past visualizations helped analysts filter, organize, and abstract overwhelming control flow graphs [17,18], delocalized data flow relationships [19,20], historical animated views [21] and hierarchical interactive views [22], and even hypothesis-driven understanding [23,24], but many of those visualization mechanisms do not appear to be implemented in the common reverse engineering platforms of today [9,25,26].

Visualizations of program dependence graphs (PDG) [27], annotated system dependence graphs (interprocedural PDGs) [28] and static value flow graphs [29] provide a reasonably intuitive view of many important data flow relationships. However, these are statically computed graphs that are not designed to be updated, they are cognitively overwhelming, and they tend to ignore values. One visualization of a dynamic data flow graph shows location, execution time, and certain values [7], making some relationships easier to understand than in other representations. However, these dynamic representations cover *one* potential set of relationships associated with a single execution, and thus they do not generalize well to static analyses. Other recent work provides insight into values [30], but these visualizations support source code understanding around variables rather than locations. Such work complements our proposed requirements by exposing more information about value sets.

Decompilers such as HexRays [9] and Dream [31] provide the most intuitive advanced data flow representations today, encoding data flow information in automatically selected variable names. The Dream++ extension [32] even selects names to reduce cognitive load on analysts parsing the decompiled code. However, these text-based visualizations still use a control flow-based layout, encoding control flow depth using whitespace indentation just as in code development. They also display *all* of the code rather than providing code folding [33], and analysts inject knowledge at a different layer of representation than that displayed (i.e., on the disassembly).

User-Centered Design. Our work is heavily influenced by two individuals who have thought deeply about supporting user decision making and understanding: Storey [5] and Victor [34]. Storey provides a taxonomy of 14 cognitive design elements to support mental model construction during reverse engineering of source code for code maintenance, focusing on program understanding, and she points out the extensive background knowledge required by reverse engineers. Victor argues for immediate feedback, particularly from tools supporting individuals who are engaging in a creative process (such as source code development, or, in our case, reverse engineering) [34]; easy movement between multiple levels of abstraction [35]; and natural interactive control mechanisms [36]. However, our work is focused in the more limited domain of answering data flow questions about a binary.

Groups considering the human as a part of the binary or vulnerability analysis system are growing in number. For example, the angr group is exploring ways to offload analysis tasks to non-experts [4]. The DARPA CHESS program is building research to support humans and computers working together to reason about the security of software artifacts [37]. Research groups such as [38] are exploring ways to allow users who are not experts in analysis algorithms to better control the analysis. Much (though not all) of this work is focused on building analytic systems to support more targeted allocation of work; in contrast, we focus on the externalization of human analysts' mental models.

2 Approach

To begin to understand the different ways that vulnerability analyses are performed, and to derive some initial requirements for a data flow visualization, we used standard cognitive task analysis methods, including semi-structured interviews, applied cognitive task analysis, and cognitive walkthroughs. We describe these activities in more detail in Sect. 2.1.

These activities showed that vulnerability analysts need to understand a range of characteristics of data flow: to identify (1) where specific data influences the code, (2) how data is parsed and manipulated through the code, (3) how the code controls and checks data to prevent problematic effects, and (4) unintended or obfuscated data flow paths. We considered conducting additional cognitive walkthroughs to identify essential data flow characteristics across the broad range of data flow understanding tasks, but we decided not to for three reasons. First, our requirements were to enable a new type of visualization, not an analysis environment; walkthroughs of other data flow tasks required more understanding of and interaction with the analysis environment and would have yielded little specific data flow information. Second, we wanted to capture information critical to understanding data flow across a wider array of program types. Third, we wanted to utilize an analysis technique that would rely less on recall and explicit reporting of thought processes and, perhaps, reveal automatic processing associated with data flow analysis and understanding.

To develop visualization requirements that would support a range of data flow analysis tasks, we next focused on gathering information about analyst mental models from artifacts of their own projects spanning such tasks.

An activity that can reveal the mental models of users is a sorting task, a task that is more commonly used to inform the grouping and naming of categories in an interface [39]. In a typical sorting task, the elements (e.g., words or functions) to be sorted are known before the task is conducted. Each participant sorts the same elements into groups; consensus grouping, if revealed, reflects similarities in how the participants think about the given elements. We hypothesized that binary analysts might reveal general purpose data flow elements through a sorting task [39] over their own meaningful data variable and value names.

In our case, however, we did not have a consistent set of elements for analysts to sort. Instead, we had artifacts that analysts had created to record analysis-relevant information from various completed projects. These artifacts were created using specialized reverse engineering tools, which allow analysts to add comments, to rename code elements like functions and variables, and to propagate assessment-relevant names through binary code. When an analyst encounters a previously-renamed element in another context, an assigned name can provide important information that has already been discovered about that element. Assigned names might reveal the general purpose data flow elements analysts needed to see in a visualization. However, these names vary across projects and across analysts according to analysis goals and personal preference, and they include information about other program features as well (e.g., memory utilization or control flow). Thus, we needed to overcome two main challenges: analysts name both data flow elements and categories of elements according to analysis goals and personal preference, making it difficult for someone unfamiliar with all the projects to find commonalities; and analysis projects span weeks, making it infeasible for analysts to independently analyze the same binaries.

To address these challenges, we created a two-stage modified sorting task. We had analysts sort the names they gave to data flow-related functions and variables taken from diverse, previously analyzed binaries, and we had experts perform a second stage of evaluation to find the commonalities and essential data flow information shared across these analysis projects. We describe the two-stage modified sorting task in more detail in Sect. 2.2.

In Sect. 3, we present the derived requirements and an example visualization, and in Sect. 4, we describe our informal evaluation. Specifically, we evaluated our visualization through a proof of principle by using the derived static requirements to generate data flow visualizations for small binaries. We then tested the utility of one of these visualizations with an analytical test to gain confidence in the produced requirements.

This research was reviewed and approved by the Sandia National Laboratories Human Studies Board.

2.1 Requirements Development from Interviews and Walkthroughs

To begin to identify tasks, sub-tasks, important cognitive processes, and data flow elements, we conducted two rounds of semi-structured interviews with experienced binary code analysts in individual sessions.

The first round of semi-structured interviews were general cognitive task analysis interviews with three experienced analysts to identify the process steps, tools, and some of the cognitive challenges associated with binary reverse engineering, in general. Subsequent interviews and cognitive walkthroughs focused on the attack surface characterization task [40]. This data flow analysis task requires identifying where an attacker might control the data in a program and whether that data may influence security-relevant parts of code. The attack surface characterization task was chosen for the cognitive walkthroughs because it is (1) representative of many of the considerations when evaluating data flow and (2) amenable to a two-hour cognitive walkthrough.

In the second round of semi-structured interviews, three experienced analysts answered questions from an applied cognitive task analysis knowledge audit [41].

The knowledge audit revealed the most important goals of attack surface characterization, cues in the binary code that indicate possible vulnerability or that contribute to program understanding, judgments being made during analysis, and tools used to support the work.

Building on results from these interviews, we designed a cognitive walkthrough task to capture information, in situ, about attention allocation, decision making, and processes used by analysts during attack surface characterization. We selected the UNIX file utility version 5.10 [42,43], choosing from the AFL (American Fuzzy Lop) fuzzer bug-o-rama trophy case [44], a listing of vulnerabilities in real programs that were found by the program AFL-fuzz.[1] Three different experienced binary analysts with no experience with the chosen program were asked to characterize the attack surface of the file binary using static analysis only. They were tested individually. To focus our data collection on the cognitions and processes used in understanding data flow, we asked analysts to begin analysis at the file_buffer function in libmagic, treating the array argument and length as attacker-controlled, i.e., as the "inputs" for the exercise. We did not require analysts to discover the vulnerability; rather, we asked analysts to produce, as if for future analysis, (1) a ranked list of (internal) functions or program points where the inputs are processed and may affect the security of the system, including specific concerns at each point, and (2) any comments, notes, or diagrams that might support a formal report for a full vulnerability analysis. We asked analysts to focus on depth over breadth (i.e., following data flow). During the two-hour test session, analysts were observed working in their chosen analysis environment while they thought aloud and answered questions posed by the human factors expert. See Appendix A for additional protocol details for the cognitive walkthrough.

We compiled the results of the interviews and walkthrough into a preliminary list of static data flow elements and interaction requirements for our data flow visualization.

2.2 Requirements Development from Modified Sorting Task

Next, we needed to develop the list of requirements, or a list of essential data flow elements and relationships, that generalized across diverse binary programs and analysis goals. To leverage the previous work of the expert binary analysts, we modified a sorting task [39] to take analyst-specific inputs and reveal mental models shared across analysts and projects. To determine the essential data flow elements across analysts and projects, we added a second stage to the sorting task. In this second stage, experts identified the commonalities and unique data flow elements that are essential for vulnerability analysis, informing our requirements for our data flow visualization.

[1] Selecting a vulnerability found by AFL gives us the opportunity to control further testing by, e.g., providing an initial problematic input to guide the analyst. Further, programs listed in the AFL bug-o-rama trophy case are real programs rather than small, designed programs, e.g., the Cyber Grand Challenge challenge binaries.

The first stage of our modified sorting task consisted of analysts sorting the products of one of their own past projects into categories important for understanding data flow. To help the analysts in this sorting task, we created a program that pulled analyst-assigned variable names from a code base and allowed the analysts to view the contextual information from the decompiled code for each name. The program displayed the entire list of names and allowed the names to be sorted into analyst-defined categories one-by-one or in groups.

We asked seven analysts to select a completed project with data flow considerations for the sorting task. See Appendix B for instructions given to participants. Projects included a variety of applications and operating system drivers. The selected programs provided from 200 to over 500 names that had been assigned by the analyst. We asked analysts to spend up to 40 min going through the names and binning them into 7 to 10 different groups. This range of groups was recommended by the sorting task literature [39]. The groups were defined by the analyst to help teach someone else about how data values flow in the code. As expected given the time constraint, analysts were only able to categorize between 72 and 110 names into 6 to 11 categories. To ensure that the important categories of data elements had been captured, at the end of the sorting period we asked analysts to review the entire list of names for missed categories; no analyst felt that categories were missing. Analysts then assigned category names to each of their groups and explained why that group was important for understanding data flow. Our collected data consisted of these category names and their descriptions. The analyst-created sorting task category names varied across analysts; program type and analysis goal had a significant impact on the created categories.[2]

To determine which category names described similar data flow elements and which names described unique aspects of data flow, we added a second stage: an additional level of categorization by a separate group of analysts. A panel of six experienced binary analysts (one of whom had participated in the original categorization task) and one experienced source code developer reviewed the sorting task categories and descriptions; each member of the panel categorized the analyst-created categories, and then, working together, the panel identified similarities and differences across the analyst-created categories that were important for understanding data flow in binaries. We added these important similarities and differences to our preliminary list of data flow elements, creating a list of required data flow elements to be represented in our static data flow visualization as described below.

3 Results: Data Flow Visualization Requirements

We used the results from our modified sorting task, augmented with results from the semi-structured interviews and cognitive walkthroughs, to derive a data flow taxonomy. This taxonomy, or set of static visualization requirements, describes

[2] Because category names and descriptions were derived from proprietary assessments, we will not share these intermediate results.

types of data elements to be represented, types of relationships to be represented, and types of information to be conveyed via a data flow visualization to support binary analysts.

To evaluate the utility of our requirements, we assigned visual design specifications to the elements in our requirements (taxonomy). We then produced a visualization of a binary and evaluated the utility of that visualization.

Because binary analysts are very comfortable working with directed graph representations, and because the data flow elements were consistent with this type of representation, we iterated on finding visualization design elements in an elaborated directed graph representation that could convey the required information. Using our data flow taxonomy, we assigned data elements like data values and memory locations to types of nodes; we assigned information about types of influence or relationship to edges. We assigned conveyance of other types of information to grouping, layout, or annotation, or left them to be determined. Our final data flow taxonomy, including the elements and their visual representations are provided in Tables 1 and 2.

Using an iterative process of product creation and evaluation, we further developed the data flow requirements list while creating a data flow visualization for the Cyber Grand Challenge [45] binary CROMU_00034 (Diary_Parser)[3], choosing specific instantiations of visual design elements. Experienced binary reverse engineers frequently reviewed design choices and accessibility of data flow information.

4 Evaluation

Vicente recommended three ways to evaluate requirements developed through the application of human factors methods [48]: (1) a proof of principle through a demonstration that the requirements generated through the cognitive work activities can be used to create a design; (2) an analytical principle that demonstrates that the design reveals important understanding about the domain of interest, and (3) an empirical principle that uses experimental testing of the new design against an existing design or against some benchmark of task performance to demonstrate utility. We conducted proof of principle and analytical principle testing, but we decided that experimental testing was premature because the visualization was not deployed within the analysis environment and only represented a subset of the information needed for a full vulnerability assessment.

The first test of the list of data flow elements was a proof of principle: could a visualization be created from the data flow primitives and their visual descriptions for a binary program, and would that visualization represent and convey the important information about the data flow vulnerabilities in the code? For this test, a novice reverse engineer just out of an undergraduate computer

[3] CGC Challenge binaries for DECREE are provided by DARPA [46]; versions ported to standard operating systems have been released by TrailOfBits [47]. We use the DARPA challenge name for binaries, but we provide the TrailOfBits name in parentheses.

Table 1. Static requirements for information to be conveyed through nodes in data flow visualization to support vulnerability analysis of binaries. Sub-types marked with an asterisk (*) are expected to be updated by analysts throughout an analysis. NYR designates elements that are not yet represented. STDIN = standard input; STDOUT = standard output.

Type	Sub-type	Visual instantiation
Value		Oval or plus sign shape
	Constant	No incoming value flow edges
	Computed	Plus sign shape
	Constraint*	Displays constraint description
	Uncertain*	Empty or displays '?'
Location		Rectangular shape
	Local	Dotted outline, when included
	Heap	Solid outline
	Global	Filled with gray
	Shared memory*	NYR
Aggregate		General aggregate NYR
	Array	Rectangle with double lines on sides
	Structure	Vertically stacked field locations
	and constraints	Boolean AND symbol (shield)
	or constraints	Boolean OR symbol (pointy shield)
Code		Text-only nodes (no edge or fill)
Communication		Most types NYR
	Input*	STDIN: arrow shape, outgoing value flow edge
	Output*	STDOUT: arrow shape, incoming value flow edges
Annotation		
	Initial configuration	Value nodes filled with yellow
	Data type*	NYR
	Size	NYR

science program was asked to create a data flow visualization for two Cyber Grand Challenge binaries CROMU_00065 (WhackJack) and the KPRCA_00052 (pizza_ordering_system) using our list of data flow elements and visualization specifications. This test revealed several ways that the data flow primitives were not specified in enough detail to create the visualization, resulting in minor revisions to the list of data flow primitives. For example, we added STDIN and STDOUT communication nodes as a distinct type of location node, we called out that value computations and certain logical locations map to a single set of evidence (e.g., different uses of STDOUT should be represented by different

Table 2. Static requirements for information to be conveyed through edges in data flow visualization to support vulnerability analysis of binaries. Analysts are expected to be able to add and remove edges. NYR designates elements that are not yet represented.

Type	Sub-type	Visual instantiation
Value flow		Solid black line from source to destination node
Function boundary		
	Parameter	Large black dot on edge
	Return value	Large black dot on edge
Points-to		Black dashed (one long, two short) line
Comparison		Black dotted line with long spaces
Control influence		
	Positive	Black dotted line
	Negative	Gray dotted line
Length		NYR, except colocation of length (source) in top-center of destination aggregate
Sequencing		Should not be represented
Code influence		
	Allocatable	Points-to edge from code node to location
	Freeable	Points-to edge from code node to location
	Readable	Value flow edge from code node to location
	Writeable	Value flow edge from code node to location
Synchronization		
	Lifetime	NYR
	Sometime	NYR
Colocation		
	Spatial	NYR
	Subset	NYR
	Overlap	NYR
Lifetime		NYR

nodes rather than by a single node throughout the binary), we annotated edges with function boundaries, we clarified that control flow enabled edges should come from the value nodes that trigger the related control flow in the binary, and we specifically relegated sequencing information to second-class information that is represented only when convenient.

The second proof of principle task identified a third Cyber Grand Challenge binary, EAGLE_0005 (CGC_Hangman_Game). This visualization was manually created for the entire binary and did not require modifications to our set of elements (see Fig. 1); the visualization represents 408 lines of relevant decompiled binary code. With existing data flow graphs, analysts would not be able to observe the entire binary at once.

To highlight how this visualization would be useful to binary analysts performing a vulnerability assessment, Fig. 2 shows the portion of the EAGLE_0005 graph that includes the two vulnerabilities present in that code. In the upper left, up to 80 bytes are read from standard input; we denote this by showing the length of STDIN as 80 bytes. These bytes are read into name, a local array aggregate (i.e., a stack buffer) that has a length of only 32 bytes. This is an easily identifiable stack buffer overflow. The location of the name buffer is stored in the pointer &name as indicated by the black dashed line with one long line and two short dashes. The uninterrupted solid black line from this pointer to STDOUT together with the processing details indicate that the data is being passed without any checks, resulting in an easily identifiable format string vulnerability. These two vulnerabilities are relatively straight-forward to identify via a line-by-line analysis as well because they are wholly contained within a single function. However, the utility of the visualization is demonstrated in understanding how an attacker might exercise these vulnerabilities; for this task, an analyst requires interprocedural data flow understanding of nearly all of the 408 lines of code and data flow depicted in Fig. 1. Current data flow visualizations do not enable effective visualization of an entire binary in this way. This example demonstrates how such a visualization might be useful theoretically; we next wanted to gain some confidence that the visualization did, in fact, allow an analyst to answer data flow questions.

The second type of testing followed the analytical principle. For these tests, a list of questions about data flow and important considerations in reverse engineering and vulnerability assessment were derived from the initial project discussions and cognitive task analysis products (see [49] for the complete list of questions). An experienced reverse engineer who was not involved in the previous activities was given a 15-min primer on understanding the graph elements using CROMU_00034, and then he was asked to answer the questions using only the data flow visualization for the EAGLE_0005 binary. The analyst was able to answer 11 of the 14 data flow questions correctly within 40 min. The questions that could not be completely answered in the allotted time involved interpreting pointers and their edges and suggest a possible area for improvement of the visualization.[4] Overall, this result gives us some confidence that visualizations produced via our static requirements are useful for answering data flow questions. We believe that such visualizations have the potential to make larger analysis tasks more manageable without dramatically slowing smaller analysis tasks, though we have not tested this hypothesis yet.

[4] Our experienced analyst looking at the corresponding binary code had similar accuracy in the same amount of time. However, the analyst looking at the visualization tended to miss questions due to mis-interpretation of the visual elements present, while the analyst looking at the binary code tended to miss questions due to data influences or uses from other portions of the code.

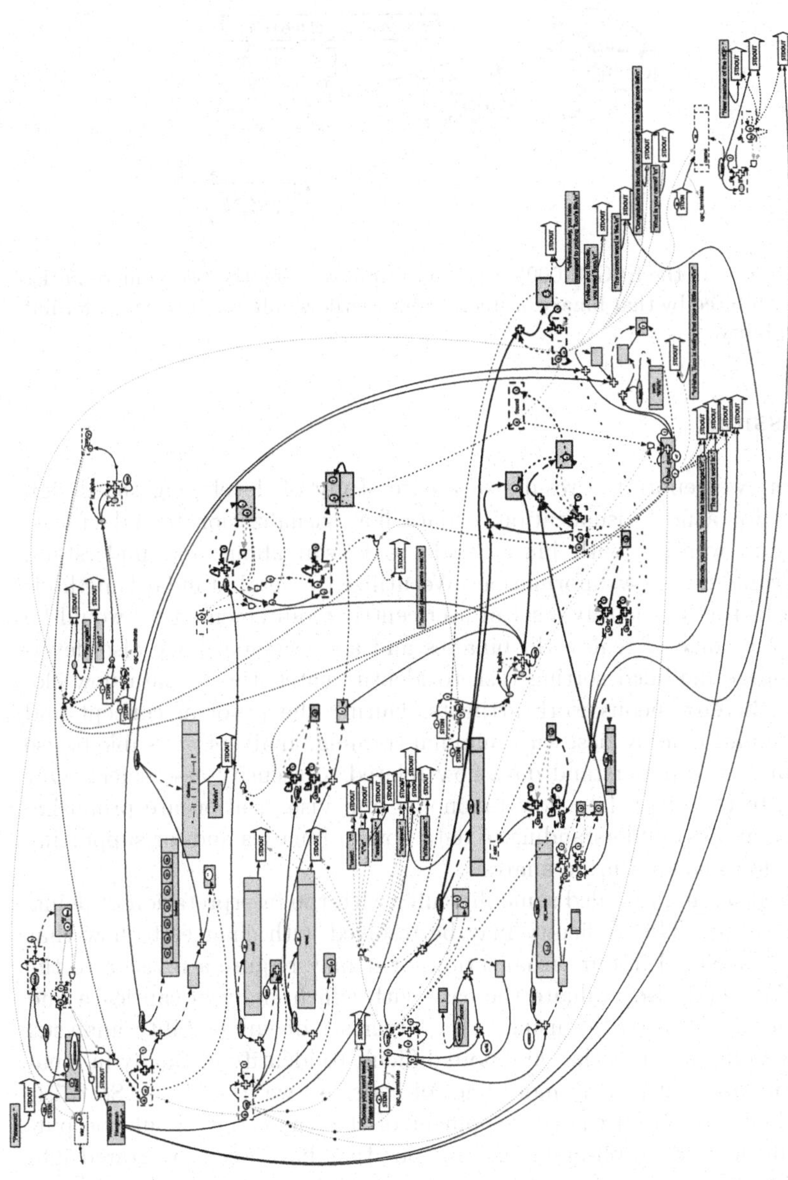

Fig. 1. A data flow graph manually constructed using our data flow requirements and final assignment to visual design elements. Generated from the TrailOfBits port of CGC challenge binary EAGLE_0005, this graph encapsulates all instructions from the binary except those from libraries.

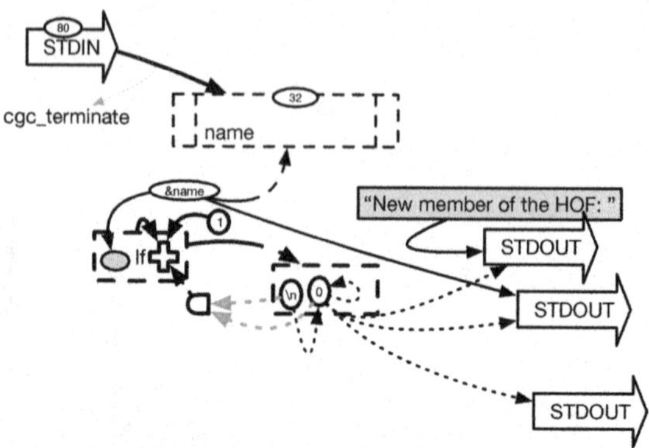

Fig. 2. The portion of the EAGLE_0005 data flow graph showing the two vulnerabilities known to be exhibited by that binary: a stack buffer overflow vulnerability, and a format string vulnerability.

5 Discussion

In this paper, we report the results of a case study of developing the design requirements for a new visualization, a data flow visualization to aid vulnerability analysts working with binary code to reason about and understand security-relevant data-flow information. We utilized several standard methods from human factors to identify a set of user-centric requirements that would be applicable to a range of real-world binaries and analysis goals. We also developed a two-stage modified sorting task to identify categories of data flow elements across heterogeneous work artifacts. During the proof of concept and analytical evaluation activities, with minimal training, analysts were able to use the visualizations to understand data flow related to security assessment. Our results indicate that this data flow taxonomy and visualization are promising for improving analyst understanding of data flow in binaries and for supporting efficient decision making during analysis.

Our limited testing revealed some difficulty with the interpretation of pointers and their edges. This difficulty may be resolved with changes to how that information is depicted in our visualization, or it may require a revision to the taxonomy. We could also evaluate the ease with which analysts can learn and use the static visualization by using (1) a larger set of vulnerability analysts, (2) data flow vulnerabilities that are more difficult to identify manually in binaries, or (3) binaries with many more lines of code. As we describe in Sect. 5.1, though, we believe that further development of this taxonomy should be pursued using automated graph-building functions that have been integrated into analyst workflows.

In this case study we utilized a new procedure to distill heterogeneous analyst categorizations into consensus about the fundamental elements of the data flow visualization across varied code and analysis goals. In our two-stage modified sorting task, we relied on domain experts to identify the similarities and differences between the categories that resulted from the first stage. The collaborative second-stage grouping revealed important sets of elements and similarities in how participants think about data flow elements. Artifact analysis, such as our modified sorting task, can be powerful for understanding the mental models of experts in a domain; artifacts can be systematically analyzed without incurring the cost of devising controlled but realistic projects with different goals. Additional artifacts that might be explored similarly include analysts' change history for names and analysts' comments in the binary code, which summarize their discoveries.

It is difficult to assess the replicability of the results generated from this work. Several factors may have influenced whether we found all the data flow elements that are important to vulnerability analysis. Our preliminary interviews and walkthroughs tested only a few people under each protocol and focused on a single type of data flow task, i.e., attack surface characterization. Further, the results of the modified sorting task may have been biased by the functionality of the programs selected or the range of potential vulnerabilities, and the judgments of our panel of experts may have been skewed by their work. Despite these concerns, we incorporated several strategies to increase the likelihood that our results are replicable. We used a range of approaches: interviews, walkthroughs, and the modified sorting task. We captured the essential data flow elements from a range of projects with different analysis goals. We used an iterative development and design process during which reverse engineers frequently reviewed the effectiveness of the data flow elements and the design choices made in the visualization. We believe that others reproducing this research are likely to develop a similar set of requirements for understanding data flow in binary analysis.

5.1 Future Work

In this case study, generating the data flow visualizations was a time-consuming, manual process. Further development of a useful visualization requires determining how graph building can be integrated into analyst workflows. Binary reverse engineers in an operational environment already maintain high cognitive loads without the added burden of creating a visualization. Manually creating the visualizations is untenable, and, although many of the data flow elements can be derived automatically, such automation is not incorporated into current workflows. Once automation can be used to derive data flow visualization components, new insights will need to be easily injectable into the visualization during line-by-line analysis. For example, the data flow visualization should support the recording of unknowns and partial insights as they become known during the analysis. Additionally, during our preliminary data gathering, analysts indicated that they required interactive features that support using the data flow graph to navigate through the code base as well as features that allow sections of the graph to be collapsed when detailed information is not necessary. We believe that these interactive requirements are most important for successful integration of this visualization into analyst workflows, but such development remains future work.

Previous human factors explorations of program understanding have identified cognitive design elements that are needed to support the construction of mental models. Storey and colleagues identified two broad classes of design elements important for helping software analysts maintaining code to build their mental model: those that support comprehension, and those that reduce the cognitive overhead of the analyst [5]. Examples of elements that support comprehension include tools and features that support the construction of multiple mental models, and tools and features that provide abstraction mechanisms. Examples of design features that reduce the cognitive overhead of the analysts include support for navigation through the code, decision making, and documentation of findings. Although these insights came from studying software maintainers, they are relevant for binary reverse engineers as well. Our work represents an attempt to create a more user-centric abstraction of data flow information to support comprehension, but further development will need to address the cognitive overhead of creating this abstraction. The insights from Storey and colleagues will continue to be important as new tools are developed, automatic analyses are advanced, and reverse engineering workflows evolve.

Another opportunity for reducing the cognitive overhead of the analyst is to provide tools that can help them to record the details of their analysis, perhaps into something like a knowledge transfer diagram [50]. These visualizations can help to externalize an analyst's understanding of both the program and the assessment. A record of this understanding can help maintain the current goal of the analysis, establishing the mental context that is required for analysis when returning to a project, or communicating the current state of understanding to other analysts or customers. Research approaches that support the design of new decision-making support tools, such as work domain analysis, could support development of these externalizations.

6 Conclusion

In this case study, we describe using human factors methods to derive requirements for interprocedural data flow visualizations that can be used to quickly understand data flow elements and their relationships and influences. To generalize requirements produced through semi-structured interviews, and through task- and program-specific knowledge audits and cognitive walkthroughs, we developed a two-stage modified sorting task that helps extract commonalities in analyst mental models of data flow across different types of programs. We used the results from the modified sorting task, augmented with results from the cognitive task analysis activities, to derive a data flow taxonomy (requirements for representation). We assigned elements of the taxonomy to visual representations in an elaborated directed graph representation, and we used these generalized requirements to manually generate and evaluate data flow visualizations for binary programs with different vulnerabilities. Analysts were able to use the data flow visualizations to answer many critical questions about data flow. Our results indicate that our data flow taxonomy is promising as a mechanism for improving analyst understanding of data flow in binaries and for supporting efficient decision making during analysis. However, future work and evaluation will require integrating the visualization into existing analyst workflows.

Acknowledgements. The authors would like to thank Danny Loffredo, Todd Jones, Doug Ghormley, Andy Wilson, Tiemoko Ballo, Bryan Kennedy, and the many binary analysts who supported this work. Their suggestions and interactions have been invaluable.

This work was supported by the Laboratory Directed Research and Development program at Sandia National Laboratories, a multi-mission laboratory managed and operated by National Technology and Engineering Solutions of Sandia, LLC, a wholly owned subsidiary of Honeywell International, Inc., for the U.S. Department of Energy's National Nuclear Security Administration under contract DE-NA0003525.

A Cognitive Walkthrough Setup

We selected the UNIX file utility version 5.10 [42,43], choosing from the AFL (American Fuzzy Lop) fuzzer bug-o-rama trophy case [44], a listing of vulnerabilities in real programs that were found by the program AFL-fuzz. We chose file version 5.10 because (1) the core processing library libmagic is vulnerable to CVE-2012-1571 [51][5]; (2) many functions in the library are involved in parsing input data from multiple sources; (3) a successful analysis requires understanding interprocedural data flow; (4) we had access to source code for both the vulnerable version 5.10 and the fixed version 5.11;[6] and (5) file is one of the smallest UNIX utility binaries listed, making it more likely that a meaningful analysis could be completed in less than two hours.

Three experienced binary analysts completed the attack surface characterization task with the file binary in their preferred binary analysis environment. The binary was compiled on a machine running Ubuntu 16.04 with llvm, creating a 32-bit binary with symbols. To focus our data collection on the cognitions and processes used in understanding data flow, we asked analysts to begin analysis at the file_buffer function in libmagic, treating the array argument and length as attacker-controlled, i.e., as the "inputs" for the exercise. We did not require analysts to discover the vulnerability; rather, we asked analysts to produce, as if for future analysis, (1) a ranked list of (internal) functions or program points where the inputs are processed and may affect the security of the system, including specific concerns at each point, and (2) any comments, notes, or diagrams that might support a formal report for a full vulnerability analysis. We asked analysts to focus on depth over breadth (i.e., following data flow) and to think aloud while performing analysis. Our human factors specialist took notes about task performance and asked for additional details to understand the thought process

[5] This known CVE in the binary could allow us to perform cognitive walkthroughs of other binary analysis tasks, e.g., determining the risk of or mitigating a known vulnerability.

[6] Having source for both versions allowed us to control the binaries analyzed, e.g., whether we provided symbols or reduced optimizations.

of the analyst, including asking for reasoning behind judgments and decisions, and asking for clarification about sources of frustration.

Walkthroughs lasted two hours including the time to set up the analysis environment. Analysts created the list of functions and concerns, but they produced few comments and no diagrams or additional notes. Although analysts often use two to four screens, we captured only the primary screen of each analyst. These artifacts were not analyzed separately.

B Modified Sorting Task Stage 1 Instructions

We would like to better understand how analysts categorize data flow elements when they are working on a VA (vulnerability analysis) or RE (reverse engineering) project. We are examining whether the symbols that you have assigned to various programming elements in a binary can reveal how you were thinking about data flow through the binary.

In order to do this, we have created a script that will scan a project file and extract the symbols that you gave to functions, data, and variables.

The script is named GroupRenamedVariables.

Using this script, I am going to ask you to sort the symbols that you assigned into categories in a couple of different ways. More details are provided below. Try to sort the symbols into 7–10 different categories. The program has extracted all of the symbols that you assigned, but we are only interested in your categorizations of data value symbols and variable symbols. To focus on these types of symbols, please sort the symbol list by type of symbol. Just ignore the function symbols.

You will be able to change and review your category assignments as you like. You can assign symbols to more than one category. You can change the name of a grouping at any time. You can split a grouping into more than one group.

Once you have completed the sorting task, we will ask you to provide descriptions of each of your categories.

Imagine that you are teaching someone else about how data values within a binary flow through a program. Organize the symbols that you have given to these variables into grouping that would help you teach that person. Try to sort the symbols into 7–10 different categories.

References

1. Somers, J.: The coming software apocalypse. The Atlantic, September 2017
2. D'Silva, V., Payer, M., Song, D.: The correctness-security gap in compiler optimization. In: 2015 IEEE Security and Privacy Workshops, pp. 73–87, May 2015
3. Song, J., Alves-Foss, J.: The DARPA cyber grand challenge: a competitor's perspective. IEEE Secur. Priv. **13**(6), 72–76 (2015)
4. Shoshitaishvili, Y., et al.: Rise of the HaCRS: augmenting autonomous cyber reasoning systems with human assistance. CoRR abs/1708.02749 (2017)

5. Storey, M.A.D., Fracchia, F.D., Müller, H.A.: Cognitive design elements to support the construction of a mental model during software exploration. J. Syst. Softw. **44**(3), 171–185 (1999)
6. Bainbridge, L.: Ironies of automation. Automatica **19**, 775–779 (1983)
7. Hu, H., Chua, Z.L., Adrian, S., Saxena, P., Liang, Z.: Automatic generation of data-oriented exploits. In: 24th USENIX Security Symposium (USENIX Security 15), pp. 177–192 USENIX Association, Washington (2015)
8. Kildall, G.A.: A unified approach to global program optimization. In: Proceedings of the 1st Annual ACM SIGACT-SIGPLAN Symposium on Principles of Programming Languages. POPL 1973, pp. 194–206. ACM, New York (1973)
9. Hex-Rays, S.: IDA pro disassembler (2008). https://www.hex-rays.com/products/ida/
10. Quist, D.A., Liebrock, L.M.: Visualizing compiled executables for malware analysis. In: 2009 6th International Workshop on Visualization for Cyber Security, pp. 27–32, October 2009
11. Zynamics: Zynamics BinNavi product description page. https://www.zynamics.com/binnavi.html
12. Rech, J., Schäfer, W.: Visual support of software engineers during development and maintenance. ACM SIGSOFT Softw. Eng. Notes **32**, 1–3 (2007)
13. Hardisty, Z.: Radia github page. https://github.com/zoebear/Radia
14. Reddy, N.H., Kim, J., Palepu, V.K., Jones, J.A.: Spider sense: software-engineering, networked, system evaluation. In: 2015 IEEE 3rd Working Conference on Software Visualization (VISSOFT), pp. 205–209. IEEE (2015)
15. Ball, T., Eick, S.G.: Visualizing program slices. In: IEEE Symposium on Visual Languages, 1994. Proceedings, pp. 288–295. IEEE (1994)
16. Eick, S., Steffen, J.L., Sumner, E.E.: Seesoft-a tool for visualizing line oriented software statistics. IEEE Trans. Softw. Eng. **18**(11), 957–968 (1992)
17. Müller, H.A., Klashinsky, K.: Rigi-a system for programming-in-the-large. In: Proceedings of the 10th International Conference on Software Engineering. ICSE 1988, pp. 80–86. IEEE Computer Society Press, Los Alamitos (1988)
18. Storey, M.D., Muller, H.A.: Manipulating and documenting software structures using shrimp views. In: Proceedings of International Conference on Software Maintenance, pp. 275–284, October 1995
19. Livadas, P.E., Alden, S.D.: A toolset for program understanding. In: [1993] IEEE Second Workshop on Program Comprehension, pp. 110–118, July 1993
20. Brade, K., Guzdial, M., Steckel, M., Soloway, E.: Whorf: a visualization tool for software maintenance. In: Proceedings IEEE Workshop on Visual Languages, pp. 148–154, September 1992
21. Baker, M.J., Eick, S.G.: Visualizing software systems. In: Proceedings of the 16th International Conference on Software Engineering. ICSE 1994, pp. 59–67. IEEE Computer Society Press, Los Alamitos (1994)
22. Orso, A., Jones, J.A., Harrold, M.J., Stasko, J.: GAMMATELLA: visualization of program-execution data for deployed software. In: Proceedings 26th International Conference on Software Engineering, pp. 699–700, May 2004
23. Rajlich, V., Doran, J., Gudla, R.T.S.: Layered explanations of software: a methodology for program comprehension. In: Proceedings 1994 IEEE 3rd Workshop on Program Comprehension- WPC 1994, pp. 46–52, November 1994
24. LaToza, T.D., Myers, B.A.: Visualizing call graphs. In: 2011 IEEE Symposium on Visual Languages and Human-Centric Computing (VL/HCC), pp. 117–124. IEEE (2011)

25. Àlvarez, S.: The radare2 book (2009). https://radare.gitbooks.io/radare2book/content/
26. Vector35: Vector 35 binary ninja product description page. https://binary.ninja
27. Würthinger, T., Wimmer, C., Mössenböck, H.: Visualization of program dependence graphs. In: Hendren, L. (ed.) CC 2008. LNCS, vol. 4959, pp. 193–196. Springer, Heidelberg (2008). https://doi.org/10.1007/978-3-540-78791-4_13
28. Deng, F., DiGiuseppe, N., Jones, J.A.: Constellation visualization: augmenting program dependence with dynamic information. In: 2011 6th International Workshop on Visualizing Software for Understanding and Analysis (VISSOFT), pp. 1–8, September 2011
29. Sui, Y., Xue, J.: SVF: Interprocedural static value-flow analysis in LLVM. In: Proceedings of the 25th International Conference on Compiler Construction. CC 2016, pp. 265–266. ACM, New York (2016)
30. Hoffswell, J., Satyanarayan, A., Heer, J.: Augmenting code with in situ visualizations to aid program understanding. In: Proceedings of the 2018 CHI Conference on Human Factors in Computing Systems, p. 532. ACM (2018)
31. Yakdan, K., Eschweiler, S., Gerhards-Padilla, E., Smith, M.: No more gotos: decompilation using pattern-independent control-flow structuring and semantic-preserving transformations. In: NDSS (2015)
32. Yakdan, K., Dechand, S., Gerhards-Padilla, E., Smith, M.: Helping Johnny to analyze malware: a usability-optimized decompiler and malware analysis user study. In: 2016 IEEE Symposium on Security and Privacy (SP), pp. 158–177, May 2016
33. Hendrix, T.D., Cross II, J.H., Barowski, L.A., Mathias, K.S.: Visual support for incremental abstraction and refinement in Ada 95. Ada Lett. **XVIII**(6), 142–147 (1998)
34. Victor, B.: Learnable programming (2012). http://worrydream.com
35. Victor, B.: The ladder of abstraction (2011). http://worrydream.com
36. Victor, B.: A brief rant on the future of interaction design (2011). http://worrydream.com
37. Fraze, D.: Computers and humans exploring software security (CHESS) (2018). https://www.darpa.mil/program/computers-and-humans-exploring-software-security
38. Mangal, R., Zhang, X., Nori, A.V., Naik, M.: A user-guided approach to program analysis. In: Proceedings of the 2015 10th Joint Meeting on Foundations of Software Engineering. ESEC/FSE 2015, pp. 462–473. ACM, New York (2015)
39. Sherwin, K.: Card sorting: uncover users' mental models for better information architecture. https://www.nngroup.com/articles/card-sorting-definition/
40. Manadhata, P.K., Tan, K.M.C., Maxion, R.A., Wing, J.M.: An approach to measuring a system's attack surface. School of Computer Science Technical report CMU-CS-08-146, Carnegie Mellon University, Pittsburgh, PA, August 2007
41. Militello, L., Hutton, R.: Applied cognitive task analysis (ACTA): a practitioner's toolkit for understanding cognitive task demands. Ergonomics **41**(12), 1618–1641 (1998)
42. Darwin, I.: Original source packages for file utility (2012). ftp://ftp.astron.com/pub/file/
43. Darwin, I.: Maintained source for file utility. https://github.com/file/file
44. Zalewski, M.: American fuzzy lop: a security-oriented fuzzer (2010). http://lcamtuf.coredump.cx/afl/. Accessed 21 June 2017
45. Fraze, D.: Cyber grand challenge (CGC) (2016). https://www.darpa.mil/program/cyber-grand-challeng

46. DARPA: DARPA CGC challenges source repository (2016). https://github.com/CyberGrandChallenge/samples/tree/master/cqe-challenges
47. TrailOfBits: DARPA CGC challenges ported to standard OS (2016). https://github.com/trailofbits/cb-multios
48. Vicente, K.J.: Ecological interface design: progress and challenges. Hum. Factors **44**(01), 62–78 (2002)
49. Leger, M., et al.: Creating an interprocedural analyst-oriented data flow representation for binary analysts (CIAO). Technical report SAND2018-14238, Sandia National Laboratories, Albuquerque, NM, December 2018
50. Zhao, J., Glueck, M., Isenberg, P., Chevalier, F., Khan, A.: Supporting handoff in asynchronous collaborative sensemaking using knowledge-transfer graphs. IEEE Trans. Vis. Comput. Graph. **24**(1), 340–350 (2018)
51. NIST: Cve 2012–1571 (2012). https://nvd.nist.gov/vuln/detail/CVE-2012-1571

Usability Evaluation of a Co-created Big Data Analytics Platform for Health Policy-Making

Brian Cleland[1(✉)], Jonathan Wallace[1], Raymond Bond[1], Salla Muuraiskangas[2], Juha Pajula[3], Gorka Epelde[4,5], Mónica Arrúe[4,5], Roberto Álvarez[4,5], Michaela Black[6], Maurice D. Mulvenna[1], Deborah Rankin[6], and Paul Carlin[7]

[1] School of Computing, Ulster University, Coleraine, Northern Ireland
{b.cleland, jg.wallace, rb.bond, md.mulvenna}@ulster.ac.uk

[2] VTT Technical Research Centre of Finland Ltd, Wellness and Living, Oulu, Finland
salla.muuraiskangas@vtt.fi

[3] VTT Technical Research Centre of Finland Ltd, Smart Health, Tampere, Finland
juha.pajula@vtt.fi

[4] eHealth and Biomedical Applications, Vicomtech, Donostia/San Sebastián, Spain
{gepelde, marrue, ralvarez}@vicomtech.org

[5] IIS Biodonostia, Donostia/San Sebastián, Spain

[6] School of Computing, Engineering and Intelligent Systems, Ulster University, Coleraine, Northern Ireland
{mm.black, d.rankinl}@ulster.ac.uk

[7] South Eastern Health and Social Care Trust, Ulster Hospital, Dundonald, Northern Ireland
paul.carlin@setrust.hscni.net

Abstract. The increasingly important role of big data in organisational decision-making brings with it significant challenges in terms of designing usable software interfaces. Specifically, such interfaces must allow users to explore, analyse, and visualise complex data from heterogeneous sources and derive insights to support management decisions. This paper describes a usability evaluation of the MIDAS Project, a big data platform for health policy-making, developed by an EU-funded Horizon 2020 project involving a number of international partners and pilot sites. We describe how a combination of heuristic and formative user-centred evaluation methods were employed, and give a summary of the key findings. We discuss key insights from the evaluation, including the importance of having diverse users, the role played by users' prior expectations, and the logistical challenge of coordinating user testing across multiple sites. Finally, we explore the relative value of each of the evaluation methods, and outline how our approach to usability testing will evolve for future iterations of the MIDAS platform.

Keywords: Big data · Health · Usability · Evaluation · Policy-making · User-centred

S. Yamamoto and H. Mori (Eds.): HCII 2019, LNCS 11569, pp. 194–207, 2019.
https://doi.org/10.1007/978-3-030-22660-2_13

1 Introduction

The impact of big data has been increasingly felt across many industry sectors in recent years. Its specific impact on the health sector was examined in 2013 in a report by McKinsey [1], which outlined several key factors that were likely to drive changes in healthcare policy and delivery. The first insight was that demand was growing for greater economic value to be generated from data, including improvements to policy-making processes, which should be linked to existing stored datasets that had not been re-used (that is, used for secondary purposes). The second factor was the expanding volumes of data being collected from organisational sources such as clinical devices and processes, as well as personal sources such as social media and mobile devices. The third point was the steady growth of open data being published by governments in order to catalyse private sector innovation. Finally, it was noted that technological change was driving predictable improvements in terms of the capture, storage and processing of data from diverse sources.

It was in this context that the MIDAS Project (Meaningful Integration of Data Analytics and Services) was funded under the EU's Horizon 2020 programme in order to capitalise on big data trends and drive policy improvements in the European health sector. The project is intended to meet the needs of citizens and policy-makers through the provision of a state-of-the-art big data platform. In this paper we present a usability study of the first iteration of the MIDAS platform, focusing specifically on the dashboard layer, which is designed to facilitate the analysis and visualisation of big data for policy-making. We begin by providing a brief overview of the project and the technical architecture of the platform, including the data integration, analytics and visualisation layers. We then explain the usability evaluation methods that were used and present a summary of the main findings from the study. Finally, we discuss the most important implications of the results, review which parts of the methodology were most useful, and outline how the usability analysis of future software development iterations will be carried out in light of the findings.

2 Background

2.1 MIDAS Project Overview

The MIDAS Project consortium consists of a variety of academic, industrial and policy experts from six European countries and the United States. A key focus of the project is ensuring that the information delivered by the MIDAS platform is relevant and actionable, and to this end the consortium has adopted a user-centred design ethos. A broad selection of experts from a diverse spectrum of backgrounds were chosen in order to effectively capture user needs and provide realistic engagement in the co-design of the system [2]. This approach has been driven by a realisation that ultimate users of the system are likely to be very diverse, and will include stakeholders with very different backgrounds and levels of technical knowledge - from statisticians and data scientists to senior civil servants and politicians.

The core elements of the MIDAS platform will include technical components to enable the collection and preparation of heterogeneous data, and an agreed architecture for data storage, data integration, data virtualization, data cleansing, deployment and management. The secure management of personal data is a key deliverable, and will be addressed through the development of a 'privacy by design' approach. This approach will enable the anonymisation and aggregation of data, while simultaneously making it interoperable to the analytics layer. The platform will also incorporate a variety of tools and algorithms that will allow meaning to be extracted from data, building on existing machine learning and other analytics methods. From the user's perspective, a key part of the platform will be the user interface (UI) layer that will draw aggregated outputs from the analytics layer for display via management dashboards and easy-to-use interactive tools.

2.2 MIDAS Platform Architecture

As stated above, a key goal of the MIDAS project is to access and integrate a range of heterogeneous datasets, located in many separate systems. A common metadata model will enable these datasets to be harmonised so that common analytics and processing can occur, but a flexible underlying data architecture is required to support the storage and processing of these disparate datasets, as well as integration of that data from diverse sources. The MIDAS platform will be based on Analytics Engines XDPTM, which is a proprietary, scalable and modular data analytics platform and Analytics Engines Unified Data View (UDV), which enables a single, unified view of data being analysed. This forms the core data storage/processing portion of the platform, upon which the analytics and visualisation layers are built.

The architecture of the MIDAS Dashboard is shown in Fig. 1. It is composed of three main layers: the User Interface, a Middleware layer and a Closed Intranet layer. The User Interface is developed with standard HTML, Bootstrap, JQuery and JavaScript technologies. It has a modular design, which will enable any third party to develop their own visualization with JavaScript. OpenVA is a Java framework developed by VTT, which is used to handle the results of the analytics that are received from the analytics layer. A Flask-based REST server manages communications between the user interface and the analytics system, allowing the frontend to retrieve specific parameters or analytics results.

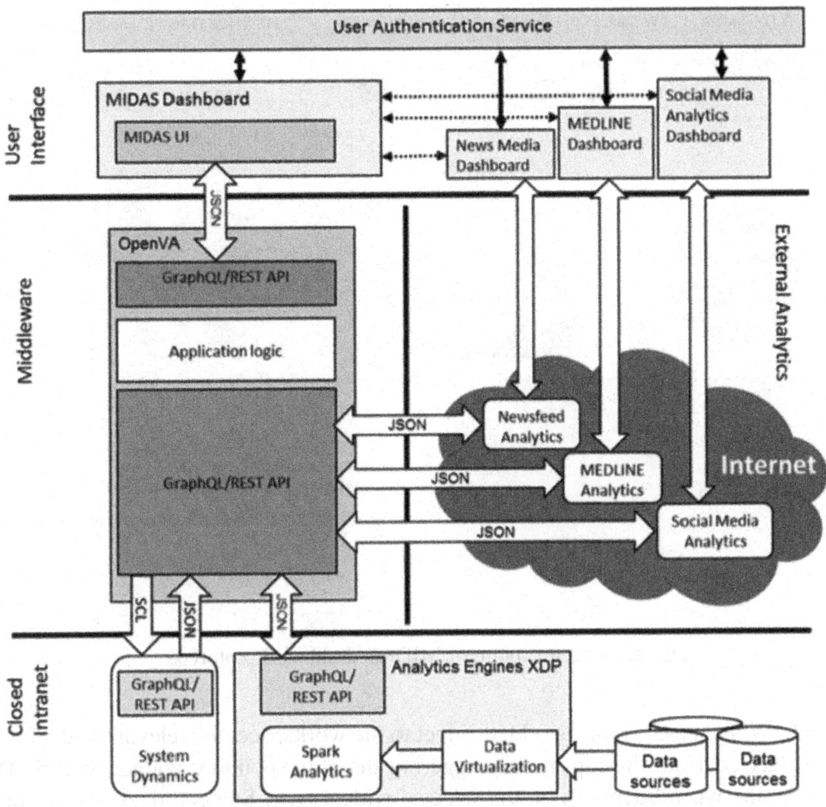

Fig. 1. MIDAS Dashboard architecture.

2.3 MIDAS Interface

In this section we describe the main components in the MIDAS Platform User Interface which were the primary focus for the evaluation.

MIDAS Dashboard. The MIDAS Dashboard has two views for the end user: the sign in page and main page. The main page is only shown to the user after they have successfully signed in. The three primary components of the main page are the menu bar at the top of the page, the name bar below the menu bar, and the workspace for the widgets. The workspace can extend outside the displayed area, and when this happens scrollbars appear on bottom and right border. This is normally triggered when there are more widgets than will fit on the current screen. An example of the MIDAS Dashboard is shown in Fig. 2.

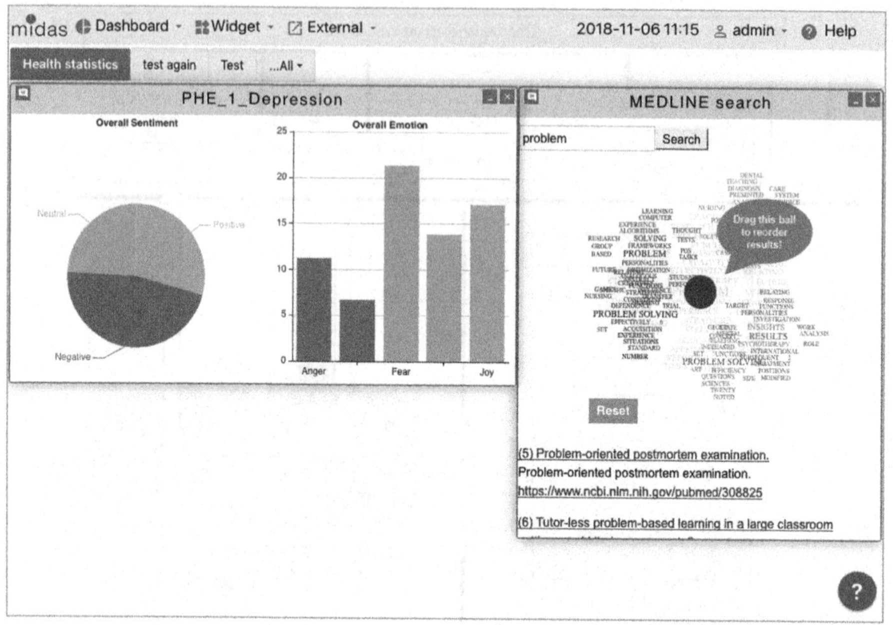

Fig. 2. Screen capture of MIDAS dashboard prototype.

Wizard. When a user wants to add a widget to the workspace, the relevant widget type can be selected from the top menu, triggering the corresponding widget wizard. The content of the wizard depends on the selected widget type. Some widget types require further input from the user. For example, the analytics widget requires the user to select the appropriate datasets and variables from a list of available datasets. Once these have been selected, the wizard asks the user to select a suitable analytics and visualization type. The available analytics and visualisation options are limited to those which are suitable for the selected data. As a final step, the wizard asks for parameters for the selected analytics and visualizations. Once these are chosen a widget will appear on dashboard, which can then be placed wherever the user sees fit.

Widgets. A widget is an object on the MIDAS Dashboard which displays the results of a specific data analytics option. Depending on the specific widget type, the data and analytics can be provided by either external or internal systems, enabling the system to support multiple information sources on the same workspace. External widgets import results from external analytics systems such as MEDLINE abstract search or the MIDAS social media platform. Internal widgets display the results of internal data and analytics. Each widget has four main functions: move, resize, update and remove. Moving and resizing can be done by clicking and dragging the edges of the widget. The update function is triggered by clicking an icon at the top right corner of the widget. This will re-open the wizard to allow the user to modify the widget parameters. Widgets can be removed by clicking the red removal button on the top right corner of the widget.

Social Media Widget. Trying to get a sense of how the public feel about a new policy can be a challenge. The MIDAS social media platform is designed to allow policy-makers to create chatbots to ask questions on their behalf. Responses are analysed using natural language processing techniques and the resulting insights can be displayed via a social media widget. This widget will enable policy-makers to get a sense of how the public feel about specific policy matters by visualising the sentiment detected in the public's responses. This will indicate, for example, whether people are responding positively or negatively to individual policy proposals.

MEDLINE Widget. The MEDLINE custom widget is an interactive visual tool that helps to surface information by re-indexing search results based on user input. More specifically, the user drags a cursor over a graph showing precomputed clusters of search terms, which triggers updates to the list of relevant documents. For example, when we enter a search term 'diabetes type 2', the system performs an elasticSearch over the MEDLINE dataset and extracts groups of keywords that best describe different subgroups of results. By moving the cursor over word-groups, the user provides the relevance criteria, thereby bringing to the top of the list the most relevant articles. The user can read its title and first lines of each abstract, and by clicking on it, open that article in the browser at its PubMed location.

External Platforms. A number of linked external analytics resources will be available to later versions of the MIDAS Dashboard. These were not included in the current evaluation study but will be included in the future UX testing iterations when the connectivity with external components has been improved.

3 Methodology

3.1 Heuristic Evaluation

This first stage of the protocol was to carry out a heuristic evaluation. This involves an expert using a series of established usability and design principles to audit the user interface. In this case, Ulster University UX lab experts used well-established usability principles such as Jakob Nielsen's 10 heuristics [3], laws from Gestalt psychology [4] and the 8 golden rules by Ben Shneiderman [5]. The test team included three specialists with extensive experience of UX testing. Each of the experts applied the whole protocol to the current system, and after these tests the severity of the problems were evaluated. Following the evaluation, usability issues were set out in a series of slides for sharing with the development team. These slides also included suggestions to improve the system. Most findings were addressed according to the suggestions prior to the formative evaluation taking place.

3.2 Formative Evaluation

For the formative evaluation a number of subjects were recruited to attempt a series of tasks using the MIDAS prototypes. It had been agreed at the outset of the MIDAS Project that the platform would tested and validated with real data and representative users of the system from across the partner countries. Twelve users in total were selected from the Basque Country, Finland, Northern Ireland and Republic of Ireland. These users were from a diverse range of technical and policy backgrounds. Although the final test protocol (see below) focused primarily on two main user personas - a data scientist and a policy-maker, it was decided that each user should perform the tasks associated with both personas in order to maximise data collection. The specific tasks for each persona are presented in Table 1.

Table 1. Tasks for each persona for usability testing protocol.

Persona	Task No.	Task Description
Data Scientist	1	Create new dashboard and give it a name
Data Scientist	2	Add an analytics widget using a specific dataset
Data Scientist	3	Add a MEDLINE search widget
Data Scientist	4	Add a social media widget
Data Scientist	5	Rearrange the dashboard layout and save your changes
Data Scientist	6	Share the dashboard with another user
Policy Maker	1	Make sense of the dashboard whilst thinking aloud
Policy Maker	2	Add 3rd widget to the dashboard, i.e. social media widget

A rigorous test protocol was jointly developed by consortium members, led by usability testers from Ulster University's UX Lab. The usability testing protocol was informed by Ulster's UX-Lab having carried out a range of usability tests on medical devices, software and data visualisations [6–16] (see Fig. 3). Each subject attempted the task whilst 'thinking-aloud'. The Think-Aloud Protocol (TAP) [17] allows the assessor to understand the user's cognitive processes hence eliciting usability issues and cognitive errors. Before and after each task, the user was asked how difficult they expected the task to be and how difficult the task was, thus measuring whether the system met the user's expectation. This is known as the Single Ease Question (SEQ) [18]. A questionnaire based on the System Usability Scale (SUS) [19] was also given to each user in order to measure perceived usability. A so-called SUS score was computed and benchmarked using a SUS distribution. In addition, after the usability test, we measured the frequency of usability errors/issues, task completion rates, and task completion times.

Testing sessions using the shared protocol took place in Northern Ireland (including Northern Ireland and Republic of Ireland users), Finland and the Basque Country. Notes were taken by moderators or a separate note taker during the sessions and video was recorded for subsequent detailed analysis. The testing data was gathered and shared on a Google Doc, and the Ulster University team carried out an analysis of the aggregated results. This analysis includes summaries of user demographics, task completion rates and times, SEQ (Single Ease Question) scores for each task, and SUS (System Usability Scale) scores for each persona. It also included a summary and analysis of the qualitative comments and insights gathered during the testing sessions.

The findings of the UX Evaluation Report were shared with developers to facilitate bugs fixes and enhance features, and to drive usability improvements as the project progressed.

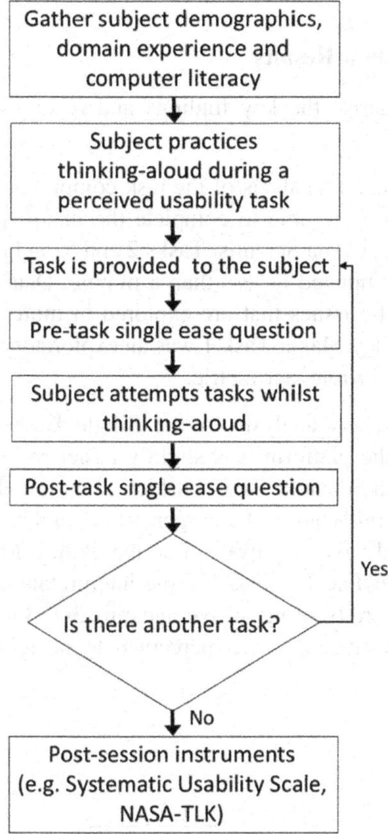

Fig. 3. Typical usability testing protocol.

4 Results

4.1 Heuristic Evaluation Results

The primary aim of heuristic evaluation in this study was to ensure that the system was ready for formative testing. Experts evaluated the MIDAS Dashboard interfaces to find the most critical problems and root causes for issues which might confuse end users. Most issues were corrected before end user representatives began the formative testing phase. Based on the heuristic evaluation the technical team fixed a number of issues, including visual fixes on boxes and text alignment, adding better search functionality, including a help menu on the menu bar, reordering menu items, and adding a "save as" option. Some problems and suggested fixes were not corrected before the formative evaluation due to time constraints, including a "forgot password" button for sign-in, better registration information on the sign-in page, an incorrect password lock on sign-in, and coloured sharing symbols for the dashboard menu.

4.2 Formative Evaluation Results

In this section we summarise the key findings and recommendations from the UX Evaluation Report.

Task Completion Times. An analysis of the task completion rates and times showed that the majority of users were able to complete the majority of tasks without assistance. With the exception of Data Scientist Tasks 2 and 5, and Policy Maker Task 1, the majority of tasks were completed in less than a minute. Data Scientist Tasks 2 and 5 raised a number of specific issues that are explored in more detail in the Qualitative Analysis (below), and Policy Maker Task 1 was an exploratory task, for which the time taken was not a particularly relevant metric.

SEQ Results Summary. An analysis of the Single Ease Question (SEQ) scores showed that in general, the platform was slightly easier to use than anticipated. One exception to this was Data Scientist Task 5, which users found more difficult that they expected. This finding is reflected in the longer task completion times, and also in the issues raised in the Qualitative Analysis. For the Policy Maker persona, the SEQ scoring indicated that user felt that Task 1 - the interpretation of shared dashboards - was not at all straightforward (scoring on average only 3/7). On the other hand, Task 2 - modifying an existing dashboard - was perceived to be relatively easy (scoring on average 6/7).

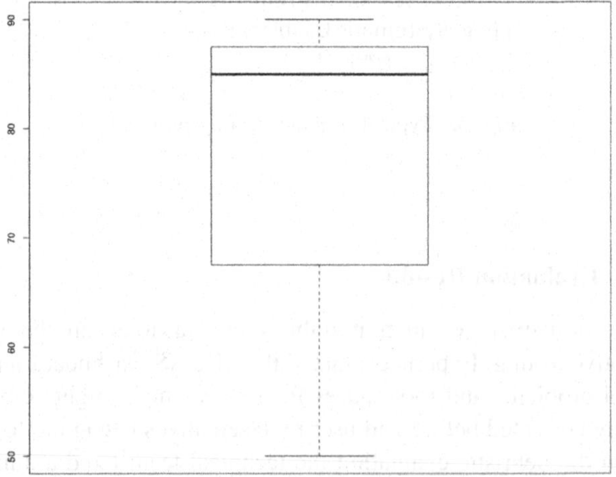

Fig. 4. Data Scientist SUS results (box plot showing overall scores for all tasks).

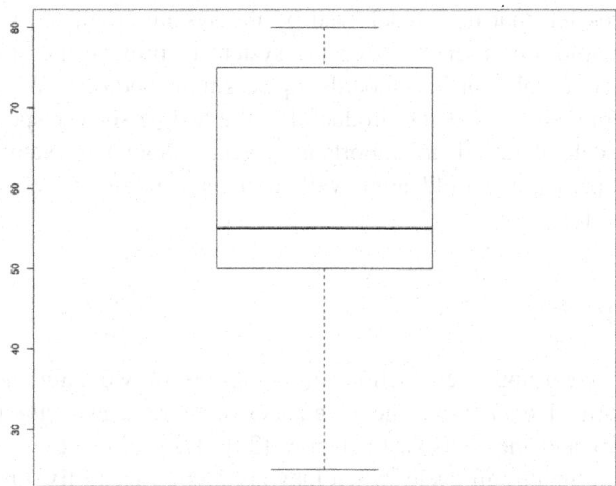

Fig. 5. Policy Maker SUS results (box plot overall scores for both tasks).

SUS Results Summary. In the context of the SUS (System Usability Scale) scores, statements 8 and 10 were outliers for both the Data Scientist and Policy Maker persona tasks. Statement 8 relates to how "cumbersome" users find the interface, although it is important to note that some studies have suggested that this score can affected by language factors with non-native English speakers [19]. The Statement 10 score suggests that users found the system easy-to-learn. Another interesting finding from the SUS analysis is that the platform scored better for the Data Scientist persona than for the Policy Maker persona (75.0 vs. 56.7), implying that users perceived that policy makers might find the current prototype more challenging to use, and in particular to interpret visualisations. Figures 4 and 5 show the distribution of the aggregated results for the Data Scientist and Policy Maker tasks.

Qualitative Results Summary. The qualitative data gives perhaps the richest understanding of the issues and insight that emerged during testing. Despite the diverse nature of the users involved in the usability testing, there were a number of clear recurring themes in the user feedback across all sites. Perhaps the most commonly identified issue was the need for more information to guide users through the system. Some options identified included more descriptive text in the menus and wizards, more hover text and pop-up hints and tips, making videos available on how to create, share and interpret dashboards, and rich user documentation. Dashboard sharing was generally seen to be a key feature for development. Many users suggested that the platform should support annotations and comments for widgets and dashboards, as well as chat functionality for dashboard creators to assist policy makers in interpreting the data. Sharing dashboards would also require some consideration of the need for effective version control, as well as user search functionality.

Alongside these and other high-level feature requests, there were numerous observations on how the interaction with individual widgets and menu items might be improved. Additionally, one user who had spent a lot of time training clinicians on how to use dashboards felt that the model used by the system conflicted with her expectations. For example, this user expected the system to provide the ability to have a number of different tabs or dashboards open simultaneously. While this user's expectations were tied to a specific product that she had personally spent a number of years working with, it raised an important question about the extent to which the MIDAS design paradigm would align with user expectations based on established products and services.

5 Discussion

As stated earlier, the usability evaluation was comprised of two main parts - a heuristic analysis and a formative analysis. The advantages of heuristic evaluations are that they are relatively fast and inexpensive to deploy [20]. They also allow problems to be identified early in the design cycle, when they are less costly to fix. One drawback is that usability experts can be hard to come by [20], although this did not apply in the case of the MIDAS Project. Most scholars agree that heuristic evaluations are best seen as a complement rather than an alternative to user testing [21]. For this reason, we decided to employ both heuristic and formative methods to the evaluation. By employing the heuristic method first, and fixing as many of the identified problems before the formative evaluation, the intention was to ensure that the maximum value was derived from the user testing. This was particularly important given the logistical challenges of engaging with relevant users from the various MIDAS sites, which in many cases required relatively senior staff giving up significant amounts of time to assist with the testing protocol.

The user-centred formative evaluation phase involved a variety of users from different backgrounds carrying out task associated with two key user personas - the Data Scientist and Policy Maker. The findings showed that there was very little overlap in results compared to the heuristic evaluation, which was perhaps not surprising given the fact that developers had already addressed most of the major concerns that had been raised by the usability experts. Task completion times were generally satisfactory, and the Single Ease Questions (SEQ) for the tasks showed that overall the system was slightly easier to use than most users had anticipated. Both the SEQ and the System Usability Scale (SUS) results indicated that the application was harder to use from a Policy Maker perspective, compared to a Data Scientist perspective.

Arguably the most valuable feedback came from the qualitative results, which were enabled by adopting a Think Aloud Protocol approach to the testing. The qualitative feedback enabled the testers to identify key issues which were common to all testing sites. These included the need for more metadata and guidance via the user interface, which many users initially found somewhat confusing. In addition to the need to make functionality more discoverable, the complexity of the underlying datasets meant that users often required help in understanding the information they were attempting to use. Another challenge was raised by one user who had already built up significant experience of an alternative dashboard-based analytics product. In their case, the UX paradigm adopted by the MIDAS platform did not align with prior expectations.

Ultimately, the researchers were able to achieve a compromise proposal in terms of how dashboards should be presented to users. This does raise an interesting question for developers, however: how can they balance the need to follow established industry practices and user expectations, with the desire to pursue more innovative and perhaps "superior" interface solutions?

6 Conclusions

Although research indicates that heuristic evaluation results tend to uncover similar problems to more user-centred methods, it is generally accepted that they should be seen as a complement to usability testing [21]. In order to reduce the potential for duplicated effort in this study, the heuristic evaluation was completed and the software was updated before the formative user-centred evaluation was carried out. This approach meant that the majority of concerns raised during the formative testing were newly identified. Testing with a variety of users across multiple sites allowed the researchers to identify recurring issues that should be prioritised for future development. While the task completion times, SEQ scores and SUS scores were useful for generating quantitative usability measures, it is worth noting that the most valuable feedback for the development team came from the qualitative feedback. This qualitative approach and analysis of user comments as they spoke about their experience using the platform provided the most valuable insights in terms of determining how ongoing development work should be targeted. This is perhaps reflective of the fact that software usability is by its nature a complex construct, requiring a depth of analysis that can only come from a qualitative approach.

It should be borne in mind that this evaluation study of the MIDAS platform was focused on an early prototype, which entailed incomplete functionality and limited access to client data. For future iterations of the platform and usability testing, it is anticipated that the functionality of the application will be significantly extended, and a richer ecosystem of datasets will be available for analysis. It is likely that large parts of the existing test protocols will be re-used for subsequent evaluation exercises. One important lesson learned through this process was the scale of the challenge in recruiting suitable users and coordinating times to attend lab-based tests. It was clear that future test events should be scheduled well in advance, preferably two to three months beforehand. Future test protocols will be adapted to focus on the specific needs of each MIDAS pilot site, and are expected to involve a richer user interface that will include external data sources and visualisation tools.

Acknowledgements. The MIDAS Consortium gratefully acknowledge the support to this project from the European Union research fund 'Big Data Supporting Public Health Policies', under Grant Agreement No. 727721 (H2020-SC1-2016-CNECT SC1-PM-18-2016).

References

1. Groves, P., Kayyali, B., Knott, D., Van Kuiken, S.: The 'big data' revolution in healthcare. McKinsey Q. **2**(3) (2013)
2. Cleland, B., et al.: Meaningful Integration of Data Analytics and Services in MIDAS Project: Engaging Users in the Co-Design of a Health Analytics Platform (2018). https://doi.org/10.14236/ewic/HCI2018.169
3. Nielsen, J.: 10 Usability Heuristics for User Interface Design, vol. 1, no. 1. Nielsen Norman Group (1995)
4. Mazumder, F.K., Das, U.K.: Usability guidelines for usable user interface. Int. J. Res. Eng. Technol. **3**(9), 79–82 (2014)
5. Shneiderman, B.: Designing for fun: how can we design user interfaces to be more fun? Interactions **11**(5), 48–50 (2004)
6. Bond, R.R., Finlay, D.D., Nugent, C.D., Moore, G., Guldenring, D.: A usability evaluation of medical software at an expert conference setting. Comput. Methods Programs Biomed. **113**, 383–395 (2014)
7. Bond, R., Mulvenna, M., Wallace, J.G., Finlay, D.D., Boyd, K., Patterson, M.: UX-handle: a cloud-based system to streamline usability testing analytics. In: Proceedings of the 31st British Computer Society Human Computer Interaction Conference, p. 2. BCS Learning & Development Ltd. (2017)
8. Boyd, K., Nugent, C., Donnelly, M., Sterritt, R., Bond, R.: A usability protocol for evaluating online social networks. In: Donnelly, M., Paggetti, C., Nugent, C., Mokhtari, M. (eds.) ICOST 2012. LNCS, vol. 7251, pp. 222–225. Springer, Heidelberg (2012). https://doi.org/10.1007/978-3-642-30779-9_30
9. Torney, H., et al.: A usability study of a critical man–machine interface: Can layperson responders perform optimal compression rates when using a public access defibrillator with automated real-time feedback during cardiopulmonary resuscitation? IEEE Trans. Hum. Mach. Syst. **46**(5), 749–754 (2016)
10. Boyd, K., Nugent, C., Donnelly, M., Bond, R., Sterritt, R., Hartin, P.: An investigation into the usability of the STAR training and re-skilling website for carers of persons with dementia. In: Engineering in Medicine and Biology Society (EMBC), 2014 36th Annual International Conference of the IEEE, pp. 4139–4142. IEEE (2014)
11. Gibson, A., et al.: Assessing usability testing for people living with dementia. In: Proceedings of the 4th Workshop on ICTs for Improving Patients Rehabilitation Research Techniques, pp. 25–31. ACM (2016)
12. Bond, R., O'Hare, P., Di Maio, R.: Usability testing of a novel automated external defibrillator user interface: a pilot study. In: Bioinformatics and Biomedicine (BIBM), 2015 IEEE International Conference, pp. 1486–1488. IEEE (2015)
13. Boyd, K., Bond, R., Gallagher, S., Moore, G., O'Kane, E.: Usability and behaviour analysis of prisoners using an interactive technology to manage daily living. In: Proceedings of the 31st British Computer Society Human Computer Interaction Conference, p. 80. BCS Learning & Development Ltd. (2017)
14. Bond, R.R., et al.: Human factors analysis of a novel engineering solution to the problem of electrode misplacement during 12-lead electrocardiogram acquisition. J. Electrocardiol. **49** (6), 933 (2016)
15. Fidler, R., et al.: Human factors approach to evaluate the user interface of physiologic monitoring. J. Electrocardiol. **48**(6), 982–987 (2015)

16. Bond, R.R., Van Dam, E., Van Dam, P., Finlay, D.D., Guldenring, D.: Evaluating the human-computer interaction of 'ECGSim': a virtual simulator to aid learning in electrocardiology. In: Computing in Cardiology Conference (CinC), pp. 409–412. IEEE (2015)
17. Peute, L.W., de Keizer, N.F., Jaspers, M.W.: The value of retrospective and concurrent think aloud in formative usability testing of a physician data query tool. J. Biomed. Inf. **55**, 1–10 (2015)
18. Sauro, J.: 10 things to know about the Single Ease Question (SEQ). Measuring U (2012)
19. Finstad, K.: The system usability scale and non-native English speakers. J. Usability Stud. **1**(4), 185–188 (2006)
20. Nielsen, J.: Chapter 2: heuristic evaluation. In: Nielsen, J., Mack, R.L. (eds.) Usability Inspection Methods, pp. 25–62. Wiley, New York (1994)
21. Paz, F., Paz, F.A., Villanueva, D., Pow-Sang, J.A.: Heuristic evaluation as a complement to usability testing: a case study in web domain. In: 2015 12th International Conference on Information Technology - New Generations, pp. 546–551. IEEE, Las Vegas (2015). https://doi.org/10.1109/ITNG.2015.92

Visualization of Component-Based Software Architectures: A Comparative Evaluation of the Usability in Virtual Reality and 2D

Meike Schaller[1,2] and Andreas Schreiber[2(✉)]

[1] German Aerospace Center (DLR), Intelligent and Distributed Systems, Linder Höhe, 51147 Köln, Germany
{meike.schaller,andreas.schreiber}@dlr.de
[2] Otto-Friedrich-Universität, 96047 Bamberg, Germany
meike-barbara-anne.schaller@stud.uni-bamberg.de

Abstract. Software visualization provides a good opportunity to explore complex software architectures. But to reach a high level of usability it is important to evaluate such visualizations properly. We present the results of an usability study that we conducted to compare the visualization of component-based software architectures in both 2D and Virtual Reality (VR), based on different representations. Study participants had to conduct five interactive tasks. The results of our study shows that users are more likely able to complete the tasks in 2D than in VR, that they are more likely able to faster complete the tasks in 2D than in VR, and that they experience more satisfaction while using 2D than VR. Because evaluations of software visualization approaches are still rare, our results might help to create further study designs and offers some advice for the development of future visualizations—especially in VR.

Keywords: Software visualization · Virtual reality · Evaluation

1 Introduction

Development of complex software architectures [13] involves—beside all the technological advances—also several challenges: Source code gets more and more extensive and thus, intangible. This hampers the comprehensibility of large software projects which costs money and time (e.g., when a new developer comes on board of a software project).

Splitting code in several components is a first step to make source code more accessible. To reach the maximum possible success on both technology and user side it is necessary to represent the software in a way which supports users in quickly comprehending the software, including all components and dependencies. *Software Visualization* exactly deals with these aspects: simplifying and accelerating the process of becoming acquainted with existing software projects.

S. Yamamoto and H. Mori (Eds.): HCII 2019, LNCS 11569, pp. 208–222, 2019.
https://doi.org/10.1007/978-3-030-22660-2_14

Several studies haven shown that humans comprehend pictures and figures more easily than plain text such as millions of lines of code [9]. Most work available focuses on evaluating 3D visualization systems in comparison to 2D ones. *Virtual Reality* (VR) as an extension of 3D is also quite well investigated [10], but the research in comparing 2D with VR and evaluating them is still rare.

Our goal was to determine if and how VR is a supportive possibility to quickly explore large software systems or if it rather overstrains users due to some well-known disadvantages of VR, such as motion sickness or cognitive overload. Therefore, we measure the main criteria for good usability such as *efficiency*, *effectiveness*, and *satisfaction*; based on ISO-9241.

We present results of a planned usability study of two different interactive visualization approaches for software architectures: VR visualization using an island metaphor [21] and Web-based 2D visualization using graph layout algorithms [22].

After a short overview about software visualization as background information (Sect. 2), we present our contributions as follows:

- Brief description of two visualizations of component-based software architectures, which we choose to compare (Sect. 3).
- The design of our user study for measuring the usability of our software visualization in 2D and VR (Sect. 4).
- Some details on how we conducted the use study (Sect. 5).
- The results of our evaluation study with respect to effectiveness, efficiency, and satisfaction (Sect. 6).

2 Software Visualization

Current research has many innovative approaches for software visualizations with different representations. These approaches are based on *visual metaphors*, which adapts objects or situations from the real world for visualizations. Especially for 3D, popular visual metaphors include:

- *City metaphor*: One of the most frequently used real-world metaphors for software visualization. The foremost reason for its popularity would be the familiarity of the city concept [24]. Most users know that a city can be organized into districts, where each district can contain multiple buildings. These three hierarchical levels are the basis for most implementations of the city metaphor. Implementations exist for different media, such as VR [11,16], or programming languages, such as Java [1] or Go [7].
- *Solar system metaphor*: A metaphor to visualize Java-based projects [12]. Each package is mapped to a sun, which is being orbited by several planets at different orbits. While the planets represent classes, the orbits represent the inheritance level within a package. The size of each planet is mapped to the number of lines of code in its underlying class and the color helps to differentiate between classes and interfaces.

We experimented with other approaches for VR headsets. For example, a naive approach where we rendered 2D graphs with bundles and dependencies in 3D space by adding third dimension [22]. Another approach was based on the visual metaphor of electrical components, where bundles are rendered as cubes in 3D space and packages are stacked on top of these cubes [20]. In both version, user could fly through the 3D space by moving their heads. While moving head, users could point with a virtual cursor to any bundle or package, which then shows dependencies to other bundles. Despite the drawbacks of the visual representations, users reported motion sickness and dizziness.

3 Visualization of Component-Based Software Architectures

In our work, we focus on the visualization and exploration of *Software Architectures*, especially component-based architectures of software based on the OSGi framework for Java. OSGi modularizes and manages software projects and their services. OSGi projects includes *bundles*. Each bundle is a Java archive (`JAR`) with Java *packages* and a metadata file (`MANIFEST.MF`), which describes different information such as *dependencies* and *services*.

3.1 Island Metaphor for Virtual Reality

We use an *island metaphor* for the visualization of OSGi-based software systems in VR [21]. The entire software system is represented as an ocean with many islands on it (Fig. 1). Each island represents an OSGi bundle and is split into multiple regions. Each region represents a Java package and contains multiple buildings. The buildings are the representatives of the individual class types which reside inside of a package. Each region provides enough space to accommodate all of its buildings without overlapping, and hence the overall size of an island is proportional to the number of class types inside of a bundle (Fig. 2(a)).

The main entities of the OSGi service layer are *service interfaces* and *service components*. As these components are linked to Java class types, we visualize them as special building types. We visualize the relationships between the service entities with a *service connection node*. These nodes hover above the service interface and service component buildings at a certain height and act as connection points for them. Each node has a visual downward connection to its parent building in order for the user to quickly locate its associated service entity (Fig. 2(b)).

Our implementation of the island metaphor in VR, IslandViz [17,18], uses repository mining on the whole source repository and data mining on source code level to get all relevant data for the visualization. We store all data in a graph database for further analysis and visualization [19].

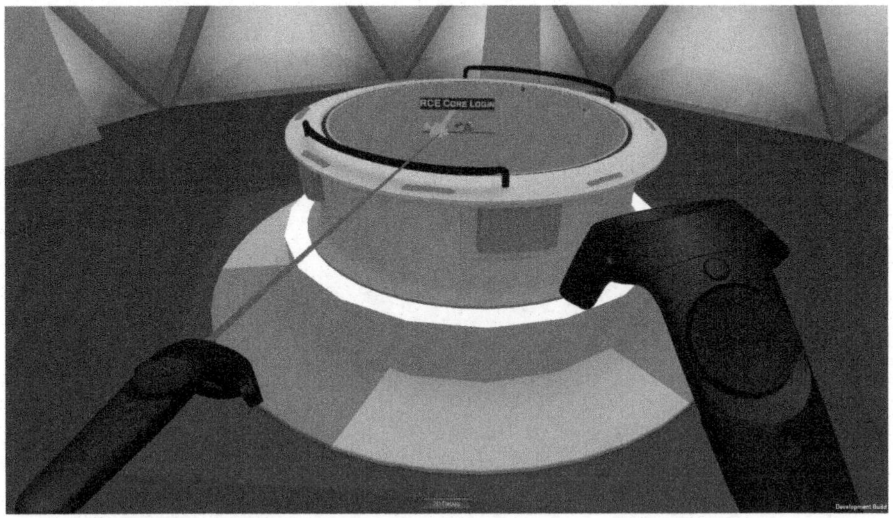

Fig. 1. IslandViz for VR: Bundles are rendered as islands on a virtual water level which is confined to extents of a virtual table. Elements of the visualization can be selected using hand controllers (HTC Vive).

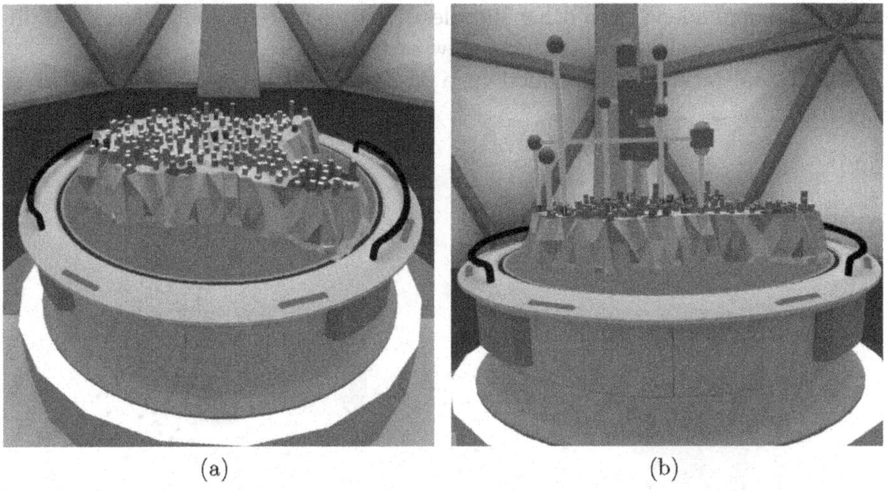

(a) (b)

Fig. 2. Details of the IslandViz visualization: (a) a single bundle (island) with packages (colored regions) and classes (buildings); (b) services and service dependencies.

3.2 Graph Visualization in 2D

We use standard graph-layout algorithms to visualize the modularization of OSGi-based applications on different abstraction levels [22]. The visualization consists of different graph views: One bundle is represented as a node whose

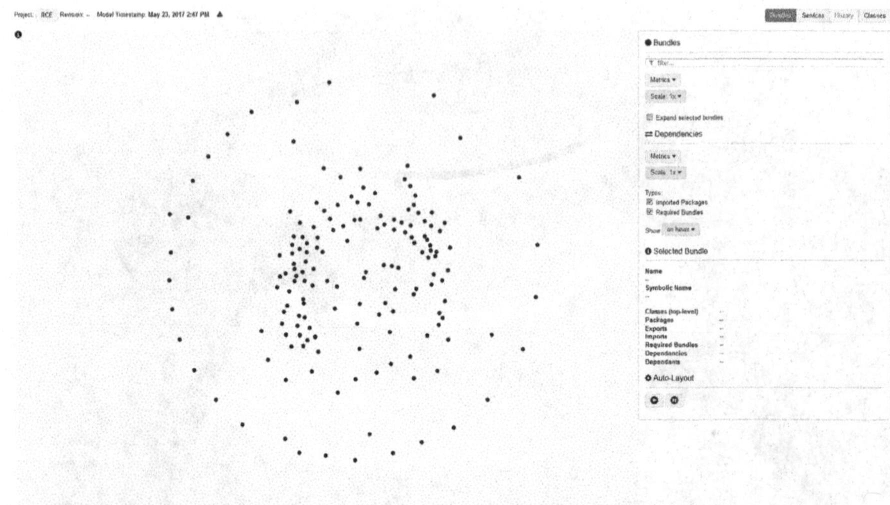

Fig. 3. Main view of interactive Web-based 2D visualization tool with visualization view (left side) and context information and configuration view (right side).

edges show dependencies to other bundles. Further-more one can change to different views (e.g., class and package view or treemap).

The visualization is embedded in a Website which consists of four areas (Fig. 3):

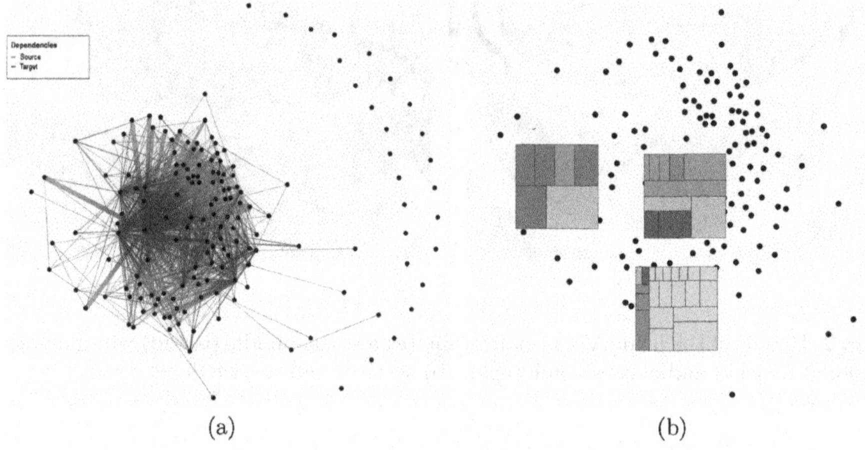

(a) (b)

Fig. 4. Examples of 2D visualization views: (a) Bundles and bundle dependencies rendered as force-directed graph; (b) bundles and package structure, rendered as treemaps where classes are assembled to packages by sharing the same color. The size of a class item is mapped to its lines of code.

1. *Project information*: static information about the OSGi-based application (e.g., name and time the model was generated)
2. *Navigation*: button-based bar for selecting the type of module that should be visualized
3. *Visualization view*: data visualization, depending on the selected module type
4. *Context information and configuration*: information about selected elements and configuration of the view (e.g., applying metrics)

Our implementation for 2D visualization uses the JavaScript library *Data-Driven Documents* (D3) [5]. It generates interactive data visualization using the Web standards HTML5, CSS, and SVG (Fig. 4).

4 Study Design

We designed our study to measure the three main aspects of usability, based on ISO-9241: *effectiveness* (accuracy and completeness with which users achieve specified goals), *efficiency* (resources expended in relation to the accuracy and completeness with which users achieve goals), and *satisfaction* (comfort and acceptability of use) [23]. Therefore, we measured both performance and self-reported metrics through two methods: *usability testing* and *questionnaires*.

4.1 Performance Metrics

In a first step of our study, users complete tasks while we measured the performance metrics *task success* and *time on task*. The overall goal of our study was to determine if the participants get a good overview of all important architectural elements (bundles, packages, classes, dependencies, and services) of the visualized OSGi-based software. Thus, the tasks needed to cover these components. Very challenging in this case was to find tasks which are feasible in both applications, because both applications had some functions which were not implemented in the other one. In the end—proved through some pretests—we determined the following five tasks:

Task 1: Select the bundle with the highest number of packages. Name the number of packages.
Task 2: Select an arbitrary bundle. Name the bundle which has the furthermost dependency and the number of its classes.
Task 3: Select the bundle `RCE Core Utils Scripting`. Name the number of its imports and exports.
Task 4: Show all existing dependencies between all bundles.
Task 5: Show all services and service components.

For each task, the success in completion was measured (i.e., giving the right answer without any help or supportive information). A task was not completed if a user gave the wrong answer or quitted the task. Time measurement started after the participant read the task description aloud.

4.2 Self-reported Metrics

In a second step, we measured self-reported metrics through two standardized questionnaires. Self-reported metrics are an effective way to gain insight into the users' subjective perception about the system and their interaction with it. The first questionnaire (*After Scenario Questionnaire, ASQ*) was developed by Lewis [14]; it measures the three main criteria effectiveness, efficiency, and satisfaction after completing a scenario or task. It consists of three items, phrased as statements which the user rates by a seven-point Likert scale from strongly agree to strongly disagree:

1. "*Overall, I am satisfied with the ease of completing the task in this scenario.*"
2. "*Overall, I am satisfied with the amount of time it took to complete the task in this scenario.*"
3. "*Overall, I am satisfied with the support information (online help, messages, documentation) when completing the task.*"

The ASQ is a good method to gain information about the three main aspects of usability: While the first statement answers the question for effectiveness, the second question focuses on efficiency. Satisfaction is measured through all three statements. Furthermore, it gives insight about which tasks the users found most difficult to find aspects in the system that still have to be improved. Additionally, the users can annotate each task.

The other standardized questionnaire that we used is the *System Usability Scale (SUS)* by Brooke [8]. It uses a five-point scale and consists of ten items which ask for the user's overall opinion about the application while half of the statements is phrased negatively and the other half positively (Fig. 5).

Please rate your level of agreement with the following statements:

	Strongly agree				Strongly disagree
I think that I would like to use the system.	O	O	O	O	O
I found the system unnecessarily complex.	O	O	O	O	O
I thought the system was easy to use.	O	O	O	O	O
I think that I would need the support of a technical person to be able to use this system.	O	O	O	O	O
I found the various functions in this system were well integrated.	O	O	O	O	O
I thought there was too much inconsistency in this system.	O	O	O	O	O
I would imagine that most people would learn to use this system very quickly.	O	O	O	O	O
I found the system very cumbersome to use.	O	O	O	O	O
I felt very confident using the system.	O	O	O	O	O
I needed to learn a lot of things before I could get going with this system.	O	O	O	O	O

Fig. 5. System Usability Scale (SUS) with ten items.

While the ASQ is evaluated through the rating's average, the evaluation of the SUS is a little bit different: Here, it is necessary to calculate a score. For this, all items' score contributions have to be summed up while the items have different contribution, dependent on its either positive or negative statement (for more information see https://www.measuringux.com). After calculating the score, the interpretation of SUS scores based on further research says that results below 50 can be assessed as not acceptable, a result between 50–70 points is marginal, and results over 70 are acceptable [23].

4.3 Hypotheses

The gathered data supports proving our three hypotheses:

H1 Users are more likely able to complete the tasks in 2D than in VR.
H2 Users are more likely able to faster complete the tasks in 2D than in VR.
H3 Users are more satisfied while completing the tasks in Virtual Reality than in 2D.

We assume that concerning effectiveness and efficiency, users of the 2D visualization gain better results. Even though VR became more popular in the last years, using a "classical" computer screen is still the preferred way to get information quickly because users are familiar with it. Concerning the third hypothesis, we assume that users will experience more satisfaction while using VR. Reasons for that are the higher level of exploration and interaction. Moreover, it is still not that common to use VR in the working environment which could bring excitement and relief to the users.

5 Evaluation

We conducted the evaluation in January 2019. The participants were all Software Engineers at the German Aerospace Center. We divided them into two groups: Group 1 completed their tasks on the VR application, Group 2 used the 2D visualization. The division was necessary to avoid learning effects while testing which minimizes the risk of biased outcomes.

We tested both visualizations in the same surrounding—the VR Lab of the Department for Intelligent and Distributed Systems in Cologne, Germany. It offers a spacious room, which was especially important for evaluating the VR version with the HTC Vive. For evaluating the 2D application, we used a laptop with a 17-in.-screen.

First, the participants had to read a short written introduction, which explained the structure of the study (i.e., conduction of tasks and answering the questionnaires afterwards). Also the participants had to read an use case description, which introduced them into the situation (i.e., being a software developer who is new to a project). After reading the paper, the participants received an introduction to the evaluated application, including the explanation of all available functions and components.

The testing started after reading the task. For the 2D application, the participants read it by themselves, while for VR we read it for them (Task 3 as an exception). A task ended with giving an answer to the question in the task. After each completed task the participants had to answer the ASQ—after completing all tasks they had to rate the whole system by with the SUS. We designed both questionnaires using the online tool https://www.soscisurvey.de.

6 Results

All in all, 14 participants (5 female, 9 male) took part in the study. 7 of them tested the VR application, 7 the 2D version while the attribution happened by coincidence.

6.1 Effectiveness

For the evaluation of the systems' effectiveness, the task success for each task has to be considered. We measured the task success with a score: 1 for success, 0 for fail. We calculated the score percentage for each task as average of 0's and 1's (Fig. 6). For both systems, the task success rates are quite high (i.e., that most of the tasks were completed successfully). Diving deeper into the diagram shows that for 2D, there is a higher success rate in two cases while for VR it is only in one case. For task 3 and task 5, the participants for both applications gained the same success rate.

With this result, the first hypothesis can be confirmed: **users are more likely able to complete the tasks in 2D than in VR.**

6.2 Efficiency

To determine how efficient an application is, measuring the time for each task is a reliable method. We measured the time with the timer function on the mobile phone—started after the participant read the respective task aloud. When the participant stated the answer of the task verbally, we stopped time measurement. To assess efficiency, we considered mean as well as median, which helps to identify possible outliers.

For both visualizations, we created a boxplot diagram to show an overview about the measured times for each task (in seconds). Comparing the boxplots for 2D (Fig. 7(a)) and VR (Fig. 7(b)), it becomes obvious that—except for task 4 and 5—the participants of the VR application need a lot more time to complete their tasks. For VR, there are two remarkable outliers, which are caused through some concentration issues by the respective participants. A remarkable difference can be found in task 3—which can be explained through the fact that the 2D version has a filtering option to find certain bundles. In VR, this function is not yet implemented. Overall, the results for efficiency also confirm the second hypothesis: **users are more likely able to faster complete the tasks in 2D than in VR.**

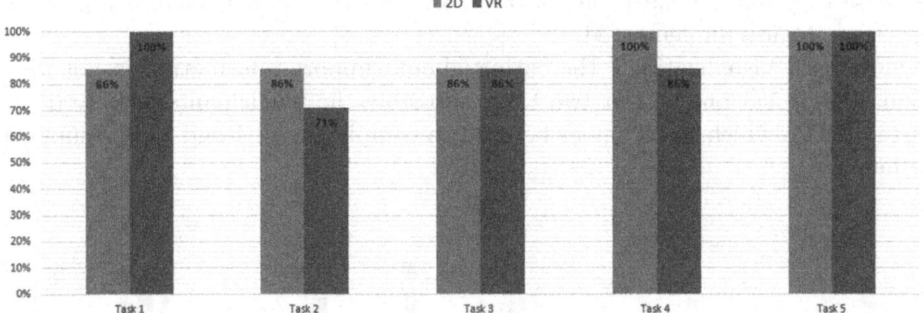

Fig. 6. Task success rates for both 2D and VR. It shows that for 2D, in two cases there is a slightly higher success percentage than in VR. In two cases the success rate is the same while VR gains only in one case better results.

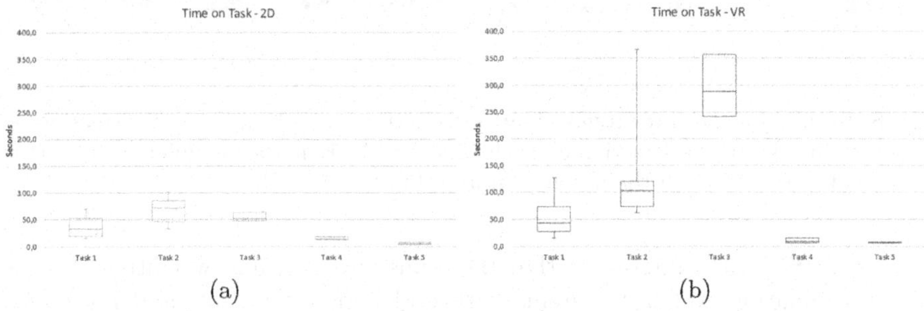

Fig. 7. Results for time measured on each task as boxplots: (a) Time on task results for 2D; (b) Results for VR with large outliers on task 1 and task 2 and remarkable more time needed to complete Task 3.

6.3 Satisfaction

We measured satisfaction through the questionnaires in two ways: satisfaction while completing a task with the ASQ and satisfaction concerning to the whole system, ranked by the SUS.

First, a closer look onto the results of the ASQ (Fig. 8). The left bar in each diagram indicates the rating about effectiveness ("Overall, I am satisfied with the ease of completing the task in this scenario"), middle one indicates efficiency ("Overall, I am satisfied with the amount of time it took to complete the scenario"). We measured satisfaction through all three statements, including the right bar ("Overall, I am satisfied with the support information when completing the task").

It turns out that concerning task completion and time on task, users seem quite satisfied for both visualizations. Remarkable high scores are on tasks 4 and 5, which are concerned with showing all dependencies and all services and service components. A large difference can be found on task 3, which required finding a certain bundle. Participants of the VR application rated it quite worse because they did not have the option to search for it. In 2D, there is a filtering function already implemented.

For both visualizations, the rating about support information is not very high, except VR on the last two tasks. Possibly the participants perceived the virtual PDA–which must has to be used to complete task 4 and 5–as a support or help.

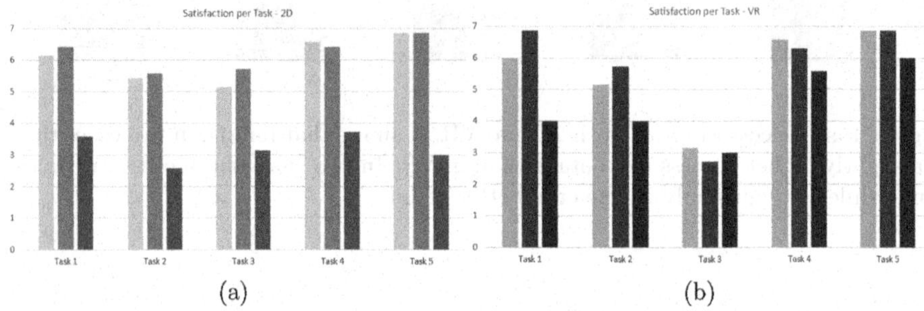

Fig. 8. Results for the three items about satisfaction on each task: (a) Satisfaction on each task for 2D; (b) Satisfaction on each task for VR. Remarkable differences on task 3 are explainable through the missing filtering function in VR.

For the SUS, it is important that the items have different weightings for the overall evaluation. While the items with odd numbers are phrased positively, the calculation is *participant's rating-1*. For items with even numbers, which are phrased negatively, it is *5-participant's rating*. The scores have to be summed up and then multiplied by 2.5 to obtain the overall SUS score (Fig. 9).

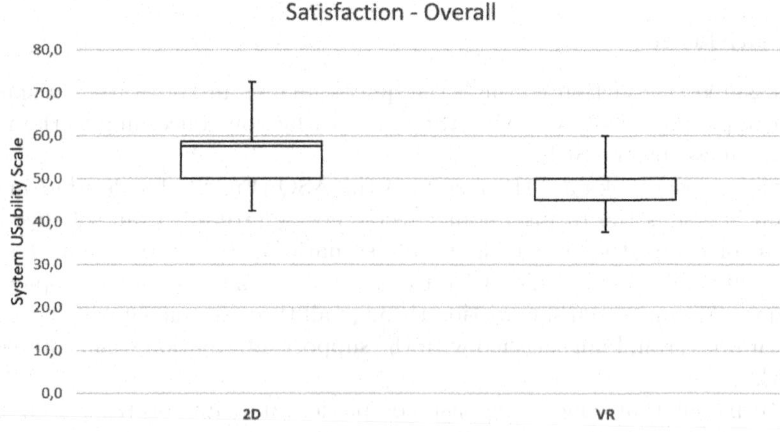

Fig. 9. Overall system satisfaction, measured by SUS. 2D is experienced slightly more satisfying than VR.

The results refute the third hypothesis: **participants experience more satisfaction while using 2D than in VR.**

For 2D, the mean value is 55.7 ($sd = 9.9$) while it is for VR 48.2 ($sd = 6.8$). Based on the interpretation of Bangor et al. [2], the usability for VR is not acceptable, for 2D it is marginal. But in both cases there are large outliers which explain the high number of standard deviations.

Taking a closer look at the ratings of the single items and the participants' comments, we found that indeed both systems seem interesting and beneficial concerning the use case (obtaining a first overview), but working with it in real life tend to be too time consuming and cumbersome, especially in VR.

7 Related Work

The research field of software visualization provides many approaches to explore software in different representations, but it is found that 62% of these approaches have never been evaluated or just offer weak evaluations (e.g., usage scenarios or anecdotal evidence). Another problem is that when there are any evaluations of a new software visualization approach, often they were conducted with participants which do not match with the target user group. Furthermore it is found that often the measured metrics are not well defined (e.g., *what does efficiency mean?*) [15].

If there are well implemented evaluations of software visualizations then they are based on different metaphors [25]. Comparing two visualizations in different representations (i.e., 2D and VR), however, is a new way for evaluating usability.

8 Conclusions and Future Work

The study's results provide a good first impression of how users perceive the two applications. Using a survey to rate each task is questionable in this case, because it seemed that it distracts the participants from their work flows. Especially in VR it turned out to be quite cumbersome, because the glasses had to be taken off and on again after each task. Furthermore, evaluating with an ASQ is not useful because concerning to the use case, the users do not have to complete tasks. The focus is more on exploring the application and gaining knowledge about the visualized project. To evaluate that, a survey with questions about the visualization would be more helpful (e.g., in VR, *for which component stands a region?*). Also, comparing a web-based 2D application with VR is not straightforward. In VR, physical constraints must be considered that do not appear while using 2D. Interpreting the results was also challenging because often the values of the standard deviation were quite high or the differences between 2D and VR were not significant enough. Even though the amount of 14 participants seems appropriate for discovering weaknesses, a higher number of participants would be helpful to get more precise results.

In summary, both applications have their advantages and disadvantages. Because VR is a relatively new field for most persons, it needs more time to become familiar with it and to complete certain tasks. Especially in the work environment the additional benefit is questionable because it still needs too much effort to gain the desired goals. Future Work should focus on the implementation of supporting functions (e.g., a filtering option for finding certain bundles). Also conversational interfaces would be helpful which leads the user through the application or gives supportive information if needed. A good approach for that could be voice assistants based on *Natural Language Processing* (NLP) and *Natural Language Understanding* (NLU). Also, it seems that *Augmented Reality* (AR) or other future 3D output devices are good alternatives for such use cases [6].

Future work include evaluation of software visualization in AR supported by voice assistant and chatbots [3] and a deeper look into the usability of conversational interfaces for all kinds of visualizations (such as chat-based interfaces for 2D visualization [4]).

References

1. Balogh, G., Szabolics, A., Beszédes, Á.: Codemetropolis: eclipse over the city of source code. In: 2015 IEEE 15th International Working Conference on Source Code Analysis and Manipulation (SCAM), pp. 271–276, September 2015. https://doi.org/10.1109/SCAM.2015.7335425
2. Bangor, A., Kortum, P.T., Miller, J.T.: An empirical evaluation of the systemusability scale. Int. J. Hum. Comput. Interact. **24**(6), 574–594 (2008). https://doi.org/10.1080/10447310802205776
3. Baranowski, A., Seipel, P., Schreiber, A.: Visualizing and exploring OSGi-based software architectures in augmented reality. In: Proceedings of the 24th ACM Symposium on Virtual Reality Software and Technology, VRST 2018, pp. 62:1–62:2. ACM, New York (2018). https://doi.org/10.1145/3281505.3281564, https://doi.acm.org/10.1145/3281505.3281564
4. Bieliauskas, S., Schreiber, A.: A conversational user interface for software visualization. In: 2017 IEEE Working Conference on Software Visualization (VISSOFT), vol. 00, pp. 139–143, September 2017. https://doi.org/10.1109/VISSOFT.2017.21, doi.ieeecomputersociety.org/10.1109/VISSOFT.2017.21
5. Bostock, M., Ogievetsky, V., Heer, J.: D3: data-driven documents. IEEE Trans. Visual. Comput. Graphics (Proc. InfoVis) **17**(12), 2301–2309 (2011). https://doi.org/10.1109/TVCG.2011.185, http://vis.stanford.edu/papers/d3
6. Brath, R.: 3D InfoVis is here to stay: deal with it. In: 2014 IEEE VIS International Workshop on 3DVis (3DVis), pp. 25–31, November 2014. https://doi.org/10.1109/3DVis.2014.7160096
7. Brito, R., Brito, A., Brito, G., Valente, M.T.: GoCity: code city for go. In: 26th IEEE International Conference on Software Analysis, Evolution and Reengineering (SANER). SANER 2019. IEEE, Hangzhou (2019)
8. Brooke, J.: SUS-a quick and dirty usability scale. Usability Eval. Ind. **189**(194), 4–7 (1996)
9. Diehl, S.: Software Visualization. Visualizing the Structure, Behaviour, and Evolution of Software, 1st edn. Springer, Heidelberg (2007). https://doi.org/10.1007/978-3-540-46505-8

10. Elliott, A., Peiris, B., Parnin, C.: Virtual reality in software engineering: affordances, applications, and challenges. In: 2015 IEEE/ACM 37th IEEE International Conference on Software Engineering, vol. 2, pp. 547–550, May 2015. https://doi.org/10.1109/ICSE.2015.191
11. Fittkau, F., Krause, A., Hasselbring, W.: Exploring software cities in virtual reality. In: 2015 IEEE 3rd Working Conference on Software Visualization (VISSOFT), pp. 130–134, September 2015. https://doi.org/10.1109/VISSOFT.2015.7332423
12. Graham, H., Yang, H.Y., Berrigan, R.: A solar system metaphor for 3D visualisation of object oriented software metrics. In: Proceedings of the 2004 Australasian Symposium on Information Visualisation, APVis 2004, vol. 35, pp. 53–59. Australian Computer Society Inc, Darlinghurst, Australia (2004). http://dl.acm.org/citation.cfm?id=1082101.1082108
13. Hasselbring, W.: Software architecture: past, present, future. The Essence of Software Engineering, pp. 169–184. Springer, Cham (2018). https://doi.org/10.1007/978-3-319-73897-0_10
14. Lewis, J.R.: Psychometric evaluation of an after-scenario questionnaire for computer usability studies: the ASQ. SIGCHI Bull. **23**(1), 78–81 (1991). https://doi.org/10.1145/122672.122692. http://doi.acm.org/10.1145/122672.122692
15. Merino, L., Ghafari, M., Anslow, C., Nierstrasz, O.: A systematic literature review of software visualization evaluation. J. Syst. Softw. **144**, 165–180 (2018). https://doi.org/10.1016/j.jss.2018.06.027. http://www.sciencedirect.com/science/article/pii/S0164121218301237
16. Merino, L., Ghafari, M., Anslow, C., Nierstrasz, O.: CityVR: gameful software visualization. In: 2017 IEEE International Conference on Software Maintenance and Evolution (ICSME), pp. 633–637. IEEE (2017). http://scg.unibe.ch/archive/papers/Meri17c.pdf
17. Misiak, M., Schreiber, A., Fuhrmann, A., Zur, S., Seider, D., Nafeie, L.: Islandviz: a tool for visualizing modular software systems in virtual reality. In: 2018 IEEE Working Conference on Software Visualization (VISSOFT), pp. 112–116, September 2018. https://doi.org/10.1109/VISSOFT.2018.00020
18. Misiak, M., Rawi85, Schreiber, A.: DLR-SC/island-viz: Islandviz 1.0, October 2018. https://doi.org/10.5281/zenodo.1464633
19. Nafeie, L., Schreiber, A.: Visualization of software components and dependency graphs in virtual reality. In: Proceedings of the 24th ACM Symposium on Virtual Reality Software and Technology, VRST 2018, pp. 133:1–133:2. ACM, New York (2018). https://doi.org/10.1145/3281505.3281602, http://doi.acm.org/10.1145/3281505.3281602
20. Schreiber, A., Brüggemann, M.: Interactive visualization of software components with virtual reality headsets. In: 2017 IEEE Working Conference on Software Visualization (VISSOFT) (2017)
21. Schreiber, A., Misiak, M.: Visualizing software architectures in virtual reality with an island metaphor. In: Chen, J.Y.C., Fragomeni, G. (eds.) VAMR 2018. LNCS, vol. 10909, pp. 168–182. Springer, Cham (2018). https://doi.org/10.1007/978-3-319-91581-4_13
22. Seider, D., Schreiber, A., Marquardt, T., Brüggemann, M.: Visualizing modules and dependencies of OSGi-based applications. In: 2016 IEEE Working Conference on Software Visualization (VISSOFT), pp. 96–100. IEEE (2016)
23. Tullis, T., Albert, B.: Measuring the User Experience: Collecting, Analyzing, and Presenting Usability Metrics, 2nd edn. Morgan Kaufmann, Bern (2013)

24. Wettel, R., Lanza, M.: Visualizing software systems as cities. In: 2007 4th IEEE International Workshop on Visualizing Software for Understanding and Analysis, pp. 92–99, June 2007. https://doi.org/10.1109/VISSOF.2007.4290706
25. Wettel, R., Lanza, M., Robbes, R.: Software systems as cities: a controlled experiment. In: Proceedings of the 33rd International Conference on Software Engineering, ICSE 2011, pp. 551–560. ACM, New York (2011). https://doi.org/10.1145/1985793.1985868, http://doi.acm.org/10.1145/1985793.1985868

A Comparison of Effectiveness Between 2-Dimensional and 3-Dimensional Data Visualization in Detecting Plant Architectural Characteristics

Thanh Van Pham[1], Byung Cheol Lee[2(✉)], and Scott A. King[1]

[1] Department of Computing Science, Texas A&M University – Corpus Christi, Corpus Christi, TX 78412, USA
tpham22@islander.tamucc.edu, scott.king@tamucc.edu

[2] Department of Engineering, Texas A&M University – Corpus Christi, Corpus Christi, TX 78412, USA
byungcheol.lee@tamucc.edu

Abstract. A new generation of crops that yield more with fewer inputs and are adapted to more variable environments is needed to secure food security. The key to breeding highly productive and tolerant crops will be the to analyze the effect of the environment on plant growth through analyzing diverse plant measurements. Plant architecture is an essential variable in plant adaptation to environment and can bring important information to understand physiological processes governing plant functioning. The factors include various images and visualized data such as leaf areas, stem diameters, plant heights and widths, intermodal lengths, color, etc. However, the development of efficient tools assessing plant architecture is still a major stake. Nowadays, due to the advance of image capturing technology, a broad range of image data and quantitative measurements can be obtained. This study explored the relative advantages of 2D versus 3D data visualization for agricultural plant architecture analysis. We compared the effectiveness and efficiency of information processing between 2D and 3D visualization by a human subject experiment. In this study, an automatic feature extraction system (AFES) was developed using the algorithms that can automatically extract plant characteristics from captured plat images. 3D plant models are constructed by height and volume measurements, leaf detection and green index. The extracted features were prepared in 2D or 3D data visualization formats (images or 3D models) for determining plant structure characteristics. The task completion times and accuracy rates were measured as performance indicators in comparison of two data visualization formats. The effect of different data visualization on human information perception were evaluated, particularly in an agricultural data analysis process.

Keywords: 2D · 3D · Visualization · Plant structural features

S. Yamamoto and H. Mori (Eds.): HCII 2019, LNCS 11569, pp. 223–236, 2019.
https://doi.org/10.1007/978-3-030-22660-2_15

1 Introduction

Genetically improved high quality crops that yield more with less inputs have been essential contributors to secure food security. However, a current bottleneck in crop research is the development of precise measurement methods to examine phenotypic traits, and major improvement in breeding data processing is required to achieve this goal [1]. Plant phenotyping is a comprehensive assessment of complex plant traits and opens challenges in the domain of data processing and analysis [2]. It also offers opportunity of precision farming with a wealth of data resources. Precise phenotyping is necessary to measure individual quantitative parameters with diverse data visualization formats and requires accurate and reliable decision-making process of researchers and scientists in agriculture and agronomy domains.

Plant architecture is an essential variable in plant adaptation to environment and is a major attribute in the plant phenotyping [3]. It also can be used in plant breeding to optimize a variety of factors in different environments. Plant architecture can bring important information to understand physiological processes governing plant functioning with various factors including leaf area, stem diameter, plant height and width, intermodal length, color, and or so. However, the development of efficient tools assessing entire plant architecture is still a major stake. Nowadays, due to the advance of image processing technology, broad range of image data and quantitative measurements can be obtained. However, when applied to large population of plants, complete image data acquisitions can be time expensive for high-throughput phenotyping, and their analysis and processing are still relying on subjective decisions.

2-dimensional (2D) and 3-dimensional (3D) visualization data formats are critical elements in scientific data analysis. Both 2D and 3D data formats have their own strengths and weaknesses, and there is still controversy about the efficiency between 2D and 3D regarding human's information processing. With 2D visualization, it is simple and has been used for a long time, but occlusion prevents full recognition and uncontrollable lighting distorts actual images while 3D visualization raises more interest and gives users the overall view of the object. However, since the visual sensory system cannot estimate precise volume and distance, 3D visualization is not recommended for accurate data processing [4]. Particularly, when applied to large population of plant architecture data, complete image data acquisitions can be time consuming for high-throughput phenotyping and require will also produce huge amount of data.

In this study, the relative advantages of 3D versus 2D visualization for agricultural plant growth models will be studied. The purpose of this experiment is to determine the proper visualized data format to improve human information perception, particularly in an agricultural data analysis process. In the experiment, the participants will answer questions about the plant parameters by 2D images and 3D models of a plant. We will investigate the effect of two visualization data formats in information processing and decision making in the agricultural area by measuring task performance including task completion time and task accuracy and evaluate cognitive workload.

Specifically, a visual data processing algorithm was developed and presented to automatically extract plant characteristics. The extracted data were compared with ground-truth data to evaluate the accuracy and reliability. Then, human subject experiments were conducted to investigate how effective plant characteristics are evaluated in 2D and 3D data visualization. Participants were presented with either plant images (2D) or 3D plant models and conducted tasks of identifying plant height and number of leaves. The outcomes will contribute to following areas: (1) accurately detecting plant phenotypes based on plant architectural structure data; (2) design of 2D and 3D visualization models to efficiently develop cultivars with superior phenotypes; and (3) comparing decision-making and information processing performance in two visualization data formats.

2 Background

2.1 Plant Feature Extraction with Image Processing Technology

Plant feature extraction is a critical process in plant phenotyping analysis. In the past, to improve the yield and quality of the crop, reduce the time-consuming, tedious, and strenuous work in the agricultural area, many automatic systems were created to support farmers in determining features and state of soil, fruit, plant, etc. Images or visualized data collected with support agriculture and agronomy researchers to make a better decision in farming, irrigating, and harvesting. Yang et al. [5] applied a Fuzzy logic decision-making algorithm into color image extraction system for precision farming. The system processed the color images of the agricultural fields affected by weeds to estimate the amount of herbicide needed, and the system could reduce the amount of herbicide use by 15–64%. A system for detecting defects on apples was developed based on the analysis of multiple images and adjusted the rotation [6]. It enables to classify 96% of correctness in finding bruises, frost damage, and scab. Jin et al. [7] suggested a system using adaptive and fixed intensity interception to detect defects on yellow-skin potatoes. The system's accuracy reached 92.1% in classification, 91.4% in recognition and 100% in inspection.

Diverse algorithms and approaches were employed in automatic plant feature extraction. 3D convexity analysis and the Canny edge detector were used to detect apples in tree images with 94% correctness [8]. Color mapping, morphological dilation, and stem and black area detection were utilized to detect 97% of red grape and 91% of white grape images [9]. Sansao et al. [10] propose a method of analysis for green index images using the Gabor filters to determine weed coverage percentage. An automatic and robust expert system was developed to analyze the greenness in an agricultural image with image histogram analysis to reflect the direct effect caused by the illumination and the contrast [11].

2.2 Comparison 2D vs. 3D Data Visualization

Prior research showed the mixed results in comparison between 2D with 3D data visualization. Risden et al. [12] examined the ease of use for 2D and 3D information visualization in web content, and the study showed the performance of interactive 3D display is better in task completion time and accuracy rate. The comparison between two visualizations was conducted in vehicle infotainment display designs [13]. Based on a multimodal architecture design concept, both visualization formats were implemented in typical key-console and touch-screen displays using speech recognition and active hand and head gestures. The study indicated that neither of the two types of the interface design were preferred, but the 3D visualization is preferable regarding the joy of use.

Information processing performance of two visualization formats has been investigated. The effectiveness of 2D and 3D graphic data presented on papers and a computer screen was investigated [14]. The results showed that the problem solving was faster in 3D data in a computer screen than 2D data on papers. Interestingly, this study also found that novice participants showed better performance in 2D presentation. Stewart et al. [15] investigated the data comprehension levels in 2D or 3D formatted graphs. The study concluded that 2D graphs are better in interpretation of complex data, and 3D graph may negatively affect participant's comprehension. Cell phone menus were examined to evaluate Information processing in different visualization formats [16]. The results showed that 3D menus that display more items with natural and intuitive interface are more favored, but the 2D menus are better in information retrieval due to low memory loading. Ware et al. [17] suggested an unique interface using 2.5D attitude, which used 3D depth selectively and focused more on a 2D layout. Using this interface, 2D interface seemed to be more appropriate in reading and editing tasks, because the texts were shown in a 2D medium. 3D display is preferred in interior design tasks which require various depth cues.

2.3 Data Presentation in Plant Phenotyping

The key to developing new high productive crops will be the analyzing of the diverse measurements in crops or plant growth in yield and the identifying of specific target environments. In addition, an understanding of how these measurements interacts with plant growth traits and the environment is another challenge. Of the measurements responsible for yield, variation in measurements associated with phenotyping play a critical role to sustainable production.

Phenotyping provides the quantitative analysis of plant structure, and it is the comprehensive assessment of complex plant traits such as growth, resistance, tolerance, physiology, yield, and ecology [18]. However, there are challenges for integrating huge amount of plant structural data to characterize plant responses to unpredictable environmental conditions [19]. Aiming at this critical challenge, efficient and accurate data processing of plant architectural and physiological data is necessary element, and visualized data format significantly affects the decision-making process of agronomy or agricultural scientist and researchers. With increasing demand to support and accelerate progress in breeding for novel traits, the plant research faces the need to accurately measure an increasing number of plants and plant parameters [20]. Though plant phenotyping has been performed by farmers and breeders for the long period of time, it was mostly based on experience and intuition, which are a process where measurement and interpretation were not clearly separated [21]. The measurement and interpretation of plant growth data were not clearly separated. This ambiguous approach lacks reliability and validity in measured data and measurements were highly depended on the individual subjectivity. The precise phenotyping data analysis is necessary to evaluate individual quantitative parameters from more complex plant structural traits.

3 Method

3.1 2D Images and 3D Model Development and Plant Feature Extraction

This study is divided into two parts. One is to develop an automatic plant feature extraction system (AFES), and the other is to compare 2D with 3D data visualization which were generated by AFES to make better decisions in plant architectural measurement tasks. In order to implement the research, plant characteristics were measured, images of plants were collected, and a 3D model was created.

Plant architectural measurements were obtained from five plant samples, and ground-truth data of plants was gathered manually. These five plant samples were chosen at random, and plant height and number of leaves were used as two architectural parameters. Plant height is a basic feature for plant growth analysis and is measured from ground to the highest point of the plant. The number of leaves gives information about the state of the plant growth at one specific time. The number of leaves were manually counted on the plants, and the height of the plant was measured by using a yardstick as reference data.

A database of plant images was created for developing 2D and 3D visualizations of plant samples. Each plant was placed in a chamber with two cameras used to take pictures of the plant (see Fig. 1). Two rotating cameras installed at different heights capture plant images every 10-degrees for a total of 72 pictures (36 pictures from each camera) per plant. Four light bulbs were used to supply enough light in the chamber. The plant features were automatically extracted, and 2D images and 3D models were generated based on the measurements of extracted features. A 3D model of each plant was generated using AutoDesk Recap Pro [22]. The features that AFES extracts are the height of the plant, the volume coverage of the plant, and the green index. The accuracy of the automatic system is determined by comparing the extracted data by the system with the measured reference data.

A between subject controlled laboratory experiment was conducted with 2D images and 3D models to investigate the effect of different data visualizations on information processing capability and the decision-making process. Data visualization presented in a well-designed format can enhance the way a human perceives and understands data. In order to suggest a suitable data visualization to improve the quality of plant characteristics understanding and analysis, an experiment was conducted to explore the efficiency between 2D and 3D visualizations on human performance in data analysis. In the experiment, participants were asked to answer questions about plant features including plant height and the number of leaves by using 2D images or 3D models.

3.2 Subjects

23 participants were recruited, and all are college students who are majoring in science or engineering. They were familiar with scientific diagrams and possessed basic knowledge of scientific or engineering measuring.

3.3 Procedure

After signing the consent forms, participants completed a survey about demographic information including age, race, and major of study. Participants then logged into a custom- built web application and learned how to navigate the application and practiced sample tasks. They were familiar with mouse controls to manipulate 3D models to find out specific plant features. After a training session, participants conducted experiment tasks which were to find the number of leaves and to estimate plant height in 2D images and 3D models given in the application. A total of 16 tasks (8 per each task type) were given to participants and the order of tasks was randomized among participants. Figures 1 and 2 show screen shots of 2D and 3D visualization tasks. The Office of Institution Research Board at Texas A&M University- Corpus Christi reviewed and approved the research procedures (ID: IRB114-17).

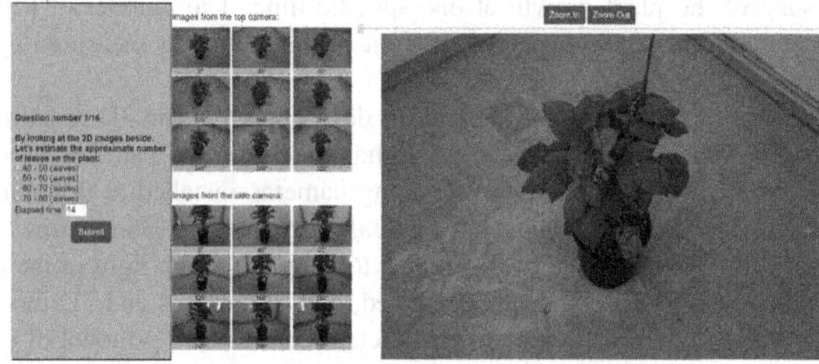

Fig. 1. An experiment screen shot of 2D visualization.

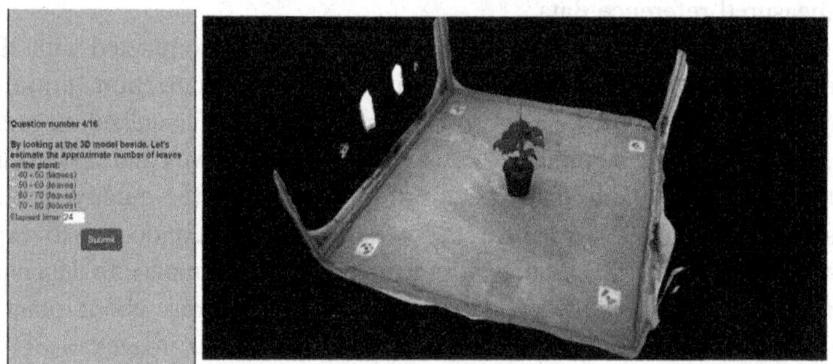

Fig. 2. An experiment screen short of 3D visualization.

4 Results

4.1 Automatic Feature Extraction System of Plant Architectural Features

The roles of automatic feature extraction system (AFES) are divided into processing 3D model files and extracting plant features including plant height, plant volume, and the greenness. Before plant features extraction, AFES crops some segments of the 3D plant model in order to separate the plant features and the background. Figure 3 shows an overall process structure of AFES.

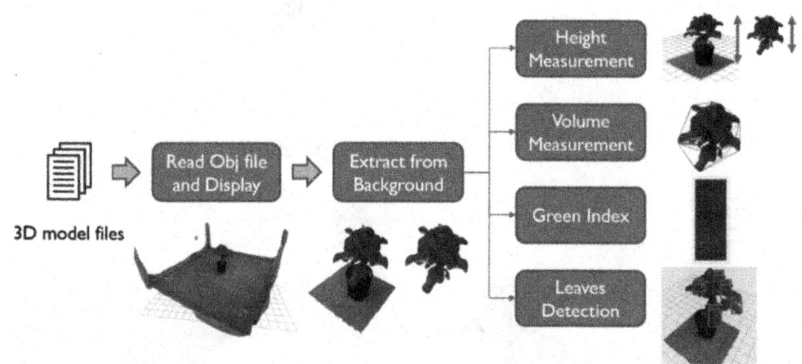

Fig. 3. Automatic feature extraction system.

This study used a topology and geometry file (.obj file) format that was developed by Wavefront Technologies for its Advanced Visualizer animation package [23]. An obj file stores 3D geometry and topology information including vertex coordinates, texture coordinates, vertex normal coordinates, and face construction data. Face construction data containing vertex indices, normal vectors and UV coordinates enable the system to build a triangular mesh to construct the 3D model. In building a 3D model, material and texture files were added to show surface detail and vertices of objects and textural information. Open GL is used to render the 3D model.

4.2 Image Data Collection

After building the 3D plant models, AFES extracts background images and plant features. The image extraction consists of three separate images: the plant with the pot, green parts of the plant, and the plant without the pot. 72 images of each plant are collected from the indoor phenotyping chamber to create an original 3D model. This model encompasses not only the plant but also the chamber and floor. Plant images and chamber environment images are separated (see Fig. 4), and green areas of the model are detected using Hue, Saturation and Value (HSV) indices. This process enables the measurement of the highest and lowest points of the plant. The plant images with the pot can be obtained in the plant image capture chamber (see Fig. 5). This process also includes floor image extraction to calculate the floor size which is used to evaluate the accuracy of algorithms. Floor image extraction is required to prevent the measurement bias of plant feature specification in extracted images.

One of main plant structural features is the leaf, and leaf detection is critical in evaluating the plant architectural features. Th leaf detection process consists of two steps. As the first step, a video file is produced by moving a virtual camera around the plant from the bottom to the top of the plant. The virtual camera is automatically moved

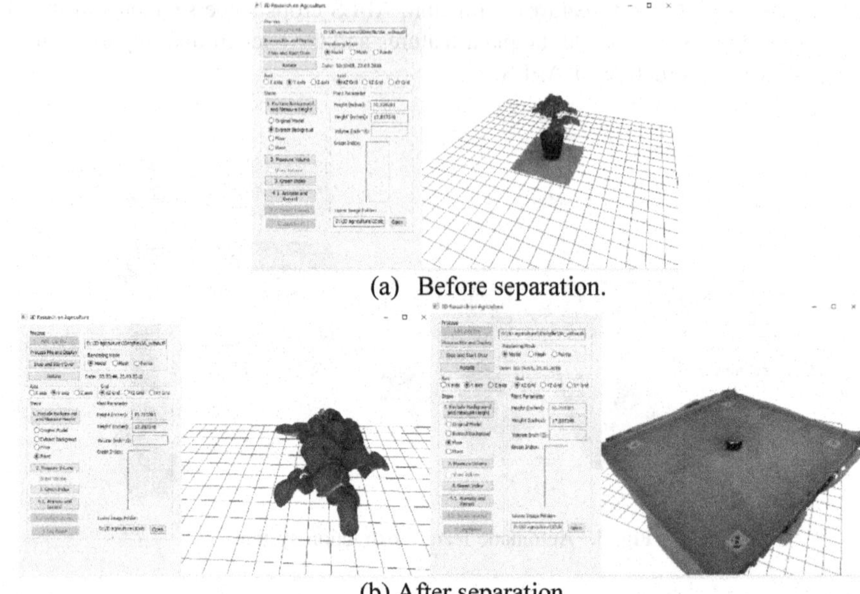

(a) Before separation.

(b) After separation.

Fig. 4. Plant-base separation process.

Fig. 5. Plant image capture chamber.

in a fixed route, and FFmpeg framework [24] is used to convert and stream the rendered animation to a video file with mp4 format. In the second step, leaf detection in the video file is processed using YOLO (You only look once) which is a real-time object detection system developed by Redmon et al. [25]. Objects are detected in the image by three processes. First, the input image is resized to 448 × 448 resolution. Second, a single convolutional network is used to analyze the image. Finally, detection results are filtered by the model's confidence.

4.3 Leaf Detection Training

Leaf detection by YOLO requires a training process with a leaf database. 213 images of leaves were collected for the database, and 90% of the images were used for training and 10% for testing. The training was conducted with about 13,000 iterations to reach the smallest error (see Fig. 6). In each iteration, 64 images were used for each batch of training. The trained system was tested on the recorded video of the plant with an example result shown in Fig. 7.

Fig. 6. Plant image examples for training and leaf detection.

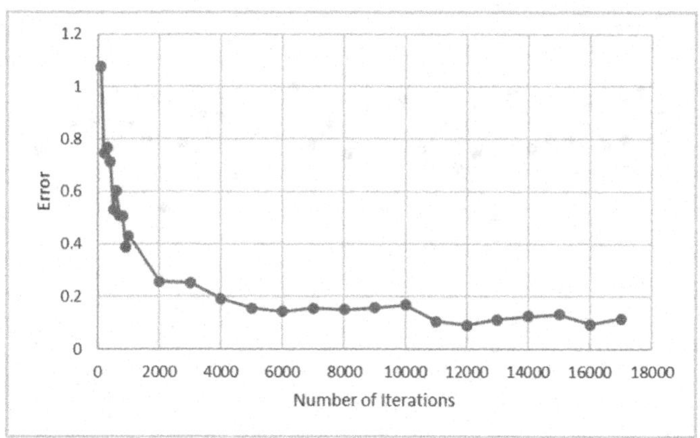

Fig. 7. Leaf detection training results using YOLO.

4.4 Validation of AFES and Trained Algorithm

Three measures were evaluated to validate 3D model extracted from previous algorithm development processes. Plant height and leaf number counts were compared to test the accuracy of the plant feature extraction algorithm. Table 1 show the comparison between extracted and actual plant heights. The average of differences is 0.44 inch (about 2.9% error compared to the actual plant heights).

Table 1. Comparison between extracted and actual plant heights

	Extracted height (cm)	Actual height (cm)	% Error
Plant 1	17.85	17.80	0.28
Plant 2	17.97	18.50	2.86
Plant 3	17.68	17.25	2.49
Plant 4	20.78	21.25	2.21
Plant 5	16.77	18.00	6.83

The leaf detection rates from 36 plant images are shown in Fig. 8. From the table, the average detection rate is 0.76. The detection rates are affected by the quality of the 3D model, the resolution of video input to YOLO detection system, and the size of the leafs in the training database. To solve the leaf size issue, the 213 images in the training databases were converted into half size and quarter size. YOLO was trained again with these resized images for about 20,000 iterations. However, the average detection rate was not much improved after the training, and the leaf size is not likely to influence the detection rates. To improve the performance of the algorithm, better quality of the 3D model, higher computing power running YOLO, higher resolution of the recorded videos, and better training database are required.

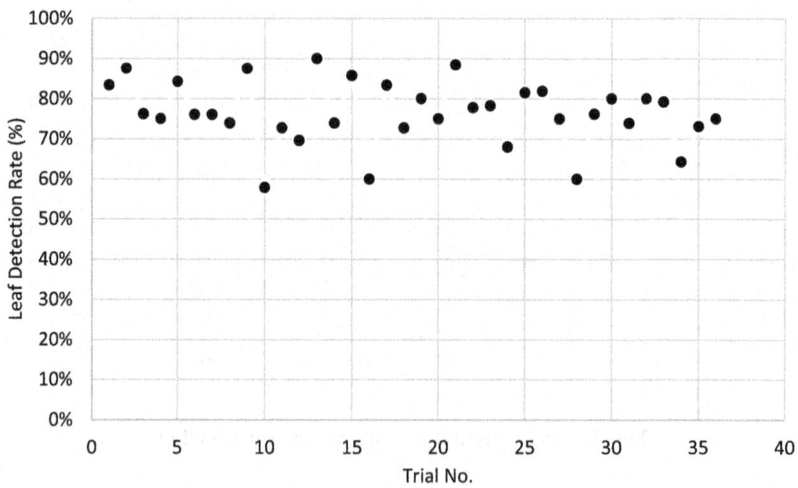

Fig. 8. Leaf detection rates with YOLO algorithm.

4.5 Comparison 2D and 3D Visualization

The average completion time and average accuracy rate of the participants were compared. Table 2 summarizes the average value and standard deviation of task accuracy and task completion time.

Table 2. Height estimation and leaf counting task performance

	Height estimation				Leaf counting			
	2D images		3D model		2D images		3D model	
	M	SD	M	SD	M	SD	M	SD
Task accuracy (%)	69.6	20	70.4		44.9		26.1	
Task completion time (sec)	42.74	15.05	53.54	17.60	84.68	31.23	82.71	33.97

With the plant height estimation, the average accuracy rate that participants obtained from 2D and 3D data visualization were not significantly different (see Fig. 9, p >> 0.05). However, average task completion time with 3D models was longer than that with 2D images (see Fig. 10, p = 0.034). Therefore, on average, the participants achieved the same accuracy rate with both 2D and 3D visualization, but they spent more time on the question using a 3D data visualization than with a 2D data visualization.

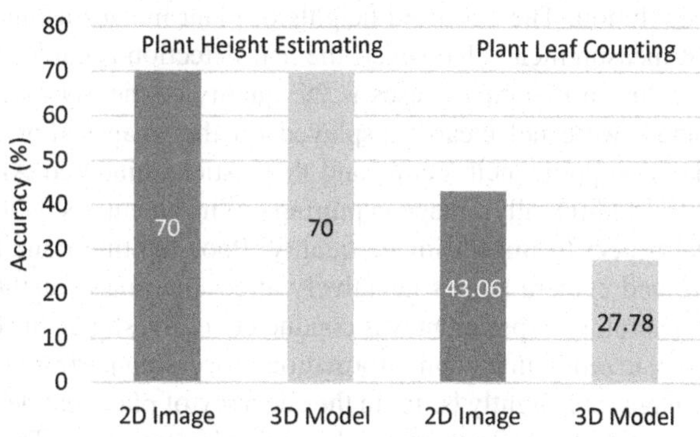

Fig. 9. Accuracy results of plan height estimating and leaf counting tasks

For leaves counting task, the average accuracy rate achieved from 2D images was higher than 3D model (p = 0.024). In detail, the accuracy rate when using 2D images was 43.06% while the accuracy rate when using 3D model was 27.78%. However, average task completion times for 2D images and 3D model were not significantly different (see Fig. 10). The completion time with 2D images equaled 84.2 s and the completion time with a 3D model equaled 82.9 s (p >> 0.05).

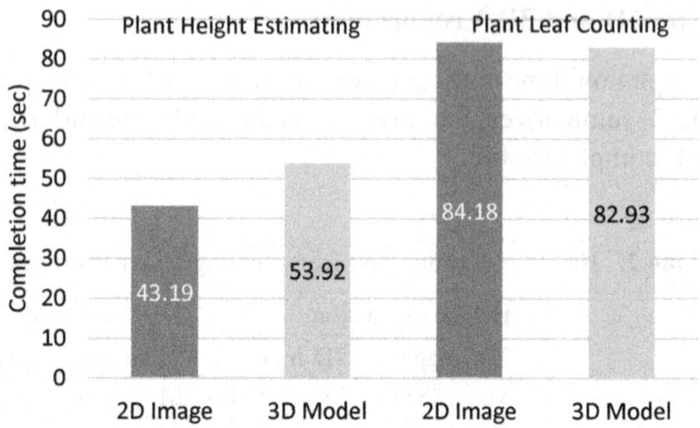

Fig. 10. Task completion time results of plan height estimating and leaf counting tasks

5 Discussion and Conclusion

In this study, 2D and 3D visualization of plant structural features were developed from an AFES and compared to evaluate effectiveness of different data visualization formats. The AFES enables building 3D models by estimated heights and volumes of plant images, and it also can detect leaves by machine learning approach using the YOLO algorithm. The algorithm was trained and improved by 213 images with 20,000 iterations. The leaf detection levels depend on the quality of the 3D model and the captured image resolution. The extracted heights of plant images using AFES are well matched to actual measurements. However, the leaf detection accuracy did not reach a satisfactory level. One of potential causes is the quality of the 3D model. Some plant structural parameters were not clearly displayed on the images. For example, some plants need sticks to support their stems, and these sticks hindered AFES to develop precise 3D models. Additionally, image capturing environment needs to be considered as another critical aspect to impact image quality. Poor lighting conditions and inappropriate aperture and camera angles negatively affect the image quality.

A controlled laboratory experiment was conducted to investigate the effectiveness of 2D and 3D data visualization in human information processing performance. The results showed that 2D images are slightly better in the accuracy of plant leaf detecting task, but similar accuracies were shown in the plant height estimating task. This indicated that data visualization dimensions do not much affect the detection of image contours, but 3D model requires more efforts in image content recognition. In task completion times, opposite patterns were appeared. Image content recognition spent similar amount time to complete tasks in both visualization formats, but 3D model needed more time to complete in the detection of image contours. Therefore, 2D images are marginally better in both accuracy and task completion time than 3D models in plant structural analysis. This study compared the impacts of two different data visualization formats on information processing performance, and 2D image format is preferred in plant feature acquisition and detection. However, the tasks used in the study are limited, and more diverse tasks should be investigated to deliver more generalizable conclusion on different data visualization formats in information perception.

References

1. Rahaman, M., Chen, D., Gillani, Z., Klukas, C., Chen, M.: Advanced phenotyping and phenotype data analysis for the study of plant growth and development. Front. Plant Sci. **6**, 619 (2015)
2. Coppens, F., Wuyts, N., Inzé, D., Dhondt, S.: Unlocking the potential of plant phenotyping data through integration and data-driven approaches. Curr. Opinion Syst. Biol. **4**, 58–63 (2017)
3. Tripodi, P., Massa, D., Venezia, A., Cardi, T.: Sensing technologies for precision phenotyping in vegetable crops: current status and future challenges. Agronomy **8**(4), 57 (2018)
4. Kosslyn, S.M.: Graphics and human information processing: a review of five books. J. Am. Stat. Assoc. **80**(391), 499–512 (1985)
5. Yang, C.C., Prasher, S.O., Landry, J.A., Perret, J., Ramaswamy, H.S.: Recognition of weeds with image processing and their use with fuzzy logic for precision farming. Can. Agric. Eng. **42**(4), 195–200 (2000)
6. Puchalski, C., Gorzelany, J., Zagula, G., Brusewitz, G.: Image analysis for apple defect detection. Biosyst. Agric. Eng. **8**, 197–205 (2008)
7. Jin, J., Li, J., Liao, G., Yu, X., Viray, L.C.C.: Methodology for potatoes defects detection with computer vision. In: Proceedings. The 2009 International Symposium on Information Processing (ISIP 2009), p. 346 (2009)
8. Kelman, E.E., Linker, R.: Vision-based localisation of mature apples in tree images using convexity. Biosyst. Eng. **118**, 174–185 (2014)
9. Reis, M.J., et al.: Automatic detection of bunches of grapes in natural environment from color images. J. Appl. Logic **10**(4), 285–290 (2012)
10. Sansao, J.P., Jnior, M.S., Mozelli, L.A., Pinto, F.A., Queiroz, D.M.: Weed mapping using digital images. In: Proceedings of International Conference on Agricultural Engineering-CIGR (2012)
11. Romeo, J., Pajares, G., Montalvo, M., Guerrero, J.M., Guijarro, M., de la Cruz, J.M.: A new expert system for greenness identification in agricultural images. Expert Syst. Appl. **40**(6), 2275–2286 (2013)
12. Risden, K., Czerwinski, M.P., Munzner, T., Cook, D.B.: An initial examination of ease of use for 2D and 3D information visualizations of web content. Int. J. Hum. Comput. Stud. **53** (5), 695–714 (2000)
13. Althoff, D.-I.F., McGlaun, G., Lang, M., Rigoll, G.: Comparing an innovative 3D and a standard 2D user interface for automotive infotainment applications. In: Mensch & Computer 2003. Berichte des German Chapter of the ACM, vol. 57, pp. 53–63. Vieweg + Teubner Verlag (2003). https://doi.org/10.1007/978-3-322-80058-9_7
14. Barfield, W., Robless, R.: The effects of two-or three-dimensional graphics on the problem-solving performance of experienced and novice decision makers. Behav. Inf. Technol. **8**(5), 369–385 (1989)
15. Henderson, M., Shurville, S., Fernstrom, K., Stewart, B.M., Cipolla, J.M., Best, L.A.: Extraneous information and graph comprehension: Implications for effective design choices. Campus Wide Inf. Syst. **26**(3), 191–200 (2009)
16. Kim, K., Proctor, R.W., Salvendy, G.: Comparison of 3D and 2D menus for cell phones. Comput. Hum. Behav. **27**(5), 2056–2066 (2011)
17. Ware, C.: Designing with a 2 1/2-D attitude. Inf. Des. J. **10**(3), 258 (2001)
18. Li, L., Zhang, Q., Huang, D.: A review of imaging techniques for plant phenotyping. Sensors **14**(11), 20078–20111 (2014)

19. Schlichting, C.D.: The evolution of phenotypic plasticity in plants. Ann. Rev. Ecol. Syst. **17** (1), 667–693 (1986)
20. Fiorani, F., Schurr, U.: Future scenarios for plant phenotyping. Ann. Rev. Plant Biol. **64**, 267–291 (2013)
21. Hoffmann, V., Probst, K., Christinck, A.: Farmers and researchers: how can collaborative advantages be created in participatory research and technology development? Agric. Hum. Values **24**(3), 355–368 (2007)
22. Autodesk, AutoDesk Recap Pro
23. McHenry, K., Bajcsy, K.: An overview of 3D data content, file formats and viewers. National Center for Supercomputing Applications, vol. 1205, p. 22 (2008)
24. Bellard, F.: “About FFmpeg,” About FFmpeg. https://www.ffmpeg.org/about.html. Accessed 14 Feb 2019
25. Redmon, J., Farhadi, A.: YOLO9000: better, faster, stronger, arXiv preprint (2017)

Interface Information Visualization of Intelligent Control System Based on Visual Cognitive Behavior

Weiwei Zhang[1], Xiaoli Wu[1(✉)], Linlin Wang[1], Yiyao Zou[1], and Hui Zheng[2]

[1] College of Mechanical and Electrical Engineering, Hohai University, Changzhou 213022, China
18362991397@163.com, wuxlhhu@163.com
[2] Trina Solar Energy Co. Ltd., Changzhou 213100, China

Abstract. A typical intelligent control system, Trina Solar MES production line, is studied in this paper. To begin with, the system information characterization and encoding method are determined through the behavior experiment. Then, the layout of interface graphic elements and system information is found through eye movement experiment. The result indicated that, visual design model of intelligent control systems is set up based on cognitive behavior process and the best layout, which provides enterprises with realizable and optimized design strategy. That is applied to the MES production line of information control system in Trina Solar Technology Company. In conclusion, it provides theoretical support, physiological analysis methods and technical means for the research of information interface design from the perspective of behavior and physiological science so as to guarantee the enterprise's safe and efficient production.

Keywords: Intelligent control system · Information interface · Visualization

1 Introduction

With the rapid development of computer technology and information control theory, the control system becomes more complex and intelligent. The complex human-computer interactive process increases the operators' cognitive load when operators perform tasks such as production, scheduling and so on. When operators consume too much cognitive load, they are prone to operating errors and may even cause fatal accidents. In order to reduce the operators' cognitive friction and improve work efficiency, it is urgent to carry out reasonable characterization; coding and layout design of the huge and complex information in intelligent control system and find out the visual design model of intelligent control system. The rational visual design of intelligent control system plays an important role in maintaining the safety and stability of production and operation in large enterprises. Based on the relationship between intelligent control system and visualization, this paper takes the interface of intelligent control system as the research object and puts forward the method of reasonable visual design in intelligent control system (Fig. 1).

S. Yamamoto and H. Mori (Eds.): HCII 2019, LNCS 11569, pp. 237–249, 2019.
https://doi.org/10.1007/978-3-030-22660-2_16

Fig. 1. Monitoring interface of intelligent control system

2 Background

In recent years, many major accidents, such as nuclear explosions and aircraft crashes, have made us aware of the importance of interface design of control system. Some scholars mainly study the design of control interface from the perspective of human cognition, and some scholars study the design method of control interface. The following is a summary of the research status and dynamics at home and abroad, from the aspects of psychological cognition process, information visualization characterization, interface layout principles and other related fields.

2.1 Research on the Psychological Cognitive Process of Intelligent Control System Operators

In terms of psychological cognition process, Chen et al. [1] uses cognitive psychology to extract interface feature elements to achieve a fast understanding of the dynamic visualization of complex data. Wu [2–5] studies the visual limitation physiological experiment method of information interaction interface and analyzes the root causes of information omission and misperception in the process of visual search. Li et al. [6] found that visual perception stratification can be performed with the degree of attentional capture. And Zeng [7] believes that the core idea of information structure design of interactive interface is to make information adapted to the regularity of human visual perception with gestalt as the guiding principle and structuration as a method. And Li et al. [8] believe that too many human-machine interfaces will cause the cognitive load becomes heavier for the operators and the selection becomes difficult. According to a study by George A. Miller, psychologists, the information amount for humans to receive cognitive knowledge at one time should be 7 ± 2 bits. Through the study of the operator's cognitive process, information visualization and interface layout design can be effectively guided.

2.2 Research on Information Visualization and Interface Layout Design

In terms of information visualization, Annie [9] and Dong [10] conducted an experimental study on the visualization of automobile navigation; Reda et al. [11] studied how to visualize heterogeneous data sets; Basole et al. [12] discussed node-based view methods for visualization of big data; Christopher et al. [13] use graphical sorting algorithms and visual similarity matrix data for visual analysis. And Wang [14] believes that interface design should enable users to form a unified system in visual cognition. Besides, in the field of information visualization, many scholars have studied the methods and principles of visualization and their theories provide a good design reference for the later visualization of the interface of the intelligent control system.

In terms of interface layout principles, Kim [15] proposed the layout of the display interface according to the idea of queue, orientation and placement. Dowsland [16] pointed out that the layout problem refers to give layout space and a number of objects to be distributed and place the objects in the given layout space in a reasonable manner that can satisfy constraints in order to reach an optimal index. Guo [17] made a general consideration of the interface design of software users and proposed the design method of the icon. Chen [18] visually divided the interface into two parts: frame structure and visual elements and proposed optimization suggestions for the reading interface. Liu et al. [19] introduced the human-machine interface design method for the main control room of nuclear power plants based on human factors engineering to prevent and reduce human error. Yang et al. [20] studied the design of the digital interface of system of nuclear power plants from several aspects, such as human-machine interface design and display screen design, etc. By studying display and control interface of the aircraft cockpit, Liu [21] found that the information transmission designed by the principle of information importance and frequency of use is more reasonable. Wang et al. [22] studied the layout design of the display and control interface of the new generation of fighters and proposed a complex system interface layout method. Li et al. [23] proposed the design criteria of the display and control interface started from the perspective of uses. Hong [24] studied how to design a set of integrated information visualization scheduling, operating and controlling platform through reasonable design. Li et al. [25] proposed an interface layout scheme based on visual cognition and interaction habits.

Kamran [26] and Lee [27] proposed that a complete layout process can be extracted through the accumulation of experience. In addition, Amadieu et al. [28–31] studied the interface color and proposed that red, yellow and blue are colors that are the most attractive. At present, there are a lot of researches on information visualization and interface layout, but there is still a lack of research on the monitoring interface layout of intelligent control systems, so the research in this paper is of great significance.

3 Information Visualization of Intelligent Control System Monitoring Interface

3.1 Information Presentation

Taking the MES production line of Trina Solar co. LTD as a sample, this paper collects the workshop information and selects 8 procedures on the workshop assembly line as samples to analyze the functional characteristics of each processes, and also refers to Chengqi's [32] design guidelines of optimization of icons, which are "identification", "normative", "aesthetic", and "style unification" and adaptation to the trend of the times to visualize icon design. And the E-prime behavior experiment is performed on the icon, and the icon is further optimized by the correct rate and reaction time. As shown in Fig. 2, the optimized process icon is shown.

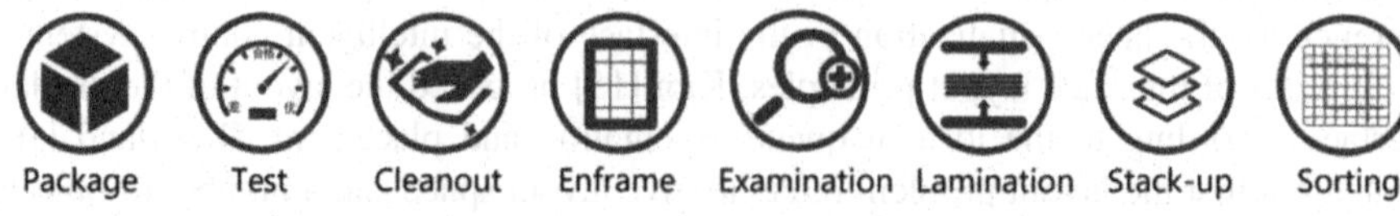

Fig. 2. Visualization of 8 process - icon design

3.2 Interface Layout

As shown in Fig. 3, the interface layout design of the monitoring interface of Trina Solar MES system takes Trina Solar MES as a sample and employs the icons showed above, which is also combined with the basic layout principles proposed by Chengqi [32]: classification principle, frequency principle, importance principle, control and display compatibility principle.

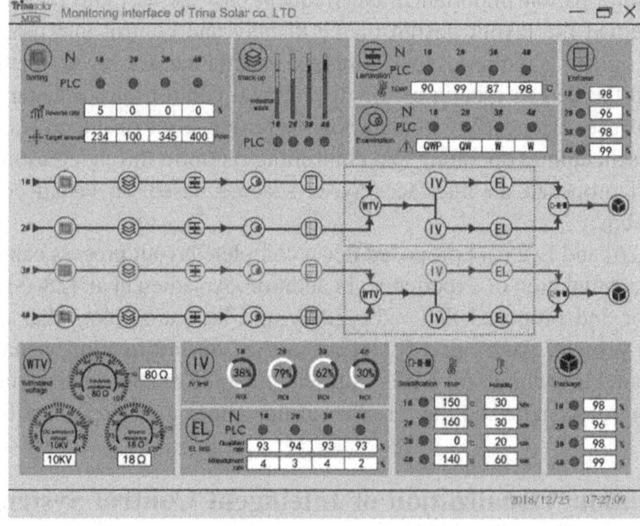

Fig. 3. Monitoring interface design of Trina solar co. LTD MES production line

4 Experiment

4.1 Experiment Objectives

The purpose of the experiment is to study the impact of changes in the layout of the monitoring interface of the production line's control system on human cognitive load.

And the experiment is to find the optimal visualization mode of the monitoring interface by analyzing the influence of the changes of three factors (layout scheme, whether there is a warning box in the fault area or not, and how information blocks are presented) of the interface on the user's cognitive effect through Trina Solar's monitoring interface.

4.2 Experiment Design

The experiment takes the Trina Solar monitoring interface as the sample and employs three factors (layout scheme, whether there is a warning box in the fault area or not, and how information blocks are presented) as independent variables to do the data analysis through behavior indexes and visual physiological indexes.

As shown in Table 1, there are three tasks in the experiment and each task has two forms. Each form has three random experimental materials with a total of 2 × 3 × 3 stimulus materials randomly presented.

Table 1. Task type

Task types of experiments					
task one : interface layout		task two : without/with warning box		task three : Presentation of information Blocks	
shown in three lines	Around center	without warning box	with warning box	the warning lights displayed horizontally	The warning Lights displayd vertically
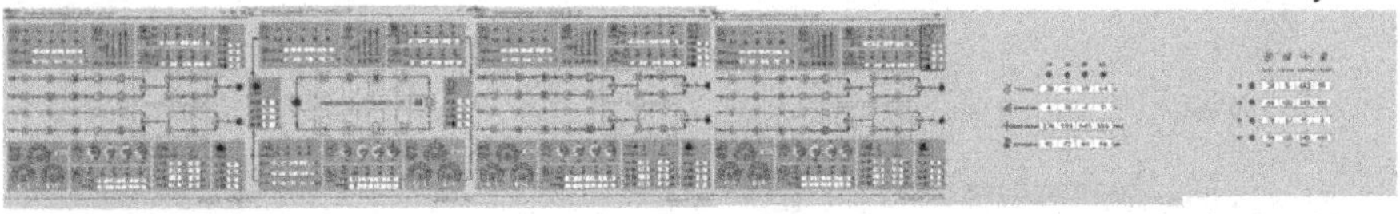					
Three search tasks: lamination2#、enframe4#、 IV test2#		Three search tasks: lamination2#、enframe4#、 IV test2#		Three search tasks:2#target amount、3# temperature、4#reverse rate	

4.3 Experimental Equipment and Participants

The experiment introduces the stimulus material into the studio system of the eye tracking device TobiiX120 and sets the target and task materials. The experiment was carried out in the Human-Computer Interaction Laboratory of Hohai University, and 15 college students of engineering were selected as the participants. The eye tracking device recorded the search time of each task material of each participant and some related physiological index of reaction of eye movement.

5 Results

5.1 Behavioral Data

A total of 15 participants were selected for the experiment, and 12 people with data collection rate greater than 80% were selected. The data of 9 people was finally used in data analysis of the experiment.

(1) Correct Rate. With no time limits, the correct rate for both task one and task two is 100%. There are differences in the correct rates of the two presentations of the information block of task three. And after analyzing the variance of the correct rate, the conclusion is that the main effects ($F = 29.469$, $p = 0.006$, $p < 0.01$) of different information presentation were significant. The correct rate of the horizontal display of the warning light is 100%, and the correct rate of the vertical display of the warning light is 89%. It is considered that the searching effect of horizontal display of the warning information in the information block is better.

(2) Total Visit Duration. After analyzing the variance of the reaction time of three different independent variables, it was found that the main effects (layout scheme: $F = 12.704$, $P = 0.023$, $p < 0.05$; with or without a warning boxes: $F = 16.522$; $P = 0.015$, $p < 0.05$, the way information blocks are presented: $F = 12.976$, $P = 0.023$, $p < 0.05$) were significant.

As shown in Fig. 4, when the layout scheme is around center with warning boxes and warning lights for horizontal display, the search time is shorter, the search efficiency better, and the presentation of the interface better.

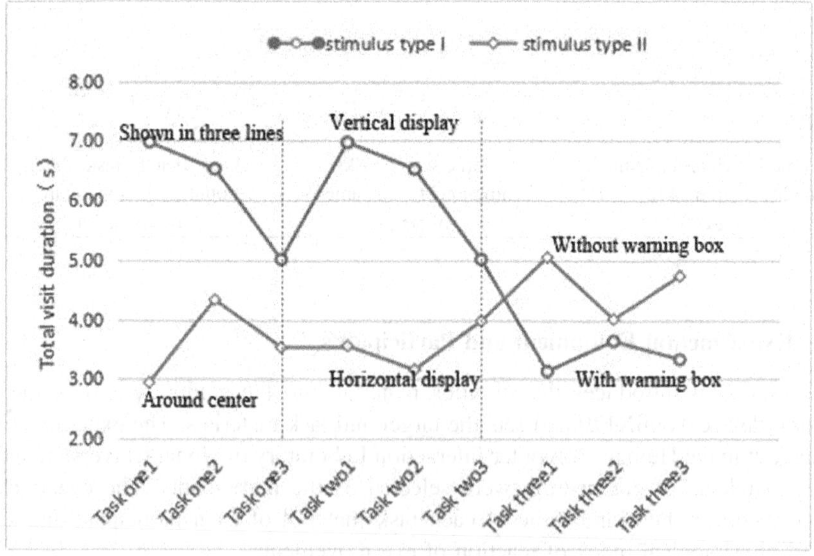

Fig. 4. Comparison of reaction time of experiment tasks

5.2 Visual Physiological Data

(1) Analysis of Index of AOI. The times of fixations refers to the total number of times of gazing, indicating the number of times the participant is looking for task information and performing cognitive processing. Fixation in AOI refers to the number of times the participants performing cognitive processing in the information area and the total fixation indicates the number of times the participants performing cognitive processing on the entire task interface. The higher the ratio of fixation in AOI, the higher the search efficiency. As shown in Table 2, through the variance analysis of fixations in AOI, it was found that the main effects (layout scheme: $F = 147$, $P = 0$, $p < 0.01$; with or without warning boxes: $F = 34.926$, $P = 0.004$, $p < 0.01$) were significant. The main effect ($F = 0.014$, $P = 0.912$, $p > 0.05$) of the warning light presentation is not significant.
Therefore, the layout scheme and the search efficiency of the warning box (with or without) can be analyzed by the ratio of fixations in AOI to the total number of times of fixations. From the ratio of fixations in AOI to the total times of fixations (shown in three lines: 36%, around center: 82%, without warning box: 36%, with warning box: 80%), it is found that the around center layout and the search box with warning boxes are more efficient.

Table 2. Analysis of variance of fixation in AOI

Variance analysis of ANOVA (dependent variable: points in AOI)						
Unit: piece		Sum of squares	df	Mean square	F	P
Layout scheme	Inter block	30.106	1	30.106	147.000	.000
	Interclass	.819	4	.205		
	Total	30.925	5			
With/without warning box	Inter block	42.667	1	42.667	34.926	.004
	Interclass	4.886	4	1.222		
	Total	47.553	5			
The way the information blocks are presented	Inter block	.054	1	.054	.014	.912
	Interclass	15.651	4	3.913		
	Total	15.705	5			

(2) Fixation. In the cognitive process, the fixation is closely related to the cognitive activities of the brain. When the brain thinks, eyes won't gaze, and the pause time will grow longer as the thinking time becomes longer. From the operator's gaze duration, the time spent on cognitive activities can be roughly observed. As shown in Table 3, through the variance analysis of gaze duration in AOI, it was found that the main effects (layout scheme: $F = 15.696$, $P = 0.017$, $p < 0.05$; with or without warning boxes: $F = 10.886$, $P = 0.030$, $p < 0.05$; the way information blocks are presented: $F = 46.486$, $P = 0.002$, $p < 0.05$) were significant.

Therefore, the search efficiency can be analyzed by the gaze time. As shown in Fig. 5, in the case that the correct target is found, the gaze duration is longer when the layout scheme is around center, with warning boxes and the warning lights are displayed horizontally, and the search efficiency and the interface presentation are better.

Table 3. The variance analysis of fixation duration

Variance analysis of ANOVA (dependent variable: fixation duration)						
Unit: MS		Sum of squares	df	Mean square	F	P
Layout scheme	Inter block	12125537.200	1	12125537.200	15.696	.017
	Interclass	3090038.802	4	772509.701		
	Total	15215576.003	5			
With/without warning box	Inter block	10881659.208	1	10881659.208	10.886	.030
	Interclass	3998260.633	4	999565.158		
	Total	14879919.841	5			
The way the information blocks are presented	Inter block	6955977.285	1	6955977.285	46.486	.002
	Interclass	598544.395	4	149636.099		
	Total	7554521.680	5			

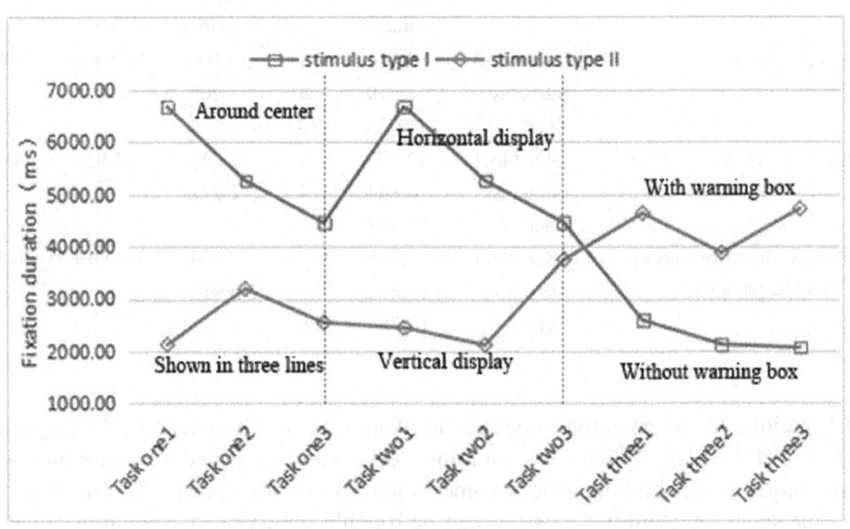

Fig. 5. Comparison of gaze duration of experimental tasks

(2) Saccade. Saccade is the process of visually finding a target. When an operator searches for a target, the movement of the eye appears as a saccade. And if the operator can quickly find the target, the number of times saccades will be less. As shown in Table 4, through the variance analysis of the number of times saccades, it was found that the main effects (layout scheme: $F = 8.699$, $P = 0.042$, $p < 0.05$; with or without warning boxes: $F = 8.017$, $P = 0.047$, $p < 0.05$; the way information blocks are presented: $F = 9.306$, $P = 0.038$, $p < 0.05$) were significant.

Table 4. Variance analysis of the times of saccades

Variance analysis of ANOVA (dependent variable: saccades times)						
Unit: time		Sum of squares	df	Mean square	F	P
Layout scheme	Inter block	76.755	1	76.755	8.699	.042
	Interclass	35.294	4	8.823		
	Total	112.049	5			
With/without warning box	Inter block	47.714	1	47.714	8.017	.047
	Interclass	23.805	4	5.951		
	Total	71.520	5			
The way the information blocks are presented	Inter block	39.784	1	39.784	9.306	.038
	Interclass	17.100	4	4.275		
	Total	56.883	5			

Therefore, the search efficiency of the interface layout form and the information block presentation mode can be compared by the times of saccades. As shown in Fig. 6, in the case that the correct target is found, saccades are lesser when the layout scheme is around center, with warning boxes and the warning lights are displayed horizontally, and the search efficiency and the interface presentation are better.

(4) Fixation/Saccade Ratio. The formula for visual search efficiency proposed by Goldberg and Kotval [33] is as follows:

$$\text{Ratio} = \frac{\textit{time for the cognation to process information}(f)}{\textit{Time to search for information}(s)}$$

In the formula, time for the cognation to process information refers to the gaze duration, which is *f*; time to search for information refers to saccade, as which is *s* therefore:

$$\text{R shown in three lines} = \frac{\text{f}}{\text{s}} = \frac{5463}{1594} = 3.4$$

$$\text{R around center} = \frac{\text{f}}{\text{s}} = \frac{2620}{547} = 4.8$$

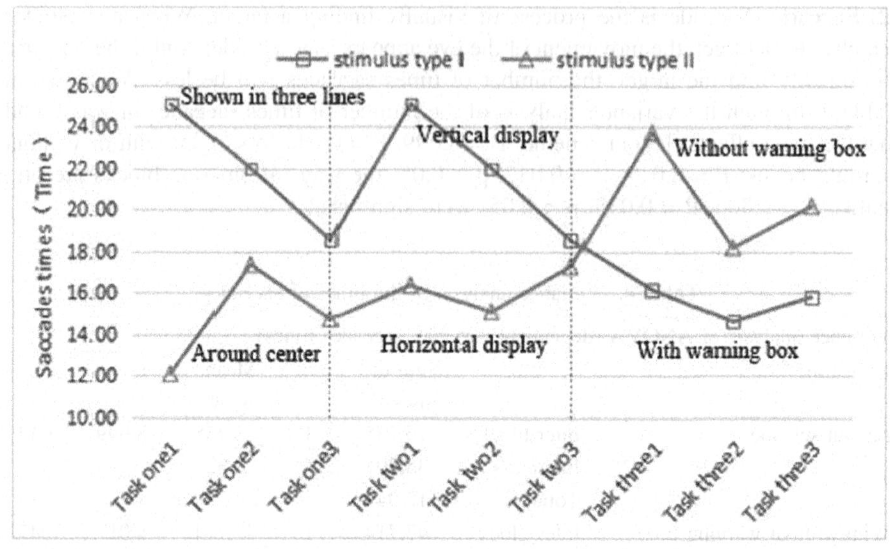

Fig. 6. Comparison of times of saccades

$$R\,\textit{without warning box} = \frac{f}{s} = \frac{5463}{1594} = 3.4$$

$$R\,\textit{with warning box} = \frac{f}{s} = \frac{2769}{738} = 3.8$$

$$R\,\text{horizontal display} = \frac{f}{s} = \frac{2257}{605} = 3.7$$

$$R\,\text{vertical display} = \frac{f}{s} = \frac{4410}{959} = 3.6$$

The search efficiency can explain the advantages and disadvantages of the information layout of the interface. The time for cognition to process should be much longer than the time for searching information, that is, the value of Ratio is greater than 1. And, the larger the number, the higher the search efficiency. It can be clearly seen from the number that when the layout scheme is around center, with warning boxes and the warning lights are displayed horizontally, the number is larger, the search efficiency is better, the search efficiency is greater than when the warning information is vertical displayed.

5.3 Optimized Design of the Interface

The experiment finds that when the interface layout is around center, warning boxes in the fault zone and warning information in the information block are arranged horizontally, the efficiency is higher. Thus, the layout of the monitoring interface is arranged in the way listed above, as shown in Fig. 7.

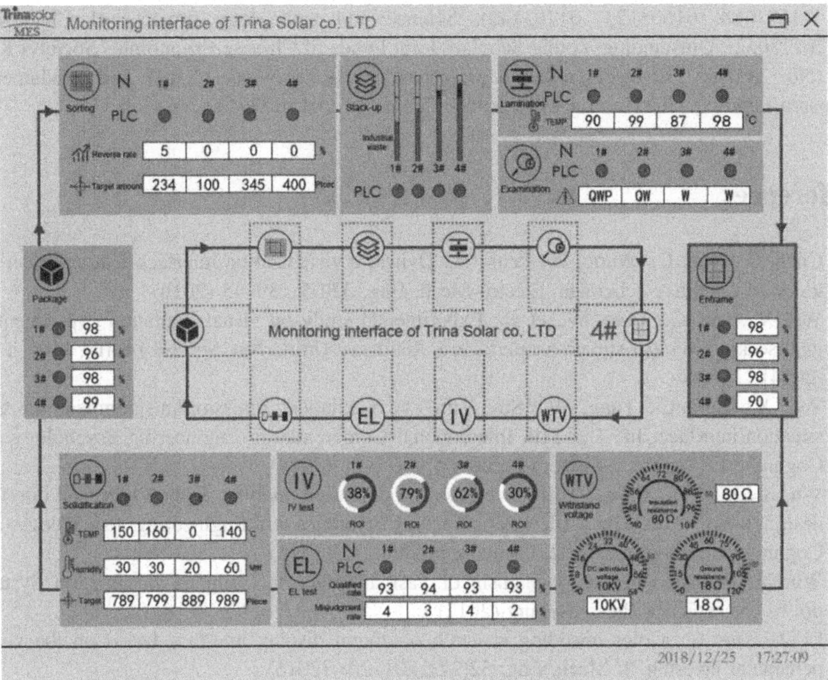

Fig. 7. Optimized design of the monitoring interface for Trina Solar co. LTD's production line

6 Conclusion

When the information icon of the monitoring interface is presented in a blue circle without shading, the search efficiency is higher; the layout of the monitoring interface is better selected as around center, and the information block should be surrounded by the annular production line, so that the search path is relatively short and the efficiency is higher; the warning boxes in the fault area is more easily found by the operators; and when the warning information in the information block is arranged horizontally, the search time is short.

According to the operator's psychological cognition process, information display and principle of interface layout, a monitoring interface in this paper is designed for Trina Solar's MES production line and a design interface is proposed for the monitoring interface of intelligent control system for large enterprises. It is hoped to provide enterprises with feasible optimization strategies and to provide theoretical support, physiological analysis methods and techniques for design and research of information interface from the perspective of behavioral and physiological science, so as to ensure the safe and efficient production of enterprises.

Acknowledgement. This work was supported by Jiangsu Province Nature Science Foundation of China (BK20181159, BK20170304), Jiangsu Province Key Project of philosophy and the social sciences (2017ZDIXM023), the National Nature Science Foundation of China (Grant No. 71601068, 61603123, 61703140), Science and technology projects of Changzhou (CE20175032), Outstanding Young Scholars Joint Funds of Chinese Ergonomics Society- King Far (No. 2017-05), Overseas research project of Jiangsu Province (2017), and Fundamental Research Funds for the Central Universities (Grant No. 2015B22714).

References

1. Chen, C., Xue, C., Wang, H., Peng, N.: Dynamic visualization interface feature under the guide of cognitive schemata. Electro-Mech. Eng. **32**(05), 39–43 (2016)
2. Wu, X., Xue, C., Tang, W., et al.: Experimental study on visual limitation experiment of goal-seeking in radar situation-interface. J. Southeast Univ. (Nat. Sci. Ed.) **44**(6), 1166–1170 (2014)
3. Wu, X., Xue, C., Tang, W.: Study on eye movement omission/misjudgment in rader situation-interface. In: The 11th International Conference on Engineering Psychology and Cognitive Ergonomics, Grete, Greece, pp. 407–418 (2014)
4. Wu, X., Xue, C., Zhou, F.: Misperception model-based analytic method of visual interface design factors. In: The 11th International Conference on Engineering Psychology and Cognitive Ergonomics, Grete, Greece, pp. 284–292 (2014)
5. Wu, X.: Error-Cognition Mechanism of Task Interface in Complex Information System, pp. 61–68. Science Press, Beijing (2017)
6. Li, J., Xue, C.: Color encoding research of digital display interface based on the visual perceptual layering. J. Mech. Eng. **52**(24), 201–208 (2016)
7. Zeng, J.: Information structure design of interactive interface based on gestalt theory. Light. Ind. Sci. Technol. **30**(06), 95–96 (2014)
8. Li, J., Xue, C., Tang, W., et al.: Color saliency research on visual perceptual layering method. In: 11th International Conference on Engineering Psychology and Cognitive Ergonomics, Crete, pp. 86–97 (2014)
9. Rydström, A., Broström, R., Bengtsson, P.: A comparison of two contemporary types of in-car multifunctional interfaces. Appl. Ergon. **43**(3), 507–514 (2012)
10. Lee, D.-S.: The effect of visualizing the flow of multimedia content among and inside devices. Appl. Ergon. **40**(3), 440–447 (2009)
11. Khairi, R., Alessandro, F., Aaron, K.: Visualizing large heterogeneous data in hybrid-reality environments. IEEE Comput. Graph. Appl. **33**(4), 38–48 (2013)
12. Basole, R.C., Clear, T., Hu, M.: Understanding interfirm relationships in business ecosystems with interactive visualization. IEEE Trans. Vis. Comput. Graph. **19**(12), 2526–2535 (2013)
13. Mueller, C., Martin, B., Lumsdaine, A.: A comparison of vertex ordering algorithms for large graph visualization. In: Asia/Pacific Symposium on Visualisation, Sydney, Australia, pp. 141–148 (2007)

14. Wang, H.-Y.: Boeing 737-Type Aircraft Cockpit Interface Concept Design. Southeast University (2017)
15. Kim, W.C., Foley, J.D.: Providing high-level control and expert assistance in the user interface presentation design. In: Conference on Human Factors in Computing Systems, pp. 430–436 (1993)
16. Dowsland, K.A., Dowsland, W.B.: Packing problems. Eur. J. Oper. Res. **56**(1), 2–14 (1992)
17. Guo, X.: Research on the Usability of Software User Interface Based On Icon Design. Nanjing University of Aeronautics and Astronautics (2012)
18. Chen, Y., Xu, M.: Comparison and optimization in digital reading interface visual design. Design **2018**(17), 132–135 (2018)
19. Liu, S., Tian, R.: Design of man-machine interface in main control room of nuclear power plant based on human factors engineering. Autom. Appl. **2014**(06), 49–51 (2014)
20. Yang, Q., Yang, Y., Bai, J.: Design of HMI for digital system of nuclear power plant. Sci. Technol. Vis. **2014**(09), 10–11 (2014)
21. Liu, X.: The Optimization of Display Interface in Light Aircraft Cokpit. Shenyang Aerospace University (2018)
22. Wang, H.-Y., Bian, T., Xue, C.: Layout design of display interface for a new generation fighter. Electro-Mech. Eng. **27**(04), 57–61 (2011)
23. Li, Y., Qian, R., Zhang, Y.: Research on one method of vehicle display and control UI design. Veh. Power Technol. **2015**(03), 35–40+59 (2015)
24. Hong, J.: Large screen display system solution in intelligent command platform. Electron. Technol. Softw. Eng. **2016**(10), 81 (2016)
25. Li, F., Gan, J., Chen, H., Luo, J., Wang, J.: Layout design of interface for scientific experimental system. Pack. Eng. **38**(12), 169–173 (2017)
26. Kamran, D., Maziar, A., Hossein, S.: FARAGAM algorithm in satellite layout. In: Proceedings of the Sixth Asia-Pacific Conference on Multilateral Cooperation in Space Technology and Applications, Beijing, pp. 120–127 (2001)
27. Lee, Y.C., Lee, J.D., Boyle, L.N.: The interaction of cognitive load and attention-directing cues in driving. Hum. Factors Ergon. Soc. **51**(3), 271–280 (2009)
28. Amadieu, F., Marine, C., Laimay, C.: The attention guiding effect and cognitive load in the comprehension of animations. Comput. Hum. Behav. **27**(1), 36–40 (2011)
29. Liang, J., Zhen, L., Zhou, Y., Liu, S.: Ergonomics of encoding color matching on display interface. Ship Electron. Eng. **36**(05), 109–111 (2016)
30. Cui, K.: The analysis of the cockpit display interface's color effects on novice drivers' visual pre-attentive progress. Chin. J. Ergon. **20**(02), 35–40+24 (2014)
31. Zhang, L., Zhuang, D.: Color matching of aircraft interface design. J. Beijing Univ. Aeronaut. Astronaut. **35**(08), 1001–1004 (2009)
32. Xue, C.: The Design Method and Application of Digitalized Human-Computer Interface on Complex Information System, pp. 169–173. Southeast University Press, Nanjing (2015)
33. Goldberg, J.H., Kotval, X.: Computer interface evaluation using eye movements: methods and constructs. Int. J. Ind. Ergon. **24**, 631–645 (1999)

Story Envisioning Framework for Visualized Collective Storytelling in Conversation

Qiang Zhang[1,2](✉), Maryam Sadat Mirzaei[1,2](✉), Hung-Hsuan Huang[2](✉), and Toyoaki Nishida[1,2](✉)

[1] Graduate School of Informatics, Kyoto University, Kyoto, Japan
zhang.qiang.84n@st.kyoto-u.ac.jp,
nishida.toyoaki.4e@kyoto-u.ac.jp
[2] RIKEN-AIP, Kyoto, Japan
{maryam.mirzaei,hung-hsuan.huang}@riken.jp

Abstract. In this paper, we introduce the method of story envisioning as an efficient approach to collective storytelling in daily conversation and training procedure. The goal of story envisioning is to provide intuitive, concrete and consistent visualization contents as interactive drama for storytellers who are not professional at storytelling. We employ graphic recording to symbolize and visualize the stories written in natural language. We built a partially automated framework TSEiA that allows storytellers to visualize and edit the stories. By traversing through the whole story structure, storytellers are also able to compare and analyze different consequences of branches. Preliminary experiments showed that using visualized interactive drama can help participants have better understanding to the conversation from culture and personality viewpoint. Simultaneously, story envisioning could help the storytellers organize the story structure in a better way and enhance the immersion of their stories. Game platform powered by TSEiA was built to illustrate how story envisioning could be considered as an effective tool for collective storytelling and content generation.

Keywords: Storytelling · Story envisioning · Conversation analysis

1 Introduction

Conversation plays an important role in sharing information, knowledge, thoughts and emotions in human society. Conversation allows people to transmit implied thoughts and experience in their mind and share them with others based on culture and knowledge background [1]. Considered as part of highest-level intelligence of human, conversation skill is frequently studied in the filed of AI. Nishida, etc looked at conversation from five viewpoints: *verbal communication* as central element, *nonverbal communication* as emotion indicators, *social*

S. Yamamoto and H. Mori (Eds.): HCII 2019, LNCS 11569, pp. 250–261, 2019.
https://doi.org/10.1007/978-3-030-22660-2_17

discourse as social implications, *narratives and content* as content structure and *cognitive process* as mental processing [2].

From these viewpoints, conversation can be considered as a process of exchanging social signals, contents as story pieces which can be represented as components of the larger story [2]. This property of conversation leads to the irregularities of order and duration which eventually constructs the complicatedly hierarchical discourses structure of conversation.

Serving as an inevitable part of conversational and cultural activities, storytelling is an essential method of sharing experience and knowledge. Storytelling entails the method that mankind organize and package their experience and personal memories as structural stories in daily conversation to help others have a better understanding of the story contents [1]. The method of storytelling has been applied into areas such as education, training, media study, language learning, etc.

In the original idea of storytelling, it also describes the procedure of multiple narrators with different culture background to generate the contents collaboratively. From the studies by Jefferson and Sacks, storytelling in conversation are *locally occasioned, recipient designed* [4] and *co-constructed* [5]. More researches have demonstrated that in conversational storytelling, collaboration among multiple participants plays an important role in content generation. Listeners collaborate with storytellers in substantial ways to exert influence on storytellers [6]. In this procedure, listeners may also provide their own experience and knowledge and add them to the original story. The update of storytelling in daily conversation helps us to create a shared space. This is frequently used to build training system which can train high-level skills containing cultural elements.

However, embedded in human evolution history, storytelling usually demands rich cultural and literal knowledge, which brings difficulties to tell stories. In conversation, inappropriate expressing methods, ambiguous meanings and hierarchical discourses usually complicate the procedures of storytelling. Background knowledge of the story are required to be provided when a third party is willing to join the conversation [7]. These problems are approached by using a method of story visualization. Story is rebuilt in a virtual world in which resources such as characters, animations and objects are used to represent the story contents. Text-to-scene systems inspired the method to generate a static visualized scenario from natural language. Simultaneously, collective storytelling and authoring tools are used to create game-based language training courses. However, using the method of visualized collective storytelling to create and analyze daily conversation remains as blank.

In our research, we claim that story envisioning can serve as both a visualization tool which can assist people to understand conversation better and a collective storytelling tool which can be used for rapid content generation. Story envisioning focuses on facilitating the contents in common ground as interactive drama by treating the conversation as an update of common ground [8]. Rather than directly translating stories into visualized scenarios, story envisioning put more emphasis on rebuilding the whole structure of a conversation to give inspirations on analyzing the high-level interpretations. By creating branches for each interpretation, story envisioning is able to create an visualized shared community in which different people can perceive others' interpretations and leave comments or modifications.

2 Related Work

There have been several systems developed that apply visualized storytelling and collective storytelling. Text-to-scene systems contributed to the initial stage of visualized storytelling. WordsEye [9] represented the approach to creating 3D static scenes by extracting semantic intent of the users. CarSim [10,11] is a program that generates short simple animations from natural language car accident reports. CONFUCIUS [12] is a multimodal systems that takes sentences containing verb as input. More researches by Chang, etc. showed that spatial relationships and objects types in different scenes can be learned from given text knowledge [13,14].

Other researches have focused on developing storytelling systems using various method to represent story. Cassell, etc. created dialogue planner based on topic coherence relations to study user trust on virtual agents [16]. Interactive storytelling system "Say Anything" described the method of providing interactive experience by acquiring large-scale knowledge [17]. Our previous work focusing on a bargaining scenario created storytelling environment in virtual reality to study how misunderstanding are brought to the surface due to culture difference [7]. On top of storytelling, earlier works on collective storytelling and collaborative authoring tools were used in Tactical Iraqi [15], a serious game for learning language and cultural elements. It has been used by a lot of trainees in US military. Recently, visualized collective storytelling and collaborative authoring are frequently embedded in games.

3 Framework TSEiA

To address the goal of story envisioning, we developed system TSEiA (The Story Envisioning Intelligent Assistant). TSEiA provides convenient approaches to story visualization, content management, story traversing and collective storytelling. The framework is designed to solve the problem of information dispersion in daily conversation. The method of using action sequences to represent the story reduced the effort to create repository database. Moreover, experiment shows that using action sequences to represent the story could could retain most of the information.

3.1 Framework Overview

TSEiA is a system mainly built on Unity3D game engine. Together with a natural language processing module and a word embedding module, the system can convert stories in natural language into an animated 3D interactive drama. Functionally, the system contains three modules: *Story Visualization Module, Story Editing Module* and *Collective Storytelling Module* (Fig. 1).

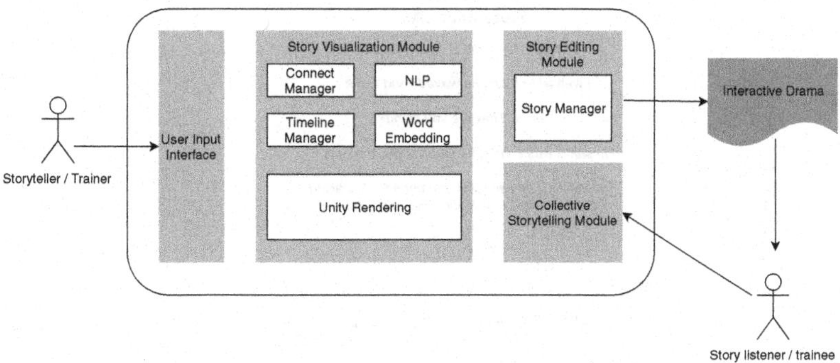

Fig. 1. Architecture of TSEiA

3.2 Story Visualization Module

This module provides services to symbolize and visualize the original story. Story visualization module accepts stories as input and outputs the visualization interactive drama.

Storytelling commonly represents stories as connected events which reveals the information flow [3]. However, on one hand, in daily conversation, the story pieces are highly dispersed throughout the whole conversation. As a result, events are connected inconspicuously and can hardly represent the information flow. On the other hand, from the experience of previous text-to-scene/animation systems, using event to represent story always bring difficulties and limitations for visualization.

In our research, we found that the content of storytelling in daily conversation tends to be more lifelike. Comparing to traditional storytelling, less fictional and legendary elements are being used in storytelling in daily conversation. Instead, storytelling in daily conversation traces a piece of past personal experience, memory or adventure. Individuals put more emphasis on the activities of each subject in their stories. We introduced the method of *action sequence* in which each action represents one activity of a certain object and the whole sequence represents the activity trajectory of this object to stand for stories in daily conversation (Fig. 2).

In TSEiA, original stories are processed by a NLP processor containing rules to extract verbs as "actions". TimelineManager (Fig. 1) dynamically initialize a Unity TimelineAsset according to the action sequences. Assets are loaded from repository database in which resources that are needed to create scenes are downloaded and stored. In order to reduce the effort to prepare for the database, we use word embedding to categorize actions into a smaller space. With the actions labeled by the word embedding module, the rendering engine can visualize the scenario (Fig. 3).

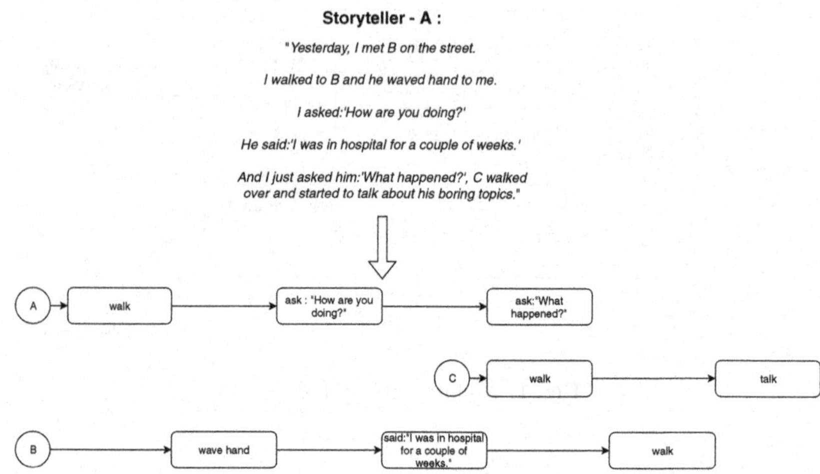

Fig. 2. Action sequence

3.3 Story Editing Module

This module can support user to edit and arrange the story branches. The intelligent story editing module allows storytellers to add, delete, embed, and compare story branches. Each branch contains the visualization of a piece of story. StoryManager (Fig. 1) is managing a story tree to organize and index the story content created by storytellers. This module also provides the function to traverse through each branch, from which storytellers can inspect mistakes and modify the content (Fig. 3). By traversing through different branches, storytellers are able to locate most important verbal or non-verbal signals that can change the direction of the conversation. TSEiA also provides API for storytellers to edit stories dynamically.

3.4 Collective Storytelling Module

As one of our main contribution, this module allows storytellers to accomplish visualized collective storytelling. All the users are considered as both storytellers and story readers. A typical collaboration flow may comply with the following order: (1) A storyteller creates the domain and topic of a conversation and gives some initial visualized branches. (2) The contents those are generated by this storyteller is synchronized through cloud. (3) Other storytellers read these content and give their modifications. (4) New contents are synchronized through cloud. The contents those are generated by all the storytellers are being stored as file and can be shared inside community. Moreover, learning from the data collected from this module, we are able to build the predictive model that can envision some possible branches.

Fig. 3. An Example UI for Story Editing. This UI contains story input area, branch editing area. Storytellers can use "←" and "→" on the keyboard to traverse through the branch.

4 Experiment

In order to show that story envisioning can be an effective method for visualized collective storytelling, an experiment was conducted to answer the following questions:

Q1. Can story envisioning help people have a better understanding of the stories in daily conversation?
Q2. Can story envisioning be helpful to create content for collective storytelling?

We built a game platform powered by TSEiA and conducted experiment with 18 participants. We used a suspense role-playing game platform with the stories that involved multiple characters and human daily relationship.

4.1 Pilot Experiment

Before the real experiment, a pilot experiment was conducted to ensure that our system meets the basic functionality requirements. The pilot experiment contains two phases. In the first phase, some short animated dramas generated by TSEiA are presented to the participants. For each drama, there were five choices containing relevant text to it. The participants need to select the choice from which the drama was generated. In the second phase, participants are requested to create their own drama clips limited to a given repository. By reviewing the final output, participants need to evaluate how much can the system meet their expectations. Participants are also requested to finish the questionnaire after the experiment. Positive results are obtained from the questionnaire.

4.2 Main Experiment

The goal of this experiment is to evaluate how much story envisioning can contribute to content comprehension of storytelling in daily conversation as well as to collective storytelling.

(a) Find Item

(b) Inquire NPCs

(c) Dramas

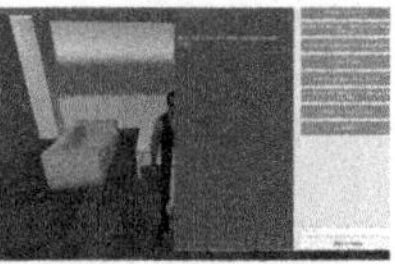

(d) Answer Questions

Fig. 4. Experiment Setting. (a) Participant explore the environment to find evidence items. (b) Participant get information by communicating with the NPC. (c) Drama are presented to the participant. (d) Participant converse to the policeman and answer the question.

Experiment Setting. In this experiment, participants are required to play a suspense role-playing game. Participants are divided into 6 groups where each group contains 3 participants. Participants in the same group independently start the game session at same time. Participant plays the role of a chemist (main character) who is working in a medicine company. The main character's boss died in the office. After investigation, the policeman found out that the boss was poisoned by someone and the poison was actually a new medicine developed by the main character. Other three characters (agents) with unique background are also involved as suspects. Participants are provided with part of background information in text format. In this game setting, the main character needs to explore the environment and search for evidences to show his innocence. The evidences are indicated as special items or agents in the environment (Fig. 4). Once the main character found an evidence, a short animated drama conveying information of the murder will be presented. All dramas are generated by TSEiA from determined stories. For example, one of the evidences in our setting is a video tape. A drama disclosing the content of the video tape is shown to participant once the main character found the tape. There are 6 evidences located at different places in the environment. Participants are not informed the total amount of the evidences prior to the experiment. The more evidences participants can find, the more information they can obtain.

Combining the information obtained from the text and dramas, participants are required to have a conversation with the policeman and answer some questions. For each question, we initially gave 1 to 2 available answers for participants to choose from. However, if participants were not satisfied with the answers being provided, they were able to add their own answers. The answers created by participants in each group were synchronized and available for participants in next group. To be noticed, participants are not informed that the answers are created by other participants prior to the experiment.

We designed two types of question to evaluate both the content comprehension and motivation to create stories of participants. The first type of question is related to the objective content of the story in game. Participants are able to answer this type of question by exploring the game environment and collecting evidence dramas provided in the game. Factual answers are required for this type of question. Half of the first type questions are related to information provided in text format as control group to show the effectiveness of visualization (Q1). The second type of question is open question without clear or determined answers. Participants can give arbitrary based on their own understanding. The quantity and quality of the answers created by participants can reflect participants' motivation to create new stories (Q2). Typical examples for these two types of questions are as following:

First type: Who was in the room when you saw the dead body?
Second type: Tell me about your family, do you have any issues in your family recently?

18 questions including 12 first type questions and 6 second type questions are required to be answered. After the session, participants are requested to finish a questionnaire. We evaluate the integrated performance based on the questionnaire.

4.3 Result and Analysis

Table 1 compares the result of questions related to text information (text-related question) versus those related to visualization information (visualization-related question) and suggests that the average score of visualization information (MEAN = 0.71) is significantly higher than that of text information (MEAN = 0.47). We evaluate answers given by participants based on the the research on question test by Hensen and Johnston. The score of an answer is decided by three attributes: *Comprehension, Accuracy* and *Consistency.* Figure 5 shows the average score of answers to text-related questions and visualization-related questions on each attribute Answers those are more relevant to fact obtain higher score (0.0–1.0). As a result, it can be inferred that the visualization dramas are more effectively and accurately in terms of conveying information in this experiment. In another word, the visualization dramas can help participants have a better understanding the stories (Q1). This is also reflected on the questionnaire (Fig. 6). Most of the participants agreed that visualization dramas helped them understand the content better.

Table 2 demonstrates some answers to second type questions given by participants. Number increment of answers quantitatively suggests that participants are more motivated to create their own content than choose from available answers (Q2). Simultaneously, available answers provided baseline, comparison and inspired participants to create new content. New answers were given somehow related to previous answers as inferences, deductions or reasons. This transfers the signal that visualized collective storytelling can support participants to

Table 1. Relevance score

	Question	Number	Mean	SD
Score	Text	6	0.47	0.08
	Visualization	6	0.71	0.06

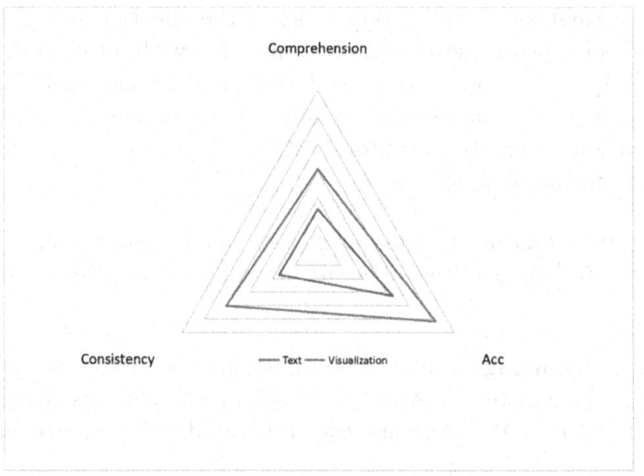

Fig. 5. Evaluation

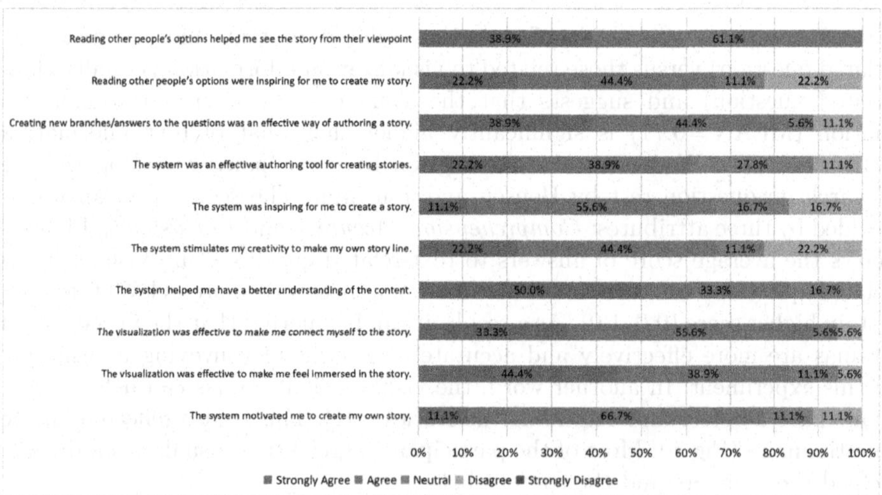

Fig. 6. Questionnaire result

analyze the situation and contribute to content generation. The questionnaire also suggests that story envisioning can stimulate, inspire participants to create more contents (Fig. 6). Moreover, contents created are derived from cultural or

Table 2. Contents created by participants

Question	Number of answers	Sample answer 1	Sample answer 2
Where were you at the time of the murder?	(1) 12	"I was walking a dog"	"I was working on my medicine in the lab."
Did you personally see anyone attempting to poison the boss?	(1) 10	"I did not. But I know there were some tensions in the office."	"Maybe Lury uses poison by himself."
Do you have any issues in your family recently?	(1) 9	"I am personally okay but I cannot say that about everyone."	"I have no problem but my son get hurt in his soccer game."
Who is your closest friend in the company and who is the least close person to you in the company?	(1) 11	"Charlie is a nice person I think, but I don't like Simons."	"Charlie has been reliable, but any people didn't trust Simons."
Explain more about your boss's family.	(1) 15	"I may have taken the ice cream from his son and threw it on the ground to show him what is mean."	"I bumped his wife to the street and got hit by a bus, lost her voice. Maybe that's why he likes me."
Do you know who has the access to the lab where the new medicine is stored?	(1) 16	"The lock's broken since 2 weeks ago, we pretended to swipe our cards until they fixed it."	"Anyone can because the door is always open."

personality elements of the participants, which indicated that the contents can be potentially used for cross-culture conversation analysis.

5 Conclusion

In this paper, we proposed the method of story envisioning to assist people envision their stories in daily conversation. The method of story envisioning considers human daily conversation as an update of common ground and uses graphic recording theory to visualize the common ground. Story envisioning describes the method of using interactive dramas to represent story pieces in order to involve not only story contents but also prior knowledge, background and other shared cultural information. We state that story envisioning could help people have a better understanding of the stories in daily conversation and could be an effective method for visualized collective storytelling. System TSEiA was built to provide story envisioning services. Experiment is conducted on a role-playing game platform powered by TSEiA to evaluate the usage and effectiveness of story envisioning. The results showed that story envisioning helped participants understand the stories more concretely and accurately. Simultaneously, the experiment showed that story envisioning inspired and stimulated participants to collaboratively generate more conversational contents. Experiment showed that the system could be used as an effective tool to train communication skills and collect cross-culture data.

The system is still under development and it has limitations. For example, the system has problem with handling stories with object interaction and descriptive information. Although the method of action sequence greatly reduced the difficulty of visualization, it cannot handle complicated input with detailed descriptions. In this sense, relationships between two or more objects in the story should also be extracted. Moreover, to create more contents for cross-culture studies, we will prepare the system for crowd sourcing. Using the data corpus created, we will be able to create predictive model that can automatically give story branches.

References

1. Nishida, T., Nakazawa, A., Ohmoto, Y., Mohammad, Y.: Artificial intelligence and conversational intelligence. In: Conversational Informatics, pp. 1–16. Springer, Tokyo (2014). https://doi.org/10.1007/978-4-431-55040-2_1
2. Nishida, T., Nakazawa, A., Ohmoto, Y., Mohammad, Y.: Conversation: above and beneath the surface. In: Conversational Informatics, pp. 17–41. Springer, Tokyo (2014). https://doi.org/10.1007/978-4-431-55040-2_2
3. Teeter, P., Sandberg, J.: Cracking the Enigma of asset bubbles with narratives. Strat. Organ. **15**(1), 91–99 (2017)
4. Jefferson, G.: Sequential aspects of storytelling in conversation. Studies in the Organization of Conversational Interaction, pp. 219–248 (1978)
5. Sacks, H., Jefferson, G.: Lectures on conversation (1995)
6. Battaglino, C., Bickmore, T.: Increasing the engagement of conversational agents through co-constructed storytelling. In: Eighth Workshop on Intelligent Narrative Technologies (2015)
7. Mirzaei, M.S., Zhang, Q., Nishida, T.: Conversation envisioning to train intercultural interactions. In: Meiselwitz, G. (ed.) SCSM 2018, Part II. LNCS, vol. 10914, pp. 68–80. Springer, Cham (2018). https://doi.org/10.1007/978-3-319-91485-5_5
8. Mirzaei, M.S., Zhang, Q., van der Struijk, S., Nishida, T.: Conversation envisioning framework for situated conversation. In: Mouhoub, M., Sadaoui, S., Ait Mohamed, O., Ali, M. (eds.) IEA/AIE 2018. LNCS (LNAI), vol. 10868, pp. 517–529. Springer, Cham (2018). https://doi.org/10.1007/978-3-319-92058-0_50
9. Coyne, B., Sproat, R.: WordsEye: an automatic text-to-scene conversion system. In: SIGGRAPH 2001 (2001)
10. Åkerberg, O., Svensson, H., Schulz, B., Nugues, P.: CarSim: an automatic 3D text-to-scene conversion system applied to road accident reports. In: Copestake, A., Hajic, J. (eds.) Proceedings of the Tenth Conference on European Chapter of the Association for Computational Linguistics, vol. 2, pp. 191–194. ACM Press, New York (2003)

11. Johansson, R., Williams, D., Berglund, A., Nugues, P.: CarSim: a system to visualize written road accident reports as animated 3D scenes. In: Proceedings of the 2nd Workshop on Text Meaning and Interpretation, pp. 57–64. Association for Computational Linguistics, Stroudsburg (2004)
12. Ma, M.: Automatic Conversion of Natural Language to 3D Animation. Ph.D. thesis, University of Ulster (2006)
13. Chang, A.X., Savva, M., Manning, C.D.: Learning spatial knowledge for text to 3D scene generation. In: Proceedings of the Conference on Empirical Methods in Natural Language Processing, pp. 2028–2038 (2014)
14. Chang, A., Monroe, W., Savva, M., Potts, C., Manning, C.D.: Text to 3D scene generation with rich lexical grounding (2015). arXiv preprint: arXiv:1505.06289
15. Johnson, W.L., Valente, A.: Tactical language and culture training systems: using artificial intelligence to teach Foreign languages and cultures. In: Proceedings of the 20th Innovative Applications of Artificial Intelligence (IAAI) Conference, Los Angeles, Alelo (2008)
16. Cassell, J., Bickmore, T.: Negotiated collusion: modeling social language and its relationship effects in intelligent agents. User Model. Adapt. Interfaces **13**(1–2), 89–132 (2003)
17. Swanson, R., Gordon, A.S.: Say anything: using textual case-based reasoning to enable open-domain interactive storytelling. ACM Trans. Interact. Intell. Syst. **2**(3), 1–35 (2012)

Information, Cognition and Learning

Impact of Compiler's Feedback on Coding Performance

Tamirat T. Abegaz(✉) and Dianna J. Spence

University of North Georgia, 82 College Circle, Dahlonega, GA 30597, USA
tamirat.abegaz@ung.edu

Abstract. One of the tasks of a computer programmer is to diagnose and debug programming errors generated by either a compiler or an interpreter. However, the ways that the feedback is composed and presented to the programmer generally result in frustration and discouragement, especially for novice programmers. In fact, almost all compilers generate cryptic feedback messages displayed using a red foreground color. The purpose of this study is to examine the effects of a compiler's feedback on programming performance. This research hypothesized that the feedback provided by the majority of the compilers hinders novice programmers in their effort to learn programming concepts. To investigate this, the research explores ways to incorporate low-level emotional design elements as part of the compiler's feedback to counterbalance the frustration caused by the cryptic compilers feedback messages. The study was a 3 by 3 repeated measures factorial design ANOVA with two independent variables: affect type (neutral, positive, and negative) and feedback design type (fColor, fPhraseValence, and fHybrid). In addition, this research defines debugging effectiveness (dependent variable) as a numerical count that depicts the number of execution attempts before correcting a programming error. The predicted result was that positive emotion could reduce frustration & help programmers correct the errors with fewer attempts. Surprisingly, this study suggested that feedback designed to evoke negative emotion tends to lead programmers to correct programming errors with fewer execution attempts. Overall, this research demonstrated that the nature and type of feedback messages could potentially affect programming performance.

Keywords: Visual stimuli · Compiler · Syntax error · Programming languages

1 Introduction

Feedback matters. During the human-computer interaction (HCI) process, feedback plays an important role, providing a way for a computer system to communicate about the success or failure of a given task (process). According to Human Factors research, there are three fundamental features that a feedback message must possess (Akamatsu et al. 1995; Wickens et al. 1998). First, the feedback message must alert the human operators and call for their attention. In other words, it should capture the human operator's attention since it is the most important thing to be addressed at the specified moment. Second, the feedback message must report the nature of the condition. It should tell the human operator what is wrong. Third, the feedback message must direct

S. Yamamoto and H. Mori (Eds.): HCII 2019, LNCS 11569, pp. 265–279, 2019.
https://doi.org/10.1007/978-3-030-22660-2_18

the human operator in an appropriate corrective action in addressing the issue. Arguably, this is the one thing most feedback messages are deficient in addressing accurately (Stanton et al. 2013). Meanwhile, a number of research findings indicate that in the course of human-computer interaction, feedback displayed by a computer system to a human operator generally affects the emotional state of the human subject (Forgas 1991; Ceaparu et al. 2004; Clore and Huntsinger 2007; Lazar et al. 2006).

Understanding the processes of software development is an essential factor to becoming successful in the computer programming field. A key to understanding computer programming is to engage oneself in the programming activities. One of the various challenges students face during programming courses is to diagnose and respond to syntax errors (Jackson et al. 2005; Sadler et al. 2012; Altadmri and Brown 2015; Reynolds 2001; Denny et al. 2014). In most computer programming languages, compilers or interpreters (special programs that convert a human-like program into machine language) are delegated to generate the syntax errors encountered during program compilation or execution (Reynolds 2001; Jackson et al. 2005). However, the ways that the feedback is composed and presented generally result in frustration and discouragement, especially for novice programmers. In fact, various research indicated that over 40% of programming time is wasted due to frustrating experiences associated with the compiler's feedback presented to the programmer (Jackson et al. 2005; Sadler et al. 2012; Altadmri and Brown 2015).

The purpose of this research is to evaluate the impact of compiler feedback on the comprehension and performance of computer programmers. The intent of incorporating emotional design elements as part of compiler feedback is to enhance positive affect, thereby promoting creative thinking. This bolstered thinking is meant to improve the programmers' performance in solving the problem at hand, rather than being stymied by frustration. To accomplish this goal, we need to examine some of the theories behind affect, exploring how affect influences programmers' abilities to diagnose and debug programming errors. This research examines some of the theoretical and methodological aspects of how low-level emotional design elements influence programmer's abilities to diagnose and debug computer programming errors.

In this study, participants were given several Java programming tasks with an Eclipse IDE (Integrated Development Environment). Currently, errors generated from the compiler use obscure phrases displayed in red text color (Jackson et al. 2005; Altadmri and Brown 2015; Saff and Ernst 2005). For this research, the compiler errors were augmented with words that can induce positive or negative emotions accordingly. In addition, the text colors were purposefully modified to serve as an emotional stimulus.

Explanatory variables in the present study are the nature and the type of feedback provided to programming students. The outcome of interest in this study is the programming students' problem-solving performance. Performance in this context includes debugging effectiveness (numerical count that depicts the number of execution attempts before correcting a programming error) and efficiency (how long does it take or students to debug the error). Following are the goals and expected outcomes of the proposed research:

(1) Exploration of low-level emotional design elements as alternative methods for compilers' feedback presentations.

(2) Seamless integration of low-level emotional design elements as part of compiler feedback to improve programmers debugging performance.
(3) Evaluation of the impact of emotional design elements on debugging performance of novice programmers
(4) Recommendations on how to write an effective compiler's feedback that reduces frustration and discouragement by students for committing syntactical errors.

The remainder of this paper is organized as follows. In Sect. 2, related works relevant to this research are presented. Section 3 discusses the methodology used for this research. Section 4 presents the experimental results. Finally, a discussion of the results and their implications are presented in Sect. 5.

2 Related Work

2.1 Effects of Color and Word Valence on Achievement Motivations

Numerous studies have reported that motivation of a person to solve a specific problem is based on that individual's emotion and achievement related goals. In particular, according to achievement motivation theory (AMT), people generally associate their achievement goals from either an approach (desire: I love to do it) or avoidance (responsibility: I have to do it) orientation. In approach motivation, people are passionate about the positive outcome and the satisfaction they will get while trying to reach their goals. On the other hand, in avoidance motivation, people fear the negative outcome if they don't meet their responsibility, therefore, they do their best to meet their goals to avoid failure. In a related study, Messer noted that individuals with approach motivation tend to focus on creative thinking by going beyond the minimum requirements to solve a given problem. By contrast, individuals with avoidance motivation tend to be more narrowly focused and detailed-oriented while trying to reach their goal, rather than being creative. Moreover, a recent line of studies indicated that color and word valence can influence individuals with avoidance or approach motivations differently (Elliot and Maier 2014; Elliot 2015).

Color. Color is one of the fundamental aspects of human perception, influencing cognition and behaviour through both innate and learned associations (Elliot and Maier, 2014; Kuhbandner and Pekrun 2013; Mammarella et al. 2016). It carries different meanings in different contexts (for example, intellectual achievement, physical achievement, relational context). Many research findings have shown how different colors have different impacts on cognition, behaviour, and task performance. Essentially, Elliot and Maier explained that color associations are the product of two foundations: innate and learned behavior, yielding a combined effect of learned associations with innate response to color stimuli (Elliot and Maier, 2014). In general, researchers tend to agree that the color red is naturally associated with anger, blood, and fire, which induce negative emotions. Similarly, it could also be a learned behavior since people use red ink to mark errors, red warning signals, red light to signal danger, etc. Similarly, green and blue are associated with positive behavior.

More interestingly, researchers demonstrated that negative emotion could potentially result in avoidance motivation, which could enforce individuals to focus on detailed tasks to achieve their goals to avoid the possibility of failure (Elliot 2015; Lichtenfeld et al. 2009). However, researchers also demonstrated that negative emotion could produce anxiety and frustration, which could impair performance (Thorstenson 2012; Xia et al. 2016). All in all, researchers demonstrated that exposure to some colors such as red could potentially impair academic performance. Various findings concur with the findings that red color has a negative effect on the academic performance of students. Table 1 summarizes research findings related to the effect of the color red on academic performance.

Table 1. Prior findings related to the color red.

Red color	Performance
Thorstenson (2012)	Marked more errors when correcting essays; Improved performance on detailed-oriented task
Lichtenfeld et al. (2009)	Undermined intellectual performance (IQ test performance)
Elliot and Moeller, Elliot (2015)	Undermined intellectual performance
Gnambs et al.	Impeded performance
Xia et al. (2016)	Enhanced the performance on a simple detail-oriented task (the proofreading task)

Word Valence. According to Affective Event theory, affect is described as "an unconscious reaction to stimuli before any cognitive appraisal of events occurs". Psychological frameworks conceptualize emotion ratings with respect to words (phrases) along three affective dimensions: dominance, arousal, and valence. Word dominance ratings range from in control to out of control; arousal ratings range from calm to excited. With respect to valence, which is the focus of this study, affective ratings range from pleasant to unpleasant. A research-based collection called Affective Norms for English Words (ANEW) contains an extensible set of more than a thousand words with their valence values (Bradley and Lang 1999a). ANEW is based on various previous works such as Center for Emotion and Attraction (CSEA: University of Florida 1999) & International Affective Digitized Sound (Bradley and Lang 1999b). ANEW provides a rating of the words using the three previously described affective dimensions (i.e., dominance, arousal, and valence). Valence ratings are numbers from one to nine, where one represents an extremely unpleasant valence and nine represents an extremely pleasant valence. Based on the work provided by Bradley and Lang, Table 2 shows some of the words used in this research and their respective affective assessment, given as the mean value for valence, followed by the standard deviation (SD).

Table 2. Affective norms for English words Bradley and Lang (1999a, b)

Description	Valence mean(SD)
Failure	1.70(1.07)
Disaster	1.73(1.13)
Crashed	2.21(1.74)
Rejected	1.50(1.09)
Terrible	1.93(1.44)
Success	8.29(0.93)
Excellence	8.38(0.96)
Satisfied	7.94(1.19)
Progress	7.73(1.34)
Improve	7.65(1.16)

Figure 1 shows the nonverbal pictographic measures of Self-Assessment Manikin (SAM) as representations of word valence.

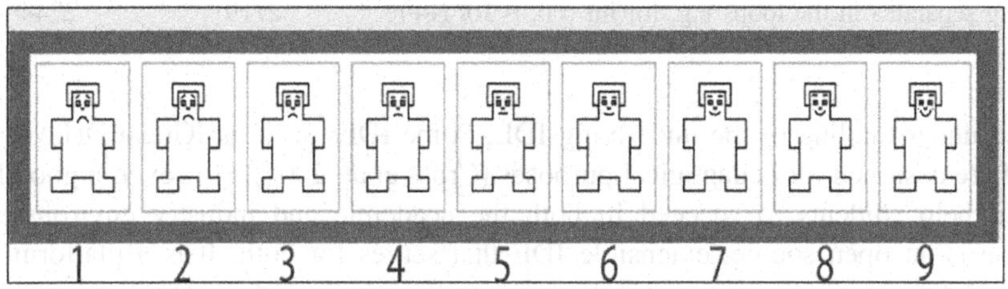

Fig. 1. SAM depictions of word valence ratings from 1 to 9

2.2 Java Errors

Various researchers and practitioners have observed and collected very similar lists of errors made by novice programmers. For instance, Jackson et al. collected more than half a million errors committed by student programmers in the course of a semester (Jackson et al. 2005). Most Recently, Altadmri Brown conducted a comprehensive study on Java errors generated by the compilers (2015). They were able to collect more than 37 million errors committed by novice programmers. Table 3 summarizes the rank, error type, number of occurrences, and number of distinct users. As shown in Table 3, most of the errors are related to simple language syntax mistakes. For instance, missing parentheses, braces, and quotations are among the top errors made by beginner programmers.

Although Integrated Development Environment (IDEs) are not part of the requirements in programming curriculum, their usage in programming courses is becoming prevalent. Choosing the right IDE requires a comprehensive study and

Table 3. Affective norms for English words Bradley and Lang (1999a, b)

Error	Number of occurrence	Distinct users
Unbalanced parenthesis, curly or square braces and/or quotation marks e.g. while(x==0}	793232	119407
Confusing the assignment operator(=) with the comparison operator (==) e.g. if(x=y)	173938	45082
Including the types when calling a method e.g. myObject. setVal(int x, string s)	52826	21904
Incorrect semi-colon after an conditional or repetition structure e.g. while(a==b);	49375	18350
Incorrect semicolon at the end of a method header e.g. public int getVal();{}	38001	19502
Confusing & with &&, or | and || e.g. if(a==b) & (c==d)	29605	8742
Forgetting parentheses after method call e.g. myObject.getVal	18955	10232
Incompatible types between return & type e.g. int x = myObject.toString();	16996	7556
Getting greater than or equal wrongly e.g. if(a=<5)	4214	
Wrong separates in the loops e.g. for(int i=0; i<10, i++)	2719	2244

deeper understanding of the underlying IDE. Some IDEs such as JGrasp DrJava, and BlueJ are designed for pedagogical purposes (Cross et al. 2004). However, a good IDE should help students to succeed in both the academic and industry environments. Eclipse is an open source, extensible IDE that serves for both. It is a platform that allows integration of various development tools which makes development more efficient and effective.

The Eclipse IDE makes program development more efficient and productive by providing three aspects of benefits to the programmers: reduction of redundant code typing, generation of Javadoc documents, and real-time compilation with syntax highlighting. Eclipse reduces code redundancy by providing wizards for generating classes, interfaces, constructors, as well as getter and setter methods. In terms of auto document generation, Eclipse typically generates useful documentation easily if the comments are written within with the standards of Javadoc (Eclipse 2007; Murphy et al. 2006). Lastly, Eclipse also provides features such as syntax highlighting, real-time compilation, and comprehensive feedback for both the syntactical and semantic errors. However, the error messages are obscure for novice programmers. Table 4 shows the error messages generated by Eclipse IDE. The sample code segments were purposefully created to align with the errors listed in Table 3. In other words, the Eclipse IDE error messages listed in Table 4 roughly correspond to the errors listed in Table 3.

Table 4. Feedback types and their respective code fragment with generic feedback message

Feedback type	Code fragment and error message
Expected (missing semicolon)	String computer = "Computer Science") Exception in thread "main" java.lang.Error: Unresolved compilation problems: Syntax error, insert ";" to complete LocalVariableDeclarationStatement
Unclosed String Literal (missing ')')	Scanner input=new Scanner(System.in; Exception in thread "main" java.lang.Error: Unresolved compilation problems: Syntax error, insert ")" to complete Expression
Illegal Start of an Expression	String 1301progammingclass = "Computer Science course"; Exception in thread "main" java.lang.Error: Unresolved compilation problem: Syntax error on token "1301", delete this token

3 Methods

Participants were given several Java programming tasks with an Eclipse IDE (Integrated Development Environment). By default, errors generated from the compiler use obscure phrases displayed in red text. In the present study, compiler error messages were altered to use different colors and different wording, both selected to evoke particular emotional responses. Specifically, compiler errors were augmented with words selected to induce positive or negative emotions. Likewise, the font color of each error message was purposefully modified to evoke a particular emotional reaction. The methods and resources constructed for this study may be a useful guideline for compiler designers and developers to create constructive feedback messages to syntax errors.

3.1 Participants

In total, sixty-three students were recruited at a public university in the Southeastern United States to take part in the experiment. All of the participants were students enrolled in an introductory programming course at the time of the experiment. The university IRB approved this study. All procedures employed in the study comply with ethical standards on human experimentation stated in the IRB application.

3.2 Protocol and Materials

Each programming task consisted of loading a small Java program file that already contained a few lines of code, constructed in advance to produce one of the errors shown in Table 4. The participant was instructed to compile the program and fix any errors detected, repeating the debug-compile process until the program compiled successfully. Each participant completed nine tasks, receiving a different customized error message for each one. To capture the number of attempt, time to complete tasks, and to verify if the participants complete a given task, Apache's Log4j tool was used (Log4j).

3.3 Design

The study is a 3 by 3 repeated measure factorial design ANOVA with two independent variables. As shown in Table 5, the first independent variables is computer affect type which includes three levels: neutral, positive, and negative. The second independent variable is feedback design type and contains three conditions: fColor, fPhraseValence, and fHybrid (i.e., combination of color and phrase). The dependent variable is debugging effectiveness, which is defined for the present study as a numerical count that depicts the number of execution attempts before correcting a programming error. However, the efficiency performance indicator (the other outcome of interest) was excluded due to data screening. The expected result was that feedback containing positive emotional content would enhance debugging effectiveness.

Table 5. Three by Three study design

Affect type	Design type	Compiler message style
Positive	fColor	feedbackGreen
Negative	fColor	feedbackRed
Neutral	fColor	feedbackBlack
Positive	fPhraseValence	feedbackPositive
Negative	fPhraseValence	feedbackNegative
Neutral	fPhraseValence	feedbackNeutral
Positive	fHybrid	feedbackGreenPositive
Negative	fHybrid	feedbackRedNegative
Neutral	fHybrid	feedbackBlackNeutral
Positive	fColor	feedbackGreen

To customize the error messages, we selected three colors (black, red, and green) and 9 affective words from ANEW (see Table 2). Table 6 shows the sample java program fragments with their respective error messages for color design type. Table 7 shows the sample java program fragments with their respective error messages for word valence design type. Table 8 shows the sample java program fragments with their respective error messages for color and word valance design types combined. Each programming task was pseudo-randomly assigned to the participants in order to counterbalance the learning effect.

Table 6. Design Type: Color only

Feedback type	Code fragment and error message
feedbackGreen	String computer = "Computer Science"; System.***out***.println(computer.substring(-1,8)); **java.lang.StringIndexOutOfBoundsException: String index out of range: -1**
feedbackRed	String datascience = "Data Science"; System.***out***.println(datascience.substring(-5,12)); **java.lang.StringIndexOutOfBoundsException: String index out of range: -5**
feedbackBlack	String year = "Superbowl 2017"; System.***out***.println(year.substring(10,15)); **java.lang.StringIndexOutOfBoundsException: String index out of range: 15**

Table 7. Design Type: Valence only

Feedback type	Code fragment and error message
feedback-Positive	String worldCup = "World cup 2018 Russia"; System.***out***.println(worldCup.substring(12,25)); **EXCELLENT PROGRESS! You have made PROGRESS, please use compiler's suggestion to IMPROVE your program: java.lang.StringIndexOutOfBoundsException: String index out of range: 25**
feedback-Negative	**int**[] age=**new int**[10]; **for**(**int** i=0; i<=age.length; i++) age[i]=i+1; **EXECUTION FAILURE! The program FAILED to work. You must fix the following errors to avoid DISASTER: java.lang.ArrayIndexOutOfBoundsException: 10**
feedbackBlack Neutral	String engineering = "Software Engineering"; System.***out***.println(engineering.substring(9,21)); **New Message! The computer has the following suggestion to make it properly work: java.lang.StringIndexOutOfBoundsException: String index out of range: 21**

Table 8. Design Type: Color and Valence combined

Feedback type	Code fragment and error message
feedbackGreen Negative	String team =""; String[] worldCup= {"Russia", "France","Spain", "Mexico", "Englad"}; **for**(**int** i=0; i<=team.length; i++) worldCup=worldCup+team[i]; **QUALITY IDEA! The computer has a suggestion to IMPROVE your program. Use your IMAGINATION skills to IMPROVE the program: The type of the expression must be an array type but it resolved to String**
feedbackRed Positive	String[] fruits= {"Apple", "Banana","Orange", "Mango", "Peach", "Grape", "Berry"}; **for**(**int** i=-1; i<=fruits.length; i++) System.***out***.println(fruits[i]); **DISASTER: The program ABORTED the execution attempt. The computer CRASHED the program. Use this FAILURE message to fix this MISTAKE: java.lang.ArrayIndexOutOfBoundsException: -1**
feedbackBlack Neutral	**double**[] score= **new double**[25]; **for**(**int** i=-1; i<=score.length; i++) System.***out***.println(score[i]) **New Message! The computer has the following suggestion to make it properly work: java.lang.ArrayIndexOutOfBoundsException: -1**

4 Results

The descriptive statistics of the influence of feedback design and affect type on debugging effectiveness is provided in Table 9. Recall that debugging effectiveness is measured by the number of debugging attempts before successfully compiling a program. Hence, lower values represent greater effectiveness. As shown in Table 9, the debugging effectiveness means of fColor feedback design type for neutral (Black), positive (Green), and negative (Red) affect levels are 4.19, 4.19, and 3.05, respectively. For fPhraseValence type feedback design, the neutralValence, positiveValence, and negativeValence affect levels have effectiveness means of 4.22, 3.67, and 3.29, respectively. Similarly, the debugging effectiveness means of fHybrid feedback design type for neutral (fBlackValence), positive (fGreenValence), and negative (fRedValence) affect levels are 3.84, 4.19, and 3.49, respectively. Of all the above conditions, the descriptive statistics suggest that negative affect type may positively influence debugging effectiveness. Furthermore, Table 9 also shows that fPhraseValence feedback design type did not follow this pattern.

Table 9. Three by Three study design

Feedback design	Affect type	Means	Std. dev
fColor	Neutral (fBlack)	4.19	2.36
	Positive (fGreen)	4.19	2.19
	Negative (fRed)	3.05	1.64
fPhraseValence	Neutral (neutralValence)	4.22	2.79
	Positive (positiveValence)	3.67	1.87
	Negative (negativeValence)	3.29	1.95
fHybrid	Neutral (fBlackNeutralValence)	3.84	2.54
	Positive (fGreenPositiveValence)	4.19	2.36
	Negative (fRedNegativeValence)	3.49	1.62
fColor	Neutral (fBlack)	4.19	2.36

Further data analysis was required to determine the statistical significance of each of the conditions. For debugging effectiveness, Table 10 shows that the analysis indicated a statistically significant result for Affect type, F (2, 76.15) = 10.37, $\rho < 0.0001$, $\eta_p^2 = 0.14$. However, Table 4 shows that the analysis result indicated that there were no statistically significant differences in debugging effectiveness based on feedback design type, or based on the interaction between affect type and feedback design condition.

Table 10. Three by Three study design

Source of variance	SS	df	MS	F	P(Sig)	η_p^2
Feedback Design Type	1.37	2	0.68	0.23	0.792	0.04
Error (Feedback Design Type)	363.74	124	2.93			
Affect Level	76.15	2	38.08	10.37	0.0000	0.14
Error (Affect Level)	454.96	124	3.67			
Feedback Design Type *Affect Level	22.02	4	5.50	2.33	0.057	0.36
Error (Feedback Design Type *Affect Level)	586.21	248	2.36			

Note: SS = Sum of Square, MS = Mean Square, Result of 3 (Feedback Design Type: fColor, fPhraseValence, fHybrid) * 3 (Affect Level: Positive, Neutral, Negative)

We conducted follow-up analysis of mean differences in debugging effectiveness by affect level. As shown in Table 11, post-hoc pair-wise comparisons of mean debugging effectiveness by affect level indicated that there was a statistically significance difference in debugging effectiveness between neutral and negative affect levels. In addition, similar post-hoc pair-wise comparisons also suggested a significance difference in effectiveness between positive and negative affect levels. However, no significance differences were found in debugging effectiveness between neutral and positive affect levels.

Table 11. Three by Three study design

Comparisons by affect level	Estimated mean difference	Standard error of difference mean	Sig (p)	Bonferroni adjustment 95% CI
Neutral* Positive	−.069	.189	1.00	−0.395, 0.533
Neutral vs. Negative	0.810*	0.207	0.001	0.301, 1.318
Positive vs. Negative	0.741*	0.196	0.001	0.259, 1.222

Note: *$p < 0.05$, where p-values are adjusted using Bonferroni method

Figure 2 displays a plot of the mean debugging effectiveness within each affect type across the three feedback conditions. The plot reflects the significant differences reported above, showing a clear and consistent gap in effectiveness between scenarios with negative affect type and both of the other affect types.

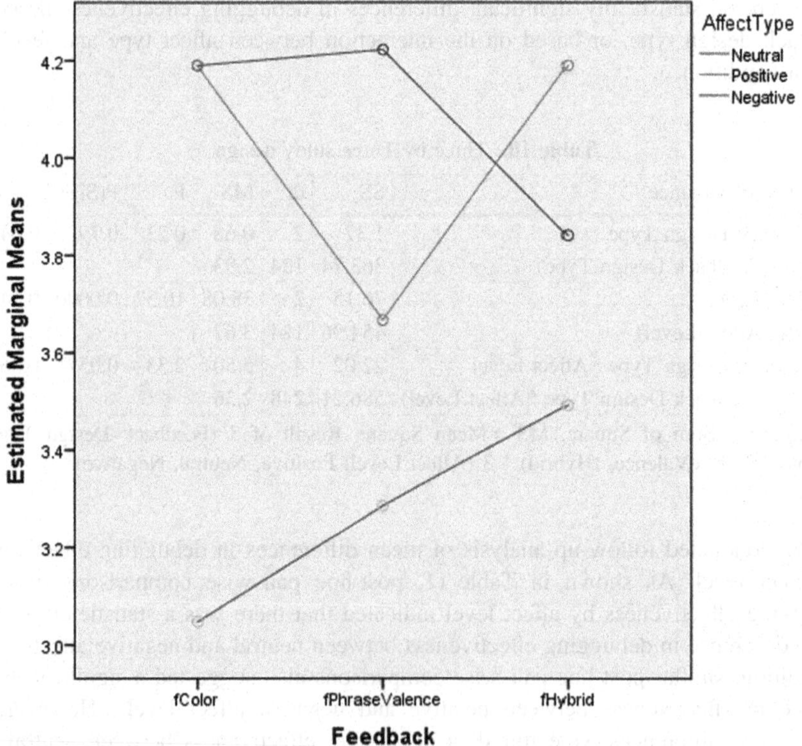

Fig. 2. Estimated means for Debugging Effectiveness across various affect level and feedback design

5 Discussion and Conclusion

The overall objective of this research was to describe the interaction between affect and problem solving, facilitated through human-computer interfaces. In the context of computer education, one of the tasks students encounter during programming courses is to diagnose and debug (correct) syntax errors. However, the ways that feedback messages are composed and presented generally result in frustration and discouragement, especially for novice programmers. Based on the premise that the feedback provided by compilers hinders novice programmers in their effort to learn programming, this study explored ways to incorporate low-level emotional design elements as part of a compiler's feedback to counterbalance the frustration caused by the cryptic compiler feedback messages. It was hypothesized that positively worded interface dialogs, specifically error messages, would promote positive user affect and the resulting positive affect would have a measurable impact on problem-solving performance.

The predicted result was that a positive emotional response could reduce frustration & help programmers correct the errors with fewer attempts. Surprisingly, this study suggested that cues designed to invoke negative emotional response are more likely to lead programmers to correct the programming errors with fewer execution attempts. More specifically, as indicated in the result section, there was a statistically significance difference in debugging effectiveness between neutral and negative affect levels, as well as between positive and negative affect levels. One possible explanation for the apparent impact of the messages designed to induce negative emotion is that these negative messages created an increased sense of urgency for the students. Additional research could be beneficial to investigate this phenomenon in greater depth.

More broadly, this research demonstrated that the nature and type of feedback messages could potentially affect programming performance. Overall, this result indicates that feedback messages affect debugging performance and gives some insight to compiler designers, developers, and computer science educators about the potential impact of feedback messages regarding syntax errors. Since the content and presentation of these messages can have an impact on a programming student's performance, it might be worthwhile for compilers and IDEs to be designed with configurable error messages. If such configurable error messages were readily available, it might be useful for programming instructors to leverage that feature when teaching programming skills. In addition, the results obtained from this research could be used in other fields of research that involves feedback messages to the human operator.

References

Akamatsu, M., MacKenzie, I.S., Hasbroucq, T.: A comparison of tactile, auditory, and visual feedback in a pointing task using a mouse-type device. Ergonomics **38**(4), 816–827 (1995)

Wickens, C.D., Gordon, S.E., Liu, Y., Lee, J.: An introduction to human factors engineering (1998)

Stanton, N., Salmon, P.M., Rafferty, L.A.: Human Factors Methods: A Practical Guide for Engineering and Design. Ashgate Publishing, Ltd., Farnham (2013)

Forgas, J.P.: Affective influences on partner choice: role of mood in social decisions. J. Pers. Soc. Psychol. **61**(5), 708 (1991)

Ceaparu, I., Lazar, J., Bessiere, K., Robinson, J., Shneiderman, B.: Determining causes and severity of end-user frustration. Int. J. Hum. Comput. Interact. **17**(3), 333–356 (2004)

Clore, G.L., Huntsinger, J.R.: How emotions inform judgment and regulate thought. Trends Cogn. Sci. **11**(9), 393–399 (2007)

Lazar, J., Jones, A., Hackley, M., Shneiderman, B.: Severity and impact of computer user frustration: a comparison of student and workplace users. Interact. Comput. **18**(2), 187–207 (2006)

Jackson, J., Cobb, M., Carver, C.: Identifying top Java errors for novice programmers. In: Proceedings of the 35th Annual Conference Frontiers in Education, FIE 2005, p. T4C. IEEE, October 2005

Sadler, P.M., Sonnert, G., Hazari, Z., Tai, R.: Stability and volatility of STEM career interest in high school: a gender study. Sci. Educ. **96**(3), 411–427 (2012)

Denny, P., Luxton-Reilly, A., Carpenter, D.: Enhancing syntax error messages appears ineffectual. In: Proceedings of the 2014 Conference on Innovation & Technology in Computer Science Education, pp. 273–278. ACM, June 2014

Reynolds, C.J.: The sensing and measurement of frustration with computers (Doctoral dissertation, Massachusetts Institute of Technology) (2001)

Saff, D., Ernst, M.D.: Continuous testing in Eclipse. In: Proceedings of the 27th International Conference on Software Engineering, pp. 668–669. ACM, May 2005

Elliot, A.J., Maier, M.A.: Color psychology: effects of perceiving color on psychological functioning in humans. Annu. Rev. Psychol. **65**, 95–120 (2014)

Elliot, A.J.: Color and psychological functioning: a review of theoretical and empirical work. Front. Psychol. **6**, 368 (2015)

Kuhbandner, C., Pekrun, R., Maier, M.A.: The role of positive and negative affect in the "mirroring" of other persons' actions. Cogn. Emot. **24**(7), 1182–1190 (2010)

Kuhbandner, C., Pekrun, R.: Joint effects of emotion and color on memory. Emotion **13**(3), 375 (2013)

Mammarella, N., Di Domenico, A., Palumbo, R., Fairfield, B.: When green is positive and red is negative: aging and the influence of color on emotional memories. Psychol. Aging **31**(8), 914 (2016)

Lichtenfeld, S., Maier, M.A., Elliot, A.J., Pekrun, R.: The semantic red effect: processing the word red undermines intellectual performance. J. Exp. Soc. Psychol. **45**(6), 1273–1276 (2009)

Thorstenson, C.A.: Effects of Color Perception and Enacted Avoidance Behavior on Intellectual Task Performance in an Achievement Context (Doctoral dissertation, Appalachian State University) (2012)

Xia, T., Song, L., Wang, T.T., Tan, L., Mo, L.: Exploring the effect of red and blue on cognitive task performances. Front. Psychol. **7**, 784 (2016)

Bradley, M.M., Lang, P.J.: Affective norms for English words (ANEW): instruction manual and affective ratings, pp. 1–45. Technical report C-1, the Center for Research in Psychophysiology, University of Florida (1999a)

Bradley, M., Lang, P.J.: The International affective digitized sounds (IADS): stimuli, instruction manual and affective ratings. NIMH Center for the Study of Emotion and Attention (1999b)

Altadmri, A., Brown, N.C.: 37 million compilations: investigating novice programming mistakes in large-scale student data. In: Proceedings of the 46th ACM Technical Symposium on Computer Science Education, pp. 522–527. ACM (2015)

Cross, J.H., Hendrix, D., Umphress, D.A.: jGRASP: an integrated development environment with visualizations for teaching Java in CS1, CS2, and beyond. In: 34th Annual Frontiers in Education, FIE 2004, pp. 1466–1467. IEEE (2004)

Eclipse IDE: The Eclipse Foundation (2007)

Murphy, G.C., Kersten, M., Findlater, L.: How are Java software developers using the Elipse IDE? IEEE Softw. **23**(4), 76–83 (2006)

Learning Support System Adapting to Multidimensionality of Knowledge Acquisition Process of Intellectual Property Law of Engineering Students

Takako Akakura[1,4(✉)], Takahito Tomoto[2], and Koichiro Kato[3,4]

[1] Faculty of Engineering, Tokyo University of Science, 6-3-1 Niijuku, Katsushika-ku, Tokyo 125-8585, Japan
akakura@rs.tus.ac.jp

[2] Faculty of Engineering, Tokyo Polytechnic University, 11583, Iiyama, Atsugi-shi 243-0297, Japan

[3] Graduate School of Innovation Management, Kanazawa Institute of Technology, 1-3-4 Atago, Minato-ku, Tokyo 105-0002, Japan

[4] Graduate School of Engineering, Kanazawa Institute of Technology, 7-1 Ogigaoka, Nonoichi, Ishikawa 921-8501, Japan

Abstract. Our previous work classified students according to several dimensions, such as by student learning style and attitude toward the study of law, and then examined how these various classifications related to attitudes exhibited by students toward learning support systems. In doing so, we were able to clarify differences in preference among student types in regard to learning support systems. In the present study, we continued that line of investigation by attempting to determine ways to provide tailored learning support systems to students who were classified according to multiple dimensions. An evaluation experiment showed that students who did not respond positively to learning support systems based on logical formulas and logic circuits were the same students who had been classified as unreceptive to two defined learning styles (information-gathering–focused and practice-exercise–focused) and who reported feeling that legal texts are both hard to read and difficult to understand. However, a subsequent survey of the same students suggested that by reexamining system functionality and making adjustments, such as by changing the order in which the systems are provided and the method in which information is presented on screen, it may be possible to optimize the systems to best serve each type of student.

Keywords: Learning support system · Multidimensionality of knowledge acquisition process · Intellectual property law

1 Introduction

Japan's level of technology has contributed to the country's development of a sophisticated information-oriented society. Japan possesses world-class technological prowess and enjoys a strong reputation as a highly developed, technology-rich country.

S. Yamamoto and H. Mori (Eds.): HCII 2019, LNCS 11569, pp. 280–291, 2019.
https://doi.org/10.1007/978-3-030-22660-2_19

At the same time, Japan possesses few natural resources, a condition which makes intellectual property (hereafter, IP) critically important to the nation [1]. A sound understanding of IP is essential for working professionals, especially those involved with technology. Bearing in mind the insufficient amount of time spent on IP education in university faculties of engineering, the authors have thus far endeavored to identify optimal IP education practices to support engineering students, develop different types of learning support systems [2–7], and examine the effects of those systems. One of our previous studies defined a model problem-solving process for the study of Patent Act (Japanese law) for engineering students and developed a learning support system based on that definition [3]; however, the study also specified that in order for the model to be applied, students would first need to possess adequate knowledge to solve the problems posed by the system. In other words, the system was output-focused, providing students with opportunities to demonstrate acquired knowledge. Another previous study [2] found that students prefer different types of learning support systems depending on their own personal learning styles. However, one limitation of the study [2] was its classification of learning styles into just two types. Furthermore, in regard to the educational process for IP law, the study clarified which types of students (when classified according to several dimensions, with a primary focus on attitude toward the subject of law) preferred which types of systems, as well as how different types of students interacted with the systems [8]. Following on the results of our previous work, in this study we attempted to define a learning support system tailored to different types of students, classified according to multiple dimensions, as well as methods for implementing such a system.

2 A Learning Support System for the Study of Legal Texts

2.1 Multi-dimensional Student Classification and System Evaluation

Our previous work [8] defined and used the following three dimensions to classify students:

(a) Learning Style – Students were divided into four categories: "practice-exercise–focused," "information-gathering–focused," "equally receptive to both learning styles," and "not receptive to either learning style."
(b) Perceived Ability to Read Legal Texts – Students were divided into the two categories: "finds legal texts easy to read" and "finds legal texts difficult to read."
(c) Perceived Ability to Understand Legal Texts – Students were divided into the two categories: "finds legal texts easy to understand" and "finds legal texts difficult to understand."

The combination of all options across all dimensions (4 × 2 × 2) resulted in 16 possible categories into which students could be classified; the study ignored categories not containing any students after classification had been performed, leaving 11 categories for potential analysis. However, of those 11, one category contained only a single student; that category was noted but not included in the final analysis.

The study also prepared three types of learning support systems:

(1) A system for studying text as-is (the "text system") (see Fig. 1)

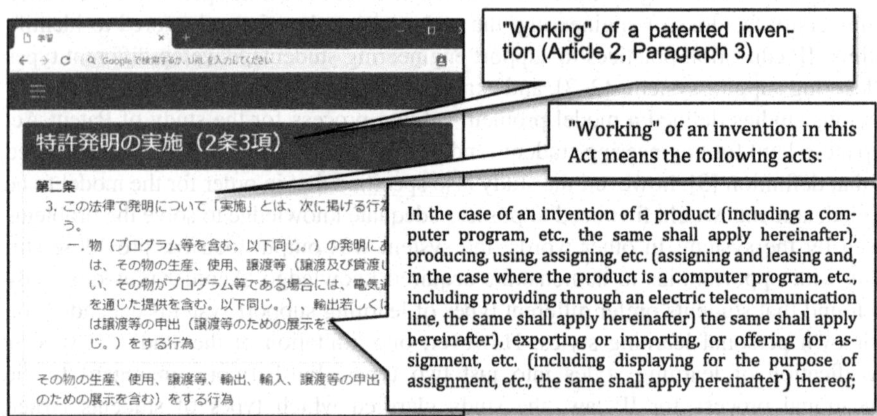

Fig. 1. Article learning screen

(2) A system employing logical formulas as a study method (the "logical formula system") (see Fig. 2)

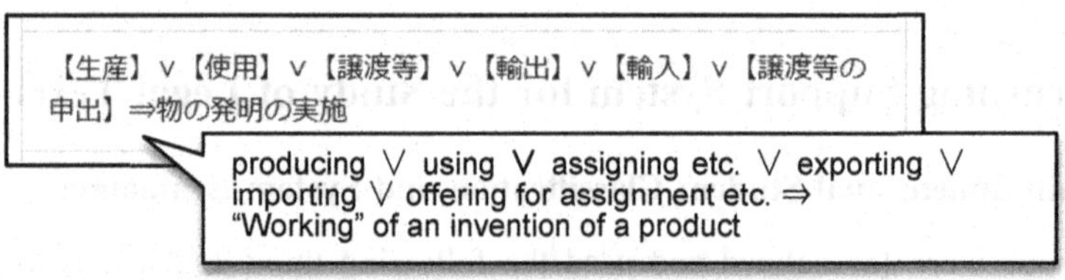

Fig. 2. Logical formula of learning screen

(3) A system in which students learn by assembling logic circuits (the "logic circuit system") (see Figs. 3, 4, 5, 6, 7 and 8).

In this way, the study also prepared three types of learning support systems, in addition to printed practice exercises (Fig. 9) and explanation (Fig. 10).

As shown in Figs. 3, 4, 5, 6, 7 and 8, the logic circuit system does not merely display exercises on the screen in a passive manner; when students study using this system, they must assemble the circuits themselves, after which they receive feedback from the system about whether each assembled circuit was correct or incorrect.

An examination of the relationship between students' system evaluations and the multi-dimensional classifications revealed that practice-exercise–focused students tended to rate the text and logical formula systems poorly, while giving favorable ratings to the logic circuit system. Furthermore, among students defined as practice-exercise–focused, stronger agreement that "law is a (relatively) easy subject" tended to

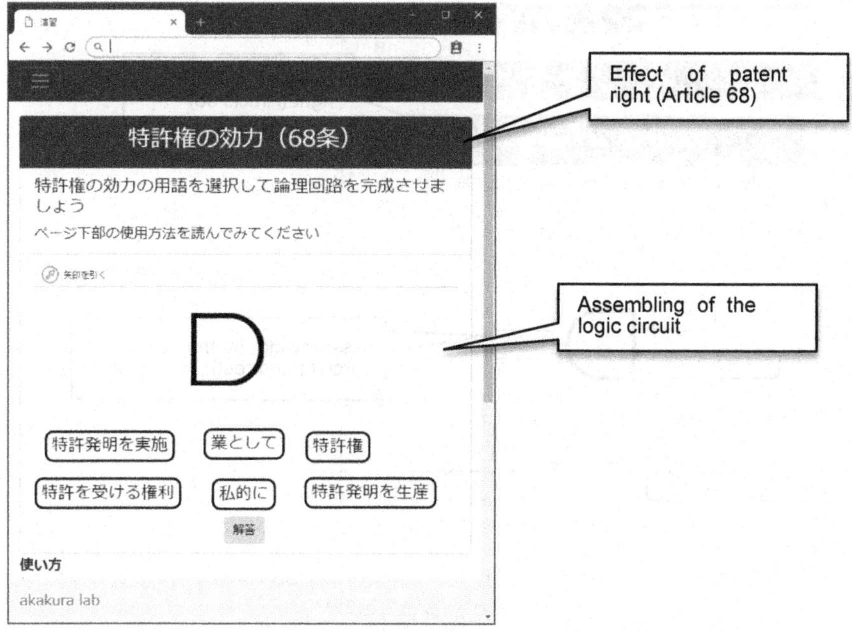

Fig. 3. Assembling of the logic circuit (initial screen)

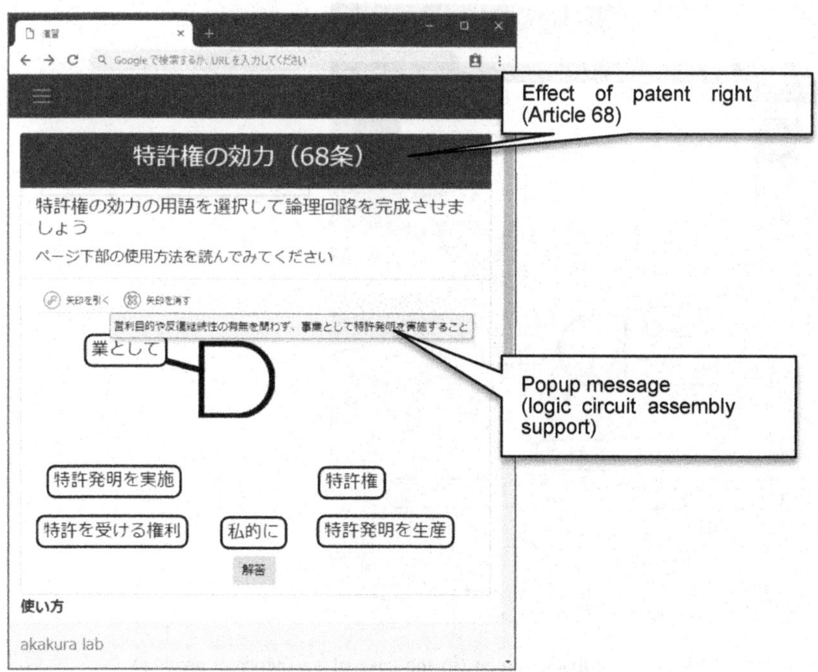

Fig. 4. Assembling of the logic circuit (operating screen)

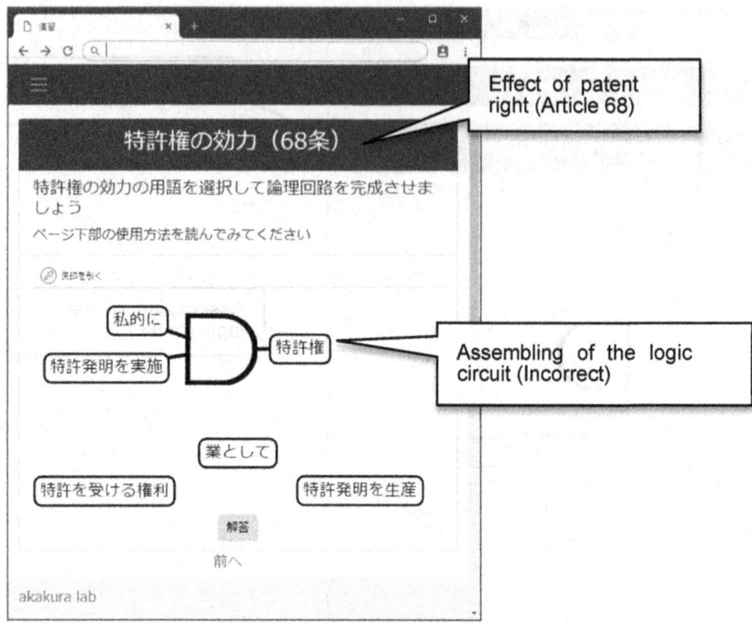

Fig. 5. Assembling of the logic circuit (incorrect operating screen)

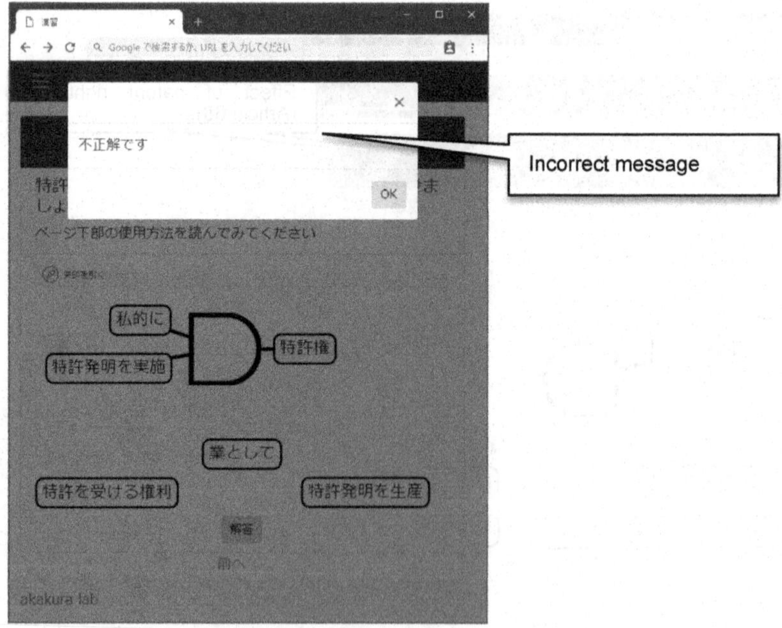

Fig. 6. Feedback screen (in the case of an incorrect answer)

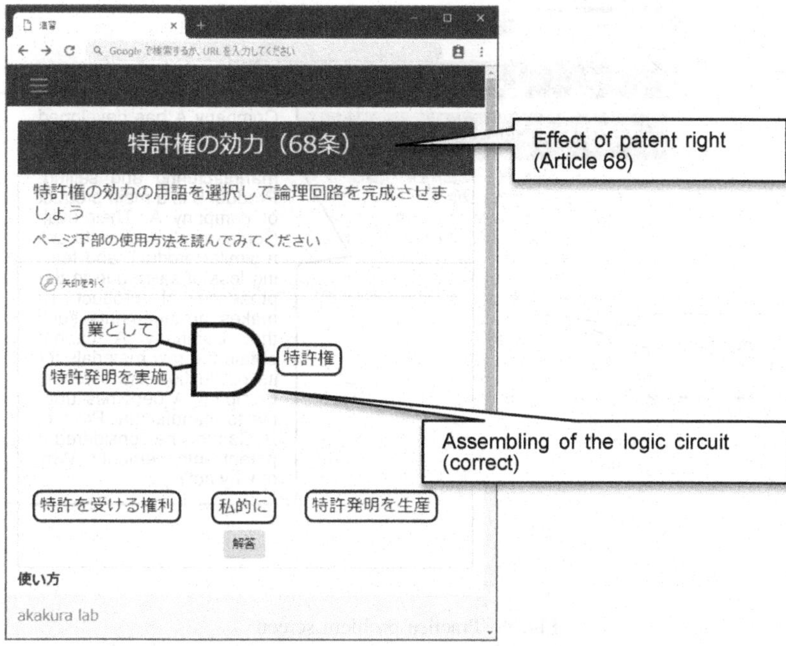

Fig. 7. Assembling of the logic circuit (correct operating screen)

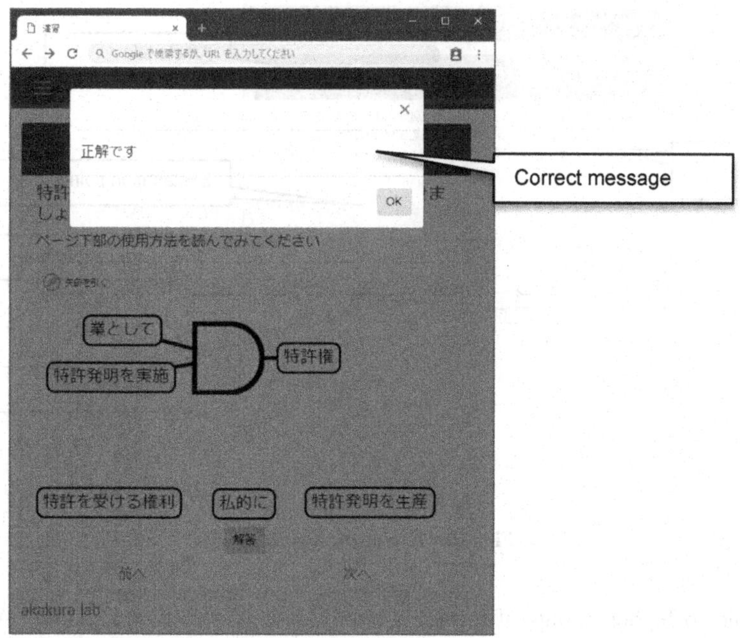

Fig. 8. Feedback screen (in the case of a correct answer)

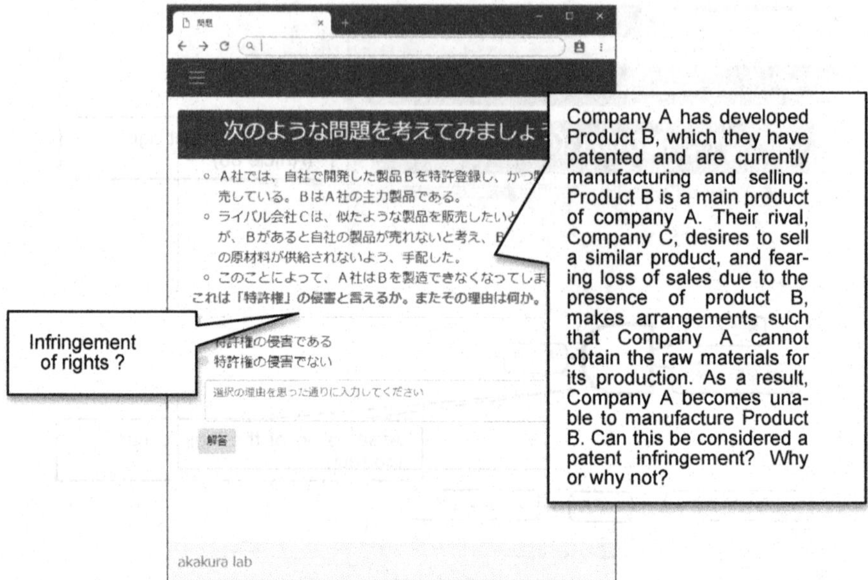

Fig. 9. Practice problem screen

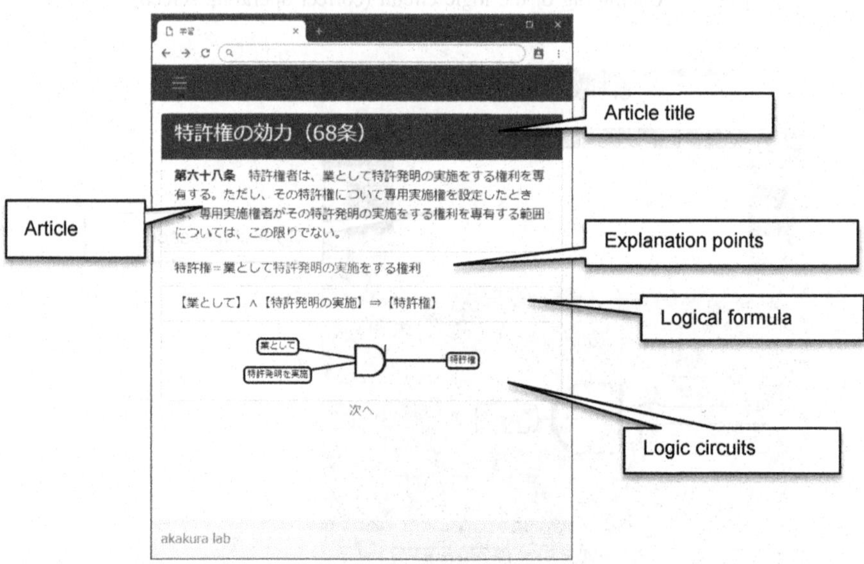

Fig. 10. Explanation screen

correspond to higher ratings of the logic circuit assembly method of study. Among information-gathering–focused students, those who perceived legal texts as difficult to read but not necessarily difficult to understand tended to ignore the text system almost entirely; however, these students made regular use of the logical formula system and tended to use that system more frequently than the logic circuit system.

Logical Based on this relational analysis, the present study hypothesized an optimal method for supporting students, as outlined below (see Table 1). The remainder of this paper examines the validity of our hypothesized method.

Table 1. Adaptive systems to multidimensionality of students' learning style

Learning style	Ease of reading law	Difficulty of law	Adaptive system			Category Number
			Legal texts (articles)	Logical expression	Logic circuit	
Knowledge-oriented problems	Easy	Difficult	○	○	◎	1
		Easy	◎		△	2
	Difficult	Difficult			◎	3
		Easy		◎	◎	4
Exercise-oriented problems	Easy	Difficult	○		○	5
		Easy	○	△	◎	6
	Difficult	Difficult			○	7
		Easy			◎	8
Neither	Difficult	Difficult	○			9
Both	Difficult	Difficult		◎	△	10
		Easy	◎		◎	11

◎: Very adaptive ○: Adaptive △: Neither Blank: Not adaptive

2.2 Evaluation Experiment

We first investigated a method for supporting information gathering, as shown in Table 1.

Subjects: A total of 86 university students studying IP infringement.

Methods: Students were twice presented with a problem that required them to combine information from texts and think critically. Between the first and second instances, students received explanations of how to solve the problem, and they also performed practice exercises. Explanations were provided according to the model problem-solving process for Patent Act (Japanese law) study (see Table 2) [3]. Generation support for surface structure and formularized structure denoted the provision of assistance in extracting terminology from texts. Generation support for conditional structures denoted assistance in the creation of logical formulae. Also, generation support for solution structures denoted assistance in the creation of logic circuits. We collected information on whether students answered the problem correctly or incorrectly on each of the two instances, and we also asked students to make subjective evaluations of the support methods on a scale of 1 to 4 points. In addition, we performed system-use analyses and other tests as shown in Figs. 3, 4, 5, 6, 7 and 8.

Table 2. Model for a problem-solving process for Patent Act (Japanese law) [3].

Surface-layer structure generation process	Surface structure	Relational representation between attributes of problem statements (e.g., structural understanding of problem statements)
Formulation process	Formulation structure	Surface structures represented by words used in statute text (e.g., substitution of terms in the statute)
Solution derivation process	Constraints structure	Logical formulas describing attributes of problem statements (e.g., representation of statute text as a logical formula using logic symbols such as $\wedge$ and $\vee$)
	Solution structure	Logical structures for deriving a solution from attributes (e.g., binary representation in a logic circuit using MIL)
	Objective structure	Solution

Results: We divided students into four groups (those who answered correctly both times [C→C], those who answered incorrectly the first time but correctly the second time [I→C], those who answered correctly the first time but incorrectly the second time [C→I], and those who answered incorrectly both times [I→I]) and then examined the relationship between these four groups and the students' own subjective evaluations. Groups C→C and I→C tended to rate the support methods used in this study more favorably than did the other two groups (see Fig. 11). For Group I→I, little difference was observed across scores given for any of the evaluation items.

The analysis revealed a positive opinion of the logical formulas and logic circuits among the I→C and C→C groups; furthermore, the fact that students in these groups were able to determine the correct answer after receiving support suggests that the systems may be useful in helping students acquire new knowledge. Conversely, the analysis also suggests that for students like those in the I→I group, who display little interest in any of the support methods, knowledge acquisition remains difficult.

With that in mind, we next looked at which of the multi-dimensionally defined categories each student belonged to. We found that students in the I→I group were the same students that had been classified as not receptive to either learning style and perceived legal texts as both hard to read and difficult to understand; this supported the findings of previous research [8]. Finally, we attempted to identify support methods for students in this particular category.

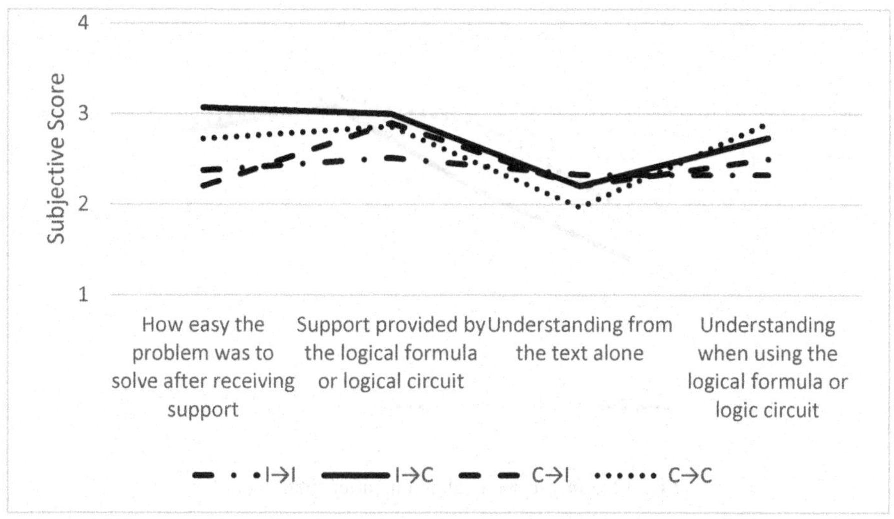

Fig. 11. Subjective evaluations from the evaluation experiment

2.3 Multi-dimensional Student Classification and System Evaluation

As shown in Table 1, the text system is the recommended system for students classified as not receptive to either learning style and who perceived legal texts as both hard to read and difficult to understand. (In previous research [8], these students had rated all of the systems poorly; however, their evaluation of the text system was less unfavorable than that of the other systems.) Bearing in mind the possibility that students in this category were poorly motivated to study law from the outset, we decided to administer an additional survey (as described below) to these students following their final exam for the term. Responses to items (1) to (4) were made using a 4-point Likert scale, from positive to negative.

(1) Was the semester term final exam difficult?
(2) Did you make use of the learning support system?
(3) Did the learning support system help you prepare for the term final exam?
(4) How did you feel about the exercise that allowed you to assemble logic circuits yourself?
(5) Free description question etc.

Analysis of this additional survey found no significant difference between these students' answers and the overall averages for items (1) to (4) (see Fig. 12). However, on the free response portion, students shared sentiments such as "I think the systems can be useful depending on how they are used," "The systems are intuitive to use," "I would be more interested in using the systems if the interfaces had more entertaining designs," and "Drawing the lines for the logic circuits requires too many clicks, making the interface feel cumbersome." This suggests that improvements made to the systems' features, along with adjustments to the order in which the systems are used, could lead to more positive system evaluations from students.

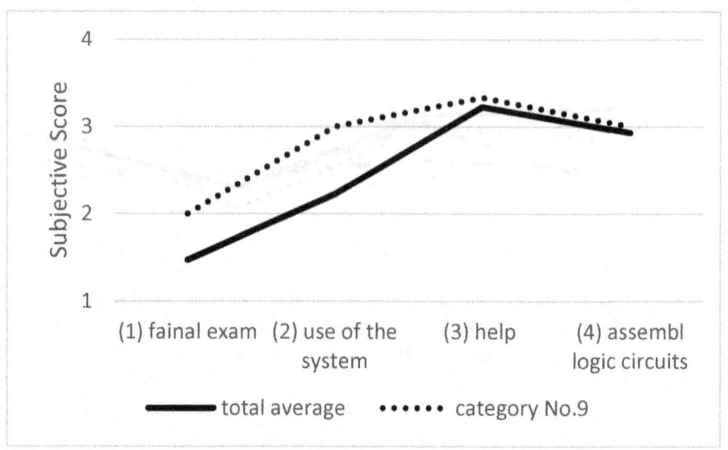

Fig. 12. Subjective evaluations after final exam

3 Conclusion and Future Work

This study attempted to determine the ideal method for implementing learning support systems so that they can best assist different types of students; the learning support systems in question were previously developed by the authors, and they are meant to aid information acquisition in the study of Patent Act (Japanese law). The study determined that adjustments to the learning support systems, such as changes made to the order in which the systems are presented, could have a positive effect on system-use outcomes, even among students for whom learning support has not had a previous significant effect. These adjustments should be made in the context of student categories determined according to a multi-dimensional classification system, including dimensions such as student attitudes toward the study of law.

Future research should endeavor to further improve the systems, as well as to determine ideal design, expansion, and usage methods for learning support systems.

Acknowledgments. This research was partially supported by a Grant-in-Aid for Scientific Research (B) (#16H03086; Principal Investigator: Takako Akakura) from Japan Society for the Promotion of Science (JSPS).

References

1. Intellectual Property Strategy Headquarters, "Intellectual Property Promotion Plan 2017" (2017). https://www.kantei.go.jp/jp/singi/titeki2/kettei/chizaikeikaku20170516.pdf. (in Japanese)
2. Akakura, T., Kawamata, T., Kato, K.: Use of learning support systems in intellectual property law education in engineering departments. Eng. Educ. **67**(1), 75–80 (2019). (in Japanese)

3. Akakura, T., Tomoto, T., Kato, K.: Self-learning support system about learning patent act based on the problem-solving process model using logical structure of legal texts. Jpn. J. Educ. Technol. **42**(2), 141–153 (2018). (in Japanese)
4. Akakura, T., Tomoto, T., Kato, K.: Development of a blended learning system for engineering students studying intellectual property law and access log analysis of the system. In: Yamamoto, S., Mori, H. (eds.) HIMI 2018, Part II. LNCS, vol. 10905, pp. 231–242. Springer, Cham (2018). https://doi.org/10.1007/978-3-319-92046-7_21
5. Akakura, T., Kawamata, T., Kato, K.: Development of a blended learning system for engineering students studying intellectual property law, and an analysis of the relationship between system usage and the knowledge acquisition process. In: Proceedings of 2017 IEEE International Conference on Teaching, Assessment, and Learning for Engineering (TALE 2017), Hong Kong, pp. 114–117, December 2017
6. Akakura, T., Kawamata, T., Kato, K.: Development and use of a video on demand e-learning system with logic circuit exercises for teaching intellectual property law. In: Proceedings of 2018 IEEE International Conference on Teaching, Assessment, and Learning for Engineering (TALE 2018), Wollongong, Australia, pp. 722–725, December 2018
7. Akakura, T., Kawamata, T., Kato, K.: Development of a learning support system for studying intellectual property law based on representing legal statements as logical circuits. In: Proceedings of 12th International Technology, Education and Development Conference (INTED 2018), Valencia, Spain, pp. 3956–3963, March 2018
8. Akakura, T., Kawamata, T., Kato, K.: Relationship between the multidimensionality of the knowledge acquisition process for law and the use of learning support systems that simulate legal texts as logic circuits. In: Proceedings of 12th International Technology, Education and Development Conference (INTED 2019), Valencia, Spain, March 2019 (accepted)

Does the Use of Tablets Lead to More Information Being Recorded and Better Recall in Short-Term Memory Tasks?

Hailey Arreola(✉), Andrea Nicole Flores, Amber Latham, Hanna MacNew, and Kim-Phuong L. Vu

Department of Psychology, California State University, Long Beach, USA
haileyarreola1@gmail.com,
{andrea.flores03, amber.latham, hanna.macnew}@student.csulb.edu, kim.vu@csulb.edu

Abstract. Cognitive offloading is the process of recording information onto an external source (i.e., a piece of paper) to reduce short-term memory demands. People engage in cognitive offloading to be able to recall more information accurately [1]. The capacity for short-term memory is typically 7+/−2 items [2], but the number of items that can be accurately remembered decreases as the complexity of the information increases. As a result, people are more likely to engage in cognitive offloading when the memory task is difficult. Most cognitive offloading studies have used paper as the External Medium [1, 3]. People, however, may not have a pen and paper readily available to record information. Due to the increase of mobile technology, though, people are more likely to carry around mobile devices such as smartphones and tablets. Mobile devices can be used as a convenient medium to offload information. The present study examined if use of mobile technology would increase participants' offloading behaviors and recall accuracy compared to using paper for recording information. Results indicated that although all tablet features were available (e.g., swiping, voice recording), participants engaged in less cognitive offloading when using tablets compared to paper, and this resulted in lower recall performance for the tablet condition. Implications of these findings are discussed.

Keywords: Cognitive offloading · Mobile technology · Human performance

1 Introduction

1.1 Background and Motivation

The creation of mobile technology within recent decades has provided users with the option of offloading, or recording, information onto their devices rather than having to remember the information using their short-term or long-term memory. For example, users can set reminders or alarms on their smartphones or tablets to aid their memory for performing a task in the future. The Pew Research Center [4] indicates that approximately 53% of Americans own a tablet and 77% own a smartphone. These percentages are typically higher for younger adults, aged 18–34, [4, 5]. This widespread ownership

S. Yamamoto and H. Mori (Eds.): HCII 2019, LNCS 11569, pp. 292–302, 2019.
https://doi.org/10.1007/978-3-030-22660-2_20

of mobile technology provides a tool that has the potential to increase human performance capabilities across a large segment of the population.

For example, a person's usage and reliance on technology can alter their behavior by influencing decisions to extend their memory into the physical world to reduce workload. College students can take pictures of PowerPoint slides with their smartphones while their professor displays the slides during class to minimize the physical and mental demands of taking notes while listening to the professor. The capturing of the information on the smartphone can also increase the accuracy of the notes that students take by preserving the source (i.e., picture of what was presented) and not just relying on the students' memory of what was shown on the slide. There can be drawbacks, however, associated with the use of technology in educational settings.

Mueller and Oppenheimer [6] examined students' note taking behaviors when using a laptop versus paper. They found that when a laptop was used for taking notes, students were more likely to take verbatim notes. Taking verbatim notes could be beneficial because it captures the information in the exact manner that it was presented, which is helpful for acquiring factual knowledge. Verbatim notes, however, can be detrimental for long term memory learning as it results in shallow processing of the information that was being presented, which leads to poorer memory of that information [7]. Mueller and Oppenheimer [6] also found that students who used a laptop for taking notes performed worse than students who used paper to take notes on a subsequent assessment for comprehension questions. Thus, Mueller and Oppenheimer concluded that use of a laptop for note-taking could negatively affect students' performance on educational assessments.

Although, use of a laptop for note-taking might not benefit delayed recall of information, Bui, Myerson, and Hale [8] found that using a computer to take verbatim notes (i.e., transcribe the lecture) was beneficial to performance when recall was tested immediately. However, Mangen, Anda, Oxborough, and Bronnick [9] found that when participants recorded words that were orally presented to them, they had better recall of the words when the words were hand-written on paper compared to when it was typed using either a conventional or virtual keyboard. Therefore, findings are mixed about whether the use of laptops and tablets for note-taking leads to better immediate recall of the recorded information. It should be noted, that in the three studies mentioned above [6, 8, 9], memory for the information was tested without the participants having access to the recorded information. For cognitive offloading tasks, though, the information is being recorded with the intent of referencing it during the recall test. Thus, use of laptops and tablets for recording information on cognitive offloading tasks can lead to information being recorded more efficiently and in verbatim, which can increase recall accuracy on both short- and long-term prospective memory tasks.

The present study uses short-term memory tasks, which require recall of information immediately, after the information was presented. People are able to retain an average of 7+/−2 items in their working short-term memory [2]. Because of this capacity limitation for short-term memory, it can be difficult for people to hold a lot of information in their mind. As a result, accuracy on short-term memory tests decreases rapidly as the number of items increase beyond 9 items. Moreover, the short-term memory span, or items that can be accurately recalled, decreases as the information becomes more complex (e.g., word length increases) [10]. Thus, the use of mobile technology might be beneficial in improving performance on short-term memory tasks by allowing people to use a convenient medium to record information. For example, if people are looking for the location of a new restaurant, they must remember the address of the location long enough to input it on Google Maps or another navigation aide. Being able to record, or offload, this information with their mobile device would allow people to simply transfer the address to the navigation aide without taxing their working memory capacity.

Previous studies of cognitive offloading behavior have used paper as the medium for participants to write down information [3]. Risko and Gilbert found that one factor that influences participants' decision to offload information is the amount of effort that is required to record the information. Since people do not typically carry around a pen/pencil and paper with them, but are often carrying some sort of mobile device, the ease in which information can be recorded using mobile technology can potentially influence cognitive offloading behaviors. Thus, the present study examines whether the medium to record information (paper or mobile device) results in different cognitive offloading behaviors and performance on short-term memory tasks.

2 Experiment 1

Participants were asked to recall pairs of words that were associated with academic studies. Participants were given the opportunity to record the word pairs as the items were presented using either pen/paper or a tablet device in the first test portion. The number of word pairs that participants were asked to recall varied in Set Sizes of 2, 4, or 6. In the second test portion, participants were asked to perform the same memory task without the option of recording information to obtain baseline measures of their working memory capacity and determine whether cognitive offloading increases the participants' performance.

2.1 Methods

Participants. Twenty-three students from California State University, Long Beach (CSULB) participated in this study. Students were recruited using the Introductory Psychology subject pool. The data from one participant was not recorded due to a program failure. Thus, the analyses were conducted using the data from 22 participants (Females: 17, Males: 5; Mean Age: 18.91; Range: 18–28 years). Participants were compensated by receiving experimental credit towards their course requirement. Informed consent was obtained from all participants, and the protocol used in this study was approved by the institutional review board (IRB) at CSULB.

Design. This experiment employed 2 (External Medium for Offloading: Paper or Tablet) $\times$ 3 (Set Size: 2, 4, and 6) mixed design. The between-subjects variable was External Medium and the within-subjects variable was Set Size. Within this larger design, the data was examined by practice condition (i.e., practice or experimental trials) and offloading condition (i.e., Choice or No Choice conditions).

Apparatus. The experiment was programmed using SuperLab 5.0 software and run on computers with Windows 10 as the operating system. The computers were Dell desktops with 24-in. monitors. Participants were seated 60 cm away from the computer and monitor. For the tablet condition, a Samsung Galaxy Tab (S2) and Apple iPad (1st Generation iPad Pro) were available for the participants to record the information as it was being presented. For the paper condition, a pen and an 8.5 × 11 piece of paper was made available to participants to record information. For both conditions, all recall responses for each trial were typed responses made on a standard QWERTY keyboard.

Stimuli. The stimuli were pairs of words that associated an academic subject with a task that students typically need to remember to do during the semester. The academic subjects were abbreviated to 3–4 letters (Math = MATH, English = ENG, History = HIST, Psychology = PSY, Biology = BIO) to make the length comparable. Similarly, the tasks that needed to be completed in the subject areas were also shortened to 4–5 letters (Paper Assignment = PAPER, Reading Assignment = READ, QUIZ, Group Work = GROUP, Exam = EXAM). Each stimulus was presented for 1 s. The words were presented in the center of the screen using Arial font at a font size of 36 points. All letters were capitalized to standardize the presentation of the stimuli. The stimuli were presented as word pairs (i.e., ENG PAPER) in Set Sizes (number of word pairs to recall) of 2, 4, and 6.

Procedure. Participants were randomly assigned to be in the Tablet or Paper condition (External Medium). In the tablet condition, participants choose between two brands of tablets (Apple or Android) before beginning the practice condition. For the Paper condition, participants were given a pen and piece of paper. When recording information, participants in the tablet condition had the freedom to use any of the capabilities provided by the tablet such as voice recording or typing. After reading the instructions for the memory task, participants began a practice condition.

The practice condition consisted of 10 trials that allowed participants to familiarize themselves with the task. Participants could record information onto their assigned External Medium while the stimuli were being presented. The order of trials in the practice condition was fixed, with two replicates at the Set Sizes of 2, 4, 6, 4, and 2. Figure 1 shows an example of a single trial with a Set Size of 2: participants were first shown a screen that indicated the Set Size for the trial, followed by the word pairs, and then a screen with "????," which was the cue to recall the items. To recall the items, the participants inputted the first letter of each subject and task needed to be recalled (e.g., PQ for PSY QUIZ, BP for BIO PAPER). The use of first letters of the word pair for recall was implemented to avoid inaccurate responses caused by typos. Participants were able to reference their recorded information on the External Medium during the recall phase and when typing the responses. For accuracy, the case (upper vs. lower) did not matter. After each trial, participants were given feedback about their accuracy.

After the practice condition, participants began the Choice experimental condition where they still had the option to offload information onto their assigned External Medium during the stimulus presentation. Participants were presented with 18 trials, with 3 repetitions of Set Sizes of 2, 4, and 6, presented in random order, in each of two blocks. Next, participants completed the No Choice experimental condition, where no offloading was permitted in order to establish baseline memory capacity and to

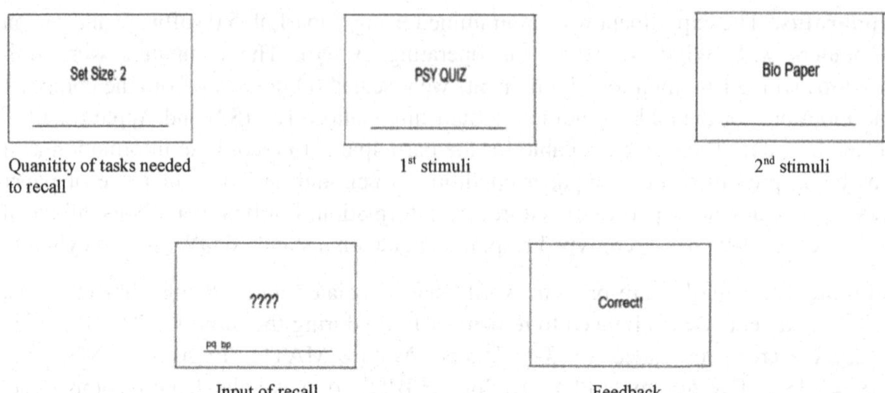

Fig. 1. Illustration of a single trial. Participants began the trial with the screen showing the Set Size (i.e., number of items to be remembered). Then, participants were shown the items and asked to recall the items when the screen displayed "????." After inputting their answers, participants were given feedback on their accuracy.

determine whether the offloading improved memory performance. Otherwise, the No Choice condition was similar to the Choice condition. After completing the No Choice condition, participants filled out two forms: a demographics questionnaire and a personality survey. The personality survey was administered for exploratory purposes and its findings will not be discussed in the present paper.

An experimenter was present in the room with each participant. The experimenter wrote down whether the participant recorded the information on the External Medium for each trial in the Practice and Choice conditions. The experimenter also ensured that participants did not record information in the No Choice condition.

2.2 Results

Practice Condition. Separate 2 (External Medium: Paper or Tablet) × 3 (Set Size: 2, 4, and 6) analyses of variance (ANOVAs) were performed on the mean proportion of offloaded trials (i.e., proportion of trials where participants recorded information) and mean accuracy (proportion of correctly recalled items). See Tables 1 and 2 for means.

For proportion of offloaded trials, there was a significant main effect of Set Size, $F(2, 40) = 29.21$, $MSE = .064$, $p < .001$, where proportion of offloaded trials increase as Set Size increases (*Ms* = .22, .55, and .80, for Set Size of 2, 4, and 6, respectively). No other effects were significant.

For accuracy, the main effect of Set Size was significant, $F(2, 40) = 9.19$, $MSE = .069$, $p = .001$. Accuracy was highest at Set Size of 2 ($M = .82$) and it decreased at Set Sizes of 4 and 6 (*Ms* = .50 and .56, respectively). No other effects were significant.

Experimental Choice Condition. Similar to the practice condition, separate, 2 (External Medium: Paper or Tablet) × 3 (Set Size: 2, 4, and 6) ANOVAs were conducted on mean proportion of offloaded trials and accuracy. See Tables 3 and 4 for means.

For proportion of offloaded trials, the main effect of Set Size was significant, $F(2, 40) = 33.04$, $MSE = .46$, $p < .001$. Similar to what was found in the practice condition, as Set Size increased, the portion of trials in which participants recorded information increased (*Ms* = .29, .72, and .91, for Set Size of 2, 4, and 6, respectively). The main effect of External Medium approached significance, $F(1, 20) = 3.93$, $MSE = .18$, $p = .061$, where participants showed a tendency to record more information when using paper ($M = .74$) than the tablet ($M = .54$). The interaction between Set Size and External Medium was not significant.

For accuracy, the main effect of Set Size was significant, $F(1, 40) = 9.32$, $MSE = .02$, $p < .001$. Accuracy was lower at Set Size of 4 ($M = .71$) than at Set Sizes of 2 ($M = .89$) and 6 ($M = .85$). The main effect of External Medium approached significance, $F(1, 20) = 3.42$, $MSE = .09$, $p = .079$, where participants showed a tendency to be more accurate when using paper ($M = .88$) than the tablet ($M = .75$). The interaction between Set Size and External Medium was not significant.

Experimental No Choice Condition. Participants in the No Choice condition did not have the option of recording information, but their accuracy was examined using a 2 (External Medium Group: Paper or Tablet) × 3 (Set Size: 2, 4, and 6) ANOVA. See Table 5 for means.

There was a significant main effect for Set Size, $F(2, 40) = 240.40$, $MSE = .016$, $p < .001$, where participants' accuracy decreased as Set Size increased (*Ms* = .82, .23, and .02, for Set Size of 2, 4, and 6, respectively). This main effect was qualified by a two-way interaction of Set Size and External Medium Group, $F(2, 40) = 4.07$, $MSE = .02$, $p = .025$, see Fig. 2. Test of simple effects were conducted at each Set Size. At Set Size of 2, participants assigned to the paper group ($M = .89$) were more accurate than those assigned to the tablet group ($M = .74$), $F(1, 20) = 8.07$, $MSE = .016$, $p = .01$. For Set Sizes of 4 and 6, the differences were not significant, $F < 1.0.7$

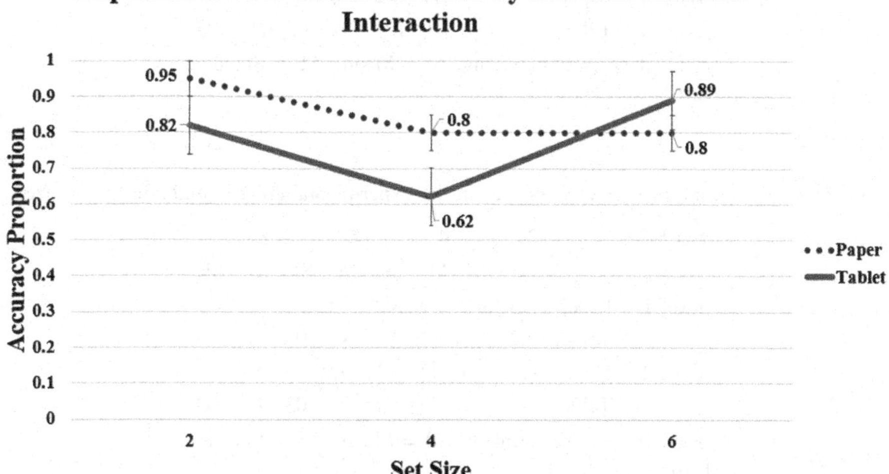

Fig. 2. An interaction between Set Size and External Medium occurring at Set Size 6.

Table 1. Proportion of trials offloaded in the practice condition by set size

Set Size		2		4		6		8	
		M	SE	M	SE	M	SE	M	SE
Exp. 1	Paper	.31	.04	.57	.03	.73	.03	-	-
	Tablet	.11	.02	.52	.03	.86	.03	-	-
Exp. 2	Paper	-	-	.75	.03	.95	.02	1.0	0
	Tablet	-	-	.39	.03	.68	.03	.91	.03

Note. Exp. = Experiment, M = Mean, SE = Standard Error

Table 2. Proportion of correct responses in the practice condition by set size

Set Size		2		4		6		8	
		M	SE	M	SE	M	SE	M	SE
Exp. 1	Paper	.82	.02	.61	.04	.61	.03	-	-
	Tablet	.82	.02	.38	.02	.50	.03	-	-
Exp. 2	Paper	-	-	.68	.02	.55	.03	.73	.04
	Tablet	-	-	.50	.03	.64	.03	.68	.04

Note. Exp. = Experiment, M = Mean, SE = Standard Error

Table 3. Proportion of trials offloaded in the experimental choice condition by set size

Set Size		2		4		6		8	
		M	SE	M	SE	M	SE	M	SE
Exp. 1	Paper	.41	.05	.85	.02	.97	.01	-	-
	Tablet	.17	.03	.59	.04	.85	.04	-	-
Exp. 2	Paper	-	-	.91	.02	.98	.01	.98	.01
	Tablet	-	-	.70	.04	.91	.03	.91	.03

Note. Exp. = Experiment, M = Mean, SE = Standard Error

Table 4. Proportion of correct responses in the experimental choice condition by set size

Set Size		2		4		6		8	
		M	SE	M	SE	M	SE	M	SE
Exp. 1	Paper	.95	.01	.80	.02	.89	.02	-	-
	Tablet	.82	.01	.62	.03	.80	.03	-	-
Exp. 2	Paper	-	-	.92	.01	.92	.01	.89	.01
	Tablet	-	-	.76	.02	.77	.03	.68	.03

Note. Exp. = Experiment, M = Mean, SE = Standard Error

Table 5. Proportion of correct responses in experimental no choice condition by set size

Set Size		2		4		6		8	
		M	SE	M	SE	M	SE	M	SE
Exp. 1	Paper	.89	.01	.20	.02	.03	.01	-	-
	Tablet	.74	.01	.26	.02	.02	.01	-	-
Exp. 2	Paper	-	-	.17	.02	.00	.00	.00	.00
	Tablet	-	-	.23	.02	.02	.01	.00	.00

Note. Exp. = Experiment, M = Mean, SE = Standard Error

2.3 Discussion

Participants engaged in cognitive offloading to maintain accuracy on the short-term memory tasks used in the present study. When the Set Size was 2, participants only recorded information during the stimulus presentation for 29% of the trials. At Set Size 4, however, offloading behavior increased to 72% of trials. At the Set Size of 6, participants recorded the stimuli on 91% of the trials. Comparing performance on the Choice versus No Choice condition, the cognitive offloading behavior resulted in increases in accuracy of 7%, 48%, and 83% at Set Sizes of 2, 4, and 6, respectively. The increase in accuracy for the different Set Sizes match the participants' cognitive offloading behavior: as cognitive offloading behaviors increased, accuracy increased. Because participants recorded the most information when the Set Size was 6, the largest benefit in performance was evident at this Set Size.

Participants tended to offload more when the External Medium was paper rather than a tablet, but this difference was not significant. Participants also showed a tendency to be more accurate in the paper condition than in the tablet condition. In the No Choice condition, participants in the paper condition had significantly higher accuracy than those in the tablet condition only when the Set Size was 2. Thus, the results of Experiment 1 only showed trends for a preference and slight benefit of paper as an offloading medium over the tablet. It is possible that the Set Sizes used in the Experiment 1, being 2, 4, and 6-word pairs, were not high enough to motivate users to use the tablet features for recording information. Therefore, we increased the Set Size by one level in Experiment 2 to examine whether making the task more difficult would motivate users to change their offloading behaviors.

3 Experiment 2

Experiment 2 was similar to Experiment 1, except that the memory task was made more difficult by using Set Sizes of 4, 6, and 8-word pairs.

3.1 Methods

A total of twenty two students were recruited from the same subject pool as in Experiment 1 (Females: 17; Males: 5; Mean Age: 18.36 years; Range: 18–22 years).

The apparatus, stimuli, and procedures used in Experiment 2 were identical to those used in Experiment 1, with the only difference being that three Set Sizes used were 4, 6, and 8, instead of 2, 4, and 6.

3.2 Results

The data from Experiment 2, were analyzed in the same manner as in Experiment 1.

Practice Condition. Similar to Experiment 1, separate 2 (External Medium: Paper or Tablet) × 3 (Set Size: 4, 6, and 8) ANOVAs were performed on the mean proportion of offloaded trials and accuracy, see Tables 1 and 2 for means.

For proportion of offloaded trials, the main effect of Set Size was significant, $F(2, 40) = 22.93$, $MSE = .04$, $p < .001$, where proportion of offloaded trials increased as Set Size increased (*Ms* = .57, .82, and .96, for Set Size of 2, 4, and 6, respectively). The main effect of External Medium was also significant, $F(1, 20) = 8.27$, $MSE = .12$, $p = .009$, where participants in the paper group ($M = .90$) offloaded more information than participants in the tablet group ($M = .66$). The interaction between Set Size and the External Medium approached significance, $F(2, 40) = 2.88$, $MSE = .04$, $p = .068$, see Fig. 3. For all Set Sizes, participants in the paper condition offloaded more information than participants in the tablet condition, with the difference being largest at Set Size of 4 ($MD = .36$), intermediate at Set Size of 6 ($MD = .27$), and smallest at Set Size of 8 ($MD = .09$).

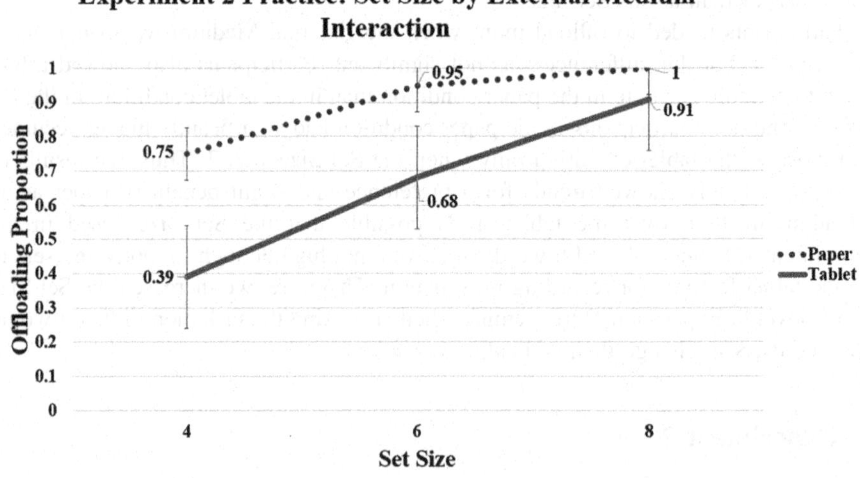

Fig. 3. For accuracy, there were no significant main effects or interactions.

Experimental Choice Condition. For the choice trials, mean proportion of trials offloaded and accuracy were analyzed using separate 2 (External Medium: Paper or Tablet) × 3 (Set Size: 4, 6, and 8) × 2 (Block: First and Second) ANOVAs, see Tables 3 and 4 for means.

For proportion of offloaded trials, the main effect of Set Size was significant, $F(2, 40) = 5.77$, $MSE = .03$, $p = .006$, where participants offloaded more trials when the Set Size was 6 and 8 ($Ms = .95$) than when it was 4 ($M = .80$). No other effects were significant.

For accuracy, only the main effect of External Medium, $F(1, 20) = 6.52$, $p = .019$, was significant. Participants were more accurate when offloading on paper ($M = .91$) than on a tablet ($M = .74$).

No Choice Experimental Trials. Accuracy scores were submitted to a 2 (External Medium Group: Paper or Tablet) × 3 (Set Size: 4, 6, and 8) ANOVA. There was a significant main effect of Set Size, $F(2, 40) = 27.13$, $MSE = .01$, $p < .001$, where accuracy decreased as Set Size increased, $Ms = .20$, .01, and .00, for Set Size of 4, 6, and 8, respectively). No other effects were significant.

3.3 Discussion

Increasing the Set Size by one level in Experiment 2 lead participants to record information on about 26% more trials compared to Experiment 1. Consequently, increasing Set Size motivated users to engage in more cognitive offloading. Additionally, participants in the present experiment were 76% more accurate in the Choice condition than in the No Choice condition. Thus, participants were using cognitive offloading as a strategy to improve their performance.

In the practice condition, participants assigned to the paper condition offloaded more information than participants assigned to the tablet condition, especially for the smaller Set Sizes. In the Choice experimental condition, participants were also more accurate when using paper to record information compared to using a tablet. Thus, similar to Experiment 1, participants preferred to use paper as the External Medium for offloading information, even though the tablet offers more features (e.g., voice recording) that could be used to effectively and efficiently record information. This may be attributed to the concept of "paper persistence," where individuals continue to use paper instead of technology due to paper's efficiency and ease of use, as well as a lack of knowledge or experience with the technology provided to them [11].

4 Conclusion

Overall, participants engaged in more cognitive offloading as task difficulty increased, which led to higher recall accuracy for more difficult trials in both Experiments 1 and 2. Thus, participants are able to effectively change their cognitive offloading behavior to adapt to task demands: offload information when the amount of items that need to be recalled exceeds short-term memory capacity. Participants also tended to engage in more cognitive offloading when assigned to the paper group compared to the tablet group. This preference for paper may be a result of its familiarity to users and quicker speed in recording information.

5 Limitations and Future Directions

This study consisted of several limitations. First, the level of knowledge and experience participants had with the tablet used during the experiment was not measured. It may be the case that the participants sampled do not use tablets for taking notes or setting reminders, which means that this aspect of the technology was novel to them. As a result, the participants were not able to take advantage of all the features of the tablet that could have led to more efficient recording of information and more accurate recall. Second, the sample size was small in both experiments, which resulted in low power for detecting group differences. Finally, the sample consisted of Introductory Psychology students, which limits the generalization of the research findings to other groups. Future studies should consider examining the use of the participants' personal mobile devices to increase familiarity of the device. In addition, larger sample sizes and more diverse user groups should be included in the sample.

Acknowledgements. We thank the students of the Center for Usability in Design and Accessibility for assistance with conducting this study. The CSULB McNair Scholar Program supported Hailey in this study.

References

1. Risko, E.F., Dunn, T.L.: Storing information in-the-world: metacognition and cognitive offloading in a short–term memory task. Conscious. Cogn. **36**(C), 61–74 (2015)
2. Miller, G., Kintsch, W.: The magical number seven, plus or minus two: some limits on our capacity for processing information. Psychol. Rev. **101**(2), 343–352 (1994)
3. Risko, E.F., Gilbert, S.J.: Cognitive offloading. Trends Cogn. Sci. **20**(9), 676–688 (2016)
4. Pew Research Center: Mobile Fact Sheet (2018). http://www.pewinternet.org/fact-sheet/mobile/. Accessed 25 January 2019
5. Smith, A., Fox, S.: U.S. Smartphone Use in 2015. Pew Research Center, Pew Internet & Technology Project site, 1 April 2015. http://www.pewinternet.org/2015/04/01/us-smartphone-use-in-2015/
6. Mueller, P., Oppenheimer, D.: The pen is mightier than the keyboard: advantages of longhand over laptop note taking. Psychol. Sci. **25**(6), 1159–1168 (2014)
7. Craik, F.M.I., Lockhart, R.S.: Levels of processing: a framework for memory research. J. Verbal Learn. Verbal Behav. **11**(6), 671–684 (1972)
8. Bui, D.C., Myerson, J., Hale, S.: Note-taking with computers: exploring alternative strategies for improved recall. J. Educ. Psychol. **105**(2), 299–309 (2013)
9. Mangen, A., Anda, L.G., Oxborough, G.H., Bronnick, K.: Handwriting versus keyboard writing: effect on word recall. J. Writ. Res. **7**(2), 227–247 (2015)
10. Baddeley, A.D., Thomson, N., Buchanan, M.: Word length and the structure of short-term memory. J. Verbal Learn. Verbal Behav. **14**(6), 575–589 (1975)
11. Saleem, J., Russ, A., Neddo, A., Blades, P., Doebbeling, B., Foresman, B.: Paper persistence, workarounds, and communication breakdowns in computerized consultation management. Int. J. Med. Inform. **80**(7), 466–479 (2011)

Human Factors Guidance for Building a Computer-Based Procedures System: How to Give the Users Something They Actually Want

Walter E. Gilmore(✉)

Sandia National Laboratories, Albuquerque, NM, USA
wegilmo@sandia.gov

Abstract. Historically, "skill-of-the-craft" was the single measure of job qualification. In those days, no one gave workers a procedure to follow. Today, large complex industries rely on procedures as a way of ensuring the job will be performed reliably and safely. Typically, these procedures provide a layer of protection to mitigate the severity of an accident or prevent it from happening. While paper-based procedures have long been the standard way of doing business, there is increasing interest in replacing this format with Computer-Based Procedures. Though, the transition from paper to paperless can be more problematic than it seems. Some issues that have led to these problems are discussed here. It is hoped that, by knowing what these issues are, the same mistakes will not be repeated in the future. Mistake avoidance begins with a well-defined set of user requirements for the proposed system. Plus, it is important to realize that Computer-Based Procedures are likely going to be placed in a facility that has never used this type of technology before. As for any new technology, a new way of thinking must come with it. Otherwise, if attempts are made to intermingle old ideas with new ways of doing business, problems are destined to occur.

Keywords: Human computer interface · Computer Based Procedures · Human factors guidelines

1 Introduction

A wide range of industries utilize procedures in some form or fashion. Whether flipping switches in a chemical processing plant, or assembling the parts for a military weapon, procedures provide a level of assurance that the task will be performed consistently, correctly, and in a predetermined sequence [1]. Procedures are typically a set of written instructions that guide the worker through a series of steps. Each step is intended to be followed in a predefined order. In this fashion, procedures augment the workers capacity to do the job reliably and safely. Procedures are particularly useful in situations when the job is complex, and the consequences associated with making an error can be catastrophic.

S. Yamamoto and H. Mori (Eds.): HCII 2019, LNCS 11569, pp. 303–316, 2019.
https://doi.org/10.1007/978-3-030-22660-2_21

It is only within recent history that procedures were accepted as a standard way of doing business. Before procedures came into use, the quality of work was almost entirely dependent upon the "skill-of-the-craft." This principle was based on the idea that written instructions of any kind were neither called for or needed. Rather than having a procedure in hand, workers relied on their skills and know-how of the rules to perform the job [2]. To "know the ropes" could be described as an early example of "skill of the craft." Its origins are believed to be a nautical expression dating back to the late 18th century. To "know the ropes" meant that sailors working on early sailing ships were qualified and ready to perform the duties assigned to them. For instance, knowing which rope raised and lowered which sail, and learning to correctly tie knots [3].

Similarly, throughout the 19th century, apprenticeships were generally the means one obtained skill-of-the-craft. For instance, the steamboat pilots in the 1800's learned how to do the job while working under the supervision of a more senior pilot. To earn their license, apprentice pilots were taught to read the river. This entailed having the mental sharpness to know what lays ahead, whether it happens to be snags, rocks, sandbars, or geographical landmarks. Most importantly, to successfully navigate the Mississippi river, the pilot had to know the depth of the water at different places as well as the nature of the currents. Ultimately, the long hours of training in the wheelhouse would give the pilot a sense of "feel" of the boat, for all seasons of the year, and all foreseeable weather conditions [4]. Mark Twain was one of those steamboat apprentices that succeeded in reading the river, and for his accomplishments, he earned a steamboat pilot license in 1859 [5].

Then beginning in the early 20th century, the basic knowledge required to interact with newer technologies became increasingly more complex. From that period, Ford Model T owners could have a manual containing diagrams for servicing their new cars. For example, one diagram provided the owner with a lubrication schedule that points out where and at what mileage interval grease should be applied [6].

Then in the latter half of the 20th century, the demand for production output particularly in the energy sector, began to expand. As a result, plants started scaling up in size and capacity to meet demand. According to Perrow [7], growth in output coincides with increasing levels of system complexity. In turn, the abrupt rise in complexity makes it harder to understand the actual risk associated with operating one of these plants. Thus, despite our best efforts at controlling risk, we are left with a limited understanding of the underlying processes. In the absence of having a comprehensive state of knowledge in terms of how a plant operates, it is difficult to recognize and anticipate what can go wrong. The cause and effect relationships between systems, subsystems, and related components are too numerous to contemplate. As a result, the risk analyst has an incomplete picture of what it takes to predict accidents and finding ways to mitigate their severity.

But, if complexity exists, it must still be dealt with in a constructive way. One approach involves building layers of safety protection against the myriad number of events that could happen. The layers can be described as defense in depth measures that increase the chances that plant mishaps both anticipated and unanticipated, can be ameliorated or stopped altogether [8]. Today, procedures significantly contribute to the defense in depth philosophy. Figure 1 [8] illustrates how defense in depth measures might be implemented to mitigate the effects of a fire.

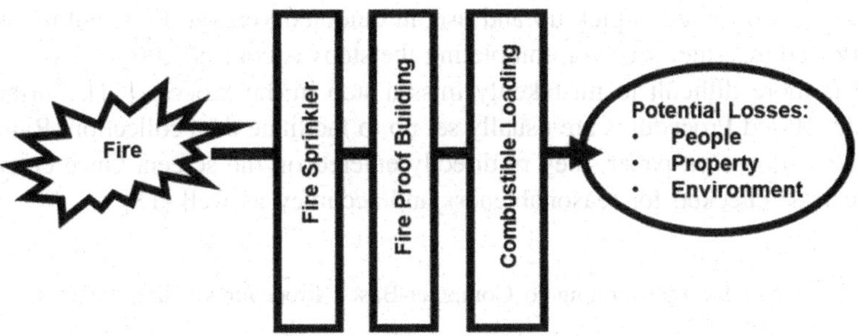

Fig. 1. Example of defense in depth measures that are in place to protect assets against the threat of a fire. (*Adapted from*: [8].)

Assuming a fire begins to propagate, the fire sprinkler provides the first layer of defense in depth. Next, the structures were built with fire proofing materials, constituting the second layer of defense in depth. Finally, a procedural control is followed to routinely pick up trash and materials that could contribute to the combustible load if a fire took place. Thus, the procedure for controlling combustibles becomes the third layer of defense in depth. Overall, the three layers act in concert to avoid or minimize potential losses if the fire happened to occur.

As increasingly more complex industries progressed into the 21st century, procedural controls were endorsed as a way of assuring that large processing facilities operate in a safe and stable configuration. Regrettably, the 1986 nuclear accident at Chernoby is a testament to the importance of having procedures, and what happens when procedures are not followed. At Chernobyl, activities were underway to test the operability of safety systems during loss of offsite power. To conduct the test, the supervisors decided to violate their own technical specifications for controlling reactivity and power. As the test continued, the reactor systems began to merge toward conditions that the personnel at the plant did not understand. Essentially, by choosing to ignore the instructions that would keep the plant in a safe state, a catastrophe ensued [9].

2 Computer Based Procedures: Why and for What Purpose?

It is fair to assume that procedures are here to stay. Procedures, particularly for complex high-risk systems, provide an added measure of protection and formality to the operations. While paper-based procedures remain a traditional mainstay of many industries, there is a growing interest in replacing paper with Computer-Based Procedures. If paper is an acceptable way of managing an industrial process, why transition to paperless? Some reasons are presented in Table 1. In Table 1, one primary motivator for going paperless is the often-held belief that it is an easier way to maintain documents. Essentially, if procedures are maintained from cradle to grave in a data base, product quality goes up and the administrative burden goes down. Additionally, a collection of documents held in a data base is searchable, and it is relatively simple to link related material [10]. At the shop floor level, Computer-Based Procedures minimize opportunities to pick up and use an outdated version. Plus, with Computer-Based Procedures, the order for completing the steps is controlled by the software. As such, it is more difficult to mistakenly miss a step in the process [11]. Furthermore, Computer-Based Procedures are usually set up to facilitate data collection. Rather than write values down on paper, they're directly entered on the screen. Once entered, the values can be checked for reasonableness and accuracy as well [13].

Table 1. Reasons for transitioning to Computer-Based Procedures. (*Adapted from*: [10, 11], and [13])

Compared to paper-based procedures, Computer-Based Procedures…
Are easier to maintain
Reduce the chances that an operator will follow a wrong procedure. (e.g., an out of date or incorrect version)
Avoid opportunities to skip a step or perform a series of steps out of sequence
Cannot be accessed remotely. Limited to local use (unless support technology is available)
Don't require physical space for storage
Facilitate recording of data and checking the accuracy of input
Hyperlinks can be used to cross reference steps to and from supporting materials

Thus, there are advantages to having Computer-Based Procedures. The same advantages are simply not possible for paper-based procedures. And it is apparent that Computer-Based Procedures could minimize human errors associated with missed steps, picking up the wrong version, and entering incorrect data. But it's less clear knowing how and to what extent overall human performance and decision making may be impacted by Computer-Based Procedures relative to paper [12]. Results gleaned from prior usability evaluations tend to suggest these concerns are warranted. In fact, there were indications that Computer-Based Procedures had an adverse impact on human performance and decision making. Specifically, these indications suggested that the path from paper to paperless environments was not as simple as it seemed. Principally, the operators reported that certain features were difficult and confusing to use [13, 14].

Over time, after observing operators and asking them questions about the problems they were having, their experiences were found to align with a few main issues. These issues are discussed in the next section.

3 Computer-Based Procedures: Issues

The issues presented here are not intended to be exhaustive, as there are different ways of looking at the problems people are having with Computer-Based Procedures. For each problem, numerous solutions are perhaps available, depending on the context of the work and goals expected to be accomplished using Computer-Based Procedures. Rather, the issues described here can be thought of as a snapshot of lessons learned that the author feels should be taken into consideration before the choice is made to transition from paper to paperless. By raising a level of awareness, it is hoped that the same mistakes and missteps that happened in the past will not be repeated in the future.

3.1 Integrate Computer Based Procedures with Current Operations

The choice to move from paper to paperless presents a brand-new way of doing business. Therefore, careful consideration should be given to the degree of impact Computer-Based Procedures may have on the organization, and the people responsible for doing the work. Referring to Moray's [15] characterization of a highly reliable organization, possible impacts could occur at the workstation, where the Computer-Based Procedures would be pulled up on the screen and acted upon. At this level, issues could arise as to whether the screen that is intended to display the procedures interferes with established work patterns. For instance, it would be of interest to know if, while reading and responding to the procedural instructions, the operators could still access the equipment, tools, and parts they need to perform the task.

Within the local environment, it would also be useful to know if the Computer-Based Procedures can be seen under current lighting conditions. Additionally, with the introduction of Computer-Based Procedures, operators may have to reconsider how they might communicate and collaborate amongst themselves, and at the same time, continue to maintain a strong sense of situational awareness in the workplace.

Finally, because a Computer-Based Procedures system is intended to replace the former paper-based system, impacts should also be assessed at the point where procedures are developed. Essentially, the basic rules for assuring the technically accuracy apply, whether the procedure happens to be presented in hardcopy or online [11]. Additional aspects, dealing with the infrastructure for producing and releasing final procedures to the shop floor, should also be reconsidered. For example, resources should be allocated to revise the local format and style guides for writing procedure. What may have worked well for paper no longer applies to Computer-Based Procedures. Other changes include the mechanisms by which procedures should be updated when new information becomes available. Above all, the processes for validation and quality assurance may also be different. As the steps taken to validate Computer-Based Procedures will likely be unique relative to paper procedures.

3.2 Affordances of Paper Are Naturally Embedded in the Flow of Work

Despite the benefits likely to be realized by Computer-Based Procedures, giving up paper also has a downside. The downside of giving up the affordances that paper provides us in daily life. Building upon the Theory of Affordances introduced by James J. Gibson, Sellen and Harper [10] describe some affordances regarding paper. When someone skims through a pile of documents, the physical paper allows for spatial flexibility. Only a short glance is necessary to know, "….where things are." [10] (p. 102). Whereas, compared to computer-based presentations, the operator is often limited to what can be viewed through the screen. Another closely related affordance with paper is the ease that users can scribble and jot notes directly on the page. It appears that the combined aid of the eye and the hand makes it easier to grasp the full meaning of the content. When completing the steps of a procedure, it is not unusual to mark up the pages for attention getting purposes, such as place keeping. As for most Computer-Based Procedures, a pen input feature is seldom available.

In short, according to Sellen and Harper [10], there are just certain things that people can do with paper that cannot be accommodated, at least not easily, with Computer-Based Procedures. Given the range of affordances that paper offers; it is important to carefully balance technological solutions with the inherent value paper naturally gives us.

3.3 Automatic Branching Doesn't Make Step to Step Navigation Any Easier

There are instances where computer-based procedure systems were developed without due consideration for the tools the operator would need to navigate through the entire range of steps [13, 14]. Nielsen [16] claims it should be just as easy to navigate the Web as it would to leaf across pages in a book. However, considering the problems operators have had navigating computerized procedures, it is expected they would find the task of leafing through a book less daunting. It appears that navigational capabilities are either added as an afterthought or overlooked entirely. This lack of emphasis on navigation may also be attributed to the perception that Computer-Based Procedures are a medium for presentation. True, the technology is intended as a device for displaying procedural content. But just being able to read content is of little value if the operators do not know if they are at the correct place in the procedure. Additionally, if they discover they are in the wrong place, there is no roadmap that shows them how to get to the correct place in the procedure.

Problems with navigation were particularly prevalent when operators encountered the automatic branching feature. The succinct definition for automatic branching is: "The procedure branches automatically to the appropriate instructions based on a choice made by the technician at the specified point in the procedure." [17] (p. 68). Expanding on this definition, automatic branching occurs when the operator is asked to read a step and, based on the information contained in the step, enter a value in an assigned field. (Typically, the value entails recording a measurement.) When the value is entered, the system advances to a next step. The action is automatic, without operator input. As a result, the operators are often left wondering why they were directed to that specific place in the procedure. Since the operators were unaware of what happened, they would occasionally believe themselves at fault for making a mistake.

The following example describes how automatic branching features are problematic for the operator. To best understand automatic branching, it is essential to first appreciate how the mechanics of branching are intended to work in a paper-based procedure. To illustrate, a paper-based procedure used to check the car's engine oil is presented in Fig. 2. In Step No. 1, the operator is instructed to read the oil level with the dipstick. This is determined by comparing the level of the oil against two marks, ranging from FULL to LOW, that are referenced on the dip stick (See Fig. 3.) In Step No. 2, the operator checks the box for the oil level that was just read. Three choices are available (Oil level > "LOW" AND ≤ "FULL"; Oil level ≤ "LOW"; and Oil level > "FULL"). In Step No. 3, the operator picks one of three columns, depending on the oil level that was previously checked off.

1. READ the oil level using the dipstick. NOTE: The oil level should show between the upper scribe mark that reads "FULL" and the Lower scribe mark that reads "LOW".

2. PLACE a checkmark in the box next to the oil level that was READ using the dipstick:

☐	Oil level > "LOW" AND ≤ "FULL"	☐	Oil level > "LOW" AND ≤ "FULL"	☐	Oil level > "LOW" AND ≤ "FULL"
☐	Oil level ≤ "LOW"	☐	Oil level ≤ "LOW"	☐	Oil level ≤ "LOW"
☐	Oil level > "FULL"	☐	Oil level > "FULL"	☐	Oil level > "FULL"

3. PERFORM the following:		
Option 1 Oil level > "LOW" AND ≤ "FULL"	Option 2 Oil level ≤ "LOW"	Option 3 Oil level > "FULL"
Oil level Acceptable	Oil level Unacceptable	Oil level Unacceptable
• Continue. • GO TO Step No. 4, "CHECK the Air Filter."	• ADD 1/4 Quart of oil. • GO TO Step No. 1.	• Using a Socket and Socket Wrench, Slightly LOOSEN the oil drain plug on the oil pan. • VERIFY that approximately 1/4 Quart of oil drains into the drain pan. • TIGHTEN the oil drain plug using a Socket and Socket Wrench. • GO TO Step No. 1.
4. CHECK the Air Filter		

Fig. 2. Checking the engine oil: A typical format for paper-based procedures.

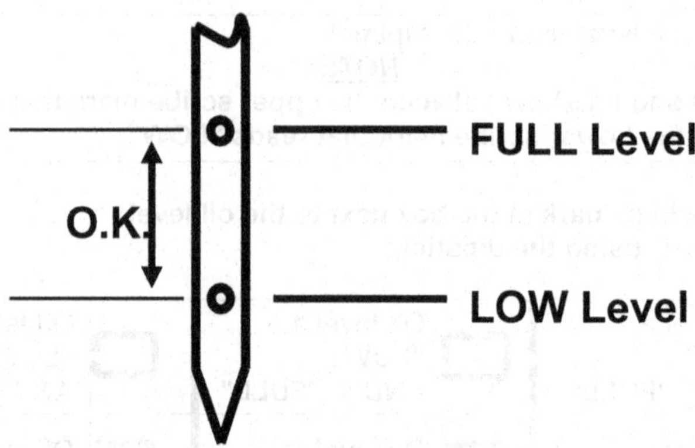

Fig. 3. Oil dipstick showing the "O.K." acceptable range between "Low level" and "Full level."

Next, a flow chart of a computer-based procedure for changing the engine oil is provided in Fig. 4. Again, same as for the paper version, the operator is directed by the procedure to read the oil level. Once the level is identified, the operator presses a button that represents the reading. Here, the choices are the same as for the paper-based procedure (Oil level > "LOW" AND ≤ "FULL"; Oil level ≤ "LOW"; and Oil level > "FULL"). If the oil level is unacceptable, the flow chart follows a pathway that is like that for the paper-based procedure. That is, instructing the operator to either add or drain oil and read the new level.

If the oil level is acceptable, the operator presses the button for > "LOW" AND ≤ "FULL". After the button is pressed, automatic branching prompts the operators to check the air filter. The system does not provide feedback that explains to the operators how or why they arrived at a step that deals with the air filter. In the absence of feedback, the operators have no way of knowing if steps for checking the oil were performed correctly or completed at all. The operators are only aware of an action taken to enter a value for engine oil. Then, without further explanation, they are directed to check the air filter. Even though automatic branching was intended to make the job easier, it was found to be confusing for the operators.

As a result, Computer-Based Procedures that utilize automatic branching, and other modes of automation as well, should be evaluated for usability before they are implemented in the field Parasraman, Sheridan, and Wickens [18] compiled a list of evaluative criteria that could help designers decide what should be automated, and if so, how and to what extent automation should be applied. One criterion having relevance to computer-based systems addressed the extent that automation affected mental workload. If, it could be determined that automation did not notably reduce the level of mental workload, then other solutions should be considered. Additionally, Parasraman, Sheridan, and Wickens [18] identified the impact of automation on situation awareness. Accordingly, if changes in system state are left up to another agent, the operator is less aware of the surrounding environment. As such, the operator loses the opportunity to

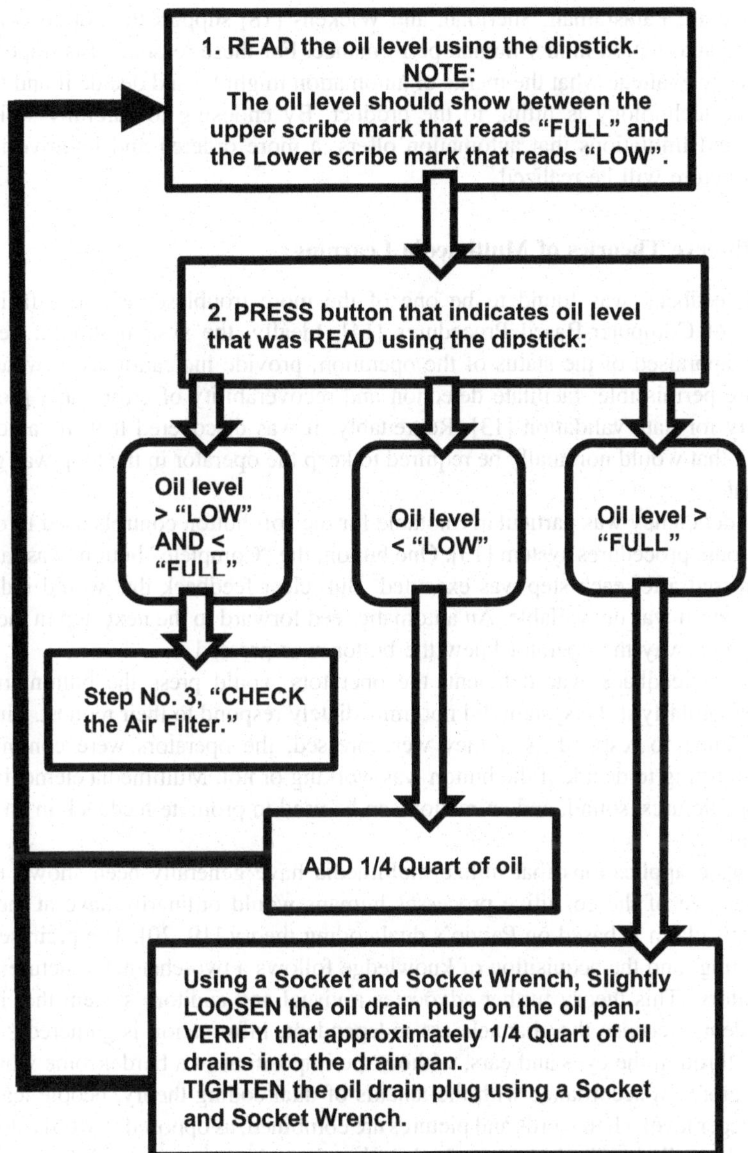

Fig. 4. Checking the engine oil: Example of automatic branching.

be actively engaged in the process. As one might suspect, loss of situation awareness can place people in the role of being a passive decisionmaker. As for applications specific to Computer-Based Procedures, if situation awareness is found to be lacking, the operators will be unable to perform the work at their fullest potential.

Above all, Parasraman, Sheridan, and Wickens [18] support the notion that some aspects of automation hinder human performance. For these reasons, it is important to thoughtfully evaluate what the merits of automation might be and decide if and to what extent the technology is fitting to the product. By choosing to carefully weigh the benefits and limitations that automation offers, a more ordered and intuitive navigational structure will be realized.

3.4 Observe Theories of Multimedia Learning

Limited feedback was found to be one of the more troublesome issues facing the usability of Computer-Based Procedures [14]. Ideally, the system should: keep the operator appraised of the status of the operation; provide indication as to what operations are permissible; facilitate detection and recoverability of errors; and provide a capability for data validation [13]. Regrettably, it was discovered that the amount of feedback that would nominally be required to keep the operator in the loop was grossly inadequate.

This deficiency was particularly notable for the soft button controls used to operate an electronic procedures system [13]. One button, the "Complete" button, was intended to be pressed after each step was executed. But, clear feedback that would indicate a pressed button was unavailable. An automatic feed forward to the next step in the series was the only way the operator knew the button was pressed.

Because feedback was deficient, the operators would press the button multiple times, particularly if the system did not immediately respond to their request. Since the buttons failed to respond as if they were pressed, the operators were continuously frustrated trying to decide if the button was working or not. Multimedia elements, such as words, pictures, sound, and animation can be used to promote feedback in an online environment.

Software applications that utilize multimedia have generally been shown to take full advantage of the cognitive processes humans would ordinarily have at their disposal. This claim is based on Paivio's dual coding theory [19, 20]. The premise being that learning, and the acquisition of knowledge follows a two-channel structure: visual and auditory. This theory further advocates a visual and auditory system that is truly independent. Because the channels are independent, information is gathered simultaneously, through the eyes and ears, without the imposition of a burdensome workload.

Therefore, in accordance with the tenants of dual coding theory, people learn at a much deeper level when words and pictures are combined, as opposed to words alone. As such, multimedia is suited to foster the learning that takes place through two-channels. Mayer [21] and other researchers over the years have extended some of these ideas. Drawing upon Paivio's dual coding theory, Mayer's model of multimedia learning is shown in Fig. 5. Starting from the left side, the operator receives the Multimedia Presentation, a format composed of pictures, words, and audio input. The signals are then transmitted to Sensory Memory where it is received by the eyes and ears. Next, Sensory Memory transfers the sounds and images gathered through the senses to a verbal and pictorial model of the user's experience. In turn, the channels are integrated in Working Memory, and the subsequent information is stored in Long-Term Memory.

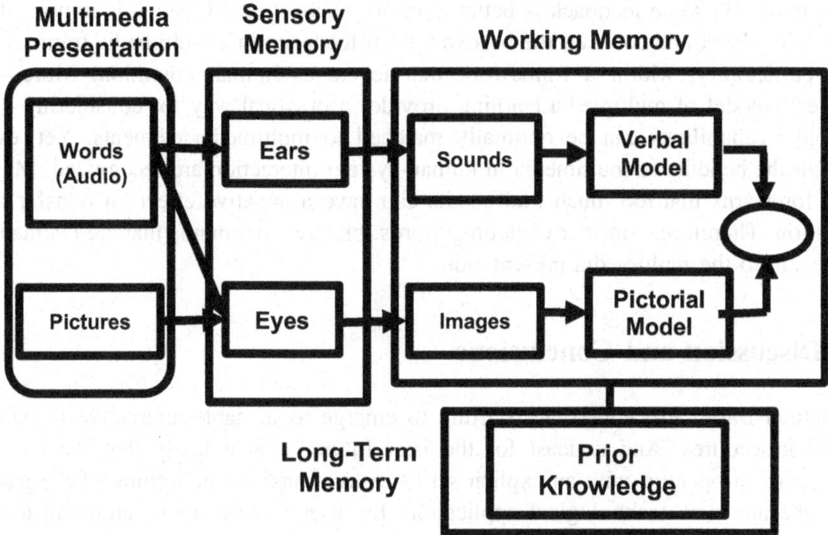

Fig. 5. A model of multimedia learning as it relates to the act of pressing a soft button on a touch screen. (*Adapted from*: [21]).

For a more concrete example, Mayer's model shows how multimedia elements were used to enhance the "Complete" button. The enhanced button is presented in Fig. 6. This button takes advantage of the two-channel structure. Visually, the button utilizes an icon that symbolically directs the operator to go forward. A text label, "Complete", was also added to supplement the icon image.

Color further enhances the level of feedback. For instance, the red background change in color (e.g., red to green), after it's been pressed. The feedback could even be augmented with an auditory cue, a "beep" to further reinforce the amount of feedback.

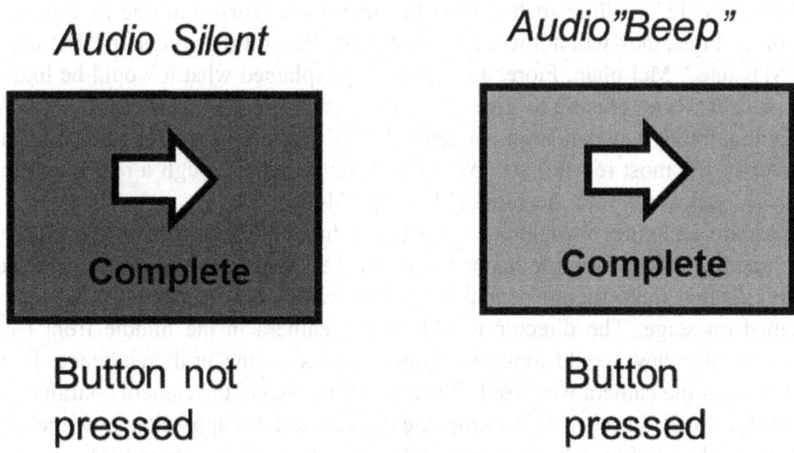

Fig. 6. A "Complete" button that's been enhanced to display the use of words and pictures. (Color figure online)

Obviously, some feedback is better than no feedback at all. But it is important to take a step back and consider the best way to fit feedback in a multimedia framework; and particularly, within a framework that leverages human cognition. Moreover, Mayer's model of multimedia learning provides a practical way for considering how people's capabilities can be optimally matched to multimedia elements. Yet, even though the benefits of multimedia in human-system interaction are recognized; Mayer [21] forewarns that too much multimedia can have a negative effect on transfer and retention. Therefore, consider excluding words, pictures, or sounds that are deemed as irrelevant to the multimedia presentation.

4 Discussion and Conclusions

Computer-Based Procedures are starting to emerge as a viable alternative to paper-based procedures. And at least for the near future, it is unlikely that the idea of providing an operator with an explicit set of instructions will be a thing of the past.

Like any new technological application, the user requirements pertaining to the design, development, procurement, and implementation for a computer-based procedure system deserves special consideration. If comprehensive user requirements are in place, there is a good chance that issues, such as those mentioned here, can be avoided. It is also important to point out that user requirements for a computer-based procedure system should not be restricted solely to the user-computer interface. Ultimately, for the project to be successful, user requirements should be included in all elements of the organization, not necessarily at the intersection between user and computer. Otherwise, without a broad comprehensive set of user requirements, project failure at the point of implementation, at the "last mile", will likely occur [22]. (p. 139).

Finally, comprehensive user requirements are not always sufficient unless the stakeholders having an interest in Computer-Based Procedures are willing to alter their thinking. To alter one's thinking entails having the flexibility to realize that Computer-Based Procedures are a new idea. As a new idea, it is unrealistic to think this technology should be forced on old trades, traditional ideas, and previously set ways of doing business [23]. While such approaches may have worked at one time for paper-based procedures, they will not work for Computer-Based Procedures. In "The Medium is the Massage," McLuhan, Fiore, and Agel [24] explained what it would be like to be in the present while refusing to give up on the past, "The past went that-a-way. When faced with a totally new situation, we tend always to attach ourselves to the objects, to the flavor of the most recent past. We look at the present through a rear-view mirror. We march backwards into the future." [24] (p. 74–75).

There are examples throughout history that have born witness to the "rear-view mirror" analogy. One example happened in the very early days of the motion picture industry. At that time, the art of making a film was drawn from the format for plays performed on stage. The director would fix the camera in the middle front row, to mimic what the view would look like from someone sitting in the audience. Because the position of the camera was fixed, if actors left the stage, the camera continued to be aimed at the vacated scene. At the time, the director did not appreciate how the camera might be used to follow the actors beyond the confines of the stage [25].

From this simple beginning, the craft of making a movie matured from a novel way to record stage plays to the form seen today. Of course, numerous other examples abound. Norman [23] cites other examples where old ideas steadfastly remained in the presence of new emergent technologies. But, as organizations move from paper to paperless, it is essential to recognize that the change forces us to see the world through a different lens. A lens that, at the end of the day, hopefully produces something the users will want.

Funding Statement. Sandia National Laboratories is a multimission laboratory managed and operated by National Technology & Engineering Solutions of Sandia, LLC, a wholly owned subsidiary of Honeywell International Inc., for the U.S. Department of Energy's National Nuclear Security Administration under contract DE-NA0003525. SAND No. 2019-1147 C.

Disclaimer. This paper describes objective technical results and analysis. Any subjective views or opinions that might be expressed in the paper do not necessarily represent the views of the U. S. Department of Energy or the United States Government.

References

1. Oxstrand, J., Le Blanc, K.: Supporting the future nuclear workforce with computer-based procedures. Nucl. Future **12**(INL/JOU-15-37135) (2016)
2. Swain, A.D., Guttmann, H.E.: Handbook of human reliability analysis with emphasis on nuclear power plant application, Final report. NUREG/CR- 1278, US Nuclear Regulatory Commission, Washington, D.C. (1983)
3. Martin, G.: The Phrase Finder, The meaning and origin of the expression: know the ropes (2019). https://www.phrases.org.uk/meanings/know-the-ropes.html. Accessed 23 Jan 2019
4. On the Water, Reading the River, Inland Waterways 1820–1940. http://americanhistory.si.edu/onthewater/exhibition/4_5.html. Accessed 23 Jan 2019
5. Mark Twain receives steamboat pilot's license, History.com Editors, A&E Television Networks, 13 December 2018. https://www.history.com/this-day-in-history/mark-twain-receives-steamboat-pilots-license. Accessed 23 Jan 2019
6. Instruction Book for Ford Model T Cars, Force Motor Company, Detroit, U.S.A. http://www.mtfca.com/books/1911_instruction_book.htm. Accessed 29 Jan 2019
7. Perrow, C.: Normal Accidents: Living with High Risk Technologies. Princeton University Press, Princeton (1999)
8. Reason, J.: Human Error. Cambridge University Press, Cambridge (1990)
9. Higginbotham, A.: Midnight in Chernobyl. Simon & Schuster, New York (2019)
10. Sellen, A.J., Harper, R.H.: The Myth of the Paperless Office. MIT Press, Cambridge (2003)
11. O'Hara, J.M., Higgins, J.C., Stubler, W.F., Kramer, J.: Computer-Based Procedure Systems: Technical Basis and Human Factors Review Guidance, NUREG/CR-6634, U.S. Nuclear Regulatory Commission, Washington, D.C. (2000)
12. Nuclear Power Engineering Committee of the IEEE Power & Energy Society: IEEE guide for human factors applications of computerized operating procedure systems (COPS) at nuclear power generating stations and other nuclear facilities. IEEE 1786, The Institute of Electrical and Electronics Engineers, Inc., New York (2011)
13. Ramos, M.V., Gilmore, W.E.: The paperless shop floor. Ergon. Des. **14**(1), 12–17 (2006)

14. Gilmore, W.E., Brannon, N.G.: Usability evaluation of computerized operating procedures in a high-consequence industrial workplace. In: Proceedings of the HCI International 2005 – 11th International Conference on Human-Computer Interaction, Los Vegas, Nevada, July 2005
15. Moray, N.: Culture, politics and ergonomics. Ergonomics **43**(7), 858–868 (2000)
16. Nielsen, J.: Designing Web Usability: The Practice of Simplicity. New Riders Publishing, Indianapolis (2000)
17. BWXT Pantex: Writer's Manual for Interactive Electronic Procedures (IEP), MNL-293088, Issue 1, Amarillo, Texas (2005)
18. Parasuraman, R., Sheridan, T.B., Wickens, C.D.: A model for types and levels of human interaction with automation. IEEE Trans. Syst. Man Cybern. Part A Syst. Hum. **30**(3), 286–297 (2000)
19. Paivio, A.: Mental Representations: A Dual-Coding Approach. Oxford University Press, New York (1986)
20. Pavio, A.: Dual coding theory: retrospect and current status. Can. J. Psychol. **45**(3), 255–287 (1991)
21. Mayer, R.E.: Multimedia Learning. Cambridge University Press, Cambridge (2001)
22. Thuemmler, C., Mival, O., Lim, A.K., Holanec, I., Fricker, S.: A social-technological alignment matrix. In: Proceedings of 2014 IEEE 16th International Conference on E Health Networking, Applications and Services (Healthcom), pp. 200–205, October 2014
23. Norman, D.A.: The Invisible Computer. The MIT Press, Cambridge (1999)
24. McLuhan, M., Fiore, Q., Agel, J.: The Medium is the Massage: An Inventory of Effects. Gingko Press Inc., Corte Madera (1967)
25. Pearson, R.: Early cinema. In: Nowell-Smith, G. (ed.) The Oxford History of World Cinema. Oxford University Press, New York (1996)

Statistical Analysis of Micro-error Occurrence Probability for the Fitts' Law-Based Pointing Task

Hikaru Gyoji[1], Tania Giovannetti[2], Rachel Mis[2], Caitlyn Vega[2], Lorena Silva[2], Atsuya Shirotori[1], Yuki Nagasawa[1], Maiko Sakamoto[3], Tetsuya Harada[4], Hayato Ohwada[5], and Takehiko Yamaguchi[1(✉)]

[1] Suwa University of Science, 5000-1 Toyohira, Chino, Nagano, Japan
h.gyoji.vrds@gmail.com, tk-ymgch@rs.sus.ac.jp
[2] Temple University, Philadelphia, PA 19122, USA
[3] Saga University, 5-1-1 Nabeshima, Saga, Saga, Japan
[4] Tokyo University of Science, 6-3-1 Niijuku, Katsushika-Ku, Tokyo, Japan
[5] Tokyo University of Science, 2641 Yamazaki, Noda, Chiba, Japan

Abstract. Identifying mild cognitive impairment (MCI) at an early stage and preventing its progression to dementia has become an important task. In order to solve this problem, we focused on micro-errors (MEs), including stagnation of behavior, as a criterion for discriminating between healthy subjects and MCI patients. According to the naturalistic action test (NAT), when the difficulty of the task (index of difficulty: ID) is increased, the occurrence frequency increases drastically. In this research, we aimed to develop a model that simplifies the virtual kitchen challenge (VKC), which reproduces the NAT task on a tablet terminal, and estimates the ME occurrence probability based on a learning difficulty model that considers shape similarity. In this study, 20 university students were asked to perform a shape task. Using the generalized linear model showing the relationship between the occurrence probability of the ME and the result of the shape task, we confirmed that the ME occurrence probability increases with the difficulty level. Moreover, as future work, it is necessary to investigate the influence of handedness and gaze and the relation between color similarity and planning with regard to the ME occurrence probability.

Keywords: Mild cognitive impairment · Micro-error · Instrumental activities of daily living

1 Introduction

It is important to identify mild cognitive impairment (MCI) in older adults at an early stage to prevent progression to dementia. As of 2018, it is estimated that the number of people suffering from dementia worldwide will increase from 50 million to 82 million by 2030 and to 152 million by 2050 [1]. It is estimated that in Japan itself, the number of people with dementia will increase to about 4.62 million in 2012 and 6.75 million in 2025 [2]. The prevalence and the disease rate of dementia markedly increases with age,

S. Yamamoto and H. Mori (Eds.): HCII 2019, LNCS 11569, pp. 317–329, 2019.
https://doi.org/10.1007/978-3-030-22660-2_22

and 40–60% of dementia is reported to be Alzheimer's disease. Neither the cause of the disease nor the treatment has been clarified; the only measure taken is to delay the progression. Therefore, it is necessary to detect the precursor stage of dementia early and to prevent the onset of dementia. Of individuals diagnosed with MCI, which is the precursor stage of dementia, up to 50% may meet the criteria for dementia within 5 years [3].

Currently, cognitive function tests such as Mini Mental State Examination (MMSE), Revised Hasegawa Type Simple Intelligence Assessment Scale (HDR-S), and Clinical Dementia Rating are widely used for screening dementia [4]. These tests are face-to-face tests intended to evaluate the subject's memory, awareness, executive function, etc. For the MMSE, though the discrimination accuracy at the severe disability stage is about 100% at the stage of moderate dementia and about 50% at the stage of mild dementia, the discrimination accuracy at the MCI stage is only about 30%. Thus, the low accuracy is a challenge. Therefore, it is necessary to develop a new screening method with higher identification accuracy.

In a previous study, an index called micro-error (ME) that models the stagnation of motion during the reaching operation has been used to describe the behavioral characteristics of MCI patients. In recent years, it has become clear that there is a significant difference between healthy subjects and MCI patients in terms of the ME occurrence frequency, and an approach to discriminate MCIs based on the occurrence frequency of MEs gained attention. MEs have a characteristic that the occurrence frequency drastically increases when the average difficulty of a subtask, which is a detailed operation constituting an IADL task, is increased [5]. The nature of IADL tasks can be simplified as reaching and selection tasks. In addition, the performance in these tasks may be influenced by information such as the shape and color of objects to be selected, their implications or functions, and the planning needed to complete the task. However, it is not clear what kind of information strongly influences the occurrence of ME.

The overarching goal of this work was to develop a model to estimate the probability of ME occurrence in everyday tasks. The aims of this study were to (1) examine the influence of reaching difficulty and distractor similarity to the target on ME and (2) determine whether the MEs can be rapidly quantified as the difference between the direct path to the target and the actual reaching path to the target, with the ME expected to generate differences greater than the accurate reaching movements.

1.1 Virtual Kitchen Challenge (VKC) System

In a previous research, we developed the Virtual Kitchen Challenge (VKC) system, which measures the performance in a VR-IADL on a tablet touch screen. The VKC was modeled after the Naturalistic Action Test (NAT), a performance-based test of everyday functions that requires participants to complete tasks using real objects that are presented on a table. The VKC addresses numerous methodological challenges associated with the NAT, including the time required for set-up and scoring. In the VKC task, actions are mapped to interactions such as touching and dragging the screen of the tablet. The Lunchbox Task consists of four main tasks: (1) make a peanut butter and jelly sandwich; (2) select and wrap cookies; (3) fill a thermos with juice; and (4) pack and close the lunchbox. Distractor objects that are not necessary for the task also are included in the task environment. Figure 1 shows the Lunchbox Task in a VKC system. Past work has shown significant correlations between the ME observed during completion of the VKC and that observed during the completion of the NAT [5].

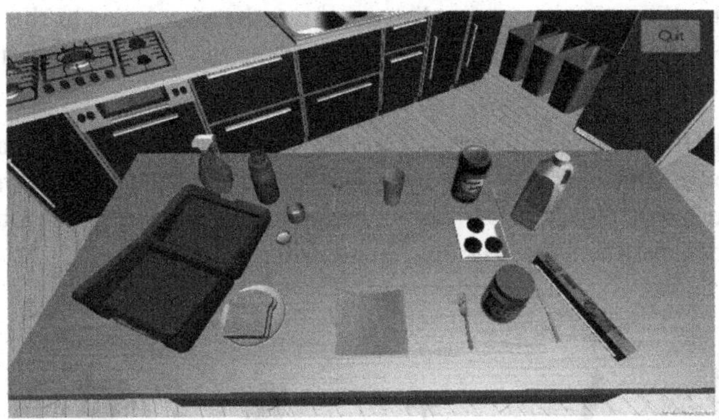

Fig. 1. VKC system.

1.2 Shape Task

The VKC is a complex, self-paced task during which the participant may sequence the task in a number of ways. To impose greater control on responses during object selection, we developed the shape task. The shape task divides each object selection into an independent trial. Trial completion time includes the time required to identify and select the target object from among an array of distractor objects and the time required to move the hand to the target object. These two aspects of each trial were modeled according to Fitts' law and Hick's law [6].

In the VKC, individuals make more ME during more difficult tasks and when there are distractor objects that are similar to the target object. Thus, we investigated the influence of trial difficulty and distractor-target similarity on ME occurrence by means of the shape task.

1.2.a. Trial Difficulty - Trial difficulty was quantified based on Fitts' law, which provides a model of human motion in the man–machine interface. Fitts modeled the relation of speed and accuracy tradeoff with the target movement. The model equation is shown in Eq. (1). Here, D is the distance to the target object; W is the size of the target object; and MT is the movement time. In addition, "a" indicates the start time or stop time of finger movement, and "b" indicates finger speed. In addition, Eq. (2) presents the index of difficulty (ID). The ID quantifies the difficulty at the time of task execution.

$$MT = a + b\,log_2\left(\frac{D}{W} + 1\right) \quad (1)$$

$$ID = log_2\left(\frac{D}{W} + 1\right) \quad (2)$$

We expect that in the shape task, ME will increase with ID. Specifically, in the shape task, the ID increases as the distance from the start point to the target object increases; we expect more ME in trials in which the target object is farther from the start point.

1.2.b. Target-Distractor Similarity - Target-distractor similarity was quantified using the correlation coefficients between the shape of each of the nine distractor objects (DO) and the target object (TO). The correspondence between each object and the correlation coefficient is shown in Fig. 2 and Table 1.

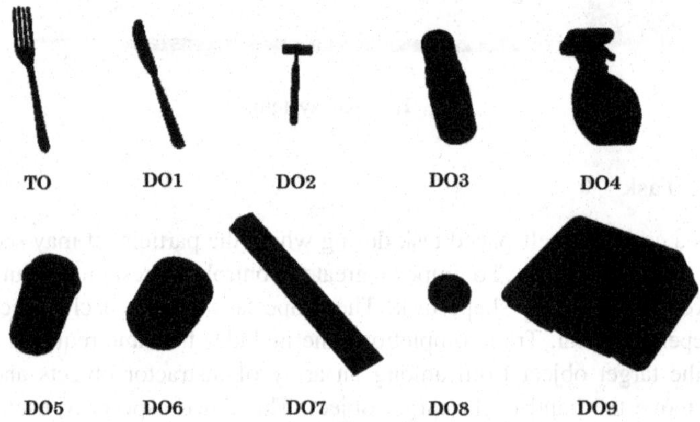

Fig. 2. Target object (TO) and nine distractor objects shown in order from the most similar to the least similar.

Table 1. Shape similarity

DO	Similarity
DO1	0.8052
DO2	0.4755
DO3	0.4328
DO4	0.4099
DO5	0.3799
DO6	0.3223
DO7	0.2976
DO8	0.2465
DO9	0.0901

Questionnaires were administered to validate the objective assessment of target-distractor similarity against subjective perceptions. The contents of the experiment show the objects in the two circles displayed slightly above the red dot and the red dot at the same time (Fig. 3). At that time, the user was asked to evaluate how much the object displayed in the second circle could be distinguished in 5 stages. Further, we evaluated all DOs based on the subjective time length difference required to discriminate. From the results of this preliminary experiment, the coefficient of determination ($R^2 = 0.5736$) and the correlation coefficient ($r = 0.759$) were obtained. We found that there exists a strong positive correlation between the similarity of the subjective form and the similarity degree of the form quantitatively calculated. The results are shown in Fig. 4.

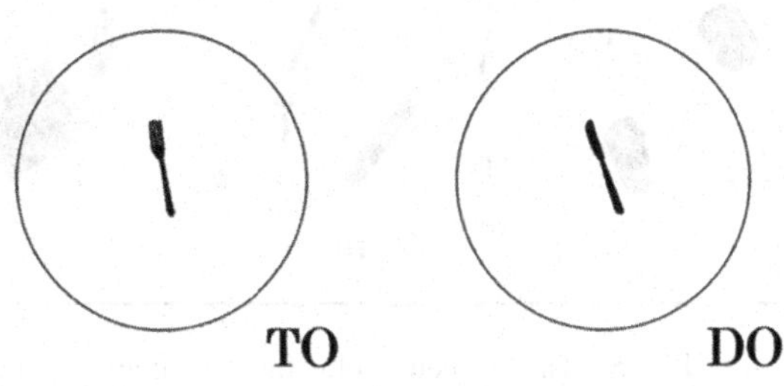

Fig. 3. Screen during the questionnaire experiment. (Color figure online)

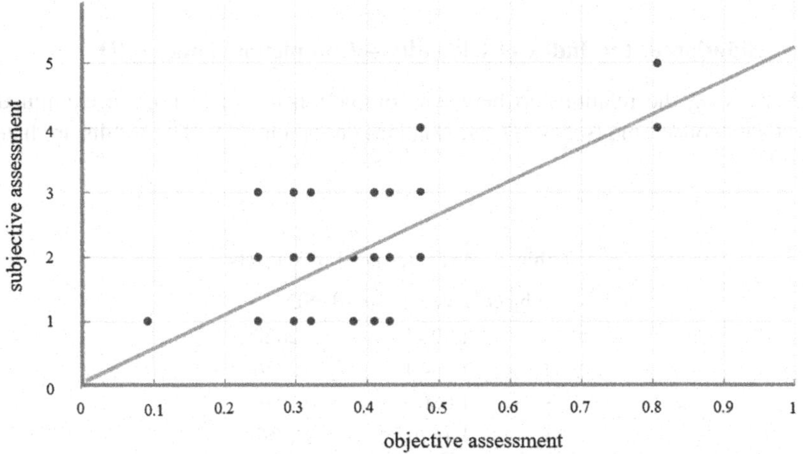

Fig. 4. Relationship between subjective assessment and objective assessment.

1.2.c. Shape Task - Twenty university students were recruited to perform the shape task. In this task, participants had to rest the index finger of their right hand on a central red start button and then reach to the fork (TO) as quickly and accurately as possible in each trial. In all, 200 trials were conducted with 10 stimulus arrays with different task IDs presented 20 times in a random order. The task screen is shown in Fig. 5.

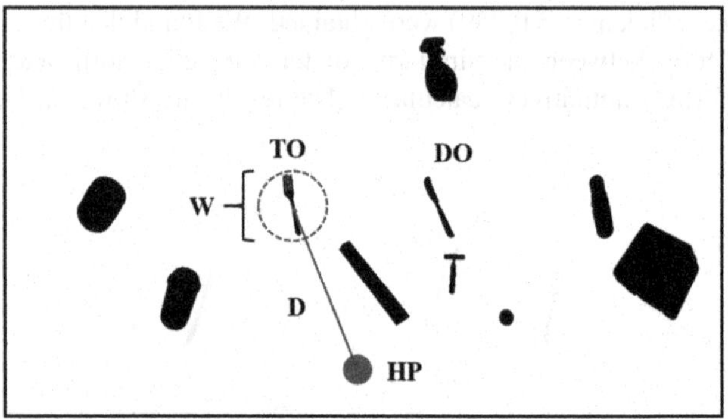

Fig. 5. Task screen (Color figure online)

Participants were video-recorded as they performed the task. Video recordings were used to code the MEs. The MEs included perturbations of reaching movements that were observable by trained human coders. Coders recorded the time when the ME occurred, the type of the ME (mis-reach or touching of a distractor object). The distractor objects that were touched were recorded. However, most ME were reaching errors where the intended object was not clear. For mis-reaching errors, the direction of the reaching error was recorded as left, right, or center.

2 Results

2.1 Validation of the Index of Difficulty – Completion Time × ID

When studying the relationship between completion time and ID, we examined the subject's response time (seconds) and standard deviation (SD). The results are listed in Table 2.

Table 2. Average speed of subjects

Subject	Average speed	SD
1	1.1237	0.2020
2	1.2440	0.2256
3	1.0861	0.1949
4	1.1679	0.1767

(*continued*)

Table 2. (*continued*)

Subject	Average speed	SD
5	1.4837	0.2354
6	1.1854	0.1661
7	1.0913	0.1468
8	1.2514	0.1264
9	1.1302	0.1808
10	1.1495	0.1379
11	1.4149	0.1451
12	1.1294	0.1497
13	1.4233	0.1848
14	1.3145	0.1203
15	1.1026	0.1544
16	1.2894	0.1787
17	1.7398	0.2146
18	1.1072	0.2083

A regression analysis was conducted to investigate whether the item difficulty in the shape task could be explained by Fitts' model. The results of the regression analysis of Subject 1 and the results of the determination coefficients (R^2) and correlation coefficients (r) of all subjects are presented in Fig. 6 and Table 3, respectively. The data of two examinees are excluded as outliers.

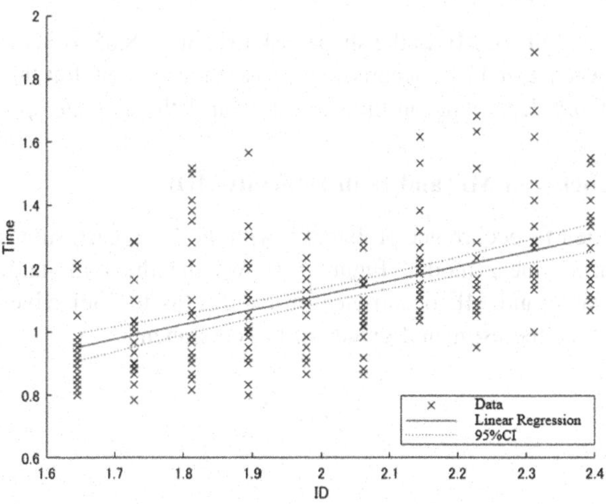

Fig. 6. Results for Subject 1.

Table 3. Coefficient of determination and correlation coefficient

Subject	R^2	r
1	0.2934	0.5417
2	0.3159	0.5620
3	0.0745	0.2729
4	0.1442	0.3797
5	0.2096	0.4578
6	0.0734	0.2709
7	0.2367	0.4865
8	0.4621	0.6798
9	0.2442	0.4942
10	0.2047	0.4524
11	0.1464	0.3826
12	0.2014	0.4488
13	0.3811	0.6173
14	0.4100	0.6403
15	0.3429	0.5856
16	0.3835	0.6193
17	0.3492	0.5909
18	0.1706	0.4130

From the data in Table 3, weak to moderate positive correlation was obtained for each subject. Thus, it is confirmed that the required time increases with the ID.

2.2 ME in the Shape Task

The mean value and SD of ME in the shape task (Mean = 48.0556 SD = 30. 6077). The relationship between speed and accuracy was also investigated, but the number of ME occurrences differed depending on the subject even if the average speed was close.

2.3 Relation Between ME and Item Difficulty (ID)

The relation of the ME occurrence probability with the ID of each subtask was modeled by the generalized linear model. Figure 7 shows the diagram modeling ID as an explanatory variable and ME occurrence probability as the objective variable in the model. Table 4 lists the estimated values of the coefficients.

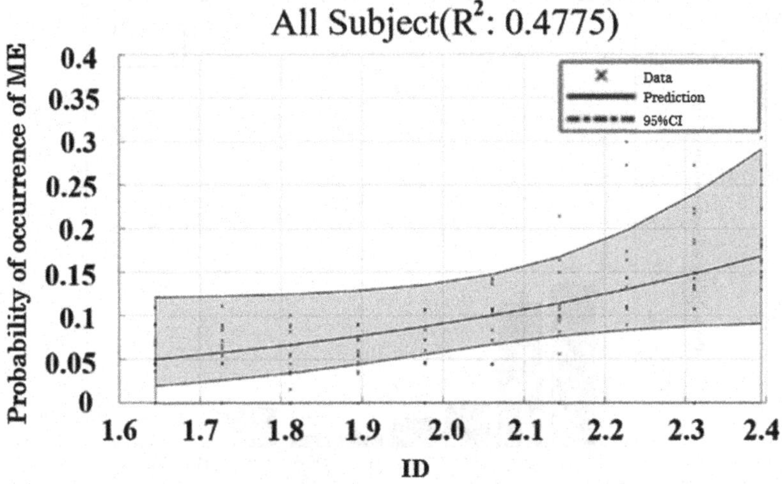

Fig. 7. Probability of occurrence of ME for ID.

Table 4. Estimated coefficients.

			95%CI			
	Estimate	STD error	Lower limit	Upper limit	t-value	p-value
Intercept	−5.8972	2.0406	−9.9181	−1.8763	−2.8899	0.0039
ID	1.7962	0.9664	−0.1080	3.7005	1.8587	0.0631

The coefficient of determination was 0.4775 (correlation coefficient: 0.6910). This result suggested that the probability of ME occurrence increased with increasing difficulty level.

2.4 Relation Between ME and Target-Distractor Similarity (DO)

Figure 8 shows the ME generation probability for each DO that was coded as the target of ME generation.

2.5 Relation Between ME Target Similarity and Reaching Difficulty (ID)

The hypothesis that ME would be likely to occur in the case of highly similar objects when the ID is especially high was evaluated by examining the occurrence of ME in trials where DO1 (i.e., the distractor most similar to the target) was on the right or left side of the target across trials that differed in terms of the reaching difficulty (ID). Figure 9 shows the probability of ME occurrence with respect to ID based on TO. Then, an analysis of variance (ANOVA; Table 5) was carried out considering the effect of ID and direction and its interaction.

The results of the ANOVA showed that the directional effect was significant ($F(1,17) = 20.31$, $p < .001$), and the interaction too was significant ($F(9,153) = 3.583$, $p < .001$).

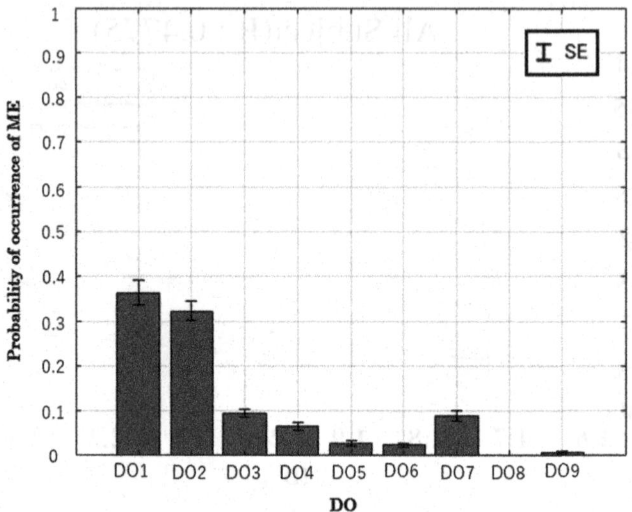

Fig. 8. Probability of occurrence of ME for DO.

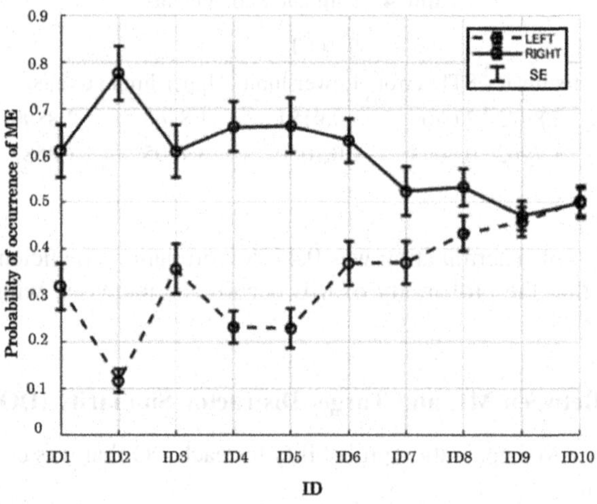

Fig. 9. Average plot of ME occurrence probability for ID.

Table 5. Result of analysis of variance

	SS	df	MS	F-value	p-value	
ID	0.3777778	9	0.04198	1.332	0.2248	
Direction	6.2020171	1	6.20202	20.31	0.0003	****
ID × Direction	3.6744323	9	0.40827	3.583	0.0005	****

+ p < .10, * p < .05, ** p < .01, *** p < .005, **** p < .001
*: significant

2.6 Relationship Between the Most Direct Path to the Target and the ME Path

Figure 10 shows a part of the figure in which the trajectory of the index finger in each trial in the shape task for Subject 1 is compared with the most direct path from the start point to the target. The difference between those paths is quantified (indicated by the area). Trials in which an ME was coded are represented by an orange background. A Support Vector Machine was applied using the area of the trajectory of each trial as learning data. The ROC curve is shown in Fig. 11.

The precision is 80.6%, and the AUC is 0.67, which is not as high as the predicted performance.

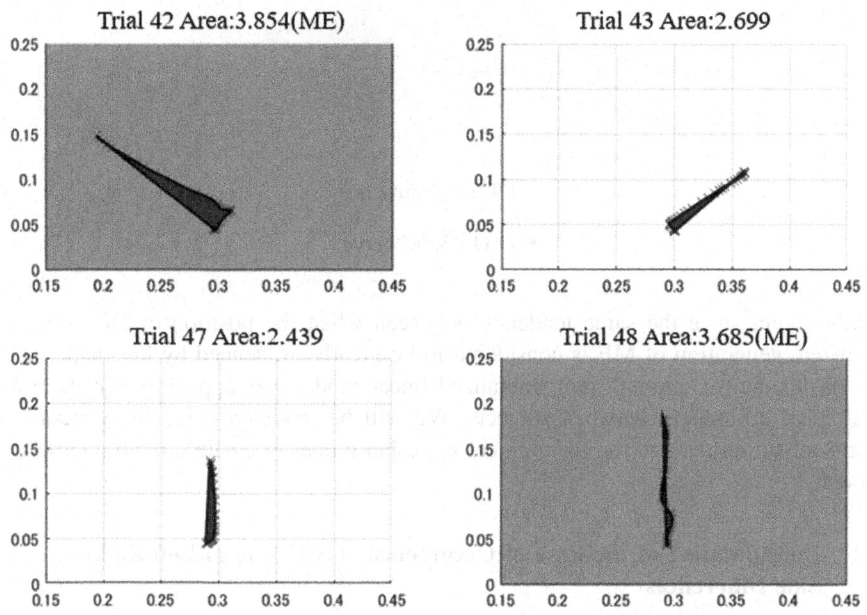

Fig. 10. Relationship between the track area and ME. (Color figure online)

3 Discussion

3.1 Consideration of the Influence of Reaching Difficulty and Distractor Similarity to the Target on ME

Using the generalized linear model, we confirmed that the ME occurrence probability increases with ID. Therefore, it is suggested that the ME occurrence probability can be quantitatively estimated from the ID. Moreover, examination of the relationship between ME and DO shows that many MEs occur in objects with high DO similarity. ME occurs when the similarity of DO is high, and this is observed equally at all IDs.

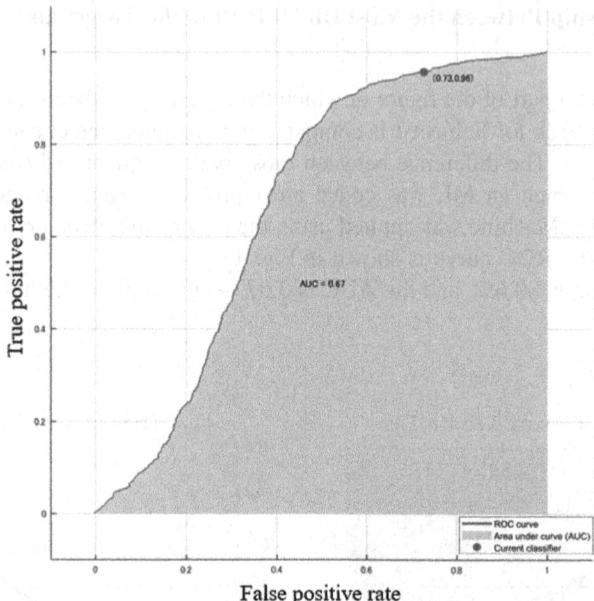

Fig. 11. ROC curve.

Furthermore, since the same tendency was seen when the position of DO was randomized, generation of ME is considered to be greatly influenced by the shape.

In this study, although the generalized linear model was applied, since there are individual differences between subjects, We will be modeled using the generalized linear mixed model and the hierarchical Bayesian model to create a more appropriate model.

3.2 Consideration of the Ease of Occurrence of ME Due to Left/Right Side Differences

If the ID is low, there are clear differences in the ME occurrence rate between the left and right sides. However, as the ID increases, the difference gradually disappears. From the results of ANOVA, significant differences were found in the factors of presenting direction of DO1 to TO; however, the interaction was also significant. The following explanations can be given: The subject's dominant hand and the fact that the task in this experiment was controlled to be performed by the right arm.

3.3 Relationship Between the Track Area and ME

The accuracy of the ROC curve is 80.6%, and the AUC is 0.67, which is not so high as the predicted performance. However, we think that it is possible to automatically discover the ME depending on the improvement. Conventionally, it is thought that coding of ME is judged by viewing the video during the task, but if we can judge the

ME from the area of the locus with high accuracy, the value can be used for early detection of MCI in a short time.

4 Conclusion

It is suggested that the degree of difficulty can be quantified by the relationship between the difficulty level on a subtask basis and the occurrence frequency of ME. This suggests that the probability of ME occurrence can be estimated from the ID value. As a future work, we will conduct comparative analysis not only for young people, but also for healthy elderly and MCI patients. Regarding the measured data, we will model not only generalized linear models, but also generalized linear mixed models considering individual differences and hierarchical Bayesian models with higher degrees of freedom. Further, the results of this experiment showed that the direction of ME was significant when TO was used as a reference. In order to investigate the cause, it is necessary to investigate relationships of gaze behaviors and dominant hands during tasks. Furthermore, in order to investigate the relationship between ME and area, investigate the relationship between area and ID, and the similarity of DO. Although this research focused on the investigation of the influence of the form, in the future, we will also investigate the relationship between color similarity and planning and the occurrence probability of ME.

Acknowledgments. This work was supported by the Grant-in-Aid for Scientific Research (C) from Ministry of Education, Japan, Grant Number: 18K12118.

References

1. World Alzheimer Report 2018: The Global Impact of Dementia, p. 34 (2018)
2. Ministry of Health: On the current situation of dementia facilities (2017). https://www.mhlw.go.jp/file/06-Seisakujouhou-12300000-Roukenkyoku/0000079008.pdf
3. Yamamoto, Y.: Psychiat. neurol. Jpn. **113**(6) (2011)
4. Kato, S., et al.: A preliminary study of speech prosody-based relationship with HDS-scores, p. 1 (2010)
5. Seligman, S.C., Giovannetti, T., Sestito, J., Libon, D.J.: A new approach to the characterization of subtle errors in everyday action: implications for mild cognitive impairment. Clin. Neuropsychol. **28**(1), 97–115 (2014)
6. Hick, W.E.: On the rate of gain of information, pp. 11–26 (1952)

The Creative Power of Collaborative Pairs in Divergent Idea-Generation Task

Risa Muraya[1], Noriko Suzuki[2], Mamiko Sakata[1](✉), and Michiya Yamamoto[3]

[1] Doshisha University, 1-3 Tatara Miyakodani, Kyotanabe, Kyoto 610-0394, Japan
msakata@mail.doshisha.ac.jp

[2] Kyoto University, Kyoto, Japan

[3] Kwansei Gakuin University, 2-1 Gakuen, Sanda, Hyogo 669-1337, Japan

Abstract. The creative power of collaborative pairs in comparison with that of individuals was assessed. Participants were 61 university students who engaged in two kinds of divergent idea-generation tasks, such as thinking of new names for specific categories, i.e. tea and rice. In the first task, new rice brand names were generated by all participants on their own, while in the second task new tea names were generated by half of the participants on their own and by the other half in pairs through brainstorming. Video sequences of collaboration by 20 pairs were annotated with the number of constructive interactions produced. Another 27 university students, as neutral third-party participants, evaluated the quality of the generated ideas with a view to originality and utility. The results suggest that pairs achieved a higher quality of ideas than did individuals and, moreover, that the greater number of constructive interactions produced by pairs contributed to the higher quality of ideas. We expect these findings to be helpful in designing relationality for improving the creativity between people as well as between people and social robots.

Keywords: Creativity · Group size · Collaboration · Divergent idea generation task · Constructive interaction · Quality of ideas

1 Introduction

Are people more creative as individuals or in pairs? We investigated the creative power of pairs in comparison with individuals by using divergent idea generation tasks.

We are sometime expected to rustle up a dinner from a few things we have on hand. At work, we are sometime expected to develop innovative products [1, 2]. In our everyday life, we need to generate new ideas to solve various kinds of problems, from immediate matters to elaborate challenging tasks.

ATC21s has addressed creativity as one of the 21st century skills for students to acquire [3]. Furthermore, engaging in creative intelligent tasks is one of the jobs expected to be left to humans after approximately 700 jobs are transferred to robots with artificial intelligence in the coming 20 years [4]. Both of these future expectations

S. Yamamoto and H. Mori (Eds.): HCII 2019, LNCS 11569, pp. 330–342, 2019.
https://doi.org/10.1007/978-3-030-22660-2_23

imply the need for people to possess creative power. How, then, can the creative power of people be improved?

In previous studies of the group-size effect in problem solving, it has been reported that group performance is generally superior to the performance of average individuals [5, 6]. However, while most studies have examined the effect of group performance on the number of ideas produced in the divergent idea generation task [e.g. 7], there has been little focus on the quality of such ideas.

In this paper, we focus on the group-size effect, i.e. individuals or pairs, on the quality of ideas by using the divergent idea-generation task of creating new brand names for tea or rice. We measured two kinds of individual abilities: (a) communication skills [8] and (b) active-learning attitudes [9]. We also measured two kinds of performance in pairs: (c) degree of conversational satisfaction as a subjective indicator [10], and (d) number of ideas and (e) number of constructive interactions as an objective indicator. In the education field, a constructive interaction in collaborative group work is regarded as an essential step in developing understanding, improving the learning effect, and solving problems [e.g. 11]. In addition, (f) the names generated in the two tasks were rated in terms of originality and utility by third-party participants.

We compared the originality and utility of ideas based on group size, that is, either individuals or pairs. We analyzed the relationship between the number of constructive interactions produced and the creativity of ideas (i.e. originality and utility) generated by pairs.

2 Method

2.1 Predictions

Group-Size Effects on the Quality of Ideas: We are interested in the relationship between group size and the quality of ideas. We predict that the quality of ideas by pairs is superior to that by individuals in a divergent idea-generation task, just as demonstrated for the number of ideas [5, 6].

Effect of Constructive Interactions Produced in Pairs on the Quality of Ideas: We are also interested in the relationship between the number of constructive interactions produced and the quality of ideas, especially by pairs. We predict that a larger number of constructive interactions produced through collaboration in pairs will achieve a higher quality of ideas, as already shown for the learning effect of problem solving in the classroom [11].

2.2 Divergent Idea-Generation Task

Participants: A total of 61 university students (M = 30, F = 31, mean age: 20.41 years, SD: 1.49) participated in two kinds of name-generation tasks based on the framework of a divergent idea-generation task [7]. In the first task of generating new rice names, all participants engaged in it as individuals. In the second task of generating new tea names, 21 participants took part as individuals, while the other 40 participants performed it as 20 same-gender pairs. Each pair consists of same gender for minimizing effects of gender differences on interaction. They were randomly assigned to individuals or pairs.

Procedure: All participants were asked to generate as many new rice names as possible within one minute to measure their own creative ability. They engaged in the rice-name-generation task as individuals and worked independently. Next, after randomly dividing participants into two groups, i.e. individuals or pairs, they were asked to generate as many new tea names as possible within three minutes to compare the creativity of individuals with that of pairs. This second task of generating tea names was repeated three times with the same groups, and their performances were video-recorded. Then, they were asked to take both a communication skills test and an active-learning attitudes test. Pairs were also asked about their degree of satisfaction in communication.

Parameters: This paper used the following subjective or objective parameters as analytical indicators for measuring the creativity of participants.

Subjective Indicators: The following three parameters were assessed by the participants on their own performance as subjective indicators.

(a) Score of communication skills test: Total score of the communication skills test for every participant [8].
(b) Score of active-learning attitudes test: Total score of the active-learning attitudes test for every participant [9].
(c) Degree of conversational satisfaction: Eighteen questions on the paired participants' degree of satisfaction with the conversation of the partner in their pair using an eight-point scale [10] for every two-person group.

Objective Indicators: The following two parameters were assessed by the three annotators as objective indicators.

(d) Number of ideas: Total count of ideas for new rice names within one minute or for new tea names within three minutes in each experimental trial.
(e) Number of constructive interactions: Total count of constructive interactions from video sequences in first and third trial of pair. A constructive interaction consists of two roles, *task-doing* and *monitoring*. A previous study reported that the exchange of roles between two participants through collaboration facilitates learning [11]. All utterances were classified into two kinds of speech acts: understanding and non-understanding. The speech acts of understanding include three labels: self-evident, proposal, and confirmation. The speech acts of non-understanding include three labels: searching, criticism, and question. One constructive interaction is counted from the first speech act of understanding and the last speech act of non-understanding.

2.3 Third-Party Evaluation of Quality of Ideas

Participants: A total of 27 university students (M = 9, F = 18, mean age: 20.48 years, SD: 1.91) who did not participate in the two name-generation tasks engaged in an evaluation experiment as neutral third-party participants.

Procedure: All participants were asked to evaluate every name of rice or tea on its originality and utility as measures of the quality of ideas.

Parameters: This paper used the following parameters as analytical indicators for measuring the quality of ideas.

Originality: In this experiment, a new name with higher originality is defined as a novel name that evaluators had never before seen. Total score of originality in every new idea for a rice or tea name was calculated using a five-point scale. Examples of tea names with higher originality are as follows: *Ikkyu-san mo tanoshinda ocha* (tea that Ikkyu-san enjoyed drinking), *Otousan no aizyou ga komotta ocha* (tea that's like a father's affection), *Shizuoka kenmin ga kirai na ocha* (tea that a citizen of Shizuoka prefecture does not like), *Sawayaka na kaze no youni* (tea like a fresh breeze), *Ochazuki ni yoru ochazuki no tameno ocha* (tea for a tea lover by a tea lover).

Utility: In this experiment, a new name with higher utility is defined as a suitable name for a product put on the actual market. Total score of utility in every new idea for a rice or tea name was calculated using a five-point scale. Examples of tea names with higher utility are as follows: *Ajiwai* (tasty), *Kaori* (aroma of tea), *Umami no shizuku* (a drop of tasty tea), *Koiuma* (strong and tasty tea), *Wa no megumi* (a blessing of Japanese style).

3 Results and Discussion

3.1 Relationship Between Group Size and Quality of Ideas

Group Size and Number of Ideas

Tables 1 and 2 show the descriptive statistics value for the number of ideas in the new tea name generation task. A three-way mixed-design ANOVA on the number of ideas for the names of tea (group sizes * gender * trials (2 * 2 * 3)) did not reveal any significant effect for group size ($F(1,37) = 2.48$, $p = .12$, $\eta_p^2 = .05$), gender ($F(1,37) = .37$, $p = .55$, $\eta_p^2 = .01$), or number of trials ($F(2,37) = 0.02$, $p = .98$, $\eta_p^2 < .01$). It also did not show significance of any interaction among factors for the number of ideas: between group size and gender ($F(2,74) = 1.43$, $p = .24$, $\eta_p^2 = .03$), between group sizes and trials ($F(2,74) = .17, p = .85, \eta_p^2 < .01$), or between gender and trials, ($F(2,74) = 1.20, p = .31$, $\eta_p^2 < .01$). Table 3 shows the ANOVA table for the number of ideas in the new tea name generation task. From the results, group size, gender and trials did not seem to affect the number of ideas.

Table 1. Descriptive statistics value for the number of ideas in the tea name generation task.

	Ave.	Median	Mode	*S.D.*	Min.	Max.
1st trial	12.32	10	10	13.04	0	83
2nd trial	12.20	10	4	10.38	0	59
3rd trial	12.31	9	6	9.44	2	38
Total	36.83	28	24	30.94	4	180

Table 2. Descriptive statistics value for the number of ideas in the tea name generation task: stratified by group size, gender and trials.

Group size	Gender	1st trial		2nd trial		3rd trial	
		Ave.	*S.D.*	Ave.	*S.D.*	Ave.	*S.D.*
Individuals	Female	10.44	4.39	11.89	7.47	12.44	6.77
	Male	18.50	21.99	16.25	16.51	17.25	14.86
Pair	Female	10.91	6.77	11.09	6.04	9.18	4.71
	Male	7.67	4.44	8.44	4.53	9.44	2.98

Table 3. The ANOVA table for the number of ideas in the new tea name generation task.

	SS	*df*	*MS*	*F*	*p*
Group size	758.73	1	758.73	2.48	.12
Gender	113.05	1	113.05	0.37	.55
Group size * Gender	438.92	1	438.92	1.43	.24
Trials	0.91	2	0.46	0.02	.98
Group size * Trials	8.14	2	4.07	0.17	.85
Gender * Trials	17.58	2	8.79	0.36	.70
Group size * Gender * Trials	58.95	2	29.47	1.20	.31

Group Size and Originality or Utility of Ideas

Table 4 shows the descriptive statistics value for the evaluation score of originality and utility of ideas in the new tea name generation task. Tables 5 and 6 shows the descriptive statistics value for the evaluation score of originality or utility of ideas stratified by group size, gender and trials.

Table 4. Descriptive statistics value for the evaluation score of originality and utility of ideas with a five-point scale in the new tea name generation task.

	Ave.	Median	Mode	*S.D.*
Originality	2.41	2.40	2.00	0.53
Utility	2.85	2.82	3.00	0.58

Table 5. Descriptive statistics value for the evaluation score of originality of ideas with a five-point scale in the tea name generation task: stratified by group size, gender and trials.

Group size	Gender	1st trial		2nd trial		3rd trial	
		Ave.	*S.D.*	Ave.	*S.D.*	Ave.	*S.D.*
Individuals	Female	2.22	0.36	2.30	0.44	2.25	0.39
	Male	2.41	0.49	2.40	0.53	2.54	0.65
Pair	Female	2.41	0.54	2.47	0.55	2.58	0.58
	Male	2.30	0.46	2.48	0.50	2.48	0.53

Table 6. Descriptive statistics value for the evaluation score of utility of ideas with a five-point scale in the tea name generation task: stratified by group size, gender and trials.

Group size	Gender	1st trial		2nd trial		3rd trial	
		Ave.	*S.D.*	Ave.	*S.D.*	Ave.	*S.D.*
Individuals	Female	3.02	0.57	2.86	0.57	2.95	0.60
	Male	2.80	0.61	2.65	0.55	2.64	0.58
Pair	Female	3.07	0.47	2.99	0.52	2.84	0.57
	Male	3.00	0.51	3.01	0.59	3.00	0.60

A three-way ANOVA on the score of the quality of ideas according to originality and utility (group size * gender * number of trials (2 * 2 * 3)) showed a main effect for trials (originality: ($F(2,1518) = 6.42, p < .01, \eta_p^2 = .01$) in Table 7 utility: ($F(2,1518) = 7.69$, $p < .01$, $\eta_p^2 = .01$) in Table 8). There were also significant differences in interaction between group size and gender (originality: $F(1,1518) = 19.94, p < .01, \eta_p^2 = .01$), utility: ($F(1,1518) = 21.78, p < .01, \eta_p^2 = .01$)). Post-hoc comparisons revealed that the score of originality of ideas in the third trial of the tea-name-generation task was demonstrated to be significantly greater than that in the first trial ($F(1,996) = 12.29, p < .01, \eta_p^2 = .01$ in Table 9), although the score of utility of ideas in the third trial was demonstrated to be significantly lower than that in the first trial ($F(1,996) = 13.45$, $p < .01$, $\eta_p^2 = .01$ in Table 10).

Table 7. The ANOVA table for the evaluation score of originality of ideas with a five-point scale in the new tea name generation task.

	SS	*df*	*MS*	*F*	*p*
Group size	3.31	1	3.31	12.08	**<.01**
Gender	1.26	1	1.26	4.62	**.03**
Group size * Gender	3.52	2	1.76	6.42	**<.01**
Trials	5.46	1	5.46	19.94	**<.01**
Group size * Trials	0.56	2	1.28	1.03	.36
Gender * Trials	0.14	2	0.07	0.25	.78
Group size * Gender * Trials	1.25	2	0.62	2.28	.10

Table 8. The ANOVA table for the evaluation score of utility of ideas with a five-point scale in the new tea name generation task.

	SS	*df*	*MS*	*F*	*p*
Group size	8.88	1	8.88	27.87	**<.01**
Gender	3.37	1	3.37	10.58	**<.01**
Group size * Gender	3.24	2	1.62	5.09	**<.01**
Trials	6.71	1	6.71	21.07	**<.01**
Group size * Trials	1.15	2	0.57	1.80	.17
Gender * Trials	0.30	2	0.15	0.46	.63
Group size * Gender * Trials	1.56	2	0.78	2.44	.09

Table 9. Descriptive statistics value for the evaluation score of originality of ideas with a five-point scale in the new tea name generation task: stratified by trials.

	Ave.	*S.D.*	Total number of evaluated ideas
1st trial	2.36	0.48	475
2nd trial	2.41	0.52	532
3rd trial	2.47	0.58	523

Table 10. Multiple comparisons in trials for the evaluation score of utility of ideas with a five-point scale in the new tea name generation task.

	SS	*df*	*MS*	*F*	*p*
Between 1st trial and 2nd trial	3.65	1	3.65	11.23	<.01
Between 2nd trial and 3rd trial	0.06	1	0.06	0.81	.67
Between 1st trial and 3rd trial	4.61	1	4.61	13.45	<.01

As a result of the simple main effect, female participants showed a higher score of originality in pairs than in individuals ($F(1,1526) = 27.67$, $p < .01$, $\eta_p^2 = .02$), although male participants did not show any significant difference between performance in pairs and in individuals ($F(1,1526) = 0.37$, $p = .54$, $\eta_p^2 < .01$) (Fig. 1). On the other hand, male participants showed a higher score of utility in pairs than in individuals ($F(1,1526) = 39.54$, $p < .01$, $\eta_p^2 = .03$), although female participants did not show any significant difference between performance in pairs and in individuals ($F(1,1526) = 0.51$, $p = .48$, $\eta_p^2 < .03$) (Fig. 2).

We did not find any correlation between the communication skills of participants and their score of idea quality (originality: r = −.10, utility: r = −.03). We also did not find any correlation between the active-learning attitude of participants and their score of idea quality (originality: r = .04, utility: r = .07).

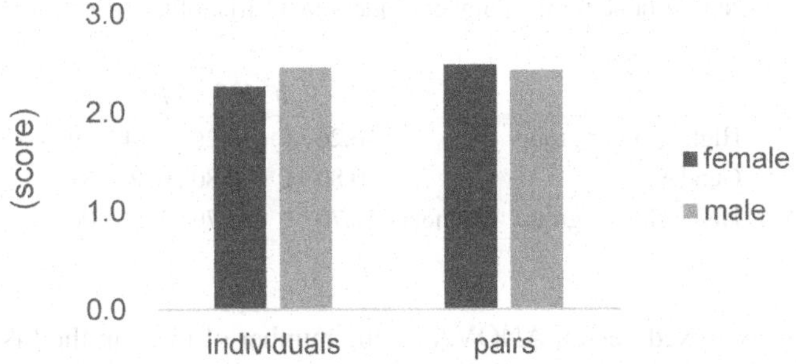

Fig. 1. Relationship between group size and the evaluation score of originality of ideas.

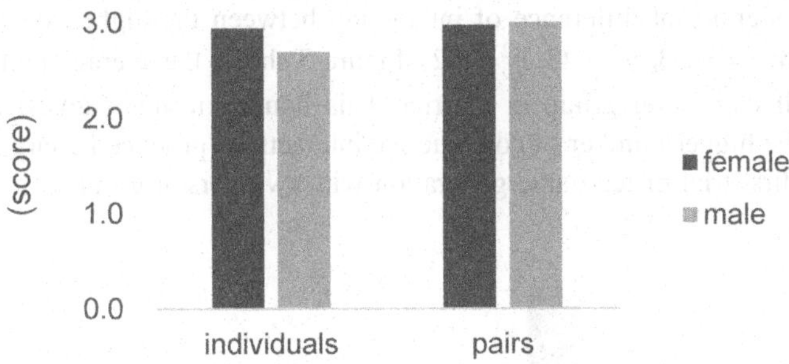

Fig. 2. Relationship between group size and the evaluation score of utility of ideas.

3.2 Relationship Between Constructive Interaction and Quality of Ideas

Twenty pair was divided into two groups by using average number of constructive interaction; (i) higher group: pair was produced larger number of constructive interaction than average, and (ii) lower group: pair was produced smaller number of constructive interaction.

Number of Constructive Interaction and Number of Ideas

Tables 11 and 12 show the ANOVA tables for the number of ideas in 1st and 3rd trials of the new tea name generation task.

Table 11. The ANOVA table for the number of ideas in 1st trial of the new tea name generation task.

	SS	*df*	*MS*	*F*	*p*
Higher/lower group	185.36	1	185.36	6.56	**.01**
Gender	97.20	1	97.20	3.44	.07
Higher/lower group * Gender	17.85	1	17.85	0.64	.43

Table 12. The ANOVA table for the number of ideas in 3rd trial of the new tea name generation task.

	SS	*df*	*MS*	*F*	*p*
Higher/lower group	16.26	1	16.26	1.14	.29
Gender	0.80	1	0.80	0.06	.81
Higher/lower group * Gender	51.70	1	51.70	3.64	.06

The two-way mixed design ANOVA on the number of ideas in the first trial of the tea-name-generation task (gender * higher/lower group (2 * 2)) showed a main effect for the higher/lower group (F(1,36) = 6.56, p = .01, η_p^2 = .15). There was no significant difference in the main effect for gender (F(1,36) = 3.44, p = .07, η_p^2 = .09). There was also no significant difference of interaction between the higher/lower group and gender (F(1,36) = 0.63, p = .43, η_p^2= .02). Figure 3 shows the average number of ideas with the higher or lower group in 1st trial. This figure's results suggest that the participants in the higher number of constructive interactions produced a larger number of ideas in the first trial of tea-name generation with two-person groups.

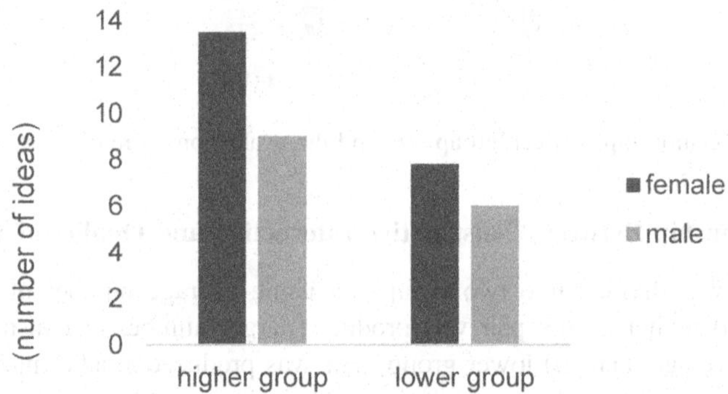

Fig. 3. Relationship between higher/lower number of constructive interactions and the average number of ideas in the first trial of the tea-name-generation task in pair.

Number of Constructive Interaction and Creativity of Ideas

Tables 13, 14, 15 and 16 show the ANOVA tables for the originality or utility of ideas in 1st and 3rd trials of the new tea name generation task.

Table 13. The ANOVA table for the evaluation score of originality of ideas in 1st trial of the new tea name generation task.

	SS	*df*	*MS*	*F*	*p*
Higher/lower group	0.02	1	0.02	0.44	.51
Gender	0.13	1	0.13	2.42	.13
Higher/lower group * Gender	0.01	1	0.01	0.01	.92

Table 14. The ANOVA table for t the evaluation score of originality of ideas in 3rd trial of the new tea name generation task.

	SS	*df*	*MS*	*F*	*p*
Higher/lower group	0.86	1	0.86	8.38	**<.01**
Gender	0.04	1	0.04	0.42	.52
Higher/lower group * Gender	0.10	1	0.10	0.94	.34

Table 15. The ANOVA table for the evaluation score of utility of ideas in 1st trial of the new tea name generation task.

	SS	*df*	*MS*	*F*	*p*
Higher/lower group	0.15	1	0.15	2.27	.14
Gender	0.05	1	0.05	0.68	.41
Higher/lower group * Gender	0.04	1	0.04	0.61	.44

Table 16. The ANOVA table for t the evaluation score of utility of ideas in 3rd trial of the new tea name generation task.

	SS	*df*	*MS*	*F*	*p*
Higher/lower group	0.12	1	0.12	1.10	.30
Gender	0.45	1	0.45	4.04	.05
Higher/lower group * Gender	0.04	1	0.04	0.37	.55

The two-way ANOVA on the quality of ideas in the third trial of the tea-name-generation task (gender × higher/lower number of constructive interactions (2 × 2)) showed a main effect for the higher/lower number of constructive interactions on the originality of ideas ($F(1,36) = 8.38$, $p < .01$, $\eta_p^2 = .19$), although there was no significant difference in the main effect on the utility of ideas ($F(1,36) = 1.10$, $p = .30$, $\eta_p^2 = .01$). There was no significant difference in the main effect for gender (originality: $F(1,36) = 3.44$, $p = .07$, $\eta_p^2 = .09$, utility: $F(1,36) = 4.04$, $p = .05$, $\eta_p^2 = .10$). There was also no significant difference in interaction between the higher/lower number of constructive interactions and gender (originality: $F(1,36) = 0.63$, $p = .43$, $\eta_p^2 = .02$, utility: $F(1,36) = 0.37$, $p = .55$, $\eta_p^2 = .01$). Figure 4 shows the average score for the originality of ideas with the higher or lower number of constructive interactions. From this figure, it can be seen that the participants with the higher number of constructive interactions produced higher originality of ideas in the third trial of tea-name generation with two-person groups.

We did not find any correlation between the conversational satisfaction in pair and their score of idea quality (originality: r = .08, utility: r = −.27).

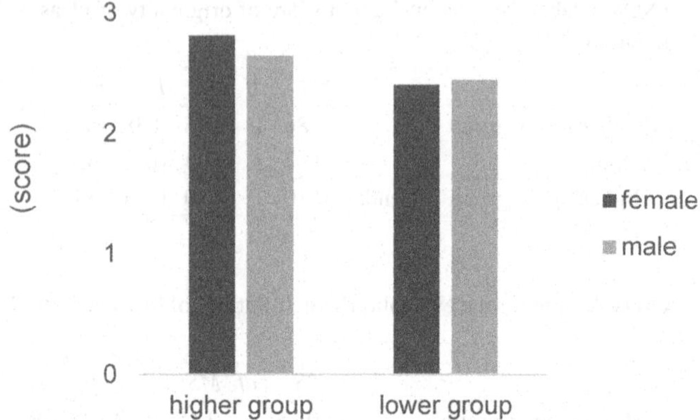

Fig. 4. Relationship between higher/lower number of constructive interactions and the average score for the originality of ideas in the third trial of the tea-name-generation task in pair.

4 Discussion

4.1 Group-Size Effects on Quality of Ideas

Group size affected the quality of ideas in terms of originality and utility in the divergent name-generation task, although it did not affect the number of ideas. The quality of ideas in pairs is superior to that in individuals. Thus, our prediction might be partly supported, even though the results on the quantity of ideas showed different tendencies from those in previous studies. This appears to be caused by participants making more contributions to the quality of ideas in the presence of others. This effect is called social facilitation [12].

4.2 Production of Constructive Interaction Affects Both Quantity and Quality of Ideas

Producing a larger number of constructive interactions increased the quality of ideas in the third trial, while it increased the number of ideas in the first trial. The production of constructive interaction includes making propositions or giving critical opinions to the partner [11]. In the first trial, a pair producing a larger number of constructive interactions affects the number of ideas. On the other hand, such a pair in the third trial might frequently change between the two roles of task-doer and monitor. This is caused by participants making more contributions to the quality of ideas with the higher quality of interaction with each trial.

5 Conclusions

In this study, we examined the creative power of collaborative pairs in divergent idea-generation tasks in comparison with that of individuals. The results suggest that the quality of ideas, i.e. originality and utility, in pairs was superior to that in individuals.

It was also suggested that a larger production of constructive interactions through the collaboration of pairs enhanced the quality of ideas. On the other hand, there was little contribution of individuals' communication skills or active-learning attitudes to the quality of ideas.

These findings could be applied to the relational design [13] between people as well as people and social robots to improve the creativity of people. When the optimal framework of relations for facilitating collaboration of pairs is established, the creativity of people would improve as a result of increasing the constructive interaction within the pair. Previous studies on human-robot learning showed that social robots provided constructive interaction to students for learning or problem solving in the classroom [11]. Similarity, social robots would support the emerging creativity of people by producing constructive interaction through collaboration with people (e.g., [14]). Robots with artificial intelligence would become support-givers for enhancing the creativity of people rather than simply competitors for jobs currently held by humans [4].

As future work, we will examine the group-size effect [15] on the quality as well as number of ideas. In particular, we are interested in how larger group size induces social loafing [12, 16] from the viewpoint of the quality of ideas.

Acknowledgements. The findings of this study are based on the first author's graduation thesis. We thank 88 students of Doshisha University for their participation in the experiment. This work was supported by JSPS KAKENHI Grant Number JP16H03225.

References

1. Burkus, D.: The Myths of Creativity: The Truth About How Innovative Companies and People Generate Great Ideas. Jossey-Bass, San Francisco (2013)
2. Shenk, S.W.: Power of Two: Finding the Essence of Innovation in Creative Pairs. Eamon Dolan/Houghton Mifflin Harcourt, Boston (2014)
3. Care, E., Griffin, P., Wilson, M. (eds.): Assessment and Teaching of 21st Century Skills: Research and Applications. EAIA. Springer, Cham (2018). https://doi.org/10.1007/978-3-319-65368-6
4. Frey, C.B., Osborne, M.A.: The future of employment: how susceptible are jobs to computerisation? Technol. Forecast. Soc. Chang. **114**(C), 254–280 (2017)
5. Hill, G.W.: Group versus individual performance: are N + 1 heads better than one? Psychol. Bull. **91**(3), 517–539 (1982)
6. Laughlin, P.R., Hatch, E.C., Silver, J.S., Boh, L.: Groups perform better than the best individuals on letters-to-numbers problems: effects of group size. J. Pers. Soc. Psychol. **90** (4), 644–651 (2006)
7. Dijksterhuis, A., Meurs, T.: Where creativity resides: the generative power of unconscious thought. Conscious. Cogn. **15**(1), 135–146 (2005)
8. Kikuchi, A.: Scale of Social Skills: Handbook of KiSS-18. Kawashima-shoten (2007). (in Japanese)
9. Hatano, K., Mizokami, S.: The examination of student' type based on active class attitude and learning time in university students. Jpn. J. Educ. Technol. **37**(1), 13–21 (2013). (in Japanese)

10. Bernieri, J.F., Gillis, J.S., Davis, J.M., Grahe, J.E.: Dyad rapport and the accuracy of its judgment across situations: a lens model analysis. Pers. Soc. Psychol. **71**, 110–129 (1996)
11. Miyake, N.: Constructive interaction and the iterative processes of understanding. Cogn. Sci. **10**, 151–177 (1986)
12. Harkins, S.: Social loafing and social facilitation. J. Exp. Soc. Psychol. **23**(1), 1–18 (1987)
13. Shimohara, K.: Relationality design. In: Proceedings of 2008 International Congress on Humanized Systems (HRI 2012), pp. 365–369 (2008)
14. Kanda, T., Shimada, M., Koizumi, S.: Children learning with a social robot. In: 2012 ACM/IEEE International Conference on Human-Robot Interaction (HRI2012), USA, pp. 351–358. ACM (2012)
15. Suzuki, N., Imashiro, M., Shoda, H., Ito, N., Sakata, M., Yamamoto, M.: Effects of group size on performance and member satisfaction. In: Yamamoto, S., Mori, H. (eds.) HIMI 2018. LNCS, vol. 10905, pp. 191–199. Springer, Cham (2018). https://doi.org/10.1007/978-3-319-92046-7_17
16. Latane, B., Williams, K., Harkins, S.: Many hands make light the work: the causes and consequences of social loafing. J. Pers. Soc. Psychol. **37**, 822–832 (1979)

Interactive HMI for Qualification and Programming in Process Automation EduBrain 4.0

Sebastian Schmitz and Daniel Schilberg(✉)

Institute of Robotics and Mechatronics, University of Applied Sciences Bochum, Lennershofstr. 140, 44801 Bochum, Germany
{sebastian.schmitz,daniel.schilberg}@hs-bochum.de

Abstract. The following article deals with the topic of interactive qualification and programming in industrial applications. Due to the constantly increasing demands on the employees of a company, it becomes necessary to support the employees with new tools for training and further education. The interactive human – machine – interface (HMI) EduBrain 4.0 offers the user an optimized further education option via a cloud-based information model and provides the user with application information. The first part of this thesis discusses the current possibilities and methods of personnel training and further education as well as the use of digital devices and tools in the field of automation technology, especially during troubleshooting. Furthermore, the advantages and effects of optimized further education are discussed. In the second part of this thesis the concept of the information model of HMI is presented. The third part shows the construction and technical development of a robot training factory in detail. The robot training factory is to serve as the basis for testing the HMI in a man-machine collaboration plant, further projects and experiments in the area of man-machine cooperation. All current techniques are combined here, so that the information model can be tested optimally and the distance increased.

Keywords: Education · HMI · Knowledge · Deep learning · Human – machine – interface · Collaboration · Robotic · Cloud · Information

1 Introduction

The level of automation of production facilities is increasing steadily. According to the "International Federation of Robotics" there will be roughly 1.4 million new industrial robots applied in the industry by 2019 [2], just in the area of material handling. By now industrial robots have been applied in almost all areas of production, from "simple" material handling, over welding and coating, to other highly complex tasks. Due to the fact that the technology in the area of robotics and automation is being developed further every year, by the research activities of numerous scientists and companies worldwide, the question arises how the average shop floor worker is supposed to acquire all the crucial knowledge needed for the operation and programming of those complex systems and machines. Nowadays several companies already run relevant systems simultaneously. In order not to be dependent on one particular supplier, most

S. Yamamoto and H. Mori (Eds.): HCII 2019, LNCS 11569, pp. 343–351, 2019.
https://doi.org/10.1007/978-3-030-22660-2_24

companies apply systems with the same properties, like industrial robots, gluing controllers or welding machines from different manufacturers. Hereby the number of systems that have to operated and controlled rises significantly. Because, due to the progress made in technology and the constantly increasing demands on the systems, even trivial devices are equipped with programmable controllers which do not have a uniform programming language, the requirements to the programmer and operator are increasing as well. While programmers are mostly trained for a particular amount of systems, the operator theoretically has to be familiar with every single system, in order to be able to react appropriately in case of errors or malfunctions, which is in fact almost impossible. The economy demands "Industry 4.0" and everybody has a different opinion what "Industry 4.0" actually is. But regardless of the contentwise meaning and the extent of "Industry 4.0" one thing is for sure, the requirements to the employees involved will increase. By the new development of so called collaborative industrial robots [3], on the one hand a new field of activity for the application of those systems arises and now tasks can be carried out, that have not been feasibly before, where robots assists the human directly, but on the other hand again the need for further training regarding the programming, operating and safety of those systems arises. Many of the collaborative robots applied in the industry are used as assistance systems at assembly tasks in order to accomplish time saving for the worker or to relief the human by taking over strenuous tasks like the handling of heavy objects. An area that has not been really developed yet is the fixture construction, where often fixtures are assembled that have a high variance, but which components are relatively trivial.

The information model of EduBrain 4.0 is based on an extensive database which is continuously updated by the manufacturers through the implementation of the most recent technical documentations of their products. The user can variably select the topics that are important for his company and define an individual training program. With the subject areas selected by the user the algorithm chooses the specific topics and generates an information model and a training program. The users are provided with important system information over the HMI and can acquire knowledge about the applied technologies online. Thereby the time needed for training employees on a new production facility or system is reduced significantly. Through the systematic selection of information downtime caused by error diagnosis is minimized as well. The information model is based on the Deep Learning Technology. Gathered information and optimizations in the information model are saved in a cloud and are globally accessible. The software recognizes all participants in the network and automatically loads there specifications into the HMI. The user sees at a glance which components and technologies are applied in the plant. If the users wants to inform himself about one of the topics the software makes the demanded information available via drag and drop.

2 State of the Art

2.1 Education

There are basically two strategies that companies can pursue in the area of continuing training. The first strategy is to regularly send employees to train and educate the various manufacturers and suppliers. The leading manufacturer of industrial robots Fanuc Robotic alone trains around 3000 participants in Germany each year in the fields of robotics and CNC programming and CNC operation. The second strategy is learning through action. Many companies pursue this strategy for cost and time reasons. But the problem with this strategy is the inaccurate or undetailed knowledge of the employees. Most of the current training courses are often carried out through the rather outdated frontal instruction. Although this method has been tried and tested for a long time, it is no longer quite up-to-date. Intuitive, independent working out of questions and topics under expert guidance is clearly more future-oriented and optimal. Furthermore, conventional hardcopy manuals are still used today in many areas of training, from which the lecturer lectures. In the digital age of tablets and smartphones electronic documentation should be used here. A universal digital tool for training and further education which learns by the input and requirements of the user and adapts its interface and information output for the user should represent a clear optimization here.

2.2 Process Automation

Outside of the learning environment, for example in the field of automated operations, documentation for troubleshooting can also be found in analog form. Especially in the area of troubleshooting, a quicker reaction in the event of an emergency is necessary. It is therefore of great advantage if the corresponding manual is available on an electronic device at short notice without any effort. Some companies with a high degree of automation have already reacted. They use a local cloud to store technical documentation and troubleshooting manuals. Most production plants have machine - human - interfaces on several parts of the plant where the operator controls and monitors the plant. From these HMI he has access to the local server and can load information in case of an error. In some cases, the individual departments even have a kind of local Wikipedia where they store information, experience or advices to help them deal with problems. The problem here is that this information is usually only available to a small part of the workforce. This information is passed on to other parts of the company or even to other company locations that often have identical systems in use is practically not practiced in almost any company. Due to the variety of technologies and manufacturers used, it is usually very difficult to find the right document in the local cloud. If the requested document is not in the cloud, the user usually cannot use the HMI to search for it on the internet, as the ports are blocked for security reasons. In many cases, the user has to leave the system and go to the office to search the file online. A solution here would be a terminal device that is decoupled from the safety circuit, such as a tablet on which I can see the process data and obtain information about the system.

3 Conception and Layout

3.1 Information Model

In order to be able to provide the user with the desired information and to be able to offer the right topics for further training, an information model must first be created in order to clearly identify which information has which prioritisation. Especially in a constantly changing field such as automation technology, this is not a trivial process. There are a multitude of technologies, products and manufacturers and thus a gigantic number of documents. For structuring purposes, categorisation must first be carried out. For this purpose, the individual components of the system are considered in the first step and divided into different main categories (Fig. 1). Then the components of the main categories are looked at and further detailed. This is done as long as the last component has been categorized. For the creation of the logarithm which shall carry out this classification in the later software, this is carried out once by hand. On the basis of the terms, manufacturer names and abbreviations, the software will make suggestions to the user during the next categorization into which new, but components with similar manufacturing or designation could be integrated. Here the user makes the decision. All categorization decisions are forwarded to the cloud that will share this information with other users (Fig. 2).

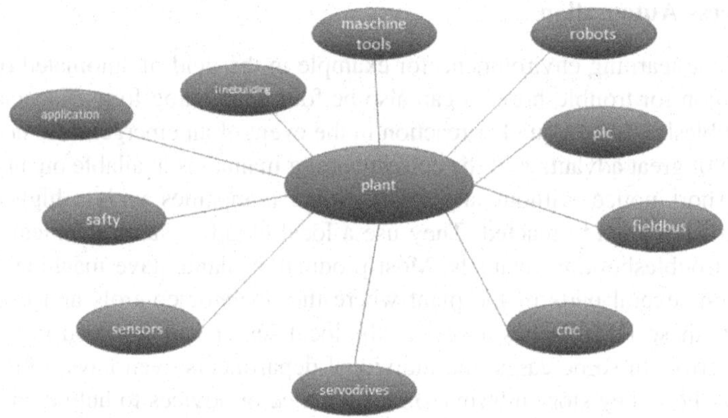

Fig. 1. Schedule line process

When uploading the information, the software differentiates between confidential information that is stored only for the company in cloud and only intended for the users of the company or information that is made available globally and therefore all users benefit from this information. If all categories have been created at one time, the information such as manuals, tutorials, datasheets and for example drawings have to be loaded into the cloud and the corresponding parts have to be stored here, manufacturers of components are provided with the possibility of an interface for information sharing. They can store all their products under a QR code. If a user is called to an installation where, for example, a robot shows a defect, he can use his tablet to read the QR code. The software immediately provides the user with the necessary manuals and information stored under this QR code. If the user so wishes the software can also install apps from the manufacturer that are also stored under the code. For example, these can be a diagnostic tool that establish a connection to the product and simplify the diagnosis.

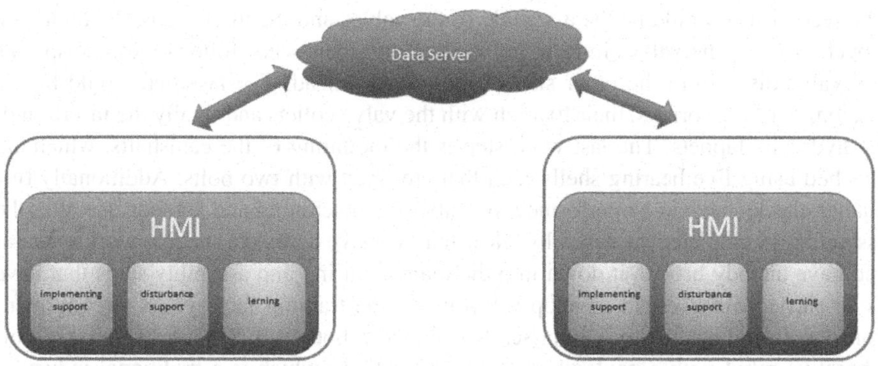

Fig. 2. Networking of multiple devices

With the final software it should be possible that for example service technicians who are called to a defect can work with the software, no matter which factory of the company they are located in. If it is not a matter of plant-specific details, but for example an S7-1500 PLC from Siemens, then everybody who uses the software after reading the QR code has all the information to this plc which he needs, independent of country and language. If the tablet is not used to read the individual components of the QR code, but rather the individual components of the system, the user is presented with an overview of the system, a list of the used and components and the system status on the tablet. This QR code is created by the operator or the system builder and loaded into the cloud. As there is no update tool for most industrial systems or components, the software has a further advantage. If there is an update from the system manufacturer, it is immediately displayed to the end user at the next contact. There is no need to inquire about updates on the internet. Since the software knows exactly which components are installed, it can automatically recognize which technologies and thus which topics are present in the system. This diagnosis enables the software to create a learning environment that is optimized for the user's needs, with which he or she can further train himself or herself.

3.2 Robotic Training Factory

In the considerations for a suitable work scenario to test the software. Since robotic, especially collaborative robotic is currently and in the future very important, it is obvious to plan an application with such a robot. Firstly the parts worked on should be big and heavy in order to emphasize the strengths and advantages of the collaborative robot, which is the core of the whole training factory. Secondly the workpieces had to provide enough possibilities for assembly and handling tasks since these form the interface between the human, the robot and the HMI. Finally the choice was made for cylinder heads for motor vehicles, since they have a high weight and offer various possibilities for manufacturing, assembly and handling tasks. There are basically three main work steps the cylinder head has to walk through. The first step is the machining, where the different contact surfaces are finished, holes are drilled and taps are cut etc.

The second step would be the assembly of the valves and the insertion of the hydraulic tappets. At first the valves have to be inserted into their seats, followed by the springs and valve discs from the other side of the cylinder head. The last step would be the tensioning of the springs, their fixation with the valve collets and finally the insertion of the hydraulic tappets. The last work step is the mounting of the camshafts, which are attached using five bearing shells each that are fixed with two bolts. Additionally two quality checks have to be performed, one after the machining and another one after the assembly is completed successfully. Now that we have defined a specific work scenario and have already broken it down into the manufacturing and assembly steps that have to be carried out, we can develop a layout for the training factory. As already mentioned the training factory comprises two Fanuc robots. A CR-35iA, which is a collaborative robot with a payload of 35 kg and a M20, which is a traditional industrial robot with a payload of 20 kg. Both robots have a reach of 1800 mm. Another important element of our training factory is a CNC-machining center, the Fanuc Robodrill. Apart from that a workstation for the assembly tasks, a storage for material and finished parts as well as a rack between the two robots are further components.

The first draft of the training factory is shown in Fig. 3. The collaborative robot is placed right next to the machining center and the workstation. It is responsible for the automatic machine tending and of course for the handling of the cylinder heads during their assembly in HRC. The M20 is placed in close proximity to the material and finished part storage. It is responsible for storing the finished parts and handing out components for the assembly process.

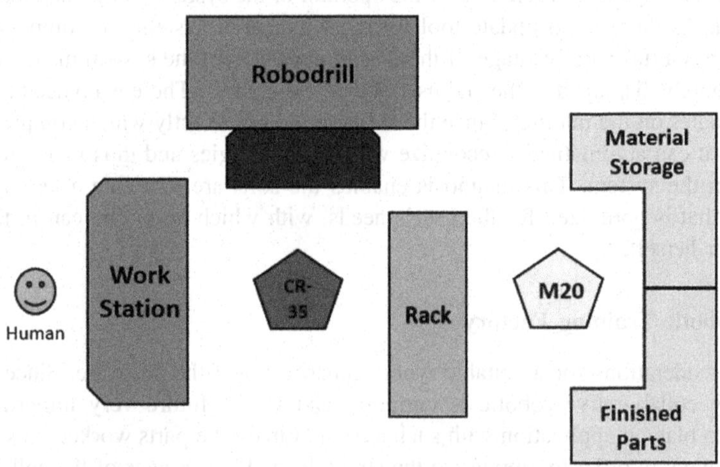

Fig. 3. Rough design of the training factory

Figure 4 shows the final draft of the training factory created with the simulation software Fanuc Roboguide. The floor space needed for the factory as it is shown in Fig. 4 amounts to approximately 5.5 × 3.5 m. The final draft does not differ very much from our first draft apart from the fact that it is more compact in order to adapt to the given floor space and the fact that the M20 is placed inside a robot cell which contains the material and finished part storage. The cell has two open entrances. One on the left between the robots that is needed for the handover and another one on the lower side of the cell which is used for handing out the finished parts that are stored inside the cell. The collaborative robot does not need any safety fences, however when the robot is intended to be run with different speeds depending on whether an operator is present in its workspace or not, the robot's workspace has to be monitored accurately. For example by using light curtains or safety mats.

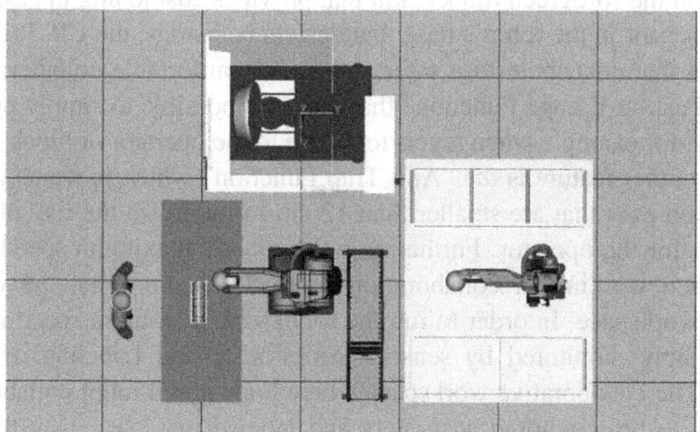

Fig. 4. Detailed design of the training factory

With our layout completed we can now take a closer look at the individual work steps, especially at the ones that are carried out in human-robot-collaboration. After the machining process of the cylinder head in the Robodrill is successfully completed, the workpiece has to be checked. This quality check is performed in collaboration with the CR-35 handling the part and the operator inspecting it. A voice or gesture control or a HMI could be used to communicate with the robot and give commands to make the robot present the part in different perspectives. When the part has successfully passed the quality check the first assembly step which is the insertion of the valves is next. The CR-35 holds the part in front of the operator in a height that is comfortable to reach so that the operator can insert the valves into their seats. Next the robot rotates the cylinder head by 180° so that the valve heads are facing the tabletop and places it into a nest. Then the operator would place the springs and disc on the valve shafts, followed by the tensioning and securing of the valves. This could either be done using a fixture attached to the nest that pushes the springs down, while the operator secures them with the valve collets. Or by the CR-35 with a special end-of-arm-tool and the operator's assistance. Either way the process of tensioning the springs has to be designed in a way that reduces the risk of clamping or shearing for the operator, for example by using low forces first and higher forces after one can be sure that everything is safe. Afterwards the camshafts have to be mounted. Here the CR-35 could again handle the cylinder head during the process, while the operator places the camshafts on their seats and attaches them with the bearing shells and bolts. When a second collaborative robot would be added to the workstation it could take over the screw-driving process and the operator would only have to position the shells and bolts in the right places. Finally another quality check has to be carried out to verify the correct assembly of the cylinder head.

3.3 Safety Measures

Just like in each and every application of industrial robots or other machines the safety of the human always has the highest priority. So it is in our training factory.

Beside from the soft green rubber skin that provides cushioning in case of a contact and the force sensor in the robot's base that detects collisions, the CR-35iA has further safety features that contribute to a safer and more comfortable collaboration. One of those is the "Push-to-Escape Function" that makes it possible to simply push the robot out of the way, for example when it gets too close to the operator or blocks the human's workspace. Another feature is the "Anti-Trap Function" which prevents gaps between the robot's main axes that are smaller than 12 cm to minimize the risk of clamping or getting caught for the operator. Furthermore the robot's maximum speed is limited to 250 mm/s when working in collaboration or to 750 mm/s when no operators are present in its workspace. In order to run the robot with maximum speed its workspace has to be reliably monitored by sensors. Monitoring and Labeling of the Robots' Workspaces. The collaborative workspace where human and robot collaborate directly with each has to be monitored accurately and labeled in a clear way that is easy to understand. The workspace of the M20 also needs to be monitored and labeled since it has open entrances that pose a considerable threat (Fig. 5).

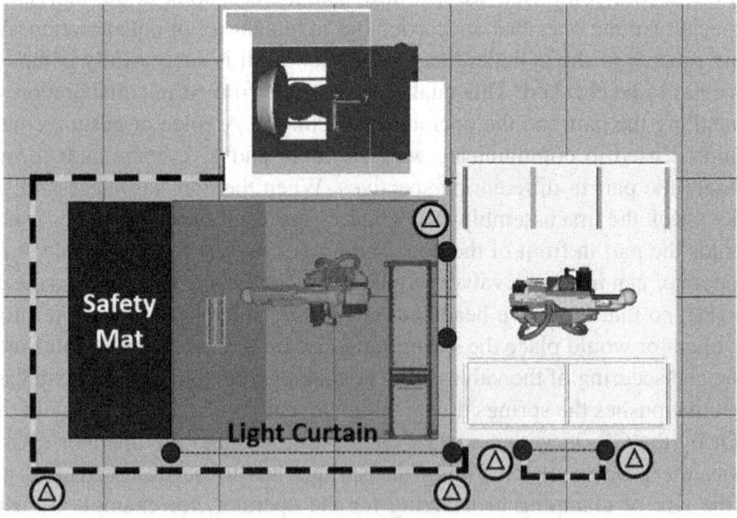

Fig. 5. Labeling and monitoring of the robots' workspaces

The CR-35's workspace is monitored by a light curtain that covers the area between the workstation and the rack and a safety mat placed in front of the workstation. When either the safety mat or the light curtain is activated the robot's maximum speed is set to 250 mm/s. In operations where no human assistance is needed like the automatic machine tending, the robot can work with a maximum speed of 750 mm/s. In order to give information about the current state of the collaborative robot, an additional visual display is required that indicates whether the robot is operating in collaborative or automatic mode. The two open entrances to the work cell of the M20 are monitored by light curtains that stop the robot immediately when activated. Apart from the monitoring of the robots' workspaces their correct and unambiguous labeling is also very import to make sure that even people who are not familiar with the training factory are aware of the prevailing risks and dangers. The whole collaborative workspace as well as the areas in front of the open entrances to the robot cell are marked using yellow/black safety tape. Additionally signs that indicate the use of industrial robots, collaborative robots and the risk through the automatic start of machines are put up in several locations around the robots' workspaces.

4 Conclusion

The aim of this article was to show the possibilities that a cloud based information system offers if it is communicated to the user via a suitable human machine interface. Working interactively with such a system has great potential in education and training. Both in the area of information provision and in the area of further education, such an HMI with the right and stable software solution is a very efficient tool for accelerating or extending processes. In the first part, the current applications of HMI were presented and optimizations described. In the second part, the robotic cell specially developed for the HMI software test series was described in detail and the research possibilities in this area were presented.

References

1. International Federation of Robotics (IFR): Executive Summary World Robotics 2016 Industrial Robots (2016)
2. Knauer, H.: Conception of heterogeneous robotic training factory. In: REM 2017 (2017)
3. Betschon, S.: Collaborative Robots: Die Befreiung der Roboter (2015)

Investigation of Learning Process with TUI and GUI Based on Protocol Analysis

Natsumi Sei[1(✉)], Makoto Oka[2], and Hirohiko Mori[1]

[1] Graduate Division, Tokyo City University,
1-28-2 Tamadutumi, Setagayaku, Tokyo, Japan
G1791801@tcu.ac.jp

[2] Tokyo City University, 1-28-2 Tamadutumi, Setagayaku, Tokyo, Japan

Abstract. In this paper, we evaluated learning process of tangible user interface and graphical user interface. We investigate the effect of the user interface on learning process when user learn by using computer. When TUI and Graphical User Interface (GUI) were used, how an adopted interface may affect learning process was focused. We conducted the experiment to clarify the effect on learning process when a specific interface was used, difference in learning process is to be reviewed by using TUI and GUI. An analysis was conducted for the verification using a protocol analysis. Strategy of problem-solving by using two systems were similar in case of early in the experiment.

Adopting other measures when getting familiar with such problems, however, it has been proved that participants find out a correct answer by accumulating sub-goal achievement in case of GUI and they figure out a correct answer while taking various measures such as searching of clues and accumulation of sub-goal achievement in case of TUI.

Keywords: Tangible User Interface (TUI) · COCOM · Cognitive process · Interface

1 Background

The types of interfaces have become diversified in association with the popularization of computers. Among them, TUI is a type of interfaces through which we can operate computers by directly touching physical objects. One of the advantages of TUI is its easy operation procedures as it enables us to operate computers in an intuitive manner. For this reason, it is thought that we can solely focus on learning activities without paying much attention to how to operate a computer. Researches using TUI in a learning environment have been conducted. However, while some researches have showed that using TUI has an impact on learning environments, how it affects learning processes has not been verified yet substantially.

S. Yamamoto and H. Mori (Eds.): HCII 2019, LNCS 11569, pp. 352–361, 2019.
https://doi.org/10.1007/978-3-030-22660-2_25

2 Purpose

In this paper, how an interface in use influences the learning process will be examined for TUI and GUI. Revealing such influences enables us to provide an interface suitable for learning activities.

3 Related Works

Tablets and notebook PCs are the interfaces frequently used in the learning activities using computers like those making use of ICT. Tablets and notebook PC are featured by their capability to adapt themselves to various classes by changing an application to be used in them. Also, Yokoyama et al. [1] conducted a class using tables PCs for elementary school and junior high school students, the results of which suggested that their ability to think was improved. In addition, Akahori et al. [2] examined the influences on learning by using the three media: papers, PCs and tablets. It was revealed that with papers learners had a high understanding of basic problems and clearly recognized letters, while with tablets they showed a deep understanding of applied problems and a high-level recognition of images. As such, it was demonstrated that influences given on learning vary by a media to be employed for it. Some researches have used TUI in the learning making use of ICT. Kuzuoka et al. [3] utilized a globe as a tangible interface for the learning of astronomy, consequently proposing a learning environment under which we can learn about the relationships between the earth and the sun. It was indicated that learners tended to depend on a system in learning activities so that they were unable to gain an essential understanding and accordingly misguided to a wrong thought. Also, Cuendet [4] conducted a class using TUI. It was found that while the learners became more willing to learn there was no difference produced in terms of their learning effectiveness. Cuendet [5] conducted a class with the use of TapaCarp, meaning that the students could use TUI in the class. It was indicated that using TapaCarp enabled them to gain more positive attitudes toward the class and also to come up with flexible ideas. In the meantime, he said that there was a problem in terms of its versatility for classes. From the above facts, it is understood that using TUI produces a positive effect of their getting motivated to learn. On the other hand, however, it was suggested that TUI was unable to cause a powerful effect in respect of their performances and skills. However, I believe that TUI has not demonstrated a significant result just because there has been no research that verifies how much effects TUI can cause on what kinds of learning activities. Therefore, I think that learning activities using TUI would produce effective outcomes by closely looking at the learning process such as how learners will address their own problems in their learning process and by investigating the influences TUI exerts on them, rather than evaluating outcomes only through their performances.

4 Experiment

4.1 Objective of Experiment

We conducted the experiment to clarify the effect on learning process when a specific interface was used, difference in learning process is to be reviewed by using TUI and GUI.

4.2 Experimental Policy

As a learning task, logical circuit learning was selected in which GUI and TUI showed the same appearance. Subjects were asked to prepare a logic circuit based on a truth table. The three logical symbol used in this experiment was the "AND", the "OR" and the "NOT". In addition, the lead wire objects and the lamp objects, to connect among each gate and to confirm the output of the circuit respectively, were also prepared.

GUI is operated with a mouse using "click" and "drag" while watching on a PC screen. TUI is operated using cube- shaped blocks to create a logic circuit by applying them in 2-dimensional place. Asking subjects to voice what the subjects asked to "think aloud", and, their behavior and verbal protocol data were recorded by VCR.

4.3 Experimental Methodology

Subjects were asked to solve problems using a system to learn logic circuit. Operation manual of the interface was written out on a paper for subjects to be able to read again during experiment and instruction of the logic circuit was also written on a paper likewise.

Experiment was performed for 6 weeks (6 times) by increasing the difficulty every week. Subjects were asked to solve problems taking for around an hour in each experiment. A personality assessment test was conducted in the first week in order to recognize their original strategies. They were asked to solve problems regarding a logic circuit in the second and later experiments. In the second week, such problem was set for them to fill in an output part in a truth table in reference to a logic circuit in order for them to get familiar with a way to read truth tables. From the third and later week, they were asked to solve problems to create a logic circuit from a truth table. The problems of 3th are make logic circuit from truth table. Logical symbol of 3th is 2 pieces, 4th is 3 pieces, 5th and 6th are no specified pieces for increase the difficulty level.

In the 6th, number of available logic symbols was not designated for the problem with a setting of two lamps for output. Because of the increased two output lamp, subjects were required for applied skill different from the case of problems provided in the 5th or before.

5 Analytical Methods

Analyses will be made from three perspectives. The first analysis is to, based on quantitative data, examine how many research participants could solve problems. The second one is a protocol analysis that perform analyses from the narrations and behaviors of the participants. The third analysis a one using the contextual control model being a type of the recognition model. These three analyses are going to be made from their individual perspectives.

5.1 Learning Process

We analyzed the subjects' mode transition based on COCOM by dividing the whole period of the experiment into 3 stages to focus on their learning process as follows:

Initial stage: The third week
The subjects learn the basis of the logic circuits.
Latter stage: The 4th and 5th weeks
The subject becomes accustomed to solve the problems of the logic circuit.
Practical stage: The 6th (using 2 lams)
The subjects are asked to solve some advanced problems.

5.2 Contextual Control Model

In order to analyze what kinds of subject behavior will take, an analysis is made in reference to Contextual Control Model (COCOM) [6] by Hollnagel. There are five modes for COCOM.

Scrambled control mode: A control to select of random or panic.
Opportunistic control mode: A control to select next action just based on the current situation.
Explorative control mode: A control to seek for new ways at a venture without any other option available.
Tactical control mode: A control to select next action according to regulations provided in advance.
Strategic control mode: A control at high level in consideration of overall situation.

An analysis was conducted using an applied model which was adapted for problem solutions in reference to five modes advocated by COCOM.

Scramble control: The state that the user has no idea of what to do to solve the problem.
Explorative control: Their sub-goal is not clear and not to go toward the goal directly but to just try to find something tentatively.
Opportunistic control: Though subjects think looking at only one or a few sub-goals toward the goal, they do not know what kind of action should be done to achieve them.
Tactical control: Subjects think several sub-goals sweeping some part of path to the goal and knows what kind of action is needed to achieve sub-goals though they

have not found the whole Tactical control: Subjects think several sub-goals sweeping some part of path to the goal and knows what kind of action is needed to achieve sub-goals though they have not found the whole path for the goal yet. Strategic control: The path toward the goal is established more detail than tactical control, and subjects know what action are required to achieve it.

Then, we focus how the five modes of COCOM may transit in problem solving process. It was frequently observed that subjects tried ideas different from thoughts they had in the process of problem solving. With a concept to regard these thoughts as a cluster, how they bring about a transition in the cluster is reviewed.

Without any time limit for the experiments required, such a scrambled control mode to work on problems in panic did not occur. In addition, because the strategic control mode occurred when they were working on an easy problem and did not transit to other mode, the mode was excluded from the current analysis.

6 Results of the Analysis

6.1 Analyses Based on Quantitative Data

The number of the participants who had solved six problems within an hour was organized in Table 1. At the third stage, the participants in both groups were able to solve all problems. At the 4th stage, one participant in TUI group failed to solve problems. One participant in GUI group couldn't answer problems at the 5th stage, while all of the participants belonging to GUI group were unable to solve them at the most difficult 6th stage. At the 3rd stage, as the difficulty level of the problems had been set lower, the participants in both interface groups succeeded in solving them.

Table 1. The number of the participants who had solved six problems. (persons)

	3rd	4th	5th	6th
GUI	3	3	2	0
TUI	3	2	3	2

At the 4th stage, one participant in TUI group failed to answer problems. This is because such participants couldn't handle their increased level of difficulty. One participant in GUI group couldn't solve problems at the 5th stage where the difficulty level of problems had been further raised, while all the participants in GUI group failed to answer them, for they couldn't catch up with their difficulty level. Meanwhile, all the participants in TUI group succeeded in solving problems at the 5th stage at a higher difficulty level and two of them could answer them at the sixth stage being the most difficult. This can be explained by an assumption that TUI enabled them to use a solving method applicable to the problems at a higher difficulty level.

6.2 Protocol Analysis

Looking at the initial stage for GUI group (Table 2), a participant said, "AND and OR cannot be used together, so would it be a reversed flow if connecting them?" This shows that such participant predicts the outcome of a logic circuit to be designed. At the initial stage for TUI group (Table 3), a participant commented, "It lights up only with ONON. Reverse it after turning it around." Such comment suggests that this participant also projected the result of a logic circuit he would design.

At the later stage for GUI group (Table 4), a participant said, "Oh, this is not going to work." which indicates that such participant experienced a result different from the one he had expected and also that his expectation was not accompanied by a proper method. At the later stage for TUI group (Table 5), a participant commented, "I will remember this as it was the other way around.", which tells us that this participant designed a logic circuit for checking its result rather than designing it after making a prediction of its result. At the practical stage for GUI group (Table 6), a participant said, "Light this one and then both. I guess this looks good", which shows that the participant designed a logic circuit while expecting its outcome. Then, soon after, he added, "I wish it will light up", which suggests that his expectation was not a convincing one to him. At the practical stage for TUI group (Table 7), a participant quickly said, "It is AND not OR", which demonstrates that the participant designed a logic circuit for the purpose of using logic symbols occurring to his mind instead of determining them to be used based on a prediction of the result. Taken all together, it was revealed that at the initial stage the participants in both GUI group and TUI group designed a logic circuit while expecting its result. However, at the latter stage, the participants in TUI group demonstrated a different approach to the problems. It was found that those in TUI group would design a logic circuit without predicting its result. Meanwhile, those in GUI group, like the initial stage, designed a logic circuit with predicting its result. At the practical stage as well, there were many comments made by the participants in TUI group suggesting that they were designing a logic circuit without expecting its result, while there were lots of comments made by those in GUI group indicating that they were designing a logic circuit with expecting its result.

Table 2. GUI in initial stage

Time	Action	Protocol
1:45		AND and OR cannot be used together
1:52		So would it be a reversed flow if connecting them?
2:08	Move	
3:13		Not, good?
3:25	Check	
4:04		I want to connect AND

Table 3. TUI in initial stage

Time	Action	Protocol
7:10		It lights up only with ONON
7:11	Move	Reverse it after turning it around
7:22	Check	
7:29	Move	AND …
7:33	Check	

Table 4. GUI in later stage

Time	Action	Protocol
0:01		ONON, OFFOFF, OFFON
0:06	Move	
0:22	Check	
0:27		OFFON
0:32		Light in ONOFF
0:40	Move	
0:51		This is not going to work

Table 5. TUI in later stage

Time	Action	Protocol
9:16	Check	
9:23	Move	It is the other way around
9:27	Check	I will remember this
9:31		

Table 6. GUI in practical stage

Time	Action	Protocol
3:55	Move	
3:57		Light this one and then both
4:02		Like this
4:03	Move	I guess this looks good
4:19	Check	

Table 7. TUI in practical stage

Time	Action	Protocol
27:25		I wonder what about
27:35	Move	It is AND not OR
27:45	Check	Are different
27:50	Move	
27:52	Check	

6.3 Probability of Transition of Mode by COCOM

It was found that research participants tried more than one method in solving one problem. Their strategy is going to be discussed by examining how they made mode transitions in a single trial. Figures 1 and 2 illustrate the probability of mode transitions. The color gets thickened as the probability gets higher; The color goes white as the probability gets lower. Whereas the transition to the tactical control mode was frequently observed with the use of GUI at the initial stage, the transition between the tactical control mode and the opportunistic control mode as well as that to the opportunistic control mode were seen very often at the later stage and the practical stage (Fig. 1). With TUI, many research participants made transitions from the opportunistic control mode as with GUI at the initial stage, while they evenly made transitions among the three modes at the later stage and the practical stage (Fig. 2).

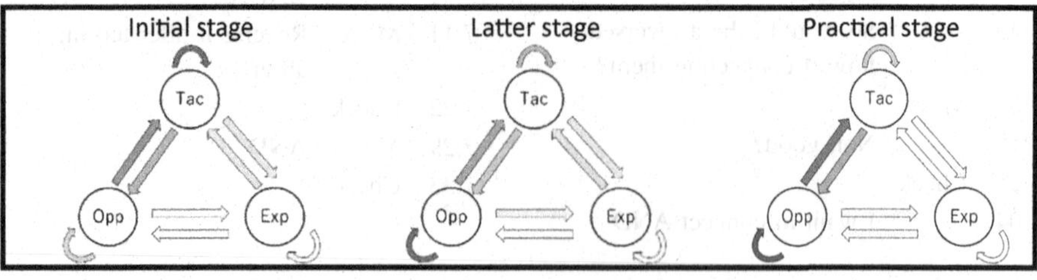

Fig. 1. Transition in GUI

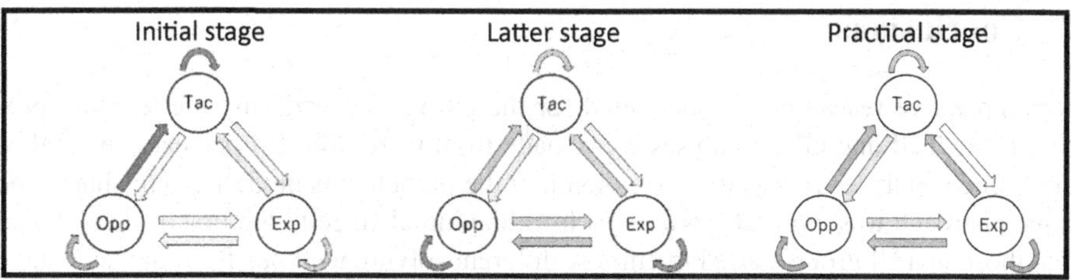

Fig. 2. Transition in TUI

These facts demonstrate that many transitions were made to the tactical control mode at the initial stage. This can be explained by their common idea that they would solve a problem with utilizing their knowledge before getting used to it. In addition, it was revealed that the participants in both interface groups employed the same strategy at the initial stage. At the later stage with GUI, the transition between the tactical control mode and the opportunistic control mode as well as that to the opportunistic control mode were frequently observed. Many transitions to the opportunistic control mode show that they tried to address a problem using their own knowledge without a proper method. In the meantime, their essential strategy had not changed from the initial stage and those in TUI group evenly made transitions among the three modes. This suggests that they not only embraced a strategy to use their own knowledge for addressing problems at a higher difficulty level but also acquired new knowledge by making a transition to the challenging explorative control mode and that they, by interface, employed a different strategy against the problems at a higher difficulty level at the stages where they got used to solving problems. At the practical stage, not a few participants made a transition to the opportunistic control mode. This can be explained by their policy to address the problems requiring an applied skill with the same tactic used at the later stage. As for TUI group, they evenly made a transition among the three mode even at the practical stage. This fact suggests that they tried to take various strategies including the one to use their own knowledge and the one to obtain new strategies for solving a problem requiring an applied skill as they did at the later stage. It was found that they employed different strategies by interface even at the practical stage.

In summary, both GUI group and TUI group addressed the problems using their own knowledge at the initial stage. In addition, while GUI group worked on the problems with utilizing their own knowledge at the later stage as they did at the initial stage, TUI group tried to take a strategy to gain new knowledge, which shows that TUI group used another strategy in addition to the one they employed at the initial stage. At the practical stage, GUI group addressed the problems with taking advantage of their own knowledge as they had done at the initial stage and the later stage. In short, GUI group used the same solving method from the initial stage through to the stage requiring an applied skill. On the other hand, TUI group embraced a strategy to obtain new knowledge even at the practical stage. This demonstrates that TUI group approached problems by employing a new strategy from the later stage and the practical stage on which they became used to solving the problems.

7 Conclusions

A comparative research was conducted for the purpose of verifying the learning process using TUI and GU. Analyses were made from three different perspectives. All of these three analyses revealed in common that the participants in GUI group shared the same approach to solving the problems from the initial stage to the practical stage and that those in TUI group started to employ different solving methods from the later stage when they became familiar with the problems.

It was revealed that the participants in GUI group solved problems while predicting results with the use of their knowledge. For this reason, the participants were unable to solve the problems requiring an applied skill because they approached the problems only with a solving method using their knowledge even if their difficulty level had been raised. Like GUI group, the participants in TUI group addressed the problems while expecting results with the use of their own knowledge. However, at the later stage, in addition to the approach to the problems taking advantage of their knowledge, the participants demonstrated a strategy to design a logic circuit without predicting results for acquiring new knowledge. This fact suggested that the participants in TUI group would develop a different strategy as they got accustomed to solving the problems. Accordingly, it is thought that many participants in TUI group were able to solve all the problems requiring an applied skill since they could get close to correct ones by tentatively designing a logic circuit instead of only using their own knowledge.

8 Application

In normal times, the participants in GUI group approach a problem by utilizing what they have learned as far as possible. In addition, it was revealed that they handled a situation with their acquired knowledge without trying any other method even if encountering an unexpected one that they hadn't learned about. Consequently, they are unlikely to cause errors but may not improve the situation. Meanwhile, in normal times, the participants in TUI group, like GUI group, deal with a situation by taking advantage of what they have learned to the maximum extent possible. However, although they might cause errors when encountering an unexpected situation they have not learned about as they will try various methods in order to remedy it, they are likely to find a method to remedy it eventually. For these reasons, it can be said that while GUI is suitable for routine problems like regular processing, TUI is recommended for the problems frequently requiring irregular processing.

Further, as another utilization method of TUI, it was found that TUI enabled participants to extensively learn how to approach application cases as well as the situations they had previously learned or been trained for. It can be concluded that TUI is suitable for pre-learning and pre-trainings. In actual operations, GUI is appropriate as those using it can handle a situation while taking advantage of the knowledge and experiences obtained through TUI.

References

1. Yokoyama, T.: Influence on the student's of the tablet PC in elementary and junior high schools, vol. 29, no. 2, Issue 2, pp. 45–50 (2014)
2. Akahori, K., Wada, Y.: Characteristics comparison of iPads, paper and PCs as learning devices, vol. 6, no. 1, pp. 15–34. Hakuoh University (2012)
3. Hideaki, K.: Thoughts on design principles for tangible learning environment for astronomy education. J. Sci. Educ. Jpn. **38**(2), 65–74 (2014)
4. Cuendet, S.: An integrated way of using a tangible user interface in a classroom. Int. J. Comput.-Support. Collab. Learn. **10**(2), 183–208 (2015)
5. Cuendet, S.: The benefits and limitations of distributing a tangible interface in a classroom (2013)
6. Hollnagel, E.: Human Reliability Analysis: Context and Control. Academic Press, London (1994)

User-eXperience Values of Automatic Driving to Consider from Dual Tasks

Naomichi Terazawa[1(✉)], Takeo Ainoya[2], and Keiko Kasamatsu[1]

[1] Tokyo Metropolitan University, Asahigaoka 6-6, Hino, Tokyo, Japan
naoterazawa@gmail.com
[2] serBOTinQ, Tokyo Metropolitan University, Asahigaoka 6-6, Hino, Tokyo, Japan

Abstract. Aiming at an automated driving society in the near future, not only automobile manufacturers, but also many companies, research institutes, and administrations are active engaged in various initiatives. In order to realize automatic driving, problems such as technical problems and social acceptance system still have many problems. Meanwhile, there is great expectation for its attractive concept proposal. In society today, a lot of tragic traffic accidents are reported. The public's interest is high in anticipation of a decrease in the number of traffic accidents caused by automatic driving. Automatic driving as a means of creating a safe automobile society is highly attractive. In this research, we focus on new experiential value by realizing automatic driving. In past driving of the car, it has been regarded as a dangerous act that the driver performs other work at the same time as driving. In this thesis, we consider the experiences by doing driving work and other work using the dual task method.

Keywords: Automatic driving · User-eXperience · Dual tasks

1 Introduction

1.1 Background

According to the development of technology, public interest in mobility automation has been increasing more and more. As expected from the near future, Toyota Motor announced the "e-Palette Concept" in 2018, the proposal of future automatic driving mobility will make us hopeful for the future that is not so far. These attractive proposals are located "level 4" within the level of automatic driving. If the next level 4 automatic driving society is the period of maturity, today's automobile society where level 2 technology-equipped general cars are spreading to the market is the early stage. It seems that there will be a "transition period" of Level 3 automatic driving in which a car having the function of automatic driving and a situation where automobiles which are not so will be disturbed on the road will be created between them. The concept proposal that depicts the prospect of the period of maturity is beyond existing stereotype "cars are made by automobile manufacturers", and it is made by many companies, research institutes, or administrations both domestically and abroad. On the other hand, however, the flexibility about proposals of automobiles in transition period

S. Yamamoto and H. Mori (Eds.): HCII 2019, LNCS 11569, pp. 362–370, 2019.
https://doi.org/10.1007/978-3-030-22660-2_26

is lower than in proposals of the period of maturity, and it seems that research on user experience in the interior space changed by the automatic operation seems not to be sufficient.

The average car age in Japan (the average of elapsed years since the car was first registered) is said to be 8.6 years at 2018. In today's automotive society, cars with automatic driving functions and cars that are not doing are intertwined on the road. In the process of realizing a fully automated driving society expected in the future, it is important that how to coexist an automatic driving vehicle and a non-automatic driving vehicle. As an example, it is conceivable to provide lanes dedicated to automatic driving vehicles on highways.

In the proposal for the concept of an automated driving vehicle at the period of maturity, the driver is released from the constraints of driving, and the appearance of taking various actions other than driving inside a car is expressed by a concept movie released by automobile manufacturers. On the other hand, it is a dangerous act that the driver does other doing than driving while driving today's car, it is not legally permitted. And there is not much debate on the possibility of what we can do about the behavior of the driver in the interior space during the transition period.

Looking at the drivers of automobiles running on public roads, we often see drivers who are driving while operating smartphones. Such an act called so-called "distract driving" is an act prohibited by the Road Traffic Act because there is a danger of leading to a traffic accident, and in case of a violation penalties are imposed. Despite these legal backgrounds, there are a lot of people who drive.

Automatic driving shifts the driving entity from the human being to the system, and the attention resources of human beings in driving work are reduced, so driver on automatic driving-car is bored, this time the risk of dozing during driving increases. In such a situation, if you can do other work at the driver's seat, it will lead to more efficient living while preventing dozing. From the above, the possibility of a new experience value is felt for driving with dual tasks under automatic driving.

1.2 Purpose

In past theory of driving a car, the so-called "distract driving" which carries out a dual task during driving is considered dangerous and should not be done. On the other hand, however, when automatic driving is put to practical use in the future and widely penetrated into society, new rules on dual tasks during driving which are not confined by the existing legal framework may be developed. In this research, we examine the influence of dual tasks on human perception by using dual tasks with driving task as the main task against Level 3, which is considered to be the transition period in automatic driving technology, and the automatic level 3 environment Consider the possibilities in driving (Fig. 1).

Fig. 1. Conceptual diagram of this research

2 Hypothesis

In the multiple resource theory Wickens advocates, it is stated that not only a plurality of information processes performed at the same time necessarily share a single resource pool, and in a dual task situation, tasks in which processing resources compete and there are combinations that do not compete at all. [1] In this research, when processing

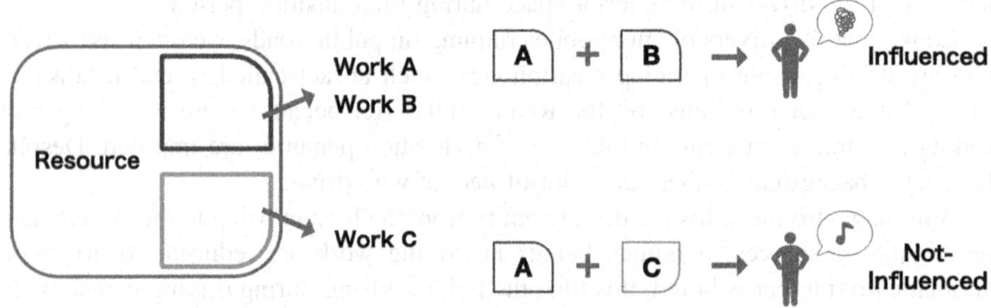

Fig. 2. Conceptual diagram of the multiple resource theory

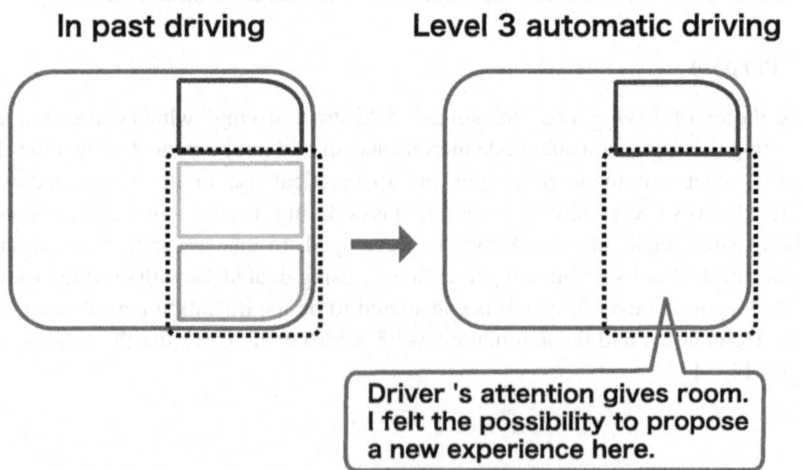

Fig. 3. Hypothesis about automatic driving of level 3 based on multiple resource theory

sub-tasks that are performed at the same time as the main task of driving, we conduct experiments under the hypothesis that there is an influence on driving work due to differences in processing resources (Figs. 2 and 3).

3 Experiment

3.1 Experimental Environment

For the experiment, racing game software "Gran Turismo 6" was used as a simulator, and operating environment was established by corrugated board assuming steering controller, seat and center console. Regarding the dimensions (Fig. 4), we referred to the interior packaging of a middle sedan type Japanese car (Fig. 5).

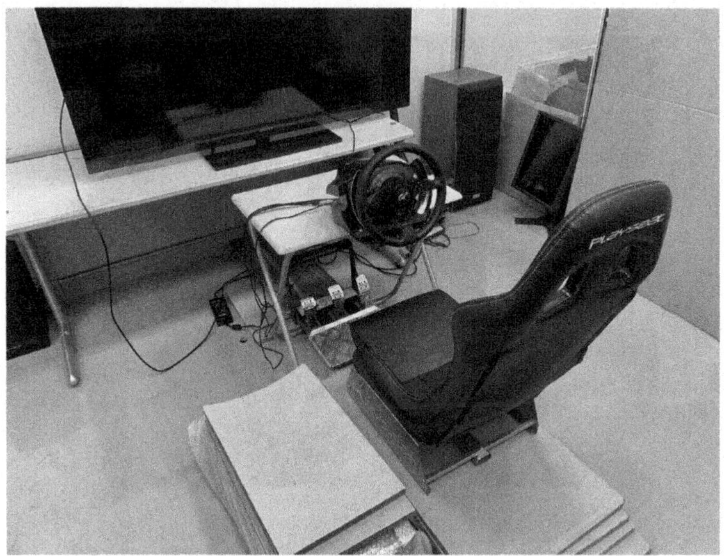

Fig. 4. Driving simulation environment

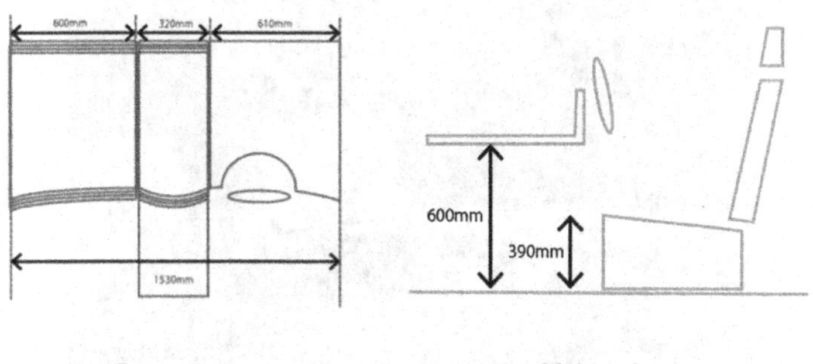

Fig. 5. Dimensions of center console

3.2 Participants

The participants were 4 students in their twenties, 2 men and 2 women. In addition, one of the participants in the experiment possessed the same racing game software as the driving simulator described later, and the skill level for the simulator was high.

3.3 Experimental Method

Participants wear a wearable eye tracker "Tobii Pro Glass 2". First of all, They go around a course simulating an urban area on the simulator as usual. After that, as you go around the course as well, ask the sub tasks (Experiment 1, Experiment 2) designated at the same time as driving work. In order to operate the driving simulator, Experimenter asked to run on the course while maintaining the speed at 50 [km/h] from 40 [km/h] to 60 [km/h] on the speed display (Fig. 6) Measure the gaze point during

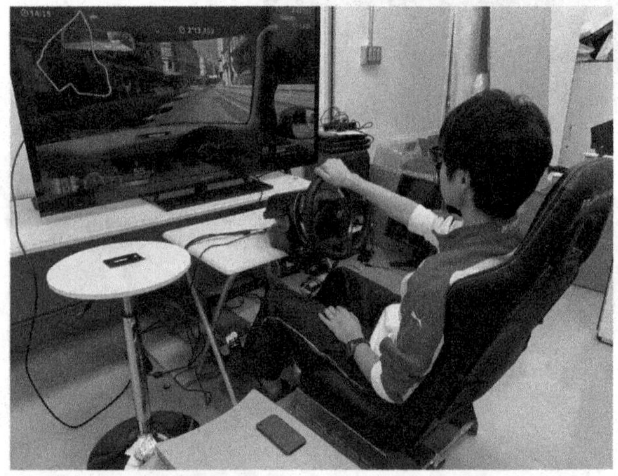

Fig. 6. Experimental method

that and observe the behavior of the driver. Data obtained through experiments were analyzed with analysis software "Tobii Pro Lab", and a heat map was prepared based on the gaze point measurement results obtained.

3.4 Experiment 1: Influence on Operation Task When Smartphone Operation Is a Sub Task

Participants wearing an eye tracker goes around a course simulating an urban area on the simulator as usual. In the same way after getting around the course in the same way, ask the smartphone of the experiment participant to send a call once without notifying it beforehand, and ask the conversation to respond. After the end of the conversation, another message of the question format was transmitted in the message application "LINE", and a response was requested to it. Measure the gaze point during that and observe the behavior of the driver.

3.5 Experiment 2: Influence on Operation Task When Drinking and Eating Are Sub Tasks

Participants wearing eye tracker go around the course. Among them, as a drinking action, they open a PET bottle drink placed on the center console from an unopened state and have it drink properly.

After that, we asked the experiment participants to go around the course again and let opened the bag confectionery placed on the center console as an act of eating and eat as needed.

4 Results

4.1 Results of Experiment 1

The measurement result of the fixation point during normal operation is shown. (Figure 7) Next, the measurement results of gazing points by the dual task of driving operation and smartphone operation are shown. (Figure 8) The results showed that the gazing point was on the traveling road. But tended to increase to the speed indication at the lower left of the screen compared with the case of only the driving work. Also, from the behavior, there was a tendency that the speed adjustment in the operation accompanying the smartphone operation became more difficult than in the case of the driving operation alone.

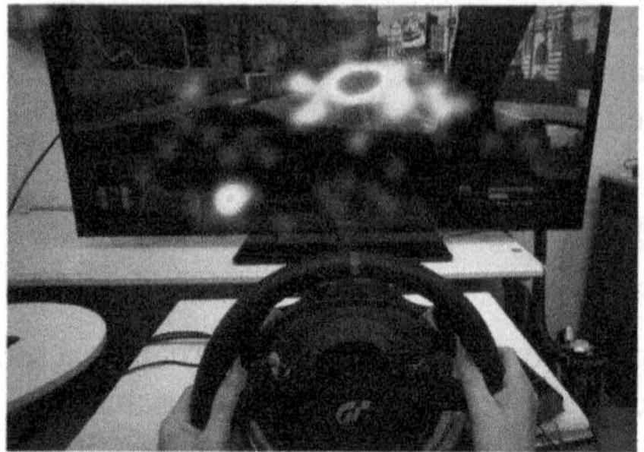

Fig. 7. Driving

Fig. 8. Driving with smartphone operation

4.2 Results of Experiment 2

The measurement results of the gaze point by the dual task of driving operation and act of drinking PET bottle drink (Fig. 9) and eating bag confectionery (Fig. 10) are shown. From the results, no change in gaze point like the previous experiment was seen, and behavior did not have a big influence on driving work by eating and drinking even from the behavior.

Some experiment participants tended to increase the speed display in the lower left of the screen of the simulator and the gaze point of the speedometer in the lower center. Some of the participants in the experiment also gazed at the map display on the upper left of the screen of the simulator.

Fig. 9. Driving with drinking

Fig. 10. Driving with eating

5 Discussion

In common with driving tasks not involving dual tasks and driving tasks involving smartphone operations, gaze points are gathered in the speed indication, and they were making a travel that adjusts the speed a little by conscious of the speed maintenance instruction Conceivable.

Also, due to reception of incoming calls and messages, the influence on the speed adjustment of the car was seen. Compared to when only driving work was done, in addition to not being able to confirm the speed display on the screen constantly in the field of view as a line of sight directed to the smartphone, in addition to the consciousness of operation of the accelerator/brake by the operation of the smartphone It is thought that it is caused by the fact that it became unclear. Drivers who did not see a collision against the course wall due to wobbling associated with the use of smartphones had operated the smartphone at the middle of the steering wheel and the body. One of the factors is that the line-of-sight trace on the simulator screen and the smartphone screen was short.

In Experiment 1, when performing a dual task of simultaneously executing subtasks of operation of a smartphone against a main task of operation task including operation of steering wheel and adjustment of accelerator/brake, problems with operation of the accelerator and the brake However, no obstacles were found in steering wheel operation and smartphone operation. In the level 3 automatic driving environment, the problem in this experiment may be solved by entering system control for steering wheel operation and accelerator/brake adjustment. From this, it can be said that driving is possible while operating the smartphone in the level 3 automatic driving environment if the driver can always return to operation (Figure 11).

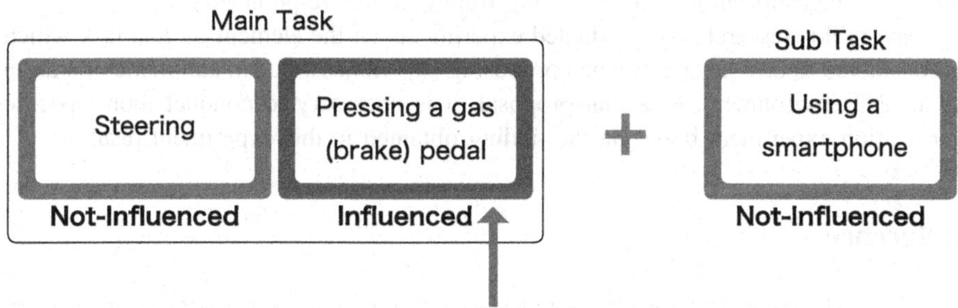

Fig. 11. Result of dual task in Experiment 1

As a result of the dual tasks of driving tasks on the driver, the possibility that the difference in resource pool to attention may be related is obtained. The influence appeared on the adjustment of the speed in the main task of driving task was a sub-task of "operation of smartphone" conducted as a dual task. This is due to the fact that these two tasks are working with the same caution resource, and because it was a resource pool different from the "drink" and "eat" actions of sub tasks. It seems that the influence did not appear in the dual task (see Fig. 12).

Fig. 12. Result of dual task in Experiment 1 and 2

6 Conclusion

In this research, when proposing new experiential value in level 3 automatic operation, we investigated and studied what kind of actions and actions affect the driving from the gazing points and behaviors of the driver at the time of driving. Then, we aimed to consider the new experience value obtained under automatic driving situation.

In past driving, humans assumed a variety of events for safe driving and paid a lot of attention. However, along with the practical use of Level 3 automatic operation in the near future, new experience value can be found there by the system control that the clearance in attention is born more than ever. By thinking over these verifications on sub-tasks against the main task of driving, we thought that we could connect to driver's interface suggestion in automatic driving from a cognitive point of view.

And in this research, we conducted experiments on the element of dual task which is considered to be a key point when proposing experience value in automatic operation of level 3 environment. In actual proposal, it is necessary to conduct more specific verification experiment based on the finding obtained in this experiment result.

Reference

1. Shigeru, H.: Theory and Measurement of Mental Workload, p. 16. Japan Publishing Service, Japan (2001)

Research of Human-Machine Interface Evaluation Based on Cogtool

Lu Wang[1], Qing Xue[1(✉)], Jia Hao[1], and Hongyan Yu[2]

[1] Beijing Institute of Technology, Beijing 100081, China
xueqing@bit.edu.cn

[2] Beijing Electro-Mechanical Engineering Institute, Beijing 100074, China

Abstract. Along with the development of interactive interface design technology, interface display becomes increasingly dynamic, multi-functional and logically-complex that increases the difficulty of interactive interface evaluation. The traditional evaluation methods of interactive interface cannot meet the requirements of interface evaluation due to its poor objectivity and economy. However, it is possible to predict the cognitive process of users by constructing human cognitive model as the development of cognitive psychology, and the interactive interface evaluation method based on the cognitive process of users is of feasibility and utmost urgency. This paper proposed a Cogtool-based interactive interface evaluation method that predicts the interactive process in terms of human's cognitive characteristics, which significantly improves the objectivity of interface evaluation and has the advantages of economy and convenience.

The Cogtool-based interactive interface evaluation method was studied in this research. (1) Interactive tasks were designed according to the main functions of the interface and Cogtool was adopted to predict the performance in completing the interactive tasks. Various data were collected such as the time required, action sequence, and the times of page turn. (2) A vague set evaluation system was established, and the vague value of each interface design scheme was calculated. The TOPSIS method was adopted to rank the multiple interfaces. (3) Taking three automotive audio and video navigator interfaces as example, the feasibility of the Cogtool-based interactive interface evaluation method was verified, and suggestions on the optimization of layout and structural logic were proposed in the end.

Keywords: Human-machine interface evaluation · CogTool · Human performance predictions

1 Introduction

User-centric design and product design in combination with user cognitive theory will become a new trend. Nowadays, user-centric design concept, user experience, psychological model of user, emotional design, human-computer interaction, user research, usability test, visual design and other design terms are gradually appearing in public view. Interface design does not only refer to how to build vision and framework of user interface in a narrow way, but also involves the psychological cognitive model, behavioral expression mode, and emotionalization of user operation [1].

S. Yamamoto and H. Mori (Eds.): HCII 2019, LNCS 11569, pp. 371–391, 2019.
https://doi.org/10.1007/978-3-030-22660-2_27

The "user-centric" design concept has been applied to the fields of interface design that are directly related to human life, such as flight instrument interface [2], mobile phone interface [3], and electronic signpost interface [4], etc. A new research trend has been emerged that integrates cognitive psychology, computer science and other disciplines to study user cognitive behavior and thereby guide product design [5].

The traditional human-computer interface evaluation methods are over subjective, and it is necessary to improve the objectivity of the evaluation method. Human-computer interface is the mediation for transmitting information in human-computer interaction, and a desirable interface design can enhance the rationality and efficiency of human-computer interaction. The traditional interactive interface evaluation methods mainly employ the means of questionnaire, user interview, behavioral record, and expert assessment [5]. Whereas, most of these methods are too subjective, which are subject to user or expert's memory, thought, experience, growth environment, preference, cognitive difference and so forth, and at the same time lack of scientific and objective quantitative evaluation. Additionally, designers typically need to obtain evaluation data through certain user test experiments when designing the traditional methods of user interface interaction, e.g. eye tracker [6]. Since these experiments and detecting instruments interfere with the interactive process between user and interface, it is very difficult to accurately collect interactive data in the natural state.

In consideration of the inadequacies of the traditional evaluation methods, an increasing number of researchers turn their sights on the interface evaluation methods based on cognitive theories. At the current, the emerging evaluation methods based on cognitive theories are divided in two major categories.

The first category is to construct mathematical models to directly evaluate interface design solutions by combining the research achievement of cognitive psychology. For an instance, Wang Changqing set pen-based User Interface as the research object. He established the user interface model ERM that complies with human characteristics on the basis of the distributed cognition theory, and applied the model to the design and evaluation of interface system [7]. Furthermore, Erik Frøkjær designed a set of MOT evaluation model focusing on mankind's habit, thought, consciousness and association, and verified the superiority of the method compared to the traditional usability testing techniques via three groups of experiments [8]. Wang Haibo explored the generation mechanism of cognitive load during the using process of interface. He combined with the cognitive resource constraint theory to analyze the generation quantity of external cognitive load, internal cognitive load, and associated cognitive load in interface use, thereby to evaluate interface design solutions [9].

The second category is to capture and evaluate the cognitive characteristics during the process of user interaction in terms of the existing models that describe human cognitive behaviors and thinking activities, and thus to evaluate interactive interface according to the capturing and predicting results. On the one hand, such category of method requires no cumbersome experiment of behavioral measure, and simultaneously reduces the interference of measuring process on user's operational process. On the other hand, the measurement or prediction based on the latest research of human body science such as cognitive physiology and neurobiology has the advantages of high accuracy and strong applicability. The common theories and methods include: the GOMS cognitive theory [10, 11], the EPIC theory [12], the Fitts law [13, 14], the Hick law [15] and the ACT theory [16–21]. In particular, the ACT theory provides a relatively well-developed cognitive framework and model, which is one of the most valuable theories for reference in the research field of human-computer interaction [22]. However, there are still some deficiencies in the current research. The existing cognitive-based interface evaluation method mainly focuses on simple interfaces. It studies the interaction process of a single task, does not further study the complex interfaces with rich functions.

Thereupon, this paper adopted the CogTool analysis tool to predict the interactions of multiple tasks from three aspects: "time", "motion characteristic" and "times of page turn", and comprehensively evaluated these multi-functional interactive interfaces by combining the multi-target vague set evaluation method, in order to identify the optimal design interface and offer suggestions on the optimization of sub-optimal solutions.

The specific steps are as follows: 1. the cognitive model embedded in CogTool (an interactive prototype design software) was used to predict and analyze user's interactive process in accordance with the cognitive characteristics of users; 2. an interactive interface evaluation system was constructed relying on the vague set theory, the evaluation results were produced by using the predicted "time" index of interactive interface and the TOPSIS method, and suggestions on interface optimization were finally proposed in terms of the analysis results of "motion characteristic" and "times of page turn". It is evident that this method has the advantages of convenience and economy, improves the objectivity of interface evaluation solutions, and significantly contributes to the quantitative evaluation and design decision of multi-functional interactive interface.

2 Evaluation Method

2.1 User Interface Prototyping Tool (Cogtool)

CogTool is designed by researchers at Carnegie Mellon University, USA. It is a user interface (UI) prototyping tool that can produce quantitative predictions of how users will behave when the prototype is ultimately implemented [23, 24]. It offers a quick and inexpensive way to explore a wide variety of user interface solutions and replaces user experience testing to a large extent [23]. Moreover, CogTool can be adopted to simulate the cognitive, perceptual and motor behaviors of human interaction with interface, reliably predict the interaction process as skilled users fulfill tasks [24–27], and predict the interaction process of novice users' exploratory behavior [28–30]. Therefore, the practical application of cognitive models becomes much easier by using CogTool [25].

CogTool's quantitative prediction is based upon a wide range of transcendental studies in the field of cognitive psychology. More precisely, it is developed according to the information foraging theory SNIF-ACT. The SNIF-ACT theory compares the behavior of user's search for information through using interface to animal's foraging behavior [31]. Animals continuously receive external information stimuli and make decisions by assessing the matching degree between external information and internal targets when foraging. In the meantime, they also measure the cost of abandoning the known information to search for new information, so as to acquire the optimal benefit. This is similar to the behavioral process of users searching for information concerning their intentions by using interactive interface. In fact, the judgment and selection of users largely depend on the semantic similarity between the target and options, which is referred to as information scent (info-scent). Before conducting information search activities, users will firstly define their task intentions and have a general cognitive understanding of the target. The SNIF-ACT model has taken the cognitive thinking time before behaviors and the shortening of thinking time when becoming skilled into consideration [32]. It is reflected in the CogTool software as following: the software generates a "thinking" operation before each act or behavior that ends as the act or behavior occurs, and the operating time of the "thinking" is calculated by the thinking operator model; the "thinking" operation will be deleted before the act or behavior if the same button is pressed for several times. Thus, the CogTool analysis tool based on the cognitive model SNIF-ACT can be used to well describe the cognitive process of users performing a certain information search task, which provides software support for the study of interface evaluation under multi-tasks.

2.2 Vague Set Theory

Since Vague set was put forward in 1993, many scholars have been interested in it, and great progress has been made in its theory and application in multi-attribute decision making. Chen, Hong and Choi. applied Vague sets to fuzzy decision making [33, 34], and proposed the concept of similarity measures between Vague sets. Vague sets have also been well applied in the multi-objective fuzzy decision making [35–37], and solving multi-attribute decision making problems [38].

Let A be the universe of discourse, and that is $A \subseteq R$. x is any element in domain A, and that is $x \in A$. For another Vague sets B, there must be either $x \in B$ or $x \notin B$. The real membership function t_B and a false membership function f_B are used to express the relation between the real number x in A set and the Vague set B [34].

The elements in the true membership function are between 0 and 1, $t_B : A \rightarrow [0, 1]$; t_B denotes the degree of support for $x \in A$.

The elements in the false membership function are between 0 and 1, $f_B : A \rightarrow [0, 1]$; f_B denotes the degree of opposition to $x \in A$.

Besides, $t_B(x) + f_B(x) \leq 1$. In particular, when $t_B(x) + f_B(x) = 1$, the Vague set B degenerates into a general fuzzy set.

Thus, the information about whether x in A set belongs to B set can be located in $[t_B(x), 1 - f_B(x)]$. This interval is regarded as the membership degree of x with Vague set B, that is the Vague value of x with Vague set B, which can be written as $V_{B(x)} = [t_B(x), 1 - f_B(x)]$. Among them, $\lambda_B(x) = 1 - t_B(x) - f_{B(x)}$ is the unknown degree of x with Vague set B. The larger the value of $\lambda_B(x)$, the more ambiguous it is whether x belongs to Vague set B; and the smaller the value of $\lambda_B(x)$, the more precise it is to know that x belongs to/does not belong to Vague set B.

When the universe of discourse A is continuous, a vague set B can be written as

$$B = \sum_{i=1}^{n} [t_B(x_i), 1 - f_B(x_i)]/x_i \tag{1}$$

$$x_i \in \mathrm{A}$$

When the universe of discourse A is discrete, a vague set B can be written as

$$B = \int [t_B(x), 1 - f_B(x)]/x \tag{2}$$

$$x_i \in \mathrm{A}$$

2.3 Evaluation Method Process

The process of the interaction interface evaluation method based on CogTool is shown in Fig. 1. The figure shows the process of data transmission. There are two key technologies involved in the flow of the CogTool-based interactive interface evaluation method: the ACT-R cognitive model embedded in CogTool was employed to predict user's interactive behavior, and the vague set theory was adopted for multi-objective evaluation.

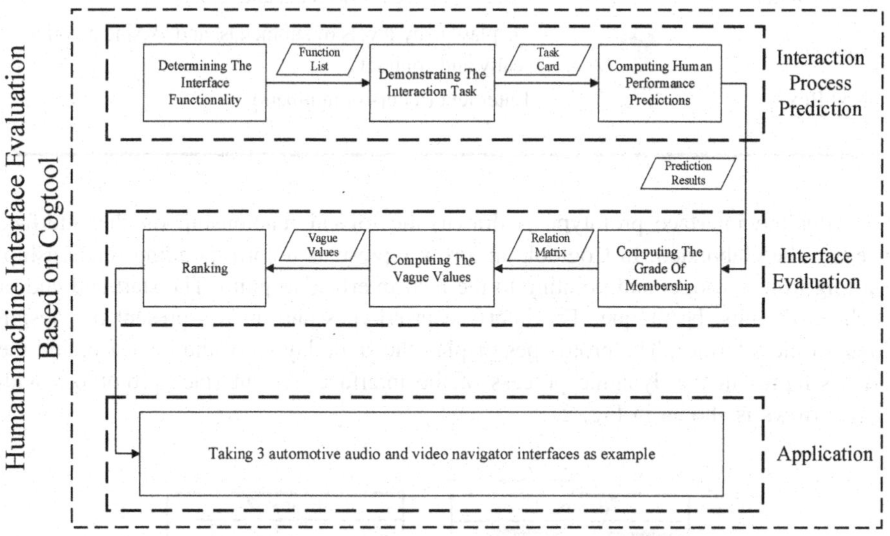

Fig. 1. Evaluation method process

3 Interaction Process Prediction

3.1 Creating the Interface Prototypes

The interactive interface prototype is a simulation interface which can represent the important components such as elements, layouts, colors and interactions on the interface through the modeling tool [39]. It is the research object of interface analysis, design and evaluation. To start using CogTool, a storyboard that illustrates the design and the way users interact with it need to be created. If the design already exists on the web, it can be imported into Cogtool from HTML. But if the interface is an entity interface, it needs to be imported in the form of pictures, and manually mark the various interaction widgets on the interface. A Widget is an element on a Frame with which a user may interact, such a button, checkboxes, a hierarchical menu, etc.. CogTool provides an extensive set of widgets to represent interactive elements, and several widgets are shown as examples in the Table 1 below.

Table 1. Types of widgets

Name	Shape	Usage
Button		Toggle from unpressed to pressed
Checkbox		Toggle from unchecked to checked
Radio Button		Toggle between unselected and selected
Menu		Display many levels of submenus, and expand automatically and contract
Text Box		Enter text (letters or numbers)
…	…	…

After the interface prototype is drawn, the logical relationship on the interface needs to be elaborated. In Cogtool, an arrow represents a corresponding relationship, starting from a widget and pointing to the next interface to jump. The start and end of each arrow must be unique. The interface prototypes and arrows present the design logic of the interface. The prototypes display the static layout of the interface, and the arrows represent the dynamic process of the interface. An interface prototypes with logic arrows is shown in Fig. 2.

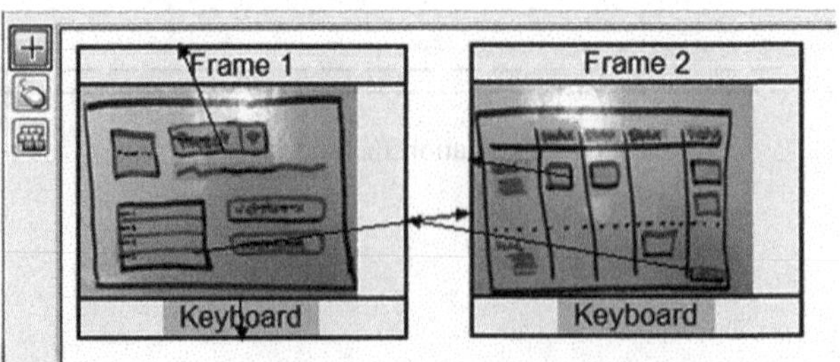

Fig. 2. An interface prototypes created in CogTool

3.2 Determining the Interface Functionality

Before the interface evaluation, the main functions of the interface should be sorted out. For the interface with user's manual, the main functions of the interactive interface can be summarized by referring to the user's manual. For the interface without relevant design data, the main functions of the interface can be inversely speculated by its layout. Through the analysis of the main components of the interface, we can divides them into multiple main functions and sub-functions in the form of a tree diagram or a list [40]. The common functions in the interactive interface include login/registration function, search function, download function, and information display function. In summary, the next step in interface evaluation is based on a clear understanding of the main functions of interfaces.

3.3 Demonstrating the Interaction Tasks

Tasks are a series of instructions that drive users to perform a series of operations in the prototype interface. Tasks must have clear execution intentions. For example, collecting favorite songs on music websites, setting ringtones on mobile phone interfaces, searching stations on public subway indicator board, etc. can be called tasks. Cogtool can keep a record of them for computational prediction. Description of interactive tasks can be filled in the following task cards (Table 2).

Table 2. Interactive task card

	Task name
The initial interface	The first interface in the task
The terminating interface	The last interface in the task
Description	A detailed description of the task, such as procedures
Requirement	A standard to weigh the completion situation of the task
Task objectives	The reason for setting up this task (which functionality is evaluated in this task)

Then, a user's workflow for accomplishing a task need to be demonstrated. During this process, CogTool automatically builds a keystroke-level model (KLM) by incorporating operators such as hand movements and mental preparation. Building a KLM by hand can be a tedious and error-prone activity; however, CogTool makes the technique accessible to anyone who can imagine a design.

3.4 Computing Human Performance Predictions

CogTool uses a cognitive architecture called ACT-R to predict the time it would take a skilled user to complete a task in seconds [29, 30]. It also produces a visualization of this performance model, as shown in Fig. 3, which shows the following components:

- Visual encoding (light purple)
- Eye movement (dark purple)

- Cognition (gray)
- Hand movement (red)

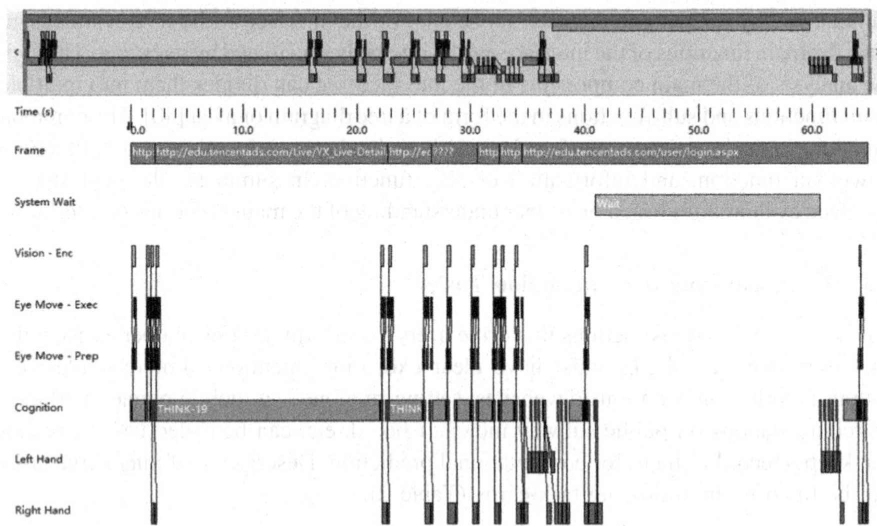

Fig. 3. A visualization for an interactive process (Color figure online)

First, Cogtool can calculate the total task time, which can gather the statistics of time to finish several tasks in an interface. Second, Cogtool can present users' actions that users take in completing each task, such as eyes movement and hands movement, and make an action analysis by the action sequence. For example, in the visualization below, you can see that the design on the bottom forces the user to do significantly more eye movement than the design on the top. This eye movement adds enough time to a user's workflow to decrease efficiency by several seconds in comparison to the other design (Fig. 4).

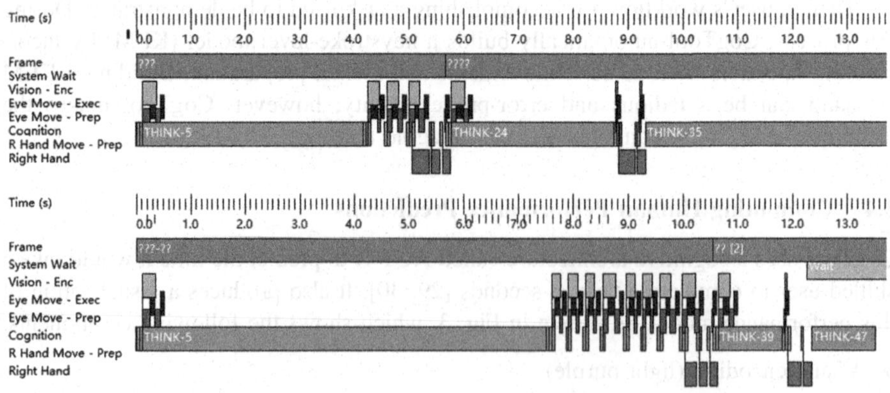

Fig. 4. Comparison of two action sequences of interface

Third, Cogtool can predicate required jumps to complete those tasks, thus optimizing design plans with repeating jumps.

4 Interface Evaluation

4.1 Evaluation Criteria

This essay mainly focuses on time indicators by using total task time of different designs as statistics of quantitative analysis and taking results of action analysis and interface jumps as basis of qualitative optimization. First, the interface evaluation based on multitask completion is actually a multi-objective decision-making issue. Besides, the completion of any interactive tasks that have been set is fuzzy for evaluating the weight of a design plan. Namely, the degree of membership of the pros and cons completed by each task to that of the designed plan is uncertain. Consequently, vague set evaluation is adopted.

4.2 Multitask Relationship Matrix

First, establish an objective decision matrix. Suppose there are m kinds of interface design schemes, recorded as Set I = $\{I_1, I_2, \ldots, I_m\}$; and n evaluation results of interactive tasks based on Cogtool, recorded as Set R = $\{R_1, R_2, \ldots, R_n\}$. With m interface designs and n tasks count form an original evaluation matrix A:

$$A = \begin{bmatrix} a_{11} & a_{12} & \cdots & a_{1n} \\ a_{21} & a_{22} & \cdots & a_{2n} \\ \vdots & \vdots & & \vdots \\ a_{m1} & a_{m2} & \cdots & a_{mn} \end{bmatrix} \tag{3}$$

Where a_{ij} is the evaluation value of the ith interface design in jth task. And i = $1, 2, \ldots$, m, j = $1, 2, \ldots$, n. Then normalization this matrix to get relationship matrix B.

$$B = \begin{bmatrix} \vartheta_{11} & \vartheta_{12} & \cdots & \vartheta_{1n} \\ \vartheta_{21} & \vartheta_{22} & \cdots & \vartheta_{2n} \\ \vdots & \vdots & \vdots & \vdots \\ \vartheta_{m1} & \vartheta_{m2} & \cdots & \vartheta_{mn} \end{bmatrix} \tag{4}$$

Where ϑ_{ij} is the relative membership of the evaluation value of the ith interface design in jth task. There are many ways to calculate the relative membership [0].

For the benefit-oriented objectives (the more, the better), its relative membership is expressed as Eq. (5).

$$\vartheta_{ij} = \frac{a_{ij}}{a_{jmax}} \tag{5}$$

For the cost-oriented objectives (the less, the better), its relative membership is represented as Eq. (6).

$$\vartheta_{ij} = \begin{cases} 1 - \left(\frac{a_{ij}}{a_{jmax}}\right), a_{jmin} = 0 \\ \frac{a_{jmin}}{a_{ij}}, a_{jmin} \neq 0 \end{cases} \tag{6}$$

For the fixed objectives ((approaching to specific value), its relative membership is written as Eq. (7).

$$\vartheta_{ij} = \frac{a_0}{\left(a_0 + \left|a_{ij} - a_0\right|\right)} \tag{7}$$

4.3 The Vague Values of Interfaces

Firstly, affirm the lower limit of the better scheme as σ^L and the upper limit of the worse scheme as σ^U, then

- If $\vartheta_{ij} \geq \sigma^U$, the completion situation of the jth task in the ith interface design is good, or in other words, the completion situation of the jth task is in support of the ith interface.
- If $\vartheta_{ij} \leq \sigma^L$, the completion situation of the jth task in the ith interface design is poor, or in other words, the completion situation of the jth task is against the ith interface.
- If $\sigma^L < \vartheta_{ij} < \sigma^U$, the completion situation of the jth task in the ith interface design is neutral, or in other words, the completion situation of the jth task does not support or oppose the ith interface.

Then, the support set S, the opposition set O and the neutral set N of the interface are determined according to the σ^L and σ^U.

- Let $S = \left\{\vartheta_j \in \theta \middle| \vartheta_{ij} \geq \sigma^U\right\}$ is the support set of the ith interface, and it indicates that the jth evaluation result supports the ith interface.
- Let $O = \left\{\vartheta_j \in \theta \middle| \vartheta_{ij} \leq \sigma^L\right\}$ is the opposition set of the ith interface, and it indicates that the jth evaluation result oppose the ith interface.
- Let $S = \left\{\vartheta_j \in \theta \middle| \sigma^L < \vartheta_{ij} < \sigma^U\right\}$ is the neutral set of the ith interface, and it indicates that the jth evaluation result neither supports nor oppose the ith interface.

Next, m interfaces are evaluated. Let β be the weight of evaluation index, where $\beta = \{\beta_1, \beta_2, \ldots, \beta_n\}$, and n is the completion situation of n tasks. a vague value (interval) v_i can be used to express the pros and cons of any interface.

$$v_i = [t_i, 1 - f_i] \tag{8}$$

Where,

$$t_i = \frac{\sum_{i \in \eta_1} \beta_j \vartheta_{ij}}{\sum_{j=1}^{n} \beta_j \vartheta_{ij}} \tag{9}$$

$$\eta_1 = \{j | a_j \in S_i\}$$

$$f_i = \frac{\sum_{i \in \eta_2} \beta_j \vartheta_{ij}}{\sum_{j=1}^{n} \beta_j \vartheta_{ij}} \tag{10}$$

$$\eta_2 = \{j | a_j \in O_i\}$$

The evaluation vague value of the ith interface v_i can be obtained:

$$v_i = \left[\frac{\sum_{i \in \eta_1} \beta_j \vartheta_{ij}}{\sum_{j=1}^{n} \beta_j \vartheta_{ij}}, 1 - \frac{\sum_{i \in \eta_2} \beta_j \vartheta_{ij}}{\sum_{j=1}^{n} \beta_j \vartheta_{ij}} \right] \tag{11}$$

$$\mathrm{i} = 1, 2, \ldots, \mathrm{m}; \mathrm{j} = 1, 2, \ldots, \mathrm{n} \tag{12}$$

4.4 Ranking Multi-interfaces Based on Topsis

The vague value of each interface contains uncertain information about support, opposition and neutrality to the interface scheme, which indicates that the design of the scheme is good or bad. Next, the Topsis method is used to rank the design schemes.

The proposal of Topsis is to define a positive ideal value X^+ and a negative ideal value X^- [41, 42]. The positive ideal value X^+ is the upper limit of the ideal scheme, and the negative ideal value X^- is the lower limit of the ideal scheme [41, 42]. Both X^+ and X^- are vague values, and they can be given as:

$$X^+ = [maxt_i, 1 - minf_i] \tag{13}$$

$$X^- = [mint_i, 1 - maxf_i] \tag{14}$$

Next, benchmark every interface design plan to the ideal scheme, calculating the approaching degree d_i^+ and d_i^- from interface design scheme to ideal scheme.d_i^+ is the distance from the vague value of the ith interface design scheme to X^+, and d_i^- is the distance from the vague value of the ith interface design scheme to X^-, as shown in Eqs. (15) and (16).

$$d_i^+ = d(x_i, X^+) = \sqrt{(t_{ij} - t^+)^2 + (f_{ij} - f^+)^2} \tag{15}$$

$$d_i^- = d(x_i, X^-) = \sqrt{(t_{ij} - t^-)^2 + (f_{ij} - f^-)^2} \tag{16}$$

Let λ be the approximation index from interface design to ideal scheme. The larger the λ is, the better the interface scheme is. The λ is calculates based on the Eq. (17).

$$\lambda_i = \frac{d_i^-}{d_i^+ + d_i^-} \tag{17}$$

According to the value of λ, the multiple interface design schemes can be ranked from the best to the worst. In particular, when the values of σ^L and σ^U are different, the evaluation ranking of multiple will be affected [41]. when the designer holds a strict criterion, the values of σ^L and σ^U are higher, while σ^L and σ^U are smaller. when the designer holds a loose criterion, the values of σ^L and σ^U are the opposite.

5 Application

5.1 Introduction

This essay adopts automotive audio and video navigator as the evaluation object for the following reasons. On the one hand, automotive audio and video navigator are widely used in high-end cars today, making it a universal object for evaluation; on the other hand, they are so abundant in styles and similar in functions that users often find it difficult to choose among them. Therefore, evaluation based on the 7600 series, Changxin 3 and CE4K01212A, products of FlyAudio, Road Rover and ADAYO respectively, which are the three largest manufacturers of automotive audio and video navigator in China, will be made from the perspective of interface design.

These three automotive audio and video navigator are greatly similar and replaceable in function, but their interface design styles are significantly different. The main interfaces of the three products are as follows (Fig. 5):

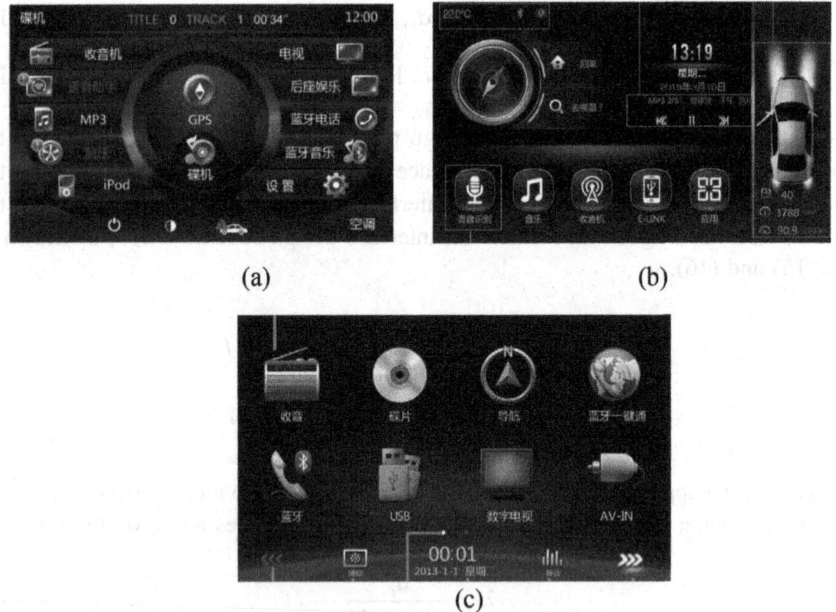

Fig. 5. The main interfaces of 3 automotive audio and video navigators

The scheme A, B and C is FlyAudio 7600 series, Road Rover Changxin 3 and ADAYO CE4K01212A separately.

5.2 Procedure

First, the three automotive audio and video navigators interface are created in CogTool, and the logical relations among each widget and interface are marked. Five corresponding interactive tasks are designed according to the main functions of the automotive audio and video navigator, namely, navigating, music playing, Bluetooth dialing, radio listening and settings modifying. Then CogTool automatically simulates the user's interaction of the five tasks on each of the three interfaces, and obtains the data of the action sequence, page jumps, task time, etc. (Table 3).

Table 3. Task card.

Tasks	Task I: Navigating to the destination	Task II: Music playing	Task III: Bluetooth dialing	Task IV: Listening to the Radio	Task V: Time setting
The initial interface	The main interface	The main interface	The main interface	The main interface	The main interface
The terminating interface	Navigation starting interface	Music playing interface	Dialing interface	Radio broadcasting interface	The main interface
Description	1. Navigate from Nanjing University of Aeronautics and Astronautics to Beijing Institute of Technology 2. 'Recommended route' by default	Choose and play a specific song	1. Connect the phone and make a match 2. Dial the phone number 15313658969	Listen to Jiangsu Communication Broadcasting FM101.1	1. Replace 'April 03, 2018' with 'May 30, 2018' 2. Exit the modification page and return to the main interface to check the time
Requirement	Start navigating correctly	Play the music at the right volume and mode	Dial the correct number	Dial the correct number	Set the time successfully
Task objectives	Test the interactive effect of a series of operations such as selecting a destination and a route	Test the interactive effect the user playing the music and making custom modification	Test the interactive process of the user dialing the phone	Test the convenience of the interactive process of the user searching for channels and listening to the broadcast	Test the time-setting function

CogTool automatically simulates the user's interaction of the five tasks on each of the three interfaces, and obtains the data of the action sequence, page jumps, task time, etc.

Table 4. Data of time completed for each task of each plan (unit/seconds).

Tasks	Navigating	Music playing	Bluetooth dialing	Listening to the Radio	Time setting
FlyAudio 7600 series	236.912	140.327	55.072	85.453	55.543
Road Rover Changxin 3	247.447	133.832	75.046	72.540	42.634
ADAYO CE4K01212A	239.235	142.511	54.341	117.212	39.036

The three design interfaces complete 5 interactive tasks, producing a total of 15 interactive data. Table 4 demonstrates the time for the three automotive audio and video navigator to complete the five tasks. The performance of each interactive interface shows different pros and cons when completing each task. No single one can complete every single task within an optimal span of time (least time). Thus, vague set evaluation system shall be established subsequently. In addition, the navigation in the five tasks generally consumes the most amount of time, while the time setting tasks, the least, which can reflect the complexity/difficulty of these tasks to a certain extent.

Table 5. Numbers of clicks completed for each task of each plan (unit/times).

Tasks	Navigating	Music playing	Bluetooth dialing	Listening to the Radio	Time setting
FlyAudio 7600 series	21	9	15	4	10
Road Rover Changxin 3	18	8	19	4	9
ADAYO CE4K01212A	21	9	17	9	9

Table 5 presents the numbers of clicks for the three automotive audio and video navigator to complete the five tasks. The performance of each interactive interface shows different pros and cons when completing each task. No single one can complete every single task with optimal (the least) operating actions.

Table 6 presents the numbers of clicks for the three automotive audio and video navigator to complete the five tasks. The performance of each interactive interface shows different pros and cons when completing each task. No single one can complete every single task with optimal page-jumping actions. Page jumps involve more interface logic, and a reasonable page jump will produce the greatest information effect.

Table 6. Numbers of page jumps completed for each task of each plan (unit/times).

Tasks	Navigating	Music playing	Bluetooth dialing	Listening to the Radio	Time setting
FlyAudio 7600 series	15	4	4	2	5
Road Rover Changxin 3	12	5	6	2	4
ADAYO CE4K01212A	15	5	4	4	4

5.3 Evaluation Result

Construct the evaluation matrix:

$$A = \begin{bmatrix} a_{11} & a_{12} & \cdots & a_{15} \\ a_{21} & a_{22} & \cdots & a_{25} \\ a_{31} & a_{32} & \cdots & a_{35} \end{bmatrix}$$

Substitute the evaluated value, namely:

$$A = \begin{bmatrix} 236.912 & 140.327 & 55.072 & 85.453 & 55.543 \\ 247.447 & 133.832 & 75.046 & 72.540 & 42.634 \\ 239.235 & 142.511 & 54.341 & 117.212 & 39.036 \end{bmatrix}$$

Transform the evaluation matrix into the relationship matrix, according to the relative membership calculation method:

$$B = \begin{bmatrix} 1.000 & 0.954 & 0.987 & 0.849 & 0.703 \\ 0.957 & 1.000 & 0.724 & 1.000 & 0.916 \\ 0.990 & 0.939 & 1.000 & 0.619 & 1.000 \end{bmatrix}$$

It is determined that the better lower bound that user can accept is $\sigma^L = 0.95$, the acceptable worse lower bound is $\sigma^U = 0.80$, and the supporting set, opposing set, and neutral set of each interface are as follows:

$$\begin{array}{lll} S_1 = \{\vartheta_1, \vartheta_2, \vartheta_3\} & O_1 = \{\vartheta_5\} & N_1 = \{\vartheta_4\} \\ S_2 = \{\vartheta_1, \vartheta_2, \vartheta_4\} & O_1 = \{\vartheta_3\} & N_1 = \{\vartheta_5\} \\ S_3 = \{\vartheta_1, \vartheta_3, \vartheta_5\} & O_1 = \{\vartheta_4\} & N_1 = \{\vartheta_2\} \end{array}$$

The weight of evaluation index $\beta = \{0.3, 0.3, 0.1, 0.2, 0.1\}$. And the vague value of the three interface schemes are calculated based on the Eq. (11).

$$v_1 = [0.740, 0.924]$$
$$v_2 = [0.828, 0.924]$$
$$v_3 = [0.551, 0.863]$$

According to the Eqs. (13).and (14)., The positive ideal value X^+ and the negative ideal value X^- are set as $X^+ = [0.828, 0.924]$ and $X^- = [0.551, 0.863]$. So the approximation index λ can be obtained, following the approaching degree d_i^+ and d_i^-.

$$\begin{array}{lll} d_1^+ = 0.088 & d_2^+ = 0 & d_3^+ = 0.284 \\ d_1^- = 0.199 & d_2^- = 0.284 & d_3^- = 0 \\ \lambda_1 = 0.693 & \lambda_2 = 1 & \lambda_3 = 0 \end{array}$$

In the light of the closeness with the ideal interface scheme, the three interface of automotive audio and video navigator interface were ranked from excellent to inferior as below: RoadRover Changxin 3 > FlyAudio 7600 Series > ADAYO CE4K01212A. It indicates that RoadRover Changxin 3 is the most convenient and efficient automotive navigator interface solution that conforms to the cognitive logic of users when considering five main functions. The evaluation results greatly contribute to manufacturers' design and user choice, due to that other manufacturers can set this product as the benchmarking to constantly improve the performance of their products and users can thereby choose a relatively suitable automotive interface.

5.4 Suggestions on Interface Optimization

The complicated operation sequence and repeated interface jump were identified in terms of predicting results of motion and interface jump. The operations and the corresponding page structures can be optimized by cancellation, merging, and rearrangement. Taking the Bluetooth dial-up task as example, the task-fulfilling processes of three automotive audio and video navigator interface Schemes are shown as the following figures.

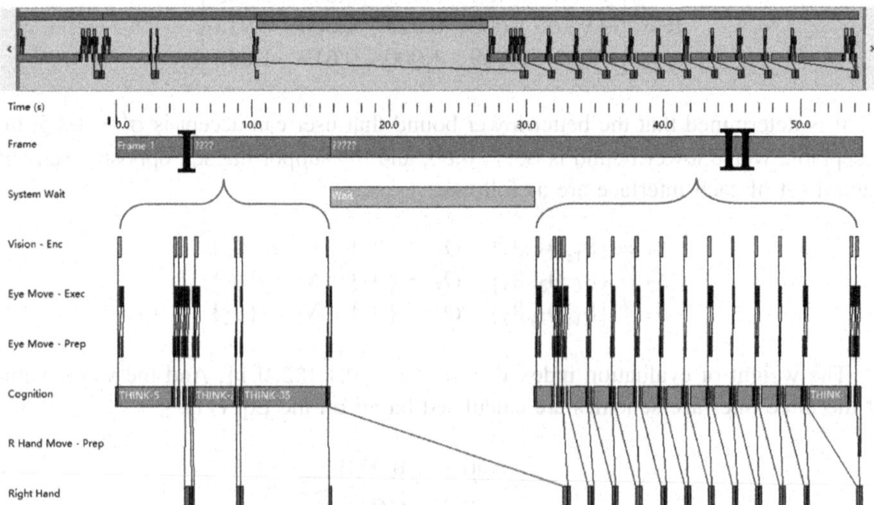

Fig. 6. The Interaction process of the bluetooth dialing task in the FlyAudio7600 series interface (Scheme A)

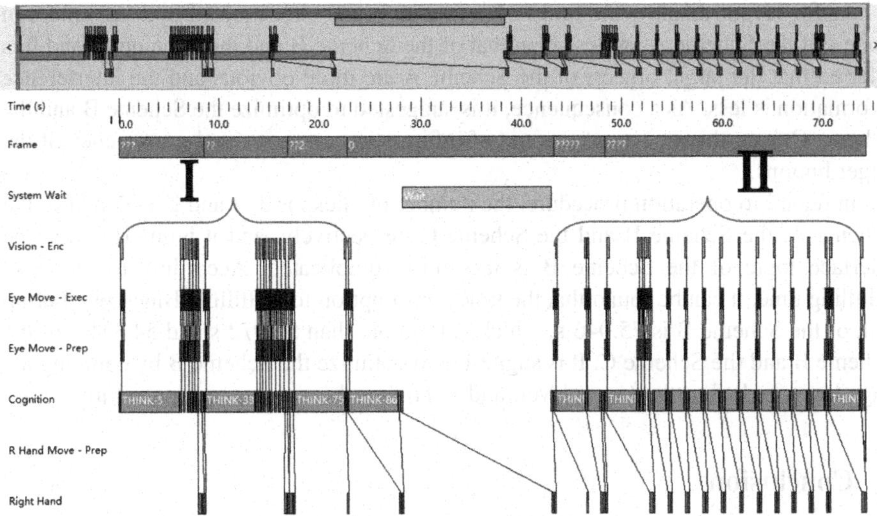

Fig. 7. The Interaction process of the bluetooth dialing task in the Road Rover Changxin 3 interface (Scheme B)

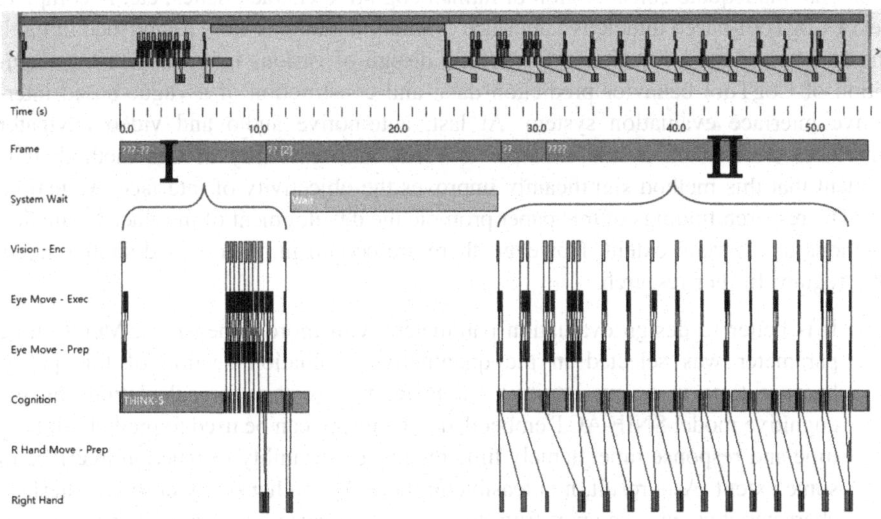

Fig. 8. The Interaction process of the bluetooth dialing task in the ADAYO CE4K01212A interface (Scheme C)

It is obvious that to dial out the eleven-digit number "15313658969" on the digital dial plate is a necessary operation. While the dialing process of the three Schemes are very similar (Zone II in Figs. 6, 7 and 8), Zone I (Zone I in Figs. 6, 7 and 8) is the analyzing and optimizing area where the major difference is located. The analysis was carried out from the perspectives of layout display and operation procedure.

As for layout display, the times of preparation and execution of eye movement in Zone I of the Scheme A are less than that of the Scheme B and the Scheme C, and it is inferred that the target objects of the Scheme A are more obvious and the interference information is less. As a consequence, it is suggested to optimize the Scheme B and the Scheme C from the aspects of amount of information on pages and prominence of the target buttons.

In regard to operation procedure, the number of clicks is 3, 4 and 2 in Zone I of the Scheme A, the Scheme B and the Scheme C, respectively, and it is inferred that the interface logic of the Scheme B is the most complicated. According to the task-fulfilling time, it can be found that the time consumption for fulfilling Bluetooth dial-up task of the Scheme B is 75.046 s, which is far more than 55.072 s and 54.341 s of the Scheme B and the Scheme C. It is suggested to optimize the Scheme B by combing the page logic, reducing the target level, and removing the unnecessary page turns.

6 Conclusion

The CogTool-based interactive interface evaluation method was studied in this research aiming at the inadequacy of interactive interface quantitative evaluation methods, time and labor consuming of user experience testing, the conventional interface evaluation methods' inadequate consideration of human cognitive characteristics, etc. A complete set of CogTool-based interactive interface evaluation methods were established through the analysis of main functions of interface, design of various interactive tasks, acquisition of CogTool behavior prediction data, and construction of a vague-based interactive interface evaluation system. At last, automotive audio and video navigator interfaces were taken as the example to verify the feasibility of this method. It is evident that this method significantly improves the objectivity of interface evaluation.

The research findings of this paper promote the development of interface evaluation methods to a certain extent. However, there are certain limitations and shortcomings that require further research:

(1) It is better to design evaluation parameters with more dimensions. Merely time parameter was selected in the quantitative evaluation section of this paper, because time is a very intuitive parameter that is easy for calculation and the cognitive model SNIF-ACT embedded in CogTool can be used to predict thinking time and response time, namely time reflects the usability of reaction interface to some extent. As a result, it is feasible to more comprehensively describe interface characteristics, in case apart from time other parameters are adopted, e.g. amount of information on the interface.

(2) Novice users who frequently make errors should be taken into account when designing interactive interface evaluation methods. At present, CogTool's prediction program is essentially based on skilled users who seldom make errors. The interface evaluation method based on different users' cognitive characteristics can be further improved via the calculation of error rate, in case the procedures where errors occur are considered.

(3) Develop a CogTool-based interface evaluation prototype system. The CogTool-based interface evaluation method proposed in this paper will be implemented in practice more conveniently, if CogTool's prediction process and vague set evaluation process are linked by an integral software system.

References

1. Bellotti, V., Fukuzumi, S., Asahi, T., Suzuki, S.: User-centered design and evaluation – the big picture. In: Jacko, J.A. (ed.) HCI 2009. LNCS, vol. 5610, pp. 214–223. Springer, Heidelberg (2009). https://doi.org/10.1007/978-3-642-02574-7_24
2. Alppay, C., Bayazit, N.: An ergonomics based design research method for the arrangement of helicopter flight instrument panels. Appl. Ergon. **51**, 85–101 (2015)
3. Lalji, Z., Good, J.: Designing new technologies for illiterate populations: a study in mobile phone interface design. Interact. Comput. **20**(6), 574–586 (2008)
4. Choocharukul, K., Sriroongvikrai, K.: Road safety awareness and comprehension of road signs from international tourist's perspectives: a case study of Thailand. Transp. Res. Procedia **25**, 4522–4532 (2017)
5. Shneiderman, B.: Designing the user interface - strategies for effective human-computer interaction. J. Assoc. Inf. Sci. Technol. **39**(1), 1073–1074 (1988)
6. Rashid, S., Soo, S., Sivaji, A., et al.: Preliminary usability testing with eye tracking and FCAT analysis on occupational safety and health websites. Procedia - Soc. Behav. Sci. **97** (2), 737–744 (2013)
7. Kieras, D.E., Meyer, D.E.: The EPIC architecture for modeling human information-processing and performance: a brief introduction. Cognitive Processes, p. 22 (1994)
8. Frøkjær, E.: Metaphors of human thinking for usability inspection and design. ACM Trans. Comput.-Hum. Interact. (TOCHI) **14**(4), 1–33 (2008)
9. Wang, H., Xue, C., Huang, J., Song, G.: Design and evaluation of human-computer digital interface based on cognitive load. J. Electro-Mech. Eng. **29**(05), 57–60 (2013)
10. Ramkumar, A., Stappers, P.J., Niessen, W.J., et al.: Using GOMS and NASA-TLX to evaluate human-computer interaction process in interactive segmentation. Int. J. Hum.-Comput. Interact. **33**(2), 123–134 (2017)
11. Rim, R., Mohamed Amin, M., Adel, M., Mohamed, A.: Evaluation method for an adaptive web interface: GOMS model. In: Madureira, A.M., Abraham, A., Gamboa, D., Novais, P. (eds.) ISDA 2016. AISC, vol. 557, pp. 116–124. Springer, Cham (2017). https://doi.org/10.1007/978-3-319-53480-0_12
12. Yang, H., Wang, Y., Zhang, L.: Comparison of human-computer interaction model of GOMS and EPIC. J. Packag. Eng. **8**, 96–99 (2015)
13. MacKenzie, I.S.: Fitts' law as a research and design tool in human-computer interaction. Hum.-Comput. Interact. **7**(1), 91–139 (2009)
14. Fitts, P.M.: The information capacity of the human motor system in controlling the amplitude of movement. J. Exp. Psychol. Gen. **47**(3), 262–269 (1954)
15. Tang, S., Zheng Qin, L.: Usability study of menus on Fitts's law and Hick's law. J. Comput. Eng. Appl. **52**(10), 254–258 (2016)
16. Anderson, J.R., Matessa, M., Lebiere, C.: ACT-R: a theory of higher level cognition and its relation to visual attention (1997)
17. Anderson, J.R., Matessa, M., Lebiere, C.: ACT-R: a theory of higher level cognition and its relation to visual attention. Hum.-Comput. Interact. **12**(4), 439–462 (1997)

18. Byrne, M.D.: ACT-R/PM and menu selection: applying a cognitive architecture to HCI. Int. J. Hum.-Comput. Stud. **55**(1), 41–84 (2001)
19. Marquis, Y., Chaoulli, J., Bordage, G., et al.: How to integrate time-duration estimation in ACT-R/PM. Mol. Ecol. **17**(24), 5177–5188 (2005)
20. Jo, S., Myung, R., Yoon, D.: Quantitative prediction of mental workload with the ACT-R cognitive architecture. Int. J. Ind. Ergon. **42**(4), 359–370 (2012)
21. Oh, H., Jo, S., Myung, R.: Computational modeling of human performance in multiple monitor environments with ACT-R cognitive architecture. Int. J. Ind. Ergon. **44**(6), 857–865 (2014)
22. Atashfeshan, N., Razavi, H.: Determination of the proper rest time for a cyclic mental task using ACT-R architecture. Hum. Factors **59**(2), 299 (2017)
23. Shankar, A., Lin, H., Brown, H.F., et al.: Rapid usability assessment of an enterprise application in an agile environment with CogTool (2015)
24. Ritter, F.E., Rooy, D.V., St Amant, R.: A user modeling design tool based on a cognitive architecture for comparing interfaces. In: Kolski, C., Vanderdonckt, J. (eds.) Computer-Aided Design of User Interfaces III. Springer, Dordrecht (2002). https://doi.org/10.1007/978-94-010-0421-3_10
25. Swearngin, A., Cohen, M.B., John, B.E., et al.: Human performance regression testing. In: International Conference on Software Engineering (2013)
26. Bellamy, R., John, B., Richards, J., et al.: Using CogTool to model programming tasks. In: Evaluation & Usability of Programming Languages & Tools (2010)
27. Harris, B.N., John, B.E., Brezin, J.: Human performance modeling for all: importing UI prototypes into CogTool. In: International Conference on Human Factors in Computing Systems (2010)
28. Hong, K.W., St Amant, R.: Novice use of a predictive human performance modeling tool to produce UI recommendations (2014)
29. Teo, L.H., John, B., Blackmon, M.: CogTool-Explorer: a model of goal-directed user exploration that considers information layout (2012)
30. Teo, L., John, B.E.: CogTool-Explorer: towards a tool for predicting user interaction. In: Extended Abstracts Conference on Human Factors in Computing Systems (2008)
31. Zhao, L., Huang, J., Zhong, N.: A context-aware recommender system with a cognition inspired model. In: Miao, D., Pedrycz, W., Ślęzak, D., Peters, G., Hu, Q., Wang, R. (eds.) RSKT 2014. LNCS (LNAI), vol. 8818, pp. 613–622. Springer, Cham (2014). https://doi.org/10.1007/978-3-319-11740-9_56
32. Pirolli, P., Fu, W.-T.: SNIF-ACT: a model of information foraging on the world wide web. In: Brusilovsky, P., Corbett, A., de Rosis, F. (eds.) UM 2003. LNCS (LNAI), vol. 2702, pp. 45–54. Springer, Heidelberg (2003). https://doi.org/10.1007/3-540-44963-9_8
33. Hong, D.H., Choi, C.H.: Multicriteria fuzzy decision-making problems based on vague set theory. Elsevier North-Holland, Inc. (2000)
34. Chen, S.M., Tan, J.M.: Handling multicriteria fuzzy decision-making problems based on vague set theory. Elsevier North-Holland, Inc. (1994)
35. Zhou, X.G., Zhang, Q., Wang-Bin, H.U.: Research on TOPSIS methods based on vague set theory. Syst. Eng.-Theory Methodol. Appl. **14**(6), 537–541 (2005)
36. Qiang, Z., Ying, M.: A note on handling multicriteria fuzzy decision-making problems based on vague set theory. In: IEEE International Conference on Systems (2006)
37. Peng, F., Xing, Q., Wang, S.: Threat assessment of aerial targets based on TOPSIS method and vague set theory. Electron. Opt. Control **17**(10), 23–27 (2010)
38. Gossen, T., Nitsche, M., Vos, J.: Adaptation of a search user interface towards user needs: a prototype study with children & adults. In: Symposium on Human-computer Interaction & Information Retrieval (2013)

39. Ravid, A., Berry, D.M.: A method for extracting and stating software requirements that a user interface prototype contains. Requir. Eng. **5**(4), 225–241 (2000)
40. Leavitt, M.O., Shneiderman, B.: Research-based web design & usability guidelines (2006)
41. Shih, H.S., Shyur, H.J., Lee, E.S.: An extension of TOPSIS for group decision making (2007)
42. Olson, D.L.: Comparison of weights in TOPSIS models. Math. Comput. Model. **40**(7), 721–727 (2004)

A Support System for Viewing Lecture Contents Adapted Students Understanding - Study on Question Behavior to Grasp Learner's Understanding Situation -

Tomoki Yabe[1(✉)], Teruhiko Unoki[2], Takayuki Kunieda[3], Yusuke Kometani[3], Naka Gotoda[3], Ken'ichi Fujimoto[3], Toshihiro Hayashi[3], and Rihito Yaegashi[3]

[1] Graduate School of Engineering, Kagawa University, Hayashi-cho 2217-20, Takamatsu, Kagawa 761-0396, Japan
s18g479@stu.kagawa-u.ac.jp

[2] IMAGICA GROUP, Uchisaiwai-cho Tokyu Bldg. 11F, Uchisaiwaicho 1-3-2, Chiyoda-ku, Tokyo 100-0011, Japan

[3] Faculty of Engineering and Design, Kagawa University, Hayashi-cho 2217-20, Takamatsu, Kagawa 761-0396, Japan

Abstract. We developed a lecture content viewing system using lecture content metadata. The lecture content viewing system developed by us has the function to reproduce the lecture contents based on the index and the function to reproduce the unit and learning contents of the lecture contents. However, it is necessary to grasp the scene that the learner himself/herself wants to learn, then it has not reached support of adaptive learning. In this research, we develop a lecture content recommendation system that supports adaptive learning based on learner's understanding. In this paper, we focus on the learner's questioning behavior as a method of grasping the learner understanding. We describe the survey of learner experiences using journey map and the chat function that encourages question behavior in learning using lecture contents.

Keywords: Lecture contents · Adaptive learning · Question behavior

1 Introduction

We developed the lecture contents viewing system using lecture contents metadata [1, 2]. The system which we developed has three functions, index function, unit/content viewing function and playlist function. The index function can view lecture contents from utterance time of indexing term by using index metadata. The unit/content viewing function can be played back selected unit and learning content of lecture content by using syllabus metadata generated from the syllabus. The playlist function can view plural units and learning contents continuously. This system provides various mechanism of viewing lecture contents on learning.

In recent years, attention has been paid to adaptive learning which provides learning according to learner understanding situation. Adaptive learning is a form of

S. Yamamoto and H. Mori (Eds.): HCII 2019, LNCS 11569, pp. 392–401, 2019.
https://doi.org/10.1007/978-3-030-22660-2_28

learning that measures learning progress and understanding degree of each learner and provides learning according to learners. There are quizzes and reports as methods for measuring learner understanding situation after learning. There are questions behavior as a method to measure understanding of learners during learning.

The lecture content viewing system developed by us does not have much function on support of adaptive learning. For example, there is a function to recommend learners learning next, and a function to encourage learning of units which is the premise of learning. In this research, we develop a lecture content recommendation system that supports adaptive learning based on learner's understanding.

In this paper, we describe the survey of learner experiences using journey map and the results of the survey using the journey map. In addition, we describe the psychological burden on the learner's question behavior and the chat function that encourages question behavior in learning using lecture contents.

2 Lecture Contents Viewing System Using Lecture Contents Metadata

Lecture contents metadata consist of index metadata and syllabus metadata. The index metadata is generated from text data, which is converted by teacher's utterance in lecture contents using a voice recognition technology. Figure 1 shows index metadata. In Index metadata, the information of lecture contents describe contents tags, indexing term describe term tags and utterance time of indexing term describe time tags. Figure 2 shows that the user can directly enter in the input form if the word which user wants to search is clear. Figure 3 shows the result, when it is stored in the database. In order to realize the index system, the contents created by this system don't need the play back from the beginning but from the midstream. The Syllabus metadata is generated from the Syllabus. Figure 4 shows the Syllabus metadata. Ac-cording to Fig. 4, the lecture contents JAD02 consists of various units and learning contents. This Unit consist of encoding of information and information content. This learning content consist of information transmission and symbol and code. The lecture contents can be played back selected units and learning contents by using syllabus metadata. In this research, the authors use SMIL (Synchronized Multimedia Integration Language) [3] of markup language. Using SMIL, we can create a video combined various multimedia such as moving image data, image data, sound data, and text data. Figure 5 shows SMIL file generated by playback of units and learning contents function. According to Fig. 4, the lecture contents JAD02 playback unit of information content from 1905 s to 3008 s. These information are based on syllabus metadata which the author defined in this research.

3 Measurement Method of Learning Achievement

The syllabus is a learning plan for lectures and lessons. It is a memo which incorporates all the necessary information concerning each lecture attendance. For example, the name of the lecture, the name of the teacher in charge, the number of credits to be

```
<contents name="JAD02">
   <index>
      <term name="Encoding">
         <time>00:04:39</time>
      </term>
      <term name="Symbol">
         <time>00:07:32</time>
         <time>00:14:12</time>
         <time>00:46:08</time>
         <time>01:07:29</time>
         <time>01:07:54</time>
      </term>
      <term name="Codeword">
         <time>00:08:03</time>
         <time>00:12:11</time>
         <time>00:46:08</time>
      </term>
      <term name="Length of code">
         <time>00:10:23</time>
      </term>
      <term name="Average code length">
         <time>00:10:37</time>
         <time>00:25:46</time>
      </term>
      …
   </index>
</contents>
```

Fig. 1. The index metadata

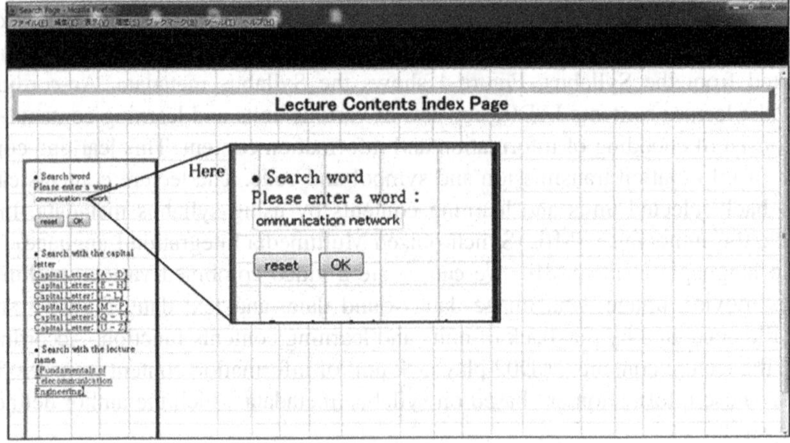

Fig. 2. Search

taken, the period during which the lecture is held, the textbook, the purpose of the lecture, the subject of the lecture, the goal by the lecture, the grading evaluation method, etc. are described in syllabus of the university. Also, most universities are

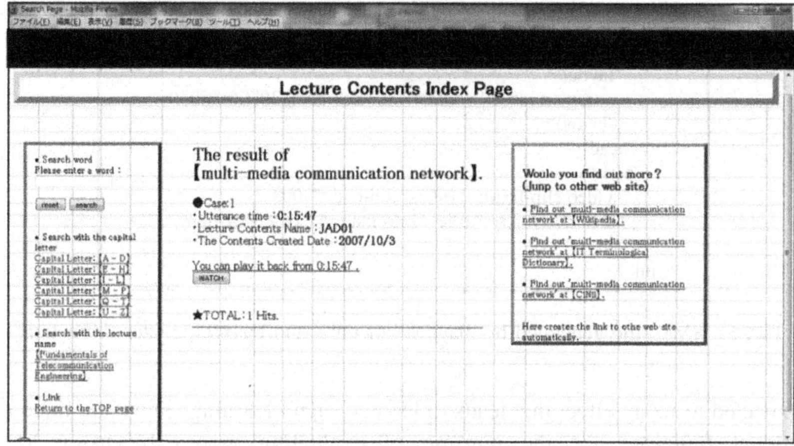

Fig. 3. Result

```
<lecture title=" Fundamentals of Telecommunication Engineering">
  <unit id="1">
    <unitstart>00:00:00</unitstart>
     <unitend>00:31:45</unitend>
     <unittitle>Encoding of Information</unittitle>
     <content id="1">
       <contentstart>00:00:00</contentstart>
         <contentend>00:06:41</contentend>
       <contenttitle>Information Transmission</contenttitle>
    </content>
    <content id="2">
       <contentstart>00:06:41</contentstart>
       <contentend>00:09:57</contentend>
         <contenttitle>Symbol and Code</contenttitle>
    </content>
...
  </unit>
  <unit id="2">
    <unitstart>00:31:45</unitstart>
    <unitend>00:50:08</unitend>
    <unittitle>Information Content</unittitle>
...
  </unit>
...
</lecture>
```

Fig. 4. The syllabus metadata

currently publishing the contents of syllabus on the Web. Therefore, it is an effective tool for students to select lectures.

Learning achievement is an index which can show how much students achieved the goal of the lesson set for syllabus by learning. Learning achievement is used to verify whether students achieve the goal set for syllabus. The result of learning achievement is

```
<smil>
    <head>
      <layout>
        <region id="1" width="480" height="320"fit="fill"/>
      </layout>
    </head>
    <body>
      <video clip-begin="1905s"clip-end="3008s"
        src="JAD02.rm" title="Information Content"region="1"/>
    </body>
</smil>
```

Fig. 5. SMIL file generated by playback of units and learning contents function

also expected to be an effect that leads to learner's next learning. There are three major educational functions for the purpose of evaluating grades by using learning achievement. The first purpose is to provide opportunities for students to review themselves and to verify understanding of the lecture. The second purpose is to provide opportunities for students to confirm their level of understanding. The third purpose is to provide opportunities for students to acquire more motivation to learn. Also, lectures at universities are generally conducted based on syllabus. This also applies to educational video content (lecture content) such as e-learning.

In the measurement method of learning achievement, appropriate methods are used for measuring the knowledge area, the attitude area, and the skill area, respectively. In addition, the measurement method of learning achievement has several methods depending on the learning objectives. These methods are classified into two major types: tests (objective test, in-class essay exam, oral test, practical test) and reports (paper, report). Table 1 shows the types of the measurement method of learning achievement according to learning objectives. There are objective tests and in-class essay exam and reports as the measurement method of learning achievement used in general e-learning. Quiz tests (objective tests, in-class essay exam) can measure knowledge, understanding, ability to solve problems, etc. Reports can measure knowledge, analytical skills, descriptive power, logic, information gathering ability, creativity and so on [4]. In addition, the measurement method of learning achievement is not only implemented after lecture execution but also it may be used to grasp learner understanding during lecture. For example, it is also possible to grasp the learner understanding from question behavior that the learner performs during lecture as a method similar to the oral test, or the attitude and atmosphere of the learner during lecture as a method similar to the practical test. It is possible to grasp learner understanding by the score of the quiz. On the other hand, it is difficult to grasp learner understanding by question behavior, because there is existence/nonexistence of implementation of question behavior for each learner. It is stated that there are four steps in the process until the learner performs question behavior. The first step is "perception of learning tasks" that individuals understand learning tasks in lectures. The second step is "question raising" that is suspicious of what learners are learning. The third step is "Generate Question" to convert questions that are occurred into languages and generate questions. The final step is to "act behaviors of questions" that actually makes the generated questions words to other people [5]. In this research, we focus on a method (question behavior etc.) to grasp learner understanding.

Table 1. The measurement method of learning achievement according to learning objective.

Measurement method of learning achievement		Learning objective
Objective test	O × Format, Multiple choice question	Knowledge, Understanding, Ability to solve problems
In-class essay exam	Drawing problem	Knowledge, Understanding, Ability to solve problems
Paper/Report	Discussion along the theme	Knowledge, Analytical skills, Descriptive power, Logic, Information gathering ability, Creativity
Oral test	Examination by interview	Knowledge, Understanding, Ability to solve problems, Communication skills
Practical test	Evaluation by observation record of actual behavior	Ability to solve problems, Skill, Perspective, Custom, Creativity, Applied skill, Communication skills

4 Survey of Learner Experiences Using Journey Map

4.1 Journey Map

In this research, we created a journey map to investigate learner experiences in lecture. A journey map is one of methods for examining the design of the entire service by visualizing the user image (persona) and the overall image of the service, the experience used between the user and the service [6]. In this survey, three students from Faculty of Engineering, Kagawa University were conducted as subjects. Subjects created a journey map by replacing the service with a lecture. Table 2 shows the set persona. By creating a journey map, it was possible to express the flow from the start of lecture to the end of lecture about a set persona as a chart. In addition, subjects described the specific touchpoints (points of contact between the user and the service) during lecture on the journey map and the interaction at touchpoints. In the journey map, it was possible to express the user's emotions as interaction and a result of interaction. Figure 6 shows a journey map which created in this survey.

4.2 Consideration of Learner Experience Using Journey Map

Table 3 summarizes some of learners' action, thoughts/emotions, tasks, and solutions for each touchpoint of a journey map. Figure 7 shows overview of journey map created. In this survey, each subject changed the emotional change from the start of lecture to the end of lecture by curves (emotional curves). At this time, the start of the emotional curve starts from 0, and it doesn't specifically designate the way of finishing and quantitative index. In touchpoints from the emotion curve set by the persona before

Table 2. Persona set up.

Sex	Man
Age	21 years old
Organization	College student
Department	Faculty of Engineering
Part time job	Kitchen staff of the restaurant (the third year)
Hobby	Social gaming, Web surfing
Room layout/Living arrangements	1K/Alone
Relations with teacher	Relations that can't be greeted
Q&A session during a lecture	He has a question but he can't hand it
Reasons	He is concerned about the evaluation of the surroundings
Motivation of lecture	He seats a seat before starting lecture He is sitting alone in the seats and listening to music with earphones until the beginning of the lecture

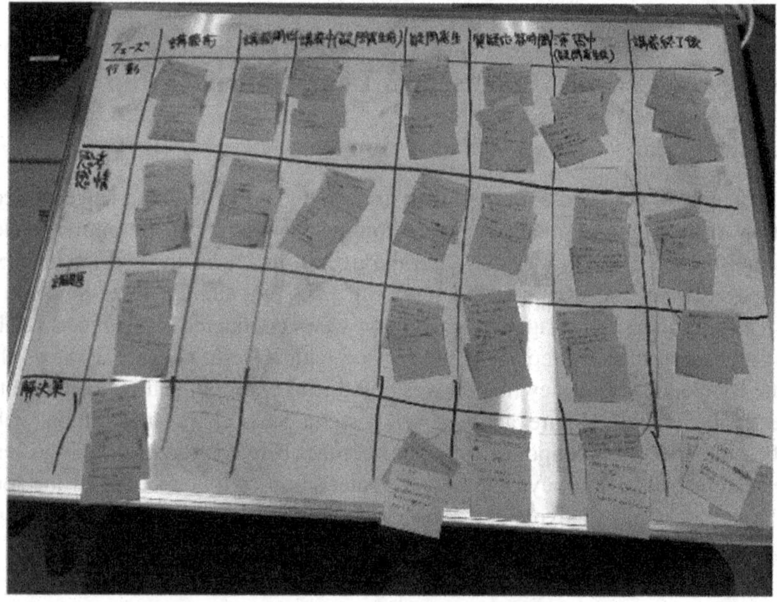

Fig. 6. Journey map

lecture to the end of lecture, it was able to be read that the feelings were biased in the minus direction in common with them at the stage when learner noticed a question. From this here, it is conceivable that some sort of psychological burden exists at the question generation stage during learning in this persona. Table 3 extracts more detailed behavior, thought/emotion, problem, solution of persona from the journey

Table 3. Journey map excerpt

Touchpoint	Before lecture	Start lecture	During lecture (Before doubt)	Doubt
Action	Sit in the corner of the classroom.		Learn according to the pace of the lecture.	Don't understand but do a board work.
Thoughts / Emotion				Let's revisit a little before because they don't know.
Problem				Not good at standing out.
				There is no one who can consult around.
Solution				

Touchpoint	Q & A time	During exercises (After doubt)	After the lecture ends
Action	Wait for someone to ask a question.		
Thoughts / Emotion	Hate it being my own doubt. Don't want to be watched. Don't want my teacher getting angry.		They are ashamed to go and ask the teacher's teacher. Let's review it at home.
Problem		Despite being able to ask questions individually during exercises, they can't question by carefully evaluating teachers.	They can't ask the teacher individually for questions.
			They left the classroom right away.
Solution	There is no need to ask questions during the lecture.	Ask someone other than the teacher.	They ask questions individually to the teacher at the time other students return so as not to be noticed.
	It would be nice if there was a way to ask the teacher anonymously.		Ask questions by means other than meetings such as e-mail.

map. It is stated that learners set for persona are not going to solve the problem due to gaze from others in each touchpoint. In particular, touchpoint such as questioning, questioning and answering time, after the end of lecture can be mentioned. Based on Fig. 7 and Table 3, the learner is able to clarify the question and language of the question. However, it has been shown that there are cases where they hesitates questioning behavior (questioning by the learner to the teacher) due to a psychological burden caused by consciousness of other people think and evaluation etc.

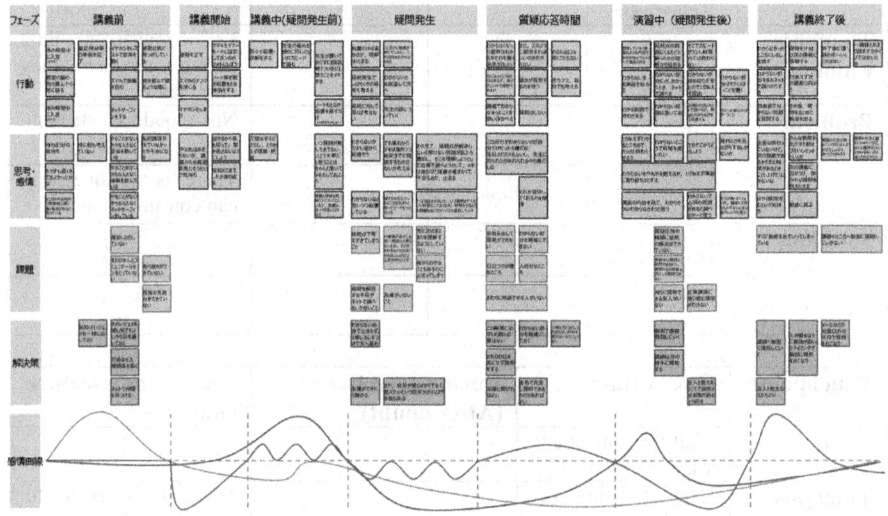

Fig. 7. Overview of journey map

5 Chat Function to Encourage Questions Behavior

In a general lecture, learners compensate for their understanding by asking teachers about the content of which understanding is insufficient. Learners are reported to worry about other people's thought and evaluation, and it is reported that there are cases where they may hesitate asking quest by psychological burden [5]. In this research, we propose a chat function in order to reduce the psychological burden of learners and promote question behavior in learning using lecture contents.

The scenario of the chat function will be described below. In the chat function, the chat bot will ask the learner about questions on lecture at an arbitrary scene of lecture contents. Next, the learner answers the question from the chat bot. After lecture content viewing, the chat bot asks the learner about questions about lecture contents. If the chat bot function can automatically answer questions, the chat bot will automatically answer. When the chat bot function can't answer automatically for questions, the chat bot records as learner understanding data, and the teacher in charge answers questions. The purpose of the chat bot function is to reduce the psychological burden on question behaviors of lecture contents by making dialogue with the chat bot before questioning lecture contents to the learner.

6 Conclusion

In this paper, the results of the survey using the journey map and the journey map aiming at grasping the psychological situation during lecture of the learner were described. In addition, we described the psychological burden on the learner's question behavior and the chat function that encourages question behavior in learning using lecture contents.

References

1. Saitoh, T., Hayashi, T., Yaegashi, R.: The lecture contents with index for self study and its system. In: Proceedings of International Conference on Information Technology Based Higher Education and Training 2012 (ITHET2012), 6 p. (2012)
2. Saitoh, T., Hayashi, T., Yaegashi, T.: Self-study support system using the lecture contents/creation of study ontology from syllabuses. In: Proceedings of International Conference on Information Technology Based Higher Education and Training 2012 (ITHET2012), 6 p. (2012)
3. Synchronized Multimedia Integration Language (SMIL 3.0). http://www.w3.org/TR/SMIL/
4. Hisa Nomoto Introduction to grading method. SPOD-Ehime university (2019). https://www.spod.ehime-u.ac.jp/wp/wp-con-tent/uploads/2015/02/%E8%B3%87%E6%96%99%E3%80%90%EF%BC%B0%EF%BC%A4%EF%BC%A6%E3%80%9117.pdf
5. www.hues.kyushu-u.ac.jp/education/student/pdf/2001/2HE00061P.pdf
6. Banfield, R., Todd Lombardo, C., Wax, T.: Design Sprint-A practical Guidebook for Building Great Digital Products, O'Reilly Japan, Inc., Tokyo (2016)

Modeling Pilots' Operation Error Based on Fitts' Law

Qianzheng Zhuang[1], Xiaoyan Zhang[2(✉)], Hua Zhao[2(✉)], Hongjun Xue[2(✉)], and Tao Li[2(✉)]

[1] China Aviation Radio Electronics Research Institute, Shanghai, China
[2] School of Aeronautics, Northwestern Polytechnical University, Xi'an, China
zxyliuyan@163.com, 1046445923@qq.com, lt940826@qq.com, xuehj@nwpu.edu.cn

Abstract. Pilot error has long been a threat to aviation safety. Predicting pilot error can provide cockpit designers with useful information to reduce the possibility of pilot error and cost of training, improve the safety and performance of systems, and increase operator satisfaction. We present a theoretical model of pilot error based on review investigations of how effectively cockpit layout predict pilot error. The validity of the model was confirmed based on data collected from pilot operation experiments. Experiments were performed on five different operation tasks. Results showed that predicted values from the proposed model were highly correlated to actual error rates from the experiments. The findings indicate that the proposed error analysis model appears to be effective in the prediction of pilots' error over time. The model thus can be used to find out the potential safety problems of cockpit layout to improve the design of cockpit.

Keywords: Fitts' law · Pilot error · Positioning movement · Error rate · Error model

1 Introduction

While the development of manufacturing technology leads to great improvement in mechanically safe aircraft design, pilot error has long been a threat to aviation safety [1–3]. An aircraft is a large class of systems that require active interaction or continuous control by pilots [4]. Cockpit is the main workstation for pilots. In cockpits, pilots need to perform various operations, such as pushing a button, twisting a knob, and pulling a handle [5]. Every different type of operation mistake will lead to a pilot error. Pilots' operational mistakes are the main cause of pilot error [6]. Therefore, quantifying the operation mistakes and reducing pilot error are of great urgency.

There are two methods of studying error indicators: user testing and heuristic evaluation [7]. User testing is generally a direct measure of user's error rates [8]. But there exists a relatively large standard deviation in user testing when the number of testers is insufficient. Heuristic evaluation measures error indicator with usability inspecting method, which focus on the formulation of evaluation criteria [9]. Because heuristic evaluation is based on subjective investigation and analysis instead of

S. Yamamoto and H. Mori (Eds.): HCII 2019, LNCS 11569, pp. 402–411, 2019.
https://doi.org/10.1007/978-3-030-22660-2_29

quantified model, it is difficult to obtain a comprehensive evaluation criterion and find out the essence of pilot operation mistakes.

In contrast, Human reliability analysis (HRA) is a more feasible model to analyze operation mistakes. HRA relates to methodologies for anticipating and assessing the effect of those failures which relate to human action or inaction, and not the failure of some physical component [10, 11]. HRA usually corrects the probability of human error with correction factor, or calculates the probability of a system error as part of the probability of correctly diagnosing events [11]. However, in the actual calculation process, the formation factor is difficult to determine, so that the correction coefficient of the error probability is not accurate enough. Thus the accuracy of the HRA model may be compromised.

Moreover, the above model cannot describe the relationship between cockpit layout and pilot error. We aimed to address this limitation in the present study. Fitts' law is a positioning movement rule describing motion characteristics. It was reported that Fitts' Law mathematically imply a predictive error rate model [12]. Therefore, we proposed a novel pilot operation error assessment model based on Fitts' law. This model used basic operation conditions such as task distance, target angle, and target position and so on as the input data and the operation error would be output.

2 Modeling Pilot Operation Error Based on Fitts' Law

Positioning movement is the basic operation in the cockpit, such as pushing a button, which had been certified for compliance of Fitts' Law [13, 14]. Fitts's law predicts the movement time MT to acquire a target of size W at distance A (shown in Fig. 1). Starting point is the point where finger is before operation. Target is a button (or a handle, knob) that you need to operate. End point is the center of target in a positioning movement. Typically, MT is the dependent variable in Fitts' law. The basic law is written:

$$\mathrm{MT} = \mathrm{a} + \mathrm{b}\log_2\left(\frac{2A}{W}\right) \tag{1}$$

In Eq. 1, *a* and *b* are empirically determined regression coefficients, which vary among user and devices. Hoffmann [15] suggested that *a* and *b* represents decision time and positioning movement efficiency respectively.

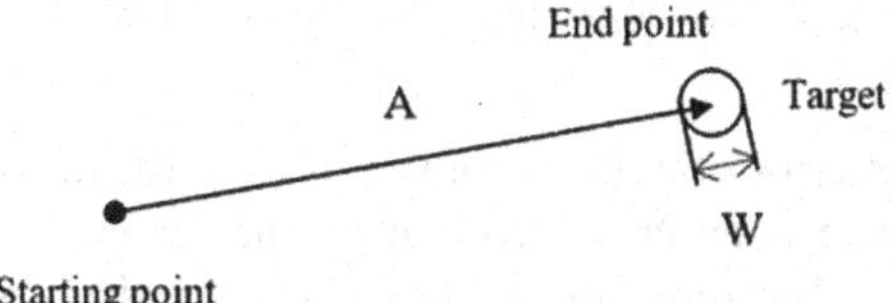

Fig. 1. Variables involved in Fitts' Law

Note that Fitts' Law is used to calculate the average motion time, and cannot obtain other statistics such as variance and maximum deviation in the positioning movement [16]. Besides, Fitts' law applies only to the starting point and end point of the positioning movement, and cannot predict the intermediate process [17]. To address these two problems, this paper will derive the logarithmic Fitts' Law.

Logarithmic Fitts' Law divides a positioning movement into several steps and describes the characteristics of variables in each step. Suppose the distance to target after ith moving is A_i, and the remaining distance after each movement is λ times of the remaining distance of the previous step. Suppose τ is the time that each step takes, and *a* is the initial time before the movement starts. The specific derivation is as follows (Fig. 2).

$$A_{i+1} = \lambda A_i \tag{2}$$

$$A_n = \lambda^n A = \frac{W}{2} \tag{3}$$

$$n = -\log_2\left(\frac{2A}{W}\right)/\log_2(\lambda) \tag{4}$$

$$T = a + \tau \times n \tag{5}$$

Positioning movement error comes from two aspects. The first type of error exists in logarithmic Fitts' Law. Because logarithmic Fitts' Law describes a continuous movement towards target instead of target center, end point may not be at the center of target but with a certain error in last move (shown in Fig. 3). It is considered that this error does not exceed W/2, which is within the tolerance of the target's width W. So this error will not lead to the pilot positioning movement error independently.

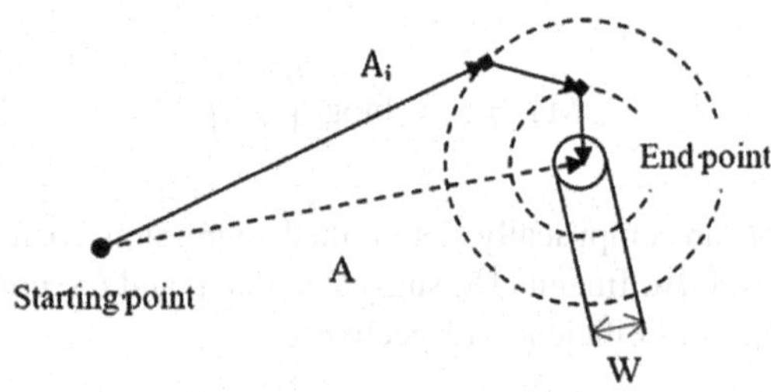

Fig. 2. The logarithmic derivation of Fitts' Law

The second type of error originates from decision mistakes (shown in Fig. 4). This paper assumes that there is an error between planned target and actual target during positioning movement. The direction of the error is random, and the mean of error distribution is proportional to the distance from end point (shown in Fig. 5).

According to logarithmic Fitts' Law, the first type of error is $\lambda^n A$, where *n* is the number of times the pilot moves. For *i*-th move, the Fitts' law shows that the remain

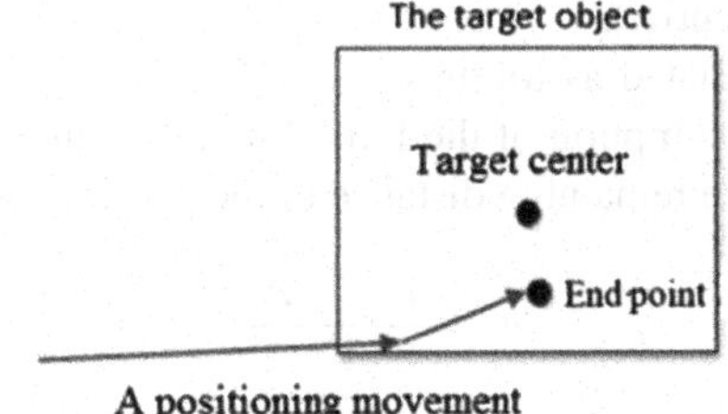

Fig. 3. The first type of error

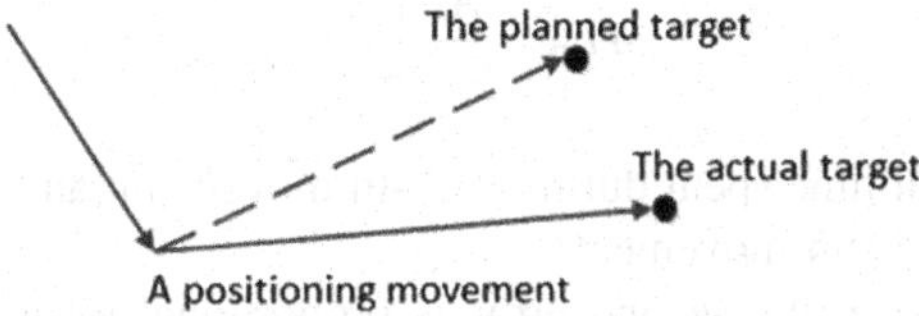

Fig. 4. The second type of error

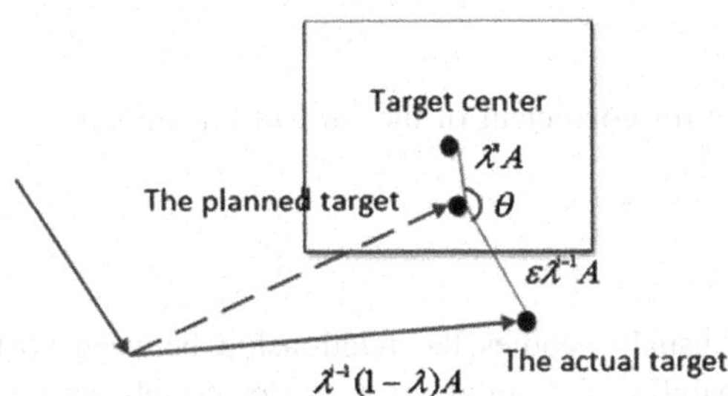

Fig. 5. The type of errors

distance from end point is $\lambda^{i-1}A$ before moving. Suppose the second type error of the i-th move between actual target and planned target is $\varepsilon\lambda^{i-1}A$, where ε is coefficient and $\varepsilon \sim N(0, \sigma^2)$.

Due to the feature of positioning movement, the target of next movement is corrected after each movement. Although the second error exists in each moves, these errors will not accumulate and will be corrected in next movement. Therefore, we only need to consider the second type of error caused by last move. In last move, the superposition of two types of errors is the total error of positioning movement. The direction of these two errors is random and independent. Suppose the angle between the two is θ, where $\theta \sim U(0, \pi)$. The total error can be obtained by cosine theorem.

$$d = \left[\lambda^{2n}A^2 + \varepsilon^2\lambda^{2(n-1)}A^2 - 2\varepsilon\lambda^{2n-1}Acos\theta\right]^{\frac{1}{2}} \tag{6}$$

If $d \geq w/2$, error occurred.

Where, ε can be calculated as follows.

According to basic assumption of the Fitts' Law, the remaining distance after each movement is λ times of the remaining distance of the previous step (in Eq. 2). And then

$$\tau = \frac{A_{i-1} - A_i}{V_i} \tag{7}$$

Where, A_i is the ideal remaining distance after i sub-movements; V_i is the speed of the i-th movement.

$$MT_{ei} = \frac{A_{i-1} - A_i^{'}}{V_i} \tag{8}$$

where, MT_{ei} is the real time spent during the i-th movement, and $A_i^{'}$ represents the real remain distance after i sub-movement.

As mentioned above, the second error is proportional to the distance to the end point.

$$\varepsilon_i = \frac{A_i^{'} - A_i}{A_{i-1}} \tag{9}$$

Where, ε_i is the error coefficient of the i-th sub-movement.

3 Method

The existing model usually studies the relationship between positioning movement time and error probability. The pilot error model established in this paper mainly involves the following variables: the number of moves n, angle θ, distance A, error coefficients (λ and ε).

3.1 Participants

Six male master students with an average age of 23.5 ± 1.1 participated in the study. They were all recruited from Northwestern Polytechnical University and had experience of flying C919 simulator as a captain. This research was approved by the local ethics committee at NWPU. Informed consent was obtained from each participant.

3.2 Apparatus

The experiment was conducted in C919 simulator in Northwestern Polytechnical University. Motion data was recorded by an optical motion capture system (Shape-WarpIII) with sampling rate set at 93 Hz. Raw data was collected and processed by ShapeRecorder software (SensoMotoric Instruments GmbH, Teltow, Germany) in real time (Fig. 6).

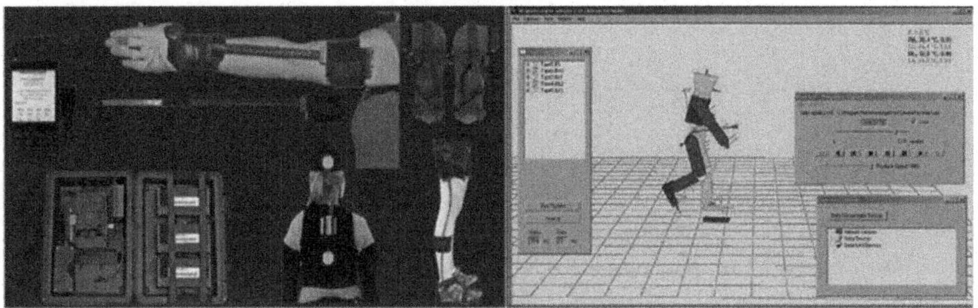

Fig. 6. Motion capture system

3.3 Task

There are five different operation tasks for participants: push/pull landing gear handle, flap lever, brake pad handle, throttle lever, and center console button. Each operation should be repeat 10 times.

3.4 Results

The speed-time curves describing the characteristics of each movement from starting point to target were shown in Fig. 7. The peaks of curves represent different steps of pilot positioning movement. According to logarithmic Fitts' Law, there are three distinct steps during a positioning movement in the cockpit.

The distribution of the unknown variable ε in the model can be obtained from the experimental data. And this paper finally took $\varepsilon \sim (0, 0.0762)$ from the data.

Wobbrock [12], and HCR [18] models are both well-known error models of positioning movements. The simulation condition is consistent with the experiment of Wobbrock [12]. The simulation results of the three models and experimental results are shown in Fig. 8. The error rate of the model built in this paper is not significantly different from the experimental data and the other two models ($F(3, 28) = 0.08$, $p = 0.97 > 0.05$). At the point MTe/MT = 1, the error probability is respectively 4.23%, which is close to the 4% rate that Fitts's Law recognizes [19].

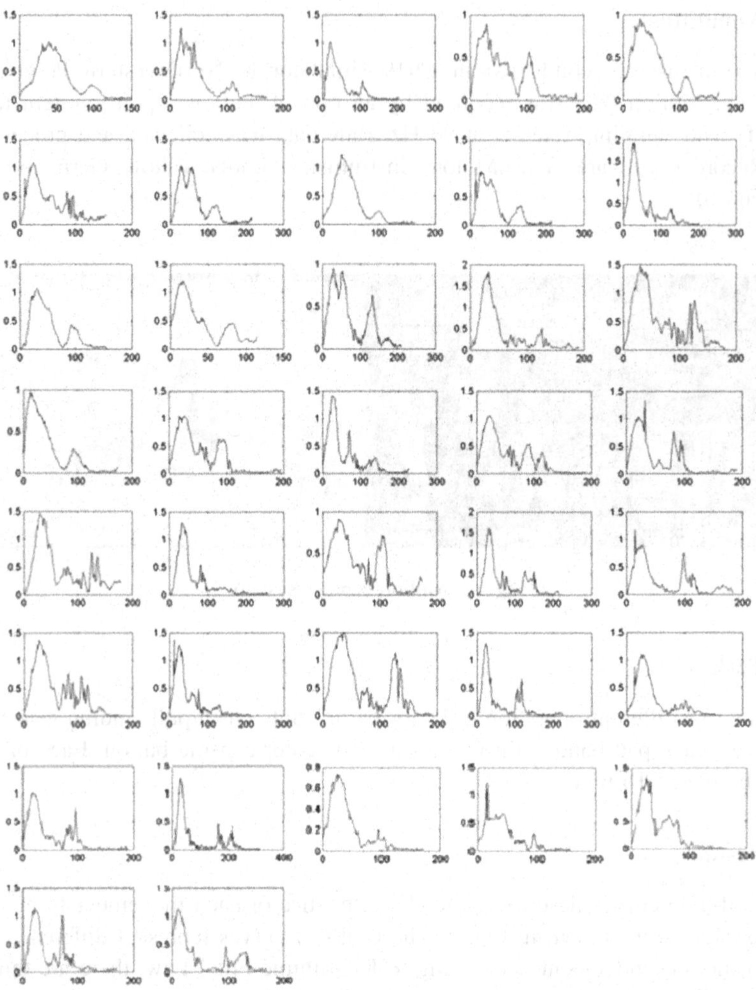

Fig. 7. Speed-time curve of positioning movement

The results of Wobbrock and HCR [12, 18] model are generally higher than the experimental data when the actual time is less than the theoretical time, and are generally less than the experimental data when the actual time is greater than the theoretical time.

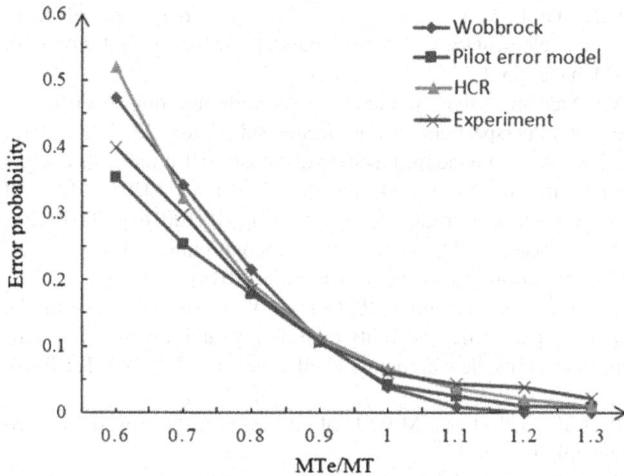

Fig. 8. Comparison of simulation results

4 Discussion and Conclusion

Error model of target-pointing in the cockpit provides good error-rate predictions (Fig. 8). Although models are always imperfect and measurements noisy, the match between error rate predictions and observed error rates is strong, especially given the contrived nature of experimentally controlled movement times.

Compared with existing models, the model proposed in this paper has the following advantages. There is no significant difference between pilot error model and the other two models. So the pilot error model is of great value for deepening pilot error study. Secondly, existing models only focused on the relationship between error probability and time. In this paper, the relationship between error probability and other characteristics of positioning movement can also be studied. Moreover, pilot error model can also be used to calculate the correction coefficient of the error probability, which is of great importance for improving accuracy in HRA.

Pilot error resulted in a series of aviation accidents, but there is still a lack of a systematic quantitative model of pilot error probability. Based on the logarithmic derivation of Fitts' Law, this study constructs a quantifiable pilot error model that can accurately analyze error probability. This model is of great importance to reduce pilot error and improve flight safety.

References

1. Naranji, E.: Reducing human/pilot error in aviation using augmented cognition and automation systems in aircraft cockpit. Neuroscience **117**(3), 557–565 (2015)
2. Sun, R., Zhao, K., Zhang, X.: Research on error proofing design of boeing and airbus cockpit from pilots survey. In: Harris, D. (ed.) EPCE 2015. LNCS (LNAI), vol. 9174, pp. 492–504. Springer, Cham (2015). https://doi.org/10.1007/978-3-319-20373-7_47

3. Coursaris, C.K., Osch, W.V.: A cognitive-affective model of perceived user satisfaction (campus): the complementary effects and interdependence of usability and aesthetics in is design. Inf. Manage. **53**(2), 252–264 (2016)
4. Al-Wardi, Y.: Arabian, Asian, Western: a cross-cultural comparison of aircraft accidents from human factors perspectives. Int. J. Occup. Saf. Ergon. **23**, 1–29 (2016)
5. Thomas, P., Biswas, P., Langdon, P.: State-of-the-art and future concepts for interaction in aircraft cockpits. In: Antona, M., Stephanidis, C. (eds.) UAHCI 2015. LNCS, vol. 9176, pp. 538–549. Springer, Cham (2015). https://doi.org/10.1007/978-3-319-20681-3_51
6. Dumitru, I.M., Boşcoianu, M.: Human factors contribution to aviation safety. Scientific Research & Education in the Air Force-AFASES (2015)
7. Fayollas, C., Martinie, C., Palanque, P., Deleris, Y., Fabre, J.C., Navarre, D.: An approach for assessing the impact of dependability on usability: application to interactive cockpits. In: Tenth European Dependable Computing Conference, pp. 198–209. IEEE Computer Society (2014)
8. Afonso, A.P., Lima, J.R., Cota, M.P.: Usability assessment of web interfaces: user testing. Inf. Syst. Technol. **3**, 1–7 (2013)
9. Toribio-Guzm, J.N., et al.: Study of the usability of the private social network SocialNet using heuristic evaluation. In: Proceedings of Xvii International Conference on Human Computer Interaction (2016)
10. Simon, F., Adhikari, S., Bayley, C., Bedford, T., Busby, J., Cliffe, A., et al.: Human Reliability Analysis: A Review and Critique. Social Science Electronic Publishing (2009)
11. Abbassi, R., Khan, F., Garaniya, V., Chai, S., Chin, C., Hossain, K.A.: An integrated method for human error probability assessment during the maintenance of offshore facilities. Process Saf. Environ. Prot. **94**, 172–179 (2015)
12. Wobbrock, J.O., Cutrell, E., Harada, S., Mackenzie, I.S.: An error model for pointing based on Fitts' law. In: SIGCHI Conference on Human Factors in Computing Systems, pp. 1613–1622 (2008)
13. Zhang, W.: Usability Evaluation Model of Civil Aircraft Cockpit in Detailed Design Phase. Master dissertation, Northwestern Polytechnical University (2016)
14. Liu, X.: Experimental and Simulational Research on Manipulation Performance of Pilot. Master dissertation, Northwestern Polytechnical University (2012)
15. Hoffmann, E.R.: Fitts' law with an average of two or less submoves? J. Mot. Behav. **48**(4), 1–13 (2016)
16. Guiard, Y., Halla, B., et al.: Fitt's law as an explicit time/error trade-off, pp. 1619–1628. ACM (2011)
17. Rioul, O., Guiard, Y.: Power vs. logarithmic model of fitts' law: a mathematical analysis. Math. Soc. Sci. **199**, 85–96 (2012)
18. Nakayasu, H., Nakagawa, M., Miyoshi, T., Patterson, P.: Human cognitive reliability analysis on drivers using simulator experiments (theory and methodology, the 40th international conference on computers and industrial engineering (cie 40). J. Japan Ind. Manage. Assoc. **62**(6), 278–285 (2012)
19. Soukoreff, R.W., Mackenzie, I.S.: Towards a standard for pointing device evaluation, perspectives on 27 years of Fitts' law research in HCI. Int. J. Hum.-Comput. Stud. **61**(6), 751–789 (2004)
20. Ballard, S.B., Osorio, V.B.: U.S. civil air show crashes, 1993 to 2013: burden, fatal risk factors, and evaluation of a risk index for aviation crashes. Transp. Res. Rec. **2471**, 1–13 (2015)
21. Burno, R.A., Wu, B., Doherty, R., Colett, H., Elnaggar, R.: Applying fitts' law to gesture based computer interactions. Procedia Manufact. **3**, 4342–4349 (2015)

22. Cockburn, A., Gutwin, C.: A model of novice and expert navigation performance in constrained-input interfaces. ACM Trans. Comput.-Hum. Interact. (TOCHI) **17**(3), 1–38 (2010)
23. Lüdtke, A., Osterloh, J.-P., Mioch, T., Rister, F., Looije, R.: Cognitive modelling of pilot errors and error recovery in flight management tasks. In: Palanque, P., Vanderdonckt, J., Winckler, M. (eds.) HESSD 2009. LNCS, vol. 5962, pp. 54–67. Springer, Heidelberg (2010). https://doi.org/10.1007/978-3-642-11750-3_5
24. Rioul, O., Guiard, Y.: The power model of Fitts' law does not encompass the logarithmic model. Meeting of the European Mathematical Psychology Group (2011)
25. Rozenberg, R., Socha, V., Socha, L., Szabo, S., Nemec, V.: Critical Elements in Piloting Techniques in Aerobatic Teams. Transport Means (2016)
26. Stepniczka, I.: Human-machine interaction in aircraft cockpits-situational awareness and mental workload in highly complex environments. J. Fire Sci. **30**(6), 511–534 (2012)
27. Stone, R.W., Baker-Eveleth, L.: Students' expectation, confirmation, and continuance intention to use electronic textbooks. Behav. Inf. Technol. **34**(10), 992–1004 (2013)
28. Vetter, S., Bützler, J., Jochems, N., Schlick, C.M.: Fitts' law in bivariate pointing on large touch screens: age-differentiated analysis of motion angle effects on movement times and error rates. In: Stephanidis, C. (ed.) UAHCI 2011. LNCS, vol. 6766, pp. 620–628. Springer, Heidelberg (2011). https://doi.org/10.1007/978-3-642-21663-3_67

Information, Empathy and Persuasion

Presenting Low-Accuracy Information of Emotion Recognition Enhances Human Awareness Performance

Shinichi Fukasawa[1(✉)], Hiroko Akatsu[1], Wakana Taguchi[2], Fumio Nihei[2], and Yukiko Nakano[2]

[1] Oki Electric Ind. Co., Ltd., Warabi-shi, Saitama, Japan
{fukasawa856,akatsu232}@oki.com
[2] Seikei University, Musashino-shi, Tokyo, Japan
{dm186205,dd166201}@cc.seikei.ac.jp,
y.nakano@st.seikei.ac.jp

Abstract. We examined the effectiveness of presenting emotion recognition information with accuracy information to enhance awareness on audio-visual telecommunication systems. Sixteen participants observed an experimenter whose emotion was induced by picture stimuli. The participants then evaluated the valence emotion of experimenters across 4 environmental conditions: face-to-face (F2F), remote audio-visual environment without accuracy information (Remote-None), remote audio-visual environment with emotion recognition information and 70% accuracy information (Remote+70%), and the same with 90% accuracy information (Remote+90%). The level of emotional transmission and observation time were measured. Results showed that the level of emotional transmission did not significantly differ between F2F and Remote-None conditions, but was 10% higher in Remote+70% than in other conditions. Moreover, observation time was significantly shorter in the Remote+70% condition than in the Remote-None condition. These data indicate that presenting low-accuracy information as well as emotion recognition effectively enhanced human awareness performance.

Keywords: Emotion recognition · Recognition accuracy · Emotional transmission · Telecommunication · Awareness

1 Introduction

Telework, which enables workers to connect remotely between distant offices, has drawn attention due to its advantages in flexibility, energy savings, business continuity planning, and other benefits. However, compared to direct face-to-face (F2F) environments, teleworkers encounter persistent difficulties in achieving "awareness" [1] of coworkers' emotions, situations and workplace atmosphere from the remote location [2]. Pirola-Merlo et al. [3] reported a significant positive correlation between an index of the team members' emotions (team climate) and team performance. If there are

The original version of this chapter was revised: The affiliation of authors 'Shinichi Fukasawa' and 'Hiroko Akatsu' was incorrect. The correction to this chapter is available at https://doi.org/10.1007/978-3-030-22660-2_48

S. Yamamoto and H. Mori (Eds.): HCII 2019, LNCS 11569, pp. 415–424, 2019.
https://doi.org/10.1007/978-3-030-22660-2_30

inherent barriers to awareness or comprehension of coworkers' emotions due to their remote environment, teleworkers will experience difficulties in team communication or collaboration. Such problems would limit the viability of widespread adoption of telework.

To address such potential drawbacks, technological advancements have been made toward real-time recognition of humans' physical and emotional states (situations). In particular, sensors such as cameras, microphones, and wearable devices have been used to recognize emotional states [4]. These emotion recognition technologies present an opportunity to solve the problem of awareness of others posed by telework. When audio-visual telecommunication systems can be employed in telework (e.g., conventional video conference systems or "Ultra-Realistic telework system" [5]), systems with emotion recognition capabilities may effectively facilitate awareness of remote coworkers' situations.

This study sought to examine factors related to the accuracy of emotion recognition via a technological solution. Recognition error generally occurs in stochastic recognition processing using sensor data. Thus, it is highly unlikely that recognition accuracy will reach 100% in the wild. Emotion recognition poses significant difficulty in achieving high recognition accuracy compared to mature recognition technologies. Speech recognition, for example, is currently able to achieve better than 90% accuracy. Meanwhile, the recognition accuracy of positive emotional "valence" [6] ranges from 60 to 70% [7]. If a teleworker is provided with emotion recognition information of their remote coworkers via telecommunication systems, but is aware of the low accuracy of this information, such information is likely to be disregarded due to its low reliability.

Despite the significant implications of such concerns very little research has examined the effectiveness of presenting accuracy information alongside recognition information. Dixon, Wickens, and McCarley [8] examined the influence of false alarms and misses of diagnostic automation, and reported that false alarm-prone automation hurt the overall performance of operators more than miss-prone automation. Nevertheless, their study did not examine "human" emotion recognition system, but rather a diagnostic automation "machine" system.

The purpose of this study was to examine the effectiveness of presenting emotion recognition information with added accuracy information to enhance awareness via audio-visual telecommunication systems. The evaluation experiment was designed to test the following hypotheses:

H1: Although the level of emotional transmission between remote audio-visual environments is lower than that found in direct F2F environments, presenting stochastic emotion recognition information improves the emotional transmission across remote audio-visual environments.

H2: The effectiveness of presenting stochastic emotion recognition information varies in response to presenting high or low recognition accuracy information.

2 Experiment

To summarize the experiment, participants were exposed to 4 environmental conditions: face-to-face (F2F), remote audio-visual environment without accuracy information (Remote-None), remote audio-visual environment with emotion recognition information and 70% accuracy information (Remote+70%), and the same with 90% accuracy information (Remote+90%). They observed an experimenter whose emotional valence state was induced to be pleasant, neutral, or unpleasant. Further, participants evaluated the valence emotion of the experimenter. Level of emotional transmission and observation time were compared across these 4 conditions.

Figure 1 depicts the configuration of the experimental environment, and Fig. 2 shows an experimental scene (details are described below).

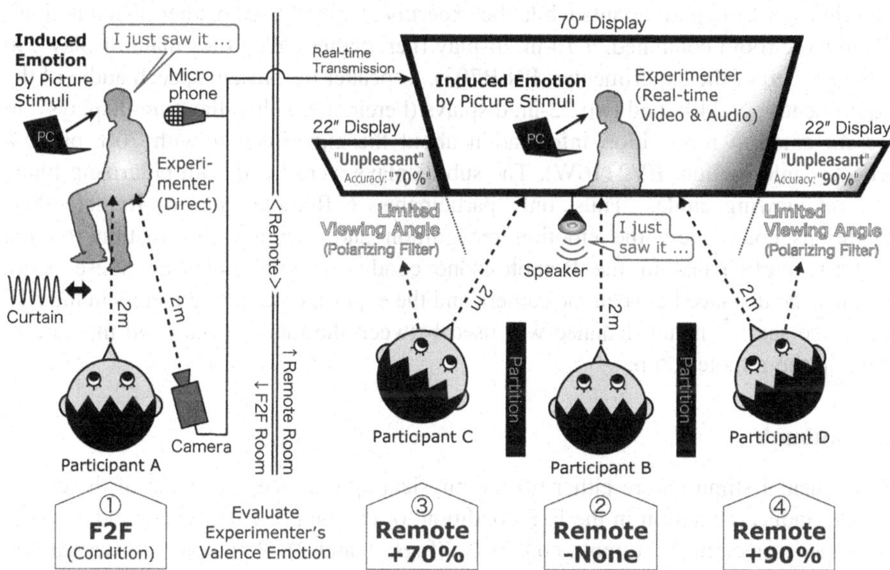

Fig. 1. Configuration of the experimental environment

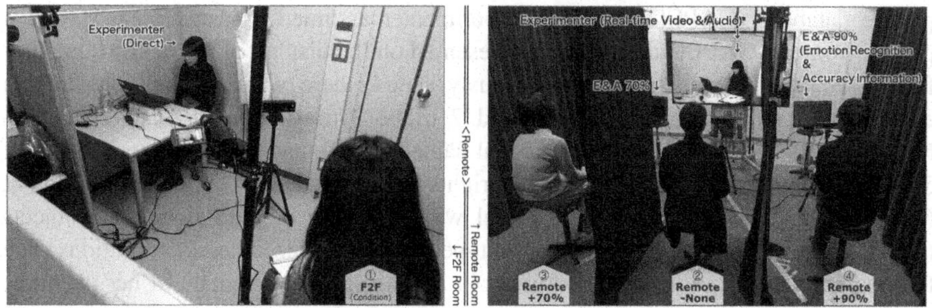

Fig. 2. Experimental scene

2.1 Participants

Sixteen Japanese undergraduate and graduate students (mean age ± SD: 22.3 ± 1.3 years; 9 males and 7 females) participated in this study after providing informed consent. All participants had normal vision (i.e., above 20/28) and hearing ability.

2.2 Experimental Environment

The experiment was carried out using two rooms (Figs. 1 and 2). One was the F2F room, where the participant was with an experimenter in the same space. By contrast, the other was the remote room, where 3 participants were presented real-time video and audio of the experimenter in the F2F room. In the F2F room, there was a camera (to transmit video of the experimenter; HDR-CX900), a microphone (to transmit speech audio of the experimenter; ECM-66B), a laptop computer (to induce the experimenter's emotion by presenting affective pictures; Dynabook R82) and a curtain (to conceal the experimenter from participants while the experimenter evaluated his/her own emotion). The remote room contained, a 70-in. display (hereinafter called the "main display"; to present video of the experimenter; PN-R703), a speaker (to present speech audio of the experimenter; X-240), and two 22-in. displays (hereinafter called the "sub-displays"; to present emotion recognition information about the experimenter with 70% or 90% accuracy information; EV2116W). The sub-displays were fitted with polarizing filters to limit viewing angles. Thus, only participants in Remote+70% or Remote+90% conditions could view the emotion recognition and accuracy information (on the contrary, participants in the Remote-None condition could not view these data). Because the distance between the camera and the experimenter was 2 meters in the F2F room, the same 2-meter distance was used between the main display and the participants in the remote room.

2.3 Stimuli

Experimental stimuli were either (a) the physical appearance and voice of the experimenter induced emotion in the F2F condition, or (b) the presented video and audio of the experimenter in the remote conditions (Figs. 1 and 2). Participants observed and evaluated the valence emotion of the experimenter.

The emotional state of the experimenter was induced to pleasant, neutral, or unpleasant through the presentation of affective pictures from the Geneva affective picture database (GAPED) [9]. The experimenter assumed a seated posture, and a picture from the GAPED database was presented on the display of the laptop computer for 45 seconds in each trial. As previously stated, there were 4 conditions in this experiment, and each condition included 7 trials: 3 trials with pleasant pictures—human babies (GAPED No. P035), animal babies (P114), and nature sceneries (P070); 3 trials with unpleasant pictures—human rights violations (H074), animal mistreatment (A075), and spiders (Sp136); and 1 trial with a neutral picture—inanimate objects (N061). The order of presentation of trial types was randomized across conditions. The two experimenters involved were a male in his thirties and a female in her twenties.

Participants' contact with experimenters was limited to prevent them from becoming acquainted. The order of observation and evaluation of components for the experimenters was counter-balanced across participants.

Additional experimental stimuli were emotion recognition and accuracy information on a sub-display during Remote+70% or Remote+90% conditions. The representation of the information was character strings: 3 forms of emotion recognition information ("Pleasant," "Neutral," or "Unpleasant"), and 2 levels of accuracy values ("Accuracy: 70%" or "Accuracy: 90%"). The emotion recognition information came in the form of existing valence rating of pictures from GAPED. Additionally, to produce accuracy of emotion recognition close to 70% or 90% in this experiment, we intentionally manipulated recognition error (e.g., presenting "Unpleasant" character string in the trial with pleasant picture). The produced ratio of error was 2 of the 7 trials.

2.4 Measurement

The level of emotional transmission, observation time, and level of referring to recognition information were measured.

The level of emotional transmission was defined as the response accuracy to 3 categories of valence emotion (pleasant, neutral, or unpleasant) by the participants with the experimenters. Participants evaluated the experimenter's valence emotion using the Self-Assessment Manikin (SAM) scale [10] (including a 9-point Likert scale between unpleasant and pleasant). The experimenter also evaluated his/her own valence emotion.

Observation time was the latency from the participant's initiation of observation (precise time of the opening of the curtain in the F2F room) to initiation of filling in the SAM scale. Observation time was analyzed by coding video of participants. However, because videos were recorded during only the second half of the experiment, the sample size of observation time was 7.

The level of referring to recognition information was rated on a 4-point Likert scale that ranged from "not at all" to "very much" referring to emotion recognition information.

The measurements above were averaged across male and female experimenters.

2.5 Procedure and Design

The experimenter concealed him/herself behind the curtain before the start of the experimental sessions. When each trial began, the experimenter's emotion was induced via presentation of a picture from GAPED. Concurrently, the curtain was opened, allowing participants to observe and evaluate the emotion of the experimenter. The experimenter viewed the GAPED picture, and repeated the spoken phrase "I just saw it." five times across the following 45-second period. Next, the curtain was closed (i.e., participants could not observe), and the experimenter evaluated his/her own emotion. After this evaluation, the experimenter was presented with the GAPED picture (inanimate objects, N091) for 15 seconds to induce a neutral emotion. Each participant was exposed to a total of 56 trials (7 trials $\times$ 4 conditions $\times$ 2 experimenters).

One-way repeated measures analysis of variance (ANOVA) was applied to the induced 3 valence emotion of the experimenters (pleasant, neutral, and unpleasant; within-subject factor) and 4 environmental conditions (F2F, Remote-None, Remote +70%, and Remote+90%; within-subject factor). The order of the 4 environmental conditions was counter-balanced across participants. When any significant main effect was found in the factors, parametric multiple comparisons were performed using the Bonferroni procedure. The level of statistical significance was set at 0.05.

3 Results

3.1 Verification of Emotion Induction of Experimenter

Figure 3 shows the SAM valence rating of the experimenters per 3 valence emotion. The main effect of the SAM valence rating was significant ($F_{(2,30)} = 966.11$, $p < 0.001$). Further multiple comparisons of SAM valence rating found significant differences ($p < 0.01$) between the 3 valence emotions (pleasant, neutral, and unpleasant). This indicates that we successfully induced the experimenters' emotions as intended using GAPED according to the described procedure.

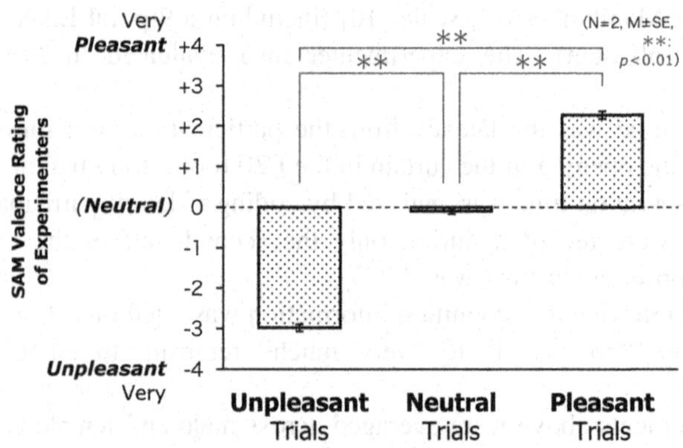

Fig. 3. Verification of emotion induction of experimenters

3.2 Level of Emotional Transmission

Figure 4 shows the level of emotional transmission across the 4 environmental conditions. The main effect of level of emotional transmission was significant ($F_{(3,45)} = 3.92$, $p = 0.014$). Further multiple comparisons (Bonferroni) found that level of emotional transmission in the Remote+70% condition was significantly higher than in the F2F, Remote-None, and Remote+90% conditions ($p = 0.047$, 0.049, and 0.039, respectively).

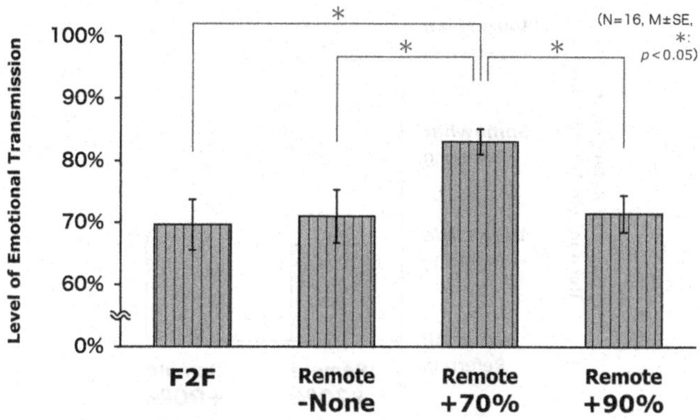

Fig. 4. Level of emotional transmission

3.3 Observation Time

Figure 5 shows observation times according to environmental conditions (except for F2F, because no such data were collected). The main effect of observation time was significant ($F_{(2,12)} = 5.36$, $p = 0.022$). Further multiple comparisons (Bonferroni) found that observation time in the Remote+70% condition was significantly shorter than in the Remote-None condition ($p = 0.022$).

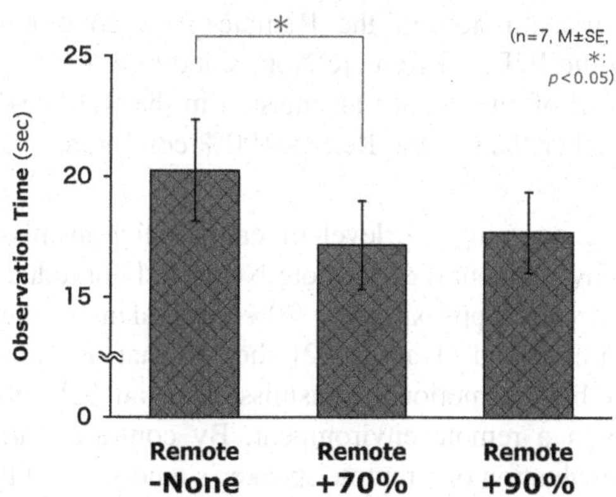

Fig. 5. Observation time

3.4 Level of Referring to Recognition Information

Figure 6 shows the level of referring to recognition information across environmental conditions (except for F2F and Remote-None, because no such data were collected). Two-sided Student's t-test of level of referring to recognition information found no significant difference between Remote+70% and Remote+90% conditions ($t_{(15)} = 1.31$, $p = 0.210$).

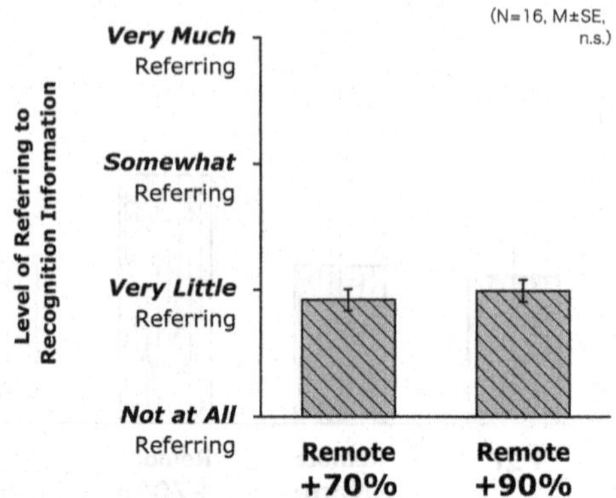

Fig. 6. Level of referring to recognition information

4 Discussion

The purpose of this study was to examine the effectiveness of presenting emotion recognition information with added accuracy information to enhance awareness (emotional transmission) facilitated by an audio-visual telecommunication system. The results of this experiment provided support for the previously stated hypotheses.

H1: Partially supported. Although level of emotional transmission showed no significant difference between in the F2F and Remote-None conditions, the level of emotional transmission in the Remote+70% condition was significantly higher than in the F2F and Remote-None conditions.

H2: Supported. Level of emotional transmission in the Remote+70% condition was significantly higher than in the Remote+90% condition.

First, the results concerning the level of emotional transmission showed that a remote audio-visual environment (i.e., Remote-None) did not reduce level of emotional transmission. Degrees were approximately 70% equivalent in the F2F and Remote-None conditions. Arimoto and Okanoya [2] showed that the number of participants who felt subjectively better emotional transmission in an F2F environment was significantly more than in a remote environment. By contrast, correlation coefficients between a listener's evaluation of a remote speaker's emotion and the remote speaker's self-evaluation of his/her emotion showed no significant difference. Hence, deficits in awareness of another person's emotion in remote environments seem to occur via "subjective" cognition troubles rather than objective reduction of transmission of emotion.

Second, the Remote+70% condition yielded levels of emotional transmission that were significantly higher than the Remote-None condition. On the other hand, the Remote+90% condition did not produce such improvement. This indicates that the effective improvement of emotional transmission requires more than simply presenting stochastic emotion recognition information; low accuracy of information is also necessary. In their interview immediately following the experiment, one participant commented, "I reminded myself to not rely too much on emotion recognition information in the Remote+70% condition, but did not attempt to do so in the Remote+90% condition." Another participant commented, "Because about one third of emotion recognition information was incorrect in Remote+70%, I rarely referred to the recognition information while evaluating the remote person in that condition." Thus, awareness of low-accuracy information is presumed to induce more attentive observational behavior because of attempts to precisely evaluate a person's emotion.

Observation data showed that presenting emotion recognition information could shorten the time spent evaluating emotion. Presenting emotion recognition information seemingly expedited judgments when evaluating emotion. However, as previously stated, we should consider that only the Remote+70% condition significantly improved level of emotional transmission. Consequently, presenting accuracy information as well as emotion recognition information effectively increases awareness performance. Namely, improved emotional transmission and decreased observation time can be predicted, especially in the case of low accuracy.

To gain further insights into the effectiveness of presenting accuracy information, additional researches needed to address several limitations of this study. First, the measurements employed in this study require refinement. For instance, added gaze-tracking data could provide clarity for understanding how the recipient of information prioritizes various forms of information, such as emotion recognition information, accuracy information, and the physical appearance of a remote person on video. Moreover, concentration on presented information, as estimated by electroencephalogram or pupillary reaction, would provide additional meaningful data. Another limitation is the influence of representation of presented information, including user interface design. Because we had considered this study a fundamental examination, we adopted character strings as the simplest representation of presenting information. Meanwhile, the influence of richer representations such as graphical charts, avatar-like agents, or communication-robots has not been investigated. For example, such a communication-robot can express gestures representing uncertainty in cases of low accuracy of recognition. Finally, the range of emotion types used presents a limitation to the generalizability of our findings. We placed an emphasis on examining "valence" emotion in this study due to perceived ease of application to business settings. However, additional examination is needed to assess whether similar effectiveness is found with respect to other emotions such as arousal, the six basic emotions [11], and complex emotions.

5 Conclusion

We examined the effectiveness of presenting emotion recognition information along with accuracy information to enhance awareness when using audio-visual telecommunication systems. Effectiveness was compared between 4 environmental conditions (F2F, Remote-None, Remote+70%, and Remote+90%). Consequently, level of emotional transmission was significantly higher in the Remote+70% condition than in any other condition. Furthermore, observation time was significantly shorter in the Remote +70% than in the Remote-None condition. Honestly disclosing and presenting accuracy data of recognition functions or technologies could enhance human awareness performance with respect to evaluating a remote person's emotion. This is particularly true in the case of low-accuracy information. This study showed the effectiveness of presenting accuracy information as well as emotion recognition information in addition to audio-visual information of a remote person. These findings will contribute to improving telecommunication systems for teleworkers.

References

1. Greenberg, S., Gutwin, C., Cockburn, A.: Awareness through fisheye views in relaxed-WYSIWIS groupware. In: Proceedings GI 1996, pp. 21–24 (1996)
2. Arimoto, Y., Okanoya, K.: Comparison of emotional understanding in modality-controlled environments using multimodal online emotional communication corpus. In: Proceedings LREC 2016, pp. 2162–2167 (2016)
3. Pirola-Merlo, A., et al.: How leaders influence the impact of affective events on team climate and performance in R&D teams. Leadersh. Quart. **13**(5), 561–581 (2002)
4. Picard, R.W.: Affective Computing. MIT Press, Cambridge (1997)
5. Kuno, Y.: OKI's R&D through Industry-government-academia collaboration. OKI Tech. Rev. **84**(1), 1–4 (2017)
6. Russell, J.A.: A circumplex model of affect. J. Pers. Soc. Psychol. **39**(6), 1161–1178 (1980)
7. Valstar, M., et al.: Depression, mood, and emotion recognition workshop and challenge. In: Proceedings AVEC 2016, pp. 3–10 (2016)
8. Dixon, S.R., Wickens, C.D., McCarley, J.S.: On the independence of compliance and reliance: are automation false alarms worse than misses? Hum. Factors **49**(4), 564–572 (2007)
9. Dan-Glauser, E.S., Scherer, K.R.: The Geneva affective picture database (GAPED): a new 730-picture database focusing on valence and normative significance. Behav. Res. Methods **43**, 268–277 (2011)
10. Bradley, M.M., Lang, P.J.: Measuring emotion: the self-assessment manikin and the semantic differential. J. Behav. Ther. Exp. Psychiatry **25**(1), 49–59 (1994)
11. Ekman, P.: Basic emotions. In: Dalgleish, T., Power, M.J. (eds.) Handbook of Cognition and Emotion, pp. 45–60. Wiley, New York (1999)

Approach for Communication Design for Motivation to Health Behavior

Shigeyoshi Iizuka[1(✉)], Takanori Takebe[2], Shozo Nishii[2], and Asuka Kodaka[2]

[1] Kanagawa University, Tsuchiya 2946, Hiratsuka, Kanagawa 239-1293, Japan
iizuka@kanagawa-u.ac.jp

[2] Communication Design Center, Yokohama City University, Fukuura 3-9, Kanazawa-ku, Yokohama, Kanagawa 236-0004, Japan

Abstract. It is well known that the implementation of physical activity/exercise is extremely important in preventing diseases and maintaining and promoting physical and psychological health. Therefore, we thought to realize a communication design that integrates medical care and communication and makes people actively want to behave, or behave unconsciously, so that they will become healthy. "AD-MED" is a new academic system aiming at solving various medical problems from the viewpoint of consumers by studying "communication" that realizes Behavior Change of people by incorporating an advertising viewpoint that is easy to understand and that affects people, such as design and copywriting. As part of this, the authors carried out the "Shoes Want to Walk" tour. This is an effort to realize enjoyment in the health behavior "walking" enjoyment by applying gimmicks on the walking path and moving forward while clearing them. As a result, it was found that quizzes and mail instructions during walking induced pleasure, but that alone was insufficient, and further motivational elements were needed.

Keywords: Communication design · Health behavior · Behavior modification

1 Introduction

It is well known that the implementation of physical activity/exercise is extremely important in preventing diseases and maintaining and promoting physical and psychological health. It is meaningful for individuals to voluntarily and continuously engage in health maintenance activities not only for their own good but also for society as a whole. It is impossible for people who are indifferent to health behaviors to suddenly perform health actions unless there is a strong impact. Therefore, behavioral science is cited as a prior study. Behavioral science is the science that studies human behavior scientifically and elucidates its rules. Attempts are also being made in the "Mibyou" to maintain a non-sick condition, but effective measures have yet to be realized. This is a concept to prevent lifestyle conversion and to prevent it in advance before being violated by serious diseases. In the medical system so far, there has been a premise that "it becomes the target of intervention for the first time in the midst of illness." There are many studies on the treatment of disease itself, but there is not much

S. Yamamoto and H. Mori (Eds.): HCII 2019, LNCS 11569, pp. 425–436, 2019.
https://doi.org/10.1007/978-3-030-22660-2_31

research activity aimed at urging improvement of lifestyle of the consumer for prevention. Therefore, we thought to realize a communication design that integrates medical care and communication and makes people actively want to behave, or behave unconsciously, so that they become healthy. We are working on "AD-MED [1]," which naturally motivates health behavior while incorporating an advertisement viewpoint into the communication design method. We conducted a walking tour that utilized "Shoes that want to walk" as an effort to be carried out while enjoying the health behavior of "walking." In this paper, we introduce our preceding efforts of "AD-MED" and show the contents and results of the "Shoes that want to walk" tour.

2 Preceding Efforts for Health Behavior

Conventional medical research has aimed to establish a coping method (treatment) for diseases and symptoms. Meanwhile, nowadays, entities dealing with medical and health information are rapidly shifting to the general public, and the importance of activities to communicate with people before the disease, so to speak—the so-called lifestyle—is increasing.

To change people's lifestyle, it is necessary to change their behavior. In addition, to persistently induce people's health behavior, it is important to design measures based on human characteristics. Therefore, we focused on the concept of "advertisement." People's behavior is often decided based on sensibility/instantaneous judgment rather than rational judgment. To that end, it is important to communicate in accordance with various target attributes from the perspective of ordinary people in sustainable induction of people's health behavior. We thought that the points of policy design accumulated empirically in the advertising industry provided an extremely effective viewpoint even for the purpose of actually guiding people to health. In other words, advertisement was aimed at bringing attractive messages and visuals to actual actions. When people see and listen to them, they evoke the spontaneous feeling of "Want to do ~." For example, it can be thought that applying this to "lifestyle" and considering "how to change lifestyle habits" should be a clue for a solution.

"AD-MED" is a new academic system aimed at solving various medical problems from the viewpoint of consumers by studying "communication" that realizes Behavior Change of people living by incorporating an advertising viewpoint that is easy to understand and that affects people, such as design and copywriting. In other words, it is a design system that naturally produces healthy behavior from the viewpoint of the consumer by trying "communication," making use of the advertisement's creativity.

Until now, in collaboration with municipalities, mainly in Yokohama City, various social experiment-type projects and product development in parallel with several related companies have been conducted. Some specific cases from idea of AD-MED are below.

(1) Kokoromachi Project
The waiting time at the hospital is long and boring. "Have a fun time at the hospital so that it will soon pass away." This is a project born from such thought. In collaboration with young creators of the design office aiming to change the time spent in the hospital

to "Kokoromachi Time [2]," 5 projects involving space (Fig. 1), graphic, and web design were conducted.

Also, in this project, a questionnaire was conducted including general question items on hospitals. Figure 2 shows the evaluation of this project (even if you choose what you think is good). This project was also carried out from December 10 to 26, 2018, by changing the content (plans) (at Yokohama City University Hospital 2F lobby).

(2) Stairs that you want to climb
In response to a request from the Yokohama City Health and Welfare Bureau, we conducted a health staircase project to encourage daily light exercise by choosing the stairs from January 20 to March in 2015. In this project, by changing from the conventional viewpoint of serious health information presentation, and decorating like an advertisement, a mechanism to climb the stairs while enjoying it was constructed (Fig. 3). Since the installation station was Kanazawa Hakkei Station of Keihin Electric Railway Company, we adopted a design that took advantage of the location near Hakkeijima Sea Paradise and increased the affinity with the place and the mood. As a result, more than 20% (Total 4,000 people/month) selected the staircase rather than the escalator.

(3) ALERT PANTS
In collaboration with the Yokohama City corporate health insurance association and others, we developed "ALERT PANTS" (Fig. 4), a product that is beneficial to the health promotion of workers working for SMEs. These pants can "manage health every day only" with the function of changing the color when the waist perimeter exceeds 85 cm. It is a product that promotes dieting in users by alerting the user to metabolic changes. They become yellow, which is an attention-drawing color.

(4) Reduced-salt project
Overdose of salt, which is common in Japan, hurts the blood vessels and leads to stroke and heart disease. Based on this background, we carried out a salt-reduction experiment at a company employee cafeteria with the aim of being conscious of the amount of salt consumed in everyday living. Utilizing various touchpoints on the flow lines of people in the dining room, we made attractive awareness items that bring out changes in eating behavior using posters (Fig. 5), POP, and so on. As a result, salt intake per day was reduced by 10% or more.

In addition to these, as an example of achieving behavior change of consumers through introduction of measures to the community, there is the "Smile Matsuyama Project," which realized the health score of residents on the application platform of the area.

In this way, behavior patterns are influenced by daily living spaces through design at contact points with various surrounding environments in everyday spaces. By extrapolating these concepts and conducting experiments extensively, we believe that we can cover not only information design but also products, infrastructure/space design, education, and so on as well.

Kokoromachair

Art photo on the back of the chair. A photo gallery that can be healed and enjoyed just by sitting.

Kokoromachi Tree

Patient-participating art Christmas tree created with stickers and messages

Kokoromachi Lounge

Refurbished on the 1st floor interior with interior decorating the forest, more relaxing space

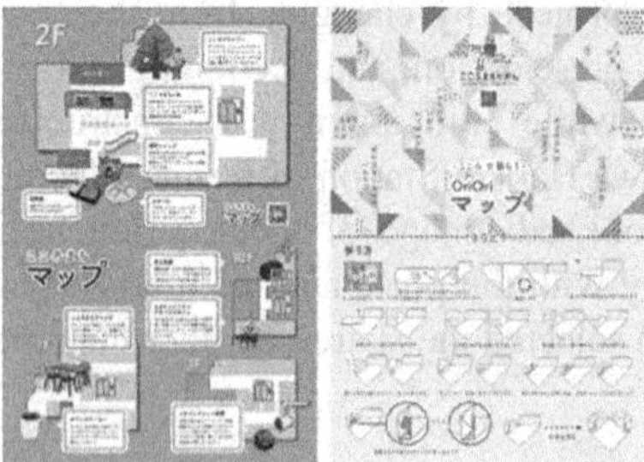

Kokoromachi Map

Brochure of map form for introduction of this project

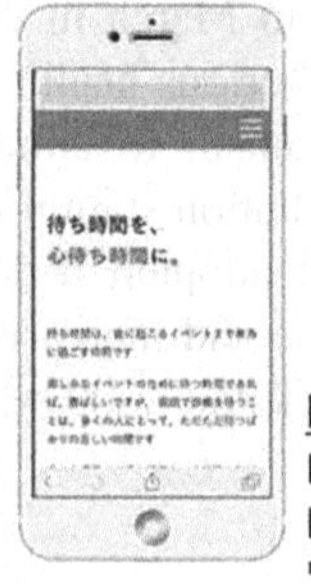

Kokoromachi Web

Dedicated information linked with "Kokoromachi Map" on dedicated website

Fig. 1. Kokoromachi project

Which plan was good?

N=161

(Multiple answers included)

Plan	Count
Kokoromachi Tree	24
KokoromaChair	15
Kokoromachi Map	11
Kokoromachi Lounge	6
Kokoromachi Web	2

Fig. 2. Questionnaire result of Kokoromachi project

Fig. 3. Stairs that you want to climb

Fig. 4. ALERT PANTS

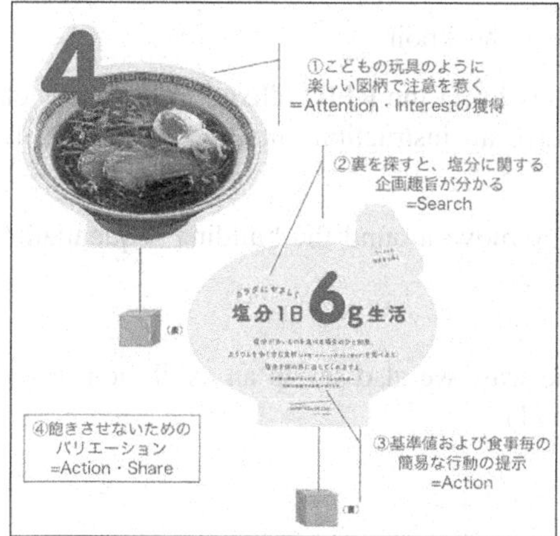

Fig. 5. Poster of reduced salt-induction package

3 "Shoes that Want to Walk" Tour

The "Shoes that want to walk" tour is an attempt to promote "walking," which is a healthy behavior, by setting incentives to "want to walk" with one project of AD-MED. This chapter shows the method and results of this tour.

3.1 Method

This tour was held in a building inside the Yokohama City University Kanazawa Hakkei Campus on February 13, 2018 (Fig. 6).

Nineteen men and women in their 20s to 40s participated. Some groups of 3 to 4 people were formed and took a group tour. One group had a tablet for receiving emails as necessary during the tour. In addition, the RFID for this tour was pasted one of the shoes in the group (Fig. 7).

Regarding participants in this effort, after enough information was given regarding the purpose and expected effect of the study, the presence or absence of disadvantage incurred by the participants, protection of privacy, and so on, the participants gave written consent. Only those studied are subject to research. A rough circling story is shown below.

1. Departure
   - On the tablet, participants receive an instruction email for the first checkpoint.
2. Checkpoint passing
   - Shoes (RFID) are near the installed receiver (Figs. 8 and 9).
   - Participants receive an email with a quiz (instructions on how to solve) on the tablet.
3. Search the panel (correct answer of the quiz) while climbing the stairs (Fig. 10)
   - On the tablet, participants receive an instruction email for the first checkpoint.
4. Pass through the next checkpoint
   - Again, participants bring the RFID affixed to the shoes close to the receiver.
   - Participants receive an instruction email (code to be solved after this) on the tablet.
5. (Even after this, they move around the building sequentially, solving quizzes and following commands.)
6. Goal

As an accent on the way, we also set up an exhibition (experience) section of the new technology[1] (Fig. 11).

[1] A mirror display system "Mirrorge" that is compatible with AGC's bright mirror image of the same level as ordinary mirrors and high visibility quality. Provide a new expression by Augmented reality.

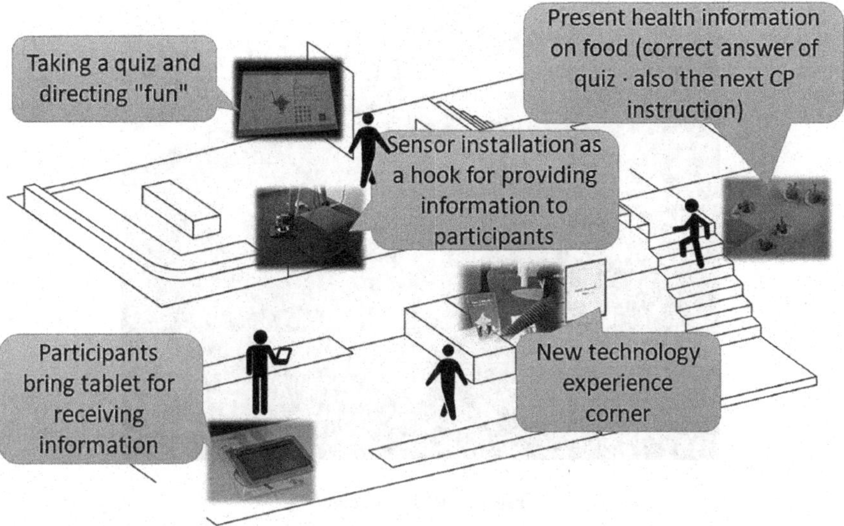

Fig. 6. Overall image of "Shoes that want to walk" tour

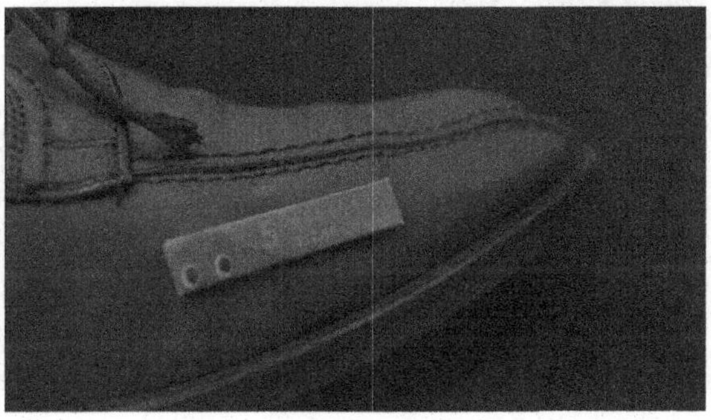

Fig. 7. RFID attached to shoe

3.2 Result

We conducted a questionnaire to let participants of the tour described in the previous section give their impressions and so on later. A Google Form was used to present actual question items and was the mechanism of data collection. As a result, 14 out of 19 participants responded.

Below, the results are shown with 14 people as a population.

First, sensuous (participant's own subjective) time and fatigue are shown. As shown in the upper graph of Fig. 12, in response to the question "How long did you feel like walking," more than half of the participants answered, "30 min." This is a value close to the real walking time on the actual tour (of course, the required time is different for each group). In addition, it seems that most of the respondents did not feel

Fig. 8. RFID receiver

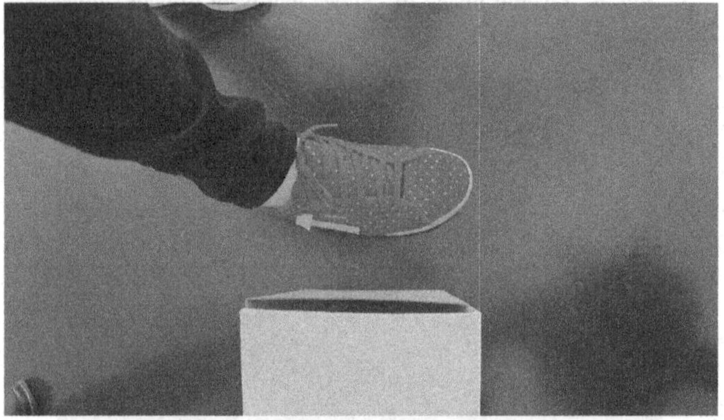

Fig. 9. The shoe (RFID) is approaching to the receiver

the required time was long or short (middle graph in Fig. 12), and most of the respondents did not feel fatigue, as shown in the lower graph in Fig. 12. Prior to the tour, we were hoping that "the sensory time would be shorter than the actual time (i.e., I walked better than I thought/I did not get tired)," but, as expected, no results were obtained. On the other hand, we also asked about participants' usual exercise frequency, but this also did not relate to sensory time and feeling of fatigue.

Additionally, "To advance while doing a quiz," "To go forward while receiving instructions with e-mail," "To act together with group (multiple people)," and "Interaction with Yotchy[2]" were cited in response to the question "What kind of place was fun?" (Fig. 13).

[2] Character of Yokohama City University.

Fig. 10. Panels attached to the walls of the stairs

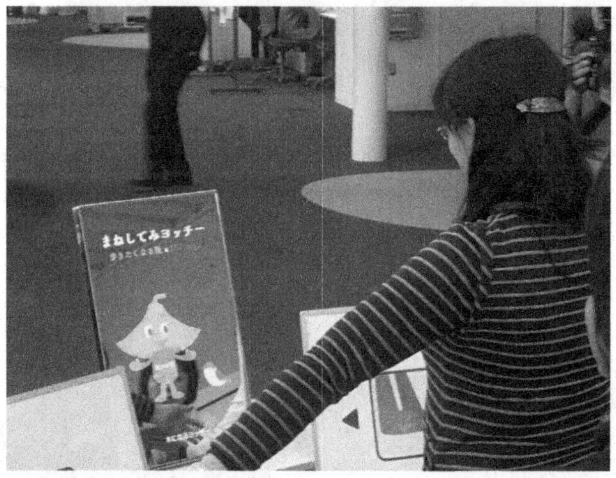

Fig. 11. Technology exhibition (Experience) corner

For these reasons, factors such as "taking quizzes" and "while receiving instructions via email" that were incorporated into this tour may be factors that add pleasure to walking, which is about 30 min long. Since fatigue was not a major factor, it can be said that this attempt was generally good. However, further motivation is still needed before reaching the stage of having the impression "I walked better/than I thought/I did not get tired" (it got the expected result).

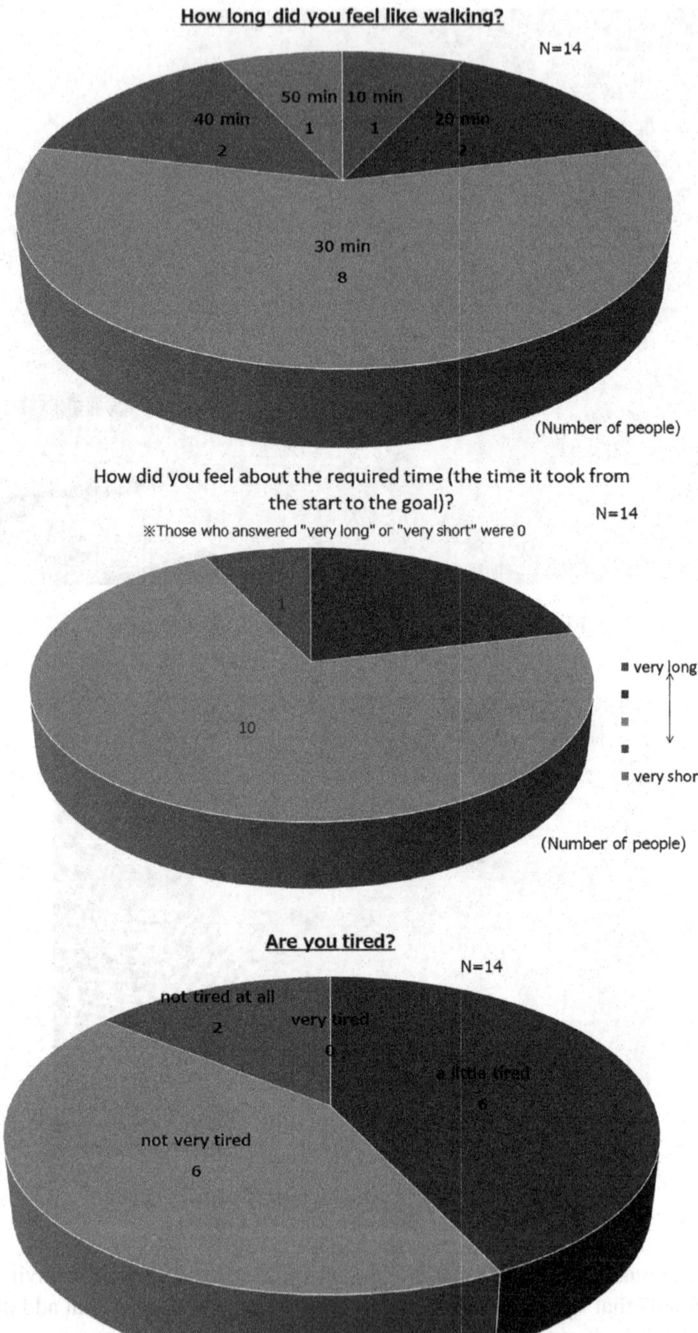

Fig. 12. Results on sensory time and fatigue

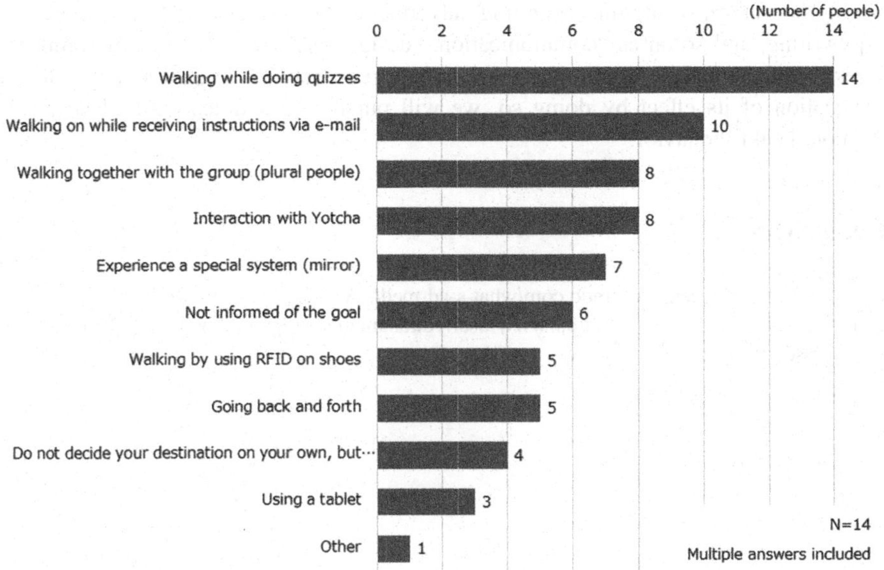

Fig. 13. Results on fun things

4 Conclusion

We have studied "communication" that realizes behavior changes in how people live by incorporating advertising viewpoints that are easy to understand, such as design and copywriting, which affect people. Various studies are conducted from the viewpoint of consumers, and we are working on "AD-MED," which is a new academic system aimed at solving medical problems. For the prevention and treatment of many chronic diseases, including lifestyle diseases, it is important to take and maintain actions that people regard as good for health. In addition, we must correct behavior that is considered bad for health and maintain that as well. Changing and maintaining both will lead to health. As part of that, we took a tour of "shoes that wanted to walk," traveling through the buildings on the university campus. This is an effort to realize a healthy behavior of walking by enjoying while applying some gimmicks in the walking path and progressing while clearing them. As a result, it was found that quizzes and email instructions during walking induced pleasure in walking, but that alone was insufficient, and motivational elements were further needed. This is a one-shot initiative, but the original behavioral change, as described above, "to transform and maintain behavior" is important. Factors such as "enjoyment," "familiarity," and "succession" are indispensable for behavior change and its sustenance.

In the future, while incorporating advertising viewpoints such as art, design, copywriting, and so on as "communication," designing personal living environments, items, services, and so on from a more human perspective and proceeding with the verification of its effect by doing so, we will pursue communication and design to promote health behavior.

References

1. AD-MED. https://admed.jimdo.com/what-s-ad-med/. Accessed 01 Feb 2019
2. Kokoromachi Time. http://www-user.yokohama-cu.ac.jp/~admed/cocoromachi-time/. Accessed 01 Feb 2019

New Habits to Increase 5 Times the Annual Chocolate Consumption of Japan

Kaori Kawasaki[1(✉)] and Yumi Asahi[2]

[1] School of Information and Telecommunication Engineering, Course of Information Telecommunication Engineering, Tokai University, Tokyo, Japan
5bjm2215@mail.u-tokai.ac.jp

[2] School of Information and Telecommunication Engineering, Department of Management System Engineering, Tokai University, Tokyo, Japan
asahi@tsc.u-tokai.ac.jp

Abstract. Chocolate has been used as a fatigue recovery and energy source as a food having various effects not only from luxury items but also from the nutrition side in the past history. In recent years, studies of ingredients contained in cacao have progressed, and excellent physiological functions of antioxidant polyphenols and other ingredients have been revealed to be useful for health. However, the annual consumption of chocolate in Japan is only about 2 kg, which is about one fifth as large as the top three countries. In this research we consider a strategy to fill this gap of one fifth. In this research, attention was paid to students (university students/graduate students), and in this research, chocolate products of a confectionery company A, which provided data for analysis, we aim to increase in the sales volume consumed by students five-fold. Using the WEB quantitative survey conducted in June 2013 (raw data), we analyzed the two points of students' 'good image for chocolate' and 'information source for chocolate', by using the correspondence analysis method. The analysis of the 'good image for chocolate' is plotted near the university students, in respect to the college student, and the category 'easy to carry • suitable for distribution' is plotted in the vicinity and 'a substitute for meal' was plotted in the vicinity of the category of graduate students. In addition, the analysis result of 'information source for chocolate' shows that categories such as 'Reputation', 'SNS', 'video sites' are plotted in the vicinity of 'college students' and near 'graduate students' are 'Advertisement', 'Radio CMs' plotted. From the above results, we set up three hypotheses; place importance on friendship compared to other occupations, graduate students live such a busy student life that they save meal time, and students tend to dislike physical advertisements which are conveyed with letters, that is, they prefer digital information and auditory information. Based on the above analysis results and hypothesis, we developed a product of tablet type chocolate (10 capsules) referring to 'a Bottle type package of a breath-care product of A company', and appointed YouTubers as a video advertisement medium. The amount of contents of the product advertised is 27.4 g, and if one package can be consumed, per day, the goal of increasing the annual consumption by five-fold can be achieved. Moreover, by advertising on YouTube, it is possible to reduce advertising expenses, and that you can draw interest of students through the effect of YouTubers popular among students. If we provide rental service of tablet type chocolate replacement servers and

S. Yamamoto and H. Mori (Eds.): HCII 2019, LNCS 11569, pp. 437–448, 2019.
https://doi.org/10.1007/978-3-030-22660-2_32

increase the number of variations of bottle type chocolate, as an increasing sales promotion plan, we can promote the habit of eating chocolate every day without ending the proposed product with a temporary trend. Since it is a problem that there is an idea which incurs expenses in the promotion plan, we need to carry out the sales promotion plan step by step. Then, even if the sales target is not reached, the deficit can be minimized by stopping the product development. In this way, we aim to increase the Japanese chocolate consumption by 5 times from a long-term perspective.

Keywords: Chocolate · Marketing · Correspondence analysis · New product proposals · Strategy for selling

1 Introduction

Japan's chocolate annual consumption is 2.0 kg for 11.7 kg: chocolate annual consumption of the top country, Germany, and Japan's chocolate consumption has about 5 times as much gap as that of the top two countries [1]. Therefore, Japan's chocolate consumption can potentially be increased five-fold.

In Japan, however, there has already been a market size of about 495 billion yen until now, so it is not easy to catch up with the consumption of those country. Therefore, it is necessary to think about strategies to create new markets and customs that have not existed so far (Fig. 1).

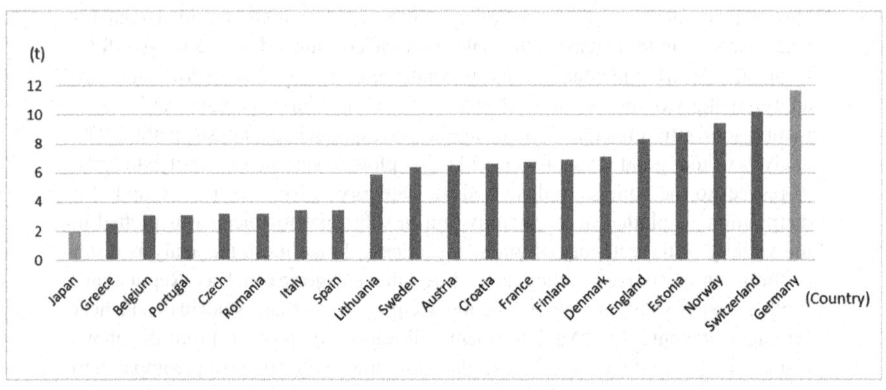

Fig. 1. Annual per capita consumption of chocolate (2015) [1]

Also, looking at the amount per sexual age purchaser, the purchase amount of chocolate for men and women aged 15 to 24 including students is small. Therefore, in this research, we focus on 'students' and consider proposals to make students' consumption of chocolate five times. Based on the questionnaire data from a Japanese confectionery company, we will offer a proposal reflecting the student's awareness by confirming the characteristics of the students. For this aim, we will analyze the student's 'image for chocolate' and 'information source for chocolate' to carry out the process (Fig. 2).

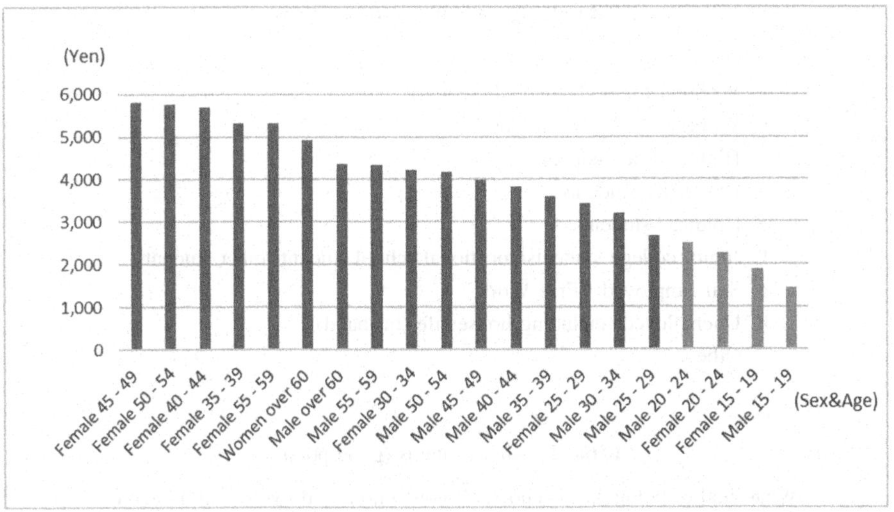

Fig. 2. Amount of one purchaser by sex and age (2017/4/1–2018/3/31)

2 Outline of Usage Data

In this research, we use data from a Japanese confectionery company. The outline is as follows.

Period: Executed in 2018 June

Target: 18 to 69 years old men and women (1030 people), including students (university students/graduate students)

Details: WEB Quantitative Survey (Low Data)

Consumer purchase history data (sexual age/annual purchase amount/period: April 1, 2017 to March 31, 2018 (graph of basic aggregation)),

Data format: Category data

The questionnaire items used in the analysis of this research are "What kind of point of chocolate confection do you think is good? Please choose all that apply", "Please select all that apply as information sources for you to know and buy chocolate confectionery" and "Please select your occupation". Details of answer items are described in the tables below (Tables 1, 2 and 3).

3 Analysis Result

3.1 Analytical Method

The analysis contents of this research are described. We aimed to grasp student values by correspondence analysis. Based on the questionnaire data from a Japanese confectionery company, we grasp the characteristics of students by clarifying the relationships between students and "chocolate image" and "information source for

Table 1. Answer items (occupations)

Occupation	
a	Working for (Full time • Dispatch)
b	Working for (part-time job)
c	High school students
d	University students
e	Graduate students
f	Junior college students/vocational school students/other students
g	Self Employed • Free Work
h	Unemployed (including housewife (husband))
i	Others

Table 2. Answer items (good points)

What kind of points in the chocolate confectionery do you think is good? and please choose all applicable items respectively			
1	Fill the small belly	11	I can eat easily
2	Instead of meals	12	Mouth lonesomity is distracted
3	Stress relief	13	Suitable for single serving
4	Relax	14	Suitable for distribution
5	Change of pace	15	Clue to communication
6	I can get rid of my brain fatigue	16	Can not get tired of it
7	Progress in my studies	17	The price is reasonable
8	In a happy mood	18	It fits well with alcohol
9	There is little sense of guilt	19	It fits tea etc.
10	Good for health and beauty	20	Easy to carry

Table 3. Answer items (information sources)

Please select all that apply as information sources when you get to know or buy chocolate confectionery			
1	TV commercials	11	Free paper
2	TV programs	12	Store's departments
3	Radio CMs	13	Store's advertisements
4	Radio programs	14	Reputation
5	Newspaper articles	15	Maker's homepage
6	Newspaper advertisements	16	SNS
7	Magazine articles	17	Video sites
8	Magazine advertising	18	Blog etc.
9	Train advertisement signboards	19	Not in particular
10	Advertisements of the Internet		

chocolate" to the two points. Correspondence analysis is one of the methods to quantify qualitative data without external standards and is an analytical method for mapping row variables and column variables together and exploring their positions and their relationships (positioning). That is, similarity and correlation between categories (items) can be visually grasped. Strong related categories are nearby, weak categories are located far away.

3.2 Analysis Result: Occupation – Good Point of Chocolate Relations

First of all, we will describe the analysis result of correspondence analysis 'good image for student's chocolate'. Input variables are 'Occupation' in the line variable, 'Question item' in the column variable; what kind of points in the chocolate confectionery do you think is good? and please choose all applicable items respectively. Details of the input variables are described in the following table.

Analysis results; it was read that '20: Easy to carry' and '14: Suitable for distribution' are plotted near 'd: College students', meal replacement category near the 'e: Graduate students' (Fig. 3).

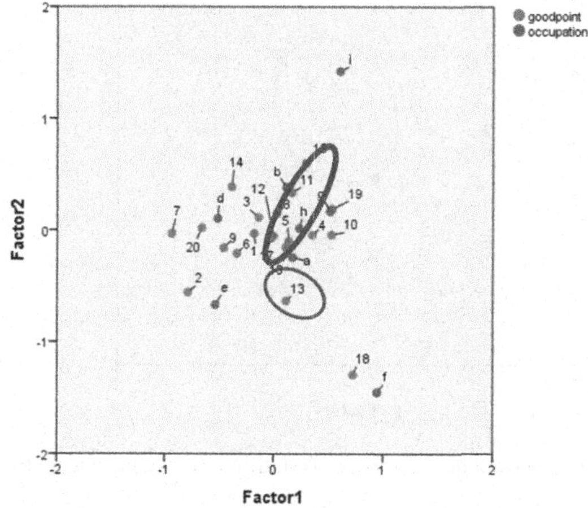

Fig. 3. Result of correspondence analysis (relations between occupations and good points of chocolate)

We thought of the images associated with these analysis results and hypotheses based on them. From the results of college students '20: Easy to carry', '14: Suitable for distribution' embraced the image that it is hard to melt, small package, small quantity, many (quantity more than quality) and easy to put in and out. Also, as a result of graduate students '2: Instead of meal', we received the impression that they think it is nutritious, it is filling, it has a variety of kinds, it is easy to eat in a hurry and it does not stain their hands.

Therefore 'college students place importance on friendships, compared to people in other occupations', 'graduate students live such a busy student life that they often omit their meal time'.

3.3 Analysis Result: Occupation – Information Source

First, we will describe the analysis result of correspondence source for students' chocolate in correspondence analysis. The input variables are "Occupation" in the row variable, "Question item" in the column variable; Please select all that apply as information sources when you get to know or buy chocolate confectionery. Details of the input variables are described in the following table.

Analysis results are categorized as '14: Reputation', '16: SNS', '17: Video sites' near the college student, '10: Advertisements of the Internet', '3: Radio CMs' near the graduate student (Fig. 4).

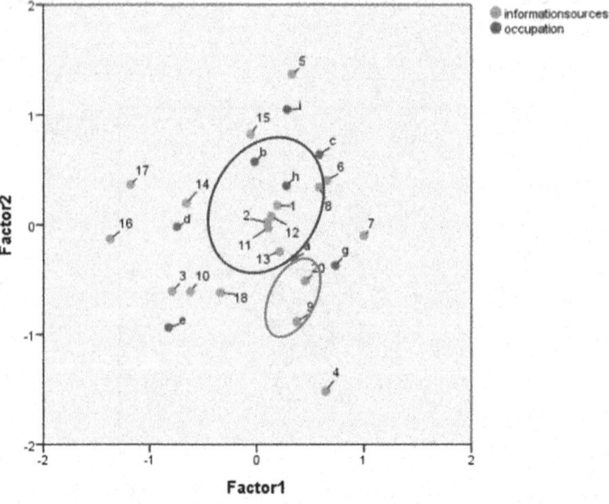

Fig. 4. Result of correspondence analysis (relations between occupations and information source)

Based on the above analysis results, we made a hypothesis that students tend to dislike analog advertisements conveyed by letters, but they rather like digital information and auditory information.

4 Proposal Based on Analysis Results

4.1 Suggested Items

The purpose of this research is 'to think about suggestions to make students' consumption of chocolate 5 times.' In order to achieve that purpose, we focused on a confectionery company (hereinafter referred to as Company A) that provided data and proposed an idea that 'Company A's chocolate products would increase sales volume consumed by students 5 times.' Based on the analysis result and hypothesis described in the above 3, we devise an item that makes use of know-how of Company A.

Packages of Company A's existing chocolate products were found in many types of bags and boxes. Therefore, we thought that we wanted to make a new package type of chocolate, reflecting the results of 'easy to carry' and 'suitable for distribution' which are the reasons for the students of the correspondence analysis results to choose chocolate.

Therefore, the product proposed in this research is tablet type chocolate with reference to 'a bottle type package' of Company A's product, a breath care product. The reason for suggesting this product is that a tablet type chocolate in the bottle package is a new form which has not been found in Company A so far, therefore we thought it was possible that since Company A had acquired the method of manufacturing a bottle type package, the new product would be manufactured at low cost.

4.2 Specific Proposal on the Proposed Package for Goods

As a concrete proposal, we propose a cylinder size ($1.4 \times 1.4 \times 3.14 \times 10 = 61.544$ cm^3) of about 61.5 cm^3 in volume with a bottom diameter of 2.8 cm and a height of 10 cm. And the content of the tablet type chocolate is 27.4 g in total, and 10 pieces of chocolate of 6.1544 cm^3 size ($1.4 \times 1.4 \times 3.14$) are included.

The reason for setting the content amount to 27.4 g will be described. In order to achieve the goal of 'making annual consumption 5 times: 10 kg,' it is necessary to consume 27.4 g per person per day. Therefore, the content of this product must be 27.4 g which is the target consumption amount per day. The reason for deciding the volume to make the content amount to 27.4 g to be about 61.5 cm^3 is because the size of the box package of about 50 g of commercially available board chocolate in Japan is about 123 cm^3. Therefore, it could be made to contents amount close to the target consumption amount of the day by making it half (about 61.5 cm^3).

If one person can consume one suggested item per day, it will be possible to achieve the goal of '5 - fold annual consumption of 10 kg' (Fig. 5).

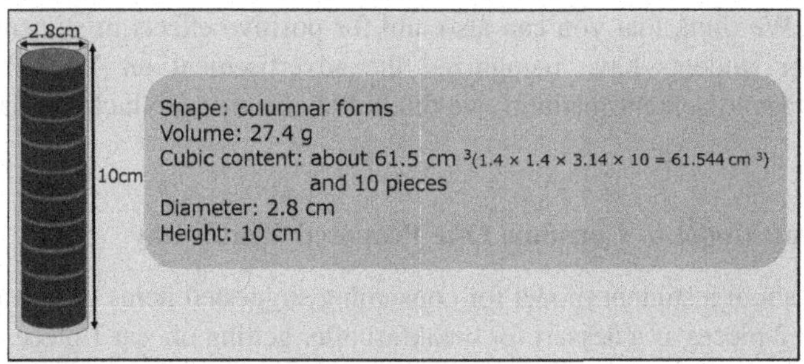

Fig. 5. Specific proposal on the proposed package for goods

4.3 PR Method for Selling Proposal Products

We suggest PR method for selling proposal products, reflecting both analysis results of correspondence analysis of students: '14: Reputation', '16: SNS', '17: Video sites', '10: Advertisements of the Internet', '3: Radio CMs', which are information sources about chocolate for students and student characteristics.

Based on the analysis results, we made a hypothesis that students tend to dislike analog advertisements conveyed by letters, but they rather like digital information and auditory information. As a recent trend, 'YouTubers' have become popular and students feel them closer than TV personalities active on television [2, 3].

From the above, as a PR method of products combining this hypothesis and recent student characteristics, we propose that 'YouTubers are appointed as advertisement talents, making use of YouTube video advertisement as advertising medium.' Next, we will write about details of the PR method of products and its effect.

For example, let's say that you put advertisement content on YouTube with YouTuber A's 'One day this one! We eat this way' and closely attached to how to eat 10 chocolates per day. Three benefits can be obtained by advertising on YouTube in this method.

First, the advertisement posting fee on YouTube only occurs when the user takes a voluntary action 'to watch the ad for 30 s/watch the ad to the end/click on the advertisement'. Therefore, it means that advertisements will always stay in the user's eyes free of charge (although there is a possibility that skipping may be done 5 s after the advertisement flows). Secondly, it is possible to reduce unnecessary advertising expenses because it is possible to narrow down the number of users who are going to be advertised on YouTube to 'students' who are the target layers, rather than an unspecified number of users. Third, we think that it is expected to attracting users who did not know the product until now or were not instead in the consumption, because the advertisement always remains in the eyes of the user [4].

Also, from the sensitivity of students to fashion, we think that we can expect to spread the product by driving the consciousness that 'we will eat 10 chocolates per day, imitating YouTuber'. Furthermore, by multiplying 'popular YouTubers', 'catchphrases' and 'unusual advertisement contents', students can share conversation with friends at schools such as 'Have you been that ad which has recently flowed on YouTube?'. We think that you can also aim for positive effects in student life etc.

And after students have recognized the advertisement on YouTube, you can increase the advertisement medium, we think that effective product popularization can be expected.

4.4 Student Model to Consume One Proposed Item a Day

We thought about a student model for consuming suggested items one item a day. For example, eat 2 pieces as a dessert for breakfast after getting up, eat 1 piece as activation of morning brain before class starts, 1 piece as sugar supplement between the first period the second period, eat 1 piece as a dessert after lunch, We will eat 2 pieces between 3 and 4, 1 piece as a reward after classes, after going home and finishing the university's tasks eat 2 pieces as a refreshment of the tired brain. In this way, you can consume 10 pieces of chocolate per day (Fig. 6).

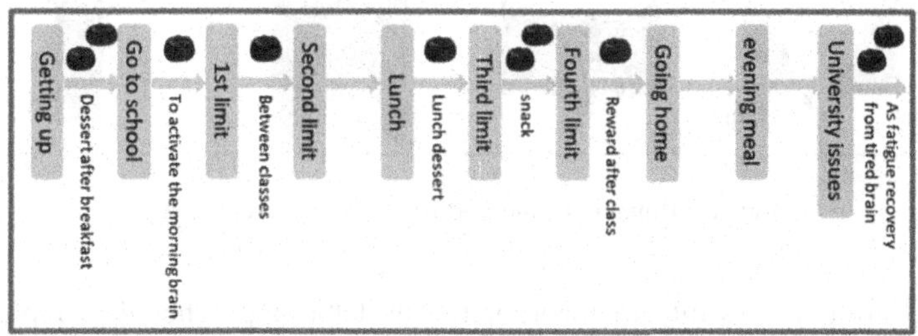

Fig. 6. Student model of time schedule to consume one proposed item a day

As another way to eat 10 pieces chocolate, for example, it can be assumed that you can dissolve chocolate tablet in milk to make chocolate juice, melt it in curry, use as a seasoning or eat as an energy charge before club activities.

Also, we think that there is a merit for students by eating chocolate one day in this way. For example, you can enjoy chocolate exchanges with a friend, imitate the timing of talent for advertising eating, enjoy each other, if graduate students choose chocolate with ingredients instead of snacks and can have eating time the advantage of being able to supply sugar by eating in between studies can be mentioned.

In addition, chocolate is rich in flavanols (cocoa flavanols) such as catechin • epicatechin and is thought to bring various benefits to our health [5]. And it is said that people with higher frequency of intake of chocolate tend to have higher cognitive function [6, 7]. Therefore, by developing the habit of eating chocolate every day, it is considered to have a positive influence on the health and academic ability of students [8, 9].

4.5 Proposal for Rentals of Replenishment Servers

We present three promotional proposals of products in this research.

The first one is "Start rental service of replenishment server". We explain the replenishment server. The replenishment server is a machine for easily refilling tablet type chocolate. The mechanism of the replenishment server is that bottles are set in the server and 10 pieces of tablet type chocolate are replenished to the bottle (Fig. 7).

With this replenishment server, we encourage a habit of consuming 10 tablets of chocolate every day, and think that consumers can use bottles repeatedly to reduce the cost of the container and give consideration to the environment.

As a server operation method, we think that it is better to install it in university laboratories, clubrooms, convenience stores and so on. By doing so, it will be easy for students easily to use replenish tablet type chocolate. As a result, we expect that consumption of chocolate tablet can be increased. Furthermore, we think that it will be a place for students to deepen friendship between them.

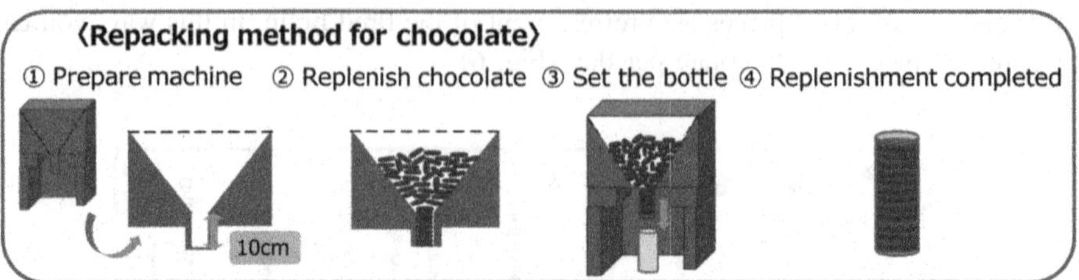

Fig. 7. Repacking method for tablet type chocolate

Moreover, it is possible to incorporate this tablet-type chocolate replenishment server into the service of renting a confectionery box containing more than dozens of sweets in offices that A company is doing, other than students.

4.6 Proposal for Promotion

We present two sales promotion proposals proposed in this research.

The first proposal is to sell bottles of various designs and functions. The aim of this proposal is to make topics in SNS (social networking sites) and the like and to become a detonator for products to hit.

We present five examples of bottle type package. The first one is a bottle package of the same design with different colors. If friends have the same design different color, it makes us feel like our familiarity with them is up, and maybe it will make our time with friends more enjoyable. The second one is a bottle type package with limited designs. By thinking of seasons and limited designs like spurring a situation that you can buy them only now, which will lead to encouraging consumption behavior. The third is to hold a bottle-shaped package design contest and commercialize outstanding works. We think that it contributes to creating topicality as a PR event of products. The fourth one is a bottle type package that collaborated with luxury brands. By doing this we think that as targeting is not limited to students, more consumers can be acquired. The fifth is sales of highly functional bottles. It aims to have the product carried around on a daily basis by making it a package that emphasizes functionality such as a bottle with a structure that raises the bottom like a lip cream and is easy to take out and one with high cold insulation properties.

The second proposal is to enrich chocolate variations and increase effective chocolate according to students' life. The aim of this proposal is that eating chocolate will not end with a temporary fashion. Also, if the shape and size of tablet type chocolate are unified, flexible targeting becomes possible by taste and function.

An example of variation of tablet type chocolate will be given.

The first one is a chocolate with enhanced nutritional value that can be supplemented with energy. We think that this is an item that can be 'a substitute for meal' which is the result of the graduate student of "correspondence image of student's chocolate" of correspondence analysis. The second one is a chocolate mixed with caffeine and having an effect of shaking off a drowsiness. We think that it can be expected purpose of chocolate other than 'enjoying the taste of chocolate' by blending caffeine. The third one is chocolate with fruits and nuts. You can enjoy tactile sensation by mixing ingredients in chocolate. Also, think that it can be 'a substitute for meal' because it can expect chewy response and satisfaction feeling.

The fourth one is chocolate containing various tastes randomly. By doing this, we think that it is possible to consume 10 tablet type chocolate without getting bored. The fifth one is calorie-off chocolate. We believe that it is expected that consumers who care about calories will be attracted as new customers by this product. The fifth one is a chocolate that melts in a drink and enjoys it. We think that not only enjoying chocolate alone but also enjoying chocolate mixed with something else can lead to an increase in the appeal of products.

5 Issues and Measures

The problems and countermeasures of products proposed in this research are described.

In carrying items outside, there are points that the temperature inside the bottle rises and melts easily, and the hands get dirty because they touch the chocolate directly. As a countermeasure to these problems, we think that we can solve by coating each tablet type chocolate one by one or selling bottles with high cold insulation. In addition, there is a possibility that it may end with a temporary fashion and there is a problem of cost. As a countermeasure of this problem, set a sales target and increase design bottles and variations of taste after every achievement. By using a stepwise promotion strategy, we can prevent it from ending with a temporary fashion.

If we do not reach sales targets, we think that we can keep the deficit to a minimum if we stop product development.

6 Conclusion

Finally, as a summary of this research, we will describe the long-term plan and its effect of our proposal.

Initially, we make PR of the proposed product, and start selling tablet type chocolate after the student's awareness has increased. After that, we start rental service of installed type replenishment servers. By doing this, we aim to habituate the act of eating chocolate on a daily basis. After customs settled, sell limited bottles and aim for being in fashion. After that, increasing taste variations prevents consumers from getting tired of chocolate and prevent it from becoming a temporary fashion. As a result, most of the students will come to carry the goods and we think that it is possible to aim for the goal of 5 times the consumption of chocolate. The difficulty degrees will rise as the level goes up, but if you can't achieve the sales target you can stop producing the goods it from becoming a big loss, and it aims to increase the chocolate consumption of Japanese students five-fold from a long-term perspective It aims to.

If we can establish the custom for eating chocolate in Japan, it will be a great opportunity for the confectionary market, which is struggling with the declining birthrate of Japan [10]. Also, not only the merit of the chocolate for the student life, but also, in health aspect, various effects which cocoa polyphenols of chocolate hold are expected [10]. Research on the prevention of high blood pressure, dementia and arteriosclerosis, skin beauty and allergy improvement etc. is progressing [11–15].

Therefore, in modern Japan where dementia and other diseases are becoming a social problem as the aging progresses, by encouraging the habit of eating chocolate on a daily basis from a young generation of students, we will expect to raise the health level and contribute to Japan's healthy future.

References

1. Nihon Chocolate Kokoa Kyoukai (Japanese Association of chocolate & cocoa). http://www.chocolate-cocoa.com/lecture/index.html. Accessed 24 Dec 2018
2. Nihon Keizai Shimbun (Nikkei). https://style.nikkei.com/article/DGXMZO07972210U6-A001C1NZBP00. Accessed 03 Oct 2018
3. Nihon Keizai Shimbun (Nikkei). https://www.nikkei.com/article/DGXMZO34044840Q8-A810C1SHA000/. Accessed 03 Oct 2018
4. YouTube's advertisement routing. https://www.youtube.com/intl/ja/yt/advertise/running-a-video-ad/. Accessed 03 Oct 2018
5. Nikkei Gooday, People who eat chocolate often tend to have a higher cognitive function (2017). https://style.nikkei.com/article/DGXMZO20977920R10C17A9000000?channel=DF130120166093. Accessed 13 Feb 2019
6. Crichton, G.E., et al.: Chocolate intake is associated with better cognitive function: the main-syracuse longitudinal study. Appetite **100**, 126–132 (2016)
7. Langer, S., et al.: Flavanols and methylxanthines in commercially available dark chocolate: a study of the correlation with nonfat cocoa solids. J. Agric. Food Chem. **59**(15), 8435–8441 (2011)
8. Scholey, A.B., et al.: Consumption of cocoa flavanols results in acute improvements in mood and cognitive performance during sustained mental effort. J. Psychopharmacol. **24**(10), 1505–1514 (2010)
9. Field, D.T., et al.: Physiol. Behav. **103**(3–4), 255–260 (2011)
10. Nihon Keizai Shimbun (Nikkei). Chocolate popularity, momentum momentum sold seasonally for the seventh consecutive year (2018). https://r.nikkei.com/article/DGXMZO28790080Q8A330C1XQH000. Accessed 13 Feb 2019
11. Bayard, V., Hollenberg, N.K., et al.: Int. J. Med. Sci. **4**, 53–58 (2007)
12. McCullugh, M.L., et al.: J. Cardiovasc. Phamacol. **47**(Suppl 2), S103–S109 (2006). 119-21
13. Grassi, D., et al.: Am. J. Clin. Nutr. **81**(3), 611–614 (2005)
14. Heinrich, U., Neukam, K., Tronnier, H., Sies, H., Stahl, W.: Long-term ingestion of high flavanol cocoa provides photoprotection against UV-induced erythema and improves skin condition in women. J. Nutr. **136**, 1565–1569 (2006)
15. Sukie, N.: The effect of improving blood fluidity of cocoa and chocolate. J. Jpn. Hemorheol. Soc., 75–78 (2002)

Meals to Make a Healthy Diet Successful

Hayato Kohama(✉) and Yumi Asahi

School of Information and Telecommunication Engineering, Department of Management Systems Engineering, Tokai University, Tokyo, Japan
6bjm2220@mail.u-tokai.ac.jp, asahi@tsc.u-tokai.ac.jp

Abstract. Dieting in Japan is aimed at reducing weight. In particular, many women in Japan are seen by people who care about their appearance, and it is ideal that their weight is small with a slim body shape. There are few dieting methods such as exercise and exercise, and there are many diets substituting food diet restrictions that can be started easily and supplements for meals. This is because there is not enough time to spend exercise and exercise because there is little free time to do housework while working while doing work in modern Japan. Also, there are many people who care about the eyes of the surrounding people from the character of the Japanese, there are factors that it is difficult for one person to go to the gym and sports facilities. On the other hand, dietary supplements and diet supplements reduce caloric intake and reduce body weight, so it is easier and easier to get started and it is increasing. Due to this influence, the types of diet foods such as supplements are increasing year by year. Among them, there are things that are ineffective and those that are contained are dangerous and there are problems. In order to diet, it can be said that it is necessary to acquire knowledge of correct meal and nutrients. In recent years, a diet boom has come in Japan. It is gradually increasing awareness of obesity since 2000. As a reason for dieting [1], the weight gained, there were many reasons related to health aspects such as to change myself and their appearance. There are various kinds of diets, a method of consuming energy from exercise such as yoga and sports and dieting. There are diet restrictions and diet that deviates from meals. Because it is easier to start a diet and the cost is low, there is a high proportion of trying to improve from the diet. In particular, there is a diet that pulls out carbohydrates which are one nutrient causing the increase in energy intake. This diet takes carbohydrates and increases blood sugar level. It is a diet focusing on the fact that when insulin becomes active and saccharides are sent to adipocytes and are not consumed by exercise etc...., it accumulates in fat as it is. However, if carbohydrates are the only source of energy in the brain, they can cause concentration and ability to think down. Other nutritional proteins are nutrients that make up the body and become built-in and blood vessel materials. Lipids become energy sources of the body and become energy sources when exercising. Vitamins serve to help each nutrient work, basically it must be ingested from the diet. Minerals have a role to arrange and make physical condition and can only be ingested from meals [2]. In other words, nutrients have their own roles, all of which are indispensable for healthy living. If one of these is lost, the physical condition of the body will deteriorate or it will be in a state of inactivity. This is considered to be one of the causes of the problem that the intake of nutrients is insufficient in the modern dietary life.

S. Yamamoto and H. Mori (Eds.): HCII 2019, LNCS 11569, pp. 449–461, 2019.
https://doi.org/10.1007/978-3-030-22660-2_33

Continued lack of nutrients leads to injuries and diseases such as osteoporosis and anemia, physical condition management problems such as not being able to maintain body temperature well, thinking ability and declining concentration. In other words, excessive dietary diet is dangerous from a physical condition. Moreover, we will not continue to eat dish forcibly or diet to examine the same dish every day. Therefore, we need to think about a meal that makes a diet successful while enjoying the balance of nutrients.

Keywords: Protein · Carbohydrate · Vitamin · Lipid · Inorganic · Energy

1 Introduction

1.1 Background

Interest in diet and awareness to improve meals are increasing year by year.

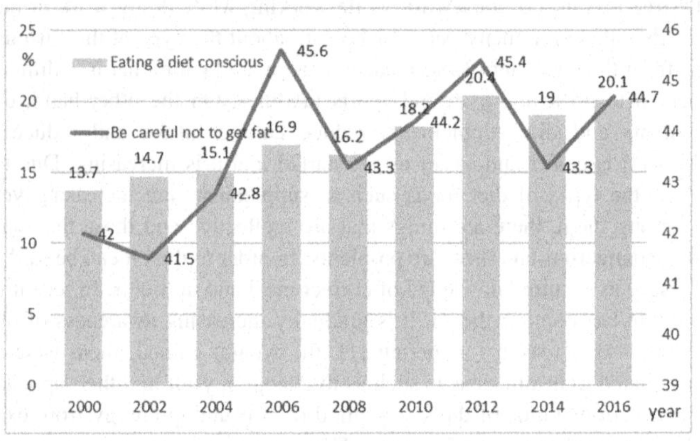

Fig. 1. Diet and meal

From Fig. 1, the proportion of people who are eating conscious diet is 13.7% in 2000, 20.1% in 2016, and 6.4% higher. In 2002, the proportion of those who are paying attention not to get fat has increased by 4.2%, or 44.7%, from 41.5%. In other words, you can see that we are rethinking from improving meals by way of dieting.

Also, in Fig. 2, the protein, vitamin B, vitamin C drops remarkably. On the other hand, there was no change in the proportion of lipid carbohydrates. In other words, since the total intake of nutrients is decreasing, we can see that today's meals are not enough for nutrients.

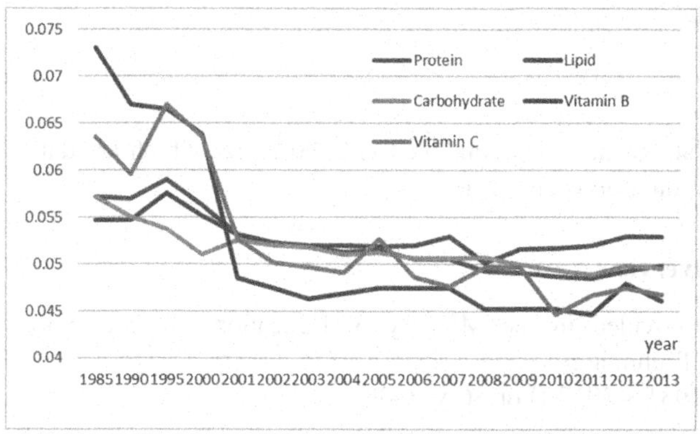

Fig. 2. Shows the trend of intake of 5 major nutrients.

It takes energy from protein, carbohydrate, fat and it is consumed by exercise and brain function. However, nutrients not converted to energy are accumulated as fat, and their condition continues to become obese. Therefore, obesity causes overdose of energy, so if you reduce the amount of protein, lipid, carbohydrate, diet will be considered successful [3]. However, if you do not keep the balance of nutrients it is harmful to your health and it will be unhealthy even if your diet succeeds. So, you need to think about meals that keep calories down while maintaining the balance of nutrients.

1.2 Propose

In the study of the structure of the meal pattern and the intake situation of nutrients [4], we focused on home cooking and studied the structure of the meal pattern and its nutritional intake. The meal pattern becomes 16 patterns, 1 juice three vegetable pattern etc. are extracted. As a result, excessive ingestion of lipid, salt and protein was seen with one juice three vegetables, and insufficiency of minerals and vitamins was seen in the pattern without side dishes. Also, in the pattern without main dishes, protein and lipid deficiency was seen. Therefore, it was found that one broth and three vegetables were not necessarily good, but overdose. On the other hand, it was a conclusion that nutrition can not be balanced and healthy if it passes through side dishes and main dishes. From this, it is necessary to review the diet which makes healthy diet succeed from the balance of nutrition of cooking in this research, so consider a dish model to make healthy diet succeed.

2 Analysis

2.1 Data

This data is data on nutrients contained in 2190 items, which are data on food names and numerical data on each nutrient.

2.2 Data Overview

Provide : provided in the Ministry of Education, Culture, Sports, Science and Technology.
Period : 1931 ~ 2017 (For 86 years).

Data is nominal data of food name. Energy intake and nutrient data classified as protein, lipid, carbohydrate, vitamin, mineral.

2.3 Basic Aggregate

It is a histogram of lipid and saturated fatty acids every 100 kcal. From here, it is found that 900 kcal of food is contained a lot. In addition, 100 kcal of food contains few ones. That is, it is understood that lipid and saturated fatty acid are factors that increase energy intake (Figs. 3 and 4).

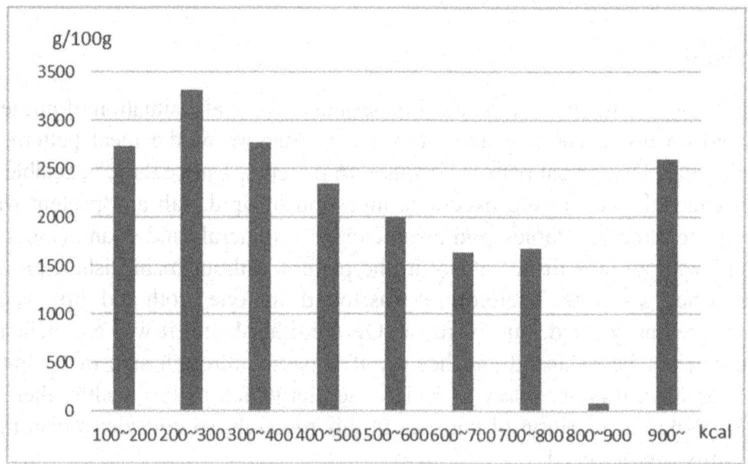

Fig. 3. Lipid.

Next is a histogram of retinol activation equivalent and vitamin B1 every 100 kcal. From this it can be seen that retinol activation equivalent and vitamin B1 contain very much of 100 kcal of food. On the other hand, it can be seen that it is not contained in food of 800 kcal to 900 kcal. In other words, retinol activation equivalent and vitamin B1 are foods that can be expected to suppress energy intake (Figs. 5 and 6).

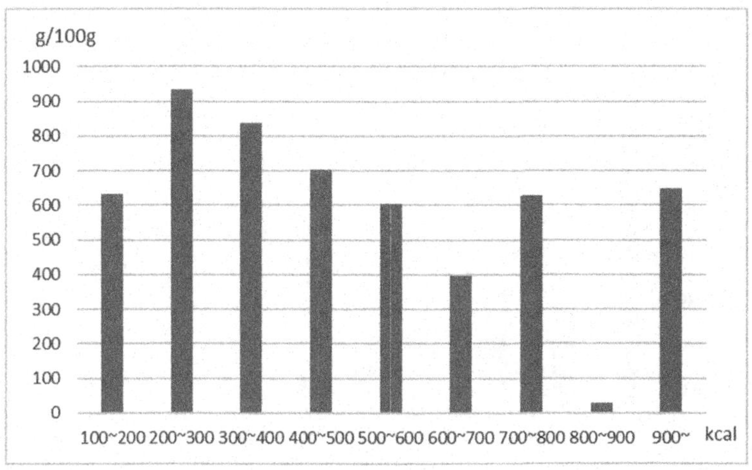

Fig. 4. Saturated fatty acid.

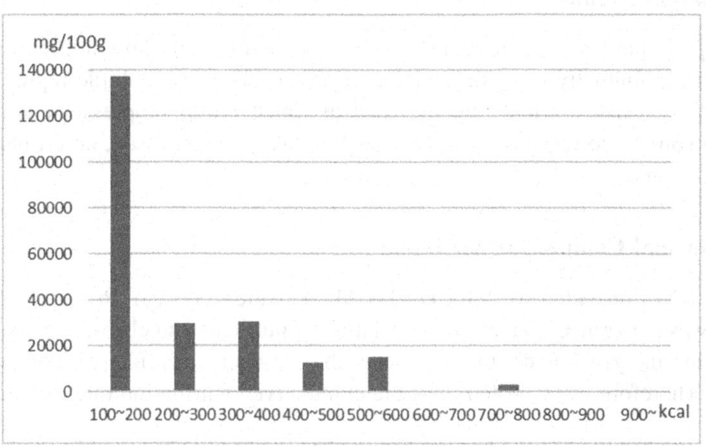

Fig. 5. Retinol activation equivalent.

From this basic counting, there are things that work to reduce energy intake by nutrients and those that increase. Also, as there is a possibility that the nutrients are affecting each other, it is necessary to analyze what kind of influence is given to energy intake by grouping by nutrient characteristics. Then create a dish model that will make a healthy diet successful.

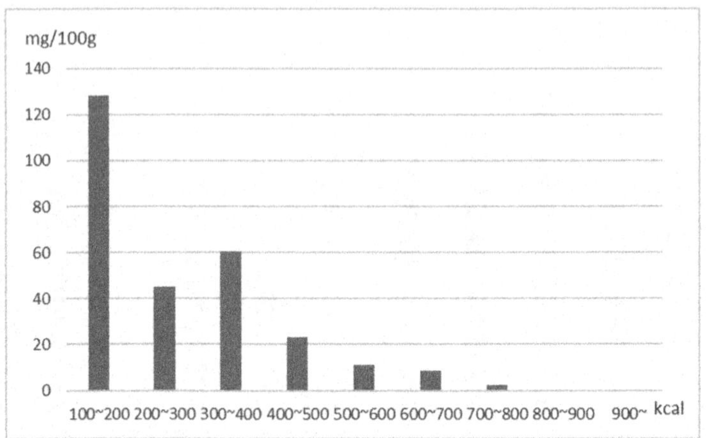

Fig. 6. Vitamin B1.

2.4 Analysis Method

Perform principal component analysis to analyze and classify how nutrients work and how nutrients mutually exert influence each other. Next, by multiple regression analysis, analyze which nutrients are included in which group suppresses energy intake. Then, by combinatorial optimization, energy intake is suppressed, and a healthy dish model is created.

2.5 Principal Component Analysis

We used VMS provided by NTT DATA Mathematical System. Principal component analysis was performed to analyze the relation of nutrients and classify foods. Principal component analysis needs to determine the number of principal components in advance. Therefore, we adopted until the cumulative contribution rate exceeds 0.7 [5].

Table 1. Principal component loading amount

	Solution 1	Solution 2	Solution 3	Solution 4	Solution 5
Protein	−0.427493486	0.11291543	0.383740863	0.09403232	0.08158626
Lipid	−0.114067621	0.60174267	−0.23237423	−0.2497604	−0.0425107
Saturated fatty acid	−0.076682276	0.60056353	−0.25604358	−0.247853	−0.0741986
Carbohydrate	0.013020355	−0.3291796	−0.19255453	−0.4721044	0.19527484
Dietary fiber	−0.24159725	−0.302753	−0.32288204	−0.4135257	0.05568202
Sodium	−0.062564077	−0.0853328	0.114806546	−0.0314738	−0.6849268
Calcium	−0.319364826	−0.0992752	0.218058161	−0.2946935	−0.3532991
Rin	−0.481680359	0.04208223	0.367231588	−0.1117959	0.03180582
Retinol active equivalent	−0.226682858	−0.0129306	−0.40230618	0.5107983	−0.124315
Vitamin K	−0.215917513	−0.2035292	−0.41321144	−0.0389258	−0.2602562
Vitamin B1	−0.338330149	−0.0100974	−0.0182209	−0.0035189	0.51520685
Vitamin B2	−0.435226447	−0.0621235	−0.25167816	0.33269318	0.03487367

Table 1 shows the results of principal component analysis. Interpretation of the number interpreted that the variable of 0.3 or more had a positive influence, while that of −0.3 or less had a negative influence. In other words, you can see which nutrients are contained in each solution and which nutrients are not much contained in foods. Protein, calcium, phosphorus, vitamin B1, vitamin B2 are low as the 1st main ingredient. Vegetables, rice and the like are included in the first principal component as food. This main ingredient is mainly vegetable, rice, staple food and fish are included. This main ingredient shall be vegetables, staple food group. The second main component is high lipid, saturated fatty acid value, carbohydrate, dietary fiber values are low. In other words, it can be said that carbohydrates and dietary fibers tend to decline in foods with many lipids and saturated fatty acids. Foods include nuts, fish, meat, vegetable oil, dairy products. Let this main ingredient be main dish, sweets group. The third principal component protein, the value of phosphorus is high, dietary fiber, retinol activation equivalents, and lower values of vitamin K. In other words, dietary fiber, retinol activation equivalent, and vitamin K tend to be low in foods containing a lot of protein and phosphorus. Food is a food containing soybean, fish and soup, and contains many ingredients of miso soup. Make this main ingredient a miso soup group. The fourth principal component is retinol activation equivalent, vitamin B2 is high, carbohydrate, and dietary fiber is low. In other words, carbohydrates and dietary fiber tend to decline in foods containing retinol activation equivalents and vitamin B2 in large amounts. Food glue that contains a built-in birds and pigs. Let this principal component be a delicacy group. The fifth main ingredient has high vitamin B1 and sodium is low value. That is, sodium containing foods containing a large amount of vitamin B1 tends to decrease. Foods include wheat, brown rice, beans, pigs and the like. We will make this principal component pan, pig group.

2.6 Multiple Regression Analysis

Multiple regression analysis was performed to analyze the degree of influence on energy intake (Table 2).

Table 2. Multiple regression analysis results

	Estimate	Std. error	t value	Pr(>|t|)
First principal component	−0.267200023	0.011715482	−22.80742977	1.84E−103
Second principal component	0.453572843	0.011715482	38.71568064	3.86E−250
Third principal component	−0.37004976	0.011715482	−31.58638914	1.07E−180
Fourth principal component	0.528000539	0.011715482	45.06861583	3.288945644e−314
Fifth principal component	−0.085192127	0.011715482	−7.271756284	4.92E−13

Table 3. Multiple regression analysis evaluation

F statistic. value	Coefficient of determination	Multiple correlation coefficient	Adjusted coefficient of determination
1020.168266	0.700103269	0.836721739	0.699417006

For the interpretation of numbers, explanatory variables with Pr (>|t|) less than or equal to 0.05 are significant. That is, it is meaningful as an explanatory variable. Both the coefficient of determination and the adjusted coefficient of determination are based on 0.7 or more.

Multiple regression analysis was performed with energy as the objective variables, from the first principal component to the fifth principal component as explanatory variables. The main component whose coefficient is negative has a low influence on energy, and conversely the main component which is positive has a high influence on energy. The evaluation of this multiple regression analysis can be said that this analysis is valid as Table 3 shows that the coefficient of determination and the adjusted coefficient of determination are higher than the standard.

The main components that have a negative influence are the first principal component, the third principal component, and the fourth principal component. The first principal component is mainly vegetables and staple food, and the degree of influence is No. 2. The third principal component is the third lowest influence degree of the miso soup group. The fourth principal component is a group of delicacies and the influence degree is the highest. These principal components commonly contain retinol activation equivalents and vitamin B2 in large amounts. In other words, it can be said that it is a nutrient that suppresses energy intake. Characteristic is that there are many healthy foods with few meat and many vegetables. By combining foods of these principal components, it is possible to prepare healthy food with reduced energy intake.

Principal components that have a positive influence are the second principal component and the fifth principal component. The second main ingredient is the main dish and the cake group and the energy intake is the most. The fifth principal component is a group of bread and pig. Common features are foods containing a lot of lipids and carbohydrates. In other words, lipids and carbohydrates can be said to be nutrients that increase energy intake. The characteristic of this main ingredient is biased to meat, sweets, bread, etc. It can be said that becoming obese if you eat too much meat dishes or snacks. In other words, if you control lipid and carbohydrates, you can say that you succeed in dieting.

2.7 Combination Optimization

From the result of multiple regression analysis, a dish model is created from the first principal component, the third principal component and the fourth principal component.

Cooking model 1 is the first principal component vegetables and staple food group, cooking model 2 is the third principal component miso soup group, cooking model 3 is made as the fourth principal component. The objective function is set to minimize the amount of energy intake and the conditional expression is limited by limiting lipids and carbohydrates.

Formulation. We used NUOPT provided by NTT Data Mathematical System. We describe Eq. (1) in this research [6].

$$
\begin{aligned}
\min \quad & \sum_{i=1}^{i} a_i \cdot x_i \\
\text{s.t} \quad & \sum_{i=1}^{i} a_i \cdot x_i \leq 720 \\
& \sum_{i=1}^{i} x_i = 7 \\
& \sum_{i=1}^{i} b_i \cdot x_i \leq 24 \\
& \sum_{i=1}^{i} c_i \cdot x_i \leq 250 \\
& x_i \in \{0, 1\}, i = 1, \ldots, n
\end{aligned} \tag{1}
$$

From Eq. (1), the objective function minimizes total energy intake. Total energy intake of the constraint formula was set as 3:3:4 for breakfast, lunch and dinner, calculated from the energy intake of the day under 720 kcal. The number of food was set referring to the balance guide of the meal. Lipids are defined as ingesting 20% of total energy intake. And as 9 kcal per 1 g of lipid, it was calculated from the dinner rate as well as the constraint of energy intake. Carbohydrates were also defined as ingesting 50% of the total energy intake, calculated as 4 kcal per g in the case of carbohydrates. Also, xi represents 0 or 1. ai is the energy intake of each food item. Also, bi and ci are lipid and carbohydrate. i = 1, …, n is the number of foods (Fig. 7 and Table 4).

Result of Analysis. It is the result of cooking model 1.

Table 4. Results of cooking model 1

Energy	Protein	Lipid	Carbohydrate	Dietary fiber	Retinol activation equivalent	Vitamin B1	Vitamin B2
607	13.2	17.6	102.6	10.2	9	0.3	0.12

Cooking model 1 is a balanced cooking model overall and foods are also selected from rice, fruits and seafood mainly vegetables. You can make staple food, main dishes, side dishes, desserts from this model, and you can make dishes from outside the soup (Fig. 8 and Table 5).

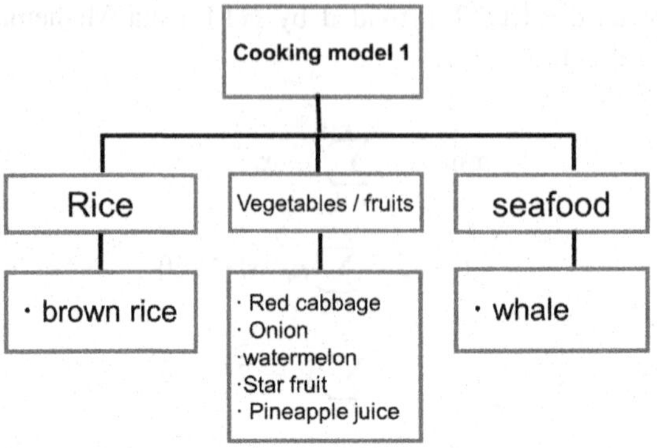

Fig. 7. Food of cooking model 1

It is the result of cooking model 2.

Table 5. Results of cooking model 2

Energy	Protein	Lipid	Carbohydrate	Dietary fiber	Retinol activation equivalent	Vitamin B1	Vitamin B2
575	124	3.8	0.47	3.8	0	140	1.84

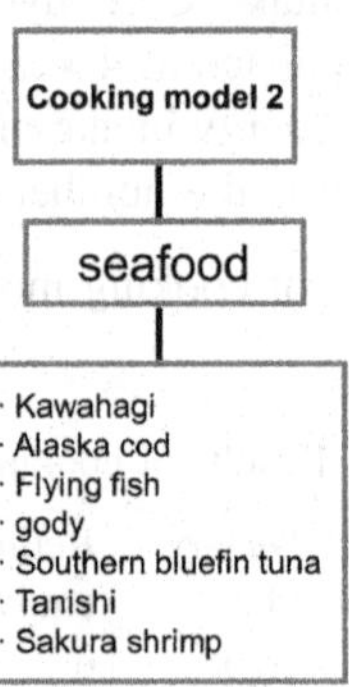

Fig. 8. Food of cooking model 2

Cooking model 2 is a dish model with no retinol activation equivalent, low carbohydrate, and high vitamin B1. Selected foods are only seafood, main dishes and soup can be made. In general, it is a disproportionate cooking model (Fig. 9 and Table 6).

It is the result of cooking model 3.

Table 6. Results of cooking model 3

Energy	Protein	Lipid	Carbohydrate	Dietary fiber	Retinol activation equivalent	Vitamin B1	Vitamin B2
622	118.4	12.5	62.8	49.9	2692	3.53	13.35

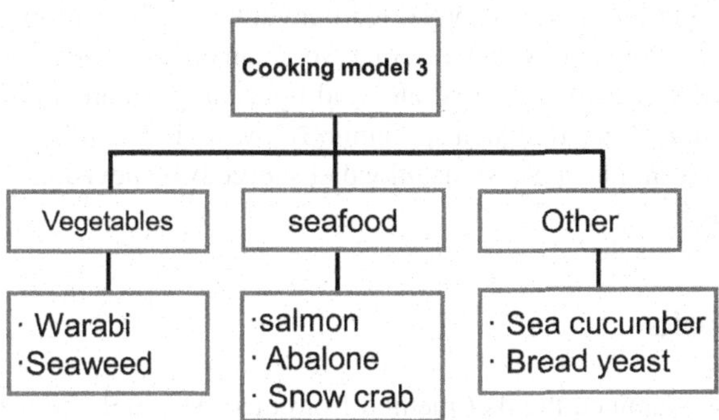

Fig. 9. Food of cooking model 3

Cooking model 3 is a model with very high retinol activation equivalent. The selected foods are mainly vegetables and seafood. From this model, staple food, main dishes, side dishes are made, and the repertoire of dishes that can be made is abundant. However, it is a model with biased nutrients.

3 Consideration

Cooking model 1 can be said to be healthy with a nutrient balanced model. It is the model with the second lowest energy intake. The variety of foods chosen is also diverse and there is no problem with the repertoire of dishes. Cooking model 2 has the lowest energy intake but the retinol activation equivalent is extremely low and biased. The selected foods are only seafood and there is little repertory of cooking. Cooking model 3 is the model with the highest energy intake. Nutrients are extremely high in retinol activation equivalents and are biased with respect to nutrients. Bread and fish and shellfish are selected for the selected food, but vegetables are few, and the repertory of the dish is inferior to the dish model 1. In other words, things like cooking model 1 are cooking models that make healthy diets successful. From here, you can diet while sending a healthy diet by devising staple foods and main dishes such as brown rice and fish and shellfish in the vegetable center. Also, it can be said that many nutrients contain a lot of carbohydrates and lipids in foods with low energy intake. In addition, it can be seen that foods not containing much carbohydrates and lipids contain a large amount of retinol activation equivalent, vitamin B1 and vitamin B2. In other words, food containing a large amount of retinol activation equivalent and vitamin B1, vitamin B2 contains less carbohydrates and lipids, and can reduce energy intake. It can be seen that staple food such as rice and bread contains a lot of carbohydrates in food. In addition, meat and fish contain a lot of lipids. In other words, excessive intake of carbohydrates and lipids can be suppressed by devising rice, bread, meat and fish. Especially in fish there are many lean fish and lipids are included. On the other hand, since white fish has few lipids and contains a lot of amino acids and proteins, it is better for white meat to eat when dieting. Regarding rice and bread, carbohydrates such as brown rice and millet rice are less suitable for healthy diet. In other words, in order to succeed a healthy diet, it can be said that if you cook carbohydrates and lipids and prepare a dish with food that contains retinol activation equivalents, vitamin B1, vitamin B2 in large amounts, it will be successful. And simple and easy healthy diet succeeds by devising staple rice, bread, main meat and fish.

4 Future Tasks

In this study, we examined the diet method from diet. Although the constraint formula of combinatorial optimization was made strict, the actual diet often exceeds the nutrient ingested. Therefore, by using fuzzy numbers as constraint expressions [7], it is necessary to analyze with constraint expressions relaxed. Also, it takes too much time to diet from meals. It is considered efficient to exercise to diet in a short period of time. Therefore, it is desirable to compare it with a dieting exercising. We also need to consider maintaining continuity of diet as well as continuing to maintain motivation. And we have to consider the most suitable diet for the individual. Although you can go on a healthy diet healthily relatively quickly by exercising, you must consider personal physical ability, body characteristics and time. If you exercise by force, you can destroy your body and troubles will arise for work and housework. There is also a problem of motivation. Diet will take a long time, so you have to manage so that your motivation lasts longer. It is necessary to do research to maintain motivation so that diet can be enjoyed while devising cooking or the like. Also, if exercising a diet is a hard and painful exercise, I will not last long and I will give up immediately. You can enjoy dieting while enjoying your own hobbies and good sports. In this way, in order to make a diet succeed in modern society, it is suitable for personal life, hobby and diet that suits what you want to challenge. Also, for those who can not exercise using the latest technology such as modern VR or AR, or who want to do but who do not have the courage to take the first step to study a new diet that can move freely even in a narrow space like home I also want to connect. I would like to build a system that supports the optimum diet suitable for individuals by finally managing diet and exercise management.

References

1. Net research Tims drive. http://www.dims.ne.jp/timelyresearch/2017/170315/. Accessed 3 Oct 2018
2. Independent administrative agency agricultural and livestock industry promotion organization. https://www.alic.go.jp/joho-s. Accessed 8 Oct 2018
3. Time of food education. http://www.chantotaberu.jp/jikan. Accessed 16 Oct 2018
4. Mitsunari, Y., et al.: The structure of meal pattern in long term dietary life survey and its nutritional status, intake status. Nakamura Gakuen University School Pharm. Sci. Res. Bull. **8**, 43–66 (2016)
5. Logics of blue. https://logics-of-blue.com/principal-components-analysis. Accessed 24 Oct 2018
6. Ministry of Health, Labor and Welfare, Final Browsing. https://www.mhlw.go.jp/stf/shingi/0000041824.html. Accessed 24 Oct 2018
7. Tsuji, A., Kurashige, K., Kameyama, Y.: Selection of dishes using fuzzy mathematical programming. Jpn. Intellect. Inform. Assoc. J. **20**, 337–346 (2008)

How to Design Adaptable Agents to Obtain a Consensus with Omoiyari

Yoshimiki Maekawa(✉), Fumito Uwano, Eiki Kitajima, and Keiki Takadama

The University of Electro-Communications, Chofugaoka 1-5-1, Chofu, Tokyo 182-8585, Japan
m1510141@edu.cc.uec.ac.jp

Abstract. This paper focuses on *Omoiyari* in Japanese as consideration/thoughtfulness for others in order to promote people to obtain a consensus among them especially in Internet society where is difficult to reach a consensus due to the limited communication/interaction, and aims at exploring the preliminary agent design that can promote people to obtain a consensus by Omoiyari. For this purpose, this paper starts by designing Omoiyari as the behaviors of filling the *numerical* and *psychological* gaps (*e.g.*, a different income as the numerical gap while a different way of thinking among people as the psychological gap), and conducts the human subjective experiment to understand what kinds of aspects should be implemented in the Omaiyari agent. In detail, we employ Barnga as a cross-cultural game which cannot determine the winner without a consensus, and analyze the behaviors of the human players in Barnga with the emotional panels expressing happy, angry, sad, and surprise, which help the players to indirectly express their feeling to the other players. The analysis of human subject experiment has derived that the emotional panels are used to express their feeling for filling the numerical and psychological gaps and derive the change of the opponent's behaviors. In detail, we found the following implications: (1) omoiyari-based behaviors are achieved by a sequence of showing the surprise/sad panels; showing the angry panel after recognizing the feeling of others; and changing the decision of the winner to the same one selected by others; (2) the surprise panel is increasingly used as the psychological gap increases; the sad panel is increasingly used as the numerical gap increases; the angry panel is used after recognizing the surprise/sad panels and contributes to changing the opponent's behaviors; and the happy panel is used when the numerical and psychological gaps are filled.

Keywords: Omoiyari · Consensus · Numerical and psychological gap · Emotional panel · Collective adaptation

---

Supported by Evolinguistics: Integrative Studied of Language Evolution for Co-creative Communication.

S. Yamamoto and H. Mori (Eds.): HCII 2019, LNCS 11569, pp. 462–475, 2019.
https://doi.org/10.1007/978-3-030-22660-2_34

1 Introduction

It is important to obtain a consensus among people in their community, but it is difficult to reach it because we cannot perfectly understand how the other persons think. This problem becomes serious in Internet society due to the limited communication/interaction. To tackle this problem, Ushida et al. focused on Human-Agent Interaction (HAI), and proposed the agents with three kinds of roles (*i.e.*, claiming; supporting; quiet agents), which needs to obtain a consensus in a human-agent group through an interaction among human and agents [1]. This research mentioned that the balance of three kinds of roles that persons/agents have is important to reach a consensus in their community. This implication is very important, but this approach limits to work well because it is difficult to change the role of human for a consensus among them due to the fact that we cannot control the mind of human. This means that one directional approach from the agents to human limits to derive the appropriate balance of three kinds of roles in a human-agent group.

From this fact, this paper focuses on *Omoiyari* in Japanese as consideration/thoughtfulness for others because human show their Omoiyari in some cases to obtain a consensus among them. This is very important because a consensus is not reached by *one* directional approach from the agents to human but by the bi-directional approach from human and agent. To promote such Omoiyari not only by human but also by agents, this paper explores the preliminary agent design based on Omoiyari from an analysis of the human subject experiment (*i.e.*, we try to understand what kinds of aspects should be implemented in the Omaiyari agent through the human subject experiment). For this purpose, we start by designing Omoiyari as the behavior of filling the *numerical* and *psychological* gaps (*e.g.*, a different income as the numerical gap while a different way of thinking among people as the psychological gap).

To investigate the effectiveness of Omoiyari and analyze it for the preliminary agent design, we employ Barnga [2] as a cross-cultural game, which is studied in the context of Gaming Simulation designed for an educational purpose. In Barnga, players cannot determine their winner without a consensus, which requires Omoiyari-based behaviors. Since the numerical and/or psychological gaps are needed to be recognized to derive Omoiyari, this paper introduces the emotional panels expressing happy, angry, sad, and surprise into Barnga to show how the other players feel. In particular, the numerical gap occurs when increasing the difference between the number of win of the winner and that of the looser, while the psychological gaps occurs when finding that other players have the different criteria of the winner selection.

This paper is organized as follows. Section 2 starts by designing Omoiyari, Sect. 3 explains Barnga, and Sect. 4 introduces the emotional panels in Barnga. The result of the human subject experiment is shown in Sect. 5 and its analysis is conducted in Sect. 6. Finally, our conclusion is given in Sect. 7.

2 Omoiyari as Filling Gaps

According to Uchida and Kitayama [3], Omoiyari consists of the following three components: intuitive understanding; sympathy; and prosocial behavior. The process to arise Omoiyari is as follows: (1) noticing about gaps; (2) sympathizing with these gaps; (3) acting appropriate behaviors for the gaps. In this research, we modeled the flow of Omoiyari as the expanded control theory [4] in the domain of social psychology. Control theory proposed that people take actions to fill gaps when minus gaps happen between ideal and reality of themselves. It means that ideal is higher than reality. However, we think that Omoiyari cannot be expressed by filling the gaps between ideal and reality of only self because people cannot live thinking about only self, and keep on getting information from environments around them. Therefore, we expand the compared object from the self to the environments around us. To fill the gaps, the following factors are needed: (1) noticing about the gaps; (2) standing the side of an opponent; (3) understanding what the opponent wants. Those requirements are included in the components of Omoiyari, so filling the gaps can be expressed as Omoiyari.

To represent Omoiyari as filling the gaps, we should define the gaps. Table 1 shows the kinds of gaps considered in this paper. This table has two clusters. The first cluster indicates the characters of the gaps: "numerical" or "psychological". The numerical gaps can be counted: weight, height, income and so on and they are visible. On the other hand, the psychological gaps are not visible. It means that the gaps of the notion, the emotions, and so on. For example, misunderstandings and differences of thought between some people are the psychological gaps. Such gaps happened between the minds is not easy to be indicated. The second cluster indicates the targets of the gaps: "between you and other people"; "between other people". In this paper, we consider the combinations of the gaps made by the two clusters.

Table 1. The clusters of the gap

Targets\Characters	Numerical	Psychological
You and other people	Gap 1	Gap 2
Between other people	Gap 3	Gap 4

3 Barnga Game

3.1 Overview

Barnga, developed by Thiagarajan [2], is a cross-cultural game, which is studied in the context of *Gaming Simulation* (GS) [5], which provides human players with a cross-cultural experience in a virtual environment. Barnga is the card game without communication (*e.g.*, speaking, writing, and utterance) among players, which requires the players to interact with other players using the non-verbal communication (*e.g.*, gesture) instead of the verbal communication. This situation simulates the situation where we have to interact with foreign peoples without knowing their language. As the other important point of Barnga, the rules of players are slightly different among the players, which reflects the cultural difference among them. From these characteristics of Barnga, the players have to understand the rules of others without communication and have a chance to discover how to cope with such a complex situation without the verbal communication. Since Barnga is designed for the educational purpose, Barnga is conducted as the following three steps:

(1) **Briefing**
The players learn the assigned rules individually. Note that each rule represents the culture of the player.

(2) **Playing**
The players play Barnga according to their own rules. They feel something difference with the other players but cannot tell it because of no communication among them. Such a situation causes a culture shock.

(3) **Debriefing**
After the players are informed that they have different rules among them, they understand the difficulty of communicating with the others who have a different cultural background and discuss how to cope with the cultural difference.

3.2 Details of Playing Sequence

The detailed sequence of (2) playing in Barnga described above is summarized as follows and its diagram is shown in Fig. 1.

1. Barnga starts.
2. The players sit down in each table. More than two tables and more than three players in each table are preferable for reflecting cultural difference.
3. The first player is determined and discards any card which s/he wants. Any number with any suite is acceptable for the first player. In this game, 28 cards (from A to 7 of each suit) are used.
4. The players discard their cards from their hands in turn. Note that the players should discard the cards with the same suit as the first card discarded by the first player.
5. The players select a winner from the cards on the table. The winner is the player who discards the strongest card in the players.
6. If all players select the same player as a winner, the winner is determined; otherwise they re-select a winner until they select the same winner.
7. The number of *game* is counted by 1.
8. The players play Barnga again (*i.e.*, return to the step 4) if the game count does not exceed the pre-determined number of the games (MAX_GAME_COUNT); otherwise proceed to the step 9.

9. The number of *round* is counted by 1.
10. Proceed to the step 11 with setting the game count as 1 if the round count does not exceed the pre-determined number of the round (MAX_ROUND_COUNT); otherwise proceed to the step 12.
11. The players move to other tables. In detail, the player who is the best winner in each table moves to a clockwise table, the player who is the worst loser in each table moves to an anti-clockwise table, and the other players remain the same table. Return to the step 2.
12. Barnga ends.

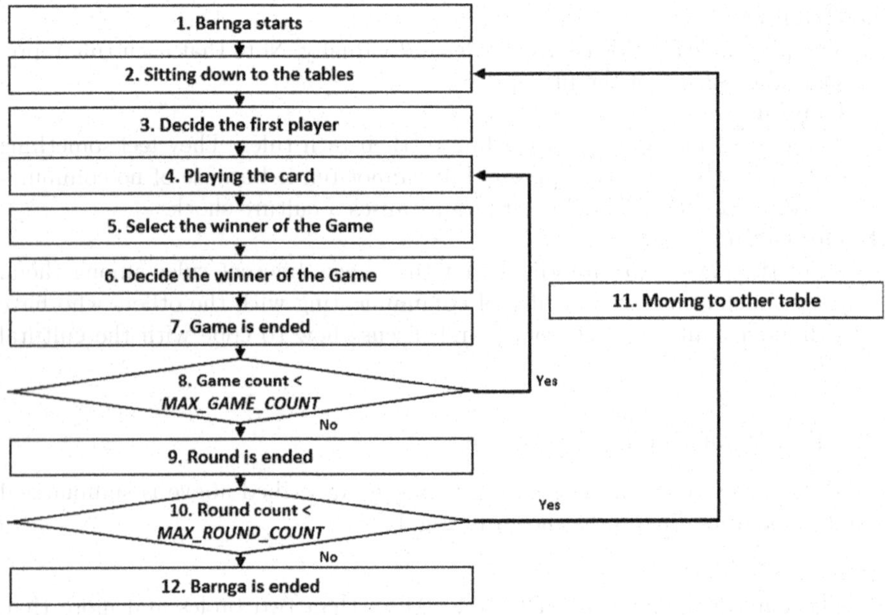

Fig. 1. Playing sequence of Barnga

3.3 Description of Rules

As a basic rule of Barnga, the bigger number the card is, the stronger the card is. However, the strength of the card changes by the two additional rules: Ace's strength and trump suit, both of which depend on the rule that the player has. First, the Ace's strength changes the strongest or the weakest. If Ace is the strongest, the strength order of the card number is $2 < 3 < 4 < 5 < 6 < 7 <$ Ace. If Ace is the weakest, on the other hand, the order becomes Ace $< 2 < 3 < 4 < 5 < 6 < 7$. Second, the trump suit decides the strongest suit. When the trump suit is HEART and you are the only player who discards the HEART card, you can win the game even if HEART is not the same as the suit of the first discarded card. However, if other players discard their HEART cards, the winner is decided by the strength of the card with the HEART suit according to the Ace's strength. To understand the winner selection, let's focus on the situation where the Ace's strength is strong and the trump suit is HEART. When the first player discards the Ace of SPADE, the second player discards 3 of DIAMOND, the third player discards 6 of SPADE, and the fourth player discards the 7 of HEART as shown in the left side of Fig. 2, the winner of the game is the fourth player. But, when the second player discards the Ace of HEART in the above case, the winner changes to be the second player as shown in right side of Fig. 2.

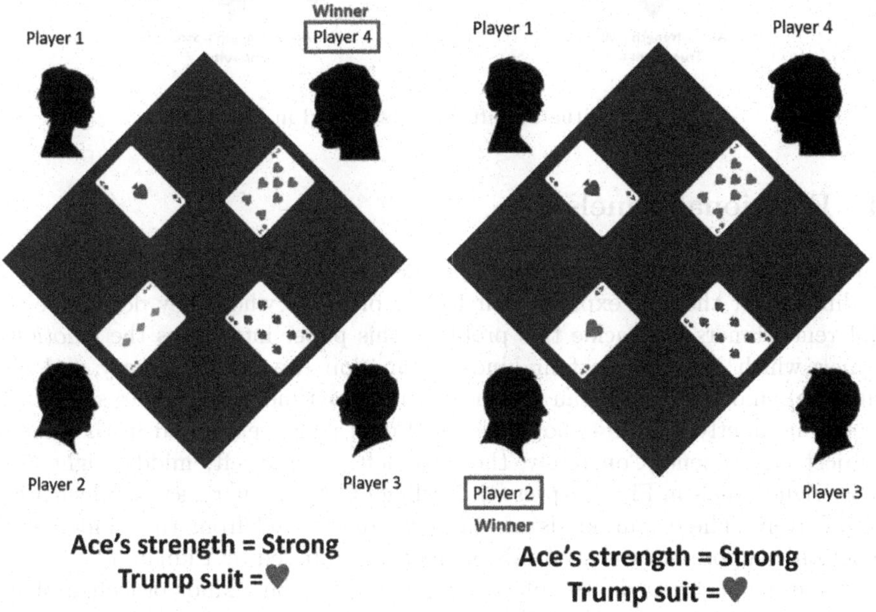

Fig. 2. The winner selection in Barnga

3.4 Moving to Other Table

In the 1st round, the players share the same rule by learning how to determine the winner from the rule instruction provided to the table. Note that one rule instruction is provided to one table but the rule instructions are slightly different among the tables, which promotes the players to learn their own rules (corresponding to their culture). From this characteristic of Barnga, the players who learn the different rules have to play Barnga at the same table from the 2nd round after the best winner and the worst loser change their table to a clockwise/anti-clockwise direction as shown in Fig. 3. Due to the different rules in the table, it is difficult for the players to determine the winner just one time after the 2nd round.

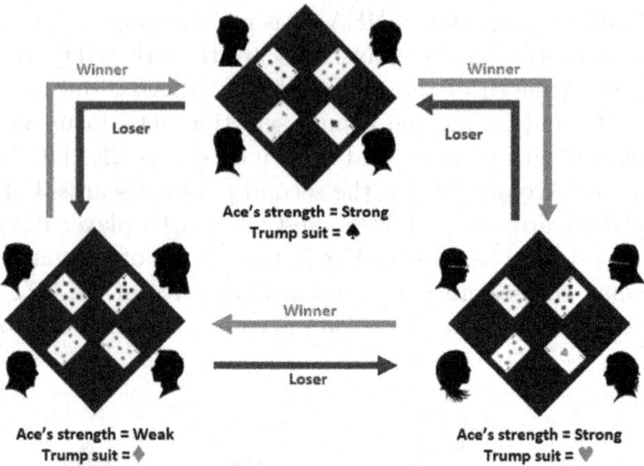

Fig. 3. Situation after the 1st round in Barnga

4 Emotional Panels

Since the verbal communication among the players is not allowed in Barnga, it is difficult for them to express their feeling precisely when they determine the different winners. To tackle this problem, this paper introduces the *emotional panels* which can express four kinds of emotion (*i.e.*, happy, angry, sad and surprise), and the players can use these panels anytime in Barnga to show their feeling indirectly. Figure 4 shows the emotional panels employed in the human subject experiment. Concretely, the most left, middle left, middle right, and most right panels in Fig. 4 express the feeling of happy, angry, sad, and surprise, respectively. These four kinds of emotion are selected from the fundamental emotion composed of the six kinds of emotion proposed by Ekman [6].

By using such panels, the players can recognize some kinds of feeling of the other players, which promote the players to change their behaviors (*e.g.*, the they may change the winner to the other winner). This contributes to selecting the same winner with a consensus among the players when the players encounter the situation where they select the different winners. From the viewpoint of the *numerical* and *psychological* gaps proposed in Sect. 2, the psychological gap in Barnga can be represented by the rule difference among the players while the numerical gap in Barnga can be represented by the difference of the number of wins among the players.

Fig. 4. Emotional panels (happy (most left), angry (middle left), sad (middle right), and surprise (most right))

5 Human Subject Experiment of Barnga

5.1 Experimental Setting

To investigate the effect of the emotional panels, we conduct the human subject experiment and explore the preliminary agent design based on Omoiyari from an analysis of the human subject experiment (*i.e.*, we try to understand what kinds of aspects should be implemented in the Omaiyari agent through the human subject experiment). Note that the players wear a mask and sun grasses in order not to show their emotions to other players, which helps to directly investigate the effect of the emotional panels. As mentioned in Sect. 4, the players can use the emotional panels when they want to use it.

In the experiment, the number of the player is four, and the rules that the players learn is shown in Table 2. For example, the player1 learns that Ace is the weakest among the cards and the trump suit is SPADE. Although many players (which is generally four players or more) separately sit down in each table in usual Barnga as shown in Fig. 3, each player in this experiment learns its own rule from the facilitator before the experiment and then four players who have the different rules play Barnga. This regards as the situation where the players start to play Barnga from the 2nd round. In this experiment, the players play Barnga in the four rounds (*i.e.*, 28 games (7 (games/round) $\times$ 4 (rounds)).

5.2 Experimental Results

Usage of Four Kinds of Emotional Panels: The human subject experiments found that the four kinds of emotional panels are used as follows:

- The *surprise* panel is increasingly used as the *psychological* gap increases (*i.e.*, as the players recognize the rule difference among them by noticing that the other players select the different winner).

Table 2. The rule of the players in the experiment

Player	Ace's strength	Trump suit
Player 1	Weak	SPADE
Player 2	Strong	SPADE
Player 3	*Strong*	*DIAMOND*
Player 4	Weak	HEART

- Although the *sad* panel is used when the player loses the game or when the different winner whom the player does not think to win is determined, but it is increasingly used as the *numerical* gap increases (*i.e.*, as the difference of wins among the players increases).
- The *angry* panel is used after recognizing the *surprise/sad* panels to express her/his claim to the other players, which provide a notice of an increase of the *psychological* and *numerical* gaps to other players. Such a panel contributes to changing the opponent's behaviors.
- The *happy* panel is used when the *numerical* and *psychological* gaps are filled (*i.e.*, when the player who often loses the games becomes the winner of the game by changing other players to select the loser as the winner after recognizing their rule difference).

Rate of Using Emotional Panels in Four Rounds: Fig. 5 shows the rate of using the emotional panels in the four rounds, where the vertical axis indicates the rate of using the emotional panels while the horizontal axis indicates the number of the rounds. Figures from Figs. 6, 7, 8 and 9 respectively show the rate of using the emotional panels in the 1st, 2nd, 3rd, and 4th round, where the vertical axis indicates the rate of using the emotional panels while the horizontal axis indicates the number of the game. In these figures, the blue, red, gray, and yellow lines indicates the happy, angry, sad, and surprise panels, respectively.

From Fig. 5, the ratio of using the happy panel increase as the number of the rounds increases while the ratio of using the surprise panel decreases until the 3rd round as the rounds increases. The rate of using the sad panel slightly increases and decreases while the rate of using the angry panel is small in the experiment. The detailed usage of the emotional panels is summarized as follows:

Round 1

From Fig. 6, the players used the surprise panel around the first several games because they noticed that the other players select the different winner. Although the rate of using the surprise panel decreases as the number of games increases, its averaged rate shown in Fig. 5 is the largest among the four emotional panels, which indicates that the players were confused by the different winner selected by the other players. From the viewpoint of the numerical and the psychological gaps, the players felt the *psychological* gap because the players recognized the rule difference among them.

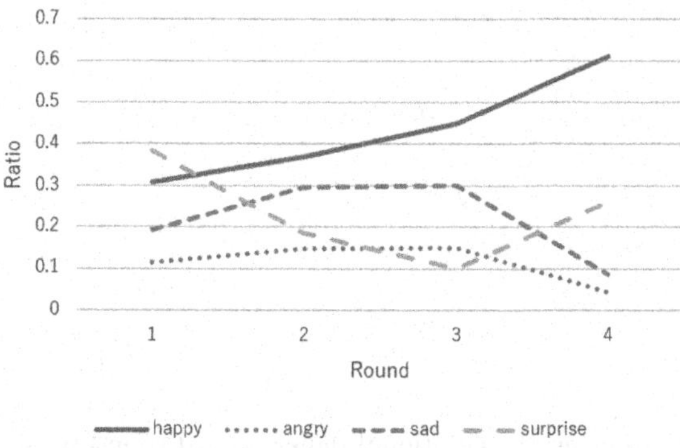

Fig. 5. The rate of using each emotional panels in four rounds (Color figure online)

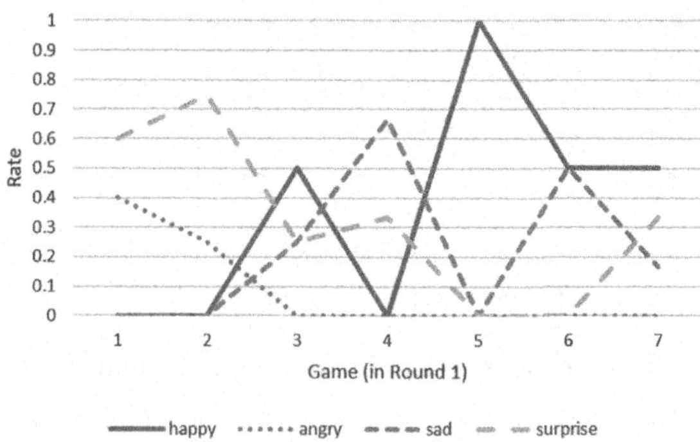

Fig. 6. The rate of using the emotional panels in 1st round (Color figure online)

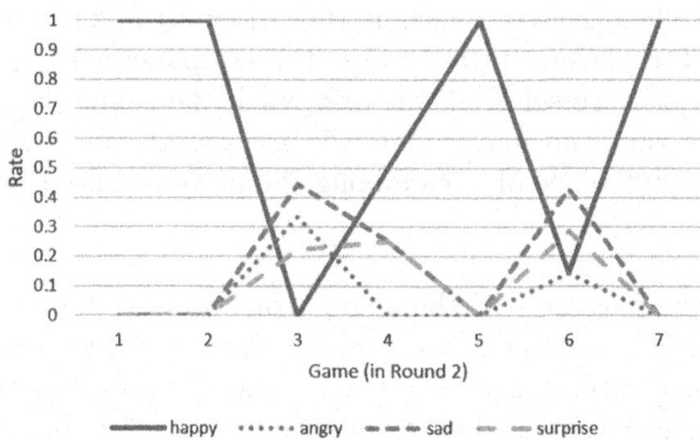

Fig. 7. The rate of using the emotional panels in 2nd round (Color figure online)

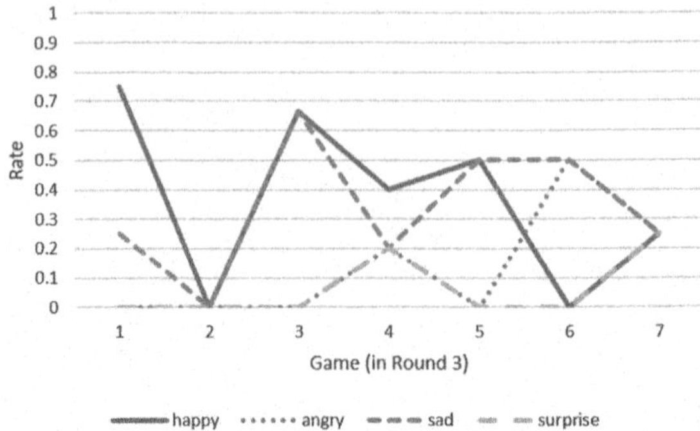

Fig. 8. The rate of using the emotional panels in 3rd round (Color figure online)

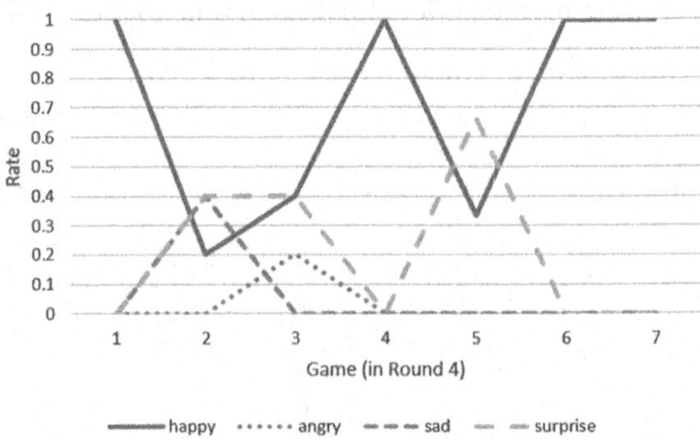

Fig. 9. The rate of using the emotional panels in 4th round (Color figure online)

Round 2

From Fig. 7, the rate of using the sad panel increases when the rate of using the happy panel decreases and vice versa, which indicates that the players were happy when the winner whom they thought to win is determined while they were sad when the winner whom they did not think to win is determined. Interestingly, the players started to use the sad panel not only when the not-expected winner were selected but also when the same players always won. This indicates that the players felt the *numerical* gap because the players recognized the difference of wins among the players caused by the win of the same players.

Round 3

From Fig. 8, the players used the angry panel around the last several games. This is because the winner was fixed (*i.e.*, the same winner was determined) around the first several games and the other players noticed that most of the players were not satisfied with this situation (caused by the psychological and numerical gaps) and some of them wanted to change this situation. In this time, the numerical and the psychological gaps become largest during the game.

Round 4

From Fig. 9, the players often used the happy panel because some players change to select the different winner after the angry panel was shown in the round 3. This derives the situation where the player who often loses the games becomes the winner of the game. As a results, the numerical and the psychological gaps are filled. In detail, the psychological gap was filled because some players sometimes accepted the different rule after recognizing the rule difference while the numerical gap was filled because the difference of wins decreases by increasing the chance of the loser to win the game.

6 Discussion

6.1 Omoiyari-Based Behaviors by Emotional Panels

According to the analysis, the emotional panels with the four kinds of the emotions express the numerical gap (*i.e.*, the difference of wins among the players) and the psychological gap (*i.e.*, the rule difference among the players) gaps. More importantly, the panels do not only express the numerical and psychological gap but also promote players to fill these gaps by changing their behaviors.

To understand this issue, let's focus on the round 3 again. In this round, the angry panel was shown to the winner players, which promotes some players to change to select the different winner. Note that the behavior of showing the angry panel was caused not only for the player's self but also for other players who may felt the same numerical and psychological gaps. In order words, this behavior has both the selfish and altruistic aspects, *i.e.*, the behavior for the player's self is selfish while the that for other players is altruistic. In particular, the latter altruistic behavior is regarded as Omoiyari.

What should be noted here is that the altruistic behavior as Omoiyari is not derived accidentally, *i.e.*, Omoiyari-based behavior requires a trigger to be derived. In this viewpoint, a recognition of both the numerical and psychological gaps of *others* becomes the trigger. As the recognition order of these gaps, firstly the player felt own psychological gap, secondly the player recognized the psychological gap of others (by looking at the surprise panel of others), and thirdly the player recognized the numerical gap of others (by looking at the sad panel of others). All of these sequence of recognition is needed to derive Omoiyari-based behaviors. In Barnga, Omoiyari-based behaviors can be achieved by a sequence of showing surprise/sad panels; showing the angry panel after recognizing the feeling of others; and changing to select the different winner, which increases to show the happy panel.

6.2 The Agents with Omoiyari

In order to implement the agent which can derive the Omoiyari-based behaviors, the agent has to know the appropriate timing and the situations when the emotional panels should be shown to fill the numerical and psychological gap of

Table 3. The usage and the effect of the emotional panels for the gaps

No.	Gap	Emotional panel	Target	Result
1	Gap 2	Happy	Other players	The situation become stable
2	Gap 3 & 4	Angry	Winning players	The situation changes
3	Gap 2	Angry	Losing players	The table lead by the user
4	Gap 2	Sad	Winning player	User's selection is adopted
5	Gap 1 & 2	Surprise	Other players	The gap is expressed

other players. Table 3 summaries the usage and effect of the emotional panels found in the human subject experiment. In this table, "Gap" column indicates the type of gaps categorized in Table 1, "Emotional panel" column indicates the type of the used panel, "Target" column indicates the target of the players for showing the emotional panels, and "Result" column indicates what is happened by using the emotional panels. For example, No. 2 in Table 3 shows the case that the angry panel shown to the winner players in Gap 3 & 4 (*i.e.*, the numerical and psychological gaps of others) results in changing the situation by promoting some players to change to select the different winner.

Even though the emotional panels are the simple tools to show the numerical and psychological gaps indirectly, the emotional panels has a potential of changing the situation of the table to fill the numerical and psychological gaps. This suggests that the agent can derive the above suitable situation if the agent shows the emotional panels at the appropriate timing and situations. Since such appropriate timing and situations are summarized in Table 2, it is easy to implement the agent by introducing them as the if-then rules. The design of such an agent and an investigation of its effectiveness will be done in the future work.

7 Conclusion

This paper focused on *Omoiyari* in Japanese as consideration/thoughtfulness for others to promote people to obtain a consensus among them, and verified the effectiveness of Omoiyari by analyzing behaviors of players in the cross-cultural game Barnga. Concretely, we designed Omoiyari as the behaviors of filling the *numerical* and *psychological* gaps and proposed the emotional panels into the Barnga in order to derive Omoiyari-based behaviors of players. In detail, the proposed emotional panels have four kinds of emotional panels expressing happy, angry, sad, and surprise, which help the players to indirectly express their feeling to the other players. The analysis of human subject experiment has derived that the emotional panels are used to express their feeling for filling the numerical and psychological gaps and derive the change of the opponent's behaviors. In detail, we found the following implications: (1) Omoiyari-based behaviors are achieved by a sequence of showing surprise/sad panels; showing the angry panel after recognizing the feeling of others; and changing the decision of the winner to the same one selected by others; (2) the surprise panel is increasingly used as the psychological gap increases; the sad panel is increasingly used as the numerical gap increases; the angry panel is used after recognizing the surprise/sad panels and contributes to changing the opponent's behaviors; and the happy panel is used when the numerical and psychological gaps are filled.

Since this paper analyzed Omoiyari-based behaviors through the human-subjective experiment but have not yet developed Omoiyari agents, we should investigate an effectiveness of Omoiyari agents through the game composed of human and agents. For this purpose, we are planning to develop Omoiyari agent by employing Q-learning as one of the machine learning algorithms, which try to reduce its own numerical and psychological gaps by estimating the rules of the other players in Barnga.

References

1. Ushida, Y., Takadama, K.: Validation of agent model in highly-dynamic environment via Barnga Game. In: The Multi-Agent-Based Simulation Workshop (MABS2012) (2012)
2. Thiagarajan, S., Steinwachs, B.: Barnga: A Simulation Game on Cultural Clashes. Intercultural Press, Yarmouth (1990)
3. Uchida, Y., Kitayama, S.: Development and validation of a sympathy scale. Jpn. J. Psychol. **72**(4), 275–282 (2001)
4. Carver, C.S., Scheier, M.F.: Control theory: a useful conceptual framework for personality-social, clinical, and health psychology. Psychol. Bull. **92**(1), 111–135 (1982)
5. Wolfe, J., Crookall, D.: Developing a scientific knowledge of simulation/gaming. Simul. Gaming **29**(1), 7–19 (1998)
6. Ekman, P., Friesen, W.V.: Constants across cultures in the face and emotion. J. Pers. Soc. Psychol. **17**(2), 124 (1971)

Does a Character's Visual Style Affect Audience Empathy and Sympathy?

Jisu Park, Nicoletta Adamo-Villani, and Robert W. Proctor(✉)

Purdue University, West Lafayette, IN 47906, USA
jspark474@gmail.com, rproctor@purdue.edu

Abstract. A believable virtual character is able to interact with the audience emotionally. To achieve believability, every component of the character from its movement to appearance must be designed carefully so that the character will elicit emotional responses such as empathy and sympathy from the viewers. However, to date, few studies have investigated what visual factors of a character trigger people's empathetic and sympathetic responses. The purpose of this experimental study was to examine the effect of visual styles of three-dimensional animated characters on audience empathy and sympathy responses. In the study, 71 participants watched three animations of three characters whose visual styles differed in the degree of stylization (i.e., lead, stylized, and iconic). In each animation, the characters showed happy, angry, and sad emotions. After viewing each character's animation, participants responded to a survey that measured their empathy and sympathy levels. Findings showed that the character's visual style did not have a significant effect on reported audience empathy and sympathy.

Keywords: Animated character · Visual style · Empathy · Sympathy

1 Introduction

Constructing a compelling character with which people can empathize is an essential process in character design [1]. Successful characters allow audiences to put themselves in the character's shoes, so to speak, and emotionally connect with the character. For this reason, a substantial body of research has focused on empathetic and sympathetic interaction between synthetic characters and users. For instance, research has shown that empathic emotions of the virtual character produced more positive feedback from people [2]. Also, another study set up a virtual classroom to teach children how to deal with bullying situations and showed that the children demonstrated empathy towards a victim character [3]. However, despite the increasing interest in virtual characters and how they can emotionally affect people, little attention has been paid to how the visual elements of a character influence people's emotional responses. In this paper, the visual style of a character is examined to determine whether it affects viewer's empathy and sympathy responses.

S. Yamamoto and H. Mori (Eds.): HCII 2019, LNCS 11569, pp. 476–488, 2019.
https://doi.org/10.1007/978-3-030-22660-2_35

2 Character's Visual Style

Characters are the direct agents with whom the audience communicates emotionally when watching an animation. In the book, *The Illusion of Life*, Thomas and Johnston discuss how designers should construct the characters carefully, considering all features a character has, from its costume, body proportions, facial features, to surrounding environment [4]. Some studies suggest that characters should be designed to look realistic [5, 6], whereas others suggest the opposite [7–10]. To investigate these contradictory ideas, we considered three visual styles of a character. The styles are based on the character hierarchy introduced by Bancroft in the book *Creating Characters with Personality* [11]. Bancroft's character hierarchy includes six visual style types: iconic, simple (stylized), broad, comedy relief, lead and realistic (see Fig. 1). Each style varies in the degree of stylization, with iconic having the highest degree of stylization and realistic having the lowest degree of stylization. In detail, an iconic character is the simplest character and, therefore, very limited in expressions. A simple character is still stylized but can convey more expressions than an iconic character because it has more facial features. A broad character can express more than the first two, with its big eyes and a big mouth for extreme facial expressions. A comedy relief character is less stylized in facial features. It conveys emotions through subtle facial and body expressions. A lead character has realistic proportions and an expressive face. Lastly, a realistic character is the character with the most realism but still possessing some degree of caricature. The three characters' visual styles selected for the present study were iconic, stylized and lead.

Fig. 1. Examples of the character hierarchy with illustrations taken from open access materials.

3 Prior Research on Virtual Characters and Audience Emotion

Prior studies have examined how virtual characters can be created to elicit emotion from the viewer. Paiva et al. highlighted the importance of the 'proximity' factor to evoke empathy in a role-playing game with 3D characters [12]. A few studies have shown that people feel empathetic towards the character if he/she is more similar to a human being [5, 6]. A study by Goetz et al. showed that the appearance of a robot influences subjects' acceptance of and cooperation with the robot [13]. Ruttkay et al.

argued that people may view realistic characters as more intelligent but may view non-humanlike characters as more appealing and entertaining [7]. McCloud, in his book *Understanding Comics*, claimed that iconic characters are more effective than realistic characters, as the audience's involvement increases [8]. For that reason, iconic characters are often used commercially. Disney characters, with their iconized look and exaggerated expressions, engage the audience. People may prefer iconic agents because iconic agents are subject to fewer social norms [9]. A study by Adamo-Villani et al. investigated whether the visual style of signing avatars (realistic vs. stylized) affected viewers' perception of the avatar's appeal [10]. Results showed that the stylized signing avatar was perceived as more appealing than the realistic one. The 'Uncanny Valley' hypothesis, according to which people feel eerie and unpleasant when a high degree of realism (but not complete realism) in a character is reached [14], may explain why iconic characters can be more appealing and engaging than realistic characters.

4 Empathy and Sympathy

Many studies define empathy differently, but all definitions agree on the concept of sharing of 'affect'. According to Eisenberg and Strayer, empathy is defined as "sharing the perceived emotion of another – 'feeling with' another" [15]. Often times, the terms, empathy and sympathy are used interchangeably, although they refer to different things. Sympathy, in contrast to empathy, is defined as "an emotional response stemming from another's emotional state or condition that is not identical to the other's emotion, but consists of feelings of sorrow or concern for another's welfare [16]". Empathy and sympathy are not mutually exclusive, but rather they are interconnected.

There are two aspects to empathy - mediation and its outcome. Mediation of empathy happens in two ways, via situations and via emotional expressions. Empathy is elicited via 'situations' when the observer interprets the emotion based on the situation another person is dealing with. Empathy is elicited via emotional expression when the observer concludes the emotional state based on the emotion the observed person is showing. These two ways of mediation produce the empathic outcome, which can be either cognitive or affective. A cognitive outcome means that the observer carries out an action to respond to empathy, for example, helping the target. An affective outcome is when the observer experiences an emotion because of the perception of the target.

In the study reported in this paper, in order to mediate via the situation, three scenarios were created, each of which could be easily understood by the audience. To mediate via emotional expressions, the audience needed to perceive the character's emotions accurately. This emotion perception was achieved through the character's body movements and facial expressions that were suitable to the story.

5 Assessing Empathic Response

Empathy can be divided into two categories: dispositional and situational. Dispositional empathy is a person's general tendency to feel empathy and is used for psychological profiling. On the other hand, situational empathy is when a person empathizes in a given situation and is used to examine if a stimulus has an effect on people. Therefore, situational empathy is what the study reported in this paper aimed to assess.

There are several methods of measuring empathy. Hogan's empathy (EM) and Mehrabian and Epstein's questionnaire (QMEE) are commonly used to measure cognitive and emotional empathy [17]. However, these scales measure dispositional empathy and, hence, were not suitable for the study. It is difficult to measure situational empathy because empathy happens internally and therefore cannot be observed [18]. Biological measures are available, for example, through devices that read heart rate or breathing rate. However, due to the difficulty of analyzing such data, self-reporting methods are suitable for most studies measuring situational empathy [18]. For our study, a scale developed by Escalas and Stern was chosen to measure empathy and sympathy because of several similarities between their work and what this research aimed to measure [19]. Escalas and Stern investigated the effect of a classical drama advertisement and a vignette advertisement on viewers' sympathy and empathy responses. The vignette ad was characterized by "multiple unconnected episodes (rather than a single unified plot), repetitive organization (rather than linear), and characters contained within each episode (rather than interacting with those in other episodes)" [19]. Those authors experimented with eight television (TV) ads, each one categorized either as a classical or a vignette ad. For the study, they created 10 survey questions and validated them by conducting two pretests with 147 participants. The first five questions tested whether subjects understood the feelings of the character and the situation happening in the TV ad, and therefore measured sympathy. The other five questions assessed whether the subjects felt like they were one of the characters or felt as though the events were happening to them, and therefore measured empathy. The underlying assumption of the survey questionnaire was that responses to the sympathy and empathy items are interconnected, not 'mutually exclusive'. The authors asked the participants, 'for the television commercial you just saw, please rate how descriptive each of the following statements is of how you personally reacted to this ad.' Participants were given a seven-point scale ranging from not at all descriptive to very descriptive. For the statistical analysis, the means of the five items of sympathy and five items of empathy were calculated.

Escalas and Stern's survey questionnaire was modified to fit the scope of this study. Questions were shortened to make them more easily readable, and a five-point scale ranging from strongly disagree to strongly agree was used. Table 1 presents the ten questions used in the study, where the first five questions assessed sympathy level and last five questions assessed empathy level. The fifth question said "last two videos" rather than all the videos because the first clip showed happy emotion, hence the character did not experience a problem.

Table 1. Modified sympathy/empathy scale used in the study

1	I understood what the character was feeling in the videos
2	I understood what was bothering the character
3	I tried to understand the events as they occurred
4	I tried to understand the character's motivation
5	I was able to recognize the problems that the character had in the last two videos
6	I experienced feeling as if the events were happening to me
7	I felt as though I was the character
8	I felt as though the events in the videos were happening to me
9	I experienced many of the same feeling that the character portrayed
10	I felt as if the characters' feelings were my own

6 Description of the Study

The objective of the study was to determine whether the degree of stylization of an animated character (e.g., lead, stylized, iconic) has an effect on viewers' empathy and sympathy. The independent variable for the experiment was the degree of stylization in the character's visual design. The dependent variables were the viewers' empathy and sympathy ratings.

The hypotheses of the experiment were the following:

H_0 = The degree of stylization of an animated 3D character has no effect on the audience empathy and sympathy levels.
H_a = The degree of stylization of an animated 3D character has an inverted U-shaped relation with the audience empathy and sympathy levels.

6.1 Stimuli

Three 3D animated characters were created with Autodesk Maya software. All three characters were of the same gender and approximately the same age. The only intended difference was the degree of stylization, which caused the proportion of the characters' bodies and facial features to be different. Several features distinguished the three characters from each other. First of all, the body proportions were different, for instance, the head size compared to the body was the largest for the iconic character. The eyeballs were modeled and textured differently: The lead character used photo realistic textures on spheres, the stylized character used a simple color texture on spheres, and the iconic character's eyes were modeled as solid-color flat disks. Facial features including eyebrow, ear, nose, lips, and hair were more detailed for the lead character and less defined for the iconic character. Textures for the lead character had the highest level of detail, as more detailed shades and wrinkles were added. For clothing, the colors and the designs were kept the same. Animation, rendering, compositing were also kept consistent across the characters. Figure 2 shows screenshots of the three characters.

Fig. 2. Neutral facial expression from the left, lead, stylized and iconic characters (face close-ups, top; full body shots, bottom)

The three characters were rigged with the same number of joints and controllers, and key frame animations were created using the controllers of the lead character. By transferring the animations of the lead character to the stylized and iconic characters, we ensured that the three characters had the same movement. When transferring the animation, the rotational values of the joints were kept, but translations of the wrist and feet IK controllers were adjusted so that the movement was proportional to the character's body. Some of the movements had to be edited slightly to avoid interpenetration issues caused by the differences in the character's body proportions. Facial animations were created with blendshapes, which is a multiple-target morphing technique. In total, three blendshapes for the eyebrows, three blendshapes of the lips, and two blendshapes for the eyelids were produced. To have equivalent facial articulations among the characters, the amount of displacement of the eyebrows and lips for the emotions was proportional to the length of the character's face. Figure 3 shows the blendshapes for lead, stylized and iconic characters.

As previously discussed, in order to mediate empathy via emotion, the audience needs to recognize the emotions the characters are presenting. The emotions represented in the animations were happy, angry and sad, which are three of the six basic emotions identified by Ekman [20]. These three emotions were selected because they are easily recognizable. The selected emotions were expressed through characters facial expressions and mainly through body animation.

The scenario was also a significant factor within the experiment because participants needed to understand the situation in order for empathy to be mediated via situation. The situations represented in the stories were easy to understand and easy for subjects to relate to. Table 2 shows a brief summary of each story, and Fig. 4 shows nine frames extracted from the 'sad animation'. The duration of each story ranged from

Fig. 3. Blendshapes for lead (top), stylized (middle) and iconic (bottom) characters

10 to 19 s. The order in which the stories were presented to the subjects was fixed (happy, angry and sad), whereas the order of presentation of the character's visual style was randomized. The final animations were rendered at a resolution of 800 × 600 pixels, with a grey background and no sound. However, the screen resolution automatically changed if a subject decided to participate using a cellphone.

Table 2. Happy, angry and sad scenarios

Happy Scenario: A character walks into the scene and sees something on the ground. He runs towards it, picks it up from the ground, and finds out that it is money. He is delighted and jumps around with happiness
Angry Scenario: A character is happily walking, holding a dish with food. Then, he trips over a rock and falls on the ground, food flying away. He sees the food on the ground, gets very upset and kicks the rock away
Sad Scenario: A character gets his exam score back. He does not see it right away because he is worried and nervous. When he finally checks it, he sees an F on the paper. He collapses on the ground with sadness

6.2 Subjects

Seventy-one subjects, both undergraduate and graduate students participated in the study. All participants were students at Purdue University and were recruited via email. The age of the participants ranged from 18 to 45; 51% were male. A total of 48 participants indicated that they majored in Computer Graphics Technology (CGT); the others were non- CGT majors.

6.3 Procedure

Subjects were sent an email containing a brief summary of the research, an invitation to participate in the study, and the http address of the web survey. Participants completed the online survey using their own computers or smartphones, and the survey remained active for two weeks. In the survey, participants first indicated their age, gender, and college major, and then watched the three characters in random order. After viewing one emotion clip, subjects were asked to select what emotion the character was feeling; four choices were provided (happy, sad, angry and other, where option 'other' allowed users to type the emotion they thought the character was displaying in the clip). After viewing all three emotion clips for one character, the participants answered a questionnaire that measured their emotional response towards the character. After completing the questionnaire, they were asked to enter the age of the character and then proceed to the next set of clips. Participants could also leave comments about the experiment in an optional comment section.

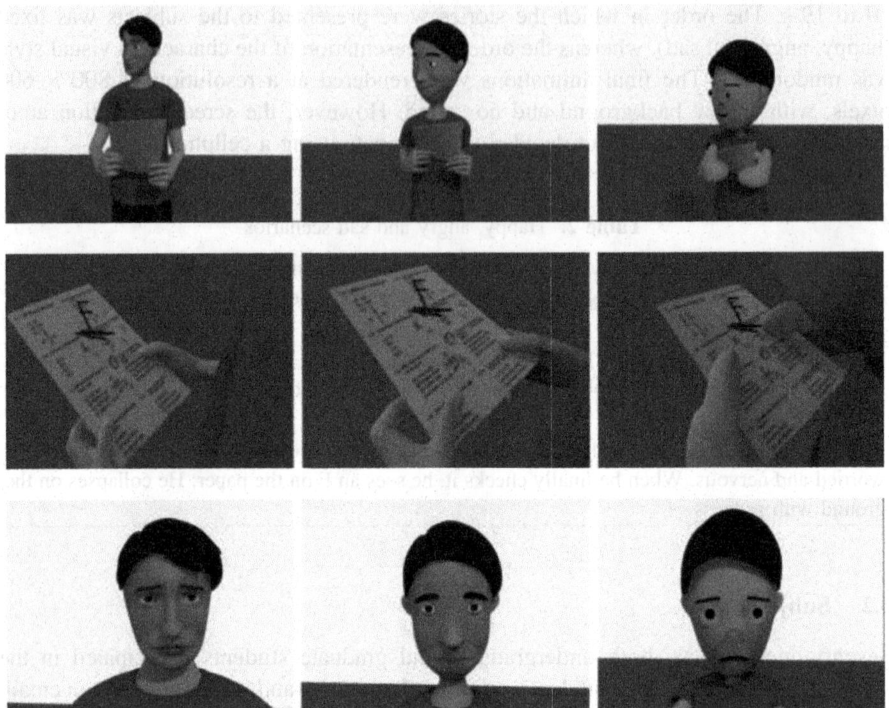

Fig. 4. Frames extracted from the "sad" animation, lead character (left), stylized character (middle), iconic character (right)

7 Results

Out of the 71 people who participated in the study, only 61 responses were analyzed; the other responses were excluded due to the following reasons. Nine responses were excluded due to incomplete participation. One participant did not answer one question (e.g., the age of the iconic character), leaving a missing response to that question.

Identification of Character's Emotion. A total of 51 participants selected the correct emotions for all nine questions. The other ten subjects selected option 'other' and entered the following answers: joy, excitement, glee, intrigue, excitement, happiness and awe for happy animation; frustration, hurt, shock, disappointment, anger and rage for angry animation; and worried, depressed, shock, anxiety, shame, sadness, embarrassed for sad animation. According to the Feeling wheel [21], those emotional words can be categorized and narrowed down to be equivalent to happy, angry, and sad. Therefore, even though participants chose the option 'other', their answers were considered to be correct.

Empathy and Sympathy Levels. The results were analyzed using a one-way ANOVA between character types and sympathy, and another one-way ANOVA between character types and empathy. These analyses showed no significant differences in subjects' empathy and sympathy levels among the three characters' visual types (sympathy: $M_{\text{lead}} = 4.46$, $M_{\text{stylized}} = 4.53$, $M_{\text{iconic}} = 4.45$, $F(2,180) < 1$; empathy: $M_{\text{lead}} = 2.64$, $M_{\text{stylized}} = 2.59$, $M_{\text{iconic}} = 2.53$, $F(2,180) < 1$). Also, a paired samples t-test was used to compare the responses between sympathy and empathy, and it was found that sympathy ratings were significantly higher than empathy ratings, $t(182) = 21.17$, $p < 0.001$).

For further analysis, a separate one-way ANOVA was used between empathy and gender ($F(1,181) = 4.280$, $p = 0.040$) and also between sympathy and gender ($F(1,181) = 1.380$, $p = 0.242$). Female participants tended to rate both sympathy, and empathy towards the characters higher than the male participants did. However, when analysis with a linear mixed-effects model for sympathy and empathy was calculated, the tendencies for gender differences were no longer evident in the statistics (Linear Mixed-Effects Model for sympathy and gender: $F < 1$ for empathy and $F < 1$ for gender).

In addition, from the same linear mixed-effects model, the effects of age, gender, college major of participants, order of characters, and characters visual type on participants' empathy and sympathy levels were analyzed. Random effect of subjects and correlation among random errors were considered in fitting the model. Probability values assuming no effect for all the factors were obtained. For sympathy, all values were nonsignificant: gender ($p = 0.365$), college major ($p = 0.986$), character type ($p = 0.219$), character age ($p = 0.975$) and subject age ($p = 0.122$). Likewise, for empathy, all values were nonsignificant: gender ($p = 0.444$), college major ($p = 0.220$), character type ($p = 0.974$), character age ($p = 0.483$) and subject age ($p = 0.733$). Hence, we found no statistically significant effects in the study.

8 Discussion and Conclusion

The paper reported a study that investigated the effect of character's visual style on audience empathy and sympathy. Findings from the statistical analyses, which included a one-way ANOVA model and a linear mixed model, revealed no significant difference in subjects' empathy and sympathy levels among the three characters. This lack of effect is similar to the finding of Gruber, Aune, and Koutstaal for judgments of trust, who reported no significant difference in perceived trust of an automated decision aid as a function of whether the recommendations were made by a low or high anthropomorphic character [22]. The results of their study and ours suggest that any influence of character visual style, at least in the laboratory setting, is relatively weak. In addition to showing no main effect of character's visual style, our study found no significant interaction between participants' age, gender, college major, characters' age and participants' empathy and sympathy levels.

Although the study failed to reject the null hypothesis, it showed that the subjects' sympathy level was significantly higher than the empathy level ($p < 0.01$). This difference could be due to two reasons. First, the short duration of the video might have prevented complete absorption needed for empathy [19]. Second, according to Escalas and Stern, it takes well-developed characters and a linear plot to evoke empathy [19].

This could explain why participants could understand the feelings and situation of the character (sympathy) but failed to completely identify themselves with the character.

The study had several limitations that future research can address. First, the characters were supposed to be the same age (to prevent age from being a confounding variable). However, the subjects' ratings of the age differed across the three style types: A one-way ANOVA with character types as independent variables and the perceived character's age as dependent variables showed that the lead and stylized characters were rated as much older than the iconic character ($M_{\text{lead}} = 21.93$ years, $M_{\text{stylized}} = 20.70$ years, $M_{\text{iconic}} = 12.71$ years, $F(2,179) = 50.151$, $p < 0.001$). This one-way ANOVA shows a significant difference in the perception of the character's age, but from the linear mixed-effects model, this difference did not affect the users' ratings of sympathy and empathy. Second, it is possible that the visual differences between the lead and the stylized characters were not sufficiently distinctive. The differences could have been more exaggerated, for example, by making the lead character look closer to a realistic one, and by making the iconic character more abstract and less humanlike. In addition, for those subjects who took the survey on their cellphones, the differences between the characters' styles might have been even less evident because of the lower screen resolution. Third, individual differences in sympathy and empathy levels exist. Some viewers may not reach the empathy stage due to the short runtime of the video clips, whereas others do. Lastly, for the optional comment section, two subjects reported perceiving the survey questions as unclear and too similar to each other. For instance, one participant commented, "Some questions are ambiguous, I think some of them just ask the same thing". The fact that some users perceived the questions as being similar may have led them to give similar ratings rather than distinguish between the components being questioned.

To summarize, a convincing synthetic character plays a critical role in keeping the audience emotionally engaged throughout animation as it exhibits strong life-like presence. To enhance this experience, we empirically tested three visual styles of the characters and their influence on audience ratings of sympathy and empathy. Because creating more realistic characters is expensive in comparison to iconized characters, the lack of significant difference in sympathy and empathy ratings between character types suggests that the cost/benefit ratio for iconic characters may be best for situations in which the animator is seeking to elicit emotional responses from the viewer. However, the strongest result of the study was the somewhat surprising finding that the age of the iconic character was judged to be much younger than that of the lead and stylized characters from which it was derived. Whether that difference in perceived age is one that will interact with the age-appropriateness of scenarios is among the work that remains to be done to test a wider variety of visual types with more extended video clips.

According to the comments on the experiment, some of the survey questionnaires on empathy and sympathy were somewhat similar to each other. The empathy questions, 'I experienced feeling as if the events were happening to me' and 'I felt as though the events in the videos were happening to me' were ambiguous to participants as to how they are different from each other. The former question could be rephrased to 'I experienced feeling because of the events'. Future research could address this issue by rephrasing the statements or better definitions and concrete examples.

In addition, future work could be performed with longer animation clips, richer scenarios, and characters that differ in visual style in a more salient way. Because research shows that characters' movements may affect the believability of a character, the relationship between style of motion and empathy/sympathy responses needs to be investigated as well.

References

1. Maestri, G.: Digital Character Animation 3. New Riders, Berkeley (2006)
2. Brave, S., Nass, C., Hutchinson, K.: Computers that care: investigating the effects of orientation of emotion exhibited by an embodied computer agent. Int. J. Hum.-Comput. St. **62**(2), 161–178 (2005)
3. Paiva, A., et al.: Learning by feeling: evoking empathy with synthetic characters. Appl. Artif. Intell. **19**(3–4), 235–266 (2005)
4. Thomas, F., Johnston, O., Thomas, F.: The Illusion of Life: Disney Animation. Hyperion, New York (1995)
5. Riek, L.D., Rabinowitch, T.C., Chakrabarti, B., Robinson, P.: How anthropomorphism affects empathy toward robots. In: Proceedings of the 4th ACM/IEEE International Conference on Human Robot Interaction, pp. 245–246. ACM, New York (2009)
6. Nass, C., Isbister, K., Lee, E.J.: Truth is beauty: researching embodied conversational agents. In: Cassell, J., et al. (eds.) Embodied Conversational Agents, pp. 374–402. MIT Press, Cambridge (2000)
7. Gulz, A., Haake, M.: Social and visual style in virtual pedagogical agents. In: Proceedings of the Workshop on Adaptation to Affective Factors, 10th International Conference on User Modeling, pp. 24–29 (2005)
8. McCloud, S.: Understanding Comics: The Invisible Art. Kitchen Sink Press, Northampton (1993)
9. Woo, H.: Designing multimedia learning environments using animated pedagogical agents: factors and issues. J. Comput. Assist. Learn. **25**(3), 203–218 (2009)
10. Adamo-Villani, N., Lestina, J., Anasingaraju, S.: Does character's visual style affect viewer's perception of signing avatars? In: Vincenti, G., Bucciero, A., Vaz de Carvalho, C. (eds.) eLEOT 2015. LNICST, vol. 160, pp. 1–8. Springer, Cham (2016). https://doi.org/10.1007/978-3-319-28883-3_1
11. Bancroft, T.: Creating Characters with Personality. Watson-Guptill, New York (2016)
12. Paiva, A., Dias, J., Sobral, D., Woods, S., Hall, L.: Building empathic lifelike characters: the proximity factor. In: Workshop on Empathic Agents, AAMAS, vol. 4 (2004)
13. Goetz, J., Kiesler, S., Powers, A.: Matching robot appearance and behavior to tasks to improve human-robot cooperation. In: The 12th IEEE International Workshop on Robot and Human Interactive Communication, Proceedings, ROMAN 2003, pp. 55–60 (2003)
14. Mori, M., MacDorman, K., Kageki, N.: The uncanny valley [from the field]. IEEE Robot. Autom. Mag. **19**(2), 98–100 (2012)
15. Eisenberg, N., Strayer, J.: Critical issues in the study of empathy. In: Eisenberg, N., Strayer, J. (eds.) Cambridge Studies in Social and Emotional Development. Empathy and Its Development, pp. 3–13. Cambridge University Press, New York (1987)
16. Eisenberg, N., Miller, P.: The relation of empathy to prosocial and related behaviors. Psychol. Bull. **101**(1), 91–119 (1987)
17. Davis, M.: Measuring individual differences in empathy: evidence for a multidimensional approach. J. Pers. Soc. Psychol. **44**(1), 113–126 (1983)

18. Seo, S., Geiskkovitch, D., Nakane, M., King, C., Young, J.: Poor thing! would you feel sorry for a simulated robot?: a comparison of empathy toward a physical and a simulated robot. In: Proceedings of the Tenth Annual ACM/IEEE International Conference on Human-Robot Interaction, pp. 125–132 (2015)
19. Escalas, J., Stern, B.: Sympathy and empathy: emotional responses to advertising dramas. J. Consum. Res. **29**(4), 566–578 (2003)
20. Ekman, P.: Facial expression. In: Dagleish, T., Power, M. (eds.) Handbook of Cognition and Emotion, pp. 301–320. John Wiley, Chichester (1999)
21. Willcox, G.: The feeling wheel: a tool for expanding awareness of emotions and increasing spontaneity and intimacy. Trans. Anal. J. **12**(4), 274–276 (1982)
22. Gruber, D., Aune, A., Koutstaal, W.: Can semi-anthropomorphism influence trust and compliance?: exploring image use in app interfaces. In: Proceedings of the Technology, Mind, and Society, Article no. 13. ACM, New York (2018)

Relationship Between Difference of Motivation and Behavior Change Caused by Visualization

Yurika Shiozu[1(✉)], Koya Kimura[2], Ryo Shioya[2], Katsunori Shimohara[2], and Katsuhiko Yonezaki[3]

[1] Aichi University, Nagoya, Aichi 453-8777, Japan
yshiozu@vega.aichi-u.ac.jp
[2] Graduate School of Science and Engineering, Doshisha University, Kyoto 610-0394, Japan
[3] Yokohama City University, Yokohama, Kanagawa 236-0027, Japan

Abstract. This study aims to verify the hypothesis that altruism makes others change their behavior. We developed an original system and application which collect global positioning system (GPS) data add photos on the maps and share them between subjects. We prepared two maps which are intended to contribute information by different motivations. The first map aims to develop a recommended course for a walk, focusing on subjects' desire for recognition as the selfish motivation. The second map is aimed at safety for children, focusing on subjects' altruism. Subjects can take pictures and upload them with an icon that they designate as the category; they are then shared among the subjects. If a subject sympathizes with the posted pictures, he/she can express approval on the picture. The results show that the map of safety for children has more pictures with multiple approvals, and some pictures on the map of recommended course for a walk have no approval. This suggests that the difference in motivation makes subjects express more approvals. With statistical analysis, we try to show that some type of visualization of GPS data may become a nudge.

Keywords: Nudge · Visualization · Photo contribution system

1 Introduction

The purpose of this study is to verify the hypothesis that altruism makes others change their behavior. Recently, in economics, the heterogeneity of human beings is considered for modelling. In computer science, the agent-based model also accounts for the heterogeneity of human beings. Heterogeneity is being considered because traditional public policy does not work well as different motivations result in different behaviors. For instance, traditional economics assumes that in a model with representative rational human beings, when the public policy to levy tobacco tax is implemented, the consumer stops smoking. However, in our society, when tax is levied on tobacco, some people stop smoking, but others do (or can) not stop smoking. Thus, as the traditional economic model faces the abovementioned limitation, researchers need to consider various types of human beings. In behavioral economics, the government can create a policy to induce the desired direction while allowing other people to have a choice. This is called "libertarian paternalism." In this example, levying a tobacco tax is a nudge.

S. Yamamoto and H. Mori (Eds.): HCII 2019, LNCS 11569, pp. 489–499, 2019.
https://doi.org/10.1007/978-3-030-22660-2_36

This research compares two maps that elicit different motivations. One map focuses on selfish motivation through the desire for recognition, while the other map focuses on altruism. The common feature of the two maps is that they are made by the residents and shared among themselves. We developed an original application to enable this feature and to clarify that visualization of information by residents brings about indirect changes in their behavior.

The remainder of this paper is organized as follows. In Sect. 2, we refer to previous studies, and we explain our model in Sect. 3. Section 4 describes the system of collecting data and our original application. Section 5 describes the results, and we present our conclusion and remarks in Sect. 6.

2 Previous Studies

In public economics, provision of public goods is an important task for the government. This is because without government intervention, households engage in utility maximization behavior, and public goods become under supplied. Private provision of public goods cannot be achieved due to the social dilemma. For example, if all the residents spend time only to do whatever they want, the utility of individuals will be maximized but no one will participate in volunteers such as regional traffic safety campaigns. The absence of traffic accidents in the area is desirable for the residents, but because traffic safety campaigns are insufficient only with police patrols, which are local public goods, traffic accidents increase and the utility of resident declines. However, Lazo et al. (1997) shows that residents supply local public goods based on selfish motivation caused by time inconsistency. Shiozu et al. (2017) shows that private provision of public goods is not successful even if there are leaders with ultra-altruism, under the condition that provision of public goods causes a financial burden on the residents.

On the other hand, Thaler and Sunstein (2003) states that households never engage in utility maximization behavior. The authors suggest that, while allowing residents to make self-decisions, the government can lead their behavior to the desired direction for the society through libertarian paternalism. Moreover, Thaler and Sunstein (2008) recommends the utilization of this nudge approach.

3 Model

3.1 Concept for Behavior Change Through Visualization and Sharing of Information

We assume that people try to share information because of two incentives. One is the selfish incentive caused by the desire for recognition, and the other is the altruistic incentive to help people. Both incentives make a person upload his/her information. But self-satisfaction is obtained when others suggest sympathy by recommending a place as a good view. This is the reason why selfish motivation makes a person upload one's information. On the other hand, sharing the information of dangerous places occurs because it seems that the information is also beneficial to others. If other people sympathize with this information, they will change their behavior. For example, someone shows agreement on a social networking service (SNS) or changes his/her behavior. Of course, these actions such as to express sympathize and change behavior may take place simultaneously. Figure 1 illustrates this concept.

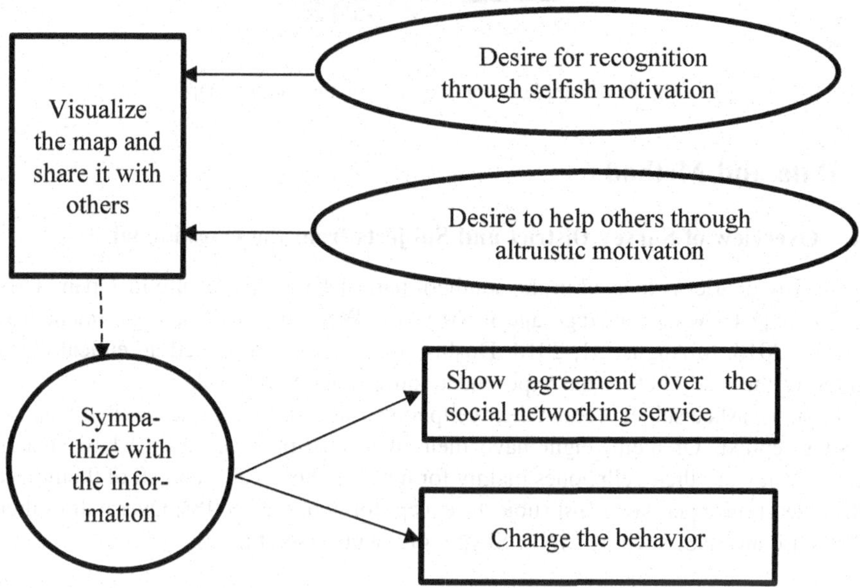

Fig. 1. Concept of our model

3.2 Nudge for This Study

In this study, we designed a nudge for the study subjects by asking them to upload a picture and an icon on two maps with two different meanings. The first map is developed to determine a recommended course for a walk. We intend this meaning to capture the subjects' need for approval. As the picture and icon on this map simply express the subjects' feelings, they do not always make others sympathize. Thus, this map focuses on the subjects' desire for approval rather than the desire for helping others. The second map involves safety for children. We intend this meaning to capture the subjects' altruism. The pictures and icons on this map show places that are dangerous for children, such as areas with heavy traffic. The information is uploaded as a call to attention. If a subject agrees with the information, he/she may change his/her behavior to avoid the danger. Figure 2 shows an example of the icon and picture on a map. We performed image processing on Fig. 2 for privacy protection. "いいね!" means "nice!" in Japanese.

Fig. 2. Example of the icon and picture on the map

4 Data and Method

4.1 Overview of Survey District and Subjects from the Questionnaire

The survey district is located in the southern part of Kyoto prefecture in Japan. There are 20 subjects, whose average age is 70 years. We conducted the experiment from June 12, 2018, to August 31, 2018. Doshisha University conducted an ethical examination of the study before the experiment and provided approval.

First, we asked subjects about their cellphone usage through a questionnaire, and 18 persons replied. Of them, eight have their own smartphones, and 10 have feature phones. They use their cellphones mainly for making phone calls, and all of them make calls at least once per day. Most subjects, except for two, send SMSs. Over half of them do not use an SNS, such as LINE, Skype, or Twitter (see Fig. 3).

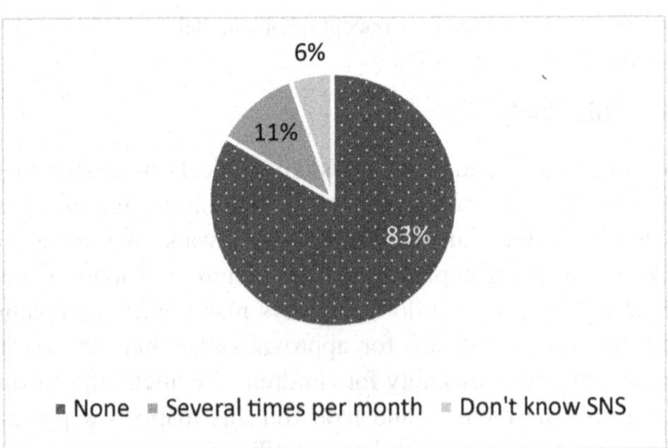

Fig. 3. Usage of social networking services (SNSs)

We asked the subjects about the type and frequency of their participation in volunteering activities. Figure 4 shows the types of volunteering activities they engaged in —five subjects do not participate in any volunteering activity. Figure 4 includes multiple answers.

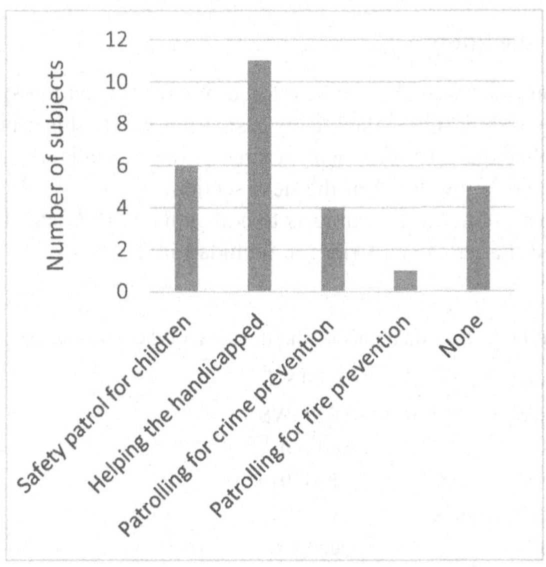

Fig. 4. Participation in volunteering activities

In Fig. 5, the frequency tends to be of three types: several times per month, once or twice per week and three or more times per week.

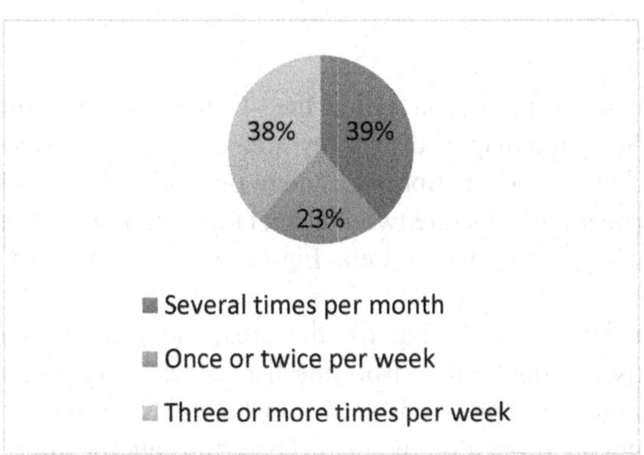

Fig. 5. Frequency of participation in volunteer activities

From these results, we find that the subjects use cellphones for making calls and sending SMSs; however, they are not used to SNSs. In addition, over 70% of the subjects participate in some type of volunteering activity. As some of these activities, such as safety patrol for children, need frequent participation, subjects may engage in it three or more times per week.

4.2 System for the Study

To confirm that our model works, we develop a photo contribution system and collect global positioning system (GPS) data using a smartphone. In this section, we describe the system for collecting GPS data with a smartphone. Details of our original photo contribution system are presented in the next section.

We loaned smartphones to the subjects to collect their GPS data. The specifications of our devices and the network carrier are included in Table 1.

Table 1. Specifications of the device and the network carrier

Manufacturer	FUJITSU
Model number	ARROWS
OS	Android ™ 5.1
CPU	MSM8916
Clock frequency	1.2 GHz
CORE	Quad Core
RAM	2 GB
Location information	GPS and GLONASS
Sensor	Direction/G-Sensor/Acceleration/Light/
	E-Compass/Proximity/Gyro Sensor
Network carrier	IIJ Mobile (MVNO of NTT DoCoMo)

4.3 Application

We developed our own application called the "Community System Design" (CSD). This application shows the map of the survey area only. For this study, the subject can upload a picture taken by the smartphone camera on two maps with different purposes. Thus, in this experiment, we operate two maps: (1) map recommending the course for a walk and (2) a safety map for children. Figure 6 shows the user interface of this application.

If no location data are available for the area, the picture cannot be uploaded. Subjects also choose a suitable icon from the list, which is uploaded with the picture. An example of an uploaded picture is shown in Fig. 2. Next, the picture and icon are shown where the pin is dropped on the map. These pins and pictures are shared among subjects. In addition, other subjects can express their approval about this picture if they tap the button called "いいね!."

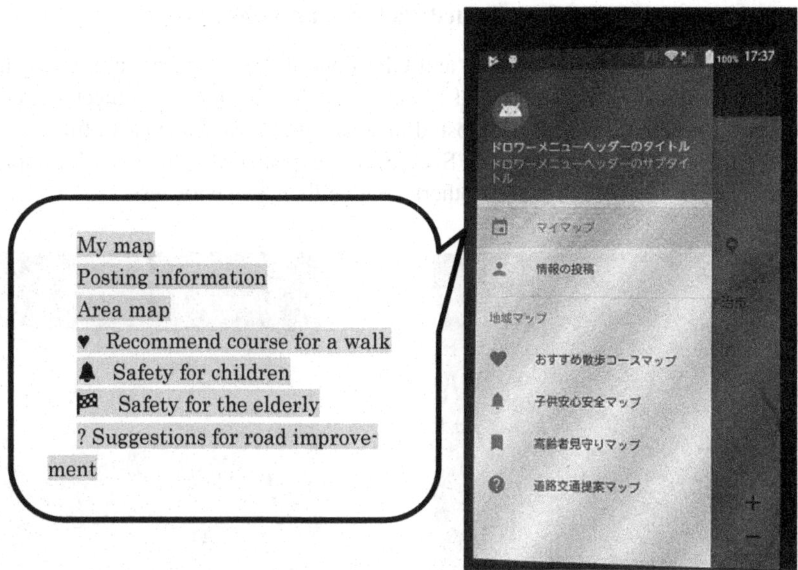

Fig. 6. User interface of the Community System Design application

5 Results

5.1 Overview of the Results

A total of 62 pictures were posted. Half of them are on the map of the recommend course for a walk. The rest of them are on the map of safety for children. Figure 7 shows the map of the recommend course for a walk[1]. This was especially significant as contributed pictures of the location of the subjects' base got 13 approvals. Moreover, four places gained three approvals, but the remaining 27 places gained only 1 or no approval.

The map of safety for children is shown in Fig. 8. This map has two types of icons: one indicates a dangerous spot, and the other indicates a good place for children. A total of 30 pictures were posted on the map of safety for children. Three places gained approval as being good, 26 places gained approval as being dangerous, and one did not gain approval. Some of them gained multiple approvals; however, three is the maximum number of approvals. This is the difference between the map of the recommended course for a walk and the map of safety for children.

Table 2 summarizes the results. More number of places gained two to three approvals on the map of safety for children than on the map of the recommended course for a walk. In addition, the map of the recommend course for a walk had multiple places that gained no approval.

[1] We performed image processing for privacy protection on Figs. 7 and 8.

5.2 Statistical Analysis of the Posted Picture and Behavior

In our system, we can obtain the time and GPS data of the posted picture. Using these data, we apply the before-after trial. If it can be confirmed that the subject visited the posted place through GPS data, the posted pictures may be considered to function as a nudge. As we assume in the model in Sect. 3, it is expected that the need for approval caused by selfish motivation makes others change their behavior less.

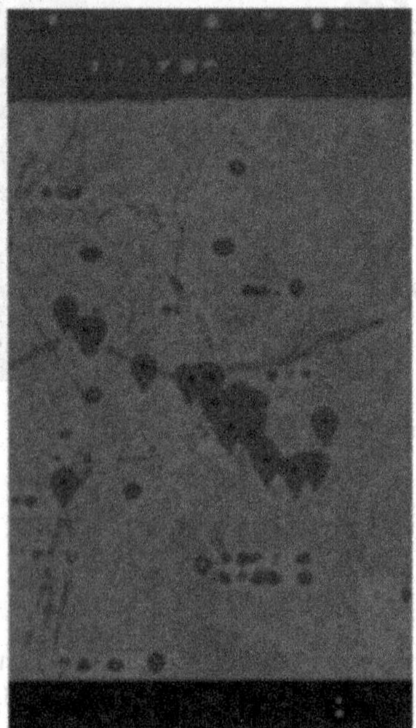

Fig. 7. Map of the recommend course for a walk

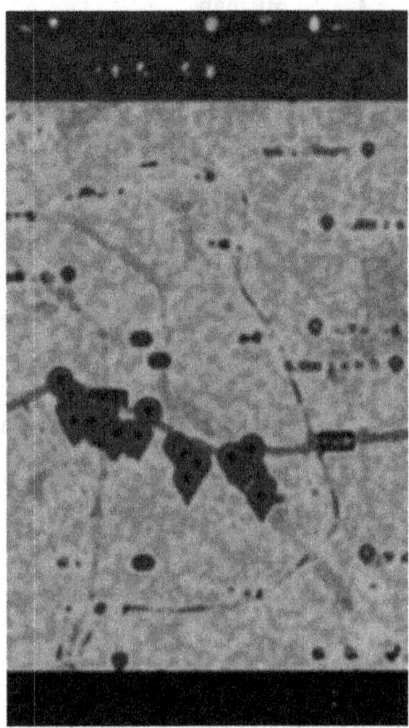

Fig. 8. Map of safety for children

First, we found the places that were contributed on the maps. Then, we determined the frequency with which other subjects visited the same place before and after the contribution date based on GPS data. We considered that other subjects had visited a place when GPS data showed they were within a radius of 5 m from that place. Table 3 shows results for the map of the recommended course for a walk. There are 35 contributed pictures on this map; however, it was observed that other subjects had visited only five of those places. As the remaining 30 pictures had no visiting records, we omitted those results from Table 3. Place Nos. 1, 2, 3, and 5 indicate the base of the research collaborator, and No. 4 is the community center.

Table 4 shows the result of the safety map for children. There are 33 contributed pictures; however, it was observed that other subjects had visited only 12 of those places. As the remaining 21 pictures have no visiting records, we omitted those results from Table 4. Except for Place No. 6, no subject had visited these places before the pictures were contributed. After the pictures were contributed, some subjects visited those places. Someone visited Place Nos. 1, 2, 11, and 12 only once. The other places recorded multiple visits.

Table 2. Summary of the results

	Recommend course for a walk	Safety for children
Number of places that gained more than four approvals	1	0
Number of places that gained two to three approvals	4	21 (dangerous place) 1 (good place)
Number of places that gained one approval	18	5 (dangerous place) 2 (good place)
Number of places that gained no approval	12	4
Total number of places	35	33

Comparison of Tables 3 and 4 show a large difference between in the number of visits. The subjects had visited all the places in Table 3 very frequently, because these places indicate the base of the Nonprofit Organization (NPO). Considering that these pictures were contributed relatively early and indicated the abovementioned base, it is conceivable that a large number of visits were recorded. The ratio of visits by other subjects to all the contributed pictures is 14.3% in Table 3 and 36.4% in Table 4.

To verify the hypothesis that altruism makes others to change their behavior, it is clarified by a *t*-test whether the number of visits of people changed before and after the subjects contributed the pictures. If the *p*-value exceeds 0.05, there is no difference between the visiting frequency before and after the picture's contribution. As the map of the recommend course for a walk is based on the desire for recognition caused by a selfish motivation, the *p*-value is expected to exceed 0.05. Similarly, since it is assumed that the map of safety for children is based on an altruistic motivation, the *p*-value is expected to be less than 0.05. The data shown in Tables 3 and 4 and data on places that were not visited are used in the *t*-test.

Table 5 shows the result of the *t*-test. As the *p*-value of the recommend course for a walk exceeds 0.05, it means that the subjects did not change their behavior. On the other hand, because the *p*-value of safety for children is lower than 0.05, it supports the hypothesis.

Table 3. Summary of the frequency of visiting the contributed place for the recommended course for a walk

Place No.	Frequency of visiting the place before the contribution date	Frequency of visiting the place after the contribution date
1	26	517
2	25	768
3	14	254
4	19	1
5	14	12

Table 4. Summary of the frequency of visiting the contributed place for safety for children

Place No.	Frequency of visiting the place before the contribution date	Frequency of visiting the place after the contribution date
1	0	1
2	0	1
3	0	6
4	0	7
5	0	5
6	1	2
7	0	3
8	0	2
9	0	3
10	0	6
11	0	1
12	0	1

Table 5. Result of the *t*-test

	Recommend course for a walk	Safety for children
p-value	0.116279204	0.003287613

6 Conclusion and Remarks

This experiment suggests that posting pictures on the map of safety for children makes subjects sympathize with the information, because much higher number of places on this map gained approvals. Especially, dangerous places pointed out on the map and shared between the members gained multiple approvals. Before this trial, the subjects made similar maps with paper. Some places were pointed out on both the paper map and our digital map; however, some places were recognized as dangerous on our digital map for the first time. Considering the average age of the subjects was 70 years, posting or expressing approval on the map of safety for children is not likely to depend on selfish motivation but on altruism. In other words, participation in making this map captures the subjects' altruism. In contrast, when making the map of the recommend course for a walk, the number of places that gained no approval suggests that, motivation is very important for solving local problems.

The result of the t-test shows that behavior could be changed if the visualization makes someone sympathize. In our study, because posting a picture on the map of safety for children made the subjects sympathize, some of them visited the place after the picture was posted. Since the subjects have a choice about whether to check the map and visit the place or not, visualization of the information can be considered as a nudge. It can be said that visualization of the map of safety for children works well as a nudge. In other words, visualization with altruism can encourage the provision of local public goods among the residents.

In this research, we did not attach short messages to pictures. However, adding short messages may cause changes in people's behavior. In addition, because we conducted experiments among acquaintances, malicious posts were not observed. Moreover, the posted picture has the possibility of be used for crime. In the future, we would like to extend the current research as well as address these issues.

Acknowledgments. We appreciate the assistance of the members of the specific NPO Corporation, Makishima Kizuna no Kai, and residents of Makishima who cooperated during our questionnaire survey. This research was subsidized by JSPS Graduate School Expenses JP 16K03718, JP 17KT0086.

References

Lazo, J.K., McClelland, G.H., Schulzde, W.D.: Economic theory and psychology of non use values. Land Econ. **73**(3), 358–371 (1997)

Shiozu, Y., Kimura, K., Shimohara, K., Yonezaki, K.: Willingness to pay for community bus services: a Japanese case study. In: 56th Annual Conference of the Society of Instrument and Control Engineering of Japan, pp. 1610–1615. CD-ROM (2017)

Thaler, R.H., Sunstein, C.R.: Libertarian paternalism. Am. Econ. Rev. **93**(2), 175–179 (2003)

Thaler, R.H., Sunstein, C.R.: Nudge: Improving Decisions About Health, Wealth, and Happiness. Yale University Press, New Heaven and London (2008)

Knowledge Management and Sharing

Knowledge Management for Rapidly Extensible Collaborative Robots

Matthew Johnson[1], Matthew Beane[2(✉)], David Mindell[3], and Jason Ryan[4]

[1] Institute for Human and Machine Cognition, Pensacola, FL 32502, USA
mjohnson@ihmc.us
[2] University of California, Santa Barbara, Santa Barbara, CA 93106, USA
mattbeane@ucsb.edu
[3] Humatics Corporation, Waltham, MA 02453, USA
[4] Aurora Flight Sciences, Cambridge, MA 02142, USA

Abstract. It is difficult – but increasingly important – to build collaborative systems that can do a range of jobs in a range of ways in a range of conditions. Much of this difficulty stems from the broad scope of contextual and collaborative knowledge required to interact productively with humans amidst uncertainty and change. With respect to physical collaboration, human-robot interaction (HRI) studies have made progress on related problems by constraining uncertainty and dynamism, thus limiting the knowledge required. Our participation in an extreme context prevented us from adopting these approaches: The Defense Advanced Research Projects Agency (DARPA) Aircrew Labor In-Cockpit Automation System (ALIAS) program has a requirement that the prototype robotic copilot system it seeks to develop must be extensible in 30 days to function in a different, unspecified aircraft in a range of flight conditions and missions. To accommodate, we developed a *knowledge management*-inspired approach and system that allowed a variety of stakeholders to curate and rely on a dynamic body of flight-related knowledge. This had significant positive implications across design, test and use of the system, crucially enabling pilots to compose a robot- and human-legible plan for their interaction with the system using familiar conventions. Our contributions promise to accelerate quality development of extensible collaborative robotic systems for settings such as general medical assistance, disaster response and construction that require collaborative problem solving in highly uncertain, dynamic and variable conditions.

Keywords: Collaborative systems · Robotics · Extensibility · Knowledge management · Design

1 Introduction

There is a strong and growing imperative for collaborative systems to jointly perform work tasks with humans in dynamic conditions marked by uncertainty [1–3]. As human workers can readily attest, interacting productively with others in such conditions requires extensive and up-to-date knowledge of the work, the setting, coworkers, and

S. Yamamoto and H. Mori (Eds.): HCII 2019, LNCS 11569, pp. 503–523, 2019.
https://doi.org/10.1007/978-3-030-22660-2_37

collaboration itself [4–7] – much of which is unknowable when the system is designed. When it comes to the collaborative performance of work tasks, prior research on human-robot interaction has generally designed related trials and experiments to significantly reduce the scope of uncertainty and dynamism in the interaction context. This has in turn usefully reduced the scope of contextual and collaborative knowledge that a given system requires to function, but it has also limited these systems' collaborative flexibility. Common examples include relying on a dedicated remote operator or supervisory control as well as holding the work task, work tools, division of labor and perception conditions very nearly constant [8–12].

Collaborative work – such as flying an aircraft with a copilot – is rarely so docile. Insofar as we hope to develop and deploy systems that can effectively collaborate with humans on even a moderate range of work types, goals and conditions, we must encode a broad scope of knowledge into these robots in a way that allows humans and these systems to better adapt their collaborative interactions to the situation. The DARPA ALIAS program focuses on human-robot collaborative flight and provided the opportunity to derive a novel approach for dealing with this knowledge-related challenge. More importantly, we found that adopting and building on prior work in knowledge management (henceforth KM) [13–18] allowed for exciting new possibilities for collaborative robotics development and deployment. We believe our work can serve as a valuable complement to design, development and deployment approaches currently in use in the HCI and HRI communities, particularly with respect to dynamic and uncertain collaborative work.

This work makes three specific contributions to research in human-computer interaction: (1) a KM-inspired approach for enabling dynamic reconfiguration of collaborative robotics systems to changing work contexts and for facilitating cross-functional engineering of those systems; (2) a system implementation of this approach for a robotic copilot; and (3) insights on the benefits and challenges associated with this novel approach to knowledge regarding human-robot collaborative performance of work in dynamic settings. These contributions promise to accelerate quality development of extensible collaborative robotic systems for settings such as general medical assistance, disaster response, mining and construction that require collaborative problem solving in highly uncertain, dynamic and variable domains.

In what follows, we review how human-robot interaction research has handled knowledge related to human-robot collaborative work (Sect. 2). We then describe our design challenge (Sect. 3), the KM-based approach for addressing this challenge and our implementation of this approach (Sect. 4). We then explore the limitations of our work (Sect. 5) and its implications for subsequent collaborative systems projects (Sect. 6).

2 Prior Approaches to Knowledge in HRI and HCI

Many in the HRI community and beyond have been trying for many years to build extensible collaborative robots: systems that can proactively and productively interact with humans across a range of jobs and changing conditions. The imperative for creating such system is strong and growing, in areas such as industrial assembly [19, 20], remote operation with poor communications [9, 21], driving [22], disaster response [23, 24] and military operations [25]. Even moderate success means developing a single system that can adapt with its human collaborators to a range of tasks in varying conditions.

But achieving this goal is very hard – the HRI literature alone demonstrates that the demands of collaborative work are broad and very difficult to accommodate [8, 11, 26–32] and related difficulties – such as joint sensemaking, understanding and assigning roles, maintaining clear lines of accountability and accounting for differences in skill and local knowledge – are evident in the Coordination [7, 33–35] and HCI literatures [36–38].

In order to make these problems manageable enough for substantive research and development, most HRI studies have focused on systems that were deliberately inextensible – the knowledge required for successful collaboration has therefore been invariant on numerous dimensions, such as actuation-related hardware, sensor suites, the configuration of those, the work goals, tactics, tasks, tools, the role complement and the conditions for each task performance [8–12]. Collaborative and contextual knowledge does not need to be dynamically encoded into a system to the extent that researchers restrict the change or uncertainty on challenging aspects of the collaborative context. By definition, taking this approach has meant that related advances in collaborative robotics have been robustly available only when there was a very high overlap of researcher-imposed constraints and those associated with the deployment context.

Beyond imposing such constraints on the requirements for collaborative and contextual knowledge, HRI researchers have more or less taken one of two approaches to managing related challenges. On the one hand, some have relied on humans for this knowledge via remote control. This has been done in a 1–1 teleoperation mode [9], many humans to one robot mode [1] and one human to many robots mode [10, 30, 31, 39]. While in most cases such systems retain some autonomy (e.g., obstacle avoidance, wayfinding, anomaly detection and flagging), by design they have not taken proactive action on the focal task that could interfere with humans doing the same. Additionally, the work roles assigned to humans and robots have not varied in these studies, so it is rare to find an example of a robotic system that maps to the dynamic requirements of real-world collaborative work.

Researchers and developers have also made progress by applying various algorithmic techniques to build collaborative robotic systems that learn their way to adaptive collaboration behaviors, for example learning through joint action demonstration [40], cross-training [8], adding low-cost communication to each task attempt [41], active learning techniques [42] and imposing hierarchical computational structure on an "ideal" task demonstration [43]. While extremely promising, these approaches rely much more heavily on contextual constraint than those relying on remote control. Beyond requiring such constraints so that they can accurately classify data, these systems have encoded causal relationships and probabilistic models and sought data to support related conclusions. To date, these relationships and models have not been able to flex to accommodate unexpected contextual or collaborative changes at runtime.

Prior work on KM [13–18] suggests a complementary route to rapidly extensible collaborative robotic systems. Research in this area treats knowledge as a dynamic, shared resource that becomes more valuable as stakeholders curate and rely on it. Researchers can treat knowledge relevant to human-system collaboration this way: the coordination literature shows that there is a bounded set of knowledge required for effective collaboration in dynamic conditions, that much of this knowledge is highly structured, and that a significant portion of this structure is known to, codified by and guides the humans involved in the work [44–46]. Flight is a good example. Manuals and training encode flight tasks (e.g., testing flaps), missions (e.g., search and rescue patterns), contingency responses (what to do when the oil light goes on), the range of possible flight conditions (e.g., day vs. night) and – crucially – timeworn role complements [47] that allow for smooth performance of interdependent work (e.g., pilot and copilot). Other critical knowledge is only available at run time (e.g., actual weather, mission specifics).

Taking a KM-driven approach to the structured knowledge associated with human-system collaborative work has several implications. First, it means building tools that allow interdependent stakeholders to encode this knowledge dynamically. Second, this encoding must be done in a way that is legible to humans and the system simultaneously. Third, it means applying such an approach from before a given system is constructed through its ongoing use. Overall, this approach treats collaborative and contextual knowledge as critical input *and* output of design and engineering work as well as planning for and actually collaborating with a given system. We detail our application of this approach to an extensible robotic copilot below.

3 Design Requirements for an Extensible Robotic Copilot

The DARPA ALIAS program envisions a tailorable, drop-in, removable kit that would promote the addition of high levels of automation into multiple legacy aircraft that lack modern flight control systems, enabling operation with reduced onboard crew. The goal is for the ALIAS system to perform many of the tasks typically performed by a copilot, even taking over the flight completely in the case of pilot incapacitation. Collaborative aviation presented unique challenges and drove us to develop novel approaches of supporting human collaboration with robotic systems and the complex engineering work required to develop such robotic systems. More importantly, the work drove us towards a novel approach to collaborative and contextual knowledge throughout the entire project lifecycle.

Building a robotic copilot required interdependent efforts across groups focused on diverse issues such as perception, actuation, operations and flight safety, and all of these teams relied on and supplied knowledge relevant to flight. Aviation is characterized by a continuous need to adapt to the variability in the environment, the flight crew and the situation. Thus, the robot and their human copilot needed the knowledge to adapt and accommodate to a wide range of situations. DARPA also mandated that we support extensibility to new missions and new aircraft.

Our primary goal was to develop a generalizable and extensible approach for managing knowledge required for a robotic system to fly multiple kinds of aircraft as a copilot to a human pilot. This knowledge needed to extend to three specific aircraft; the Diamond DA42 twin-engine with retractable landing gear, a Cessna Caravan 208B single-engine with fixed landing gear and a Bell UH-1 helicopter. Additionally, DARPA imposed an additional constraint that the system had to be extensible in 30 days to a different, unspecified aircraft. To accommodate, we built a design approach and a software tool that could manage knowledge about copiloting in a very wide range of aircraft.

Each aircraft had a unique operating manual that provided the flight characteristics, parameters, limitations and operating procedures for that particular model. Operating manuals contained essential information, but they were often vague and ambiguous, leaving the interpretation of a given step to the pilot in a given situation based on training. These manuals supplemented procedures with notes, cautions, and warnings that highlighted the importance of understanding context as these critical procedures were considered.

The operating manual was just the tip of the knowledge iceberg. Many other resources encapsulated different aspects of aviation knowledge, including Federal Aviation Administration (FAA) regulations and procedures, local course rules, weather related products and Notice to Airmen (NOTAMs). Many tasks associated with flying were undocumented. Examples include tuning radios, configuring navigational equipment, handling ATC (air traffic control) communications, and even periodically reporting the status of the aircraft. These often-mundane tasks were easily overlooked, but were an important part of the work within the cockpit, burdening pilots with additional workload. On top of this, there was often mission-level knowledge, particularly for military domains. This added another layer of procedures and constraints to those in the baseline operations manual. Expert pilots were another crucial source of undocumented knowledge; many key standards of practice were only known to these highly trained professionals.

This domain had four extraordinarily challenging features with respect to contextual knowledge required for human-robot collaborative work. First, it was complex, with a vast range of possible work scenarios, making it difficult if not impossible to develop a complete body of explicit knowledge that would encompass the copilot job. Second, it is also characterized by high uncertainty; it was impossible to foresee every possibility for any given flight. Third, it was dynamic; change happened rapidly (at least within the bounds of human perception) and consequences could be discontinuous. Fourth, it was failure-intolerant; failure on any key dimension for more than a few seconds could lead to catastrophic, unacceptable loss of life and/or resources.

4 Making Knowledge Management Work

Knowledge management required development of an appropriate system for KM, but also a process to facilitate KM.

4.1 System Implementation: Enabling Knowledge Management

Taking a KM perspective on the design challenges described above suggested acquiring and formalizing a significant amount of collaborative and contextual knowledge *before* building a collaborative robot. Such knowledge could inform critical design choices (e.g., what must be actuated, what must be perceived), and could then be used to enable and constrain robotic functionality (e.g., setting torque thresholds and ranges of motion). Unlike many repository-focused KM systems in organizations [15, 16], we formalized key knowledge in such a way that it was usable by a machine as well as a human. We did this because this knowledge had to guide both in the midst of their joint work. As with many modern KM implementations, this could not be a one-time activity, but required iterative development and ongoing management [48]. For our system, knowledge played a key role during operations. While it is common for KM tool requirements to be separate from those associated with user interfaces for activities relying on this knowledge (e.g. [49, 50]), we designed a single system to address all stages of the process. Three aspects of our context drove these design choices: the role of pilots in the process, the nature of aviation and DARPA's 30-day extensibility requirement.

In our project, pilots were a critical source of airframe-specific knowledge and would also be the end users of that knowledge when copiloting with the robot. On the front end, it was crucial that pilots be able to easily interpret, verify and edit knowledge as the engineers built the system. They were the final authority on correctness of the system. We therefore built a KM tool with the appearance and formatting of a traditional operations manual instead of a tool based on more traditional ontology development or systems engineering. Pilots were accustomed to relying on physical flight manuals to guide collaborative flight operations, so our tool's similarity to these manuals made it far easier for pilots to use in preparation for and during flight.

The dynamic, uncertain nature of aviation was also highly influential in our design choices. Aviators typically conduct a flight brief prior to any flight. This is a process by which the crew plans out, as best as possible, the details of the pending flight, taking account of up-to-date knowledge of the mission and related conditions (e.g., weather). This is a critical task to ensure effective and safe aviation and as such it was critical for our tool to be able to support KM at this phase of the work, not just during the engineering of the system. Our tool had to support KM in the midst of human-robot collaboration as well. As any pilot knows, flights rarely go exactly as planned – they adapt goals, tactics and roles to accommodate change and uncertainty as a flight unfolds. This need for our KM tool to support an ongoing and continuous process was well aligned with the view that knowledge does not culminate at some point, but is a resource that stakeholders manage over time [51]. This was an even more appropriate orientation for Aurora's work on the ALIAS program given that it included the ongoing challenge of extending the system to new missions and new aircraft types.

Finally, our tool had to enable construction of a system that was testable on a "surprise" aircraft in 30 days. To give engineers crucial information early in this 30-day period, our KM tool had to allow users to quickly generate a customized resource that allowed interdependent users to manage a great deal of the knowledge required to operate a new aircraft. In order to achieve this, we designed our system to make flight knowledge reusable across airframes. This meant our KM tool allowed the developer to capture the generalizable portions of flight activities – including what would be relevant to human-robot collaborative flight in many other aircraft – in order to build a library of reusable knowledge components. Our tool also provided a means for the developer to quickly generate a customized (digital) flight manual for specific models of aircraft.

System Architecture

We identified three distinct, sequential phases of use that our KM system needed to support, depicted in Fig. 1. The first was the "Builder" phase. Here our system had to support building a library of reusable knowledge. It also had to rapidly generate a model-specific knowledge repository – a data object we referred to as a "Flight Manual" – for new aircraft. In the second phase of use, the KM tool had to support construction of customized flight plans prior to every flight. We referred to this as the "Composer" phase. And finally, for the "In-flight Manager" phase, our tool needed to be usable during collaborative flight operations. Though there were three different phases of use, each with different requirements, supporting these with a single system offered significant benefits.

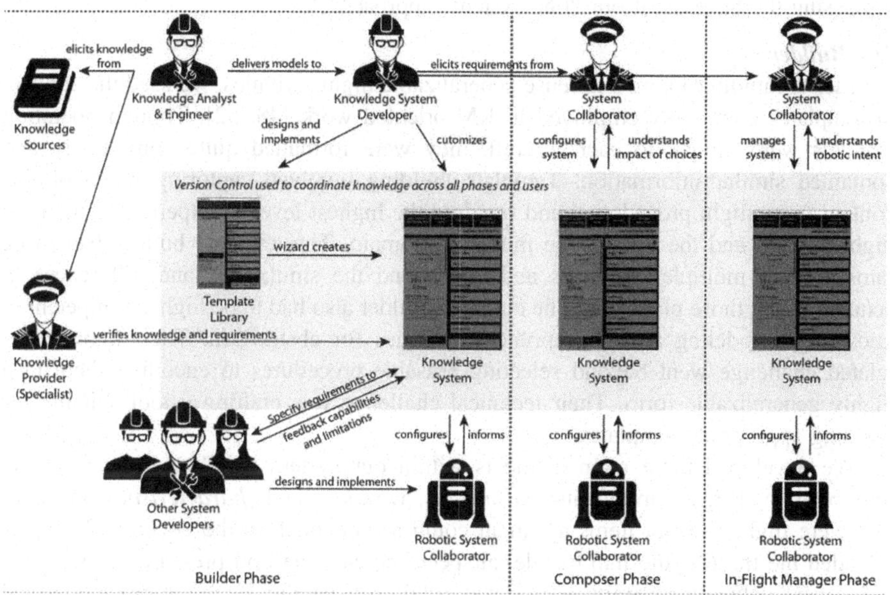

Fig. 1. KM system design. Our approach supported the development ("Builder Phase"), configuration ("Composer Phase") and operation ("In-flight Manager Phase") of the system. We treated all system developers, the robot and the pilot as users.

In our project, the KM workflow depicted in Fig. 1 began with a knowledge engineer collecting collaborative knowledge from manuals and pilots. They then delivered this information and related semantic models to a knowledge system developer, who designed and implemented our KM system. They then used the system itself to create an airframe-specific knowledge set and user interface (UI), and turned to expert pilots for further requirements, as well as validation and improvement of this system and the knowledge it contained. Teams of robotic system developers then relied on the KM system as they developed robotic subsystems (e.g., perception, actuation) – both for a clear, shared understanding of system requirements and for contributing knowledge regarding the capabilities and limitations of the robotic system as it was being engineered. From this point forward, the knowledge in the system also directly configured and was reshaped by the robotic system itself.

As pilots used the KM system to plan for a specific flight with a robotic copilot, they prefigured their interactions with the robot through the knowledge management tool, inputting knowledge only available at briefing time. Our system informed pilots in real time of the collaborative implications of their choices and inputs. This was in part possible because these choices and inputs configured their robotic collaborator, which in turn entered knowledge of its runtime-specific capabilities into our KM system. A similar dynamic played out during subsequent human-pilot interactions in flight: pilots could use the same UI to reconfigure their collaboration on the fly. In what follows, we describe in detail how our tool supported these different phases before discussing the benefits of our "one system" approach.

The Builder

In order to rapidly capture and reuse generalizable flight activities, we used the concept of templates commonly employed in KM-oriented work [48, 52]. Though operation manuals were unique to each aircraft, they were formatted quite consistently and contained similar information. Template building involved capturing much of this content (e.g., flight procedures) and required the highest level of expertise in both the flight domain and the knowledge modeling domain. The template builder had to be familiar with multiple platforms and understand the similarities and differences in actually flying those platforms. The template builder also had to be highly competent in knowledge modeling and appropriate techniques for abstraction. Their knowledge-related challenge went beyond selecting reusable procedures to encoding them in a highly generalizable form. Their technical challenge was crafting a tool suitable for building appropriate templates.

We developed three main elements within our system to allow users to create reusable knowledge components: *parameters, variables* and *characteristics*. *Parameters* were flight-relevant items a human could see or touch in the cockpit. Examples included the throttle, the flap handle, airspeed indicator and oil pressure gauge. *Variables* were values for primitives that were platform-specific. Each aircraft model had different minimum and maximum allowable airspeeds, for example. Thus, variables were a useful method of capturing invariant concepts while permitting later customization. *Characteristics* were features of an aircraft model that indicated applicability of generalized knowledge to a specific aircraft model. Parameters themselves were often characteristics of the aircraft.

For example, an aircraft may have had a condition lever or just a throttle – both tools for controlling aspects of thrust. Primitives alone were insufficient for robust generalization – our tool needed to support associating characteristics with flight procedure steps or even entire procedures as needed. Accordingly, our KM tool enabled annotating aspects of work (e.g., steps or procedures) with characteristics. All of this enabled construction of a library of reusable, modular knowledge components that supported a variety of aircraft models.

In order to generate a customized flight manual for a given aircraft, we built a "wizard" into our KM system to draw on this template-based knowledge. The knowledge system developers UI resembled a green-covered flight manual (left side of Fig. 2) and contained all of the generic template-based representations of flight-related knowledge. This wizard guided a developer through a sequence of tasks to specify characteristics of the aircraft model of interest (Fig. 2). Choices included aircraft type, landing gear configuration, flap options, power quadrant configuration and a variety of options such as the availability of chip detectors, oxygen and various cold weather operations equipment. The wizard used these characteristics to automatically produce a customized flight manual, accessible via a blue-covered flight manual UI (as shown in Fig. 2).

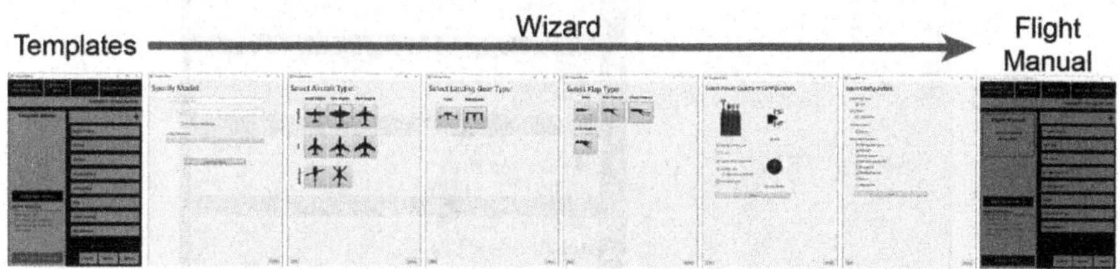

Fig. 2. The wizard process for generating a flight manual from templates. (Color figure online)

Once this customized manual was produced, the core UI (again, Fig. 3) allowed access to all other UIs (and related knowledge) in our system, typically with one click. As in the physical flight manual for many aircraft, choosing a given tab across the top of the UI provided immediate access to the requirements and capabilities of that aircraft (i.e., parameters), reference data for that aircraft (i.e., variables), missions (composed of procedures), and a list of normal procedures for that aircraft. The tabs down the right-hand side of the opening UI provided immediate access to emergency procedures for that aircraft, again mirroring the physical manuals that pilots customarily use.

The wizard customized each manual to the entered model specifications, but two manual customization steps remained before it was ready for use. The first involved resolving variables by adding model specific engine limits and other values unique to that particular aircraft model. These values were automatically grouped on a separate Reference Data page so the developer could easily set and visualize them (shown in Fig. 4) in a format familiar to anyone who had worked with standard flight manual representations of such data. Additionally, any variable not set was highlighted within procedures where they were used for easy identification. The second step involved editing template-entered flight procedures as necessary. This included tasks such as removing unnecessary steps or procedures, adding steps or procedures not covered by templates or modifying steps. Notes, cautions and warnings – specific instructions for unusual circumstances – tended to be model-specific so these were often added as well.

Figure 5 depicts an example procedure at the beginning and end of this process: on the left hand side is a template for a takeoff procedure not yet customized to a given aircraft. The general procedure for takeoff is present (e.g., setting the throttle and then checking instruments), but the aircraft-specific parameters, variables and characteristics have not yet been set. These gaps are indicated by magenta and cyan text. The left hand side of Fig. 5 has numerous instances of such gaps (e.g., unspecified takeoff power,

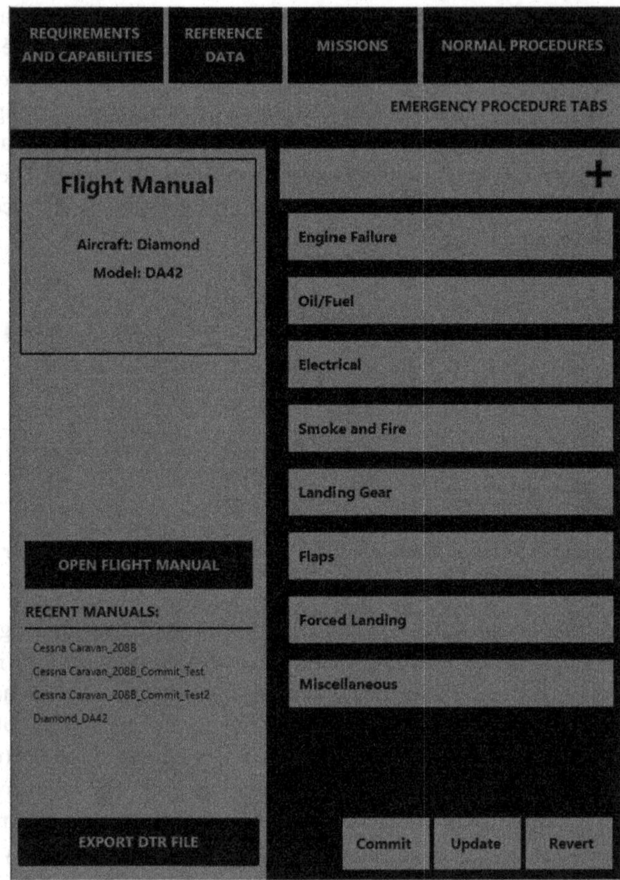

Fig. 3. Central UI for a (digital) flight manual for a DA42 aircraft.

Reference Data

Engine Limits

Instrument	Units	Minimum	Normal Min	Normal Max	Maximum
Torque	ft-lbs	0.0	0	1865	1865
ITT	°C	100	100	740	805
Ng	%	52	52	101.6	101.6
Oil Pressure	PSI	40	85	105	105
Oil Temperature	°C	-40	10	99	104
Prop RPM	RPM	1600	1900	1900	1900

Fig. 4. Engine limits page for an example aircraft.

presence/absence of a flap handle undetermined), as the aircraft model had not yet been specified. The right-hand side of Fig. 5 shows a fully tailored procedure – all aircraft parameters, variables and characteristics have been entered for a Cessna Caravan 208B aircraft and is the end result of the overall process depicted in Fig. 5.

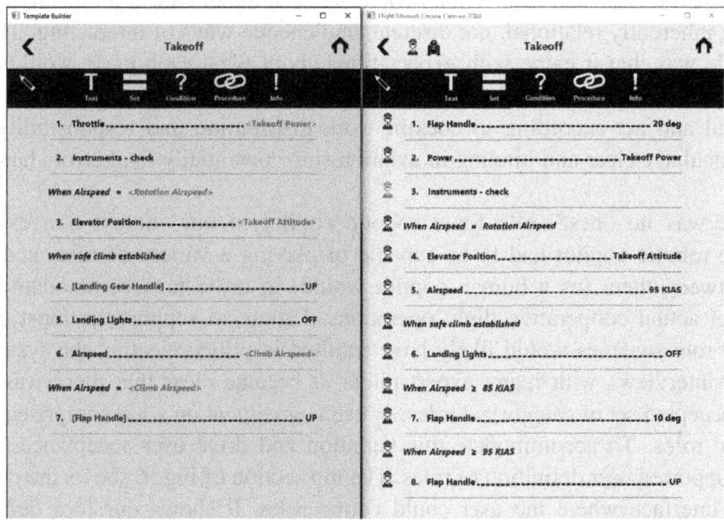

Fig. 5. Template for a takeoff procedure (on left) and a completed, specified version of that procedure for a Cessna Caravan 208B aircraft.

After building an initial knowledge corpus, we were able to complete the wizard in under one minute and finish customization for a given aircraft in approximately six hours. Our knowledge library covered 85% of the DA42 procedures leaving 15% for manual generation, and it did the same for 68% of the Cessna Caravan. The Caravan had lower coverage mainly due to non-standard equipment like a cargo pod. Given the significant differences with helicopter operations we did not expect significant coverage, but a second helicopter would have provided us with the generalization needed to obtain more reusability for helicopters.

The Composer

The composer stage focused on how users (i.e., pilots) "composed" a plan for a particular mission, using entered and new knowledge. The best metaphor for the composer stage was the flight brief: a well-known, mandated routine used to prepare for flight. Flight briefs tend to focus on building missions phase by phase, and our KM tool supported this approach. Specifically, we allowed creation and reuse of flight phases which could be composed of procedures or other phases. Flight does not proceed according to a single sequential series of steps, so our KM tool supported adding multiple activities that would likely be executed in parallel. For example, flight activities not covered in procedures but found in flight manuals such as reporting status (e.g., instrument and gas checks) were typically performed periodically in parallel to other flight procedures.

One of the most important aspects of building a mission plan was role assignment – settling which crew member would be responsible for certain tasks during different phases of flight. Roles are well-defined, well-followed bundles of rights and obligations that indicate the tasks and results that people are accountable for in joint activities [47]. Roles are inherently relational, not discrete, and encode ways of interacting. The value of the role was that it came with expectations about what each party would be contributing, as well as what they lack. In short, roles were a useful means in our context to understand and act according to cockpit work distribution and responsibility. Roles were particularly clear and binding in aviation since potentially fatal errors hang in the balance.

There was no "best" role for a robotic copilot in our context. An extensible, adaptable robotic copilot had to be capable of playing a variety of roles and rapidly move between them (as a human copilot would) in order to accommodate the exigencies of actual cooperative flight operations. Failure to support the most common roles and role switches would likely have resulted in pilots rejecting the system.

After interviews with many expert pilots, it became clear that there was no one broadly accepted set of categorical roles, or even agreement on what comprised specific functional roles. To accommodate this variation and drive user acceptance, the KM system supported user definition of roles. The top section of Fig. 6 shows the portion of our user interface where the user could define roles. It shows our four default role categories (all, flying pilot, non-flying pilot, and observer) vertically. These were based on the four roles most commonly referred to by pilots. The categories were defined by specifying associated functional roles (e.g., primary controls, secondary controls, radio tuning, external communications, etc.), which are listed horizontally. For example, the flying pilot is defined as having responsibility for the functional roles of primary flight controls and tuning of the radios and navigation aids. There was no pilot consensus with respect to which functional roles comprise each of the four main categories, so our tool supported user customization. To make the flying pilot responsible for only primary flight controls, the user simply unchecked the tuning column. Users could thus define role categories unanticipated by designers by naming the category and selecting appropriate functional roles. They could also add new functional roles and modify the definition of each functional role using the Requirements and Capabilities tool discussed below.

Once defined, roles needed to be assigned. This process occurred with every flight brief via the lower half of the UI in Fig. 6. Mission elements were composed and represented in the left-most column. The example in Fig. 6 shows three top-level activities to be executed concurrently: aircraft status reporting, health monitoring, and the day's flight procedures. Each activity could be composed hierarchically and expanded for finer-grained role assignments. Icons indicated who is assigned – pilot or robot. When subtasks were divided between the two, both icons appeared. The UI alerted the user when they tried to assign a role that the robotic copilot was not capable of supporting. For example, in Fig. 6 the robot is not capable of tuning during takeoff so a red warning is displayed. The user could drill all the way down into procedure

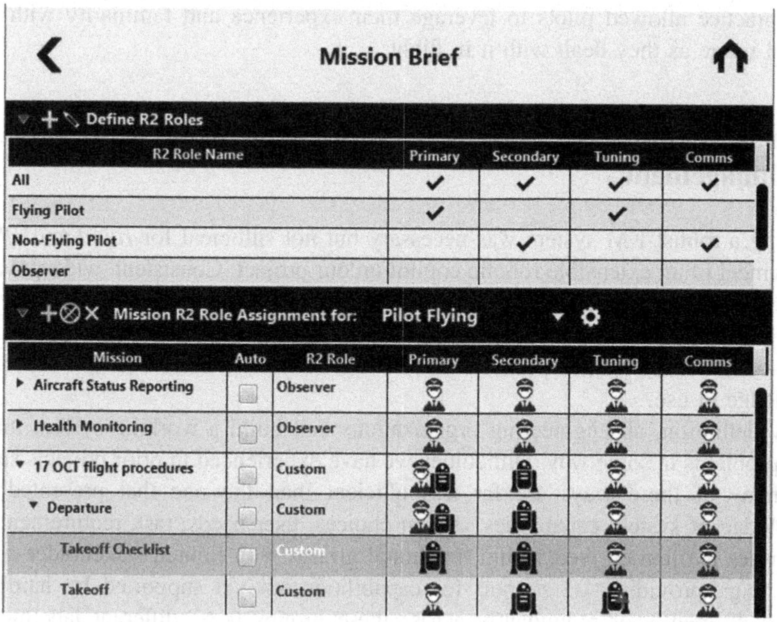

Mission Brief

Define R2 Roles

R2 Role Name	Primary	Secondary	Tuning	Comms
All	✓	✓	✓	✓
Flying Pilot	✓		✓	
Non-Flying Pilot		✓		✓
Observer				

Mission R2 Role Assignment for: Pilot Flying

Mission	Auto	R2 Role	Primary	Secondary	Tuning	Comms
Aircraft Status Reporting		Observer				
Health Monitoring		Observer				
17 OCT flight procedures		Custom				
Departure		Custom				
Takeoff Checklist		Custom				
Takeoff		Custom				

Fig. 6. Mission brief section of the KM tool. We referred to the ALIAS system as "R2." (Color figure online)

steps to thoroughly understand how the work was allocated or what specific actuation or perception limitation prevented the robot from performing a specific role.

Any role change – whether by role category or by functional role – had ripple effects throughout the mission being composed. For example, in Fig. 6, when the functional role of secondary flight controls was assigned to the robot at the top level (17 OCT flight procedures), this rippled through all procedures in that grouping, assigning all secondary flight control tasks to the robot. Similarly, if we assigned the functional role of flying-pilot to the takeoff checklist only, the effects would ripple upwards. In these cases, the high-level procedures (Departure and 17 OCT flight procedure) changed from pilot-only to a mixed icon indicating that the work was shared by both the pilot and the robot. This automation helped pilots and developers quickly understand the implications of assignments and capability limitations.

The In-Flight Manager

We designed the KM tool to resemble a traditional flight manual in form and function to support operational usage. Pilots already used small-form-factor versions of these flight manuals in flight to guide them through procedures and checklists. Our user-focused approach meant little additional effort was needed to support this. The capabilities needed to compose a flight, such as procedure composition, procedure selection, and role assignment also had to be available in flight. The key difference was the speed and urgency of the operational domain. Designing our KM tool to comply with existing work practice allowed pilots to leverage their experience and familiarity with flight manual usage as they dealt with it in flight.

5 Process Implementation: Facilitating Knowledge Management

Building a robust KM system was necessary but not sufficient for *rapid* and *efficient* deployment of an extensible robotic copilot on our project. Consistent, widespread use of our system produced speed and efficiency gains, by: (1) streamlining knowledge sharing amongst functional groups, users and subject matter experts and (2) allowing for version control with respect to the evolving body of contextual and collaborative knowledge in use.

By definition, all engineering organizations that build a working system manage these problems in some way. Difficulties we have experienced in prior projects suggest that many of these ways are far less efficient than the one that presented here. Knowledge of system capabilities, design choices, user needs, task requirements and work roles is often derived within functional groups with limited stakeholder consultation (e.g., providing UI support for capabilities not yet supported by hardware), derived differently or redundantly across these groups (e.g., different labeling conventions), encoded in ways that restrict shared access (e.g., excel spreadsheets), and modified differently and without adequate communication as a project progresses, for example.

Maintaining one knowledge management system addressed many of these problems. Relevant knowledge could be collected early and could be shared between all agents shown in Fig. 2. In this way, project teams could establish and maintain common ground [53, 54], thus counteracting one of the most destructive tendencies in any human endeavor: misunderstanding. Widespread use of our system could also reduce rework: knowledge managers and knowledge engineers could both add and modify a shared repository of airframe-specific knowledge. These groups would ordinarily work separately on the same task, producing the same (duplicative) knowledge base.

The first KM feature that assisted subsystem teams was the Requirements and Capabilities table, shown in Fig. 7. This table was automatically generated by the primitives entered as flight procedures were created. The rightmost two columns of this table contained an indicator that showed whether the capability was supported (green), not supported (red), or not necessary (gray). Here subsystem developers could update other system developers, operators and the robot itself about the availability of a given capability. The first column covered perception (P) and the second column covered actuation (A). For example, the chip detector light only imposed a perceptual requirement, while the power lever required both perception to identify it and actuation to move it. Some capabilities were not supported at all, such as seeing or actuating the flap circuit breakers. Others were partially supported. The flap handle in this example was perceivable (i.e., the robot could sense what position it was in), but it was not actuatable (i.e., the robot could not set the position). Some capabilities were not available because of development status, while others were due to the layout of the cockpit. Finally, this UI also allowed tailoring of functional roles by associating parameters with functional roles via the "Role" column.

Requirements and Capabilites

Sub	ID	Parameter	Units	Role	P	A
P	1119	Chip Detector Light	enum_on_off	ANN	●	○
A	257	Power	Foot_pounds	PRI	●	●
P	1108	Engine Fire Light	enum_on_off	ANN	●	●
P	1090	Torque	Foot_pounds(0.0, 18...	ENG	●	○
A	2006	Flap Circuit Breakers	enum_in_out	SEC	●	●
A	275	Flap Handle	enum_flaps	SEC	●	●

Fig. 7. Example requirements and capabilities table section. (Color figure online)

The second major feature of the KM tool designed to support subsystem team collaboration was version control support. The KM system integrated with Subversion to track all versions of each flight manual simultaneously. This made refreshing, retrieving, committing and undoing (reverting) – capabilities familiar to those with version control software experience – available with respect to collaborative and contextual knowledge. Subversion maintained a changelog, and all of this was accessible through the KM system. Each developer could see the time and date of each change and could retrieve any previous version. Further, new versions of a flight manual could be created from an existing flight manual by selecting "Save as" on the home page. This branched the current flight manual and made a new copy. This process was useful when developers wanted to make significant changes to a flight manual for temporary testing purposes.

6 Discussion

In this paper, we presented a novel *knowledge management*-driven approach to allow for collaborative systems that are rapidly extensible to different work and working conditions. We derived this approach and built a related system to meet the demands of the ALIAS project – an extreme human-robot collaboration use case in which DARPA required the same robotic system be reconfigurable within 30 days to copilot a previously unknown aircraft. Use of our system led stakeholders to curate and rely on a shared repository of flight-related collaborative and contextual knowledge from design through deployment. In addition to supporting DARPA's goal of generating the knowledge needed by our robotic copilot within 30 days, this made two key outcomes possible. First, it allowed a human pilot to intuitively compose a plan for human-robot collaboration that configured their joint work with the robotic copilot – one that could be reconfigured on the fly and at various levels of granularity. Second, it facilitated efficient engineering work across subteams – both by minimizing rework and misunderstanding. Below we discuss these findings, related limitations and the implications of our work for collaborative systems in contexts other than aviation.

6.1 Enabling Human-Robot Collaborative Flight Amidst Change and Uncertainty

Adopting a KM-driven approach and use of our related system allowed for flexible, dynamic and intuitive work planning, including role and task allocation. Pilots could use our Composer UI as an interaction planning tool, and configure their robotic copilot's capabilities to suit the mission at hand. They could do so via familiar conventions (e.g., roles, procedures). Our system converted these inputs into robot-readable requirements and constraints, ensuring that the ALIAS system acted in ways that the pilot expected and preferred. Additionally, pilots had a wide range of planning discretion within the Composer: much as with a human copilot, they could delegate work to the robot at various levels of granularity over time (e.g., primary flight controls for entire phases of flight, select subtasks for portions of short procedures). All of this was critically reliant on knowledge of flight operations gathered from other expert pilots.

6.2 Enabling Collaborative Engineering Amidst Change and Uncertainty

Adopting a KM-driven approach and use of our related system allowed for rapid extensibility to new aircraft in two ways. First, adopting a wizard- and template-driven knowledge entry system allowed for maximum generalizability and thus reuse of knowledge that was entered into the system. Second, integrating a version control system (Subversion) and providing our Requirements and Capabilities tool allowed engineering teams to verify and contribute to a shared repository of collaborative and contextual knowledge and to focus their development efforts more effectively.

There is a sizeable body of work on the challenges and benefits of working in larger, cross-functional engineering teams [44, 55, 56], yet no HRI- or HCI-related paper addresses the implications of these issues for the capabilities of the resulting system. Relatedly, no HRI or HCI study has made explicit links between the knowledge required for successful design and engineering of collaborative systems and the knowledge that those systems require to function effectively. This study contributes to these literatures by showing that these links may be quite strong, and that considering them explicitly and early can improve the effectiveness of both efforts.

Overall, through careful attention to managing knowledge that allows for humans and robots to cooperate in real time, this work both addresses a number of the standing research questions in the maturing KM community [13] and suggests new directions. The KM literature has dealt exclusively with knowledge curated and used by humans, and has overwhelmingly focused on knowledge as a guide to asynchronous, deliberate decision-making processes. Research on KM has therefore not considered the possibility that KM systems could be used to gather knowledge that humans and increasingly-autonomous technologies rely on to accomplish joint physical work in dynamic, uncertain conditions. Nor has this literature focused on KM processes as critical coordination device for designing, building and testing of such technologies. Further research along these lines promises to enrich KM theory and practice well beyond our specific context.

6.3 Limitations

Several aspects of our project will likely limit the generalizability of our approach. First, actuation and perception targets did not move during the work: conditions and goals occasionally changed, but the cockpit wasn't reconfigured in flight. This will clearly not be true in other forms of human-system collaborative work (e.g., mining, construction). More broadly, however, our system had to flex to accommodate known, codified variation in the work context, so our techniques should be applicable to a degree in such contexts. Clearly more research is required to explore when and how this may be the case.

Relatedly, work procedures, roles and technological capabilities were exceptionally well documented and agreed upon in our failure-intolerant work setting. Applying our approach may take more and different effort in contexts where such collaborative and contextual knowledge is more tacit and contested (e.g., disaster response). Likewise, our work setting only involved one human and one collaborative system; applying a KM approach to multi-human and/or multi-system work settings will at best require significant adaptation of the work we have presented here.

Finally, this work focused on the implementation of a KM tool in support of a robotic copilot and did not include sufficient evaluation or measurement of the impact of our design approach or the software KM tool itself. As more HCI and HRI research explores KM, such evaluations will provide a more rigorous analysis of the strengths and weaknesses of such an approach.

7 Implications

Despite the limitations above, we believe this work has important implications for HCI research and collaborative robotics in particular. First and foremost, we believe our KM approach and related system can enable and facilitate rapidly extensible collaborative systems in very different situations. Replacing aviation-specific terms (e.g., cockpit, pilot, flight manual) with generic work-related terms (e.g., work area, leader, knowledge source) in our paper offers a crude but productive first step towards a generalizable template for collecting a shared repository of human and system-legible knowledge about a wide range of collaborative contexts.

We believe the two main benefits of a KM-driven approach are achievable elsewhere. First, taking this approach promises an intuitive means for expert workers to configure their nonhuman collaborators (e.g., according to familiar role and task divisions), both preemptively and in the midst of work. This can serve as a powerful complement to various algorithmic and remote control-based techniques for enabling collaborative work with collaborative systems. For example, if a system "knows" that it is in a given role with certain phases of work and goals and its human collaborator *chose* these parameters in advance of a challenging task, then related perception and action constraints should allow the system to more productively and intelligibly apply algorithmic methods to act effectively in that role, and the human will likely expect and react productively to that system's action.

Second, this project taught us that proactive management of collaborative and contextual knowledge can have significant value well beyond planning for and actually collaborating with systems. In particular, our study shows that building a shared digital repository of such knowledge before building a collaborative system can usefully inform key design choices in areas such as perception, actuation and safety. Taking a KM-driven approach to such knowledge also promises to reduce rework and miscommunication across functional and disciplinary boundaries in team-based engineering work, allowing for more rapid and effective deployment of a given collaborative system to varying contexts, coworkers and goals.

Acknowledgements. We would not have had the opportunity to do this work without the generous support of Aurora Flight Sciences, and DARPA. This work was conducted by Humatics Corporation [in partnership with IHMC] as part of a subcontract to Aurora's work on DARPA's ALIAS program, for which David Mindell was Chief Scientist. Thanks also to all of the pilots and engineers who contributed to our efforts and to the building and testing a truly innovative robotic system. This research was developed with funding from the Defense Advanced Research Projects Agency (DARPA), and is approved for public release with unlimited distribution. The views, opinions and/or findings expressed are those of the author(s) and should not be interpreted as representing the official views or policies of the Department of Defense or the U.S. Government.

References

1. Yanco, H.A., Norton, A., Ober, W., Shane, D., Skinner, A., Vice, J.: Analysis of human-robot interaction at the DARPA robotics challenge trials. J. Field Robot. **32**(3), 420–444 (2015)
2. Murphy, R.R.: Human-robot interaction in rescue robotics. IEEE Trans. Syst. Man Cybern. Part C Appl. Rev. **34**(2), 138–153 (2004)
3. U. S. Government, Department of Defense, U. S. Military: Unmanned Systems Integrated Roadmap FY2013-2038 - Unmanned Aircraft Systems (UAS), Drones, Unmanned Maritime Systems, Technologies, Logistics, Sustainment, Training, International, Foreign Sales. Progressive Management (2014)
4. Bagosi, T., Hindriks, K.V., Neerincx, M.A.: Ontological reasoning for human-robot teaming in search and rescue missions. In: The Eleventh ACM/IEEE International Conference on Human Robot Interaction, Piscataway, NJ, USA, pp. 595–596 (2016)
5. Strohkorb, S., Scassellati, B.: Promoting collaboration with social robots. In: The Eleventh ACM/IEEE International Conference on Human Robot Interaction, Piscataway, NJ, USA, pp. 639–640 (2016)
6. Stubbs, K., Hinds, P., Wettergreen, D.: Challenges to grounding in human-robot interaction. In: Proceedings of the 1st ACM SIGCHI/SIGART Conference on Human-Robot Interaction, New York, NY, USA, pp. 357–358 (2006)

7. Okhuysen, G.A., Bechky, B.A.: Coordination in organizations: an integrative perspective. Acad. Manag. Ann. **3**(1), 463–502 (2009)
8. Nikolaidis, S., Shah, J.: Human-robot cross-training: computational formulation, modeling and evaluation of a human team training strategy. In: Proceedings of the 8th ACM/IEEE International Conference on Human-Robot Interaction, Piscataway, NJ, USA, pp. 33–40 (2013)
9. Leeper, A.E., Hsiao, K., Ciocarlie, M., Takayama, L., Gossow, D.: Strategies for human-in-the-loop robotic grasping. In: Proceedings of the Seventh Annual ACM/IEEE International Conference on Human-Robot Interaction, New York, NY, USA, pp. 1–8 (2012)
10. Zheng, K., Glas, D.F., Kanda, T., Ishiguro, H., Hagita, N.: Supervisory control of multiple social robots for navigation. In: Proceedings of the 8th ACM/IEEE International Conference on Human-Robot Interaction, Piscataway, NJ, USA, pp. 17–24 (2013)
11. Huang, C.-M., Mutlu, B.: Anticipatory robot control for efficient human-robot collaboration. In: The Eleventh ACM/IEEE International Conference on Human Robot Interaction, Piscataway, NJ, USA, pp. 83–90 (2016)
12. Admoni, H., Weng, T., Hayes, B., Scassellati, B.: Robot nonverbal behavior improves task performance in difficult collaborations. In: The Eleventh ACM/IEEE International Conference on Human Robot Interaction, Piscataway, NJ, USA, pp. 51–58 (2016)
13. Alavi, M., Leidner, D.E.: Review: knowledge management and knowledge management systems: conceptual foundations and research issues. MIS Q. **25**(1), 107–136 (2001)
14. Gold, A.H., Malhotra, A., Segars, A.H.: Knowledge management: an organizational capabilities perspective. J. Manag. Inf. Syst. **18**(1), 185–214 (2001)
15. Lee, H., Choi, B.: Knowledge management enablers, processes, and organizational performance: an integrative view and empirical examination. J. Manag. Inf. Syst. **20**(1), 179–228 (2003)
16. Kankanhalli, A., Tan, B.C., Wei, K.-K.: Contributing knowledge to electronic knowledge repositories: an empirical investigation. MIS Q. **29**(1), 113–143 (2005)
17. Newell, S., Robertson, M., Scarbrough, H., Swan, J.: Managing Knowledge Work and Innovation. Palgrave Macmillan, Basingstoke (2009)
18. Malone, T.W., Crowston, K., Herman, G.A.: Organizing Business Knowledge: The MIT Process Handbook. MIT Press, Cambridge (2003)
19. Gleeson, B., MacLean, K., Haddadi, A., Croft, E., Alcazar, J.: Gestures for industry: intuitive human-robot communication from human observation. In: Proceedings of the 8th ACM/IEEE International Conference on Human-Robot Interaction, Piscataway, NJ, USA, pp. 349–356 (2013)
20. Stenmark, M., Haage, M., Topp, E.A.: Simplified programming of re-usable skills on a safe industrial robot: prototype and evaluation. In: Proceedings of the 2017 ACM/IEEE International Conference on Human-Robot Interaction, New York, NY, USA, pp. 463–472 (2017)
21. Johnson, M., et al.: Team IHMC's lessons learned from the DARPA robotics challenge: finding data in the rubble. J. Field Robot. **34**(2), 241–261 (2017)
22. Johns, M., et al.: Exploring shared control in automated driving. In: The Eleventh ACM/IEEE International Conference on Human Robot Interaction, Piscataway, NJ, USA, pp. 91–98 (2016)
23. Murphy, R.R., Burke, J.L.: Up from the rubble: lessons learned about HRI from search and rescue. Proc. Hum. Factors Ergon. Soc. Ann. Meet. **49**, 437–441 (2005)
24. Nourbakhsh, I.R., Sycara, K., Koes, M., Yong, M., Lewis, M., Burion, S.: Human-robot teaming for search and rescue. IEEE Pervasive Comput. **4**(1), 72–79 (2005)
25. Blackhurst, J.L., Gresham, J.S., Stone, M.O.: The autonomy paradox. Armed Forces J., 20–40 (2011)

26. St. Clair, A., Mataric, M.: How robot verbal feedback can improve team performance in human-robot task collaborations. In: Proceedings of the Tenth Annual ACM/IEEE International Conference on Human-Robot Interaction, New York, NY, USA, pp. 213–220 (2015)
27. Hayes, B., Shah, J.A.: Improving robot controller transparency through autonomous policy explanation. In: Proceedings of the 2017 ACM/IEEE International Conference on Human-Robot Interaction, New York, NY, USA, pp. 303–312 (2017)
28. Devin, S., Alami, R.: An implemented theory of mind to improve human-robot shared plans execution. In: The Eleventh ACM/IEEE International Conference on Human Robot Interaction, Piscataway, NJ, USA, pp. 319–326 (2016)
29. Dragan, A.D., Thomaz, A.L., Srinivasa, S.S.: Collaborative manipulation: new challenges for robotics and HRI. In: Proceedings of the 8th ACM/IEEE International Conference on Human-Robot Interaction, Piscataway, NJ, USA, pp. 435–436 (2013)
30. Gao, F., Cummings, M.L., Bertuccelli, L.F.: Teamwork in controlling multiple robots. In: Proceedings of the Seventh Annual ACM/IEEE International Conference on Human-Robot Interaction, New York, NY, USA, pp. 81–88 (2012)
31. Rule, A., Forlizzi, J.: Designing interfaces for multi-user, multi-robot systems. In: Proceedings of the Seventh Annual ACM/IEEE International Conference on Human-Robot Interaction, New York, NY, USA, pp. 97–104 (2012)
32. Dragan, A.D., Bauman, S., Forlizzi, J., Srinivasa, S.S.: Effects of robot motion on human-robot collaboration. In: Proceedings of the Tenth Annual ACM/IEEE International Conference on Human-Robot Interaction, pp. 51–58 (2015)
33. Hinds, P.J., Bailey, D.E.: Out of sight, out of sync: understanding conflict in distributed teams. Organ. Sci. **14**(6), 615–632 (2003)
34. Beane, M., Orlikowski, W.J.: What difference does a robot make? The material enactment of distributed coordination. Organ. Sci. **26**(6), 1553–1573 (2015)
35. Malone, T.W., Crowston, K.: The interdisciplinary study of coordination. ACM Comput. Surv. CSUR **26**(1), 87–119 (1994)
36. Kraut, R.E., Gergle, D., Fussell, S.R.: The use of visual information in shared visual spaces: informing the development of virtual co-presence. In: Proceedings of the 2002 ACM Conference on Computer Supported Cooperative Work, pp. 31–40 (2002)
37. Kiesler, S., Sproull, L.: Group decision making and communication technology. Organ. Behav. Hum. Decis. Process. **52**(1), 96–123 (1992)
38. Dourish, P., Bellotti, V.: Awareness and coordination in shared workspaces. In: Proceedings of the 1992 ACM Conference on Computer-Supported Cooperative Work, New York, NY, USA, pp. 107–114 (1992)
39. Kolling, A., Nunnally, S., Lewis, M.: Towards human control of robot swarms. In: Proceedings of the Seventh Annual ACM/IEEE International Conference on Human-Robot Interaction, New York, NY, USA, pp. 89–96 (2012)
40. Nikolaidis, S., Ramakrishnan, R., Gu, K., Shah, J.: Efficient model learning from joint-action demonstrations for human-robot collaborative tasks. In: Proceedings of the Tenth Annual ACM/IEEE International Conference on Human-Robot Interaction, pp. 189–196 (2015)
41. Oudah, M., Babushkin, V., Chenlinangjia, T., Crandall, J.W.: Learning to interact with a human partner. In: Proceedings of the Tenth Annual ACM/IEEE International Conference on Human-Robot Interaction, New York, NY, USA, pp. 311–318 (2015)
42. Myagmarjav, B., Sridharan, M.: Knowledge acquisition with selective active learning for human-robot interaction. In: Proceedings of the Tenth Annual ACM/IEEE International Conference on Human-Robot Interaction Extended Abstracts, New York, NY, USA, pp. 147–148 (2015)

43. Mohseni-Kabir, A., Rich, C., Chernova, S., Sidner, C.L., Miller, D.: Interactive hierarchical task learning from a single demonstration. In: Proceedings of the Tenth Annual ACM/IEEE International Conference on Human-Robot Interaction, New York, NY, USA, pp. 205–212 (2015)
44. Bailey, D.E., Leonardi, P.M., Barley, S.R.: The lure of the virtual. Organ. Sci. **23**(5), 1485–1504 (2012)
45. Bechky, B.A.: Gaffers, Gofers, and Grips: role-based coordination in temporary organizations. Organ. Sci. **17**(1), 3–21 (2006)
46. Faraj, S., Xiao, Y.: Coordination in fast-response organizations. Manag. Sci. **52**(8), 1155–1169 (2006)
47. Hackman, J.R.: Groups That Work and Those That Don't. Jossey-Bass, San Francisco (1990)
48. Schreiber, G.: Knowledge Engineering and Management: The CommonKADS Methodology. MIT Press, Cambridge (2000)
49. Gennari, J.H., et al.: The evolution of Protégé: an environment for knowledge-based systems development. Int. J. Hum.-Comput. Stud. **58**(1), 89–123 (2003)
50. Tyndale, P.: A taxonomy of knowledge management software tools: origins and applications. Eval. Program Plann. **25**(2), 183–190 (2002)
51. Ford, K.M., Bradshaw, J.M., Adams-Webber, J.R., Agnew, N.M.: Knowledge acquisition as a constructive modeling activity. Int. J. Intell. Syst. **8**(1), 9–32 (1993)
52. Barrett, E.: Sociomedia: Multimedia, Hypermedia, and the Social Construction of Knowledge. MIT Press, Cambridge (1994)
53. Bechky, B.A.: Sharing meaning across occupational communities: the transformation of understanding on a production floor. Organ. Sci. **14**(3), 312–330 (2003)
54. Carlile, P.R.: Transferring, translating, and transforming: an integrative framework for managing knowledge across boundaries. Organ. Sci. **15**(5), 555–568 (2004)
55. Bailey, D.E., Barley, S.R.: Teaching-learning ecologies: mapping the environment to structure through action. Organ. Sci. **22**(1), 262–285 (2011)
56. Bailey, D.E., Leonardi, P.M., Chong, J.: Minding the gaps: understanding technology interdependence and coordination in knowledge work. Organ. Sci. **21**(3), 713–730 (2010)

A Practical Study on the Information Sharing System for Producers

Tomoko Kasihma[1(✉)], Shimpei Matsumoto[2], and Takashi Hasuike[3]

[1] Kindai University, Hiroshima, Japan
kashima@hiro.kindai.ac.jp
[2] Hiroshima Institute of Technology, Hiroshima, Japan
[3] Waseda University, Tokyo, Japan

Abstract. Previous researches have shown that the environment of agricultural producers needs to be enriched, and factors that help agriculture to become attractive and rewarding need to be pursued. One such approach is believed to be an audible connection with the consumers. However, there remains a need to determine how such connections between producers and consumers will be established. By identifying, planning, and shaping the environment in which information from both sides is presented, the QOL and the value of products may be improved for producers, while providing reassurance to and building trust with the consumers. Past efforts have involved the development of a network involving producers and local roadside stations. Therefore, in this study, we conducted interviews with producers as well as performed a nationwide online survey. We developed the design of a new information system with which various types of producers and consumers are connected. Then, we performed a proof-of-concept test, after which we set numerical assessment baselines for the improvement in the QOL, and designated and measured the value of produce, reassurance, and trust. Finally, we verified the effectiveness of the proposed system.

Keywords: Agricultural IT tool · Relation building · Agricultural direct sales station

1 Introduction

In recent years, the average age of agricultural workers in Japan is over 60 years old. In addition to the aging of the population, due to the lack of successors and the increase in abandoned cultivation land, the environment surrounding Japanese agriculture is a serious situation (see Table 1) [1]. Therefore, revitalization of agriculture is positioned as an important issue throughout the country. Under these circumstances, cheap agricultural crops are imported from overseas, which has seriously affected Japanese agriculture. Currently, domestic products are more than 30% higher at retail prices than imported items. Since imported goods cheaper than domestic goods are accepted by consumers, imported goods will increase more and more. As domestic agricultural products must compete with imported goods in price, Japanese agriculture has to face this difficult situation. On the other hand, the evaluation of domestic agricultural

S. Yamamoto and H. Mori (Eds.): HCII 2019, LNCS 11569, pp. 524–534, 2019.
https://doi.org/10.1007/978-3-030-22660-2_38

products is higher than imported goods because its safety, quality, and taste are relatively higher than imported goods. Therefore, it is important to make these invisible factors easy to utilize as added value so that anyone can recognize.

There have been various efforts to ensure food safety and to gain consumer confidence. However, the burden to progress these such as monetary cost and labor is not small. Also, since farmers must be familiar with how to use advanced equipment such as IoT devices, the burden on aged producers is particularly high. As agricultural prices are sluggish, it is not easy to reflect expenses at these production stages in market prices. However, these efforts may be key to consciousness reform of domestic producers and local productions, branding, and differentiation. Therefore, aggressive efforts are indispensable while considering cost-effectiveness.

Therefore, in this research, we propose a communication application "Vegescan" aiming at improving the value of domestic products. This will convey the safety, quality, and taste of crops to consumers instead of producers. By using Vegescan, producers can easily register the information of products utilizing the idle time of agricultural work. Registered information can be sent to consumers on-demand. The consumer can check the registered information by simply taking the barcode attached to the product onto the camera of tablet device located at a market. Vegescan tells consumers various data, such as the information of agricultural crops, personal information of producers, the state of fields with pictures. In addition to this basic information, consumers can also check recommended recipes using vegetables recognized by the camera, as well as other vegetable information shipped from this producer. Consumers can know the producer's information through the use of Vegescan, so they can discover their favorite producers. It will lead to opportunities to pick and purchase secure and safe crops. This interaction is indirect communication, but it can be a function to build a trust relationship. Since today trust relationships are propagated to other people through social media, the trust relationship will contribute to generating the added value of agricultural products which will lead to sales promotion.

Table 1. Agricultural working population and average age

Year	Working population (million)	Average age
2010	260.6	65.8
2016	192.2	66.8
2017	181.6	66.7
2018	175.3	66.8

2 Previous Study

As IT has progressed and high-performance IT devices are now available at a low cost, smart agriculture has been implemented in many places as it aims to improve the quality of domestic agricultural systems and to stabilize production; achievements in this regard are reported by newspapers on a daily basis. Of the smart agriculture approaches, the focus has been to acquire knowledge held by experienced persons through the accumulation of agricultural work history using sensing technologies, and for some time, large-scale, large-volume network server technologies have been the focus of attention as one of the major challenges for a long time. For example, Takatsu et al. focused on an implementation of ICT in agriculture as a means to address the falling number of descendants of farmers who are in agriculture, and they discussed the revitalization of agriculture, solving the problem of a shortage of successors, determining harvesting seasons for agricultural produce and prediction of yield, and improving the income of the producers [2]. As with the challenge associated with inheriting skills and knowledge, improvements with respect to the efficiency in logistics for agricultural produce and improvements in the added value of agricultural produce have been regarded as major challenges in smart agriculture. For example, Satake et al. reported the importance of information sharing for consumption, production, and logistics in the agricultural supply chain [3]. For the agricultural workforce, including producers, information sharing in the agricultural supply chain not only leads to a reduction in excess such as produce waste, but can also contribute to realizing enhanced freshness in shipped produce.

For the above-mentioned pair of challenges, i.e., the "fixation of agricultural knowledge" and "information sharing in agricultural logistics," the authors have investigated the IT-based support for the improvement of both efficiency and added value in agricultural logistics since 2010 [4–9]. First, in order to optimize the supply period, there is a need to understand the conditions of agricultural produce, manage production of agricultural produce that meets the demand of clients, and control excess production and supply shortages owing to changes in the growth periods for outdoor cultivation and unevenness in shipment. To do this, we developed an agricultural information system capable of video streaming, an information system that connects producers and consumers as well as supports the development of relationships between the two, and a system that shares information between food production, logistics, and consumption. Using these systems, producers can obtain information regarding the purchasers of specific kinds of agricultural produce, while customers can be provided with information on the types of agricultural produce being grown by different types of producers, and the different methods employed. In addition, the developed system enables producers to have a direct point of connection with consumers. In light of the above, for the producers, we developed a sales model that aims to guide decisions regarding the production of what sells, rather than selling what is produced, as well as a mechanism that contributes to the improvement of marketing capabilities.

However, there remain many challenges. While there has been progress in terms of the development of convenient and multi-functional systems, they have also become difficult and complicated for elderly producers. Therefore, in this study, we added the essence of communication science to these systems that were already developed and built systems that expanded on the concept. They are essentially information-sharing systems for producers with a focus on user-friendliness interface. In particular, systems are built with an emphasis on usability without incurring an additional burden to the producers. Such systems will be implemented at a roadside station, and a proof-of-concept test will be conducted to verify their validity. As a result, even workers who are new to agriculture can obtain indexes for agricultural work, and these systems would help reduce the burden by increasing the efficiency in agricultural work and developing successor's talents.

3 Similar Products

Various systems and applications are actually being introduced. Even a major supermarket can print 2-dimensional barcodes (QR codes) on goods and can view producer's information and his/her comments. However, although the cutting-edge technology has been utilized, many customers do not recognize these systems and also do not use them. The reason might be that the same information is always presented, and there is no difference in an advertisement. As another reason, any information that cannot be thought of as a high utilization rate is also published. The features of the existing systems are summarized below (see Table 2).

1. Osaka-Ainou food center (http://www.osaka-ainou.jp/)
2. Rakuten Ragri (https://agriculture.rakuten.co.jp/)
3. Itoyokado (http://look.itoyokado.co.jp/kao/movie/movie.php)
4. OISIX (https://www.oisix.com/)
5. Topvalue (https://www.topvalu.net/)

Table 2. The features of the existing systems

Feature	1	2	3	4	5
Media	Web store	Web	Web store	Web store	Store
Method	URL	URL	QR search	URL	QR URL
Producer's information	Yes	Yes	Yes	Yes	Yes
Producer's voice	No	Text	Movie	Text	Movie
Producer's face	Picture	Picture movie	Picture movie	No	Picture
Product's information	Picture	Picture movie	Picture movie	Picture	Picture movie
Growing process	No	Picture movie	Picture movie	No	Picture
Recipe	Picture	Picture	Picture movie	No	Picture movie

4 Proposed System

We attempt to enable the source of crops to be identified, while enabling producers to deliver tasty products to consumers with confidence. In addition, this system can provide information on food safety to customers via the Internet at anytime and anywhere, which allows producers to gain the broad trust of customers. For farmers, the ability to specify the source of produce lie means that they accept responsibility for the produce. However, disclosing the growth process for crops and receiving responses directly from individual customers may contribute to increased motivation for production.

4.1 Functions

The system has the following two functions.

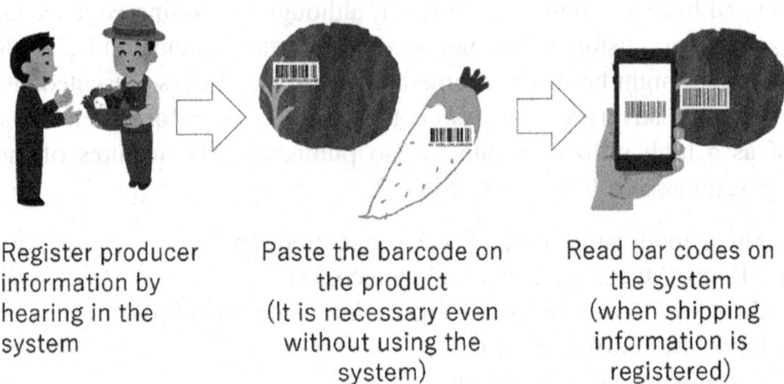
Register producer information by hearing in the system
Paste the barcode on the product (It is necessary even without using the system)
Read bar codes on the system (when shipping information is registered)

Fig. 1. How to use information browsing system.

(1) Input System

Data input is for sending out information, and it is assumed that employees of producers and shops use it. In using the input system, it is necessary to register the producer information in advance. For example, a producer number, personal information of a producer (name, face photograph, production place, information on other producers and shipping agricultural products) is input. For those other than preregistration, issue and paste a barcode (price tag) for selling the goods in the same way as the previous work. Also, register the vegetables to be shipped to confirm that there is a shipment. Registration can be done by scanning (recognizing) the issued barcode with a dedicated application (see Fig. 1).

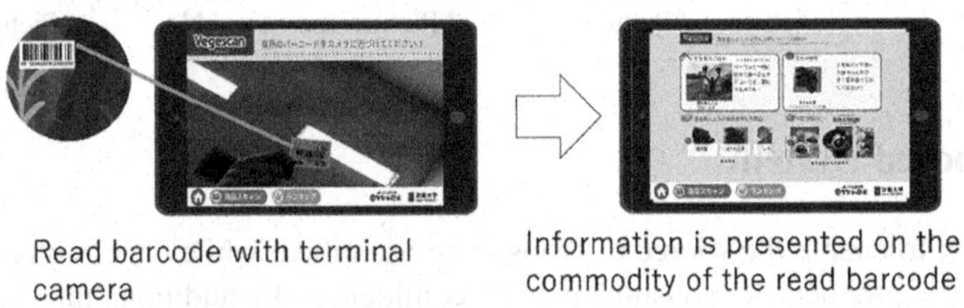
Read barcode with terminal camera
Information is presented on the commodity of the read barcode

Fig. 2. How to use information browsing system.

(2) Browsing System

It is for viewing information and supposed to be used by consumers. We set up tablet in store so that we can view freely. For browsing, you can browse product information by holding the bar code of the product on a dedicated terminal. The contents that can be viewed by the browsing system are largely three items, the details of which are as follows (see Fig. 2).

Producer's Crop Information

- Crop name
- Crop image
- Efficacy icon
- Producer name
- Producer image
- Producing area
- Producer's unique characteristics of agricultural crops
- Recommended way to eat for producers
- Recipe
- List of agricultural crops of producers shipped within 7 days

Crop Information

- Crop name
- Crop illustration image
- Agricultural crop species
- Season's icon
- Seasonal calendar
- Nutrients, efficacy icon
- Features of agricultural crops
- Impression of agricultural crops
- Preservation method
- List of other producers producing this agricultural crop

Producer's Information

- Producer name
- Producer image
- Producing area
- Commitment during production
- Producer's diary
- Question to producers
- List of recently shipped agricultural crops

Ranking information

- Suggested vegetables ranking (1st to 10th place)

4.2 Interface

The system designs with a bright image so that housewife's consumers can enjoy shopping. Consumers make the system available as if they were browsing magazines. We have created an interface so that you can easily transition to the screen of page 5.

Design evaluation of the system is done by gaze measurement (see Fig. 3). Multiple designs are created, and the subjects adopt the design which makes the screen transition the simplest.

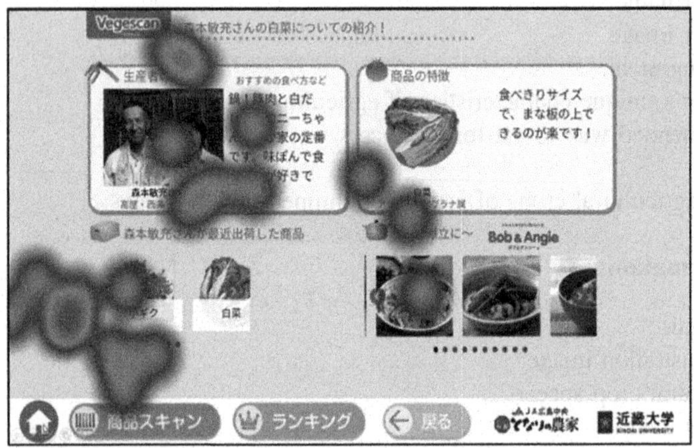

Fig. 3. Evaluation of UI by gaze movement

5 Substantiated Experiment

We conduct a demonstration experiment to confirm the effectiveness of this system. The experiment will be conducted for 1 month with the cooperation of the market (farm takaya store which is JA central) (see Fig. 4). The market to conduct this experiment is located in the center of the area where approximately 30,000 people live (see Fig. 5). There is a shopping center of a large shop near the shop where the experiment is conducted. Many consumers in this store have many elderly consumers wanting to buy local ingredients.

We conducted a questionnaire survey for consumers when introducing the system. Consumers frequently saw positive responses to the use of the system. However, problems on the operability of the system, the size of letters, and the trouble of using the system became clear. Many consumers have experience in reading bar codes at self-registration etc. at shopping centers. However, aged consumers felt it was difficult to scan barcodes on tablet cameras.

We confirmed the number of browsing and average viewing time of each page in the operation test in the store for one month. Approximately 1000 views of each page were confirmed browsing (see Table 3). The time zone in which the system was used is shown in Fig. 6. The transition ratio of each page is shown in the Fig. 7.

Fig. 4. A state of demonstration experiment

Table 3. Number of views and average time

Contents	Number of views	Average browsing time (minutes)
Bar code scan	537	
Product crop page	538	1.25
Crop pages	334	0.78
Product page	108	1.89
Ranking	362	1.7

Table 4. Percentage of total view

	Number of view	Percentage of total
Scan a barcode	301	27%
Ranking list	361	33%
Crop pages	334	30%
Producer page	107	10%
View of all pages	1103	100%

Many of the users were more interested in ranking than on specific items (see Table 4). Many users browsed the producer page rather than the crops page after barcode scanning and seeing specific product pages. Also, we confirmed the staying time of each page. Consumer stay time is long for producer page and ranking page.

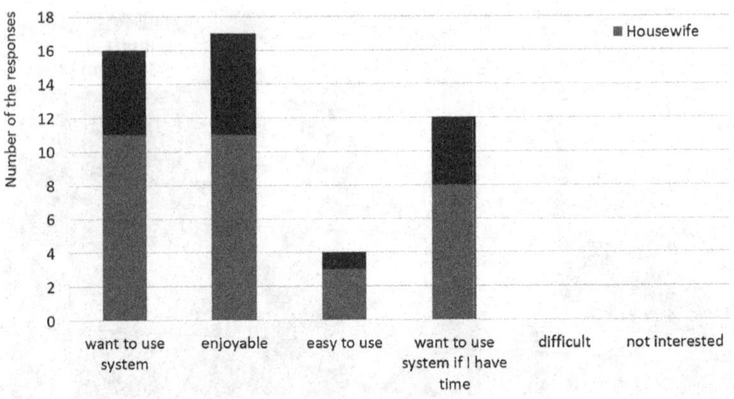

Fig. 5. Impression using the system

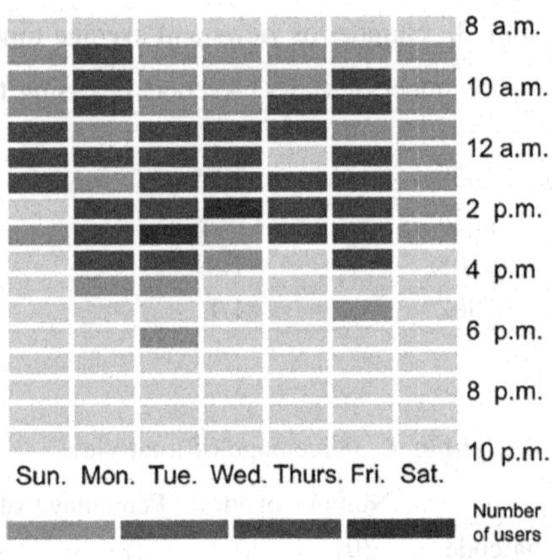

Fig. 6. Number of users by time zone

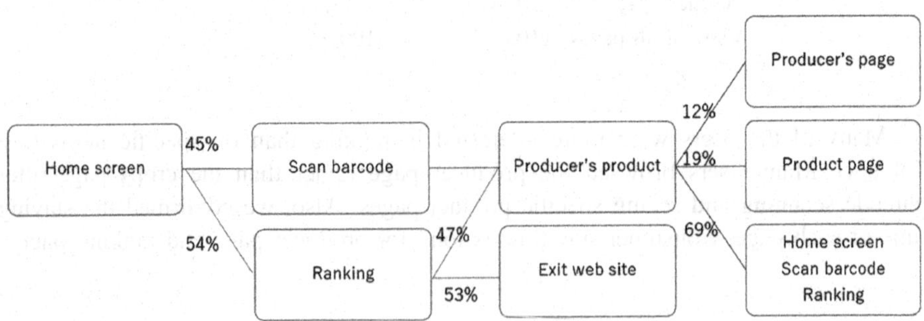

Fig. 7. Percentage of screen transition

6 Conclusion

Many systems have been previously proposed, but challenges that faced these sys-tems were overcome, and new systems were built. Currently, the authors are working on an initiative that supports the local production and consumption in Hiroshima. When the disclosure of information is seen as the source of the added value, it was difficult for them to be executed using the existing model because consumer tier and climatic conditions are considered. However, we also found that stores in Hiroshima desire to have local and fresh agricultural produce available, while consumers had a high degree of willingness to purchase local agricultural produce as long as there was no significant difference in price. In light of these findings, we focused on ideas whereby the value of agricultural produce is determined by the consumers them-selves, rather than by standards set by experts. Further, there is no portal in which information on the production of local agricultural produce can be obtained easily. We are now in the process of developing a CMS that is unique to Hiroshima, where information sharing is enabled between agricultural producers and consumers. In the case of Hiroshima, there is limited land available for agricultural production, and it is difficult to provide information on creativity with respect to ingredients when developing creative ingredients. In spite of the narrow land space, there is a great possibility that culture and ingredients have survived in the land over the years, and there is likely to be a great need to provide and share such information.

Acknowledgments. This work was partly supported by Artificial Intelligence Research Promotion Foun-dation, Japan Society for the Promotion of Science, KAKENHI Grant-in-Aid for Young Scientists, 18K18321 and Grant-in-Aid for Scientific Research(B), No. 17H02043.

References

1. Ministry of Agriculture, Forestry and Fisheries, Study group for realization of smart agriculture. http://www.maff.go.jp/j/kanbo/kihyo03/gityo/g_smart_nougyo/. Accessed 2 June 2018
2. Takado, S., Murakawa, H., Ohata, T.: Utilizing M2M service platform in agricultural ICT. Nec. Tech. J. **64**(4), 31–34 (2011)
3. Satake, Y., Yamazaki, T.: How food and agricultural clouds should improve food chain. FUJITSU **62**(3), 262–268 (2011)
4. Kashima, T., Matsumoto, S., Iseida, H., Matsutomi, T., Ishii, H.: Information system for urban agricultural crops direct sale using cloud. In: Conference on Electrical and Information Engineering Conference Chinese Branch Conference Papers Proceedings, pp. 51–52 (2011)
5. Kashima, T., Matsutomi, T., Matsumoto, S., Iseida, H.: Agricultural information system for production information sharing, In: The 24th Annual Meeting of the Institute of Electrical Engineers of Japan, vol. 3, p. 45 (2012)
6. Kashima, T., Matsumoto, S., Iseda, H., Ishii, H.: A proposal of farmers information system for urban markets. In: Watada, J., Watanabe, T., Phillips-Wren, G., Howlett, R., Jain, L. (eds.) Intelligent Decision Technologies. SIST, vol. 1, pp. 225–234. Springer, Heidelberg (2012)

7. Kashima, T., Matsumoto, S., Matsutomi, T., Iseida, H.: Development of two-way information dissemination infrastructure in the field of agriculture and reduction of environmental burden by introduction. In: Proceedings of the 20th National Convention of Artificial Intelligence Conference, 3 K 3 - OS - 08 b - 3 (2013)
8. Kashima, T., Matsumoto, S.: Development of interactive information transmission infrastructure for regional revitalization in the field of agriculture. In: Papers of the 5th Conference on Confederation of Interscience Conference, In CD - ROM, 1 A - 2 - 2 (2013)
9. Kashima, T., Matsumoto, S., Hasuike, T.: Formation of a recycling-oriented society using the content management system for the food industry. In: Proceedings of the 20th National Convention of Artificial Intelligence (28th) Conference, 1 B 3 - OS-02b-4 (2014)

Development of "Aruite Mi Mai," A Walking Application for Crime Prevention for Safe and Secure City Development

Yusuke Kometani[1(✉)], Tomoaki Isono[1], Tomoki Yabe[1], Tomoo Okubo[1], Yuya Takeshita[2], and Rihito Yaegashi[1]

[1] Kagawa University, 1-1 Saiwai-cho, Takamatsu, Kagawa, Japan
kometani@eng.kagawa-u.ac.jp
[2] Terimukuri, 1-540-3 Dokichonishi, Marugame, Kagawa, Japan

Abstract. To realize city development that allows people to live safely and securely, (1) citizens should have accurate perspectives on safety, (2) local stakeholders such as administrators, companies, and residents should share various kinds of risk information based on these perspectives, and (3) local stakeholders should create a safe community and tackle necessary problems. Therefore, we developed a mobile app to support users in learning perspectives on crime prevention through city patrol activities and in sharing the contents as risk information. In this paper, we discuss the usefulness of the app based on data from practical use and describe the prospects for supporting the formation of safe communities in the future.

Keywords: Safe and secure city development · Perspective · Crime prevention · Situational crime prevention theory · Information sharing · Community formation

1 Introduction

Japan frequently experiences natural disasters such as earthquakes, typhoons, torrential rains, flood and sediment disasters, tsunamis, volcanic eruptions, and blizzards. However, in addition to ensuring public safety and security on a daily basis through measures such as crime prevention and traffic safety, the need for a social system that guarantees safety and security has been recognized [1].

The Japanese Ministry of Land, Infrastructure and Transport [1] has noted the following: "To develop cities that allow people to live safely and securely, (1) citizens should have accurate perspectives on safety, (2) local stakeholders such as administrators, companies, and residents should share various kinds of risk information based on these perspectives, and (3) local stakeholders should build their community and tackle necessary problems."

In this paper, with the aim of promoting crime prevention during the development of safe and secure cities and communities [2], we devise a system that supports users in learning perspectives about crime prevention through city patrol activities by stakeholders such as local residents.

S. Yamamoto and H. Mori (Eds.): HCII 2019, LNCS 11569, pp. 535–544, 2019.
https://doi.org/10.1007/978-3-030-22660-2_39

As this research aims to involve a wide variety of age groups, from young people to the elderly, in crime prevention, this system is developed as a user-friendly mobile app for use on smartphones and tablets. In addition, we examine the usefulness of patrol activities for crime prevention, which involve walking around and therefore provide health benefits for users. With this background, and because a function for recording walking history is planned to be included in the app in the future, we decided to call this crime prevention walking app "Aruite Mi Mai" (which means "Let's walk" in the local Sanuki dialect of Kagawa Prefecture, Japan).

In this paper, we detail the design of risk information sharing and other functions for learning safety perspectives of crime prevention. Here we describe our newly developed app's home screen, usefulness (based on data from practical use). We conclude with a discussion of prospects for the development of a community formation support function.

2 App Design

2.1 Learning Perspectives from the Creation of a Regional Safety Map

Users of this app will carry out crime prevention patrol activities in their city to report on and share information about safe and dangerous locations. In this research, we utilized a regional safety map as a means of coordinating information recorded by individual users. A regional safety map shows photographs of places where crime is more likely to occur, with a location assessment ability (i.e., the ability to predict dangerous locations) that can be improved based on data from the user [3, 4]. Therefore, for our app, we developed a user interface (UI) that allows users to create regional safety maps.

An important aspect of this app is that it allows users to master the use of different perspectives on safety. In the process of creating a regional safety map, users not only judge whether a location is safe or dangerous, but they also explicitly evaluate the risks of that location based on correct perspectives. Therefore, our app incorporates reliable perspectives based on situational crime prevention theory [4, 5] that can be selected by users, as mentioned in Sect. 2.2.

2.2 Selection of Perspectives on Safety Within the App

To enable users to evaluate the risks of a location when reporting, the selection buttons in our app are labeled with keywords about perspectives on safety. When users share information about their perspectives, the keywords they select are tagged to their report, which can then be seen by other users.

Komiya argued that eliminating opportunities to commit crime is an optimal strategy for deterring crime, and proposed three elements of crime deterrence that allow anyone to practice the theory anytime, anywhere [4]. In addition, Komiya devised keywords that express perspectives and can be used by anyone, even elementary school students [5].

In this research, we use the keywords devised by Komiya [6] based on situational crime prevention theory [4]. Keywords for safe and dangerous locations are "easy to monitor" and "difficult to access", and "easy to access" and "difficult to monitor", respectively. "The location is easy/difficult to monitor" is a measure of monitoring ability by pedestrians or residents, and "easy/difficult to access" is a regional measure. For example, "difficult to access" means a lower likelihood of kidnapping because a car cannot easily access the location, or "easy to monitor" means a lower likelihood of mugging, etc. The app provides check boxes that enable users to select keywords after judging whether a location is safe or dangerous during patrol activities.

3 App Implementation

While our plans are for this app to eventually include a walking support function aimed at recruiting a wider range of users and supporting community formation, in this research we have implemented and evaluated only the most basic functions corresponding to the design described in the following sections. In this paper, we examine the effectiveness and usefulness of these functions using the implemented system.

3.1 Basic Specifications of the App

Our app operates on a smartphone or tablet running the Android operating system. The login screen is shown in Fig. 1. Users can sign up for an account by registering with a valid e-mail address and providing their real name, a username (viewable by other users), height, weight, and age; these data will be used to calculate calorie expenditure in the walking support function in the future.

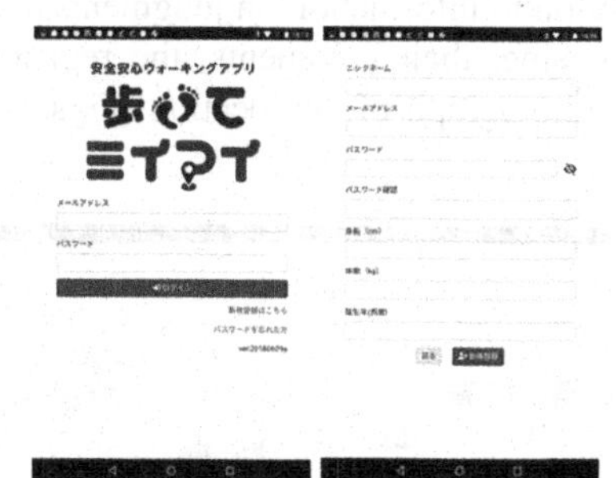

Fig. 1. Login and user registration screens.

3.2 Safe/Dangerous Location Reporting Function

The safe/dangerous location reporting function allows users to register safe/dangerous locations found during crime prevention patrols in their city. Users can take photos of locations and judge whether it is safe or dangerous. The UI is shown in Fig. 2. The app includes a GPS function that automatically attaches the longitude and latitude of the location to the content added by the user.

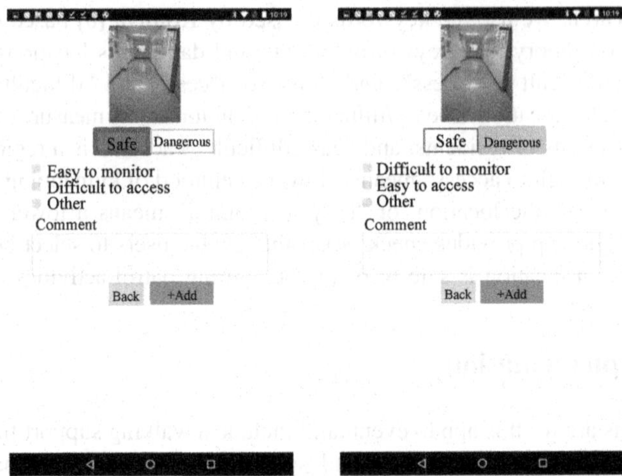

Fig. 2. Safe/dangerous location registration function: tags change (perspectives on safe/dangerous) according to user judgments of "Safe" or "Dangerous."

3.3 Safe/Dangerous Location Sharing Function

Reports registered using the safe/dangerous location reporting function can be viewed using the safe/dangerous location sharing function. Reports registered with longitude and latitude are visualized as a regional safety map. Figure 3 shows the UI of the regional safety map when using the safe/dangerous location sharing function. In this UI, a report is visualized as a flag. Blue and red flags indicate safe and dangerous locations, respectively. Users can browse through the content registered by other users by selecting a flag. In addition to information on judgments and perspectives, users can view the registrant's nickname, their comments, the registration date, the time the report was entered, and a photograph of the location (Figs. 4 and 5).

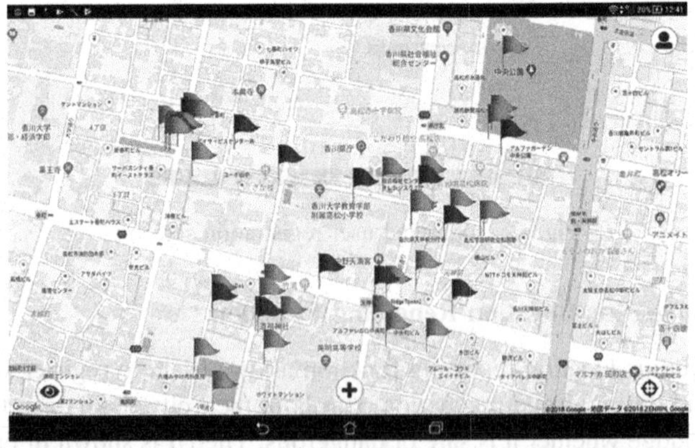

Fig. 3. User interface (UI) of the regional safety map when using the safe/dangerous location sharing function. (Color figure online)

Fig. 4. UI of a report confirmation when using the safe/dangerous location sharing function (shown is an example of a dangerous location report).

Fig. 5. UI of a report confirmation when using the safety/dangerous location sharing function (shown is an example of a safe location report)

4 Practice

4.1 Purpose

We examined the usefulness of our app based on usage logs and a questionnaire survey. We also considered whether this app could be utilized in lessons at local educational institutions or in events promoting crime prevention. Data obtained from the use field testing were then used in university and elementary school lessons.

4.2 Method

The development of this dual-function app as described in Sect. 3 was completed on June 19, 2018, after which three lessons were conducted at universities and elementary schools. Table 1 shows the contents and conditions of the lessons. In addition to usage logs, a questionnaire survey for which the students were required to provide their name was conducted after lesson B. The question items are shown in Table 2. For Q1–Q3 and Q5, users responded on a four-point Likert scale, from "1. Strongly disagree" and "4. Strongly agree", and Q4 was a free-answer question (Table 4).

Table 1. Contents of the lesson

Date	Lesson	Users	Course content
July 17, 2018	Lesson A: Kagawa University lesson "Theme C" (first year)	Kagawa University students 24 people	• Android users installed the app and registered in the week before the practice day • On the day of the class practice, about a 10-min lecture on perspectives was given. After that, fieldwork was carried out for about 50 min using the app. Finally, the regional safety map was reviewed in the room for about 10 min
November 16, 2018	Lesson B: Kagawa University lesson "Personality psychology" (second year or higher)	Kagawa University students 64 people	
December 3–5, 2018	Lesson C: Kagawa University attached to Takamatsu Elementary School (fourth graders) Class practice by Kagawa University students belonging to the Faculty of Education	Kagawa University attached to Takamatsu Elementary School (fourth graders) About 30 people	• December 3: A 60-min lecture on perspectives • December 4: About 60 min of fieldwork using the app • December 5: A 60-min group presentation by elementary school students using the regional safety map

Table 2. Questionnaire items (in lesson B)

Question item
Q1 Are you usually aware of safe places while walking around the city?
Q2 Are you usually aware of dangerous places while walking around the city?
Q3 Have your views towards the city and your aware about crime prevention changed as a result of using the app?
Q4 Regarding Q3, what specific changes have you experienced?
Q5 Did you enjoy the crime prevention walking activities using this app?

Table 3. Usage logs in lesson A (first-year university students)

Group	Member	Reported number		Selected number of perspectives on safety			Selected number of perspectives on dangers		
		Safe	Dangerous	Easy to monitor	Difficult to access	Others	Difficult to monitor	Easy to access	Others
A	3	6	7	5	1	1	7	3	2
B	3	5	7	5	1	0	5	2	0
C	3	4	10	4	0	0	7	1	0
D	3	1	2	1	0	0	2	2	0
E	3	2	8	2	0	2	8	4	8
F	3	2	4	2	0	0	2	0	1
G	3	0	4	0	0	0	2	0	2
H	3	0	10	0	0	0	9	5	0
	Total	20	52	19	2	3	42	17	13

5 Results and Discussion

Tables 3 through 5 show the numbers of reports and tags given in each lesson. Focusing on the total reported numbers in each table, for all of the demonstration lessons, there were more than double the number of reports of dangerous compared with safe places, which suggests that users tend to pay more attention to dangerous locations.

Focusing on the selection of keywords, the highest number were chosen for "difficult to monitor", followed by "easy to access", "easy to monitor", and "difficult to access". Because these values also depend on structural aspects of the city, we cannot directly discuss any associations with individual cognitive ability; however, we believe that we can clarify the possibility of further improvement based on the data, such as accounting for bias in viewpoints and requesting additional examples of judgements such as "difficult to access" to further clarify their intended meaning.

Table 6 shows the results of the questionnaire survey for demonstration lesson B. The participants stated that they were not particularly aware of safe and dangerous locations while walking through the city. However, after using the app, they reported experiencing a change in awareness of safety and noted that they enjoyed the sense of security provided by the app while walking.

Table 7 shows the views of the city held by the users in lesson B and their changes in awareness of crime prevention based on their free responses, which were categorized and aggregated by category. In total, 54 respondents answered "3. Agree" or "4. Strongly agree". In addition, 50 respondents provided free responses. The authors classified and extracted the changes in awareness among the users after they had used the app. The most common type of description (N = 22/50) involved "Awareness during usual street walking" (e.g., "There are plenty of dangerous places, I just had not noticed", "I thought that I should be careful because I understood that it was dangerous", "I think I became more sensitive to dangerous places."). This suggests that the

Table 4. Usage logs in lesson B (second-year university students and higher)

Group	Member	Reported number		Selected number of perspectives on safety			Selected number of perspectives on dangers		
		Safe	Dangerous	Easy to monitor	Difficult to access	Others	Difficult to monitor	Easy to access	Others
A	4	3	6	3	0	0	6	6	0
B	4	0	4	0	0	0	4	2	0
C	4	0	3	0	0	0	3	0	0
D	4	0	6	0	0	0	3	3	4
E	4	0	3	0	0	0	1	0	2
F	3	1	5	1	1	0	5	4	0
G	4	2	2	2	0	0	2	1	0
H	4	1	8	1	1	1	7	4	1
I	4	0	5	0	0	0	3	5	5
J	5	0	2	0	0	0	1	2	0
K	3	0	6	0	0	0	5	2	0
L	3	0	3	0	0	0	3	0	0
M	3	0	5	0	0	0	3	2	0
N	3	4	5	4	0	0	3	0	0
O	3	1	10	1	0	1	4	4	8
P	3	0	5	0	0	0	3	1	0
	Total	12	78	12	2	2	56	36	20

Table 5. Usage logs in lesson C (fourth-grade elementary students)

Group	Reported number		Selected number of perspectives on safety			Selected number of perspectives on dangers		
	Safe	Dangerous	Easy to monitor	Difficult to access	Others	Difficult to monitor	Easy to access	Others
1	1	5	1	0	1	3	4	3
2	3	5	1	0	0	4	4	0
3	0	3	0	0	0	2	0	1
4	3	4	3	0	1	4	1	3
5	0	5	0	0	0	4	5	0
6	2	3	2	2	0	2	2	1
7	1	4	1	0	0	3	0	0
8	3	3	2	0	0	2	3	0
9	2	3	2	0	0	2	1	0
Total	15	35	12	2	2	26	20	8

Table 6. Questionnaire results from lesson B (four-point Likert scale, H_0: $\mu = 2.5$, H_1: $\mu \neq 2.5$)

Question item	Average	SD	*t*	*p*
Q1	2.03	0.77	−4.60	0.000**
Q2	2.28	0.79	−2.16	0.035*
Q3	3.36	0.61	10.72	0.000**
Q5	3.16	0.50	10.10	0.000**

* significance level of 5%
** significance level of 1%

app motivated the users to be more aware during usual city walking. The next most common type of description (N = 16/50) involved "Reflection/improvement of behavior" (e.g., "I was taking a dark and narrow road to go to the convenience store around midnight, but then I thought it would be better to walk along a well-lit street instead", "I noticed that some of the places I usually walk through are dangerous."). The third most common type (N = 10/50) of description involved a "Quantitative grasp of safe/dangerous locations" (e.g., "I learned that there are many dangerous places in the neighborhood", "It seems that there are fewer safe places"). The safe/dangerous location sharing function of the app allows users to view the content that was shared in each group in real time on the map, allowing them to quantitatively grasp the safe/dangerous locations in the city; this suggests that the app could potentially increase interest in the entire region.

Table 7. Change in awareness of app users in lesson B

Category	N
Awareness of usual walking behavior	22
Reflection and improvement of behavior	16
Quantitative grasp of safety/danger points	10
Use of keywords for dangerous spots	8
Perception of importance of scenery assessment ability	1

Furthermore, the importance of the "Use of keywords for dangerous spots" and the "Perception of the importance of location assessment ability" were recognized. The purpose of this app is to train attitudes in terms of gaining an understanding of an area by making judgements about safety. The data obtained in this suggest that the app has the potential to fulfill this purpose.

6 Conclusion

In this research, we developed a walking app for crime prevention, "Aruite Mi Mai", with a safe/dangerous location reporting function as a method to implement safe and secure city development. The results of field testing suggest that users of the app support other users based on usage trends and that this app is useful for learning about crime prevention perspectives. However, we could not evaluate the extent to which the app is useful in terms of learning perspectives. Therefore, in a future study, we will study feedback methods based on accumulated usage logs and consider practical models that can evaluate user performance in multiple ways.

This research established an environment for risk sharing in relation to safe and secure city development. Therefore, to develop a function for summarizing reports, as in the study by Hayakawa et al. [7], and for grouping users, as in the study by Nakamura et al. [8], Hirunuma et al. [9], we plan to add new functions to the app to enhance awareness of group activities, such as the abilities to organize crime prevention events and to record and share results on a per event basis by any user. We expect these functions to promote the growth of community crime prevention. We also plan to improve the usefulness of this app by analyzing its growth, and the factors that contribute to its growth, and by monitoring long-term changes in individual performance.

Acknowledgments. This research is supported by Seeds Development and Industry-Academia Collaboration Fund for 2018 of Kagawa University Research Promotion Program (KURPP).

References

1. Japanese Ministry of Land, Infrastructure and Transport: What is safe and secure city development. (in Japanese). http://www.mlit.go.jp/crd/city/sigaiti/tobou/1syou.pdf
2. Japanese Ministry of Land, Infrastructure and Transport: City crime prevention. (in Japanese). http://www.mlit.go.jp/toshi/toshi_bouhan_000001.html
3. Komiya, N.: Komiya Nobuo's criminology room: reference materia. (in Japanese). http://www.nobuokomiya.com/?page=menu3
4. Komiya, N.: Community safety maps for children in Japan: an analysis from a situational crime prevention perspective. Asian J. Criminol. **6**(2), 131–140 (2011)
5. Komiya, N.: Crimes can be predicted. Shincho-Shinsho (2013). (in Japanese)
6. Komiya, N.: Komiya Nobuo's criminology room: virtual fieldwork. (in Japanese). http://www.nobuokomiya.com/?page=page6
7. Hayakawa, T., Matsuda, K., Ito, T.: Prototype of community safety map system that can collaboratively edit using openstreetmap. J. Inf. Process. Soc. Jpn. **59**(3), 1095–1105 (2018). (in Japanese)
8. Nakamura, D., Hirunuma, T., Amalia, M., Yoshimoto, S.: Education support application of crime prevention, disaster prevention, and road safety for elementary school – improvement of user interface. JSiSE Res. Rep. **33**(5), 15–18 (2019). (in Japanese)
9. Hirunuma, T., Nakamura, D., Amalia, M., Yoshimoto, S.: Education support application of crime prevention, disaster prevention, and road safety for elementary school – improvement of functions. JSiSE Res. Rep. **33**(5), 19–22 (2019). (in Japanese)

Value-of-Information Driven Content Presentation and Filtering in Military Geographic Information Systems

James Michaelis(✉)

U.S. Army Research Laboratory, Adelphi, MD 20783, USA
james.r.michaelis2.civ@mail.mil

Abstract. Military C3I (Command, Control, Communications and Intelligence) operations at the tactical level have come to rely upon Geographic Information Systems (GIS) to access geotagged information relevant to mission needs. Management of Information Objects within military GIS applications presents a number of known research challenges, tied both to selection of mission-appropriate information and management of Soldier attention. Towards supporting prioritized content delivery and filtering within tactical networks, methods based on the estimated Value of Information (VoI) specific to mission context have demonstrated prior performance benefits (e.g., conservation of network bandwidth). However, limited HCI-themed research has been conducted to-date on Soldier interaction with VoI-augmented GIS applications, including assessment of their impact on situational awareness over areas of operation. This paper presents foundational work for studying Soldier interaction with VoI-augmented GIS applications, covering: (1) a supporting experimental platform based on the Android Tactical Assault Kit (ATAK); (2) a pilot study conducted with Soldiers, to assess the impact of VoI-based content prioritization on user experience and Information Object review.

Keywords: C3I · GIS · Value of Information

1 Introduction

Military C3I (Command, Control, Communications and Intelligence) operations at the tactical level have come to rely upon Geographic Information Systems (GIS) made accessible through a variety of Portable Electronic Devices (PEDs). Similar to commercial mapping applications, military GIS software commonly offers functionality to access geotagged information (e.g., imaging feeds, personnel reports) for areas of operation. These units of geotagged information, termed *Information Objects*, can provide Soldiers with expanded knowledge over areas of operation for routine decision support tasks. Management of Information Objects in military GIS software presents a number of research challenges, including [1]: (1) Content dissemination with limited networking resources and infrastructure; (2) Content selection strategies that account for Soldier cognitive load under varying mission conditions.

In prior research (e.g., [1–3]), challenges in network management for C3I operations have been addressed through adoption of policy-based content dissemination,

S. Yamamoto and H. Mori (Eds.): HCII 2019, LNCS 11569, pp. 545–554, 2019.
https://doi.org/10.1007/978-3-030-22660-2_40

centered on assessment of Value of Information (VoI) specific to the needs of consumers. These efforts have focused on identifying methods for assessment of VoI specific to mission tasking and environmental context [4, 5], as well as development of systems to support policy-based content dissemination [6]. Within tactical networking research, VoI enhancements have demonstrated support for conservation of resources such as bandwidth [6]. By contrast, from an HCI perspective, limited research has been conducted to assess the impact of VoI functionality on Soldier interactions with GIS software and any corresponding effects on Situational Awareness [7]. As such, new research becomes desirable to investigate: (1) The utility of VoI for supporting Soldier situational awareness over areas of operation; (2) Methods for conveying VoI of Information Objects to Soldiers in a readily understandable manner.

This paper presents foundational work being applied towards studying Soldier interaction with VoI-enhanced GIS applications, covering: (1) a supporting experimental platform based on the Android Tactical Assault Kit (ATAK); (2) a pilot study conducted with Soldiers, to assess the impact of VoI-based content prioritization on user experience and Information Object review.

2 Background

2.1 Value of Information

In prior research, Value of Information has been defined along the notion of intrinsic vs. extrinsic attributes of Information Objects. Intrinsic attributes can be viewed as measuring the inherent quality of an Information Object, and will vary based on the type of content considered. For instance, an Information Object corresponding to audio data could have intrinsic quality attributes of bit rate and sample rate. Here, intrinsic attributes can be viewed as establishing the Quality of Information (QoI) for a particular Information Object. By contrast, extrinsic attributes measure the utility of an Information Object to meet a specific consumer's needs. Within the context of tactical operations, examples of extrinsic attributes could include temporal relevance (*will I need this information soon for my mission tasks?*), geographic relevance (*is this information from a mission-relevant location?*), and source reliability (*did the information come from a sufficiently trustworthy source for mission needs?*). Additionally, extrinsic attributes could measure presence of relevant information (*does this image contain mission-relevant features?*). Prior work has viewed VoI as inherently building upon QoI [1], while emphasizing the inherent difference between these assessment classes (i.e., an Information Object with high image quality may not have mission-relevant information, thereby having low VoI).

Within tactical networking systems (e.g., [1, 3]), quantitative VoI assessment has previously been applied to prioritize Information Object delivery to Soldiers, through weighted averages of *evaluation metrics* each corresponding to particular Information Object attributes. An example of a weighted metric average for VoI assessment [4] takes the following form:

$$VoI = (GR * w_{GR}) + (T * w_T) + (E * w_E) + (I * w_I) + (IC * w_{IC}) + (SR * w_{SR})$$

For each evaluation metric, a *quantitative value* is calculated along with a corresponding *weighting of importance*. In turn, the metrics listed in this equation can be defined as follows:

- **GR (Geographic Relevance):** Based on where the data for a particular Information Object was obtained, relative to a consumer's mission location(s). For example, the distance between where an image was taken and a location of mission relevance.
- **TR (Temporal Relevance):** Based on when an Information Object will be needed by a consumer for mission tasks.
- **E (Expiration):** Estimates when the content of an Information Object will become too stale for mission needs.
- **I (Importance):** A value provided by a Subject Matter Expert (SME) or automated process, denoting an individual Information Object's importance specific to particular consumers and mission tasks.
- **IC (Information Content):** An assessment of the intrinsic significance of an Information Object's content for particular mission needs, as defined by an SME or automated process.
- **SR (Source Reliability):** An assessment of the reliability/trustworthiness of an Information Object's source or provider, as defined by an SME or automated process.

VoI assessment systems are seen as having a particularly rich set of research challenges, which include development of effective models for both Soldier context (e.g., concerning environmental/physiological factors) as well as mission state. Towards representing mission state, including mission tasks and events, recent efforts tied to semantic models of mission planning and execution (e.g., [8]) are of particular relevance.

2.2 Tactical GIS Platforms

Growth in availability of mobile computing platforms has prompted their increased usage in military operations [9]. Under these conditions, a number of C3I-oriented GIS systems have been developed for Android-based devices, which include: Android Tactical Assault Kit (ATAK) [10], Kinetic Integrated Low-cost Software Integrated Tactical Combat Handheld (KILSWITCH) [11], and the Tactical Ground Reporting System (TIGR) [12]. Common features of these platforms include:

- Presentation of map-based information using interfaces similar to available commercial software (e.g., Google Maps), as depicted in Fig. 1.
- Support for communication amongst Soldier teams.
- Support for downloading/uploading information corresponding to a geographic area of operations.

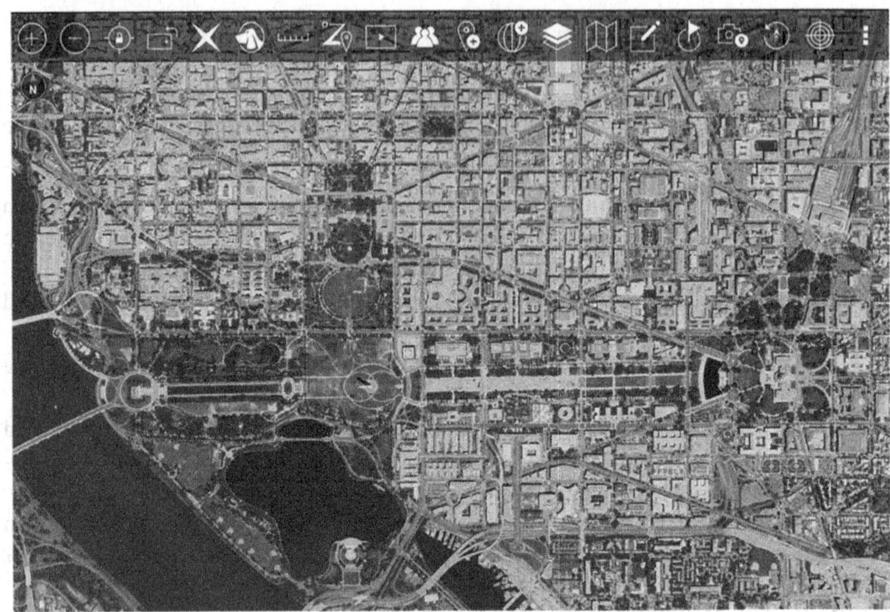

Fig. 1. ATAK user interface.

3 Experimental GIS Platform for VoI Assessment

Towards investigating the utility of VoI in military GIS systems, a prototype experimental platform was defined and implemented for usage in mission simulation based user studies. The platform implementation was based upon prior work with VoI extensions to the Android Tactical Assault Kit [3], and supports the presentation of mockup geotagged Information Objects across simulated areas of operation.

The purpose of this experimental platform is to support user studies centered on two functional uses of VoI:

- **VoI-based Filtering**, where VoI acts as a filter over a set of available Information Objects (i.e., reducing the number of Information Objects displayed).
- **VoI-based Prioritization**, where VoI acts as a mechanism to support ranking or binning of Information Objects by their estimated value.

In both cases, supported experiments center on two phases: (1) experimental trials, in which participants review a set of Information Objects displayed over an area of operations; (2) recall tasks, in which participants receive a set of questions to test their acquired knowledge of the Information Objects.

3.1 Experimental Platform Design

Figure 2 depicts the system architecture for the experimental platform, which consists of the following components:

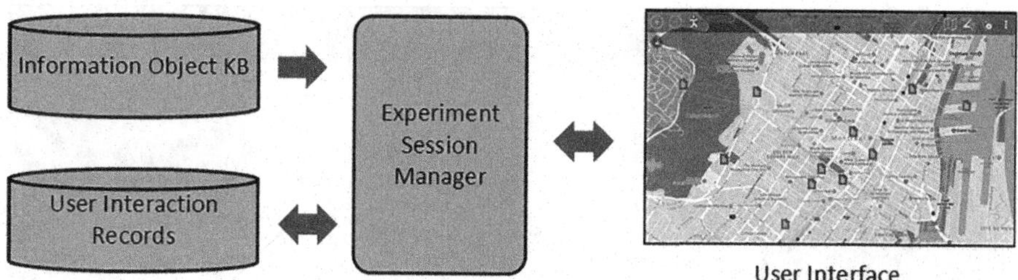

Fig. 2. System architecture for the experimental platform.

- **User Interface:** Based on the ATAK platform, this presents Information Objects during experimental trials, and sets of corresponding questions during recall tasks. Further details are provided in Sect. 3.2.
- **Experiment Session Manager:** This manages content displayed on the user interface, and processes inputs received from study participants (e.g., interface interactions, question responses).
- **Information Object KB:** This supports the generation of mockup Information Objects for experimental trials. Further details are provided in Sect. 3.3.
- **User Interaction Record KB:** This stores user responses to questions during the recall tasks, and additionally logs user interactions with the interface from the experimental trials (e.g., Information Objects clicked).

3.2 User Interface – Information Object Review

The user interface for the experimental platform (as depicted in Fig. 2) consists of three components:

- **The Map Display**, in which an area of operations is presented along with icons depicting locations for Information Objects
- **Information Object Popups (bottom right)**, which presents text-based details on an Information Object
- **Timer (bottom left)**, indicating remaining time to review information from the area of operations. The timer may be enabled or disabled, depending on the type of experiment carried out.

Similar to current usage of ATAK, user interaction is driven through point-and-click selection of Information Objects within the Map Display to review their content, as presented through Information Object Popups. Experimental trials are designed to stop under one of the following conditions: (1) non-timed: a participant indicates through the interface that they have completed their review; (2) timed: a participant runs out of time to continue reviewing. Following completion of the Information Object review, study participants are given a set of questions corresponding to the Information Object content they reviewed (types of questions supported by the experimentation platform are listed in Sect. 3.2) (Fig. 3).

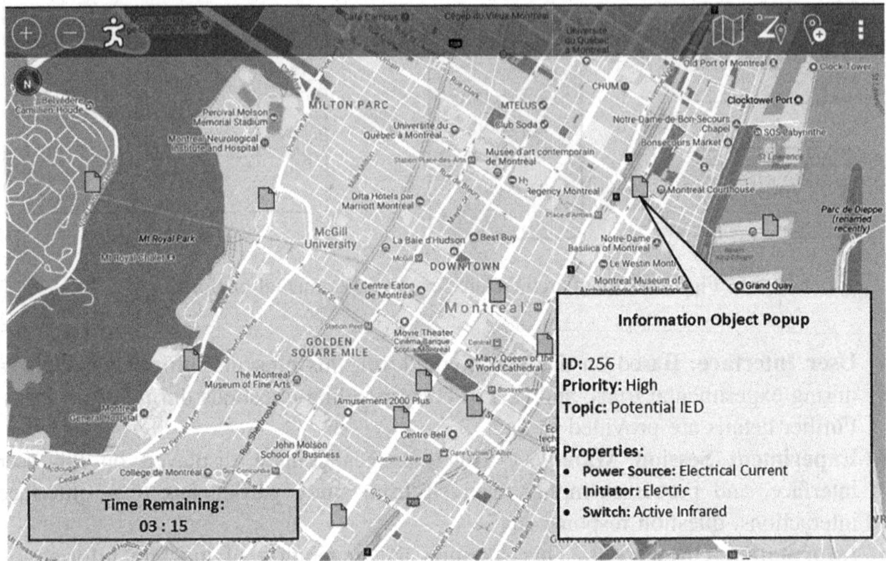

Fig. 3. User interface for the experimental platform, based on ATAK implementation.

VoI Binning for Information Objects: Within the user interface, VoI for Information Objects can be binned into three scoring categories: *High VoI*, *Medium VoI*, and *Low VoI*. Figure 4 depicts icons for each VoI binning category.

Fig. 4. VoI binnings implemented in the experimental platform, corresponding to Low, Medium, and High importance VoI categories.

3.3 Information Object Knowledge Base

To support generation of Information Objects for experimental trials, the Information Object Knowledge Base supports generation of Information Objects organized in the form of bulleted lists corresponding to pre-determined topics. From the Map Display, Information Objects can be accessed by clicking on a corresponding icon (as depicted in Fig. 2). Upon clicking, the following Information Object content is presented:

- A Numeric ID
- A Priority Level (Low, Medium, High)
- A Topic
- A Bullet List of 3–5 corresponding properties, each described in one to ten words

At present, Information Object content has been generated corresponding to the following topics:

- **Potential IEDs:** Sightings of possible IEDs, along with their visual properties.
- **Infrastructure Damage:** Descriptions of damage to infrastructure including as buildings and roads.
- **Vehicles:** Descriptors (e.g., make, color) for a particular vehicle.
- **Persons:** Descriptors (e.g., appearance, objects carried) for a particular person.
- **Signage:** Visual descriptors for signage.
- **Potential Events:** Sightings of potential events such as demonstrations.

3.4 Supported Recall Task Types

At present, the following types of recall task modes are supported by the experimental platform:

Free Recall Questions: For this, participants are asked to recall as much detail as possible about the Information Objects they reviewed. Following from the Information Object topics discussed in Sect. 3.1, these questions can include:

- What IEDs were detected?
- What infrastructure damage was detected?
- What vehicles were detected?
- What persons were detected?
- What signage was detected?

Figure 5 illustrates a portion of the free recall interface, in which text-based responses are obtained for the listed questions.

What IEDs were detected?
IED #1: Power Source: Electrical Current, Initiator: Electric
What infrastructure damage was detected?

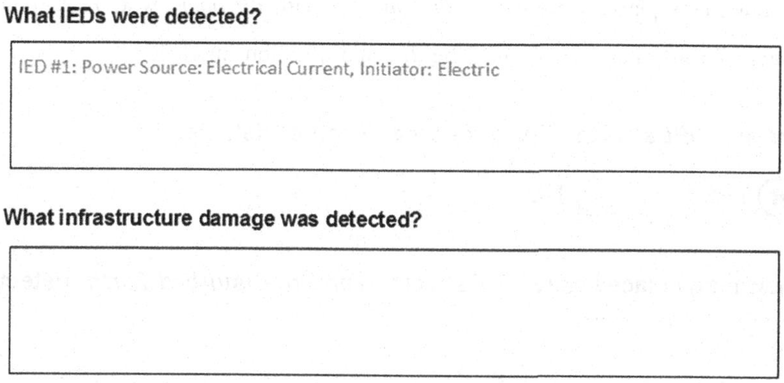

Fig. 5. A portion of the free recall interface, in which text-based responses are obtained for the listed questions.

Map Markup: For this, participants are asked to mark locations on a map where Information Objects were located, and provide the following details: (1) the Information

Object topic; (2) priority level; (3) any remembered properties of the Information Object. Figures 5 and 6 illustrates the map markup interface.

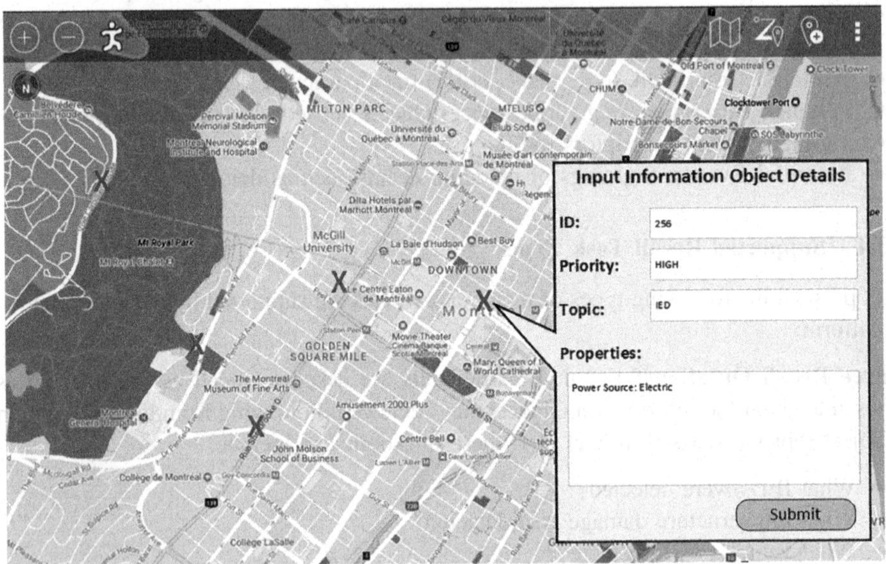

Fig. 6. The map markup interface.

Directed Questions: For this, two types of questions are considered:

- Was any *<IO with Topic T>* with *<Properties X, Y, Z>* detected?
- In how many places were *<IO with Topic T>* with *<Properties X, Y, Z>* detected?

Figure 7 illustrates a portion of the directed question interface.

Were any *"IEDs"* with *"Power Source: Electric"* detected?

◉ YES ○ NO

In how many places were *"IEDs"* with *"Terrain: Disturbed Earth"* detected?

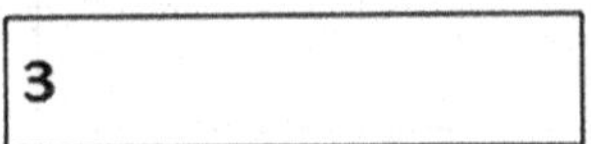

Fig. 7. A portion of the directed question interface.

4 Pilot Study

Towards testing the experimental platform for supporting VoI based studies, an initial pilot study was conducted with 44 participants from the Canadian Royal 22nd regiment. For each participant, a sequence of two experimental trials for a simulated mission were conducted, each followed by a recall task. In the experimental trials, a series of Information Objects were depicted on the Map Display, where each could be clicked to produce an Information Object Popup. Experimental trials were timed, such that participants had 3 min per trial to review the Information Objects. Following each experimental trial, a recall task was given based on the free recall question mode. Following completion of both experimental trials and recall tasks, a post-experiment questionnaire was provided, which asked participants for general feedback on ways to potentially improve VoI presentation within the ATAK platform.

Analysis of the pilot study focused on review of: (1) Logs of Information Objects clicked by Soldiers during the simulated route review; (2) Responses provided during the recall task; and (3) Responses provided during the post-experiment questionnaire. Findings from (1) and (2) indicate general inclination by participants to focus on review of higher-priority Information Objects, combined with a greater likelihood of recalling details about them.

5 Considerations for Future Studies

The pilot study represented an initial attempt at assessing the impact of VoI on Soldier Situational Awareness, in addition to testing the experimental platform. At present, several follow-on studies are envisioned, each involving separate extensions to the experimental platform and centering on the following themes:

VoI Presentation Mode: For the pilot study discussed in Sect. 4, the Information Object binning discussed in Sect. 3.2 was used, featuring three categories of importance (High, Medium, Low). Reflecting on previous implementation strategies for VoI systems (e.g., [1]), two alternative presentation approaches to compare against include: (1) Presentation of Information Objects labeled based on ranking of importance (e.g., 1st, 2nd, 3rd); (2) Presentation of Information Objects labeled with a raw VoI scoring (a numeric value calculated based on determined VoI factors).

Information Object Type: While the experimental platform has focused on supporting text-based Information Objects so far, other types of Information Objects are worth considering in future work. In particular, Information Objects based on images and other sensing data would reflect current usage scenarios for ATAK [3].

6 Conclusion

Military C3I (Command, Control, Communications and Intelligence) operations at the tactical level have come to rely upon Geographic Information Systems (GIS), which commonly offer functionality to display geotagged units of information such as imaging feeds and personnel reports. Management of Information Objects within military GIS applications presents a number of known research challenges tied both to selection of mission-appropriate information and management of Soldier attention. Towards supporting content filtering and prioritization within tactical networks, methods based on the estimated Value of Information specific to mission and environmental context have demonstrated prior benefit (e.g., conservation of bandwidth). By contrast, limited research has been conducted to-date on Soldier interactions with VoI-based GIS applications. This paper presented foundational work being applied towards studying Soldier interaction with VoI-enhanced GIS applications, covering: (1) a supporting experimental platform based on the Android Tactical Assault Kit (ATAK); (2) a pilot study conducted with Soldiers, to assess the impact of VoI-based content prioritization on user experience and Information Object review.

References

1. Suri, N., Benincasa, G., Lenzi, R., Tortonesi, M., Stefanelli, C., Sadler, L.: Exploring value-of-information-based approaches to support effective communications in tactical networks. IEEE Commun. Mag. **53**(10), 39–45 (2015)
2. Bisdikian, C., Kaplan, L.M., Srivastava, M.B.: On the quality and value of information in sensor networks. ACM Trans. Sens. Netw. (TOSN) **9**(4), 1–26 (2013). Article no. 48
3. Johnsen, F.T., et al.: Application of IoT in military operations in a smart city. In: 2018 International Conference on Military Communications and Information Systems (ICMCIS), pp. 1–8. IEEE (2018)
4. Sadler, L., et al.: A distributed Value of Information (VoI)-based approach for mission-adaptive context-aware information management and presentation. Technical Report No. ARL-TR-7674. US Army Research Laboratory Adelphi United States (2016)
5. Hanratty, T.P., Newcomb, E.A., Hammell, R.J., Richardson, J.T., Mittrick, M.R.: A fuzzy-based approach to support decision making in complex military environments. Int. J. Intell. Inf. Technol. (IJIIT) **12**(1), 1–30 (2016)
6. Benincasa, G., et al.: Bridging the gap between enterprise and tactical networks via mission- and network-sensitive adaptation. In: 2018 International Conference on Military Communications and Information Systems (ICMCIS), pp. 1–8. IEEE (2018)
7. Endsley, M.R.: Designing for Situation Awareness: An Approach to User-Centered Design. CRC Press, Boca Raton (2016)
8. Deitz, P.H., Michaelis, J.R., Bray, B.E., Kolodny, M.A.: The missions & means framework ontology: matching military assets to mission objectives. In: Proceedings of the 2016 International C2 Research and Technology Symposium (ICCRTS 2016), London, UK (2016)
9. Trethan, J.F., Brannsten, M.R., Elstad, A., Bloebaum, T.H., Mancini, F.: SMART: situational awareness experiments with the Norwegian home guard using Android (2017). https://publications.ffi.no/handle/20.500.12242/1152. Accessed 31 Jan 2019
10. Gillen, M., et al.: Beyond line-of-sight information dissemination for force protection. In: Military Communications Conference (MILCOM 2012). IEEE (2012)
11. Staten, D.: Marines use tablet technology to advance war fighting skills (2015). http://www.marines.mil/News/News-Display/Article/624674/marines-usetablet-technology-to-advance-war-fighting-skills/. Accessed 31 Jan 2019
12. Evans, J.B., Ewy, B.J., Swink, M.T., Pennington, S.G., Siquieros, D.J., Earp, S.L.: TIGR: the tactical ground reporting system. IEEE Commun. Mag. **51**(10), 42–49 (2013)

Evaluation Index to Find Relevant Papers: Improvement of Focused Citation Count

Tetsuya Nakatoh[1(✉)] and Sachio Hirokawa[2]

[1] Faculty of Nutritional Sciences, Nakamura Gakuen University, Fukuoka, Japan
nakatoh@nakamura-u.ac.jp

[2] Research Institute for Information Technology, Kyushu University, Fukuoka, Japan
hirokawa@cc.kyushu-u.ac.jp

Abstract. During a research survey, it is very important to quickly find suitable papers. It is common practice for researchers to select relevant papers by searching using query keywords, ranking those papers by citation number, and checking in order from the highest ranked papers. However, if a paper that had a query keyword as a non-primary word had many citations, it would hinder any attempt to quickly find the appropriate paper. We have already proposed a Focused Citation Count (FCC) that supports the finding of suitable papers by setting the number of citations as a more appropriate evaluation index by properly focusing on cited papers which are the sources of citation counts. In this study, we propose an improved method of FCC. Since FCC is easily affected by the size of the cited number, this proposal aims to reduce its characteristics. We evaluate the proposed method using actual paper data and try to confirm its effectiveness.

Keywords: Bibliometrics · Citation count · Index · Research survey

1 Introduction

When promoting their own research, researchers need to show their own research and superiority by studying related research. From an enormous number of academic papers, it is necessary for researchers to quickly and appropriately find existing studies related to their own research, that is, in a way that emphasizes the important papers. Studies of research facilities and researchers that we know as rivals are capable of checking papers, but there is always a need to further investigate related papers. Many academic paper databases provide a search function using query keywords, and it is possible to select papers according to the query. For example, Scopus provides citation numbers of papers obtained through searches as additional information for paper selection. Many papers are still selected, but since selected papers can be ranked using citation counts, many researchers check papers according to their ranking. It is necessary to check the

S. Yamamoto and H. Mori (Eds.): HCII 2019, LNCS 11569, pp. 555–566, 2019.
https://doi.org/10.1007/978-3-030-22660-2_41

author, title, and abstract and to obtain the main body of the paper if necessary to determine the relevance and importance of the research. The appropriate ranking of papers is an important technique that reduces waste. While there are some criticisms, the number of citations still holds an important position as a method of directly evaluating the value of a paper.

However, there is no guarantee that the number of citations is an appropriate criterion. Even if a paper has an unimportant word as a query keyword, many citations will give it a high evaluation. We need to read such a paper and remove it. Investigation of a paper will become more efficient if there is an evaluation index that is more appropriate than the number of citations.

We propose the Focused Citation Count (FCC) [9] that utilizes only appropriately cited papers in order to find other relevant research. We propose this method because we think that a paper cited from ones without appropriate content is inappropriate. Of course, such a judgment is not always easy to make. However, it is possible to make a statistical decision from many citations.

However, the FCC is easily affected by the size of the original number of citations. In the case of a paper with a large number of citations, even if the relevance is relatively small, the FCC value tends to be large. For example, we can simply show the relationship with the field you are looking for in a percentage and assume that it denotes the proportion of citations from that field. I would like to evaluate paper (A) when there is a paper (B) with a relation of 90% to paper (A) with a 10% relationship. However, if the citation number of paper (A) is 10 and the citation number of the paper (B) is 100, the FCC is 9 in paper (A) and 10 in the paper (B), and the evaluation is reversed.

In this study, we propose an enhanced method of FCC which improves this point. In order to strengthen the evaluation of relevance between the field under investigation and the thesis, we aim to reduce the influence of the number of citations by emphasizing the proportion of quotations from related fields. Experiments are carried out using actual thesis data, and the effectiveness of the proposed method is tested.

2 Focused Citation Count and Its Improvement

2.1 Focused Citation Count

FCC [9] is an evaluation index that modifies the number of citations to values useful for the proper selection of papers, by limiting the papers used for counting citations to only papers suitable for research purposes. Various methods are considered for restricting papers for this purpose, but in this study, we limit papers cited using query keywords used to search for papers. This is formulated as follows.

Let $FP(q)$ be a set of papers selected by the query keyword q in the target where all papers are set as A. Next, let $CP(p)$ be a set of papers citing the paper p. That is, $PF(q) \subset A, CP(p) \subset A$.

The total citation count $cc(p)$ of paper p is: $cc(p) = |CP(p)|$.

Let $CFP(p, q)$ be the paper set selected by the query keyword q out of the paper set $CP(p)$ citing the paper p. That is, $CFP(p, q) = CP(p) \cap FP(q)$.

The value $fcc(p, q)$ of the FCC which is the evaluation index is obtained by Eq. (1).

$$fcc(p, q) = |CFP(p, q)| = |CP(p) \cap FP(q)|. \tag{1}$$

2.2 Basic Idea of Improvement

Let us suppose that we are looking for related papers in a certain field. With respect to the research field of the papers citing the finished paper, I will show the proportion in which the field of both papers is the same with a simple numerical value. Suppose there is a paper (A) with a citation rate of 90% from the same field and a paper (B) with a rate of 10%. If the citation number of paper (A) is 10 and the citation number of paper (B) is 100, the FCC is 9 for paper (A) and 10 for paper (B). That is, the FCC of paper (B) is higher. However, from the viewpoint of expertise, I would like to evaluate whether paper (A) is more useful.

To make this possible, we propose using the ratio of citation counts from related fields for evaluation. In other words, since a paper with a high proportion of FCC to CC (citation count) is a paper that ought to be highly evaluated, we think that an evaluation combined with FCC and percentages could solve the problem described in this section. Proposals for concrete calculation methods are provided in the next section.

2.3 Improvement of Focused Citation Count

First, we calculate the ratio r of the number of $CP(p)$ and $CFP(p, q)$ as the rate of the relevant field of the paper citing paper p. That is,

$$r(p, q) = \frac{|CFP(p, q)|}{|CP(p)|} = \frac{fcc(p, q)}{cc(p)}.$$

In order to combine the FCC with the r as weight, we propose a new evaluation index, Revised FCC (RFCC), by multiplying $F(p, q)$ by $r(p, q)$ raised to α. The value $rfcc(p, q)$ of the RFCC is given by the following equation:

$$rfcc(p, q) = fcc(p, q) \times r^{\alpha}(p, q).$$

However, α is a parameter for adjusting the weight. In this paper, we set $\alpha = 1$.

3 Evaluation

3.1 Gathering Paper Data and Basic Analysis

In this section, we explain the collection method of the papers used for analysis, and conduct basic analyses of the data.

The data was gathered from Scopus. In this experiment, "bibliometrics" was chosen as a query keyword, and 10,186 papers published from 1976 to 2015 were gathered using search API. This data is written in JSON format. The items are as

Table 1. Number of papers

Cited by	Number of Papers	Cited by	Number of Papers
0	4533	:	:
1	2213	1113	1
2	1522	1157	1
3	1057	1170	1
4	845	1220	1
5	711	1477	1
6	614	1573	1
7	575	1587	1
8	435	2026	1
9	403	2343	1
:	:	4483	1

follows: "Content Type," "Search identifier," "Complete author list," "Resource identifiers," "Abstract Text," "First author," "Page range," "SCOPUS Cited-by URI," "Result URL," "Document identifier," "Publication date," "Source title," "Article title," "Cited by count," "ISSN," "Issue number," and "Volume."

Although 4,533 papers have no citation at all, there is also a paper with 4,483 citations. They are cited from 258,332 papers in total. Table 1 shows a part of the number of citations of the papers. It has the number of citations of the top 10 papers, and of the bottom 10 papers.

Figure 1 plots the data of Table 1 as a log-log graph. In this graph, the frequency of citations seems to follow the power law.

Next, I gathered papers citing each paper stated in the acquired JSON data. Information on citing papers is posted in the URL indicated in the "link" of a JSON item. Since information on the URL cannot be acquired with the API, we obtained the HTML file using the "wget" of the UNIX command. Information on 20 citing papers is published in one HTML file. However, as can be seen from Table 1, there were also citing papers exceeding 20. Regarding those, it was necessary to repeatedly obtain HTML files while changing the "wget" parameters.

Since there were 4,533 papers without a citation, we obtained the papers that cited 13,667 papers. The information on 116,743 papers on 13,667 cited papers was obtained through the execution of 10,719 wget. There were 62,265 papers when duplication was removed.

3.2 Evaluation of Revised Focused Citation Count

For the papers collected by Sect. 3.1, the following three rankings were applied. First, the top 20 papers are shown in Table 2 with the citation count indicated by Scopus. Additionally, Table 3 shows the top 20 papers in a ranking using

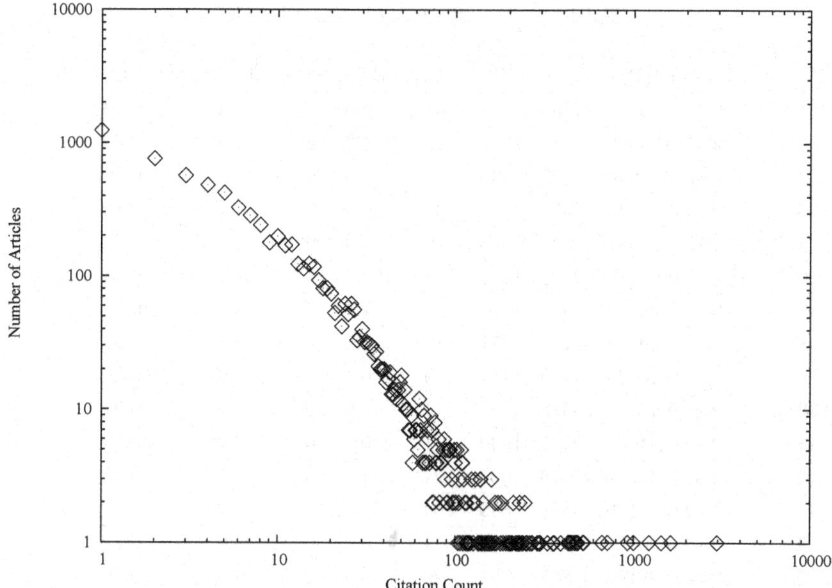

Fig. 1. Number of papers in each citation count

FCC [9]. Furthermore, Table 4 shows the top 20 papers in the Revised Focused Citation Count (RFCC) proposed in this study. In these tables, "Paper ID" is the paper ID (eid) of Scopus. By replacing the <eid> part of the URL[1] with this ID, it is possible to acquire the data of the corresponding thesis.

The extraction precision of the top 20 papers extracted by CC, FCC, and RFCC was evaluated as follows. Two testers judged whether they were appropriate as papers on "bibliometrics." They gave a rating of "1" to appropriate papers and "0" to inappropriate papers. We totaled the judgments as the number of votes, and calculated Precision@N.

The result of the CC is shown in Table 2, the result of the FCC is shown in Table 3, and the result of the RFCC is shown in Table 4. Moreover, the graph of Precision@N is shown in Fig. 2.

The result of CC was shown in Table 2, the result of FCC was shown in Table 3, and the result of RFCC was shown in Table 4. Moreover, the graph of Precision@N is shown in Fig. 2.

4 Discussion

Despite having good results in preliminary sample experiments, the RFCC could not demonstrate performance exceeding the FCC in the experiment conducted in this study. This seems to be due to the fact that the FCC shows sufficient

[1] http://www.scopus.com/record/display.url?eid=⟨eid⟩&origin=resultslist.

Table 2. Top 20 Papers sorted by CC

Ranking	Paper ID	CC	FCC	RFCC	Testee1	Testee2	Precision@N
1	2-s2.0-4243148480	4512	31	0.0	0	0	0.00
2	2-s2.0-0000994704	2361	11	0.0	0	0	0.00
3	2-s2.0-33846834126	2034	2	0.0	0	0	0.00
4	2-s2.0-39549086558	1587	27	0.5	0	1	0.12
5	2-s2.0-0033721503	1573	46	1.3	0	0	0.10
6	2-s2.0-0031049280	1477	554	207.8	1	1	0.25
7	2-s2.0-0032256758	1220	41	1.4	0	0	0.21
8	2-s2.0-29944438252	1171	416	147.8	1	1	0.31
9	2-s2.0-10944272139	1157	9	0.1	0	0	0.28
10	2-s2.0-47749113622	1114	1	0.0	0	0	0.25
11	2-s2.0-84903289127	1090	1	0.0	0	0	0.23
12	2-s2.0-34249309179	1034	124	14.9	0	1	0.25
13	2-s2.0-0016996037	849	164	31.7	1	1	0.31
14	2-s2.0-0035021707	848	1	0.0	0	0	0.29
15	2-s2.0-22144431885	762	20	0.5	1	0	0.30
16	2-s2.0-3142699221	723	164	37.2	1	1	0.34
17	2-s2.0-85008492587	656	0	0.0	0	0	0.32
18	2-s2.0-0032047559	649	274	115.7	1	1	0.36
19	2-s2.0-27144502742	611	97	15.4	0	1	0.37
20	2-s2.0-0030960168	594	39	2.6	0	0	0.35

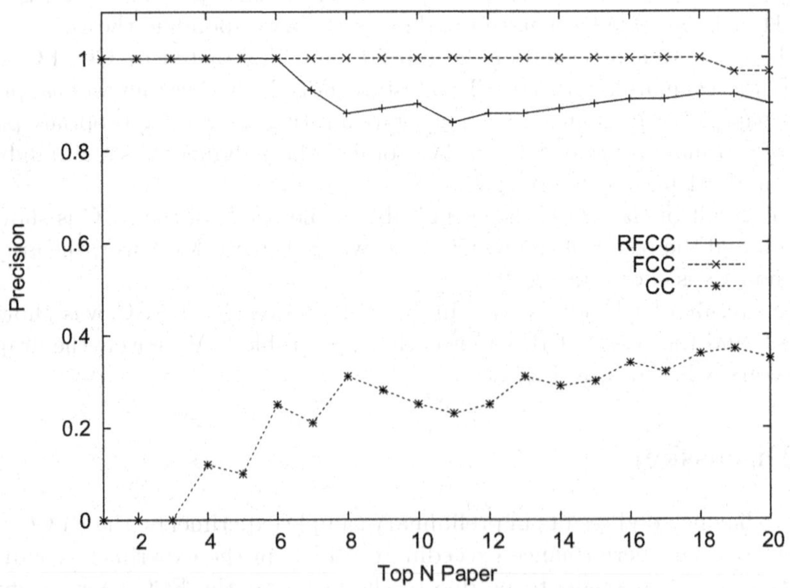

Fig. 2. Presicion@N by CC, FCC, and RFCC

Table 3. Top 20 Papers sorted by FCC

Ranking	Paper ID	CC	FCC	RFCC	Testee1	Testee2	Precision@N
1	2-s2.0-0031049280	1477	554	207.8	1	1	1.00
2	2-s2.0-29944438252	1171	416	147.8	1	1	1.00
3	2-s2.0-33748074153	458	329	236.3	1	1	1.00
4	2-s2.0-0035981386	375	319	271.4	1	1	1.00
5	2-s2.0-0032047559	649	274	115.7	1	1	1.00
6	2-s2.0-84928532180	356	233	152.5	1	1	1.00
7	2-s2.0-36849014874	548	230	96.5	1	1	1.00
8	2-s2.0-15444370852	253	214	181.0	1	1	1.00
9	2-s2.0-38549127657	500	210	88.2	1	1	1.00
10	2-s2.0-84989591524	463	202	88.1	1	1	1.00
11	2-s2.0-37649007281	450	190	80.2	1	1	1.00
12	2-s2.0-0033584703	469	180	69.1	1	1	1.00
13	2-s2.0-0029783235	363	175	84.4	1	1	1.00
14	2-s2.0-3142699221	723	164	37.2	1	1	1.00
15	2-s2.0-0016996037	849	164	31.7	1	1	1.00
16	2-s2.0-70149091772	292	158	85.5	1	1	1.00
17	2-s2.0-15444371414	375	157	65.7	1	1	1.00
18	2-s2.0-0000742089	370	157	66.6	1	1	1.00
19	2-s2.0-0035079213	178	155	135.0	0	1	0.97
20	2-s2.0-0001327392	205	155	117.2	1	1	0.97

performance, rather than the RFCC not working well. Moreover, in this experiment, using a single query keyword "bibliometrics" with a wide range of subjects may be a contributing factor.

Depending on the academic field to be searched and the kind and number of query keywords, the performance of the FCC and RFCC may differ from the results of this study. Furthermore, having two testers is a small number and may lead to biased results. As a future task, it is necessary to conduct more detailed evaluation experiments.

5 Related Work

Objective evaluation of a paper by the contents is difficult. Therefore, it is common to instead perform an evaluation using the following data of a paper: the evaluation of the journal in which the paper was published, and the paper's citation count.

The Journal Impact Factor (JIF) [2,3] is one of the most popular evaluation measures of scientific journals. Thomson Reuters updates and provides the scores for journals in annual Journal Citation Reports (JCR). The JIF of a journal describes the citation counts of an average paper published in the journal. JIF

Table 4. Top 20 Papers sorted by Revised FCC

Ranking	Paper ID	CC	FCC	RFCC	Testee1	Testee2	Precision@N
1	2-s2.0-0035981386	375	319	271.4	1	1	1.00
2	2-s2.0-33748074153	458	329	236.3	1	1	1.00
3	2-s2.0-0031049280	1477	554	207.8	1	1	1.00
4	2-s2.0-15444370852	253	214	181.0	1	1	1.00
5	2-s2.0-84928532180	356	233	152.5	1	1	1.00
6	2-s2.0-29944438252	1171	416	147.8	1	1	1.00
7	2-s2.0-0035079213	178	155	135.0	0	1	0.93
8	2-s2.0-78650989464	171	142	117.9	0	1	0.88
9	2-s2.0-0001327392	205	155	117.2	1	1	0.89
10	2-s2.0-0032047559	649	274	115.7	1	1	0.90
11	2-s2.0-27844542383	148	125	105.6	0	1	0.86
12	2-s2.0-0011001807	213	144	97.4	1	1	0.88
13	2-s2.0-36849014874	548	230	96.5	1	1	0.88
14	2-s2.0-38549127657	500	210	88.2	1	1	0.89
15	2-s2.0-84989591524	463	202	88.1	1	1	0.90
16	2-s2.0-70149091772	292	158	85.5	1	1	0.91
17	2-s2.0-0029783235	363	175	84.4	1	1	0.91
18	2-s2.0-37649007281	450	190	80.2	1	1	0.92
19	2-s2.0-78951494661	105	89	75.4	1	1	0.92
20	2-s2.0-84859429914	91	81	72.1	0	1	0.90

is considered to be the de facto standard to evaluate not only a journal, but also a researcher, research organization, and paper.

However, some problems were pointed out with JIF. Pudovkin and Garfield [8] pointed out that JIF is not appropriate to be used as a measure to compare different disciplines. Modification of JIF by normalization has been studied as one of the key issues [6,8]. Bergstrom proposed EigenFactor [1] which solves the problem of JIF by adjusting the weight of citations. Nakatoh et al. [7] proposed to combine the relatedness of a journal to the user's query with JIF.

The citation count is used as more direct criteria of a paper. However, some researchers have pointed out problems. Martin [5] reported that the citation count gained support as criteria. Kostoff [4] showed that the citation count as a criterion of research evaluation has the following characteristics: (a) theoretical correlation is not necessarily between a citing paper and the cited paper, (b) incorrect research may be cited, (c) a methodical paper is easy to cite, and (d) the citation count will be raised by self-citation.

Our concern is the citation count not as criteria of performance evaluation, but as criteria for selecting papers. However, the problem noted by Kostoff is common to both. The solution proposed by our study is including the quality of a citation in the evaluation. Eliminating the citation from papers with a low relation decreases the influence of the problems of (a) and (b). We think that this enables the selection of more appropriate papers.

6 Conclusion

When conducting a research survey, it is very important to quickly find suitable papers. It is common practice by researchers to select relevant papers by searching with query keywords, ranking papers by citation number, and checking in order from the highest ranked papers. However, if a paper that had a query keyword as a non-primary word has many citations, it would impede a researcher's ability to quickly find the appropriate paper. We have already proposed a Focused Citation Count (FCC) that supports the finding of suitable papers by setting the number of citations as a more appropriate evaluation index by properly focusing on cited papers which are the sources of citation counts. In this study, we proposed an improved method of FCC. An empirical evaluation of "bibliometrics" related to 10,186 papers showed that the FCC method was effective, but that the proposed RFCC method was not as effective. As a future task, a more detailed evaluation is necessary.

Acknowledgement. This work was partially supported by JSPS KAKENHI Grant Number 18K11990.

Appendix

List of papers used for evaluation.

2-s2.0-0000742089 Garfield E.: "Is citation analysis a legitimate evaluation tool?," *Scientometrics*, 1(4), pp.359–375, (1979)

2-s2.0-0032256758 Kleinberg Jon M.: "Authoritative sources in a hyperlinked environment," *Proceedings of the Annual ACM-SIAM Symposium on Discrete Algorithms*, pp.668–677, (1998)

2-s2.0-0033584703 Garfield E.: "Journal impact factor: A brief review," *CMAJ*, 161(8), pp.979–980, (1999)

2-s2.0-0033721503 Broder A., Kumar R., Maghoul F., Raghavan P., Rajagopalan S., Stata R., Tomkins A., Wiener J.: "Graph structure in the Web," *Computer Networks*, 33(1), pp.309–320, (2000)

2-s2.0-0035021707 Gambhir S.S., Czernin J., Schwimmer J., Silverman D.H.S., Coleman R.E., Phelps M.E.: "A tabulated summary of the FDG PET literature," *Journal of Nuclear Medicine*, 42(5 SUPPL.), pp.1S–93S, (2001)

2-s2.0-0035079213 Cronin B.: "Bibliometrics and beyond: some thoughts on web-based citation analysis," *Journal of Information Science*, 27(1), pp.1–7, (2001)

2-s2.0-0035981386 Borgman C.L., Furner J.: "Scholarly communication and bibliometrics," *Annual Review of Information Science and Technology*, 36 3 72 (2002)

2-s2.0-10944272139 Adamic L.A., Adar E.: "Friends and neighbors on the Web," *Social Networks*, 25(3), pp.211–230, (2003)

2-s2.0-15444370852 Weingart P.: "Impact of bibliometrics upon the science system: Inadvertent consequences?," *Scientometrics*, 62(1), pp.117–131, (2005)

2-s2.0-15444371414 Van Raan A.F.J.: "Fatal attraction: Conceptual and methodological problems in the ranking of universities by bibliometric methods," *Scientometrics*, 62(1), pp.133–143, (2005)

2-s2.0-22144431885 Ioannidis J.P.A.: "Contradicted and initially stronger effects in highly cited clinical research," *Journal of the American Medical Association*, 294(2), pp.218–228, (2005)

2-s2.0-0000994704 Lane P.J., Lubatkin M.: "Relative absorptive capacity and interorganizational learning," *Strategic Management Journal*, 19(5), pp.461–477, (1998)

2-s2.0-27144502742 Lee S., Bozeman B.: "The impact of research collaboration on scientific productivity," *Social Studies of Science*, 35(5), pp.673–702, (2005)

2-s2.0-27844542383 Larson R.R.: "Bibliometrics of the world wide web: An exploratory analysis of the intellectual structure of cyberspace," *Proceedings of the ASIS Annual Meeting*, 33 71 78 (1996)

2-s2.0-29944438252 Garfield E.: "The history and meaning of the journal impact factor," *Journal of the American Medical Association*, 295(1), pp.90–93, (2006)

2-s2.0-3142699221 King D.A.: "The scientific impact of nations," *Nature*, 430(6997), pp.311–316, (2004)

2-s2.0-33748074153 Daim T.U., Rueda G., Martin H., Gerdsri P.: "Forecasting emerging technologies: Use of bibliometrics and patent analysis," *Technological Forecasting and Social Change*, 73(8), pp.981–1012, (2006)

2-s2.0-33846834126 Josang A., Ismail R., Boyd C.: "A survey of trust and reputation systems for online service provision," *Decision Support Systems*, 43(2), pp.618–644, (2007)

2-s2.0-34249309179 Wuchty S., Jones B.F., Uzzi B.: "The increasing dominance of teams in production of knowledge," *Science*, 316(5827), pp.1036–1039, (2007)

2-s2.0-36849014874 Meho L.I., Yang K.: "Impact of data sources on citation counts and rankings of LIS faculty: Web of science versus scopus and google scholar," *Journal of the American Society for Information Science and Technology*, 58(13), pp.2105–2125, (2007)

2-s2.0-37649007281 Hirsch J.E.: "Does the h index have predictive power?," *Proceedings of the National Academy of Sciences of the United States of America*, 104(49), pp.19193–19198, (2007)

2-s2.0-38549127657 Bornmann L., Daniel H.: "What do citation counts measure? A review of studies on citing behavior," *Journal of Documentation*, 64(1), pp.45–80, (2008)

2-s2.0-0001327392 Narin F.: "Patent bibliometrics," *Scientometrics*, 30(1), pp.147–155, (1994)

2-s2.0-39549086558 Rosvall M., Bergstrom C.T.: "Maps of random walks on complex networks reveal community structure," *Proceedings of the National Academy of Sciences of the United States of America*, 105(4), pp.1118–1123, (2008)

2-s2.0-4243148480 Kleinberg J.M.: "Authoritative sources in a hyperlinked environment," *Journal of the ACM*, 46(5), pp.604–632, (1999)

2-s2.0-47749113622 Abraham C., Michie S.: "A Taxonomy of Behavior Change Techniques Used in Interventions," *Health Psychology*, 27(3), pp.379–387, (2008)

2-s2.0-70149091772 Kulkarni A.V., Aziz B., Shams I., Busse J.W.: "Comparisons of citations in web of science, Scopus, and Google Scholar for articles published in general medical journals," *JAMA - Journal of the American Medical Association*, 302(10), pp.1092–1096, (2009)

2-s2.0-78650989464 Chen Y.-C., Yeh H.-Y., Wu J.-C., Haschler I., Chen T.-J., Wetter T.: "Taiwan's National Health Insurance Research Database: Administrative health care database as study object in bibliometrics," *Scientometrics*, 86(2), pp.365–380, (2011)

2-s2.0-78951494661 D'Angelo C.A., Giuffrida C., Abramo G.: "A heuristic approach to author name disambiguation in bibliometrics databases for large-scale research assessments," *Journal of the American Society for Information Science and Technology*, 62(2), pp.257–269, (2011)

2-s2.0-84859429914 Aguillo I.F.: "Is Google Scholar useful for bibliometrics? A webometric analysis," *Scientometrics*, 91(2), pp.343–351, (2012)

2-s2.0-84903289127 Rodriguez A., Laio A.: "Clustering by fast search and find of density peaks," *Science*, 344(6191), pp.1492–1496, (2014)

2-s2.0-84928532180 Hicks D., Wouters P., Waltman L., De Rijcke S., Rafols I.: "Bibliometrics: The Leiden Manifesto for research metrics," *Nature*, 520(7548), pp.429–431, (2015)

2-s2.0-84989591524 MacRoberts M.H., MacRoberts B.R.: "Problems of citation analysis: A critical review," *Journal of the American Society for Information Science*, 40(5), pp.342–349, (1989)

2-s2.0-0011001807 Hood W.W., Wilson C.S.: "The literature of bibliometrics, scientometrics, and informetrics," *Scientometrics*, 52(2), pp.291–314, (2001)

2-s2.0-85008492587 Todeschini R., Consonni V.: "Molecular Descriptors for Chemoinformatics," *Molecular Descriptors for Chemoinformatics*, 2 1 252 (2010)

2-s2.0-0016996037 Price D.D.S.: "A general theory of bibliometric and other cumulative advantage processes," *Journal of the American Society for Information Science*, 27(5), pp.292–306, (1976)

2-s2.0-0029783235 Garfield E.: "Fortnightly Review: How can impact factors be improved?," *BMJ*, 313(7054), pp.411–413, (1996)

2-s2.0-0030960168 Wenneras C., Wold A.: "Nepotism and sexism in peer-review," *Nature*, 387(6631), pp.341–343, (1997)

2-s2.0-0031049280 Seglen P.O.: "Why the impact factor of journals should not be used for evaluating research," *British Medical Journal*, 314(7079), pp.498–502, (1997)

2-s2.0-0032047559 White H.D., McCain K.W.: "Visualizing a discipline: An author co-citation analysis of information science, 1972-1995," *Journal of the American Society for Information Science*, 49(4), pp.327–355, (1998)

References

1. Bergstrom, C.: Eigenfactor: measuring the value and prestige of scholarly journals. Coll. Res. Libr. News **68**(5), 314–316 (2007)
2. Garfield, E.: Citation indexes for science. Science **122**(3159), 108–111 (1955)
3. Garfield, E.: The history and meaning of the journal impact factor. J. Am. Med. Assoc. **295**(1), 90–93 (2006)
4. Kostoff, R.N.: Performance measures for government-sponsored research: overview and background. Scientometrics **36**(3), 281–292 (1996)
5. Martin, B.R.: The use of multiple indicators in the assessment of basic research. Scientometrics **36**(3), 343–362 (1996)
6. Marshakova-Shaikevich, I.: The standard impact factor as an evaluation tool of science fields and scientific journals. Scientometrics **35**(2), 283–290 (1996)
7. Nakatoh, T., Nakanishi, H., Hirokawa, S.: Journal impact factor revised with focused view. In: Neves-Silva, R., Jain, L.C., Howlett, R.J. (eds.) Intelligent Decision Technologies. SIST, vol. 39, pp. 471–481. Springer, Cham (2015). https://doi.org/10.1007/978-3-319-19857-6_40
8. Pudovkin, A.I., Garfield, E.: Rank-normalized impact factor: a way to compare journal performance across subject categories. Proc. ASIST Annu. Meet. **41**, 507–515 (2004)
9. Nakatoh, T., Nakanishi, H., Baba, K., Hirokawa, S.: Focused citation count: a combined measure of relevancy and quality. In: Proceedings of the 4th International Congress on Advanced Applied Informatics (IIAI-AAI), pp. 166-170 (2015). https://doi.org/10.1109/IIAI-AAI.2015.282

Barriers Against the Introduction of Teleworking and Survey for Workers on Their Work Contents

Miki Numano[1], Fuko Oura[1], Takeo Ainoya[2], Keiko Kasamatsu[1,2(✉)], Akio Tomita[3], and Kunika Yagi[3]

[1] Tokyo Metropolitan University, Asahigaoka 6-6, Hino, Tokyo, Japan
numano-miki@ed.tmu.ac.jp, kasamatu@tmu.ac.jp
[2] Serbot inQ, Tokyo Metropolitan University, Asahigaoka 6-6, Hino, Tokyo, Japan
[3] Misawa Homes Institute of Research and Development Co., Ltd., Tokyo, Japan

Abstract. Telework is attracting attention as one of new ways of working in Japan. Telework is a way of working that works without entering the company, but some companies are actually introducing it based on its merits, but the telework's notoriousness and penetration rate is still low in Japan. We conducted two surveys in companies that are considering introducing telework. First of all, I investigated anxiety, frustration, etc. concerning employees' introduction of telework. Next, we conducted an investigation on the actual work content. It aimed to clarify the barriers of teleworking by knowing the tendency of business contents. As a result, it was shown that insufficient infrastructure development, concern about dilution of communication, and a decrease in work efficiency are the major causes of introduction barriers, and the work contents can be classified into seven categories.

Keywords: Teleworking · Workplace · Work contents

1 Introduction

1.1 Background

Telework is being promoted as one of new ways of working recently in Japan. Telework is a flexible way of working to effectively utilize time and place to work without leaving the company such as home or cafe using ICT (information communication technology). The merit of teleworking is that employees are able to save time in commuting and to make it easier to balance work with childcare or nursing care, for employers to spread their risks during disasters, and to lower the turnover rate by optimizing work-life balance And the like. Japan has characteristic problems such as a decrease in the productive age population due to the aging of the birthrate, a commuting rush due to population concentration in the urban areas, and many earthquakes in comparison with other countries, so the introduction of new ways of working should be promoted It can be said. In Japan, the goal of telework dissemination has been set up

S. Yamamoto and H. Mori (Eds.): HCII 2019, LNCS 11569, pp. 567–574, 2019.
https://doi.org/10.1007/978-3-030-22660-2_42

in the "World's most advanced IT nation creation declaration public and private data utilization promotion basic law" decided in June, Heisei 30, and introduction of telework is being promoted. [1] In addition, following the success example of avoiding traffic congestion during the convention by incorporating telework at the 2012 London Olympics, it is being promoted towards the Tokyo convention in 2020. However, it is unlikely that it is clearly indicated at what place the business should be performed at the time of introduction of telework, and the user falls into a situation in which it is impossible to see where the business should be performed even if telework is introduced There is a current situation that may not exist.

1.2 Purpose

Therefore, in this research, we aim to clarify the introduction barriers of teleworking that the user has, and to analyze and investigate environmental factors in actual teleworking place. With the increase of choices of workplace, we aim to investigate and research what space is suitable for each work content and if so, if there is space.

2 User Survey on Introduction of Telework

2.1 Survey Method

Survey Purpose
It is the purpose of this survey to obtain opinions on current work style, office and workplace.

Survey Target
Under the cooperation of housing manufacturers, a hearing survey was conducted. We interviewed the current work style and opinion to the workplace based on the fact that free addresses will be introduced to people in work environments where working methods such as teleworking and time saving s are recognized. It was an employee of a house maker, with a total of 24 people, including 14 research workers, 6 projects, 3 management positions and 1 bookshelf. However, since it was a survey at a research facility, it is assumed that there are times when you are engaged in research on other tasks as well.

Process
We divided 24 employees into two groups and hear each hour.

There were two interviewers per group. In the interview contents of the interview, we prepared things related to how to work normally, opinions on new ways of working such as free addresses, flexible, teleworking, and opinions on the current workplace (Fig. 1).

Fig. 1. Interview scenery

Table 1.

Positive	Negative
• If you have an environment where you can focus on cafes and more, you can do digital work quickly • Productivity is higher for travel time than for me • I feel a merit in reducing the burden of securing time/moving • It is good for you to shift jobs at your own convenience and circumstances etc.	• The terminal is not maintained • The WEB meeting is hard to speak • If I am at home I will skip my work • Distance is born with colleagues and juniors, making it difficult to consult • I can not feel the merit • Regarding management of subordinates, it is difficult to confirm whether or not you are working etc.

2.2 Result and Analysis

We classified opinions that actually appeared as positive and negative with respect to introduction of new ways of working. The table below is an example of actual opinion (Table 1).

The negative opinion here is considered to be a barrier in the introduction of new ways of working and the barriers can be classified into “infrastructure improvement”, “communication”, “work efficiency”. Depending on the company and operations, it is considered that some measures can be taken depending on the barrier classification.

3 Survey for Workers on Their Work Contents

3.1 Interview on Work Experience

Survey Purpose
It aimed to clarify the work experience from the aspect of behavior and emotion and to extract intervention points of working way reform by interview.

Survey Target
The survey target was a total of 12 employees of the housing maker. Breakdown was 2 salespeople, product development 2, design 2, construction 2, after-maintenance 2, management 2.

Survey Procedure
First of all, we interviewed each work individually on the work of each industry and the work flow of the day, and the recording person wrote on the UX sheet while listening to the contents of the remarks. The UX sheet is used to summarize the work experience from the aspect of action and emotion in time series, specifically concretely fill the flow of work, place, persons involved, usage, subjective work efficiency, subjective emotional curve After that, it became a group of investigators with 2 to 3 people to be surveyed and conducted group interviews.

Survey Record
For the content of the interview, the investigator fills in the UX sheet on the spot and takes notes as necessary. With survey permitted, recording by voice recording was also done.

3.2 UXmap Analysis

UXmap is derived from the UX curve devised by Kujala et al. (2011) and is a qualitative user aimed at helping to retrospectively report on how and why the user's experience with the product has changed over time It is one of the survey methods. In the interview, the UX sheet entered with the survey target and the information on the work contents obtained from the interview were summarized as a UX map, and the work experience was visualized (Fig. 2).

3.3 Categorization of Business Contents and Its Mapping

Purpose
UXmap analysis suggested that the way the user searched for depends on the content of the work, and the requirements required for telework were also different.
Therefore, in order to make a telework proposal suitable for the characteristics of each business, it is necessary to first grasp what kind of work is involved and what kind of properties each business is. In this phase, the purpose was to map and categorize tasks based on the nature of work.

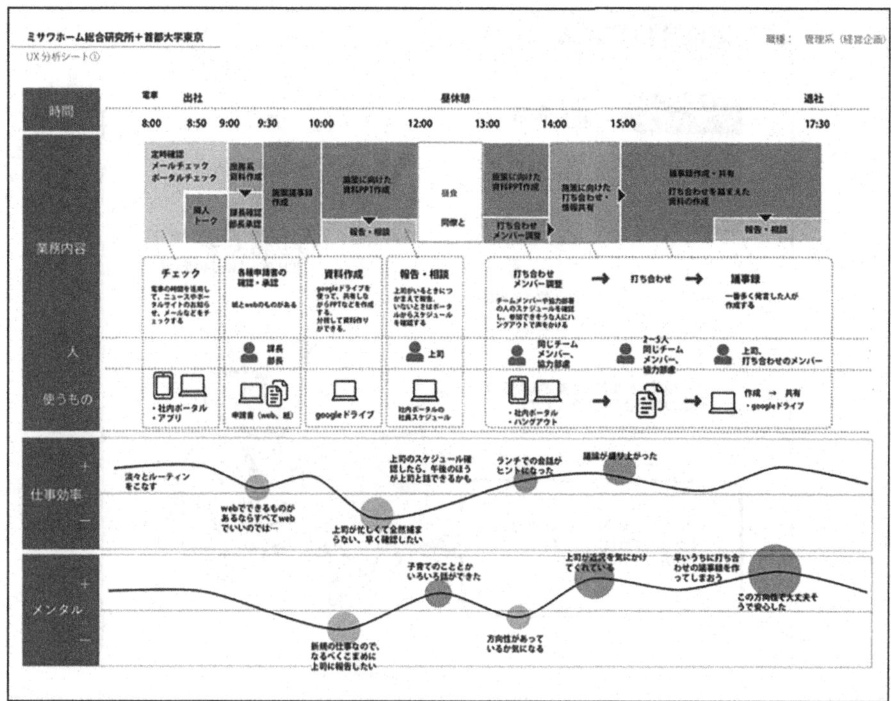

Fig. 2. Examples of UX map created

Procedure

First of all, I transcribed several tasks listed in the work content item in UXmap as a business scene card. In the card, the contents of rough work, tools used, people involved, and what kind of situation were described (Fig. 3). About 50 to 60 business scenes cards were prepared.

Following the KJ Law, categorization was carried out using a business scene card by three experts. With awareness of the nature of the work, we placed the cards so that similar things are nearby. Each group of cards was categorized and named (Fig. 4).

Result

Analysis by three experts created seven categories. The categories created are "Hearings", "Negotiations", "Construction Sites", "Reports, Consultations and Contact", "Meetings", "Inquiries" and "Material creation". In addition, in categorization, two axes of "diffusion - contraction" and "public - personal" were set as axes characterizing the work properties. In "diffusion - contraction", focusing on intellectual activities conducted in the work, "information convergence" was set to "converge" and knowledge creative activities to be "diffusion". "Public - Personal" focuses on differences among people involved in communication and workers involved in the work, "Personal" the work done by individuals, "Public" the work that diplomatically exchanges from customers and stakeholders did.

Fig. 3. Examples of business scene cards created based on interview contents

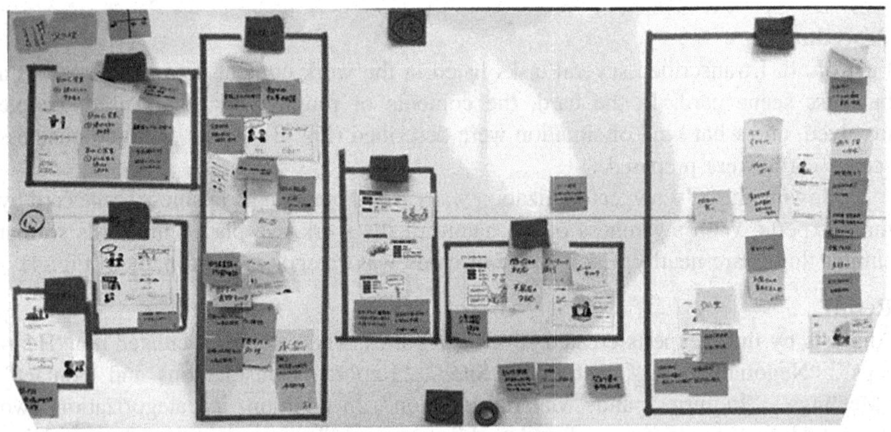

Fig. 4. Categorization and mapping using business scene card

Figure 5 summarizes the results of categorization and mapping. The contents of each category created are as follows.

Hearing (brown) …It refers to the part that mainly deals with direct customer interaction and listens to customers' opinions.

Negotiation (red) …It refers to negotiating work with real estate and customers.
Construction Site (yellow) …On-site witness and inspection work.
Report/Contact/Consultation (light green) …Report, contact, and consultation with the people around the boss and the department.
Meeting (green) …The vertical axis varies depending on whether the aim is for decision of things, for the purpose of making ideas or discussion on the agenda, or for reporting.
Inquiry (blue) …Work to handle correspondence from the outside, mainly telephone/mail correspondence.
Material Creation (purple) …The work related to the preparation of documents and various drafts will be relatively personal work.

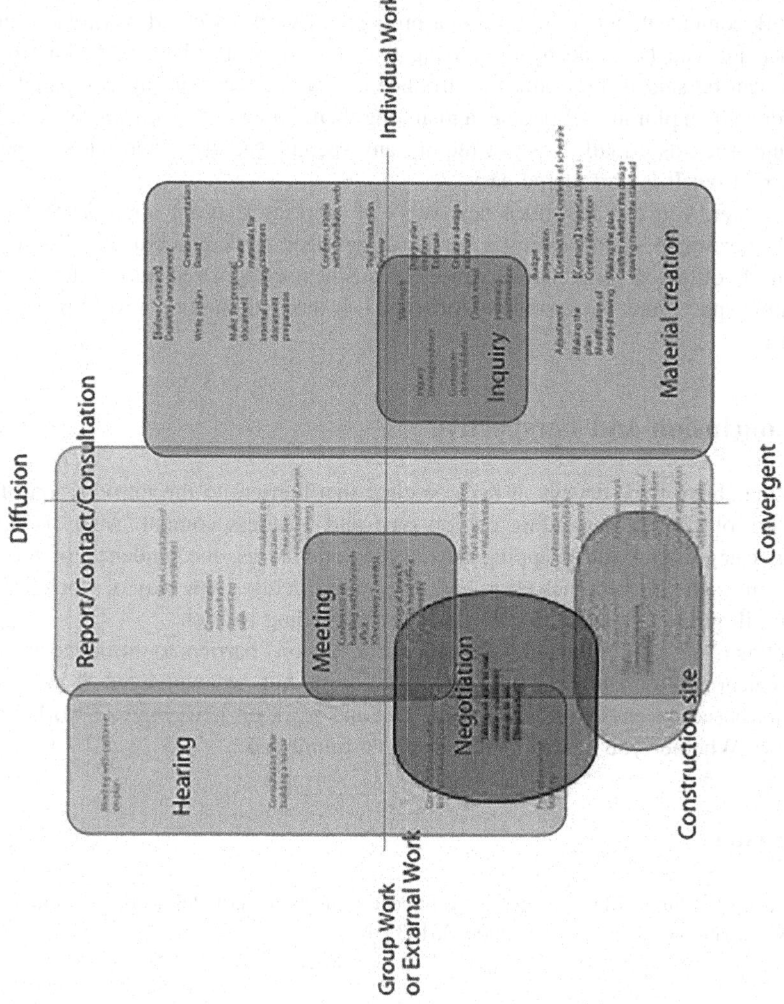

Fig. 5. Categorization of business contents and its mapping (Color figure online)

4 Consideration

From the user survey on the introduction of telework, users' barriers regarding the introduction of new ways of working can be classified as "communication", "infrastructure improvement" and "work efficiency", but there are countermeasures respectively. Although it can be said that the barriers categorized as "infrastructure improvement" are largely dependent on corporate efforts, the barriers classified as "communication" and "work efficiency" are designs of the workplace environment and contrivances between users It can be said that we can hope for improvements by. For example, with regard to "communication", designing a usual workplace in a low space of thresholds makes it possible to make it easier for workers to speak to each other even if opportunities to work by working way reduction are reduced.

In addition, although it was possible to categorize the user's work by user survey on the work content, it can be inferred that proposal of workplace and workplace suitable for each job can be made by organizing the trend of work. The work done by one person can be said to be easier to introduce a new way of working compared to the work done by a plurality of people, and among them, the work to be done by a personal computer such as e-mail does not require any specific facilities, and teleworking etc. are carried out It is considered easy.

Together, you can introduce new ways of working that are appropriate for each task. For example, by designing a barrier categorized as "communication" in consideration of "diffusion" and "convergence" of business categorized into "external" when designing space, new work suitable for work It is thought that one's work place can be proposed.

5 Conclusion and Perspective

From the above two surveys, it became clear that barriers to the introduction of telework are obstructed depending on job type and business content. Also, by investigating, categorizing and mapping the current operations, the tendency of the work content in each task becomes clear, and when introducing a new way of work, we think that it will guide guidelines for working corresponding to each.

In this issue, we conducted independent surveys on "barriers to introduce telework" and "categorization and mapping of operations", but we wondered if we can tie together based on environmental factors etc. and work on new ways of work suitable for work Whether you can propose Place is a future task.

Reference

1. Ministry of Public Management: Government's efforts towards telework promotion. http://www.soumu.go.jp/main_content/000433143.pdf

Development and Usability Evaluation of a Prototype Conversational Interface for Biological Information Retrieval via Bioinformatics

Walter Ritzel Paixão-Côrtes,
Vanessa Stangherlin Machado Paixão-Côrtes, Cristiane Ellwanger,
and Osmar Norberto de Souza(✉)

LABIO - School of Technology,
Pontifical Catholic University of Rio Grande do Sul (PUCRS),
Porto Alegre, Brazil
{walter.paixao-cortes,
vanessa.stangherlin}@acad.pucrs.br,
cristianeellwanger@gmail.com, osmar.norberto@pucrs.br

Abstract. Bioinformatics is an interdisciplinary area strongly driven by the advancement of technology and data generation. It applies concepts and methodologies derived from computer science, engineering, and statistics to the study of problems in the medical and biological areas. Bioinformatics users need to deal not only with large amounts of data but also with numerous resources to retrieve them. Furthermore, bioinformatics tools are known for their lack of usability. In this paper, we propose a service-oriented architecture-conversational interface called Maggie, which serves as the gateway to access and retrieve diverse sets of biological information based on BioCatalogue. We also discuss the usability evaluation of Maggie's prototype. Overall, the results show that a conversational interface has a great potential to become a valuable and productive tool to retrieve biological information from multiple sources if it is capable of understanding the context of the dialog maintained with the user.

Keywords: Bioinformatics · Database · Information retrieval · SOA-conversational interface · Usability

1 Introduction

Bioinformatics is an interdisciplinary and multidisciplinary area strongly driven by the advancement of technology and data generation. It applies concepts and methodologies derived from computer science, engineering, and statistics to the study of problems in the medical and biological areas [1]. Bioinformatics develops and applies computational algorithms and tools for the execution of costly and complex processes, using computers to store, organize, analyze and visualize large complex sets of biological data such as DNA, RNA, and proteins sequences and three-dimensional structures [2].

S. Yamamoto and H. Mori (Eds.): HCII 2019, LNCS 11569, pp. 575–593, 2019.
https://doi.org/10.1007/978-3-030-22660-2_43

Studies [3, 4] point out that bioinformatics is a complex field of study because it demands a series of skills such as ability to manage, interpret and analyze large data sets; extensive knowledge of data analysis methodologies - specialization in bioinformatics most common software packages and algorithms - and familiarity with genetic and genomic data [5]. For example, it is estimated that only in GenBank [6], a database of DNA sequences, whose number of nitrogenous bases doubles every 18 months, are stored approximately 10 trillions of deposited bases. This enormous amount of data and its inherent complexity generates challenging usability [7] and accessibility [8] problems for its analysis [9]. Bolchini et al. [10] state that usability barriers consume researchers' time with tasks that are not aligned with their ultimate goal.

There has been an increase in the search for methods and techniques that can make this data less complicated and easily accessible [11, 12]. An example is the study of Shaer et al. [13], which reports an initiative to reduce the complexity of the data, using an interactive visual interface. While visual interfaces are great at helping to understand the abstraction used to represent the data, it still creates some restrictions to people not familiarized with the abstraction in question (students).

Natural language interfaces to databases have been proposed by many authors as the solution to retrieve information easily, allowing their use by people who are not experts in computer programming languages, thus unlinking the formulation of a query from the specific programming language knowledge required to write it [10]. Although this type of interface is known since the '60s [14], just recently they started to gain traction through its use in business intelligence, which provided good results. However, its configuration process is a nontrivial issue. Moreover, the efficient exploration of biological data is limited also by the accessibility and usability difficulties of bioinformatics tools.

This article presents a conversational interface called Maggie for natural and easy retrieval of biological data by bioinformatics users. Maggie is based on a service-oriented architecture (SOA), and the name is a homage to Dr. Margareth Oakley Dayhoff (1925–1983), a bioinformatics pioneer. For this, we studied a specific type of conversational interface, the chatbot, which connects to biological databases through an orchestration service (via BioCatalogue [15] service mapping), simply and intuitively. The presentation of the information in an integrated and automated form in a single interface is important, as it does not require tedious, low-level coding.

We performed usability assessments with 8 area specialists who compared the performance of tasks in standard interfaces such as GenBank [6], PDB (Protein Data Bank) [16], and PubMed [17] and the Maggie interface presented in this study. The tasks were selected within a defined usage context and represent a workflow commonly performed by bioinformatics users.

2 Background

2.1 Bioinformatics

Bioinformatics conceptualizes biology in terms of molecules in the physical-chemical sense and, using computational techniques, statistics, mathematics, and computer science, allows us to store, organize and understand, on a large scale, this biological data explosion [1]. The use of computer programs to analyze DNA, RNA, and protein information has become critical to life science research and development [12].

Early bioinformatics activities included building databases. Knowledge of the structure and content of primary databases, such as NCBI, is essential as much as the ability to manipulate and process large amounts of data. As the "omics"[1] produce more data with the next generation sequencing (NGS) techniques, a more significant amount of new data is expected [18].

Several factors contribute to the explosive growth of data: more affordable hardware, new computational concepts and better software, just to name a few. The problem has become more visible with the spread of the internet, where individuals, companies, governments, non-governmental institutions are producing potential content, turning the world into a massive database that is updated by thousands of people. In the field of bioinformatics, this is no different, because data are generated by scientists and researchers when doing experiments and accessing computational services [19].

Bioinformatics is in full growth. Its most significant challenge is the management of vast amounts of data generated daily from the workbenches of researchers worldwide. The most advanced algorithms then process these data, analyze and visualize them from different perspectives. Finally, the knowledge generated is published for the benefit not only of the scientific community but also of the entire world population (through advances in medicine, the creation of new drugs) [9].

The bioinformatics databases emerged in response to a need - where to store experimental data - and their concept was thought through and executed rudimentarily (through punch cards) even before the technology that made it possible existed. Some databases even started as printed publications [20], serving the purpose of making information public. They then became modest technologies such as a simple backend to support some applications and quickly developed to the current level: complete platforms for global sharing of data generated by researchers, an ecosystem of tools that help in the tasks of analysis, processing, query, and visualization of the information.

Thanks to the technological evolution, which has brought us the electronic storage capacity, and to the database technology itself, they now occupy a prominent place among bioinformatics tools, since they are the standard (together with the internet) found to share information with the entire scientific community. The journal Nucleic Acids Research annually publishes a Database Issue[2], which presents to the scientific community new databases created to share this biological information. Only in 2018 were published 82 articles on new databases and 84 articles that feature updates that appeared in previous editions [21].

With the growing number of databases, the question of how to access these banks and how to integrate data becomes more relevant. The first response came in the form of specialization of bioinformatics databases. While the databases responsible for storing protein and DNA sequences or entire genomes are classified as primary databases because they have raw information coming from the bench, there are banks of

[1] omics - neologism used to informally reference the fields of bioinformatics study: genomics, proteomics, transcriptomics, metabolomics.

[2] NAR Database Issue - https://academic.oup.com/nar/issue/46/12.

data classified as secondary and tertiary, which deliver more enriched and specific information resulting from workflows (scientific workflows) that process information from various sources [22]. The most recent response takes advantage of these databases being made available on the internet and providing access to data through web services. These are the service-oriented architectures (SOA), which allows researchers to integrate information from different sources through the composition of web services [23].

2.2 Service Oriented Architecture

Service-oriented architecture (SOA) is the new generation of distributed computing platforms, with its own paradigms and principles [24]. The SOA is built from the technologies that preceded it (like the client-server architecture or CORBA) and added new layers of design, governance considerations, and best-in-class technologies for implementation. The purpose of this type of architecture is to enable reuse of small portions of code (services) in a highly decoupled way, ensuring end users the ability to build more complex solutions from these small pieces.

The first mention of the SOA was made in an article published by the IBM web services development team at developerWorks[3]. Since then it has been of great interest among researchers in the scientific environment and has received a strong acceptance in the software development market. Although the architecture was originated in a web development team, it does not presuppose the use of this technology, being much more comprehensive than this one.

Serman [25] defines SOA as a software architecture concept made up of components available through generic interfaces and standardized and preferably license-free protocols (services), designed to achieve the least possible level of dependence on information systems that consume them and the technical part of the development, stimulating its reuse and taking advantage of the existing functionalities. In bioinformatics, SOA proposals focus on standardization of interfaces, query, validation and analysis of biological data, and integration of new tools [26–28]. These works will be discussed in Sect. 3.

2.3 Natural Language Processing and Databases

For conversational interfaces to be able to understand human beings, they need what is now called the language understanding engine (LUE). The most well-known LUE is ALICE, based on AIML (Artificial Intelligence Markup Language) [29]. During our literature research on conversational interfaces, we observed that the interfaces mentioned in the articles used the same engine or a variation of it, and only 1 used a more modern engine (Telegram Bot) [30].

But this is not the only option: Google and Microsoft have made their LUE, called DialogFlow and LUIS (Language Understanding Internet Services), respectively, available as services in the cloud. These engines have some advantages over AIML, such as recognition of entities (variables, subjects, verbs) in sentences, a vast base of

[3] IBM developerWorks - http://www.ibm.com/developerWorks.

predefined entities, and greater ease of configuration. Its major disadvantage is that they are not free. During this research, we performed a comparative study of several natural language comprehension engines, to select the one that best fit our architectural proposal. Also, the integration of engines into a service-oriented architecture requires that the characteristics of the other components that compose it and their behavior be observed together.

Conversational interfaces are often referenced as bots or chatbots. A chatbot is a software that interacts with a user through natural language dialogues, such as in English [31]. This technology began in the '60s with the objective of verifying that the chatbots could pass for real humans in dialogues between users [32]. Thus, software ELIZA [33] appeared, the first program for natural language processing that simulated the conversation between man and machine, with human characteristics similar to feelings.

Since then, chatbots development technologies have evolved, increasing their ability to dialogue with humans. Starting with an algorithm that analyzed keywords and returned preprogrammed responses [33], evolving to natural language processing via semantic mapping, using ontologies [34] to the machine learning application such as Recurrent Neural Networks (RNN) [35].

However, chatbots are not built to mimic human conversations and entertain users. They are used in different domains, such as customer service, information retrieval, e-commerce, contextual help for websites, and education [31, 32]. There are personal assistants like Siri, Google Assistant, and Cortana who virtually help their users perform daily tasks on computers and smartphones through voice commands.

The analysis and visualization of biological data through a suitable interface, facilitated by the availability of data to scientists, is a central factor for the understanding of biological research, possessing, in addition to the vast production of information, a technological gap, with a view to obtain the meaning and value of these data [36]. We believe that conversational interfaces are an emergent feature that can provide improved user interaction in bioinformatics systems.

2.4 Usability in Bioinformatics Tools

The technical characteristics of bioinformatics tools, coupled with the importance they exert for the daily activities of researchers in the field, requires alternative ways of thinking about the aspects of their use and of better taking advantage of their results.

Usability is a feature that aims to ensure that interactive systems are easy to learn to use and remember, effective, efficient, safe and enjoyable from a user's perspective [37]. Javahery et al. [38] report that usability is a key feature for bioinformatics tools because the biomedical research community involves high-cost scientific personnel, laboratory experimentation to generate bioanalytical data, and techniques to analyze this data.

Researchers in the area take the problems related to the usability of web applications in the context of bioinformatics under different approaches [10, 39, 40]. Some focus their attention on the context of use and the way these applications are used, relying on user tests as they interact with them [8, 41, 42]. In another approach, experts rely on inspection techniques on the usability problems of these applications and on how to best solve them [8]. For example, Bolchini et al. [10] reports that usability problems compromise scientists' ability to find the information they need for their daily research activities. Even if we consider that the applications available on the web have certain advantages when compared with their desktop versions, issues like the incompatibilities between browsers are counterproductive, often preventing the creation of custom interaction components [43].

Therefore, providing resources with good usability or ensuring the usability improvement of bioinformatics resources allows researchers to find, interact, share, compare and handle important information more effectively and efficiently. Hence, they gain improved insight into biological processes with the ultimate potential to produce new scientific results [20].

The usability of a system is a qualitative metric that depends on two factors: the combination of the system interfaces and the ability of its users to pursue specific objectives for certain tasks [43]. Systems and their interfaces must be cognitive tools that facilitate perception, reasoning, memorization, and decision making [44].

3 Related Work

There are papers that describes methods to facilitate the integration of bioinformatics tools and access to various sources of biological data, without requiring the researcher to have advanced knowledge in bioinformatics. Lemos [45] addresses the construction of systems (SGABios) that facilitate the bio sequencing analysis phase and approaches the use of workflows to compose bioinformatics processes. She proposed a framework that decomposes an SGAB into two sub-systems: a bioinformatics workflow management system, which helps researchers in the definition, validation, optimization and execution of workflows needed to perform the analyzes; and a data management system in bioinformatics, which deals with the storage and manipulation of the data involved in these analyzes. Galaxy [26] is a framework that stands out for presenting features such as unified interface, validation of data types, possibility of integration of new tools, development of pipelines graphically and extensive documentation. CelOWS [27] is an SOA for the storage, reuse and composition and execution of biological models, expressed in CellML, and its representation through an ontology, which provides a natural language for the semantic description of biological models. BioGraphBot [28] is a conversational interface based on the ALICE framework for access to a bioinformatics graph database, BioGraphDB, with the Gremlin query language. It allows the translation of queries expressed in natural language to queries expressed in Gremlin, simplifying the interaction with BioGraphDB. The authors mention that the chatbot was incorporated into the BioGraphDB Web interface, but it was not possible to verify the availability of the chat.

The differences between the Maggie architecture and the related works mentioned above are in the scope and degree of evolution. In the scope aspect, it differs from the SGABio, CelOWS and BioGraphBot architectures due to their restricted availability of specific topics: bio sequencing, biological models and graph databases. Maggie proposes to be more open and to provide a comprehensive range of services. To do so, instead of pre-selecting services, we are proposing to make the discovery and mapping of services based on a catalog (BioCatalogue).

Regarding the degree of evolution when comparing Maggie to Galaxy, the main difference is that our architecture was developed to be continually evolving in the sense of learning to use new services, which results in new knowledge. In addition, although Galaxy offers a considerable set of pre-installed tools, it requires the user to develop scripts/interfaces for new programs to be integrated into the framework [26]. Another point to consider is that Galaxy provides the structure to perform the orchestration of services, but not the services themselves.

Also, it is important to note that while Maggie uses natural language to provide the resources and assist users in the search for information, the Galaxy interface requires specific programming knowledge to enable the services to be used.

Finally, BioGraphBot has some limitation on scope and technology. The content-related limitation occurs because one can only query the contents in the database. The technological limitation lays in the fact that the database must be of the type that supports graph storage, which requires specific knowledge so that the contents can be formatted appropriately.

The use of a SOA that integrates a conversational interface, using bots, addresses the problems discussed in Sect. 2.4, since the responsibility for capturing and delivering information is left to the search engine itself.

4 Materials and Methods

Based on the scientific literature presented in Sect. 2, bioinformatics scientists have a variety of databases and services available to create their own research workflows. In fact, there are so many available, that it can be difficult for users to select the most suitable ones. With that in mind, we chose BioCatalogue[4] [15] as our source of services metadata.

The next goal was to learn about tools that could use this catalog. The research has identified the tools mentioned in our related work section: Galaxy, CelOWS, SGABIO and BiographBOT. We experimented with them to identify their main features to build a more flexible solution that could be easy to use and that could incorporate more data and services over time, with minimum user intervention.

For the data collection, with the application of a questionnaire[5], we performed usability tests with 8 HCI and bioinformatics experts. The objective was to collect their opinion on the performance of bioinformatics tasks employing standard interfaces and Maggie to identify benefits, problems, and new requirements to further the development of Maggie.

The USE-based [46] questionnaire was composed of 8 closed questions: 4 on the profile (age, gender and academic background), and 4 on the Likert 5-point scale. It covers aspects of usefulness, ease of use, ease of learning and user satisfaction. Also,

[4] BioCatalogue - https://www.biocatalogue.org/.

[5] Questionnaire - https://goo.gl/forms/Uq4ta9kOYnWpIkvv2.

we have included 3 open questions: (1) In your experience, what other tasks do you believe could be performed by Maggie?, (2) In which scenario would you use Maggie? Please describe (e.g. it is more suited for executing specific tasks or as classroom resource), and (3) Please provide suggestions and list the main positive/negative points of Maggie.

In the usability evaluation, the participants performed 2 tasks using both the standard interfaces and Maggie. Table 1 summarizes the integrated tools, links and the activities performed for the tasks.

Table 1. List of tools and activities executed by respondents of the usability evaluation questionnaire.

Tool/Service	Type	Activities
NCBI[a]	Portal	- Navigate to the website
GenBank[b]	Sequence database	- Retrieve one sequence from the database, using its accession number: NP_037228.1 - Retrieve the sequence in FASTA format
RCSB PDB[c]	3D structure database	- Retrieve one protein by PDB ID: 1ENY - Navigate to subsites inside PDB: Molecule of the Month, PDB-101
PubMed[d]	Literature database	- Retrieve one scientific publication by PMID

[a]NCBI - National Center for Biotechnology Information - https://www.ncbi.nlm.nih.gov/
[b]GenBank - https://www.ncbi.nlm.nih.gov/genbank/
[c]RCSB PDB - Research Collaboratory for Structural Bioinformatics Protein Data Bank - https://www.rcsb.org/
[d]PubMed - https://www.ncbi.nlm.nih.gov/pubmed/

In Sect. 6 we will discuss the results of the data collection and what we have learned to apply in further development efforts of Maggie architecture.

5 Approach

Here we will describe the architectural and implementation levels of the Maggie conversational interface.

5.1 Architecture

Our proposed architecture is composed of 5 built and 2 external components distributed in 3 layers: front-end (F), middleware (M) and back-end (B), as seen in (Fig. 1). The external components are the Language Understanding Engine and the BioCatalogue. The details of each component are as follows and can be visualized in (Fig. 1):

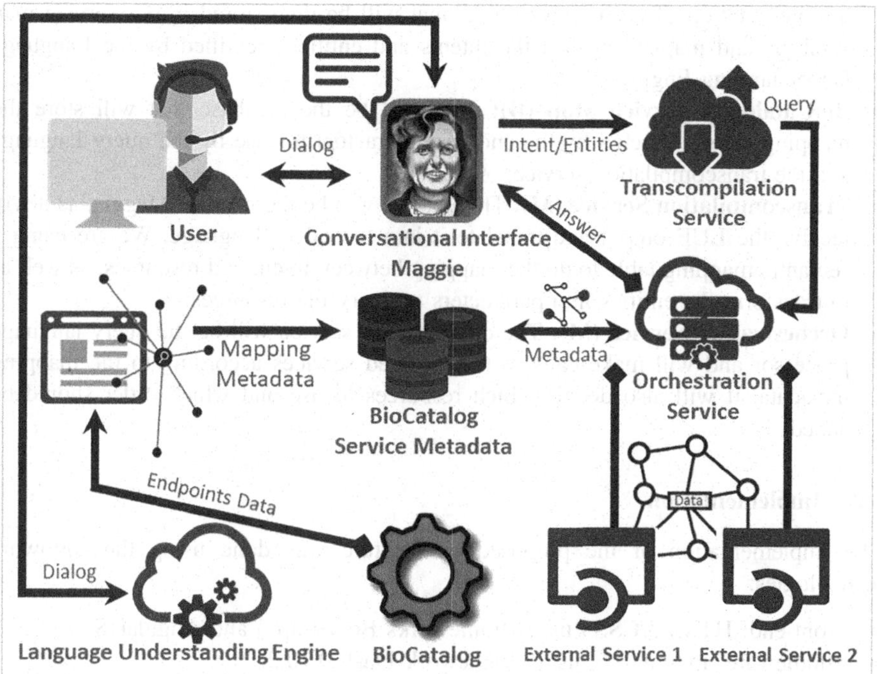

Fig. 1. The proposed SOA-based architecture for the Maggie conversational interface.

- **Conversational Interface (F):** It will be the entry point for users. This interface should allow the user to request biological data through typing or talking natural language sentences and receive the answers. It can be implemented in different formats: as a chatbot or as a search interface or integrated with virtual assistants such as Google Assistant, Siri or Cortana;
- **Language Understanding Engine (LUE) (M):** Used by the conversational interface, it will be responsible for translating a natural language sentence into the intention that represents it, along with the entities involved. This is one of the external components chosen to take advantage of the machine learning capabilities to interpret the conversation. Right now, based on criteria evaluation, we have opted for the use of MS LUIS;
- **BioCatalogue (B):** It is a catalogue of life science web services maintained by EMBL-EBI and it will be used as the source of our endpoints that will compose our services mapping layer;
- **BioCatalogue Endpoint Extractor (M):** The endpoint extractor will navigate the BioCatalogue list of services to generate the mapping metadata that will be required for the query language and transcompilation process to work properly. Here is where Maggie will be different of the solutions cited on the related work: we will navigate through the catalogue and generate, based on their documentation,

a representation of each web service, that will be then stored in our service map database and mapped against the intents and entities identified by the Language Understanding Engine;

- **BioCatalogue Service Map (B):** This will be the database that will store the mapping data (extracted by the endpoint extractor) for use by the query language and the transcompilation service;
- **Transcompilation Service (M):** This service will be the heart of Maggie, as it will receive the LUE output and translate it into the query language. We are using a semantic mapping table to do the mapping between intent and resources, as well as to transform the entities into parameters to query the resources;
- **Orchestration Service (M):** The orchestration service will be the query language processor and will make calls to the required services according to the mapping metadata. It will also decide which resources to use and which order should be called.

5.2 Implementation

The implementation of the proposed architecture was done using the following technologies:

- Front-end: HTML5/CSS3 using frameworks Bootstrap 3 and AngularJS;
- Middleware: Python 3.6, using framework Flask 0.10.2;
- Application Container: Gunicorn server 19.9.0;
- Language Understanding Engine: Microsoft LUIS with Programmatic API v2.0;
- Back-end: Python 3.6 using SQLAlchemy and Marshmallow, with a SQLite database

Since we were creating the prototype of the architecture, we did not have split the solution into individual services: instead, we have used the concept of blueprints in Flask to create individual subsets of endpoints within the same worker thread. This decision was taken to make it easier for the coding/testing approach. The final version of the architecture will split the blueprints into different services, as proposed in the architecture.

We will detail below how the 3 main components of our architecture are implemented: the language understanding engine, the transcompilation service, and the conversational interface.

Language Understanding Engine (LUE)

This component was implemented using Microsoft LUIS. In LUIS, we need to define 3 main concepts: the intents, the utterances and the entities. Those 3 are related in a way that when configured, a machine learning algorithm can receive a sentence in natural language and can classify it against the intent with identification of the entities involved.

The intent is a class of utterances and is the label that is returned from the LUE. The utterances are examples of sentences, marked with special notation to identify entities. For example, a Greeting intent could have utterances for the many ways we can greet someone: Hi, Hello, Howdy, etc. Entities are the variables or parameters that could appear on utterances and that we need to receive back so we can decide what action to execute. For example, we have an entity for PDB ID (the PDB unique identifier). So, in every intent that have utterances that contain words that represents a PDB ID, it will be tagged automatically.

After all the 3 elements were identified and configured, we trained the model and made it available as a REST service to be used from the middleware. When training the model, we aim the maximization of the prediction precision – the accuracy in classify an utterance sent by the user against the intents. Because of this, we had to find a way to generate as many examples as possible, without them being manually inputted: we have developed a script based in an Excel file that generates the MS LUIS configuration based on some patterns. Figure 2 shows an example of one intent worksheet with the list of the utterances and entities identified. The script merges the intent worksheet with the entities worksheet, generating for each line in the intent worksheet several utterances based on the entities samples.

		Entities			
Implemented	Utterance	ValidSites	PDBID	GBID	PMID
Y	can you get the [PDBID] pdb file for me, please		x		
Y	download [PDBID]		x		
Y	download pdb file for pdbid = [PDBID]		x		
Y	retrieve the [PDBID] pdb file for me, please		x		
Y	get the [PDBID] file in pdb		x		
Y	I want the pdb file for [PDBID]		x		
Y	please, retrieve the [PDBID] pdb file for me		x		

Fig. 2. Configuration of an intent worksheet, with utterances and entities identified.

Transcompilation Service

The transcompilation service was implemented as a REST API and implements a semantic mapping table that receives the result of the LUE - intent and entities and, based on this mapping, indicates what kind of execution should be done. For example, when it receives the GetPdbFileIntent and a PDB ID entity (Fig. 3), the semantic table indicates that it should be transcompiled into a call to _return_pdb_file_url function, using the PDB ID as the parameter. The result is then passed to the front-end.

```
{
    "intent": "GetPdbFileIntent",
    "type": "WS",
    "query": "_return_pdb_file_url('{PDBID}')",
    "answer1":["Here is the pdb file you requested:\n "],
    "answer2_plural": [""],
    "answer2_singular": [""]
},
```

Fig. 3. Semantic table entry for GetPdbFileIntent

Conversational Interface

The conversational interface was implemented as a single page app that represents a chat window (Fig. 4). The user can enter the sentences in the text box and the bot will answer back. The text box keeps the history of the current conversation, so the user can repeat sentences without having to type them again.

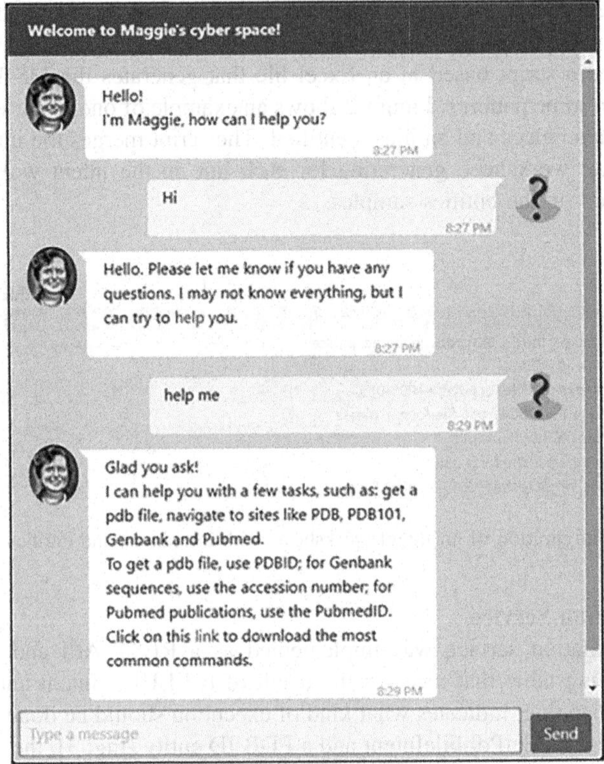

Fig. 4. Maggie's screen.

6 Usability Evaluation

As mentioned in Sect. 4, we have requested 8 specialists in HCI and/or bioinformatics to execute 2 tasks both on the traditional way (using browser and other tools if needed) and using Maggie, the conversational interface. Afterward, they answered a questionnaire. In this section, we analyze and discuss their answers. We have divided our analysis in 2 subsections. In the respondents' background, we detailed their demographics to understand how much experience they have in bioinformatics. In the usability aspects, we will describe their impressions about the use of Maggie to fulfill the tasks requested.

6.1 Respondents' Background

The majority (75%) of our respondents were in the age range of 25 to 35 years (Fig. 5, left), with a few (12.5%) under and above that range. This reflects in their educational background – most of them (62.5%) had at least a master's degree (Fig. 5, right) and an overall experience with bioinformatics averaging approximately 5.7 years (Fig. 5, bottom). Only one of them had less than one year of experience.

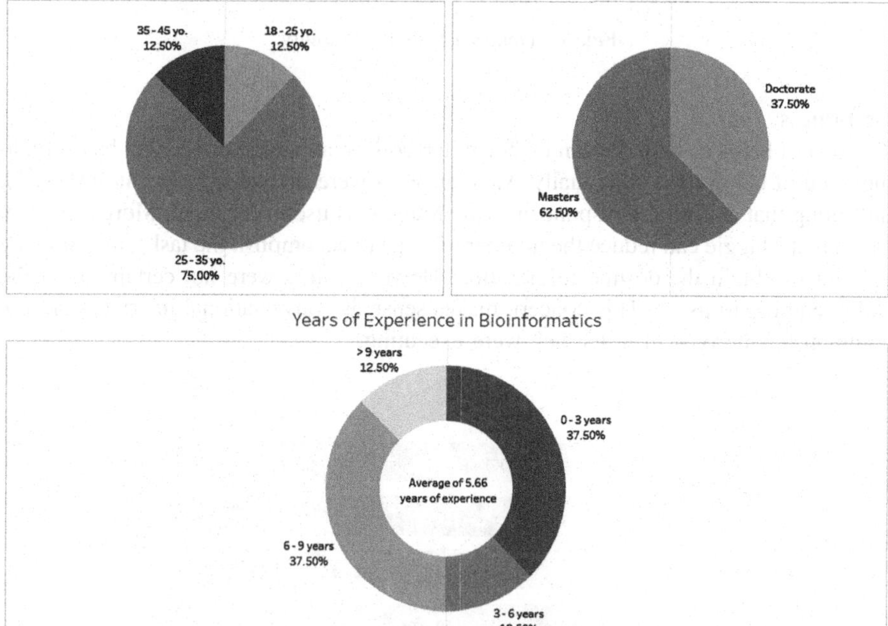

Fig. 5. Demographics distribution charts by age range, education level, and experience with bioinformatics.

6.2 Usability Aspects

The usability was analyzed according to 4 aspects: usefulness, ease of use, ease of learning and user satisfaction. For each one, we presented the respondents with statements and they should answer using a Likert 5-point scale ranging from Totally Disagree (1) to Totally Agree (5).

As we can see in (Fig. 6), the trend stablished for Maggie is favorable in all usability aspects. We will see the details of each one in the subsections below.

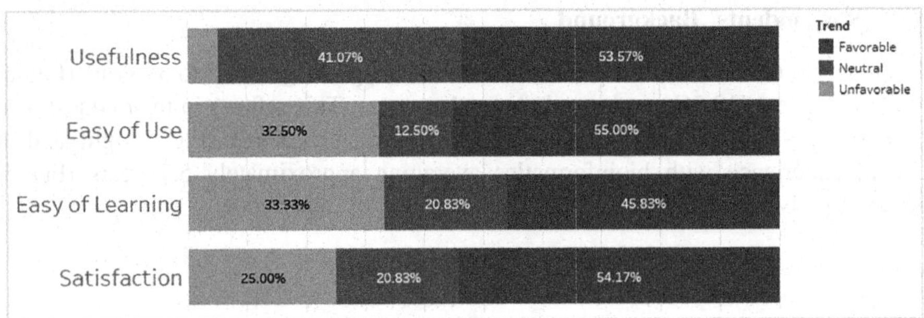

Fig. 6. Trend analysis for usability.

Usefulness

This aspect helps us to understand whether the conversational interface will be useful to the point of being used continually. Most answers were favorable and neutral (Fig. 7), indicating that overall the respondents saw Maggie as useful for them. Moreover, they stated that Maggie can reduce the number of steps to accomplish the tasks, thus making it faster to obtain the desired information. However, they were not certain about the skills required to use it. This concern makes sense as conversational interfaces are not common for the type of tasks they were executing.

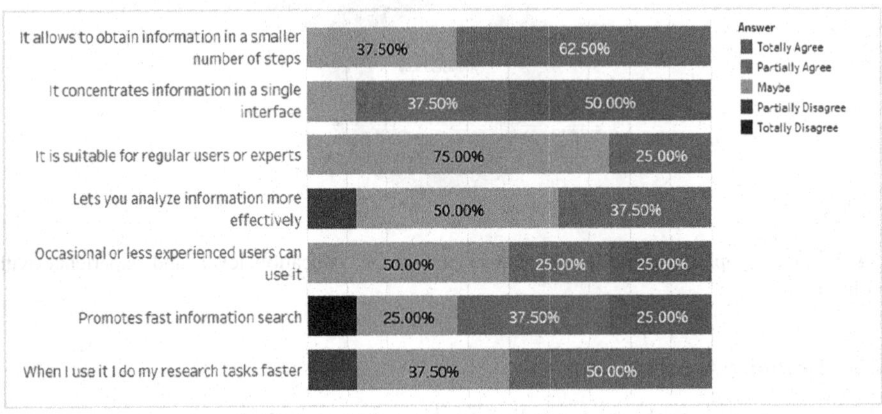

Fig. 7. Trend analysis for usefulness.

Ease of Use

This aspect evaluates if Maggie is easy to use. The results again show a favorable trend, but it is important to highlight the statement about the written instructions: Maggie has a help function that is activated when one types “help me” or “help”, but there is no indication that it is available. The respondents wrote that it was difficult to discover the help function and that example for its use were missing (Fig. 8).

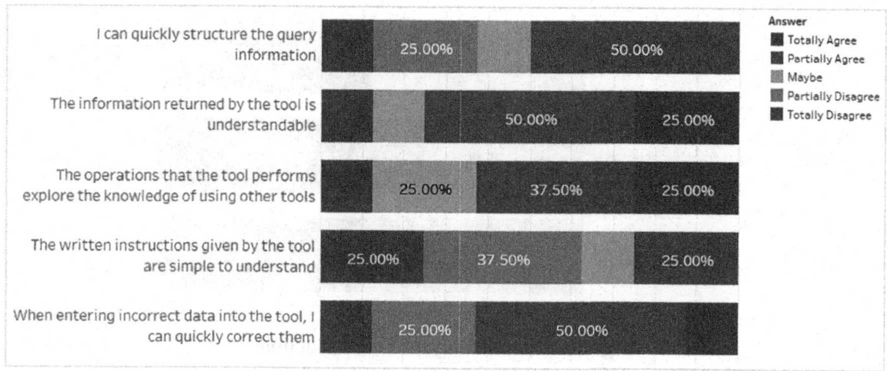

Fig. 8. Trend analysis for ease of use.

Ease of Learning

This aspect is about how easy it is to learn to use Maggie. Figure 9 shows that most users do not greet Maggie as an intuitive tool, even though they consider easy to remember how to use it. Conversational interfaces are simple and one only needs to talk with Maggie, so that explains why it is easy to remember. Maggie's current difficulties seem to be related to the way it starts and keeps the dialog.

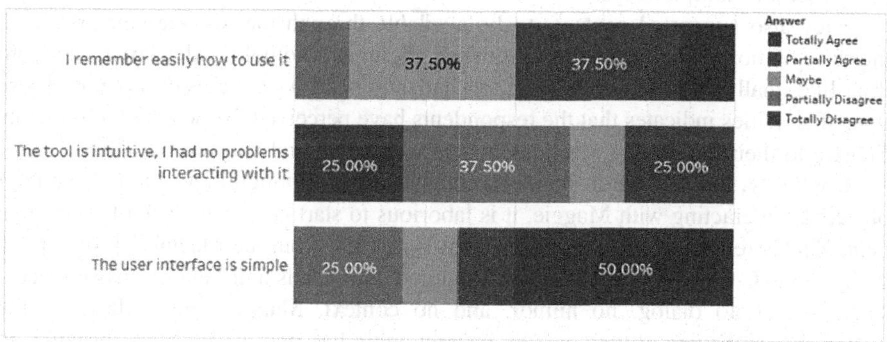

Fig. 9. Trend analysis for ease of learning.

Satisfaction

This feature measures the satisfaction of the respondents towards Maggie. Despite the issues related to the ease of use and ease of learning, the overall experience using Maggie was considered positive. However, Fig. 10 shows that about 38% of the respondents had expectations that were not met. This is not surprising given that they tested Maggie's first version.

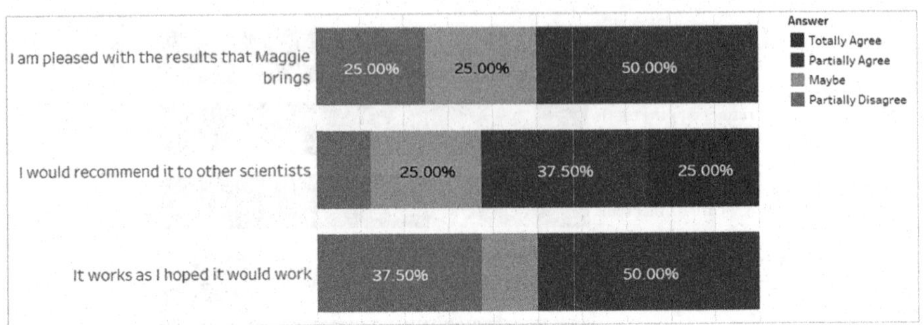

Fig. 10. Trend analysis for satisfaction.

7 Discussion

The questionnaire was enlightening and confirmed that the Maggie conversational interface can be helpful in bioinformatics. It allows easy retrieval of biological information from different data sources. Here, we will discuss about the positive and negative opinions informed by the respondents.

When asked about how they would use Maggie, most of them answered that they would use Maggie in a classroom context and in scientific workflows. This is aligned with their perceptions on usability aspects. They found the interface is simple enough to be used in multiple ways.

They also suggested contents to be available through the Maggie conversational interface. Among them, it features sequence alignment, homology detection, access to drug-like small molecule database, and visualization of 3D structures of proteins. These type of activities indicates that the respondents have perceived the potential to integrate Maggie to their day-to-day activities, which is positive and very encouraging.

Contrarily, most of the respondents indicated that although they can achieve their objectives interacting with Maggie, it is laborious to start due to the lack of contextual help. This is related to one key feature that is missing from the Maggie's prototype: a dialog flow. Currently, the user types structured commands and Maggie answers back. There is yet no dialog, no humor, and no context. Maggie cannot detect if the respondent is having difficulties to interact with her and thus cannot provide an alternative. A tutorial, as mentioned by the respondents, may be a way to mitigate temporarily the lack of context in the conversation.

8 Conclusion

Conversational interfaces could be a good way to create interaction channels between users and the content they need in a way as simple as writing a text. In fact, this type of interface has being used in many areas, from consumer service to virtual classrooms and lately, as an analytical interface, it is allowing acquisition of business insights from large datasets. From a development perspective, conversational interfaces may be an easy system to create, but its complexities are not in sight. It is necessary to have a proper dialog flow, which will offer contextual help, engage, and guide the user if needed. To address these issues appropriately, it is necessary to acknowledge usability characteristics that are not related to graphical interfaces, such as intelligent interpretation, contextualization, attitude, and vocabulary, to name a few.

The results obtained from the usability evaluation were encouraging and have corroborated our assumption that a conversational interface could aggregate values to the way bioinformatics users retrieve biological information. Moreover, Maggie's prototype has revealed itself as a suitable example of both the upside and downside of the application of conversational interfaces to a non-business specific domain such as bioinformatics usage. On the upside, Maggie engaged the respondents, allowed faster and easier execution of the tasks, instigated their curiosity on how to use it in other contexts, pointing to possible new information that could be available through it. On the downside, because Maggie currently lacks an intuitive help function and the ability to understand the context of a conversation, some respondents found it unsatisfying.

With the lessons learned during this work, we will continue to develop this SOA-conversational interface to make it serviceable to bioinformatics users in their scientific workflows and classrooms. The next steps are: (i) implement the endpoint extractor and the service mapping metadata database, so more services will be made available by Maggie; (ii) implement the transcompilation service to improve the intelligent interpretation by Maggie, and (iii) implement the context management to improve the contextualization and attitude features. We are also going to perform more evaluations, including an undergraduate biological sciences' classroom, to analyze how Maggie assisted them in learning and using bioinformatics tools.

References

1. Luscombe, N.M., Greenbaum, D., Gerstein, M.: What is bioinformatics? A proposed definition and overview of the field. Methods Inf. Med. **40**, 346–358 (2001)
2. Lesk, A.M.: Introduction to Bioinformatics. Oxford University Press, Oxford (2014)
3. Neves, R.: Uma Arquitetura de Agentes para Recomendação Contextualizada de Eventos Baseada em Propagação da Ativação (2013)
4. Madlung, A.: Assessing an effective undergraduate module teaching applied bioinformatics to biology students. PLoS Comput. Biol. **14**, e1005872 (2018)
5. Welch, L., et al.: Bioinformatics curriculum guidelines: toward a definition of core competencies. PLoS Comput. Biol. **10**, 1–10 (2014)
6. Benson, D.A., et al.: GenBank. Nucleic Acids Res. **46**, D41–D47 (2018)
7. Al-Ageel, N., Al-Wabil, A., Badr, G., AlOmar, N.: Human factors in the design and evaluation of bioinformatics tools. Procedia Manuf. **3**, 2003–2010 (2015)
8. Paixão-Côrtes, V.S.M., Paixão-Côrtes, W.R., de Borba Campos, M., de Souza, O.N.: A panorama on selection and use of bioinformatics tools in the Brazilian University context. In: Antona, M., Stephanidis, C. (eds.) UAHCI 2018. LNCS, vol. 10908, pp. 553–573. Springer, Cham (2018). https://doi.org/10.1007/978-3-319-92052-8_44
9. Reichhardt, T.: It's sink or swim as a tidal wave of data approaches. Nature **399**, 517–520 (1999)
10. Bolchini, D., Finkelstein, A., Perrone, V., Nagl, S.: Better bioinformatics through usability analysis. Bioinformatics **25**, 406–412 (2009)

11. Junior, H.L.R., de Oliveira, R.T.G., Ceccatto, V.M.: Bioinformática como recurso pedagógico para o curso de ciências biológicas na Universidade Estadual do Ceará. Acta Scientiarum Education **34**, 129–140 (2012)
12. Cattley, S., Arthur, J.W.: BioManager: the use of a bioinformatics web application as a teaching tool in undergraduate bioinformatics training. Brief. Bioinform. **8**, 457–465 (2007)
13. Shaer, O., Kol, G., Strait, M., Fan, C., Grevet, C., Elfenbein, S.: G-nome surfer. In: Proceedings of the 28th International Conference on Human Factors in Computing Systems – CHI 2010, p. 1427. ACM Press, New York (2010)
14. Nihalani, N., Motwani, M., Silaka, S.: Natural language interface to database using semantic matching. Int. J. Comput. Appl. **31**, 29–34 (2011)
15. Bhagat, J., et al.: BioCatalogue: a universal catalogue of web services for the life sciences. Nucleic Acids Res. **38**, W689–W694 (2010)
16. Rose, P.W., et al.: The RCSB Protein Data Bank: views of structural biology for basic and applied research and education. Nucleic Acids Res. **43**, D345–D356 (2015)
17. Information, N.C. for B., Pike, U.S.N.L. of M. 8600 R., MD, B., Usa, 20894: PubMed Help. National Center for Biotechnology Information (US) (2016)
18. Tan, T.W., Lim, S.J., Khan, A.M., Ranganathan, S.: A proposed minimum skill set for university graduates to meet the informatics needs and challenges of the "–omics" era. BMC Genom. **10**, S36 (2009)
19. de Carvalho, A.C.P.L., de Leon, F.D.P.: Grandes desafios da pesquisa em computação no brasil–2006–2016. Sociedade Brasileira de Computação, São Paulo (2006)
20. Dayhoff, M.O. (ed.): Atlas of Protein Sequence and Structure. National Biomedical Research, Washington, D.C. (1979)
21. Rigden, D.J., Fernandez, X.M.: The 2018 Nucleic Acids Research database issue and the online molecular biology database collection. Nucleic Acids Res. **46**, D1–D7 (2018)
22. Chen, C., Huang, H., Wu, C.H.: Protein bioinformatics databases and resources. In: Wu, C. H., Chen, C. (eds.) Bioinformatics for Comparative Proteomics, pp. 3–24. Humana Press (2011)
23. Cannata, N., Schröder, M., Marangoni, R., Romano, P.: A Semantic Web for bioinformatics: goals, tools, systems, applications. BMC Bioinform. **9**, S1 (2008)
24. Erl, T. (ed.): SOA with REST: Principles, Patterns & Constraints for Building Enterprise Solutions with REST. Prentice Hall, Upper Saddle River (2012)
25. Serman, D.V.: Orientação a projetos: uma proposta de desenvolvimento de uma arquitetura orientada a serviços. JISTEM-J. Inf. Syst. Technol. Manag. **7**, 619–638 (2010)
26. Afgan, E., et al.: The Galaxy platform for accessible, reproducible and collaborative biomedical analyses: 2018 update. Nucleic Acids Res. **44**, W3–W10 (2018)
27. Matos, E.E., Campos, F., Braga, R.M.M.: CelOWS: uma arquitetura orientada a serviços para definição, pesquisa e reuso de modelos biológicos. In: SBCARS, pp. 107–120 (2008)
28. Messina, A., Augello, A., Pilato, G., Rizzo, R.: BioGraphBot: a conversational assistant for bioinformatics graph databases. In: Barolli, L., Enokido, T. (eds.) IMIS 2017. AISC, vol. 612, pp. 135–146. Springer, Cham (2018). https://doi.org/10.1007/978-3-319-61542-4_12
29. AIML: An Introduction Pandorabots Documentation. https://pandorabots.com/docs/aiml/aiml-basics.html
30. Morais, C.G., Gomes, A.F., Leite, J.N. de F., Kléber, K. de A., Barbalho, S.T.J.: Donuts: um bot como instrumento facilitador do processo de ensino-aprendizagem na disciplina Construção de Algoritmos. Revista Eletrônica Argentina-Brasil de Tecnologias da Informação e da Comunicação **1** (2017)
31. Shawar, B.A., Atwell, E.: Different measurements metrics to evaluate a chatbot system. In: Proceedings of the Workshop on Bridging the Gap: Academic and Industrial Research in Dialog Technologies (NAACL-HLT-Dialog), pp. 89–96 (2007)

32. Shawar, B.A.: A chatbot as a natural web interface to arabic web QA. Int. J. Emerg. Technol. Learn. **6**, 37–43 (2011)
33. Weizenbaum, J.: ELIZA – a computer program for the study of natural language communication between man and machine. Commun. ACM **9**, 36–45 (1966)
34. Al-Zubaide, H., Issa, A.A.: OntBot: ontology based ChatBot. In: 2011 4th International Symposium on Innovation in Information and Communication Technology, ISIICT 2011, pp. 7–12 (2011)
35. Utama, P., et al.: An end-to-end neural natural language interface for databases. Cornell Univ. Libr. **1**, 1–12 (2018)
36. da Silva, N.M.: RedeR Web: uma plataforma web para organização e análise de redes modulares (2017)
37. Preece, J., Rogers, Y., Sharp, H.: Interaction Design: Beyond Human-Computer Interaction. Wiley, Hoboken (2015)
38. Javahery, H., Seffah, A., Radhakrishnan, T.: Beyond power: making bioinformatics tools user-centered. Commun. ACM **47**, 58–63 (2004)
39. Mirel, B., Wright, Z.: Heuristic evaluations of bioinformatics tools: a development case. In: Jacko, J.A. (ed.) HCI 2009. LNCS, vol. 5610, pp. 329–338. Springer, Heidelberg (2009). https://doi.org/10.1007/978-3-642-02574-7_37
40. Machado, V.S., Paixão-Cortes, W.R., de Souza, O.N., de Campos, M.B.: Decision-making for interactive systems: a case study for teaching and learning in bioinformatics. In: Zaphiris, P., Ioannou, A. (eds.) LCT 2017. LNCS, vol. 10296, pp. 90–109. Springer, Cham (2017). https://doi.org/10.1007/978-3-319-58515-4_8
41. Paixão-Cortes, V.S.M., dos Santos da Silva Tanus, M., Paixão-Cortes, W.R., de Souza, O. N., de Borba Campos, M., Silveira, M.: Usability as the key factor to the design of a web server for the CReF protein structure predictor: the wCReF. Information. **9**, 20 (2018)
42. Pressman, R.S.: Software Engineering. McGraw Hill, Boston (2011)
43. Cybis, W., Betiol, A.H., Faust, R.: Ergonomia e Usabilidade. Novatec (2010)
44. Lemos, M.: Desenvolvimento de workflow científico para bioinformática (2004)
45. Lund, A.: Measuring usability with the use questionnaire. Usability User Exp. Newsl. STC Usability SIG **8**, 3–6 (2001)

Effects of Note-Taking Method on Knowledge Transfer in Inspection Tasks

Mallory C. Stites(✉), Laura E. Matzen, Heidi A. Smartt, and Zoe N. Gastelum

Sandia National Laboratories, Albuquerque, NM, USA
{mcstite, lematze, hasmart, zgastel}@sandia.gov

Abstract. International nuclear safeguards inspectors visit nuclear facilities to assess their compliance with international nonproliferation agreements. Inspectors note whether anything unusual is happening in the facility that might indicate the diversion or misuse of nuclear materials, or anything that changed since the last inspection. They must complete inspections under restrictions imposed by their hosts, regarding both their use of technology or equipment and time allotted. Moreover, because inspections are sometimes completed by different teams months apart, it is crucial that their notes accurately facilitate change detection across a delay. The current study addressed these issues by investigating how note-taking methods (e.g., digital camera, hand-written notes, or their combination) impacted memory in a delayed recall test of a complex visual array. Participants studied four arrays of abstract shapes and industrial objects using a different note-taking method for each, then returned 48–72 h later to complete a memory test using their notes to identify objects changed (e.g., location, material, orientation). Accuracy was highest for both conditions using a camera, followed by hand-written notes alone, and all were better than having no aid. Although the camera-only condition benefitted study times, this benefit was not observed at test, suggesting drawbacks to using just a camera to aid recall. Change type interacted with note-taking method; although certain changes were overall more difficult, the note-taking method used helped mitigate these deficits in performance. Finally, elaborative hand-written notes produced better performance than simple ones, suggesting strategies for individual note-takers to maximize their efficacy in the absence of a digital aid.

Keywords: Knowledge transfer · Visual inspection · Note-taking

1 Introduction

International nuclear safeguards are activities or agreements that provide assurance to the global community that States are using their nuclear technologies for peaceful purposes. International safeguards are designed to detect: the diversion of nuclear material from safeguarded facilities, the misuse of safeguarded facilities for undeclared nuclear purposes, and the development of undeclared facilities for undeclared nuclear purposes. The International Atomic Energy Agency (IAEA) is the agency tasked with verifying safeguards for those countries that have signed safeguards agreements. Verification of these safeguards is achieved by sending inspectors to a facility to

S. Yamamoto and H. Mori (Eds.): HCII 2019, LNCS 11569, pp. 594–612, 2019.
https://doi.org/10.1007/978-3-030-22660-2_44

perform a variety of inspection tasks, including: verifying the integrity of seals placed on monitored items, taking material measurements, and looking for anomalies in a facility that may be indicative of misuse. Inspectors are often limited in the types of note-taking activities they can perform during an inspection (details below), and often face large time delays between the time of inspection and retrieval of the information recorded, either for briefings to team members or return visits to the facility.

As such, IAEA inspectors face a unique set of cognitive and information processing challenges in the recording and transfer of information garnered from field inspections that have not been adequately addressed by extant research literature. In this paper, we describe the cognitive nature of the note-taking tasks performed by inspectors, then note the gaps in the literature on knowledge transfer in a shift-work environment as well as the cognitive science of note-taking. Finally, we detail an empirical study aimed at addressing these gaps, in order to produce recommendations for best practices for note-taking during inspections that will maximize knowledge transfer in IAEA inspectors.

1.1 IAEA Inspection Activities

Specific activities performed by IAEA inspectors range in complexity from relatively straightforward (e.g., checking seal numbers on containers of nuclear materials against lists of seals that should be present; see [1]) to more cognitively complex (e.g., keeping track of their physical location within the facility to verify facility layout is as declared). In addition to completing their circumscribed list of inspection tasks, inspectors must also maintain situational awareness regarding the environment, and make note of anything unusual going on in the facility and/or anything that changed since the last facility visit. This means that inspection notes must be complete enough to enable effective change detection across time delays that could range from several weeks to several months in duration. Moreover, different inspection teams may visit the same facility across time, and so the recorded notes must be thorough enough to transfer this information across people.

The ability to take thorough notes during an inspection is often limited by constraints placed on inspectors during visits. For example, inspectors are often limited by the types of materials they can bring into or take out of the facility. They are always allowed to make notes with pen and paper, but on some occasions, they may be allowed to bring in a digital camera or request for their host to take digital photos that can be transferred to headquarters. Inspectors must often complete their visits in a restricted amount of time because their visits typically require that all facility activities are halted, creating time pressure to complete their activities quickly. These real-world constraints create a complex operational environment in which inspectors must perform high consequence inspection tasks.

1.2 Knowledge Transfer in Shift Work

Knowledge transfer refers to the sharing of knowledge, information, and experiences between people within an organization, and provides a way to capture and maintain records of institutional knowledge accumulated over time [2]. Anytime knowledge is handed off between teams, there is a risk for loss of continuity of knowledge if the handoff is not carried out effectively. As such, much research exists that asks how to effectively transfer knowledge across teams, the bulk of which focuses on the immediate transfer of knowledge been shift workers in a variety of environments, including production [3], medical environments [4], off-shore drilling [5], and nuclear power plants [6]. Enabling more effective knowledge transfer across shifts of workers can more effectively build institutional knowledge, keeping multiple independent groups of workers from trying to independently solve the same problem. More importantly, shift handoffs have been shown to increase the likelihood of accidents [5, 7] and medical errors [8], and so creating better knowledge transfer protocols can lower the risk of potentially life-threatening situations.

Several components of a successful shift handoff have been identified across diverse environments [5–7]. First, face-to-face handoffs have been shown to help establish a shared mental model between incoming and outgoing operators. Successful handoffs are structured and consistent to ensure that information is not missed, and have well-established expectations about the types of information to report, which relate directly to the goals of the task to be performed. Finally, operators should be given as much time as possible to prepare for and conduct handoffs. Several types of high-risk handoffs have been identified that might require even more time or preparation in order to reduce the risk of errors, which include handoffs between experienced and inexperienced operators, as well as those that occur after a long break away from work.

Unfortunately, many of these recommendations cannot be implemented in the case of IAEA safeguards inspectors. For example, although handoffs between inspectors may take place in person, they often take place at IAEA headquarters before facility visits occur. As such, when inspectors access information about previous facility visits while in the field, they must rely extensively on one-way written communications instead of the preferred face-to-face communications. Inspectors are often time-limited while on facility inspections, and so the recommendation that operators are given as much time as possible to prepare for handoffs cannot be implemented. The recommendation that handoffs are clearly structured is not always possible, because inspectors do not have control over the types of note-taking materials they are allowed to carry into the facilities they inspect. Finally, handoffs regarding specific facilities typically occur after a long break away from the facility, which qualifies IAEA inspector handoffs as high-risk.

In the absence of a face-to-face handoff, transfer of knowledge can also occur via boundary objects, which are artifacts that can span the boundary between two distinct groups of workers and can serve as a formalized way to codify relevant knowledge to share between the two groups [9, 10]. In our case, the boundary exists between the inspectors who performed the original inspection and those performing the return inspection, and the notes taken during the original inspection serve as the boundary objects. Although empirical research suggests that knowledge transfer is most successful when the creation of boundary objects is supported by the organization's culture, and when boundary objects are freely available to all workers [3], there is little research into the specific features that boundary objects should contain in order to be effective. As such, one goal of the current study is to identify how IAEA inspectors can create effective boundary objects that will enable the effective and efficient transfer of knowledge to different inspectors across a time delay.

1.3 Cognitive Science of Note-Taking

Research from both the educational psychology literature on note-taking as well as the cognitive psychology literature on memory may be relevant to our question of how to create boundary objects to enable effective and efficient knowledge transfer. These concepts will be reviewed in turn below.

Educational Psychology. The field of educational psychology has a long history on the study of note-taking efficacy for learning and achievement in academic settings (for reviews, see [11, 12]). From this literature, it has been shown that note-taking generally improves students' academic achievement by benefiting two memory processes: encoding (i.e., enables creation of stronger memory traces *at the time of study*) and external storage (i.e., enables recall of forgotten information and forming of new connections between concepts *during review* of notes). However, the bulk of this previous work has focused on classroom settings, in which participants take notes on lectures and are later tested on their memory of the factual and conceptual information presented during the lecture. Some work has examined note-taking strategies outside of the classroom (for reviews, see [13, 14]), although these have also tended to focus on heavily verbal areas, such as note-taking during boardroom meetings, courtroom procedures, or counseling sessions.

Recent work looking at the integration of technology into the classroom may apply to the current question of how to integrate digital recording technologies into inspector note-taking. Mueller and Oppenheimer [15] investigated how laptop use impacted memory for information presented in a lecture. They found that taking notes via laptop resulted in lower memory performance on conceptual questions relative to taking notes by hand, although no differences were found between the two note-taking strategies for factual questions. They postulated that this was because laptops allowed students to record more content from the lecture than writing notes by hand, resulting in a near-verbatim record of the lecture, whereas taking hand-written notes forced students to consolidate concepts before writing them down.

The educational psychology literature on note-taking fails to adequately address the needs of inspectors, namely, how to capture complex visuo-spatial information during facility visits. However, Mueller and Oppenheimer's [15] findings regarding the potential drawbacks of using technology for note-taking may apply, as the current study will investigate whether a similar over-reliance on verbatim capture rather than consolidation of information may be observed when digital cameras are used in note-taking.

Cognitive Psychology. There are also several principles that can be drawn from the cognitive psychology literature on learning and memory that could come into play to evaluate what features might make effective notes. One such concept, the dual-coding theory, posits that verbal and visual (and other nonverbal) information are processed through separate channels in associative memory (for review, see [16]). Work in this domain has shown that concepts that are represented via both verbal and nonverbal associations will be remembered better than those encoded with only one or the other [17] due to the enhanced processing afforded by the dual-channel encoding. Another relevant concept from the memory literature is that of levels of processing [18, 19], which has shown that words that are encoded at a "deeper" level of processing, such as focusing on the semantic meaning of the term, are remembered better than words encoded with a shallower level of processing, such as focusing on its surface characteristics (e.g., case).

Recent work found what has been dubbed the drawing effect, in which words that were studied by drawing a picture of the object described by the word were remembered better at test than words that were studied by simply writing the word down [20]. This finding held even when controlling for effects of elaboration, as writing a list of the object's visual features was less beneficial to memory than drawing a picture of the item. These results support the dual-coding framework, because the words that were drawn at study would have both a verbal and visual memory cue, thus strengthening their memory trace, whereas words that were only written would only have been encoded via the verbal channel.

One limitation of the memory literature in its applicability to the current question is that most memory research uses either lists of words or declarative facts for stimuli, and tends to use short retention intervals (i.e., a few minutes) between study and test. There is thus a clear gap in this literature regarding how to best record information about complex non-verbal stimuli (e.g., facility layout, visual characteristics of a room full of containers) to best enable the transfer of that knowledge either to oneself during a future inspection, or to an entirely different inspector, with a time delay of several months to a year.

1.4 The Current Study

The current study addressed the gaps in the literatures on knowledge transfer and the cognitive science of note-taking, to better understand how these techniques can be applied in a safeguards-relevant environment. We compared the efficacy of different note-taking methods for knowledge transfer on a change detection task after a time delay. In the current study, participants studied four arrays of complex images, and were limited to the types of notes they could take for each array: digital camera only, hand-written notes only, digital camera and hand-written notes, or no aid. Participants were allowed to choose their own strategies for the creation of their hand-written notes —e.g., text-based notes describing the images in prose, visually-based drawing of the images, or some combination—as well as for taking photos of the display, provided that they did not take a photograph that encompassed the entire array simultaneously. They then returned approximately two days later to complete a memory task on the image arrays, during which they could use the notes they took at study. Objects in the array could undergo several types of changes: material, orientation, location within the array, or replacement by a different object, although any one object only underwent a single change (e.g., and object would not change location and orientation).

Our experimental questions of interest were as follows. First, what is the most effective note-taking method for the transfer complex visual knowledge? To answer this question, we investigated how change detection accuracy differed across study conditions, change types, and individual note-taking strategies. Secondly, how does note-taking method impact confidence in one's decision? Given that inspectors do not know the ground truth when recording observations during inspections, it is important to understand the subjective impressions of their efficacy across different note-taking strategies. This could ensure that inspectors come away with a realistic estimation of their efficacy so that they do not unnecessarily trigger additional inspection activities erroneously. Finally, do certain note-taking methods enable more efficient knowledge transfer, as measured by the time to complete the study and test sessions? Given the time restrictions on most safeguards inspections, the amount of time needed to effectively use each note-taking strategy is an important practical consideration.

2 Method

2.1 Participants

Twenty-one participants participated in the study. One participant was excluded due to experimenter error in administering the experimental materials, leaving twenty participants in the final data set (seven females). Mean age was 44 (range: 24–68). All procedures were approved by the Sandia National Laboratories Human Studies Board, and participants gave their informed consent before the session began.

2.2 Materials

Study Images. Materials consisted of computer-generated images of novel industrial looking objects (e.g., antennae, widgets, gears, etc.; see Fig. 1), which were originally created for a machine learning evaluation task. Each object had a baseline image of a default surface material and orientation that could undergo various changes, including changes in lighting, orientation, or surface material properties such as texture. Four different study boards were created, each of which consisted of 40 initial images, for a total of 160 initial images. For the test, 20 items per board were replaced with a different image: four material changes, depicting the same object in the same orientation but with a different surface material; four orientation changes, depicting the same object made of the same material but in a different orientation; six object changes, depicting a totally different object; and, six location changes, in which six original objects rotated locations on the board. This created a total of 56 replacement images, for a total of 216 unique images in the experiment.

Demographics Questionnaire. Participants optionally completed a demographics questionnaire, in which they reported their gender, age, highest degree earned, and whether they had any prior visual search experience, either professionally (e.g., x-ray operator) or non-professionally (e.g., birding, video gaming).

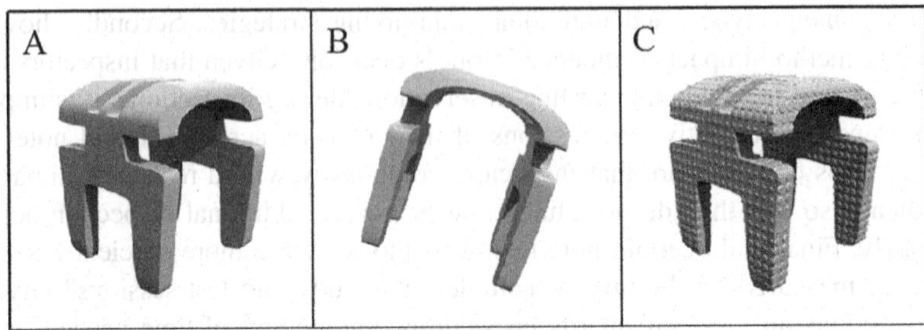

Fig. 1. Example stimuli in default orientation and material (A), with an orientation change (B), and with a material change (C).

2.3 Procedure

Study Session. Each study session began with an overview of the experimental procedure for both the study and test sessions. Participants were instructed that in the study session, their task was to learn the layout and characteristics of several sets of images presented on boards, using one of the note-taking methods allowed. They were also told that when they returned at test, they would be tested on their memory for the image layouts, and that they would be able to use the notes they took at study to help with this task. Participants were not informed of the types of changes they would be looking for at test.

Instructions for the individual note-taking conditions in the study session were as follows. In the camera only condition, participants were told: "You can take photos of the board with the digital camera provided. The only restriction is that you can't take a picture that includes the entire board, but you can take pictures of the individual items, or groups of items together." In the notes only condition, participants were told: "You can take notes in this notebook to help yourself remember the layout of the images. You can use any combination of words or pictures." In the camera + notes condition, participants were told: "You can take photos of the board with the digital camera provided (with the restriction that you can't take a picture that includes the entire board). You can also take notes in the notebook to help yourself remember anything about the layout of the images, or your strategy while taking the pictures." In the no aid condition, participants were told: "For this board, you can only rely on your own memory; you cannot take notes in any way." Participants were allowed to ask questions before the study session began.

The order of note-taking condition was counter-balanced across participants using an incomplete Latin Square design, creating four lists, each with a different order of study conditions. This ensured that each study condition appeared in each ordinal position once and that each study condition followed each other study condition once, to control for order effects. The order of presentation of the four study boards was held constant across participants, while the note-taking condition was counter-balanced as described above, ensuring that each set of images was studied equally often using each note-taking method across participants. Separate one-way between-subjects Analysis of

Variance (ANOVA) conducted on the accuracy data confirmed that there were no effects of list ($F(3,16) = .35$, $p = .79$) nor study board ($F(3,57) = 0.85$, $p = .48$); as such, these counterbalancing factors will not be included in analyses.

Participants were allowed a maximum of 12 min per study condition, although they were allowed to finish earlier if desired, and the length of time taken per study board (in seconds) was recorded by the experimenter. After all four study conditions were completed, participants completed the demographics questionnaire and were provided with a debriefing form. The experimental session lasted no longer than one hour.

Test Session. At the start of the test session, participants were informed that they would be tested on their memory of the image layouts that were studied during the test phase. For each test board, participants were given an 8 × 5 grid (on a standard 8.5″ × 11″ piece of paper), with one square per item on the board and two questions per item: (1) Did the item change? (Y/N), and (2) Are you sure? (Y/N). For each image, participants were instructed to indicate: (1) whether it changed or not (by circling "Y" or "N," respectively), (2) whether they were sure of their choice or not (again, by circling "Y" or "N," respectively), and (3) if they reported a change, the nature of the change (via open-ended response). Participants were shown a table that demonstrated an example of each of the four possible change types: material, orientation, location, or replacement. They were allowed to refer to this table during the test session. Participants were also allowed to refer to the notes and/or digital images that they took for each board during the study session. Test boards were viewed in the same order that they were studied. Participants were allowed a maximum of 12 min to complete each board, although they could choose to take less time if desired, and the time to complete each board (in seconds) was recorded by the experimenter.

Scoring. Participants received multiple scores per item. Overall accuracy was converted to binary data, in which participants received a score of 1 if they answered correctly as to whether or not the item changed, and a 0 if they answered incorrectly. For change type accuracy, participants received a score of 1 if they correctly identified the change type, a score of .5 if they responded "object" change to a location change (because a location change could be misinterpreted as an object change if only the object's original location was considered and the participant failed to see where on the board the object moved to) or for a small number of objects to which multiple participants made the same error (e.g., if an orientation change made the object look so different such that multiple participants mistook it for a new object), and a score of 0 if they reported the incorrect change type. The confidence data was also converted to a numeric value, where a "yes" response was scored as a 1 and a "no" response was scored as 0.

3 Results

3.1 Recognition Performance by Study Condition and Change Type

To answer our main experimental question of whether study condition and item change type interacted to impact accuracy, we calculated the d' statistic. The d' statistic is a measure of target discriminability, which compares the proportion of true hits and false alarms to measure a participant's ability to accurately discriminate targets (i.e., items that changed) from non-targets (i.e., items that did not change). Larger *d'* values indicated that a subject frequently responded "change" to changed items and very rarely to non-changed items, and thus were able to successfully discriminate targets from non-targets. Conversely, lower *d'* values indicated that subjects frequently responded "no change" to changed items and/or "change" to non-changed items, and thus were unable to discriminate targets from non-targets. The *d'* scores were calculated separately for each participant for each combination of study condition and item change type, by comparing the hit rate for each change type relative to the false alarm rate for the non-changed items within that study condition.

Scores were analyzed using a two-way within-subjects ANOVA, with the factors of study condition (4: camera only, camera + notes, notes only, and no aid) and change type (4: location, material, object, and orientation). Results showed main effect of study condition ($F(3,57) = 43.19$, $p < .05$) and change type ($F(3,57) = 24.35$, $p < .05$), as well as a significant interaction ($F(9,171) = 8.04$, $p < .05$). Means for each condition are shown in Fig. 2. The main effect of study condition indicated that, in general, the camera only and camera + notes conditions had the highest *d'* scores across all change conditions, followed by the notes only condition, and finally, the no aid condition. The main effect of change type reflected the fact that *d'* was highest for location and object changes, followed by orientation changes, with material changes showing the lowest overall *d'* scores. However, both of these main effects were qualified by their significant two-way interaction.

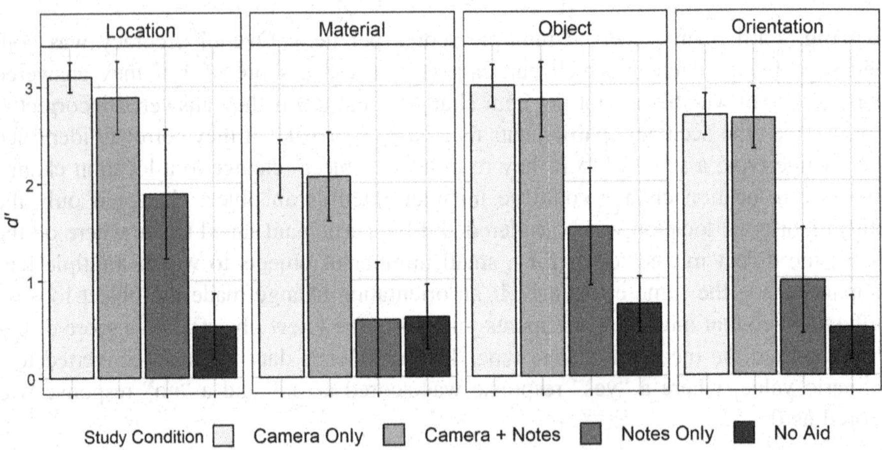

Fig. 2. Bars show the *d'* score for each study condition and item change type. Errors bars represent 95% confidence intervals around the mean.

Given the significant interaction, follow-up t-tests were conducted to compare the study conditions within each change type, to understand whether some study methods produced better knowledge transfer for certain changes. All pairwise t-tests were conducted using the Holm correction to control the family-wise Type I error rate [21], implemented by use of the "p.adjust" command in the R statistical computing environment [22]. Across all four change types, the camera only and camera + notes conditions had significantly higher *d'* than both the notes only and no aid conditions (all $t(19) > |3.66|$, $p < .05$) but did not differ from one another (all $t(19) < |1.06|$, $p > .30$). However, the notes only condition showed significantly higher *d'* than the no aid condition for location and object changes (all $t(19) > |2.75|$, $p < .05$), but did not differ from the no aid condition for either material or orientation changes (all $t(19) < |1.54|$, $p > .28$). This finding suggests that hand-written notes alone were better than no study aid in transferring gross information about the image array, like the identity and overall layout of objects, but were not effective for conveying more subtle changes, like the object's material or orientation.

3.2 Effects of Note-Taking Strategy

In the camera + notes and notes only conditions, participants were free to choose their strategy for taking hand-written notes. We will explore the hypothesis that their self-selected note-taking strategy may have impacted their *d'* scores across change types.

Camera + Notes Condition. For this analysis, we started by binning participants into categories based on the type of hand-written notes they took. These categories included various combinations of photo layout descriptions (i.e., a diagram of which images in the display each photo captured), verbal descriptions of the objects, and hand-drawn pictures of the objects. Table 1 lists the number of participants who self-selected into each note-taking strategy, as well as the average *d'* for each group. There was no significant effect of note type within the camera + notes condition ($F(6,13) = 0.33$, $p = .91$). However, there was a trend such that participants who recorded multiple types of information in their notes (e.g., photo layout + verbal description) performed better than participants who recorded only a single information type.

Table 1. The table lists *d'* scores for each participant-selected note-taking strategy within the Camera + Notes and Notes only study conditions.

Study condition	Note-taking strategy	N	*d'*	Standard deviation
Camera + Notes	Photo layout	8	2.76	0.56
	Photo layout + drawings	2	2.78	0.08
	Photo layout + verbal descriptions	1	3.12	NA
	Drawings + verbal	1	2.94	NA
	Drawings only	1	2.46	NA
	Verbal only	6	2.21	1.31
	None	1	2.81	NA
Notes only	Drawings + verbal	9	1.85	0.68
	Drawings only	8	1.12	0.74
	Verbal only	3	−0.23	2.65

Notes Only Condition. Participants' note-taking strategies in the notes-only condition were binned into three categories: combined hand-drawn pictures and verbal descriptions of the images, hand-drawn pictures only, and verbal descriptions of the objects only. We conducted an exploratory analysis to assess whether *d'* scores differed across these note-taking conditions. A one-way between-subjects ANOVA revealed a significant effect of note type ($F(2,17) = 3.91$, $p < .05$). As can be seen in Fig. 3, this effect reflected the fact that *d'* scores were highest for participants whose notes combined drawings and verbal information, followed by drawings only, with verbal notes alone producing the lowest *d'* scores. This suggests that taking more elaborative notes that included information across both verbal and visual channels (i.e., both drawing pictures *and* writing verbal descriptions) led to better recall than only using a single type of encoding (i.e., either drawings *or* verbal descriptions).

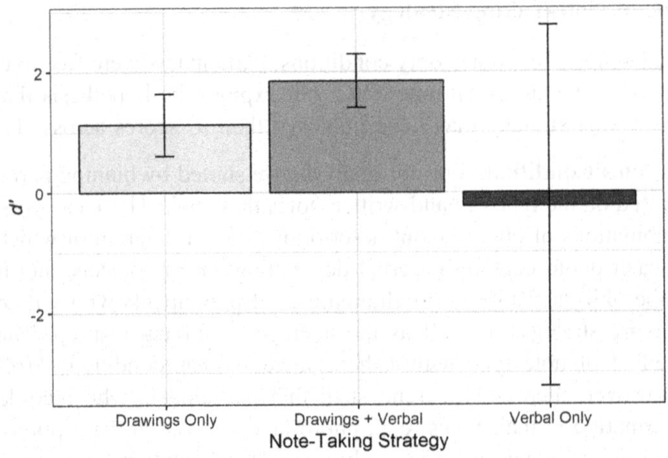

Fig. 3. The figure shows *d'* scores in the notes only study condition for each participant-selected note-taking strategy. Error bars represent 95% confidence intervals around the mean.

3.3 Change Type Accuracy

We next asked whether accuracy for identifying an item's change type differed across study conditions. This analysis only included data for items that changed *and* for which the participant correctly reported that a change took place, which comprised 1129 total observations (35% of the original dataset). One participant was excluded from this analysis due to a failure to answer any change items correctly in one condition. Change accuracy data was submitted to a one-way within-subjects ANOVA with the factor of study condition, which revealed a significant main effect of study condition ($F(3,54) = 12.55$, $p < .05$). Mean values are shown in Fig. 4. Follow-up t-tests tested all pairwise comparisons, to ask which conditions differed from each other in terms of correctly identifying the type of change. Accuracy was numerically highest for the camera + notes condition, which differed significantly from the notes only and no aid conditions (all $t(18) > |4.66|$, $p < .05$), but not from the camera only condition

($t(18) = .98$, $p = .34$). The camera only condition also did not differ from the notes only condition ($t(18) = 1.61$, $p = .25$), although it was significantly better than the no aid condition ($t(18) = 3.97$, $p < .05$). Finally, the notes only condition was significantly better than the no aid condition ($t(18) = 2.83$, $p < .05$). This pattern of findings suggests that the use of both hand-written and digital notes provided the greatest benefit in terms of transferring information about the *type* of change an item underwent (especially compared to notes alone), while the camera only and notes only conditions were not statistically different from each other.

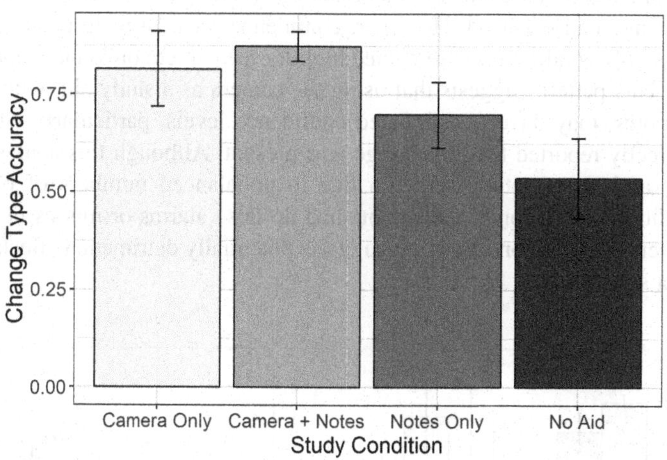

Fig. 4. Change type accuracy by study condition. Error bars are 95% confidence intervals around the mean.

3.4 Confidence

Participants reported whether or not they were sure of their answer for each item; this response was converted to a numeric value (Sure = 1, Not Sure = 0) and averaged for each participant in each study condition (see Table 2). To investigate whether confidence differed across study conditions, we submitted this data to a one-way within-subjects ANOVA with the factor of study condition, which found a significant effect ($F(3,57) = 54.67$, $p < .05$). Follow-up t-tests found that all conditions differed from one another (all $t(19) > |4.13|$, $p < .05$), except for camera only and camera + notes which were statistically indistinguishable ($t(19) = -.25$, $p = .81$). This finding shows the same pattern as overall *d'* scores did, indicating that participants had relatively good metacognition insofar as recognizing that their memory was best in the camera only and camera + notes conditions.

In an exploratory analysis, we asked whether confidence differed across different accuracy types across study conditions—that is, whether confidence differed for hits, correct rejections, false alarms, or misses. As seen in Fig. 5, confidence levels for hits were very similar for the three note-taking conditions (although slightly lower for the notes only condition). Confidence for correct rejections dropped for the notes only

Table 2. Confidence ratings for correct and incorrect trials across each study condition.

Study condition	Confidence rating	Standard deviation
Camera only	0.91	0.18
Camera + Notes	0.90	0.20
Notes only	0.64	0.26
No aid	0.30	0.22

condition, indicating that using a camera enabled participants to more confidently say when no change had occurred. However, confidence for misses dropped substantially for the notes only condition, but remained high for the camera only and camera + notes conditions. This pattern suggests that using the camera as a study aid, with or without additional notes, may have over-inflated confidence levels, particularly when participants incorrectly reported that no change was present. Although this analysis was just exploratory and no statistics were run due to unbalanced numbers of observations across conditions (e.g., some participants had no false alarms or misses in the camera only or camera + notes conditions), it suggests potentially detrimental effects of using a camera as a study aid.

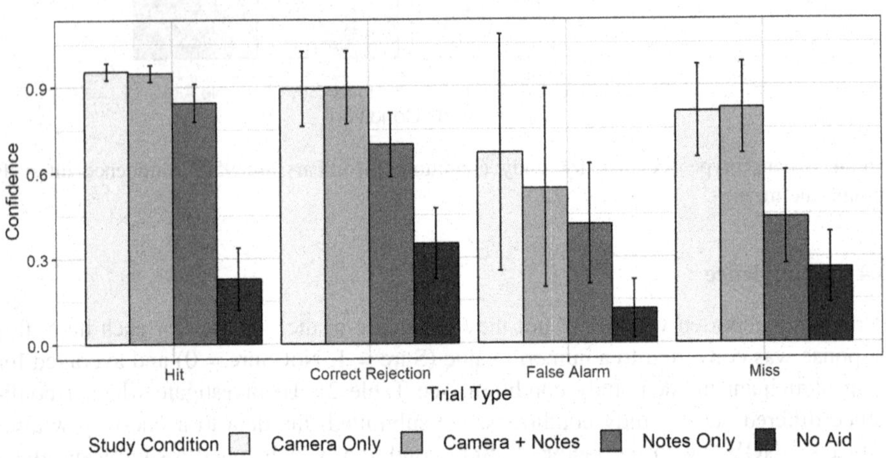

Fig. 5. Mean confidence ratings across study conditions, split by item accuracy. Errors bars represent 95% confidence intervals around the mean.

3.5 Response Times

Next, we examined whether the time that participants took either at study or at test differed by study condition. Recall that both study and test times were capped at 12 min (or 720 s), but participants could choose to take less time if desired.

Study Time. Across the four study conditions, study times were longest in the notes only condition, followed by the no aid condition, camera + notes, and finally the camera only condition (see Fig. 6). A one-way within-subjects ANOVA with the factor of study condition found a significant effect of condition, $F(3,57) = 28.50$, $p < .05$. Follow-up t-tests comparing each condition to each other showed that all conditions differed significantly from each other (all $t(19) > |3.19|$, $p < .05$), except for camera + notes and the no aid comparison ($t(19) = 0.89$, $p = 0.38$). The camera + notes took longer than the camera only condition, but did not produce any general benefits to knowledge transfer beyond a numerically higher ability to correctly detect an item's change type.

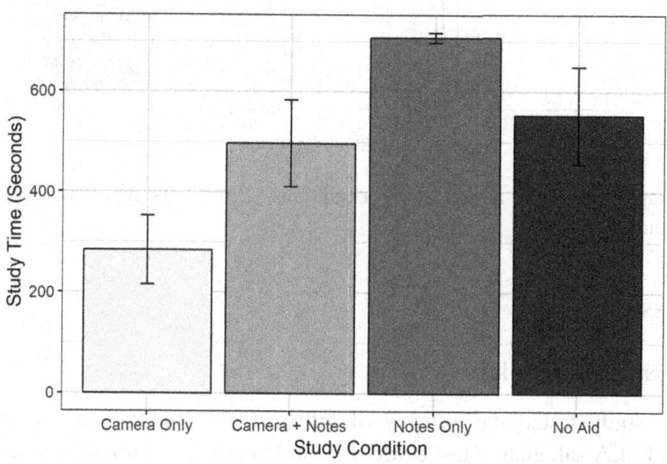

Fig. 6. Average study time across conditions. Errors bars represent 95% confidence intervals around the mean.

Test Time. Across the four conditions, test times were longest for the camera + notes condition, followed by camera only, notes only, and finally, the no aid condition (see Fig. 7). A one-way within-subjects ANOVA with the factor of study condition revealed a significant effect of condition, $F(3,57) = 5.28$, $p < .05$. Follow-up t-tests of all pairwise comparisons found that the only significant difference was between the camera + notes and no aid conditions ($t(19) = -3.65$, $p < .05$). There were, however, marginal differences between the camera + notes and the notes only conditions ($t(19) = -2.49$, $p = .09$), as well as between the camera only and no aid conditions ($t(19) = -2.65$, $p = .08$). Interestingly, the large benefit in study times observed for the camera only condition was not observed at test, suggesting that any benefits this condition may have conferred in ease of note-taking at study may have been washed out by the difficulty of accessing and using photos at test.

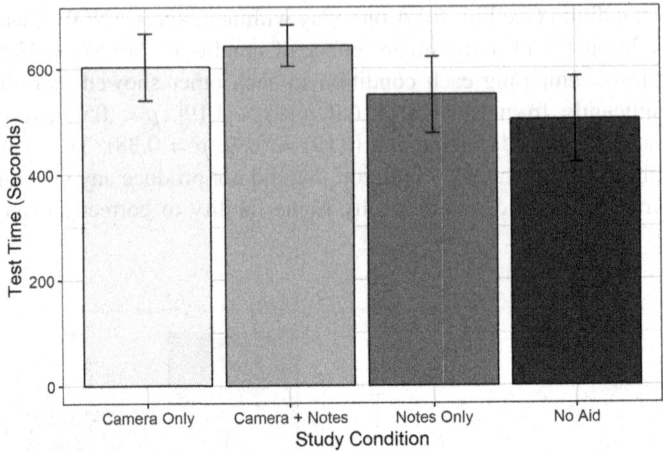

Fig. 7. Average test times across study conditions. Error bars represent 95% confidence intervals around the mean.

4 Discussion

4.1 Experimental Findings

The current study tested the efficacy of different note-taking methods that may be available to IAEA safeguards inspectors to enable knowledge transfer about a complex visual array. Our goal was to fill gaps in the literature on both knowledge transfer methods and the cognitive science of note-taking to make recommendations to inspectors on how best to utilize available note-taking methods to create boundary objects that enable effective and efficient knowledge transfer across a time delay.

Results showed that overall, the camera only and camera + notes study conditions produced the highest levels of knowledge transfer, as evidenced by their high *d'* scores, which did not differ from each other in any comparison. The notes only condition was better than the no aid condition at transferring knowledge about gross changes in the layout of images and enabled participants to notice object and location changes better, but no differences were observed between the two conditions for relaying the more subtle material and orientation changes.

When participants were only allowed to make hand-written notes, we observed a relationship between a participant's note-taking strategy and *d'* scores, such that participants who used more elaborative, dual-channel encoding strategies for their written notes (i.e., used drawings and verbal descriptions) had the highest *d'* scores, relative to participants who only made drawings or verbal descriptions. However, this comparison was made on a post-hoc basis, and could have been driven either by the elaboration effect at encoding [12] or increased ease of recall at test [11]. Regardless, it suggests that in situations in which hand-written notes are the only available study tool, recording the information in multiple ways (i.e., both visually and verbally) may be most beneficial to knowledge transfer, replicating findings from the basic memory literature in support of the dual-coding theory [16, 17].

Next, we considered what factors impacted a participant's ability to correctly detect the *type* of change an item underwent. In this analysis, the camera + notes condition had the numerically highest performance and was significantly higher than the notes only condition (neither of which differed from the camera only condition). This finding provided weak evidence that the camera + notes condition may have produced the best change-type accuracy, and moreover, highlighted a potential drawback of the camera only condition. One mechanism that may help explain this trend could be participant's over-reliance on the verbatim capture of images in the camera only condition, instead of taking the time to more deeply process and consolidate the information into their own words in order to make a hand-written note about it, as was required by both the camera + notes and the notes only conditions. This finding is similar to the over-reliance on verbatim capture when students take lecture notes on a laptop versus by hand, as observed by Mueller and Oppenheimer [15], and points to a more general drawback of technology usage in note-taking.

Unsurprisingly, the confidence data revealed that participants were most confident in their choices in the camera only and camera + notes conditions, less so in the notes only condition, and least confident in the no aid condition. However, exploratory findings showed that the use of a digital camera may have caused participants to be over-confident on incorrect trials, especially those in which they missed a change that was present.

Finally, when study and test times were considered, we found that the camera only condition had the shortest study times, but that this benefit was not present for test times. In other words, even though taking notes with the camera only was much faster than for the camera + notes condition, using the digital camera alone did not save people time at test. Anecdotally, participants often complained aloud about the difficulty of using the digital camera at test, and many appeared to struggle with the device. As such, the benefits of the camera only condition may have been outweighed by the difficulty of using the camera alone at test.

4.2 Recommendations for the Safeguards Domain

Based on our experimental findings, we would recommend that safeguards inspectors utilize a digital camera to take photos during inspections, if the option is available to do so. However, if time allows, we would recommend that inspectors make hand-written notes as well. This recommendation is based on the findings that the camera + notes condition provided at least a numeric benefit for identifying the type of change that took place relative to the camera only condition (and was significantly better than notes alone), produced test times that were equal to the camera only condition, and anecdotally reduced participant frustration at test. It is important to note that although the camera only condition elicited the shortest study times in the current experiment, the use of a camera may actually increase inspection time in the field, due to the need to obtain review and approval of photos taken in the facility.

Although no significant differences were observed in the efficacy of the type of hand-written notes that accompanied digital photos, trends in our data suggested the most effective notes both encoded information about the photo layout *and* elaborated on the images in some way, either through verbal descriptions or drawings. However, inspectors using a digital camera should be warned that they may be over-confident in their answers, especially regarding missed changes. Given the risks in the safeguards domain associated with missed targets, we would advise that inspectors use digital cameras with caution and take steps to combat their over-confidence, for example, confer with another inspector to confirm their conclusions.

If inspectors are only allowed to make hand-written notes during inspections, our findings show that it is best to take elaborative notes, as the highest d' performance was observed for participants whose notes recorded aspects of the objects in the array in multiple ways (i.e., visually and verbally). Inspectors using hand-written notes only should be warned that these notes may be less effective at transferring knowledge regarding certain types of changes, like subtle changes about surface material characteristics or object orientation. If these types of changes are critical to note, inspectors may need to put extra care into recording these details to ensure that they are accurately recorded.

4.3 Caveats and Future Work

There were several important differences to note between our experimental paradigm and an actual safeguards inspection that point to the need for future work in this domain.

First, our participant population did not include professional inspectors, who may have their own specialized strategies and domain expertise that could increase the efficacy of their notes. Future work could test whether real inspectors use different strategies or show different patterns of effects across note-taking conditions.

Next, the experimental task was necessarily simpler than real inspection activities, both in terms of the stimuli used and the lack of concurrent inspection tasks. Future work could test the efficacy of note-taking strategies during a simulated facility inspection, to understand how the other tasks performed during inspections (e.g., checking lists of seals, spatial navigation) may interfere or interact with note-taking activities. For example, we might predict that the combined camera and notes condition would provide a bigger benefit when inspectors are moving between different locations in a facility, like they would during real inspections, because it could help offload the memory demands of keeping track of where in the facility the digital photos were taken.

Our participants experienced a shorter time delay between study and test than those experienced by IAEA inspectors, which may have caused higher performance at test than would be expected after a longer delay. To make more practical recommendations for safeguards inspectors, future work should include longer delays between exposure and test to understand if the same principles for effective note-taking hold across delays of weeks or even months.

Finally, participants in our study always used their own complete set of notes and photos at test, whereas in real inspections, the inspector may not be able to take their own digital photos, or their complete set of photos may not be approved for release by the facility's review and approval process. Moreover, this study cannot address how well the notes could transfer knowledge to a different person who was not exposed to the study environment. As such, future work should test how to best integrate photos taken by someone else (e.g., the facility host) into one's own notes to maximize their effectiveness for knowledge transfer. Additionally, future work should address which aspects of notes increase their utility as boundary objects to transfer information to a different inspector. The inclusion of these variations could reduce or eliminate the likelihood that effects observed as test were due to enhanced encoding, and thus would provide more pure tests of the ability of the notes alone at transferring knowledge.

Acknowledgements. Sandia National Laboratories is a multimission laboratory managed and operated by National Technology and Engineering Solutions of Sandia, LLC, a wholly owned subsidiary of Honeywell International Inc., for the U.S. Department of Energy's National Nuclear Security Administration under contract DE-NA0003525. SAND2019-1164 C.

The authors would like to thank the IARPA MICrONS Project for generously providing the stimulus images.

References

1. Gastelum, Z., Matzen, L., Stites, M., Smartt, H.: Cognitive science evaluation of safeguards inspector list comparison activities using human performance testing. In: Proceedings of the 59th Annual Institute of Nuclear Materials Management (INMM) 59th Meeting, Baltimore, MD (2018)
2. Argote, L., Ingram, P.: Knowledge transfer: a basis for competitive advantage in firms. Organ. Behav. Hum. Decis. Process. **82**, 150–169 (2000)
3. Bosua, R., Venkitachalam, K.: Fostering knowledge transfer and learning in shift work environments. Knowl. Process Manag. **22**, 22–33 (2015)
4. Kerr, M.: A qualitative study of shift handover practice and function from a socio-technical perspective. J. Adv. Nurs. **37**, 125–145 (2002)
5. Lardner, R.: Effective shift handover: a literature review. Offshore Technology Report – Health and Safety Executive OTO (1996)
6. Patterson, E., Roth, E., Woods, D., Chow, R., Gomes, J.: Handoff strategies in settings with high consequences for failure: lessons for health care operations. Int. J. Qual. Health Care **16** (2), 125–132 (2004)
7. Wilkinson, J., Lardner, R.: Pass it on! Revisiting shift handover after Buncefield. Loss Prev. Bull. **229**, 25–32 (2013)
8. Cook, R., Woods, D., Miller, C.: A tale of two stories: contrasting views of patient safety. National Health Care Safety Council of the National Patient Safety Foundation at the AMA (1998)
9. Star, S., Griesemer, J.: Institutional ecology, 'translations' and boundary objects: amateurs and professionals in Berkeley's Museum of Vertebrate Zoology. Soc. Stud. Sci. **19**(3), 387–420 (1989)
10. Trompette, P., Vinck, D.: Revisiting the notion of boundary object. Revue d'Anthropologie des Connaissances **3**, 3–25 (2009)
11. Kiewra, K.: A review of note-taking: the encoding-storage paradigm and beyond. Educ. Psychol. Rev. **1**(2), 147–172 (1989)
12. Kobayashi, K.: What limits the encoding effect of note-taking? A meta-analytic examination. Contemp. Educ. Psychol. **30**, 242–262 (2005)
13. Hartley, J.: Notetaking in non-academic settings: a review. Appl. Cogn. Psychol. **16**, 559–574 (2002)

14. Mueller, P., Oppenheimer, D.: Technology and note-taking in the classroom, boardroom, hospital room, and courtroom. Trends Neurosci. Educ. **5**, 139–145 (2016)
15. Mueller, P., Oppenheimer, D.: The pen is mightier than the keyboard: advantages of longhand over laptop note taking. Psychol. Sci. **25**(6), 1159–1168 (2014)
16. Paivio, A.: Dual coding theory: retrospect and current status. Can. J. Psychol. **45**(3), 255–287 (1991)
17. Mayer, R., Anderson, R.: The instructive animation: helping students build connections between words and pictures in multimedia learning. J. Educ. Psychol. **84**(4), 444–452 (1992)
18. Craik, F., Lockhart, R.: Levels of processing: a framework for memory research. J. Verbal Learn. Verbal Behav. **11**(6), 671–684 (1972)
19. Craik, F.: Levels of processing: past, present… and future? Memory **19**(5/6), 305–318 (2002)
20. Wammes, J., Meade, M., Fernandes, M.: The drawing effect: evidence for reliable and robust memory effect in free recall. Q. J. Exp. Psychol. **69**(9), 1752–1776 (2016)
21. Holm, S.: A simple sequentially rejective multiple test procedure. Scand. J. Stat. **6**(2), 65–70 (1979)
22. R Core Team: R: a language environment for statistical computing. R Foundation for Statistical Computing, Vienna, Austria (2017). https://www.R-project.org/

Optimal Range of Information Quantity for Decision Making

Wenzhe Tang[1,2], Shanguang Chen[1], Chengqi Xue[1(✉)], Bo Li[2], Bingzheng Shi[3], and Yafeng Niu[1,2]

[1] School of Mechanical Engineering, Southeast University, Nanjing 211189, China
ipd_xcq@seu.edu.cn

[2] Science and Technology on Electro-optic Control Laboratory, Luoyang 471023, China

[3] Shanghai Academy of Spaceflight Technology, Shanghai 201109, China

Abstract. Information quantity is an important factor in decision making, but the relationship between them in digital interface is still unclear. This paper presents a study on the range of information quantity that is most suitable for decision making in digital interface of complex information systems. Interface image stimuli of nuclear power plant with linear change in image entropy are presented to subjects in a decision-making task. Subjects are required to make proper decision by pressing corresponding keys on the keyboard when an abnormal value appears. Results show that interfaces with image entropy between 0.4 and 0.6 have higher decision efficiency than other ranges. The decision load increases as the quantity of information increases. And different genders show differences, females prefer lower information quantity (0.4 to 0.6) and males prefer higher information quantity (0.4 to 1.2). These findings can be used to quickly control the quality of interfaces at the early stage of design and evaluate interfaces in an efficient way.

Keywords: Complex information system · Digital interface · Image entropy · Decision making · Eye tracking

1 Introduction

In the Digital Era, digital interface has played an important role in many important fields of civilian applications and national defense. For example, in nuclear power plant control room, digital interface is the main way for operators to obtain information and make response. The main task of the operator is to make decisions based on information. Some scholars have studied the impact of information on decision making. Kevin found that information can affect customers decision making through two components, quality and quantity. High quality improved decision effectiveness while high quantity decreased decision effectiveness [1]. Nicholas found that a structural approach such as information theory can better predict information overload [2]. However, few studies focus on digital interface, the relationship between information and decision making in digital interface still remains unknown.

S. Yamamoto and H. Mori (Eds.): HCII 2019, LNCS 11569, pp. 613–623, 2019.
https://doi.org/10.1007/978-3-030-22660-2_45

Among the many factors affecting information, quantity is the most basic and most important one. There are many ways to measure information quantity. One of the most efficient measurement methods is information entropy [3–5]. Image entropy, which is the amount of average information in the image. Pixels located at different positions in the image have different gradations, and image entropy is expressed as the average number of bits of the set of gray levels of an image, the same applies to static interfaces. The image entropy can be expressed by the formula as shown in Eq. (1):

$$H = -\sum_{i=1}^{L} p_i \log_2 p_i \tag{1}$$

Decision making is the main task for complex information system operators. For example, nuclear power plant operators need to switch the button accordingly when indicators reach a critical threshold [6]. Fighter pilot need to decide when to engage or escape and which tactic to use [7]. Making right decisions is the fundamental guarantee for the safety of operators and facilities.

A large amount of data and high complexity in the digital interface of complex information systems poses great challenges to users' decision making. Providing appropriate information to help user make decision is an important and promising research topic. We aim to find the image entropy limit value suitable for user's decision-making and provide effective reference and new evidence for the design and evaluation of complex information system interface.

2 Methodology

2.1 Materials

The experimental materials were a series of interfaces with linearly increasing information quantity which were designed according to the real display interface of nuclear power plant, as shown in Fig. 1. There were ten information quantity levels in the experimental materials, the image entropy of each level was proportionally increased, from 0.2 to 2.0 with an interval of 0.2. In order to facilitate the experimental record, the interface images were named as information quantity 1 to 10, the larger the number, the higher the entropy, as shown in Table 1.

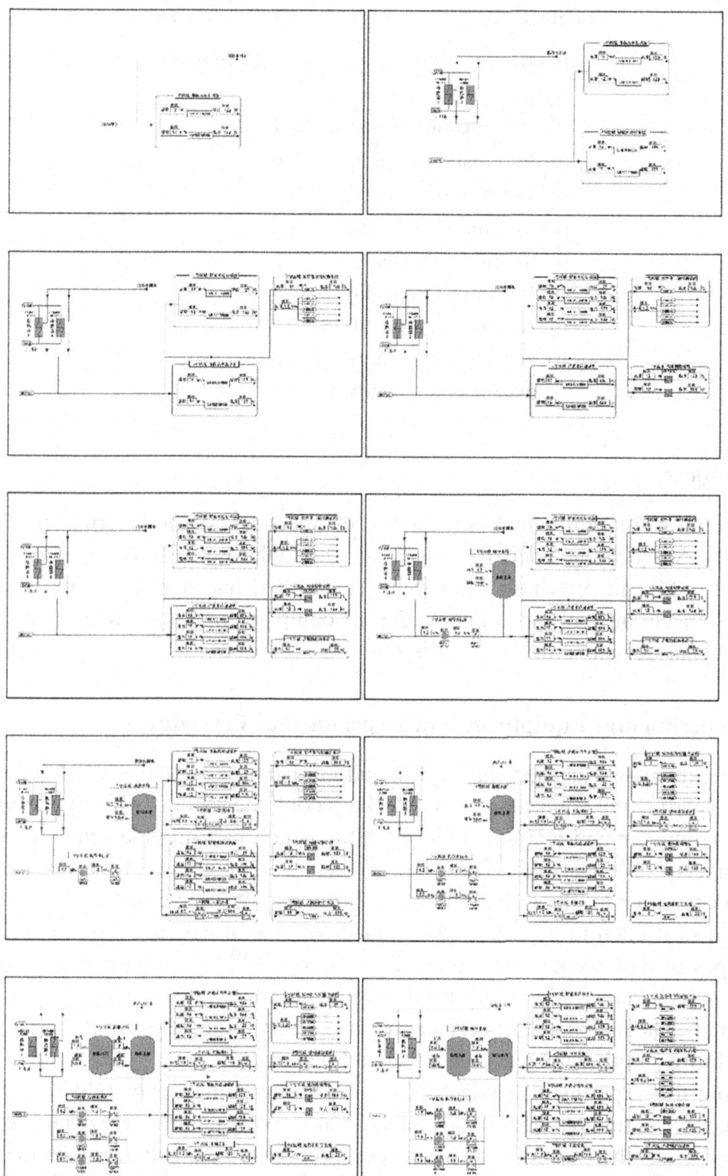

Fig. 1. Experiment interfaces with ten information quantity levels

Table 1. Image entropy of experiment interfaces

Interface	Image entropy
(a) Information quantity 1	0.2
(b) Information quantity 2	0.4
(c) Information quantity 3	0.6
(d) Information quantity 4	0.8
(e) Information quantity 5	1.0
(f) Information quantity 6	1.2
(g) Information quantity 7	1.4
(h) Information quantity 8	1.6
(i) Information quantity 9	1.8
(j) Information quantity 10	2.0

2.2 Subjects

20 subjects were enrolled from school of mechanical engineering in Southeast University. Subjects included 10 males and 10 females between the ages of 20 and 30 years (M = 24), all of whom were right handed and had normal vision or corrected vision. Subjects all had basic knowledge of computer operation and were trained to make rational decisions in the experiment.

2.3 Experimental Equipment and Experimental Procedures

The experiment was carried out in a soundproof lab under the normal lighting condition. Experimental equipment was a desktop computer and a Tobii Eye Tracker. The desktop computer had a 23-in. LCD monitor which can provide required resolution (1920 pixels * 1080 pixels). Tobii Eye Tracker was mounted at the bottom edge of computer monitor to obtain the correct recording position and angle.

The data needed to be collected included behavioral data and eye movement data. Both types of data were collected by Tobii Studio which is a supporting software of Tobii Eye Tracker. Tobii Studio needed to be installed on the computer in advance. Behavioral data included the correct rate and decision-making time. Eye movement data included pupil diameter, gaze plots and heatmaps.

Before the experiment, subject was asked to keep their eyes 620–660 mm away from the screen and both horizontal and vertical viewing angles were controlled in 2.3°. The subject was then asked to move his eyes to perform the software calibration. After the software calibration was successful, the experiment could be carried out.

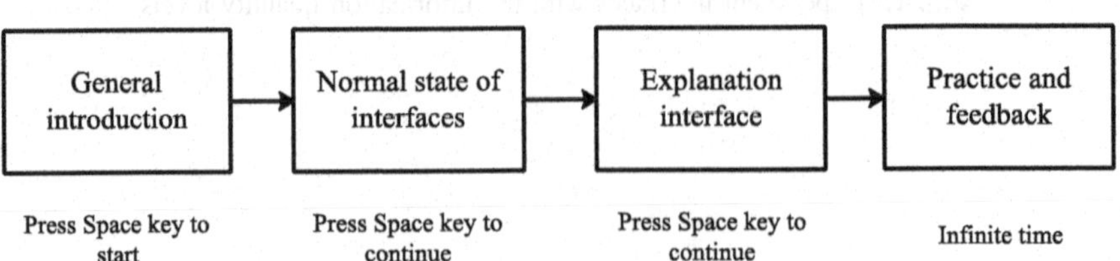

Fig. 2. Experimental flow chart: Learning part

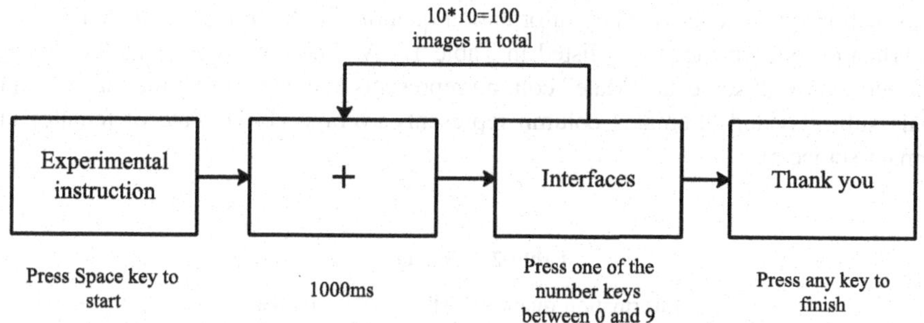

Fig. 3. Experimental flow chart: Decision-making part

The experimental tasks were divided into two parts: learning part and decision-making part. The learning part allowed subjects to achieve the level of operation required for the experiment, primarily through explanations, exercises, and feedback. The learning part began with the general introduction. After the Space key was pressed, the interface would display the normal state of the 10 interfaces of different information quantity in turn. Subjects needed to learn and remember the normal state of each interface. Then press the Space key to continue. The explanation interface would display typical abnormal values and show corresponding decision-making methods. After that came the practice, the practice would provide feedback to help subjects familiar with the operation, the learning part had no time limit. The flow chart is shown in Fig. 2.

The decision-making part was the main part of the experiment, and this part began with the experimental instruction. After the Space key was pressed, the visual guidance center appeared in the center of the screen for 1000 ms. Then subject needed to observe whether the data such as flow rate and temperature in the presented interface was normal, if abnormal data was found, press the corresponding number in the number pad. The number keys 0–9 represented 10 areas in the interface, and the subject decided which area to select by pressing the corresponding number key. Interfaces with different information quantity appeared randomly in the experiment to eliminate the influence of image changes on the subject. The flow chart is shown in Fig. 3.

The main purpose of the experiment is to study the impact of interface information quantity on user's decision-making. By analyzing user's eye movement data such as pupil diameter, gaze plots and heatmaps, the efficiency and load difference of decision making under different image entropy interfaces are explored, and the influence of interface information quantity on decision making is obtained.

3 Results

3.1 Behavioral Data

Table 2 shows the correct rate of decision-making by subjects under different information quantity levels. The correct rate is calculated by dividing the number of interfaces that are correctly responded by the total number of interfaces at the same information quantity level. The "Information quantity" column represents ten kinds of information quantity levels as listed in Table 1. "All" column represents the average correct rate of all subjects. "Male" column represents average correct rate of males (10 male subjects) and "Female" column represents average correct rate of females (10 female subjects).

Table 2. Correct rate

Information quantity	All	Male	Female
1	0.95	0.94	0.96
2	0.96	0.95	0.97
3	0.97	1	0.94
4	0.94	0.93	0.95
5	0.925	0.9	0.95
6	0.955	0.99	0.92
7	0.91	0.92	0.9
8	0.945	0.95	0.94
9	0.95	0.94	0.96
10	0.945	0.94	0.95

Table 3 shows the decision-making time of subjects under different information quantity levels. Time is presented in seconds. The decision-making time is calculated from the time when gaze point enters AOI (Areas of Interest) which is an area containing abnormal value on the interface until the keyboard button is pressed. "All" column represents the average time of all subjects. "Male" column represents average time of males (10 male subjects) and "Female" column represents average time of females (10 female subjects).

Table 3. Decision-making time (s)

Information quantity	All	Male	Female
1	0.59725659	0.68066389	0.49784127
2	0.51638767	0.59431508	0.41911905
3	0.50312212	0.59631587	0.40157143
4	0.57419478	0.63018056	0.53307143
5	0.49852952	0.51386667	0.49189484
6	0.56476807	0.61492778	0.5123381
7	0.56639999	0.64290437	0.49986786
8	0.67666863	0.80490397	0.5713877
9	0.6207059	0.68601389	0.55969762
10	0.75856422	0.82981984	0.67892937

Decision efficiency is defined as the ratio of correct rate to decision-making time. As a comprehensive indicator of decision making, the higher the decision efficiency, the better the quality of decision-making. The decision efficiency is calculated by dividing the value in Table 2 by the corresponding value in Table 3, the data is represented by a line graph as shown in Fig. 4. As can be seen from the figure, the decision-making efficiency starts to rise, reaches the maximum at the information quantity level 3, and then gradually decreases. Male and female subjects show differences.

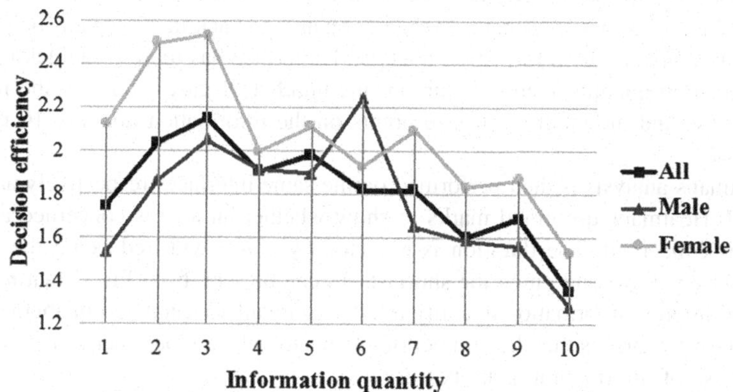

Fig. 4. Relationship between information quantity change and decision efficiency

3.2 Eye Movement Data

The change of pupil diameter is calculated from the maximum value of pupil diameter minus the minimum value. The change of pupil diameter reflects subject's decision load. The greater the change, the higher the decision load. The pupil diameter changes at each information quantity level were represented by a line graph as shown in Fig. 5.

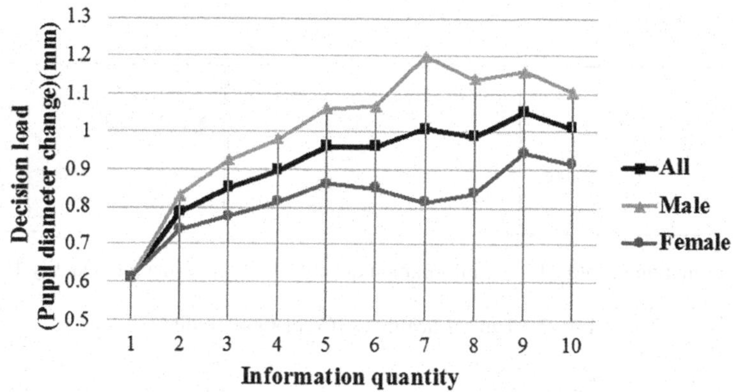

Fig. 5. Relationship between information quantity change and pupil diameter change

The decision-making load increases with the increase of information quantity generally. At the information quantity level 7, male subjects have a big increase in the value while female subjects have a drop in the value.

Gaze plots analysis is performed on the interfaces with information quantity levels of 1, 3 and 10 respectively as shown in Fig. 6. Gaze plots can present the order of the fixation point and location, the size of the dot say fixation time, the number in the dot means the order of fixation points. As can be seen from Fig. 4 that the number of gaze points on information quantity 1 interface is 20, the number of gaze points on information quantity 3 interface is 19. Although the quantity of information varies greatly, the number of gaze points is almost the same. This is mainly because the information quantity 3 interface has short paths in the region and no backtracking paths between the regions. In contrast, the information quantity 1 interface has more backtracking paths. As information quantity increases further, the number of gaze points on the interface will increase and the number of gaze points on the information quantity 10 interface reaches 47.

Heatmaps analysis is then performed on the same interfaces respectively as shown in Fig. 7. Heatmaps use cloud marks to show whether an area is concerned and how long it is concerned. The duration is reflected by color, with red being the longest, followed by yellow, and green the shortest. As can be seen from Fig. 7 that red cloud marks of different information quantity interfaces are all concentrated in abnormal data areas. The difference is that the number of green and yellow cloud marks increases with the increase of information quantity.

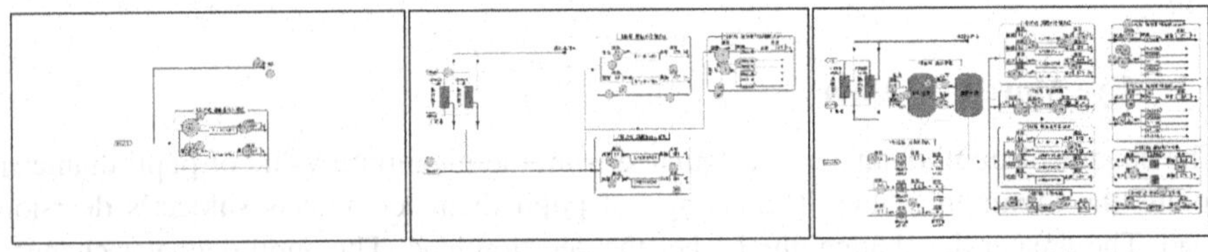

information quantity 1 information quantity 3 information quantity 10

Fig. 6. Typical gaze plots

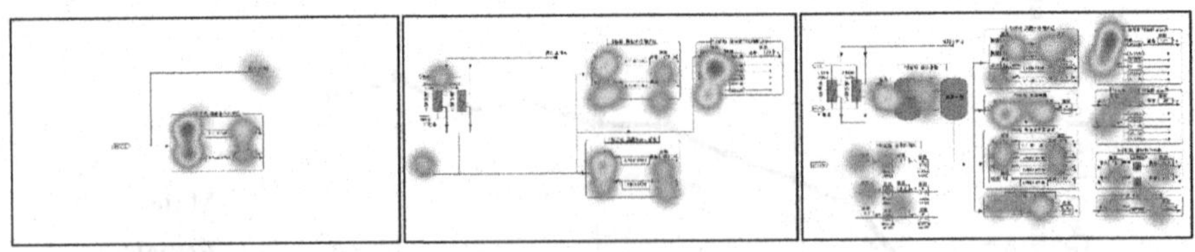

information quantity 1 information quantity 3 information quantity 10

Fig. 7. Typical heatmaps (Color figure online)

4 Discussion

4.1 Decision Efficiency

Results of decision-making efficiency indicate that the efficiency increases first and then decreases with the increase of information quantity. Information quantity has an optimal range, within this range, subjects have high decision-making efficiency. ANOVA is carried out to further analyze decision-making efficiency data, it is found that different quantity of information has no significant impact on decision efficiency ($F = 1.414$, $p = 0.194$, $\alpha = 0.05$, $p > \alpha$). Alvarez's research shows that visual short-term memory has a fixed capacity [8]. Therefore, visual short-term memory may have an influence on the reception of visual information, so that there is an optimal range of information quantity. The findings from Jie Gao seem consistent with this opinion [9]. The optimal range of information quantity may be related to the upper and lower limits at which people receive information.

4.2 Decision Load

Results of decision load show that the load increases with the increase of information quantity. ANOVA is carried out to further analyze decision load data, it is found that different quantity of information has significant impact on decision load ($F = 21.277$, $p = 0.000$, $\alpha = 0.05$, $p < \alpha$). The rise in decision load may be due to the brain calling more resources to process more information. Therefore, information quantity should not exceed a certain upper limit.

4.3 Optimal Range

According to the experimental data of decision efficiency and the questionnaire survey conducted on the subjects after the experiment, the difference between the maximum and minimum values of decision efficiency is taken as the interval, and the 80–100% of the maximum value within this interval is defined as high decision-making efficiency, the 60–80% is defined as medium decision-making efficiency, and the 60% or less is defined as low decision-making efficiency. Similarly, the difference between the maximum value and the minimum value of the decision load is taken as the interval, the 80–100% of the maximum value within this interval is defined as high decision load, the 60–80% is defined as medium decision load, and the 60% or less is defined as low decision load. Taking the intersection of the information range of high decision efficiency and that of low decision-making load, the optimal range of information quantity suitable for decision-making is obtained as image entropy 0.4 to 0.6.

4.4 Gender Differences

Subjects of different genders showed differences in the decision-making process. The maximum value of decision efficiency curve of male is more inclined to high information quantity than that of female. The difference between male and female may be because male have better ability to process high information quantity. The decision load of male is higher than that of female in almost all information quantity, which may be due to the difference in thinking mode between male and female. Therefore, for male, the optimal range of information quantity can be adjusted to 0.4 to 1.2, while for female, it is 0.4 to 0.6.

The above research provides the optimal range of information quantity for decision-making in the interface, which makes it possible to quickly judge the quality of the interface through image entropy in the early stage of interface design.

Finally, it should be pointed out that decision-making is a complex process and information quantity is only one of the influencing factors. Therefore, it is necessary to comprehensively consider various factors to determine whether an interface is suitable for decision-making. This paper provides a quick evaluation method, but it is not perfect enough, more factors such as quality and prominence need to be studied in the future.

5 Conclusions

The aim of this study is to understand the influence of information quantity on user's decision-making. Stimuli with image entropy ranging from 0.2 to 2.0 are designed by varying the number of interface information elements. Stimuli are designed to have the same size and contain the same basic elements so that they only differ in the quantity of information.

The experimental data was collected by Tobii eye tracker. By analyzing the subjects' behavioral data and eye movement data, we found that stimuli with different image entropy showed different influence on user's decision-making. As expected, decision load increased as the quantity of information increased. However, decision efficiency did not decrease as the quantity of information increased but rose first and then fell. This showed that people have lower and upper limits on the quantity of information when making decisions. Measured by image entropy, lower limit was 0.4 and upper limit was 0.6. In other words, the quantity of information suitable for user decision-making was between 0.4 and 0.6. We also found that males and females show differences in decision-making. The decision load of female was lower than that of male in almost all levels of information quantity. And female had higher decision efficiency in the range of image entropy from 0.4 to 0.6, while male is 0.4 to 1.2.

Complex information system digital interface that has high requirements for user decision-making can use image entropy method to quickly evaluate and design the interface information quantity to a reasonable range. Our research provided effective reference and new evidence for the design and evaluation of digital interface.

Acknowledgement. This work was supported jointly by National Natural Science Foundation of China (No. 71871056, 71471037, 71801037), Science and Technology on Electro-optic Control Laboratory and Aerospace Science Foundation of China (No. 20165169017), SAST Foundation of China (SAST No. 2016010) and Equipment Pre-research & Ministry of education of China Joint fund.

References

1. Keller, K.L., Staelin, R.: Effects of quality and quantity of information on decision effectiveness. J. Consum. Res. **14**(2), 200–213 (1987)
2. Lurie, N.H.: Decision making in information-rich environments: the role of information structure. J. Consum. Res. **30**(4), 473–486 (2004)
3. Crutchfield, J.P.: Information and its metric. In: Lam, L., Morris, H.C. (eds.) Nonlinear Structures in Physical Systems, pp. 119–130. Springer, New York (1990). https://doi.org/10.1007/978-1-4612-3440-1_12
4. Haussler, D., Opper, M.: Mutual information, metric entropy and cumulative relative entropy risk. Ann. Stat. **25**(6), 2451–2492 (1997)
5. Gupta, S., Ramesh, K.P., Blasch, E.P.: Mutual information metric evaluation for PET/MRI image fusion. In: 2008 IEEE National Aerospace and Electronics Conference, pp. 305–311. IEEE (2008)
6. Boring, R.L., Thomas, K.D., Ulrich, T.A., et al.: Computerized operator support systems to aid decision making in nuclear power plants. Procedia Manufact. **3**, 5261–5268 (2015)
7. Akbari, S., Menhaj, M.B.: A new framework of a decision support system for air to air combat tasks. In: SMC 2000 Conference Proceedings. 2000 IEEE International Conference on Systems, Man and Cybernetics. 'Cybernetics Evolving to Systems, Humans, Organizations, and Their Complex Interactions', cat. no. 0, vol. 3, pp. 2019–2022. IEEE (2000)
8. Alvarez, G.A., Cavanagh, P.: The capacity of visual short-term memory is set both by visual information load and by number of objects. Psychol. Sci. **15**(2), 106–111 (2004)
9. Gao, J., Zhang, C., Wang, K., et al.: Understanding online purchase decision making: the effects of unconscious thought, information quality, and information quantity. Decis. Support Syst. **53**(4), 772–781 (2012)

Analyses of Fukushima-Daiichi Accident and Other Seven Cases from Good Practice Viewpoint

Hiroshi Ujita[1(✉)] and Hiroshi Sakuda[2]

[1] Institute for Environmental & Safety Studies, 38-7 Takamatsu 2-chome, Toshima-ku, Tokyo 171-0042, Japan
kanan@insess.com

[2] Institute of Nuclear Safety System, 64 Sata, Mihama-cho, Mikata-gun, Fukui 919-1205, Japan
sakuda.hiroshi@inss.co.jp

Abstract. Fukushima-Daiichi Accident has been analyzed from the viewpoint of good practice that is from resilience engineering viewpoint. The good cases of resilience response are observed in individual base and organizational base as below: The effectiveness of insight on accident cases (inundation in Madras, 9.11 terrorism and B.5.b. order for the countermeasures) and of the risk evaluation, Decision of continuation of sea water infusion (individual base), Reflection of the experience on Chuetsu-Oki Earthquake, Improvement of seismic building which is equipped emergency power source system and air conditioning system (organizational base), Deployment of fire engines (organizational base), The effectiveness of command system in ordinary time (on-site of organizational base), and Support by cooperation companies and manufacturers (designers and site workers of organizational base). It is important to 'establish the feedback system on organization learning in ordinary time', that is to establish the system admitting violation of order. The decision at on-site are given priority than other ones. The representative example is the decision of sea water infusion continuation which was given priority at on-site, even though the official residence and the main office of Tokyo Electric Power Company had ordered to stop the infusion. As successful (good practice) cases, ten comprehensive lessons were extracted by analyzing the seven incidents, such as Return of the Asteroid Explorer "Hayabusa", US Airways 1549 Emergency Landing on Hudson River, Apollo 13 Survival, and four organizational accidents. When ten kinds of lessons are overlooked, we understood the timing of utilization of the lessons is different, so it is classified into three categories; Pre-Correspondence, Emergency Response, and Post-Correspondence.

Keywords: Resilience engineering · High reliability organization · Risk literacy · Fukushima accident · Bounded rationality · Information limitation · Time constraint · Context dependence · Near miss

S. Yamamoto and H. Mori (Eds.): HCII 2019, LNCS 11569, pp. 624–637, 2019.
https://doi.org/10.1007/978-3-030-22660-2_46

1 Introduction

In past, we often concentrated on the analysis of nonconforming events occurred. We utilized the root cause analysis method, explore the background factor, and took measures to prevent recurrence. The facility (hard side) has been improved and has become high reliable system, the interface is designed as human friendly, and for human (software) side, improvements has also observed in education and training method, working environment, and advanced management system, therefore it seems that the incidence of incompatibility is becoming lower than before.

Whereas the direction which discusses the safety from the accident analysis, a new trend of analytical methods such as resilience engineering, high reliability organization, or risk literacy research [1–3], which analyze the various events by focusing on the good practices, are becoming popular.

The results of Fukushima Daiichi Accident investigation with diversified characteristic have been released until now. Based upon the analyses of the investigation, the success cases (good practice) and failure cases for emergency responses were analyzed concerning to personal- response capability, organizational-response capability, and communication ability with external organizations, and then the problems of responses were extracted. The action of sea-water infusion on Fukushima Daiichi nuclear power plant No.1 was paid attention and analyzed based on the 'Accident Analysis Report of Fukushima Nuclear Accident' [4] (Accident Report) by TEPCO, Tokyo Electric Power Company, especially focus on the decision making of continuation of pouring sea water.

In Resilience Engineering, it is important to learn from not only failed cases but also good cases [1]. We tend to focus on non-conformities such as equipment breakdown, occupational accidents, unexpected accidents, etc., but we are trying hard to avoid such disasters and accidents. Efforts are continuing day by day, and if we compare by number, there should be more successful cases. Efforts to reduce accident occurrences are continuing day by day, and the frequency of successful cases might be more than failure cases. However, success stories are hard to touch our eyes, so it is difficult to deal with it. It is believed that the 'hiyari-hatto (near miss) activity' dealt with a good practice if it is regarded as collection and utilization cases that prevent becoming major accident beforehand by taking recovery measures.

2 Bounded Rationality in Context vs. Judge by God

As a result that the technology systems become huge, complex and sophisticated, safety issues are shifted to the problem of organization from human, and further from hardware, such socialization is occurring in every technical field [5]. For this reason, the analytical methods, as well as type and social perceptions of error or accident, are changing with the times also [6–8]. Human error and Domino accident model had initially appeared, are then changing to system error and Swiss cheese accident model, and recently move to safety culture degradation and the organizational accident.

In the field of cognitive science and the cognitive system engineering, the human being is considered as to think and judge something reasonably along context while there are information limitation and time constraint. Sometimes the decision may be judged as an error by the outside later. It is called "bounded rationality in the context" vs. "judge by God". The absurd action of the organization had been often explained in human illogicality conventionally, while the approach has recently come out to think that the human being rationality is the cause [6–8].

There are three approaches proposed from Organizational (Behavioral) Economics, business cost theory (reluctant to do), agency theory (information gap), and proprietary rights theory (selfishness) as shown in Table 1 [9]. Business cost theory analyses action of opportunity principles and sunk cost, agency theory, moral hazard and adverse selection (lemon market), and proprietary rights theory, cost externality. The common supposition is "the bounded rationality and the utility maximization".

Table 1. Three approaches by behavioral economics (The organization fails rationally: Kenshu Kikusawa 2009).

	Business cost theory (reluctant to do)	Agency theory (information gap)	Proprietary rights theory (selfishness)
Objects	Business relation	Agency relation (Principal &Agency)	Proprietary relation
Non-efficiency	• Action of opportunity principles • Sunk cost	• Moral hazard • Adverse selection (Lemon market)	• Cost externality
System solution	Business cost saving system which changes organizational style from group, via. centralization of power, and to decentralization of power	Agency cost reduction system based on mutual exchange of the information,	Internalization of the system externality based on proprietary rights distribution

The common supposition: "the bounded rationality and the utility maximization"

It is necessary to find the social context that the error is easy to occur, in the engineering for human beings hereafter. In other words, a way of thinking has changed in the direction to analyzing the social context that is easy to cause an error, from analyzing direct cause of the error. Because this direction is beyond the range of conventional ergonomic treating the contents of the error, it is very difficult. However, we should recognize it now, if we do not analyze an error in the viewpoint the relationship between safety and the environmental element surrounding human being, we can not to lead to measures. The measures should be matched with human rational characteristics.

Countermeasure on Business cost theory is business cost saving system which changes organizational style from group organization, via. centralization of power type organization, and to decentralization of power type organization, agency theory, agency cost reduction system based on mutual exchange of the information, and proprietary rights theory, internalization of the system externality based on proprietary rights distribution.

3 The Methodology on Resilience Engineering, High Reliability Organization, and Risk Literacy

Whereas the direction which discusses the safety from the accident analysis, a new trend of analytical methods such as resilience engineering, high reliability organization, or risk literacy research, which analyze the various events by focusing on the good practices, are becoming popular.

The resilience is the intrinsic ability of a system to adjust its functioning prior to, during, or following changes and disturbances, so that it can sustain required operations under both expected and unexpected conditions [1]. A practice of Resilience Engineering/Proactive Safety Management requires that all levels of the organization are able to:

- Monitor,
- Learn from past events,
- Respond, and
- Anticipate.

Organizational process defined by the High Reliability Organization is shown below. There are 5 powers in 2 situations [2].

- Preparedness for Emergency Situation in Ordinary Time:
  - Carefulness (Confirmation),
  - Honesty (Report),
  - Sensitivity (Observation),
- Emergency Response in Emergency Situation:
  - Alert (Concentration), and
  - Flexibility (Response).

Ability of Risk Literacy is also defined by followings, which is largely divided to 3 powers and further classified to 8 sub-powers [3].

- Analysis Power:
  - Collection power,
  - Understanding power,
  - Predictive power,
- Communication Power
  - Network power,
  - Influence power,

- Practical Power:
  - Crisis response power, and
  - Radical measures power.

4 The Analysis Based on Resilience Engineering, High Reliability Organization, and Risk Literacy

4.1 Chronological Analysis

The analysis for the detail of sea-water infusion to Fukushima-Daiichi No.1 unit has been performed. Chronological analysis was drawn up from "The main chronological analysis of Fukushima Daiichi nuclear power plant No.1 unit from earthquake occurrence to the next day" and "The status response relating to pouring water to No.1 unit", which came from the 'Accident Report'.

The chronological analysis shows that the preparation of sea-water infusion is decided and ordered concurrently with pouring freshwater, and also shows that continuation of sea-water infusion is decided as on-site judgment although an official residence and the main office of TEPCO directed to stop the infusion, in taking into consideration of the intention of official residence. The necessity of continuation of sea-water infusion was recognized consistently by on-site judgment, and these measures were taken. This means that the main office of TEPCO and the official residence violate the fundamental principle which on-site judgment should be preceded in emergency situation.

4.2 Organizational Factors Analysis

The process of sea-water infusion on Fukushima Daiichi No.1 unit is analyzed from the point of resilience capability, high reliability organization capability, and risk-literacy capability [1–3]. The analysis example by risk-literacy capability is shown in Table 2 from the viewpoint of risk-management, which is described in 'Introduction of Risk Literacy-Lessons Learned from Incidents' [3]. The definition of risk literacy capability which can extract communication power that is important both for ordinary time and for emergency situation is the most appropriate for analysis. The horizontal axis shows response capabilities which are suggested in each study, and the vertical axis shows each level of individual, organization, which is further divided management and on-site, and correspondence to outside such as official residence. The gothic font in green means success case or good practice, while the italic font in red means failure case.

The analysis of emergency correspondence like this kind of huge accident cannot be analyzed enough using conventional framework. As a whole of one organization, the classifications were reviewed and revised from two points. One is that the differences in correspondence and the problems in cooperation between on-site and administration department cannot be clarified. And the other one is that communication power has two sides which are the information cooperation in ordinary time and collaboration in case of emergency situation. The analysis power and information transmission power correspond to ordinary time, and the influence power and normal

Table 2. Evaluation of response capability from the viewpoint of risk literacy: The analysis of sea water infusion process on Fukushima Daiichi No.1.

Risk literacy / Analysis level	In Ordinal Time					In Emergency Situation	
	Analysis Power			Communication Power		Practical Power	
	Collection Power	Comprehensive Power	Predictive Power	Information Transmission Power	Influence power	Crisis Response Power	Radical Measures Power
Individual	•Damage of Tsunami	•Risk recognition of Tsunami damage	•Risk recognition of Power Loss	—	—	• Continuation of Sea water infusion	• Training for emergency
organization: on-site	•Collection of accidents: •Jyogan-Tsunami	•Earthquake •Tsunami •Evaluation of influence range by PSA	Recognition of accidents damage	•Information sharing at on-site	•Command system (on-site) •Centralized at seismic building •*Contact between Control Room & Emergency Response Room*	•Infusion of fresh water and sea water •Vent •Prevention of damage expansion	•Preparation of seismic building and fire engines •Command system •AM measures •Tsunami protection measures
organization: Management	•Collection of accident: Jyogan-Tsunami, JNES Tsunami PSA, Infusion at Le Blayais & Madras	•*Risk misrecognition of Tsunami damage*	•*Risk misrecognition of Power Loss*	•*Information sharing between main office and on-site*	•TV conference system (2F site) •*Confusion in command system between main office and on-site*		•Review the education and training system **Success event**
External correspondence (official residence, etc.)	•Anti-terrorism in overseas *Collection of example : 9.11 terrorism-B.5.b.*	•Classification of importance on accidents •*Risk misrecognition of earthquake and Tsunami*	•Importance of external events •*Risk misrecognition of infrastructure damage*	***Failure event***	•*Media, local government, publicity to overseas* •*Confusion of command system among official residence, main office, & on-site*	•*Delay of initial response* •*Governmental command system*	•Support by vendor and cooperation company •Support by external organizations •*Drastic measures : Structure reform (Regulation/ Electric power company*

time skill correspond to the case of emergency situation. In this analysis, the contact with official residence and the cooperation inside government are also included in correspond to external organizations.

4.3 Fukushima-Daiichi Accident Analysis from Good Practice Viewpoint

Various good cases of resilience response were observed in individual base and in organizational in Fukushima-Daiichi accident as below [7, 8]:

- The effectiveness of insight and of the risk evaluation on accident cases, such as inundations in LeBlayais and Madras, and September 11 terrorism and B.5.b.order by US Nuclear Regulatory Commission to keep the plant in safe condition even natural disasters or acts of terrorism occurred,
  - Decision of continuation of sea water infusion (individual base).
- Reflection of the experience on Chuetsu-Oki Earthquake,
  - Improvement of seismic building which is equipped emergency power system and air conditioning system (on-site of organizational base),
  - Deployment of fire engines (on-site of organizational base).
- The effectiveness of command system in ordinary situation (on-site of organizational base),
- Support by cooperation companies and manufacturers (designers and site workers of organizational base).

Table 3. Points in difference in Fukushima Daiichi and Daini, Toukai Daini, and Onagawa Plants.

Fukushima Daiichi and Daini	Toukai Daini	Onagawa
・Cold Shutdown can be achieved due to Air Cooling EDG Continue to operate in 1F5/6 Units and in 2F, 3EDGs *- Corporation based on correct information*	・New Dam at Sea-water Pump Area	・Land height determined as 14. 8m, while estimated height as 3m
・Priority to measures on Chuetuoki Earthquake	・Ibaragi Prefecture Officers estimated Enpou-bousouoki Earthquake	・Former Vice-president Decisive Judgment
・Only consideration on Tsunami affect	・Information was transferred to JAPC, Japan Atomic Power Company immediately	・Meiji-sannrikuoki and Jyogan Tsunamis considered
・No consideration on information of countermeasures on terrorism after September 11 from US	・Company managers performed safety measures	
	-Problem institution by professionals and acceptance by administration	-Problem institution by professionals and acceptance by administration
・Important Anti-seismic Building and Portable Fire Engine installed for seismic countermeasures	・No Measures	・Anti-seismic Building and Seismic Strengthening

For Tsunami countermeasures in other plants, good practices were also observed in organizational base as shown in Table 3:

- Onagawa plant level was enough high to prevent Tsunami disaster due to clear understanding of the effect and sharp decision by top management,
- Tokai-Daini plant installed water stuck for sea-water pump to protect infusion by good communication and corporation among prefecture officers and utility managers.

The many failure cases were defined under national government base and nuclear industry base which are the problems of rare event awareness and of organization culture. The ordinary time training at on-site have also worked in emergency at the accident, while the base of administration department and government didn't work well:

- Risk misrecognition of Loss of offsite power and damage by Tsunami (national government base, industry base),
- Confusion of command system (organization base- between on-site and the main office of TEPCO, and external correspondence base- among national government base, official residence, regulator, and the main office of TEPCO).

It is important to 'establish the feedback system on organization learning in ordinary time', which means that it is important to establish the system admitting violation to the order in emergency situation. The decision at on-site are given priority than other ones. The representative example is the decision of sea water infusion continuation which was given priority at on-site, even though the official residence and the main office TEPCO had ordered to stop the infusion.

4.4 Points in Common and Difference in Fukushima Daiichi and Daini, Toukai Daini, and Onagawa Plants

Points in common and difference in Fukushima Daiichi and Daini, Toukai Daini, and Onagawa Plants are summarized in Table 3. Cold Shutdown could be successfully achieved due to survive power supply, where good practices of corporation among operators and between on-site and head office were observed based on correct information. Because Air Cooling EDG (Emergency Diesel Generator) continued to operate in Fukushima Daiichi plant 5 and 6 units, and 3 EDGs in Fukushima Daini plant. Especially, TV conference system was effectively functioned in Fukushima Daini plant, because of enough information by survival indicators energized from survived batteries.

TEPCO put the priority onto countermeasures on Chuetuoki Earthquake and only considered without making countermeasures on Tsunami affect. Important Anti-seismic Building and Portable Fire Engine had been installed for seismic countermeasures in every plant of TEPCO before huge earth quake and Tsunami, and those apparatuses were used in the accident effectively in Fukushima Daiichi and Daini plants. Good practices of Tsunami countermeasures of site height decision process of problem institution by professionals and acceptance by administration performed in both Toukai Daini and Onagawa Plants.

One point we should understand is that Tsunami estimated height has drastically changed as time passed, which means it is not reliable information. At the information limitation circumstance, four plants showed good resilience examples. The difference of the correspondence is due to difference in priority policy. Fukushima made efforts on earthquake measures, on the other hand, Onagawa and Tokai Daini, efforts on Tsunami measures. It seems that the differences in suffered effect and in its correspondence between Fukushima Daiichi 1–4 and 5–6 & Daini both owned by TEPCO are due to relative relationships between actual tsunami height and site height.

4.5 Consideration on Organizational Problem

The true nature of the problem in Japanese organization that doesn't change from when the 'Substance of Failures' [10], in which Japanese military operation failures in the World War II were analyzed, was written by Tobe, Nonaka, et al. Failure cause was described as standpoint of irrationality in Japanese on this book. But the problems in organization are not able to be resolved by irrationality in Japanese. It should be explained using by bounded rationality which Kikusawa advocate in 'Absurdity of Organization' [9]. His idea is that decision making which are made under limited circumstances based on limited information will end in failure from the eye of God. He also advocates destroying the bounded rationality for failure measures. It means that it is important to 'establish the system admitting violation of order in emergency situation'. The decision at on-site are given priority than other ones. The representative example is observed in the decision of sea water infusion continuation, the decision at on-site were given priority even though the official residence and the main office TEPCO had ordered to stop the infusion. Otherwise it is the failure case that occur delay of PCV vent, for time loss to get the permission of national government and local government.

It is important to 'establish the feedback system on organization learning in ordinary time'. The continuations of emergency training in ordinary time with assuming the severe accident progression is considered to be the effective way. The emergency training is necessary in management level, in which responsibility assignment is regularly taken, the incident seriousness is evaluated, and the mode is switched from ordinary time to emergency situation.

The problems as above can be explained by "Homogeneous way of thinking" and "Concentric Camaraderie", as shown in Fig. 1, which are the hindrance on safety pursuit in Japan. 'Bottom-up decision making structure' connects to 'Absence of top management', and then becomes to 'Delay of decision making and Lack of understanding on valuing safety'. Due to the Japanese are excellent as noncommissioned officer (Soldier: Russian, Junior officer: French, Chief of staff: German, General: American), they often show their ability at emergency situation. But Japanese are short of management abilities, they often make heavy intervention or omission.

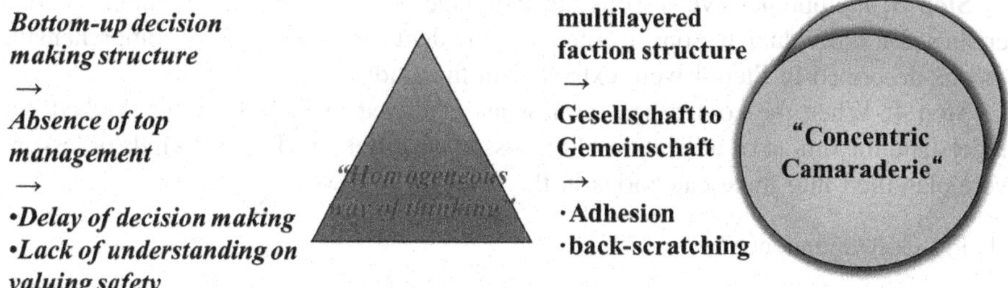

Fig. 1. "Homogeneous way of thinking" and "Concentric camaraderie", obstruction factors on safety pursuit in Japan.

'Multilayered faction structure' appeared in "Concentric Camaraderie" makes 'Organization from Gesellschaft to Gemeinschaft', and then 'Adhesion and back-scratching' are spread in the organization. For the "Concentric Camaraderie", the feedback system in organization learning leads to the failure due to be preceded to internal logic than social common sense even in national government level or nuclear industry level.

5 Lessons Learned Derived by the Analyses of the Good Practice Cases

The method to analyze the good practice cases in the incidents and to extract the lessons learned derived by the analyses has been developed, which consists following six steps;

Step 1: Incidents which are considered to include successful (good practice) cases are analyzed by human factors viewpoint. In the study, the following six incidents were analyzed, in which first three incidents are considered as famous successful stories in the world, rest three are typical organizational accidents in Japan;

1. Return of the Asteroid Explorer "Hayabusa",
2. US Airways 1549 Emergency Landing on Hudson River,
3. Apollo 13 Survival,
4. Steam Generator Heat Transfer Tube Damage Accident at Mihama Unit2,
5. Train Derailment Accident at JR Fukuchiyama Line, and
6. Shigaraki Plateau Train Collision Accident.

Step 2: Thirty four individual lessons learned are extracted based on the analysis results in Step 1 for each incident. Typical examples of individual lessons in the famous success stories such as US Airways 1549 and Apollo 13 were hard training and resilience capability in the emergency situation achieved by the training. From the experience of Fukuchiyama Line Train and Shigaraki Plateau Train Accidents, resilience responses were observed in emergency medical operations and the information system was established after the accidents in the rescue emergency medical field and the disaster medical field.

Step 3: Comprehensive lessons are extracted by searching the common characteristics for individual lessons learned for incidents in Step 2. Ten comprehensive lessons described in Step 4 were extracted in the study.

Step 4: When the comprehensive lessons extracted in Step 3 are overlooked, we understand the timing of utilization of the lessons is different. Here, ten kinds of lessons were classified into three categories in the study as follows:

"1. Pre-Correspondence":

1. Fostering expertise, non-technical ability,
2. Improvement of organizational environment for demonstrating ability,

"2. Emergency Response":

3. Sharing goals,
4. Strengthen emergency regime,
5. Enhancement of emergency response training,
6. Enhancement of hard and software countermeasures assuming emergency,
7. Understanding of human characteristics and preparing manual in emergency,
8. Flexible response by surrounding organizations and individuals,

"3. Post-Correspondence":

9. Thorough disclosure of information, and
10. Preventing weathering of lessons learned.

Step 5: When we investigate incidents in Step 1 once more by considering above ten comprehensive lessons, additional individual lessons can be extracted and identified. That is, feedback process is very important to extract good practices comprehensively and efficiently. Examples of additional lessons in aircraft accidents and railway accidents were the preservation and restoration of accident body or accident spot and the establishment of "Investigation Committee on the Accidents".

Step 6: We can analyze the new cases and extract good practices easily and effectively by using ten comprehensive lessons extracted in the study. Here, new one was considered as the rather successful response case as the organizational accident in Japan;

7. Road Collapse Accident in front of Hakata Station.

One example of good practice extracted in the case was quick response based on the decision by the former experience, which is corresponds to 'Strengthen emergency regime' of 4th comprehensive lesson. Therefore, recommended approach is that good practice case analysis would be done with reference to the ten comprehensive lessons learned shown here. Further, if additional comprehensive lesson was extracted by new case analysis, such knowledge might be extended to the former analysis cases, that is feedback process importance is emphasized again.

The future task is how to find good examples from recovery measures to prevent accidents that correspond as a matter of course in many daily tasks.

6 Discussion

Rare Event is high consequence with low frequency. Low consequence with high frequency event is easy to treat by commercial reason, while it is very difficult to handle the rare event even the risk is just the same. "Unexpected event" has been used frequently, but it is the risk-benefit issues to assume or not. Tsunami Probabilistic Risk Analysis has been carried out, and safety related personnel knew the magnitude of the effect well.

Regardless of the initiating event, lack of measures to "Station blackout" is to be asked. According to the "Defense in Depth" concept reflecting Fukushima accident, we should consider three level safety functions; usual normal system, usual safety system, and newly installed emergency system including external support functions. Anyway the diversity is significantly required for not only future reactor concept but also existing plant back-fit activities.

Swiss Cheese Model proposed by Reason, J indicates operational problem other than design problem [5]. Fallacy of the defense in depth has frequently occurred recently because plant system is safe enough as operators becomes easily not to consider system safety. And then safety culture degradation would be happened, whose incident will easily become organizational accident. Such situation requires final barrier that is Crisis Management.

Concept of "Soft Barrier" has been proposed [6]. There are two types of safety barriers, one is Hard Barrier that is simply represented by Defense in Depth. The other is Soft Barrier, which maintains the hard barrier as expected condition, makes it perform as expected function. Even when the Hard Barrier does not perform its function, human activity to prevent hazardous effect and its support functions, such as manuals, rules, laws, organization, social system, etc. Soft Barrier can be further divided to two measures; one is "Software for design", such as Common mode failure treatment, Safety logic, Usability, etc. The other is "Humanware for operation", such as operator or maintenance personnel actions, Emergency Procedure, organization, management, Safety Culture, etc.

7 Conclusion

The good practices or success cases of resilience response are observed in individual base and organizational base as below.

- The effectiveness of insight on accident cases (inundation in Madras, 9.11 terrorism and B.5.b. order for the countermeasures) and of the risk evaluation.
  - Decision of continuation of sea water infusion (individual base)
- Reflection of the experience on Chuetsu-Oki Earthquake
  - Improvement of seismic building which is equipped emergency power source system and air conditioning system (organizational base)
  - Deployment of fire engines (organizational base)
- The effectiveness of command system in ordinary time (on-site of organizational base)

- Support by cooperation companies and manufacturers (designers and site workers of organizational base)

The many failure cases are defined under national government level and nuclear industry level which are the problems of rare event awareness and of organization culture. The ordinary time training at on-site also work in emergency situation at the accident, while the level of administration department and government didn't work well.

- Risk misrecognition of Loss of offsite power and damage by Tsunami (national government level, industry level)
- Confusion of command system (organization base- between on-site and the main office of TEPCO)
- Confusion of command system (external correspondence base- national government level, and organization base- among official residence, regulation, and the main office of TEPCO)

It is important to 'establish the feedback system on organization learning in ordinary time', that is to establish the system admitting violation of order. The decision at on-site are given priority than other ones. The representative example is the decision of sea water infusion continuation which was given priority at on-site, even though the official residence and the main office TEPCO had ordered to stop the infusion.

As successful (good practice) cases, ten comprehensive lessons were extracted by analyzing the seven cases, such as Return of the Asteroid Explorer "Hayabusa", US Airways 1549 Emergency Landing on Hudson River, Apollo 13 Survival, etc. When ten kinds of lessons are overlooked, we understood the timing of utilization of the lessons is different, so it is classified into three categories:

"1. Pre-Correspondence":

1. Fostering expertise, non-technical ability,
2. Improvement of organizational environment for demonstrating ability,

"2. Emergency Response":

3. Sharing goals,
4. Strengthen emergency regime,
5. Enhancement of emergency response training,
6. Enhancement of hard and software countermeasures assuming emergency,
7. Understanding of human characteristics and preparing manual in emergency,
8. Flexible response by surrounding organizations and individuals,

"3. Post-Correspondence":

9. Thorough disclosure of information, and
10. Preventing weathering of lessons learned.

References

1. Hollnagel, E.: Safety culture, safety management, and resilience engineering. ATEC Aviation Safety Forum, November 2009
2. Weick, K.E., Sutcliffe, K.M.: Managing the Unexpected. Jossey-Bass, San Francisco (2001)
3. Lin, S.: Introduction of Risk Literacy- Lessons Learned from Incidents. In: NIKKEI-BP (2005) (in Japanese)
4. TEPCO: Accident Analysis Report of Fukushima Nuclear Accident (June 2012)
5. Reason, J.: Managing the Risks of Organizational Accidents. Ashgate, Farnham (1997)
6. Ujita, H., Yuhara, N.: Systems Safety. Kaibundo, Tokyo (2015). (in Japanese)
7. Ujita, H.: Accident analysis by using methodology of resilience engineering, high reliability organization, and risk literacy. In: Kurosu, M. (ed.) HCI 2015. LNCS, vol. 9171, pp. 358–369. Springer, Cham (2015). https://doi.org/10.1007/978-3-319-21006-3_35
8. Ujita, H.: Requirement on personnel and organization for safety and security improvement by accident and error model. In: Kurosu, M. (ed.) HCI 2017. LNCS, vol. 10271, pp. 94–102. Springer, Cham (2017). https://doi.org/10.1007/978-3-319-58071-5_8
9. Kikusawa, K.: Absurdity of Organization. DIAMOND (2000). (in Japanese)
10. Nonaka, T., et al.: Substance of Failures. DIAMOND (1984). (in Japanese)

On the Relationality Assets and Gift-and-Circulation Model in Community Problem

Katsuhiko Yonezaki[1(✉)], Kosuke Ogita[2], Koya Kimura[2], Yurika Shiozu[3], Ryo Shioya[2], and Katsunori Shimohara[2]

[1] Yokohama City University, Yokohama, Japan
kyonezaki@hotmail.com
[2] Doshisha University, Kyoto, Japan
[3] Aichi University, Aichi, Japan

Abstract. Japan is a state-of-the-art aging society of the world from the viewpoint of average life expectancy, the number of elderly people, and the speed of aging. And accompanied by a declining population, the society in Japan is facing a turning point. In Japanese society, the connection of local communities has played a very important role. However, the concentration of the population in the urban area that began in the high economic growth period has changed to the concentration in the Tokyo metropolitan area in the 2000s, and as the declining birthrate and aging population advances, regional relationships have been diluted there. In this paper, we introduce the relational assets and Gift-and-Circulation model, which are key concepts of our approach to constructing a methodology as a solution to the above problem. And from a macro-perspective, how relational assets works will be examined.

Keywords: Relationality assets · Community design · Gift-and-Circulation model system dynamics

1 Introduction

Japan is a state-of-the-art aging society of the world from the viewpoint of average life expectancy, the number of elderly people, and the speed of aging. And accompanied by a declining population, the society in Japan is facing a turning point. In 2014, a report on the Japan Policy Council "A Stop Declining Fertility: Local Revitalization Strategy" was published. It is the concept of "municipalities at risk of vanishing" that was picked up in this report. It is predicted that 896 towns and villages across Japan will no longer be viable by 2040. Furthermore, such problems are progressing not only in rural areas but also in urban areas, and it is pointed out that regional relations in the community are diluted.

In Japanese society, the connection of local communities has played a very important role. However, the concentration of the population in the urban area that began in the high economic growth period has changed to the concentration in the Tokyo metropolitan area in the 2000s, and as the declining birthrate and aging population advances, regional relationships have been diluted there. But it is not that Japanese do not want to engage in relationships and connections with the community.

S. Yamamoto and H. Mori (Eds.): HCII 2019, LNCS 11569, pp. 638–647, 2019.
https://doi.org/10.1007/978-3-030-22660-2_47

As new opportunities, various policy and events are being done, but we have not gotten the answer yet.

In this paper, we introduce the relational assets and Gift-and-Circulation model, which are key concepts of our approach to constructing a methodology as a solution to the above problem. And from a macro-perspective, how relationality assets works will be examined. This paper is organized as follows: Sect. 2, we discuss our concept for view of community. We first presented the model of relationality asset: then we discuss the Gift and Circulation model and introduce the system dynamics analysis. In Sect. 4, we presented the result of the analysis. Finally, Sect. 5 is conclusion.

2 Concept: Community as a System

We are targeting "community" as a system that does not function unless residential people are voluntarily involved. In other words, a community as a system is composed of "Hito", "Mono" and "Koto" and their relationality which residents naturally generate through making their daily lives. We are aiming to quantify and visualize relationality between "Hito", "Mono" and "Koto" in a community. Original ideas are to postulate relationality as assets the community people individually earn, and to elicit their awareness of relationality assets as trust.

We focus on the following issues: whether or not the introduction of relationality assets in a community influence the increase of acquaintance, the total amount of relationality assets, and some change in their behavior. In order to investigate those issues, we built simulation models using system dynamics (SD) to investigate how the proposed mechanisms work and influence the behaviors of the community as a system. Now, we are building a simulation model through which community people themselves are positively involved in managing and sustaining relationality assets in a community.

3 Model

In this section, we introduce the framework of Relationality asset model, and the influence of the Gift-and-Circulation model analyze from a macro perspective.

3.1 Relationality Asset Model

The relationship asset model is defined as follows. Bi is the benefit of individuals obtained from the community. *i* is a symbol representing an individual. This benefit Bi consists of three elements (Bi = {X, Y, Z}), which are the gain X obtained directly from the community and the gains Y, Z indirectly obtained. Here, we assume that the gains indirectly obtained from the community are relationality assets.

More specifically, the benefit of an individual is expressed as Bi = X + Y + Z. The direct gain X is X = D − C. D is a benefit directly obtained from activities in the community. In this case, expenses will be incurred for the activity, and the cost is C. Y is a gain indirectly obtained in the community. And Z expresses the interaction with the community members of the indirectly obtained gain. Z is as follows.

$$Z = \Sigma G_{-i} - G_i + R \tag{1}$$

G represents the amount of gift. Gi is a gift of i and ΣG−i represents the total amount of gifts other than i. R is the public account effect, representing redistribution. Therefore, the benefits from individual community activities are as follows.

$$\begin{aligned} B &= X + Y + Z \\ &= D - C + Y - Gi + \Sigma G - i + R. \end{aligned} \tag{2}$$

To summarize the conclusion derived from the above formula, if the benefit B obtained from the community is positive (B > 0), there is incentive to conduct community activities and if the benefit is negative (B < 0), there is no incentive to conduct community activities. If we categorize the formula, we get C + Gi = D + Y + ΣG − i + R, which is the threshold for participation in community activities. And, when comparing the benefits and costs directly obtained from community activities, even if they are negative, there is a possibility of conducting community activities if the indirectly obtained benefit is large (C + Gi − D < Y + ΣG − i + R).

3.2 Gift and Circulation

Concept. As one of possible approaches for revitalizing a local community, we could think of introducing LETS (Local Exchange Trading System) or local currency. The local currency plays a role of connecting person to person, activates intercommunications of them, and works as media for people to share and transmit a sense of value. The sense of value shared in a community can be regarded as sort of trust, and can work to make relationality within a community strong. Some of local currency have no interest or even minus interest so as not to be accumulated and continue to increase but to promote and activate its exchange between people. Relationality assets we proposed in this research should have the similarity with the local currency. That is, the mechanism we introduce here is for people to get some dividend by investing their assets to others, while the amount of assets is automatically decreased if people keep them, as shown in Fig. 1.

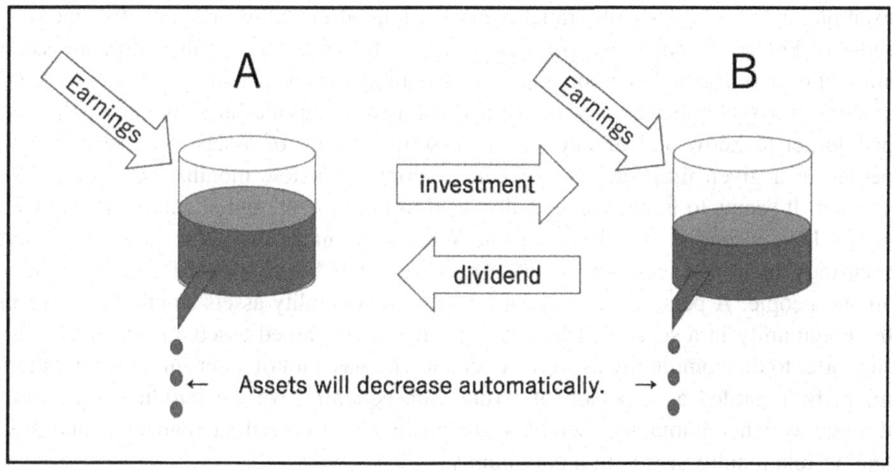

Fig. 1. A model of investment and dividends

On the other hand, there should be a big difference between relationality assets and the local currency. Relationally assets are sort of assets but not currency for equivalently exchanging something and something. Here we propose a model of gift and circulation instead of a model of investment and dividend, as shown in Fig. 2.

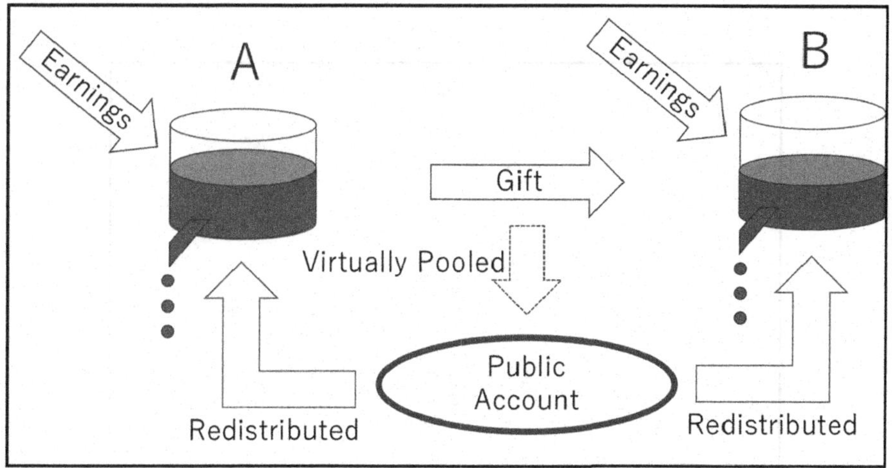

Fig. 2. A model of Gift-and-Circulation

What we want to promote is not equivalent exchange based on one-time pay-it-back relationship but gift and circulation that activate successive pay-it-forward relationship within people. For that purpose, we introduce a public account to accumulate the same amount of assets gifted from someone to someone. People could express, for example, a sort of goodwill, smile, thank, feeling of empathy or sympathy, and/or a sense of linkage to others by gifting their assets to the others. At that time, the same amount of assets gifted is automatically accumulated in the account. The accumulated amount of assets indicates how active pay-it-forward activities are among people, and people get to know and monitor it. Also, some amount of assets is redistributed to people in a given time such as a week, a month or a few months from the public account. It seems to be the same as dividend to investment, and should work to make people have incentive to such movement. What we want to emphasize, however, is that such movement is driven not by pay-it-back activities but by pay-it-forward activities among people. A person who can earn a lot of relationality assets should be active in the community in a sense that he/she can gift his/her earned assets to others as a big supporter to the community as well. A person who has a lot of assets gifted from others might be regarded as a person of virtue. Subsequently, we are building a platform through which community members are positively involved in managing and sustaining relationality assets in a community.

System Dynamics. We are building a simulation model through which community people themselves are positively involved in managing and sustaining relationality assets in a community. System Dynamics (SD) is a method to explore dynamic characteristic of a target system by modeling the internal structure of a system that fluctuates within changes over time and simulating the behavior of system. We investigated the optimal combination of the rate of redistribution and damping for Gift-and-Circulation model. We use STELLA 9.1.4 to build the stock and flow diagram of Gift-and-Circulation model. The followings are description of the diagram in Fig. 3;

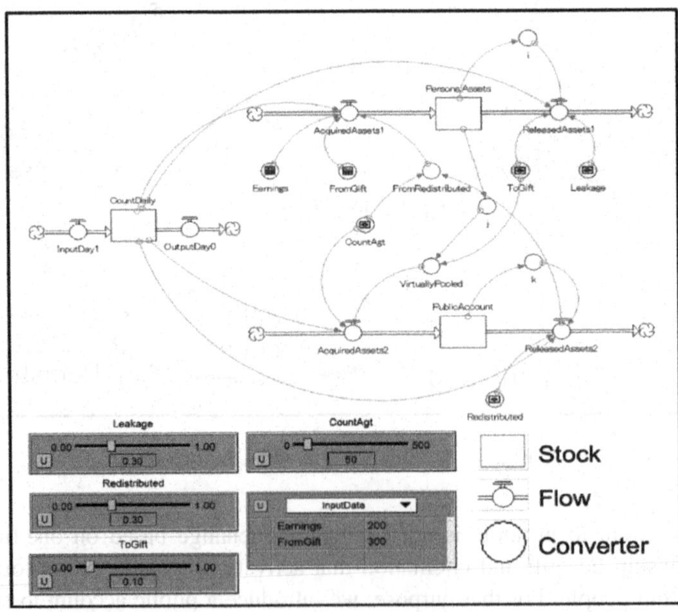

Fig. 3. Relationship between characteristics and attributes of a person agent

- Gift: People could express linkage to others by gifting their assets to the others.
- Public Account: People can monitor changes.
- Redistributed: Some amount of assets is redistributed to people in a given it every week.
- Earnings: The amount of assets that people earn individually.
- Leakage: The value of the asset falls automatically.
- Virtually Pooled: The same amount of assets gifted is automatically accumulated in the account.

In this model, relationality assets are distributed with one week as one unit (see Table 1). We set up to saturate the total amount of relationality assets for the following reasons;

- Divergence: relationality assets continue to increase = over interference World.
- Converging to 0: In a world where leakage is large and redistribution is small, no one thinks that it wants to maintain a connection.

Therefore, we assume a "saturate" that converges on somewhere other than 0, because it is not over-interference, but a relationship that can be maintained as it is.

Table 1. Distribution of relationality assets: each week as one unit

	Personal assets	Public account
Monday	FromGift	
Tuesday		
Wednesday	Redistributed (2)	Released assets (2)
Thursday		
Friday	ToGift	Virtually Pooled
Saturday		
Sunday	Leakage	

4 Results and Discussions

We discuss the results of the simulation by System Dynamics using the model of Fig. 3.

4.1 Task 1: Suitable Parameter as Dynamically Changing

If all parameters are made static, the relationality assets increase indefinitely. Therefore, one parameter is set to change dynamically. Figure 4 show simulation results of the value of personal assets and public account with gift, leakage, redistributed parameters, respectively. Here, the redistributed with a small amount of change of personal assets was set as a dynamic parameter.

Figure 4 Simulation Results of the value of personal assets and public account with gift, leakage, redistributed parameters.

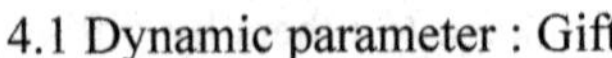

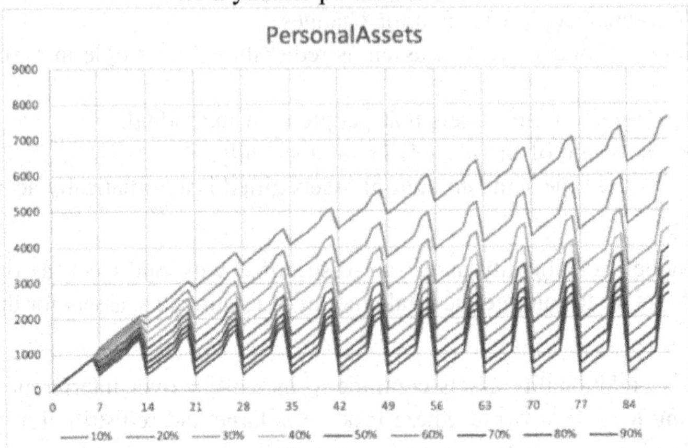

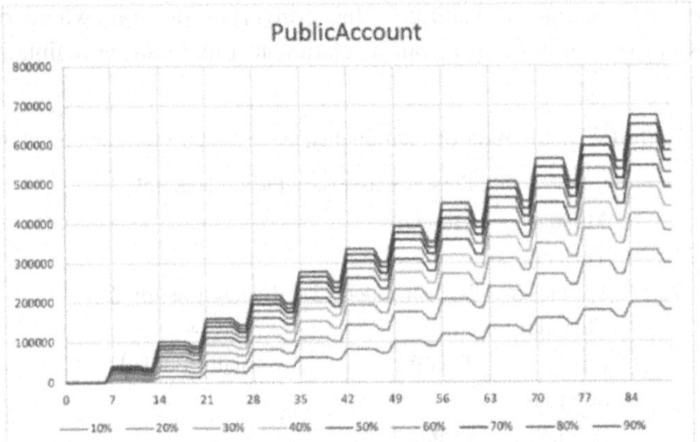

4.2 Dynamic parameter :Leakage

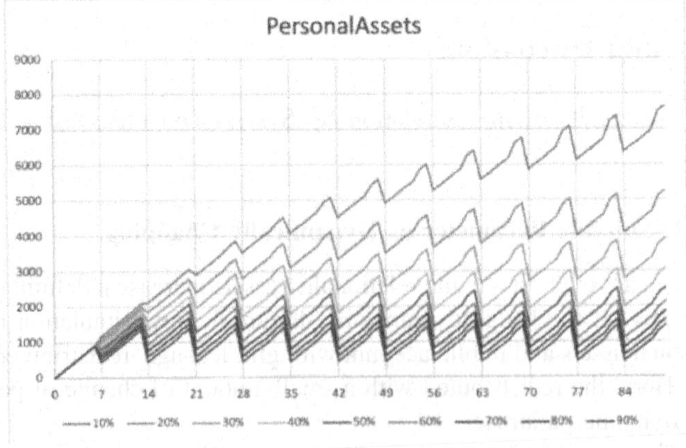

Fig. 4. Simulation Results

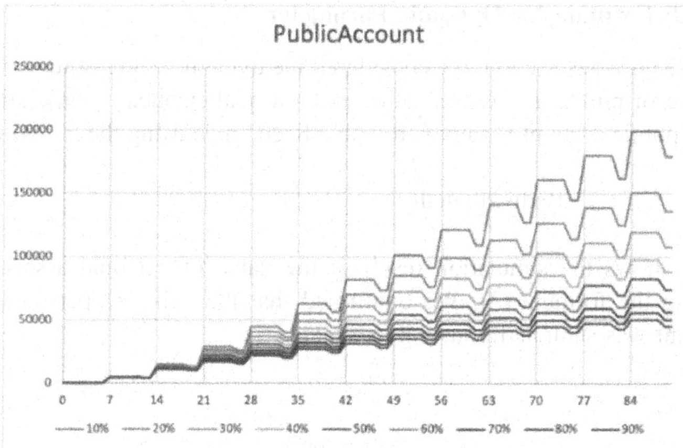

4.3 Dynamic parameter :Redistributed

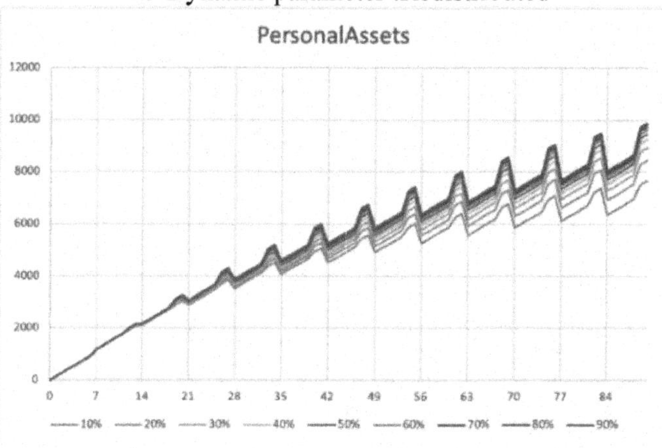

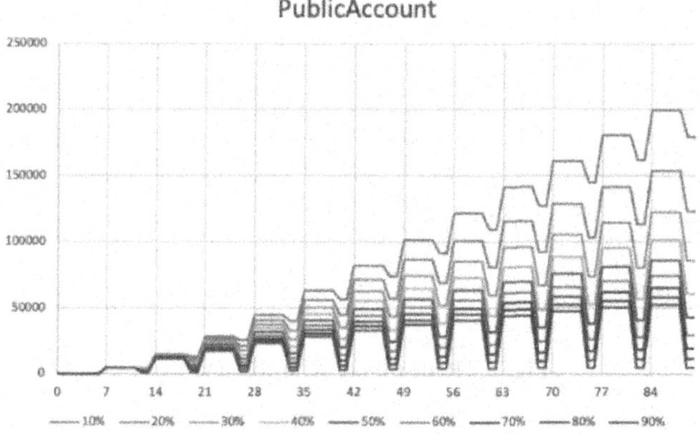

Fig. 4. *(continued)*

4.2 Task 2: Formula for Dynamic Parameter

Following the previous section, we considered the dynamic value of redistributed such that the value of public account is saturated as a mathematical expression. Here, we decided that public account is saturated with a fixed value using the following formula;

$$\text{Redistributed}(x) = 0.4\left(1 - e^{-0.000015x}\right) \quad (3)$$

Figure 5 shows the simulation result of the value of personal assets and public account using the formula (3). We confirmed that the value of personal assets and public account was saturated with a fixed value.

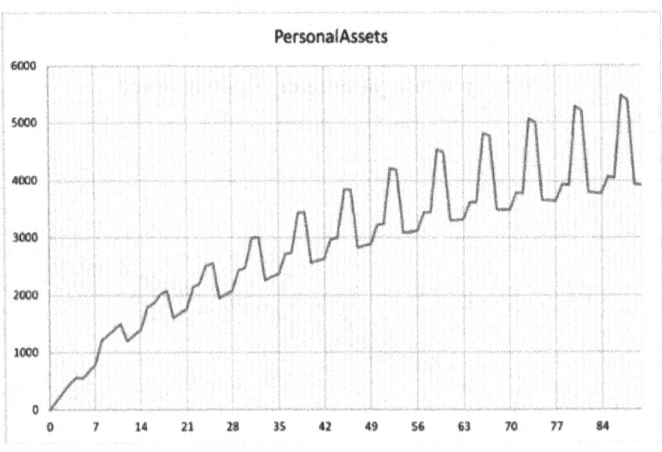

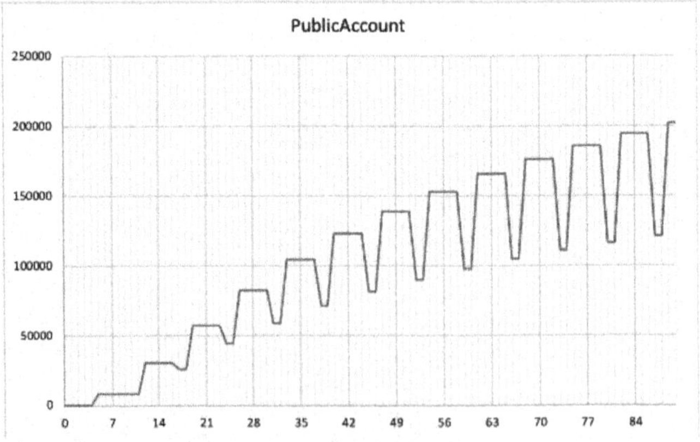

Fig. 5. Redistribute with formula (3)

5 Conclusion

A community is a system that cannot exist without community people's self-motivated involvement in itself, and that is composed of "Hito", "Mono", "Koto" and their relationality which community people naturally generate through making their daily lives. Relationality among "Hito", "Mono" and "Koto" that community people daily generate in a community should be regarded as assets in a sense that relationality should be social and economic value expected to provide some benefit to a community in the future.

Towards rebuilding of a community, we have proposed a system model to quantify and visualize relationality between Hito, Mono and Koto in a community as relationality assets that residents individually earn, and to elicit their awareness of relationality assets as trust. In order for relationality to function as assets, in addition, we have proposed a mechanism through which community people gift their assets to others and they can share a sort of common assets virtually pooled by their gifting activities among people. For modeling, we built simulation models using system dynamics (SD) to investigate how the proposed mechanisms work and influence the behaviors of the community as a system. These models were then refined by proof-of-concept in the field.

References

The Japan Policy Council.: A Stop Declining Fertility: Local Revitalization Strategy (2014)

The Ministry of Internal Affairs and Communications, Japan.: Kongo no toshibu ni okelu komyuniti no arikatani kansuru kennkyuukai houkokusyo (2014). (in Japanese)

Ogita, K., Kimura, K., Shiozu, Y., Yonezaki, K., Tanev, I., Shimohara, K.: Simulation for visualizing relationality assets in local community toward re-building of communities. In: 45th SICE Symposium on Intelligent Systems (2018)

Kimura, K.: Design of Relationality to Enable the Vitalization of Resident-centered Communities. Doctoral dissertation (2019)

Correction to: Presenting Low-Accuracy Information of Emotion Recognition Enhances Human Awareness Performance

Shinichi Fukasawa, Hiroko Akatsu, Wakana Taguchi, Fumio Nihei, and Yukiko Nakano

Correction to: Chapter "Presenting Low-Accuracy Information of Emotion Recognition Enhances Human Awareness Performance" in: S. Yamamoto and H. Mori (Eds.): *Human Interface and the Management of Information*, LNCS 11569, https://doi.org/10.1007/978-3-030-22660-2_30

The original version of this chapter 'Presenting Low-Accuracy Information of Emotion Recognition Enhances Human Awareness Performance' starting on p. 415 was revised. The affiliation of authors 'Shinichi Fukasawa' and 'Hiroko Akatsu' was incorrect. It has been updated as follows: Oki Electric Ind. Co., Ltd., Warabi-shi, Saitama, Japan.

The updated version of this chapter can be found at https://doi.org/10.1007/978-3-030-22660-2_30

S. Yamamoto and H. Mori (Eds.): HCII 2019, LNCS 11569, p. C1, 2019.
https://doi.org/10.1007/978-3-030-22660-2_48

Author Index

Printed in the United States
By Bookmasters